VIETNAM AT WAR

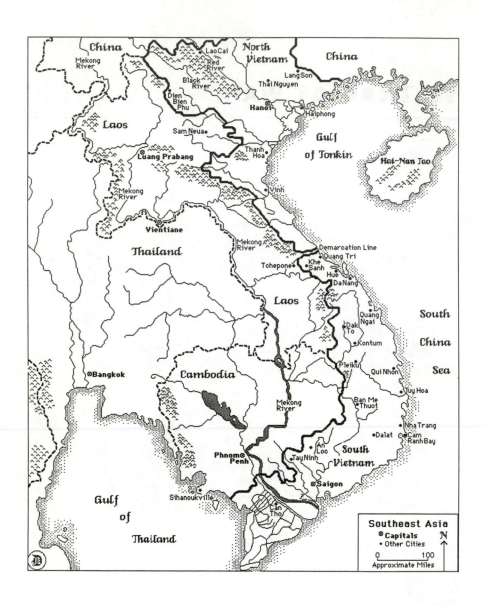

VIETNAM AT WAR

The History: 1946–1975

Phillip B. Davidson

★
PRESIDIO

Copyright © 1988
by Phillip B. Davidson

Published by Presidio Press
31 Pamaron Way, Novato CA 94949

27.⁵⁰

Library of Congress Cataloging-in-Publication Data

Davidson, Phillip B., 1915–
    Vietnam at war.

    Bibliography: p. 819
    Includes index.
    1. Indochinese War, 1946–1954.   2. Vietnamese
Conflict, 1961–1975.   3. Vietnam—History—1945–1975.
I. Title.
DS553.1.D38   1988   959.704   87–7320
ISBN 0–89141–306–5

Printed in the United States of America

2 3 4 5 6 7 8 9 10 — 90 89 88

52040

To Donna, with love—
whose encouragement and effort made this book possible.

Contents

PART II

Preface

I wrote this book to explain to my own satisfaction how the United States won every battle in and over Vietnam and yet lost the war. Such a defeat is unprecedented in the annals of military history.

And we did lose the war. Our objective was to preserve South Vietnam as an "independent, non-Communist state,"[1] and we obviously failed to do that. Refusing to accept this defeat, or saying that we won the shooting war, may assuage our bruised egos, but it oversimplifies the conflict and distorts our understanding of its true nature.

Faced with the task of finding out how we lost the war, the first decision I had to make was at what time in history I should begin my search for the answer. After some thought, the not very original answer occurred to me: start at the beginning, that is, when the Vietminh, the Vietnamese Communist Party, and the North Vietnamese Army were being formed and developed, in the thirties and forties.

If I were going to trace the United States' defeat in the seventies back to the thirties and forties, I must then find some way or some symbol to tie this lengthy scenario together. As the connecting symbol I chose Sr. Gen. Vo Nguyen Giap, longtime commander of the North Vietnamese Army and North Vietnam's minister of defense. He was a principal figure throughout the three wars which ravaged Indochina: Indochina War I between the Vietminh and the French, Indochina War II between the United States/South Vietnam and North Vietnam/Viet Cong, and Indochina War III between North and South Vietnam. Only Ho Chi Minh was more dominant in Communist affairs than Giap, but Ho died in 1969, well before the final Communist victory of 1975 and the historic events leading to that triumph.

The focus on Giap gives other insights. Through him and his associates we see how the war looked to the North Vietnamese. We can scrutinize the internal disputes in the North Vietnam Politburo about the nature of the conflict, and we can see the changes Giap made in strategy and tactics in response to shifting circumstances. Finally, a study of Giap reveals the unique strategy he and his cohorts conceived, developed, and used against us. The answer to my question—how did we lose the Vietnam War—lies in large measure, then, with Vo Nguyen Giap.

---

[1] *National Security Action Memorandum 288,* March 17, 1964.

Acknowledgments

I owe a deep debt of gratitude to those who helped me write this book. My profound thanks go to that distinguished soldier, Gen. William C. Westmoreland, the commander of United States forces in Vietnam from 1964–1968 and Chief of Staff, United States Army, from 1968–1972. He gave me many personal documents not heretofore made public and generously assisted throughout the book's preparation with advice, comment, and critical insight. Let me hasten to add that he probably does not agree with everything I have written here. I am also indebted in large measure to Dr. Walt W. Rostow, now a professor at the University of Texas, Austin, and onetime national security adviser to President Johnson during the critical period of the Vietnam War. Conversations with him were essential in clarifying several crucial points and areas. To Douglas Pike, the West's foremost authority on Vietnamese communism, I acknowledge another debt. He not only made available the invaluable resources of his Indochina Studies Program at the University of California, Berkeley, but brought a unique insight into the strategy of revolutionary war, North Vietnamese-style.

Col. John Schlight, U.S. Army, Retired, and Mr. Arthur S. Hardyman of the United States Army Center of Military History furnished valuable documents, maps, and photographs. Col. Dale E. Finkelstein, Judge Advocate General's Corps, U.S. Army, provided expert advice on the rules of land warfare, while Maj. Gen. Rathvon McC. Tompkins, U.S. Marine Corps, Retired, contributed valuable information regarding the siege of Khe Sanh and the "water point" story. My thanks go to Mr.

Alfonso J. Butcher and Miss Patricia Heaton of the Ft. Sam Houston library for their long-term assistance.

Finally, I owe a huge debt of gratitude to the late Col. Charles A. Morris, U.S. Army, not only for his assistance on this work, but for his outstanding contributions during two tours as an intelligence officer in Vietnam, during one of which I had the honor to have him as my principal assistant. RIP, Charlie.

Part I

1 Volcano Under the Snow

On 7 May 1975 the ABC evening news report showed an action shot of the North Vietnamese hierarchy celebrating its victory over South Vietnam. From a platform in front of the Presidential Palace in Saigon, Pham Van Dong, the North Vietnamese premier, pointed to Sr. Gen. Vo Nguyen Giap, the North Vietnamese minister of defense and commander in chief of its armed forces. "There," proclaimed Dong, "is the architect of our victory." This was not the usual hyperbole of triumph; this was a fitting tribute, for Giap commanded the North Vietnamese armed forces from 1944, when it consisted of one platoon of thirty-four men, until 1972 or 1973, when it became the third-largest army in the world. He made war for over thirty years, and he beat the French, the South Vietnamese, and, judged by the final results, the United States of America. What is more unusual is that Giap had no prior schooling, training, or experience to fit him for the role he played.

Vo Nguyen Giap was born in 1912 in the village of An Xa in Quang Binh province, just north of the Demilitarized Zone (DMZ). Quang Binh and the two neighboring provinces to the north, Ha Tinh and Nghe An, form the North Vietnamese "panhandle," which is one of Vietnam's most impoverished areas. Historically these three provinces have shown little respect or sufferance for their governors, be they Chinese, French, or even Vietnamese. The inhabitants revolted against the Chinese; they rose up against the French in the 1880s and again in

3

1930; and they rebelled against North Vietnam's land reform program in 1956. It is no coincidence that the area produced not only Giap, but Pham Van Dong and Ho Chi Minh as well.

Not much is known about Giap's parents. Some sources say that his father was a scholar and a teacher; others state that he was only a poor farmer. What is certain, however, is that the elder Giap was a Vietnamese revolutionary. He took an active part in the uprisings against the French in 1885 and 1888, and Giap grew up in an atmosphere filled with revolutionary fervor and hatred for the French.[1]

In 1924 Giap entered the Lycée National at Hue. It was an unusual school, founded, ironically, by Ngo Dinh Kha, the father of Ngo Dinh Diem, who would be a future leader of South Vietnam, and as such, one of Giap's many adversaries. The older Ngo, a high-ranking mandarin, wanted an institution in which exceptional Vietnamese boys could get an integrated Vietnamese/Western education free of French influence. Its alumni testify to his success, including not only the Ngo brothers and Giap, but Ho Chi Minh and Pham Van Dong as well.

Giap launched his career as a covert revolutionary at the age of fourteen. His guide into this murky underworld was Phan Boi Chau. Chau had a long history as an anti-French agitator, and for his revolutionary activities, the French Sûreté drove him out of Vietnam to China. There he came to know Ho Chi Minh, then going under one of his innumerable aliases as Ly Thuy. Each headed a different Vietnamese revolutionary group and therefore they were rivals. The French say that in June 1925, Ho betrayed Chau to the Sûreté in Shanghai for 100,000 piasters. Years later Ho justified this treachery on two grounds: Chau's arrest and trial would stir up a hotbed of resentment in Vietnam, which was something the Revolution needed; and Ho needed his share of the money to finance his Communist organization in Canton.[2]

Phan Boi Chau was returned to Hanoi, tried and sentenced to life at hard labor, but a few weeks later the French reduced his sentence to permanent house arrest in Hue. The French not only let this firebrand out of jail, but they permitted Chau to receive visits, principally from schoolboys. Giap described these visits in his collection of writings, *The Military Art of People's War:* "Often he (Chau) told us about world events. On the walls of his house were portraits of Sun Yat-sen, Lenin, and Sakyamuni. We were of those youths so eagerly searching for the truth."[3] In addition to his talks on world affairs, Chau preached to the youths what he wrote in one of his books, that ". . . the oppressed people will rise up one day and fight for their independence. And on that day, woe to the French!"[4] Sometime later Giap was pushed even deeper into the revolutionary movement after he read a pamphlet written by another nationalist in exile, Nguyen Ai Quoc or "Nguyen the Patriot." Nguyen was another alias of the ubiquitous Ho Chi Minh (that name is also an alias). Giap records that the pamphlet, entitled *Colonialism on Trial,* was passed from hand to hand among the young revolutionaries, and it ". . . inspired us with so much hatred, and thrilled us."[5]

In 1927 Giap, with other students at the Lycée, launched a "quit school" movement as a protest against some perceived French injustice. It was a "Children's Crusade" and, like the original, quickly collapsed. Giap was expelled from school and went back to his home in the village of An Xa. One day a friend from Hue visited him and they talked of revolution and politics. Before the friend left An Xa, he recruited Giap into the *Tan Viet* Party, whose aim was ". . . to carry out first a national revolution and then a world revolution."[6] Although the *Tan Viets* were not Communists, they tilted heavily in that direction.

Shortly thereafter, Giap, then about sixteen, returned to Hue as an active underground member of the party, serving with the *Tan Viets* until 1930. In the spring of that year the *Tan Viets* (including Giap) joined another nationalist group, the *Viet Nam Quoc Dan Dang,* in an abortive uprising against the French. Giap was arrested and sentenced to three years in prison, but the length of his actual stay in jail is obscure. Giap claims that he was imprisoned for two years; others believe he spent only a few months in prison. At any rate Giap has always omitted any discussion of the period between 1930 and 1932 in his accounts of his life. This imprisonment, of whatever length, was not all bad for Giap, for it provided him his first romantic interlude. In jail he met another revolutionary, a young girl named Minh Thai, who was to become his first wife.

By 1932 he had somehow ingratiated himself to the French, and with their consent he took and passed the difficult Baccalaureate in Hue and moved to Hanoi, the site of the nation's best university. Giap entered the university in 1933 and remained there until 1937 when he gained a Bachelor of Law degree. He failed to obtain the Certificate of Administrative Law the following year, however, which would have permitted him to practice. Nor did he win a Doctorate of Law, as many sources claim. His biography in the hands of the United States Army states that he also gained the equivalent of a doctorate in political science, but other sources dispute this.

About Giap's scholastic aptitude there is no dispute—he was a precocious student. One of his professors described him as "the most brilliant student at the University at that time," but noted that "he was a young man eager to learn, but introverted." During his student days at the university, Giap read every available book on history and communism. During this same period he met Pham Van Dong, now premier of North Vietnam, and Truong Chinh, the Party's leading theoretician. Chinh converted Giap to doctrinaire communism, and Giap joined the Communist Party in 1937.

In 1938 Giap continued to attend the university, studying political economy, but his academic brilliance waned. He now spent most of his time at the mundane business of earning a living and in writing articles for four underground newspapers, two in Vietnamese and two in French. In 1937–1938, with Truong Chinh, he completed a two-volume work entitled *The Peasant Problem*. Wilfred Burchett, the Red propagandist in Asia, describes the work with his usual excess of admiration for all things Communist: "Giap, together with Truong Chinh published a masterly analysis of the Vietnamese peasant . . . Giap and Truong Chinh's profound study of Vietnamese society, *The Peasant Problem,* served as the basis for the Communist Party, and later Vietminh policies toward the peasantry."[7]

To support himself during this stage of his life (circa 1938), Giap taught history in the Lycée Thang-Long, a private high school in Hanoi. He lived at the home of one of the professors, Dang Thai Mai, whose daughter was to become Giap's second wife. He gained a reputation at the school as a lecturer on history, and a student of his, who in 1954 fled to South Vietnam from Hanoi, told with awe how Giap ". . . could step to a blackboard and draw in the most minute detail every battle plan of Napoleon." His high school pupils called him "the general," a peculiarly accurate prophecy from a group of derisive children.

In either 1937 or 1938 he married Minh Thai (real name Thi Quan Than), the girl he had met during his prison term in the early thirties. Both Minh Thai and her sister, Minh Khai, were ardent Communists. The latter had studied in the Soviet Union and was a member of the Central Committee of the Communist Party of Vietnam. In his writings and interviews Giap has never discussed his life with Minh Thai. About all that is known of this relationship is that in either 1938 or early 1939 she bore Giap a daughter.

The French government outlawed the Communist Party in France and in its colonies on 26 September 1939. In Vietnam alone, the Sûreté seized more than a thousand Party members, forcing the Communists to take rapid countermeasures. The Communist Central Committee ordered Giap and Pham Van Dong to flee to China where they would be trained in guerrilla warfare. Giap's wife, Minh Thai, and her sister, Minh Khai, were ordered to stay in Vietnam as Communist liaison officers and couriers. Years later Giap would recall with anguish this parting from his young wife. He wrote, "On 3 May 1940 at 5:00 P.M., after school hours, I went directly to the Great Lake, just as if going for a walk or normal activity. Comrade Thai, with little Hong Anh (Giap's daughter) in her arms was waiting for me on the Co Ngu Road. . . . we had no idea we were meeting for the last time."[8]

Hounded by the French, Giap's wife and her sister fled Hanoi for Vinh. In May 1941, the Sûreté captured both sisters and Giap's daughter. Minh Khai, the sister, was guillotined, and Minh Thai, Giap's wife, was sentenced to fifteen years in prison. According to United States intelligence reports, the French hung her by the thumbs and beat her to death in 1943. Giap's daughter died in prison, probably from neglect, about the same time. Other reports state that in addition to Giap's wife and daughter, the rest of Giap's family—his father, two sisters, and a brother-in-law—were killed by the French between 1941 and 1943, but these executions have never been confirmed.

In May of 1940, Giap, then en route to China, could not know of the deaths and hardships which would befall his family. He and Pham Van Dong took a train from Hanoi to Lao Cai, a town in the northwestern corner of North Vietnam on the Chinese border. During this trip the French police searched the train twice, and Giap and Dong barely eluded them by jumping off the train and hiding underneath like two hoboes evading railroad "dicks." Eventually, they reached Lao Cai and crossed the Red River into China, where they contacted members of the local Chinese Communist Party who sheltered them from Chiang Kai-shek's agents. Other Vietnamese Communists who had reached Kunming ahead of Giap and Pham Van Dong told the two newcomers that they must wait for the arrival of a Vietnamese named Vuong who would tell them what to do. One day in June 1940, Giap and Dong met Vuong, who was—predictably—Ho Chi Minh using another of his aliases. Ho told the two young men that they were to go to the Chinese Communist headquarters in Yenan to study politics and military techniques. They never reached Yenan, for the German blitzkrieg smashed through France, and Ho saw that the defeat of the French army profoundly changed the situation in Indochina. He got word to Giap and Dong (along with the other Vietnamese Communists in China) to return immediately to Vietnam.

After some delay the entire Vietnamese Communist cadre, about thirty strong, returned to Vietnam and set up a crude base camp in the remote mountains along the Vietnamese/China border. There they began a program of indoctrination, training, and propaganda aimed at the primitive tribes living nearby. Coincidentally, Giap established his first "self-defense" unit made up of a few men armed with crude and castoff weapons. In 1942 with the help of these "self-defense" units, the Vietminh (as Ho had named the Communist movement) began to push south. The Vietminh ambushed a few French patrols, assassinated "reactionary" Vietnamese officials, and propagandized the population. During 1943 and 1944 the size of Giap's guerrilla band grew, but their activities consisted of little more than terrorism and organized banditry. Viewed in the light of the momentous events of 1943–1944—the Battle of Midway, Stalingrad, and the Normandy landings—the Vietminh activities were trifling. Within Vietnam both the French and the Japanese saw the Vietminh as a minor annoyance, although the French made some effort to eradicate them. It was this casual disregard which permitted the spread of the Vietminh organization and the growth of its armed bands.

In July 1944, with Ho once again in China, Giap called a special conference of Communist leaders. At Giap's urging this group concluded that the time was ripe for a large-scale guerrilla uprising in the northern Vietnamese provinces of Cao Bang, Lang Son, and Bac Thai. This was Giap's first strategic decision, and it promptly backfired. Ho returned shortly and immediately rescinded Giap's decision on the grounds that the uprising would be rash and premature.

On 19 December 1944, Ho ordered Giap to establish the first of the Vietnam Propaganda and Liberation Units, the organized forerunners of the People's Army of Vietnam (PAVN), the North Vietnamese Regular Army. Note this combination of military and political force, which was a trademark of the North Vietnamese Army. It was with these units that Giap began his career as a military leader of organized armed forces. Giap's World War II campaigns culminated in almost bloodless seizure of power throughout North Vietnam in August 1945, and these experiences of the so-called August Revolution had a strong impact on Giap's future strategic concepts and operations.

These were busy years for the young Giap. In 1945 he became minister of the interior in Ho's provisional government. In March 1946 he was appointed to the presidency of the Supreme Council of National Defense, a post which allowed him to consolidate his command of the PAVN. In 1946 or 1947 Giap remarried. This time his bride was Dang Thai Hai, the daughter of Giap's old professor at Thang-Long High School.

In 1946 The French Empire and its armed forces returned to Vietnam. Ho ordered Giap, as the commander of the PAVN, to go to the airport and welcome the French commander, the famous Gen. Jacques Le Clerc. Giap violently objected and avowed that he would never shake hands with a Frenchman. Ho—a tough old bird under his grandfatherly veneer—disdainfully told him, "Cry your eyes out, Giap, but you be at the airport in two hours." When Giap greeted Le Clerc at the airport he did shake his hand and pompously proclaimed, "The first resistance fighter of Vietnam salutes the first resistance fighter of France." Le Clerc's reaction to Giap's brazen attempt to equate their ranks and careers is unrecorded.

Giap served as vice chairman of the North Vietnamese delegation in its 1946 negotiations with the French. The French considered him to be highly emotional, but nevertheless the outstanding member of the Vietnamese delegation. Throughout the negotiations Giap distrusted French intentions and hoped that the negotiations would break down. They did, and Indochina War I came to Vietnam on 19 December 1946, when French and Vietminh forces began fighting in Hanoi.

Between Indochina War I against the French and Indochina War II against the Americans and the South Vietnamese, Giap engaged in a constant series of quarrels with other members of the North Vietnamese leadership. Sometimes the disputes were over basic questions of ideology or policy, for example, the debate which ran for years over whether priority should be given to the development of the economy of North Vietnam or to the task of bringing South Vietnam under the control of the North. Many times, however, they were only disguised power struggles to gain relative rank within the Politburo and determine control of the various agencies of the government. While the losers lost prestige and power—sometimes a great deal of both—and the winners won them, the game was played for less than lethal stakes. The loser would lose his job and perquisites (and then often only temporarily), but unlike the case in other Communist dictatorships, he stayed out of jail and escaped the firing squad.

The smoke of battle had barely cleared over Dien Bien Phu in 1954 when Giap crossed swords with the man who had converted him to communism, Truong Chinh. The battle between these two had been building for several years. Both were egocentric, contentious, ambitious, and eager to succeed Ho when "Uncle" passed on. During the war against the French, Giap bitterly resented Chinh's continual interference in military affairs, particularly Chinh's attempt in 1949 to import large numbers of Chinese troops to help the Vietminh fight the war. The quarrel intensified in 1950. Chinh manipulated the appointment of Gen. Nguyen Chi Thanh, a protégé, to be the head of the Political Section of the North Vietnamese Army. Giap saw this move correctly as a challenge to his control and command of the army, and he barely beat it off.

In 1956 Chinh authored the Land Reform Program. It was a complicated ideological-economic plan devised to give land to the peasants and to establish the complete dominance of the *Lao Dong* (Communist) Party. The program was carried out with excessive zeal and spread terror among the people with its irresponsible accusations, drumhead trials, and hasty executions in which 100,000 peasants were killed. It paralyzed agricultural production, which fell to disastrous levels. Since Ho Chi Minh and the Communist regime could not take responsibility for the failed program, Ho designated Chinh as the scapegoat and Giap as the "hatchet man" to chop him down publicly. At the Tenth Party Congress held in October 1956, Giap castigated Chinh and his program, and Chinh was dismissed from the key job of Party secretary. Chinh would later be rehabilitated, but this was clearly a triumph for Giap.

In September 1957 Giap got into a dispute with his old train-hopping colleague, Pham Van Dong, over the policy towards the unification of Vietnam. Giap took the hard line—no concessions to the South Vietnamese government—while Dong favored a more moderate approach. Dong won, and Giap dropped from public view for a few months, allegedly suffering from migraine headaches.

In 1959 another internal power struggle erupted. This time the dispute was over the role of the North Vietnamese Army. Chinh, now restored to favor, and Le Duan, the most powerful southerner in the Politburo, wanted to use the soldiers as industrial workers to increase production. Giap objected, and again, he lost. Nguyen Chi Thanh, allied with Chinh and Duan, was promoted to senior general, and now, more than ever, became a competitor of Giap's in the army. In 1960, as in the past, Giap disappeared from the public view for several months for medical reasons. Giap was soon back in Ho's good graces and General Thanh had been unhorsed for some obscure misdeed, relegated temporarily to the agriculture collectivization program. The game of "musical chairs"— always under "Uncle Ho's" direction—went on.

In 1964, Giap and the now-restored General Thanh clashed again, this time over how to counter United States military intervention in South Vietnam. As the South Vietnamese government reeled from political turmoil and military defeat, Thanh and Le Duan pressed for stepped-up military action in the South by the North Vietnamese Army. Giap and Truong Chinh objected. They wanted to build up the economy in North Vietnam. Thanh and Le Duan won, and this time Giap's loss almost destroyed his career.

By late 1965 Giap, as irrepressible as a rubber ball, was again in Ho's good graces; so much so that he and Thanh joined a rhetorical battle over the Communist strategy for waging the war in South Vietnam. In essence, Giap favored a strategy emphasizing guerrilla warfare and "protracted war" so as to erode American willpower over the long haul. Thanh wanted a "big unit," conventional war which would destroy large American units and installations. The debate raged through 1966 and ended in July 1967 when General Thanh died in his South Vietnamese headquarters, allegedly of a heart attack.

The remainder of Giap's career is intimately tied to the war against South Vietnam and the United States and the events leading to the end of Indochina War III against South Vietnam alone in 1975. After 1975 (and perhaps before that) Giap began to withdraw from leadership in the military affairs of North Vietnam. In February 1980 he surrendered his last post of authority, that of defense minister. Giap was removed from the Politburo in 1982 and now spends his time in retirement.

A photograph of Giap taken in the early seventies shows a toad-like face with thick lips, a flattened nose, no neck, a bulging forehead, and a receding hairline—a face like that of the late American actor, Edward G. Robinson. The photograph does not show the network of veins which purple Giap's nose and cheeks, nor does it reveal that his eyes are cold and piercing. It does not show that he was getting fat and above all, it does not show that Giap is a very small man, not quite five feet tall. Even by Vietnamese standards this is extremely short, and this runtiness probably accounts for some of his unpleasant personality—for Vo Nguyen Giap is definitely not your "Mr. Nice Guy."

Journalists who have talked to him, and reports in the hands of United States intelligence agencies, depict Giap as somehow combining the worst personality traits of Adolf Hitler and Benito Mussolini. First, he is arrogant. He delighted during his days of ascendancy in taking his young second wife to parties where other officials dared not take theirs. Giap's oafish greeting to General Le Clerc in 1945, where he attempted to equate their status and rank, was brazen effrontery. He treated interviewers and subordinates to marathon monologues, lecturing them like a professor talking to dim-witted students. He frequently told interviewers not to interrupt him or to "shut up." One United States reporter who has interviewed Giap called him "a peasant, a surly boor."

Like Der Führer, he is impulsive and sometimes irrational. At two official dinners given during the sixties by the Chinese Communists in Hanoi he felt himself seated below his rank. On both occasions he got up and left. When he led the Vietminh team negotiating with the French in 1946, he frequently shouted at the French delegates and stalked out of the meetings. His frequent, uncontrolled outbursts following hours of icy calm have earned him the name among his North Vietnamese contemporaries of *Nue Lua,* the "Volcano Under the Snow." Like Mussolini, he is vain and self-indulgent. While it is hard to believe, one intelligence report states that in the late forties, he alone in North Vietnam wore button shoes. He later sported tailored Western suits and luxurious uniforms. During his heyday he preached sacrifice to the people and to his troops, but he lived in a beautiful French villa and rode around Hanoi in a limousine.

Giap can be evasive and deceitful, as well. In an interview with Oriana Fallaci, the noted Italian biographer, he denied any responsibility for the Tet offensive, saying that the National Liberation Front in South

Vietnam (the Viet Cong) was responsible.[9] In the same interview he disclaimed any knowledge of the objectives of the offensive. Both are lies. After the interview, in which he made several statements damaging to himself, he attempted to retract his comments by sending Ms. Fallaci a text which had been carefully edited and contained none of his controversial remarks. This, said Giap, was the only text which could be published. Ms. Fallaci refused to accept the substitution and published the original interview, which was unfavorable to Giap.

Giap is contentious, vindictive, and ruthless. He had no friends among his peers, always viewing other members of the North Vietnamese leadership as rivals for power. Through the years he has fought with Truong Chinh, Pham Van Dong, Nguyen Chi Thanh, Le Duan, and Le Duc Tho, and in one way or another he probably settled his personal score with his old rival, Sr. Gen. Nguyen Chi Thanh. He is totally ruthless. Giap is widely reported as saying that "Every minute hundreds of thousands of men all over the world are dying. The life and death of tens of thousands in battle, even if they are compatriots, means very little." Giap denies that he ever said this, but whether he said it or not is immaterial. What is important is that he conducted his campaigns, even the victorious ones, with a callous disregard for casualties among his own troops.

Psychologists who have studied the material available on Giap speculate that his personality and character result from the psychic bruises Giap suffered. In his youth he was poor and sickly, and as a young man he suffered deeply when the French Sûreté tortured and killed his family. He is painfully sensitive about his lack of height. Psychologists conclude that these experiences have made him fearful of subjugation and humiliation. In short, he has a "runt complex." According to the psychologists, Giap feels that in any relationship he must always play the superior role, that he is uncomfortable with his peers and only at ease with subordinates.

When Giap suffered a political reversal, he left the scene. The disappearances have all been explained as required for "medical" reasons and this may be true. He has had high blood pressure since 1954, migraine headaches since 1957, and Hodgkin's disease for an unknown number of years. While some of these disappearances may have been to "save face," the psychologists see strong psychosomatic elements in them. They conjecture that defeat and humiliation bring on within Giap a rage, which he knows must be contained, so he turns it inward into actual physical symptoms.

Can no good be said of Giap? Certainly. He has a brilliant mind; he is dedicated to his country and to communism; he was resolute and tenacious in driving towards his military goals. Above all else, he had that quality which generals need most—he won. This last quality, his ability to win, only raises another question. How did this high school history teacher get the education and the training to become a victorious general?

Like many other details of Giap's early life, accounts of his formal military education are sketchy and contradictory. The Central Intelligence Agency reports that Giap attended military schools in the USSR and may even have been trained by the Chinese Nationalists at their Whampoa Military Academy. The Defense Intelligence Agency states that Giap received military training from the Chinese Communists. Both agencies are incorrect. Giap himself refutes this latter report in his book *The Military Art of People's War*.[10] Hoang Van Chi, a North Vietnamese, who claimed intimate knowledge of Ho Chi Minh, Truong Chinh, Pham Van Dong, and Giap, states in his book that "Giap had no military education other than a short training in guerrilla warfare at an American camp in Tsin-tsi during the Second World War."[11] No mention of any such episode occurs in Giap's published works. Giap does mention that he and other members of the initial Vietminh cadre arrived at Tsin-tsi in late 1940. There, according to Giap, the Vietminh set up a training course for the Nungs, a local tribal group.[12] This could be a partial truth, omitting any American participation or training.

There are routes other than West Point, St. Cyr, or Sandhurst to gain a knowledge of the officer's craft. Napoleon himself said, "Read and reread the campaigns of Alexander, Hannibal, Caesar, Gustavus, Eugene, and Frederick; model yourself upon them; this is the only way to become a great captain and to discover the secrets of war."[13] Of Napoleon's counsel, a modern "great captain," Viscount Bernard Montgomery of Alamein, wrote, "No better advice was ever given any student of war."[14] This road, the study of military history, was Giap's route to martial glory, and one which must have been particularly appealing to Giap, the former history teacher at Thang-Long High School.

Giap's extensive writings on military affairs reveal the names of the "great captains" of the past from whom he gained his ideas of strategy and tactics. First, there were the legendary warrior heroes of Vietnam, a group little known in the Western world, but, nevertheless, genuine "great captains." His next tutor was his leader and mentor, Ho Chi Minh. Under the circumstances this is to be expected, but Giap's writings reveal Ho as not only a wily and sophisticated statesman, but also as a realistic military thinker. In his writings Giap publicly credits two other giants of communism, Lenin and Mao Tse-tung, for some of his military concepts, and through Lenin and Mao, Giap picked up two more tutors—Clausewitz (a favorite of Lenin's) and Sun Tzu (400–320 B.C.), a Chinese military philosopher.

Giap had two other teachers he never mentions in his writings. The first, already cited, was Napoleon. The second was T. E. Lawrence, the fabled Lawrence of Arabia of World War I fame. In 1946 Giap confided to the French general, Raoul Salin, "My fighting gospel is T. E. Lawrence's *Seven Pillars of Wisdom*. I am never without it." Here then are the immortal masters of conflict who taught Vo Nguyen Giap: Napoleon Bonaparte, T. E. Lawrence, Carl Von Clausewitz, Vladimir Lenin, Mao Tse-tung, Sun Tzu, Ho Chi Minh, and those legendary Vietnamese heroes of countless battles against the invading Chinese and the hard-driving Mongols.

What an array of instructors! Ideologically, they range from Napoleon on the Right to Lenin, Ho, and Mao on the Left, but they are connected by a common thread—all of them were in varying degrees theorists. Some (Ho and Lenin) never commanded men in battle. The combat experience of Clausewitz was minimal. Of course, Napoleon, Lawrence, Mao, and the legendary Vietnamese heroes had taken advanced degrees in handling men under fire or steel, but they too were theorists. All conceived strategies which in their day, in their countries, against their enemies, won campaigns and wars, and each contributed significantly to Giap's development of his own strategic theories.

In his writings Giap emphasizes that his foremost teachers were his own ancestors, the Vietnamese heroes of antiquity. Time and again Giap pays tribute to his military heritage from past Vietnamese patriots. In *Banner of People's War* he writes, "Our Party's military line has inherited, developed, and improved to a new level our nation's age-old traditional strategic ability." In another passage in this work, Giap praises the

Party and the Marxist theory of war for their contribution to his "military line," but pays tribute also to ". . . the intelligence and strategic abilities of our ancestors."[15]

In chronological order, the first of Giap's Vietnamese teachers were the Trung sisters. In 39 A.D. the Chinese, then occupying Vietnam, executed a restive feudal lord as an example to the other Vietnamese leaders. To the surprise of the Chinese occupiers, the feudal lord's wife, Trung Trac, and her sister, Trung Nhi, raised an army and overwhelmed the complacent and unprepared Chinese garrisons. The unexpected success of the operation stunned not only the Chinese, but the Vietnamese as well, for they found themselves free for the first time in 150 years. In gratitude they proclaimed the Trung sisters as their queens.

The Chinese struck back in 43 A.D. The key battle took place at the edge of the Day River where the Chinese massacred the Vietnamese. The Trung sisters chose to make their last stand in an open field with their backs against a cliff, and the more experienced Chinese forces destroyed the few remaining Vietnamese troops. The Trung sisters committed suicide by drowning themselves in the river. Giap credits the Trung sisters with demonstrating the value of the continuous offensive aimed at toppling foreign rule. More realistically, the last battle of the Trung sisters should have taught Giap the folly of the static defense against a superior army.

The greatest of the legendary heroes of Vietnam were Le Loi and his advisor, the great scholar, Nguyen Trai. In 1418 Le Loi and Nguyen Trai led a revolution against the Chinese in Thanh Hoa province. They freed the province and, using it as a base, liberated adjoining Nghe An province. In 1426 Le Loi attacked the Chinese in the Red River Delta. The population rallied to his banner, and he was able to bottle up the Chinese in Hanoi. In 1427 he ambushed a Chinese army sent to relieve the beleaguered garrison in the Chi Lan mountain pass, a tactic used successfully by the modern Vietnamese against the French. When the Chinese sued for peace, Le Loi took the advice of Nguyen Trai and offered to provide the defeated force with food and transport if they would return to China. Giap credits Le Loi with the development of the strategy of what is now called "the protracted war," which is the use of time to wear down an enemy. Giap wrote, "Meanwhile the liberation war led by Le Loi and Nguyen Trai ended victoriously after ten years of hard struggle. For this reason our people inherently possess a tradition of persistent resistance, an art of defeating the enemy in protracted wars."[16]

Of particular interest to Americans, Vietnamese history has a direct precedent for the Tet offensive of 1968. Nguyen Hue, also known as Quang Trung, one of the three Tay Son brothers who led a revolution in 1771, defeated a Chinese army near Hanoi by launching a surprise attack during the height of the Tet festivities in the winter of 1789.

From his Vietnamese ancestors Giap learned that to be successful in warfare, the people—all of the people—must be mobilized to fight the invader. This had been characteristic of Vietnamese warfare through-out the ages. Giap notes this heritage in describing Vietnam's historical wars as obviously "people's wars."[17] He points out that what he calls the "strategic-offensive ideology" of modern Vietnamese wars is derived in major part from past heroes. He writes, "The present offensive ideology of our party, armed forces, and people is not disassociated from our traditional national military ideology. In our national history, generally speaking, the victorious uprisings and national liberation was led by the Trung sisters, Ly Bon, Trieu Quang, Le Loi, and Nguyen Trai, representing various processes of continuous offensive aimed at toppling the foreign feudal ruling yoke."[18]

From his ancestors, then, Giap learned two historical lessons of fundamental importance in devising his own strategic concepts. First, in a war of liberation all of the people must be mobilized to support it, not only militarily, but politically. Second, "the protracted war" takes advantage of the historical tenacity and martial spirit of the Vietnamese people. Both of these lessons he would use well.

Giap places in the second rank of his teachers his leader, Ho Chi Minh. Giap wrote, "It may be rightly said that our army, which stems from the people, has been brought up according to the ideas and way of life of the Party and Uncle Ho."[19] Ho, however, stands apart from Giap's other mentors. His forte was not so much theory, although he had plenty of that, as it was rice-paddy practicality. Ho won his place in history not primarily as a military or political theorist, but as a "doer," an operator. Ho was a pragmatic Communist leader with a tremendous breadth of practical revolutionary experience. It is this pragmatism that he passed on to Giap.

Ho Chi Minh demonstrated this pragmatism and prudence in military decisions. In 1944 Ho cancelled Giap's first planned offensive because he deemed it premature. In 1945 he settled quickly a dispute over the command of the three types of Vietminh forces—regulars, regional forces, and guerrillas—and quickly established unity of command over all three. Ho saw, more clearly than did Giap, that a political base among the people must be established before military action could begin. Ho preached another pragmatic fact of revolutionary war: base areas had to be set up and maintained, not only as a springboard for military and political action, but in Ho's words, as a "foothold in case of reverse."[20]

Thus, Giap learned from Ho several valuable lessons: practicality; the importance of propaganda work and the establishment of a political base among the people; and the need for secure base areas. Finally, from Ho, Giap learned the most valuable of a soldier's lessons—resolution. Giap writes, (it was) "A most valuable lesson for us before we went to the battlefront. That lesson was as he (Ho) often said, 'Determination, determination, with determination one can do everything successfully.' "[21]

The Communist Party meant to Giap not so much Marx and Engels as those other two great theorists of conflict, Lenin and Mao. Giap must have been uniquely drawn to Lenin, for their early lives were remarkably similar. Lenin, like Giap, had been expelled from school as a youth for revolutionary activity. Later Lenin, like Giap, took a law degree with honors (at St. Petersburg University), and, again like Giap, he never practiced.[22] What Giap learned from Lenin fitted neatly into his other strategic and political acquisitions. First, Lenin stressed the primacy of ends over means. To Lenin, and to all Communists, any means which lead to the goal of world revolution is justified. A corollary of this basic theme, which Giap apparently absorbed, was that the immediate welfare of one's own people, whether they be Russian or Vietnamese, is secondary, and a successful revolution justifies enormous sacrifices of life and liberty. Thus, Lenin ruthlessly suppressed civil liberties, installed mass terror, and seldom intervened to save former comrades from the Cheka firing squads. The pupil, Giap, in his turn could say—and then deny—that "the life and death of tens of thousands" meant little to him. So steeled, he could expend the lives of hundreds of thousands of Vietnamese to drive the French and the Americans from his native land.

Lenin pointed Giap toward the military philosopher Clausewitz. Lenin had studied the Prussian's writings carefully, often echoing in his own works Clausewitz's oft-quoted maxim that war was a continuation of politics by other means. From Clausewitz, Giap learned the interrelation of politics and combat. He (Giap) governed all of his later campaigns by Clausewitz's basic thesis that the political object, as the original motive of the war, should be the standard for determining the military objectives and the application of the force to be used.

Giap studied not only Lenin, but particularly the works of Mao Tse-tung. In Giap's student days, Mao was the foremost theoretician of "revolutionary war," and like the bond between Lenin and Giap, a special bond existed between Mao and Giap. Mao's first wife, like Giap's, had been killed by Mao's political opponents, the Kuomintang. Mao, like Giap, taught himself strategy and tactics, and he consistently extolled the value of history as a teacher of the military arts. Mao himself could and did teach a great deal about political and military strategy, and Giap's writings indicate that he absorbed many of these theories.

Mao's concept of strategy sprang from the basic Communist tenet that there are immutable laws governing all social, political, and military activities. In an offhand manner, Mao once wrote, "But there is nothing mysterious about war, which is a process governed by laws."[23] In several other passages Mao refers to the "scientific" and "unscientific" conduct of war. Giap accepted Mao's dictum that war, at least revolutionary war, is conducted in accordance with a set of laws. Giap, quoting Mao, writes, "Revolutionary armed struggle in any country has common fundamental laws. Revolutionary armed struggle in each country has characteristics and laws of its own too."[24]

Another concept which Giap gleaned from Mao is the importance of the human being, both as an individual soldier and as a part of the "masses." Both men saw the need for continuous psychological and political indoctrination. In his famous series of lectures delivered in 1938, entitled "On the Protracted War," Mao stated, "This is the theory of 'weapons decide everything,' which is a mechanist theory of war, a subjective and one-sided view. In opposition to this view, we see not only weapons but also human beings. Although important, weapons are not the decisive factor in war; it is man and not material things that decide the issue. The contest of strength is not only a contest of military and economic power but also of human power and morale."[25] Giap learned well these psychological and political concepts of Mao's. The importance Giap gave to the morale and political indoctrination of his army and of the North Vietnamese people testify to his devotion to these vital subjects and to his expertise in these areas. In addition, there were other lessons which Giap learned from Mao. Some of the more significant were: the importance of establishing base and rear areas, the value of taking the initiative and the offensive, the uses of personal military experience, the necessity for concentrating a superior force on the battlefield, and the importance of the principle of economy of force.

Of equal consequence, however, were those concepts of Mao's which Giap rejected. He discarded Mao's theory that a victorious revolutionary war had to go through a rigid three-phase strategic cycle (guerrilla war, positional war, mobile war). Giap believed that the form of combat must be chosen by an analysis of the strategic factors actually existing at any given moment. Giap also strayed from Mao on the "man versus arms" question. To Mao, the power of the human will is supreme. To Giap, human will is important, but weapons play an equally significant role. There were other conceptional differences between the two men brought about by the size of their native countries, the enemies each had to meet, and the natural factors of their respective theaters of operations. Actually, Giap, in his writings, seems to ignore Mao as a tutor. Since that is not totally possible, he seeks subtly to depreciate his conceptual debt to the Chinese leader. North Vietnamese internal politics were basically pro-Soviet and anti-Chinese, and Giap's tributes lean accordingly. Nevertheless, a great deal of Giap's strategy originated with Mao Tse-tung.

Another teacher was Lawrence of Arabia. In 1946, Giap in his kindergarten period of generalship, described T. E. Lawrence's *Seven Pillars of Wisdom* as his "fighting gospel." Lawrence taught Giap some fundamental truths about war, and Lawrence's imaginative and penetrating mind developed many of the concepts of revolutionary war as they are known today. Lawrence's first lesson for Giap dealt with the strategy and tactics of irregular war. He perceived that the Arabs' objective was not the physical destruction of the Turkish army in the field, but the ejection of the Turks from Arab lands. In Lawrence's concept, the expulsion of the Turks could be achieved by scattering their combat power and by wearing them out. This goal could be attained by the maintenance of a constant and shifting Arab threat which forced the Turks to spread their forces throughout the desert in defensive garrisons. And the Arabs had another ally—time. A prolonged period of time, coupled with a persistent inability on the part of the Turks to bring the Arabs to bay, would eventually erode the morale of the Turkish troops in the field, their generals, and finally the government itself.

Lawrence probed deeper into the fundamentals of revolutionary war. He was perhaps the first military theorist of modern times to realize that both sides in a revolutionary war fought for the "hearts and minds of the people"—a phrase which has fallen into scornful disrepute, a disrepute which cannot, however, cloud its basic truth. Lawrence wrote, "A province would be won when we had taught the civilians in it to die for our ideal of freedom."[26]

Finally, from Lawrence, Giap learned the value of the psychological element in war, particularly psychology applied to the building and maintenance of the morale of his own troops. Lawrence described this applied psychology when he wrote, "There remained the psychological element to be built up into apt shape. I went to Xenophone and stole, to name it, his word *diathetics* . . . On it we should mainly depend for the means of victory on the Arab front. . . We had seldom to concern ourselves with what our men did, but always with what they thought."[27] To Lawrence's *diathetics* Giap added modern psychological mind-altering techniques and outright Communist "brainwashing" in a carefully thought-out program which developed in his troops a fanaticism and sacrificial courage seldom seen in this century. This accomplishment was a major key to Giap's success.

Disregarding all other "great captains," a study of Napoleon's campaigns alone provides any budding general a complete course in military strategy and leadership. Also there is from Napoleon the melancholy lesson of declining powers, of waning character, and of self-delusion. If Giap copied any one trait of Napoleon's, it should have been the young Bonaparte's clear eye for facts. Napoleon said of himself that he "was obliged to obey a heartless master, the calculation of circumstances and the nature of things."[28] Carlyle said about Napoleon, "The man had a certain, instinctive, ineradicable, feeling for reality, and did base himself upon fact so long as he had any basis."[29] Finally, however, Napoleon lost his eye for facts, and they became not what they were, but what he wanted them to be. This brought, as it always does, catastrophe—the Russian campaign, the defeat at Leipzig, and finally, Waterloo.

The supreme importance of facts is presented in the teaching of most of Giap's immortal masters. A study of Giap's campaigns reveals that of all the lessons of war he learned from his tutors, he grasped *least* the transcending value of facts in war. He deluded himself in 1951, in 1968, and again in 1972, and his men paid a heavy price each time.

✓ On the other hand, from his various masters he learned most of his lessons well. The major ones were: the relationship of the political objective to the use of military force; the criticality of mobilizing all the people into an active political base; the importance of political indoctrination of the people and the soldiers; and the use of the "protracted war" to erode the enemy's will and to defeat a stronger enemy.

While a future general can gain much from a military academy or the study of military history, there is one other way to learn the profession of arms. Mao once said that the two best generals in Chinese history were both illiterate, and he also wrote, "A person who has no chance to go to school can also learn warfare, which means learning it through warfare."[30] Mao was right in extolling the virtues of experience. That is, after all, how the "great captains" of antiquity learned about war. By maxim, experience is the best teacher, and regardless of an officer's early training, experience is his graduate school. Giap respected the value of experience. In 1945 he told General Le Clerc, "I have been to a military academy—that of the bush and guerrilla war against the Japanese."[31] While Giap's statement was primarily a brassy attempt to elevate himself in the eyes of Le Clerc, it does show that Giap appreciated the educational value of his experience.

It must be said at the outset that Giap's military experience prior to the outbreak of the French/Vietminh War in 1946 was minimal. In 1941 when Ho Chi Minh ordered Giap, Pham Van Dong, and the other Communist cadremen who were then in China to return to the China/ Vietnam border, Giap began "to learn warfare through warfare," to use Mao's words. There, life was hard. Giap and the others lived in caves. Bedeviled by colds and influenza, they almost starved, and they were harried by French patrols. In spite of these tribulations, Giap organized and trained small bands of "local self-defense forces." Poorly armed, virtually untrained, this rabble had no military capability other than the laying of small ambushes and booby traps. When these guerrilla bands became too troublesome, the French officials sent out clearing parties and drove Giap's ragtag forces deeper into the mountainous jungle. During

1942 and 1943, as the Vietminh strength slowly increased, the French expanded their counterguerrilla efforts, which turned out—as they often did—to be counterproductive. The French caught few guerrillas, while their terror tactics solidified Vietnamese opposition to the Europeans. Thus, the period between 1941 and mid-1944 saw a steady, but unspectacular, growth of Giap's irregular forces.

On 22 December 1944, the Vietnam Propaganda and Liberation Unit came into existence. On Christmas Eve, two days after its activation, Giap's unit attacked two small French outposts at Phai Khat and Na Ngan, annihilating them. One account states that Giap surprised the garrisons by dressing his thirty-four men as pro-French partisans and entering by the main gate.

These successes permitted Giap to enlarge his platoon to a company, with which he intended to attack the important outpost of Dong Mu. One source claims that Giap backed off without action when he saw that the French expected the attack.[32] Giap himself writes that his company attacked Dong Mu, and that he "was injured in the leg."[33] This peculiar phraseology leaves it to the reader's imagination whether Giap was wounded or injured in some less heroic fashion. At any rate Giap was soon active again. By early spring 1945 he had expanded his one company to five. Additional recruits in sizable numbers began appearing daily, and with this force Giap began infiltrating to the south, meeting little resistance.

The big break for the Vietminh came on 9 March 1945. On that day the Japanese, who had been in Vietnam as "guests" of the French, suddenly overturned the French governing apparatus and seized the country. It was the same old story—an uneasy arrangement between two restive enemies, and each feared that the other was about to pounce. The Japanese struck first, and that gave Ho and Giap the opportunity for which they had been waiting. The Japanese coup dismantled the French administration and destroyed the French security system, while the Japanese holed up in the major cities and made no effort to control the countryside. This failure gave the Vietminh an unprecedented opportunity to move about and to gain new adherents and recruits. Giap lost no time. By mid-1945 he had an army of some 10,000 men and held large areas of the country north of the city of Thai Nguyen and the Red River. The only fight between the Vietminh and the Japanese during

World War II occurred at Tam Dao, a small outpost located some thirty-five miles northwest of Hanoi. There, in early August 1945, five hundred Vietminh attacked thirty Japanese, killing eight of them.[34]

In August 1945 the United States dropped atomic bombs on Hiroshima and Nagasaki, bringing an end to World War II. Ho moved fast to take advantage of the Japanese surrender and to consolidate his position before the French returned to Indochina. On 16 August he issued the call for a "general insurrection" throughout Vietnam as Giap moved his Liberation Army towards Thai Nguyen, a key city in northern Vietnam. But as he moved on Thai Nguyen, a grander prize beckoned. On the night of 18 August Giap learned that Hanoi, the capital, was in the hands of the Vietminh. Part of Giap's troops stayed in Thai Nguyen, while the rest, under Giap, made a forced night march into Hanoi. There, on 19 August, Giap took formal control of the city. The Vietminh had triumphed, holding power not only in Hanoi, but throughout large areas of Central and South Vietnam as well.

It is well to note that Giap's campaign, from the two platoon-sized attacks on Christmas Eve 1944 to the fall of Hanoi on 19 August 1945, had been almost bloodless. In most cases the Vietminh simply walked in and took over from the disheartened French and the bewildered, even cooperative, Japanese. The combat experience, the knowledge of actual fighting, which Giap gained from these operations was slight.

The so-called August Revolution, during which the Vietminh seized Hanoi, made a profound and lasting impression on Giap and his comrades. On their perception (or misperception, really) of this success, they would build a portion of their future strategic concepts. Giap viewed the success of the August Revolution of 1945 as a peculiarly Vietnamese victory, involving two unique Vietnamese concepts.[35] The first of these concepts is that the cities and the rural areas are equally critical to the Vietnamese revolution. Giap believes that while rural base areas are important, the cities can and must be liberated by a combination of an uprising in the city and an attack from the rural areas. This is what happened in Hanoi in 1945.

The second, and more important, concept which Giap derived from the August Revolution is the requirement for the closest coordination between military and political action. In Giap's view, political action eventually becomes a "general uprising" or a "general insurrection." Military action eventually becomes a "general offensive." The two combined result in a massive political upheaval and an all-out military offensive which will destroy the enemy. Giap would put these two strategic concepts to the test of combat in 1968, when he launched the Tet offensive. The North Vietnamese/Viet Cong name for this Tet attack, significantly, was "Great Offensive, Great Uprising," and in concept it was a direct descendent of the August Revolution.

✕ From Giap's study of the great masters of strategy and from his own sparse experiences, Giap, Ho, and Chinh fashioned a strategy for conducting revolutionary war. If the Vietnam experience from 1940 to the present is to be understood, one must comprehend the fundamentals of this North Vietnamese strategy, a strategy so invincible that "there is no known proven counter strategy," according to Douglas Pike, the foremost authority in the West on Vietnamese communism and revolutionary war.[36]

To grasp Giap's strategy for the conduct of revolutionary war, or people's war (as Giap called it), one must first define it. Revolutionary war is a political war in which a group seeks to seize political power *within* a nation-state.[37] It is a total war, which seeks to mobilize all the people behind the revolution. It involves use of the whole spectrum of power—military, political, diplomatic, economic, and psychological. Each is used in conjunction with the others, and each contributes always toward the attainment of the final goal—overthrow of the state.

Another way to define revolutionary war is to explain what it is *not*. It is not conventional war, although in its later stages it may employ conventional war as a weapon. It is not even conventional war with a psychological war adjunct, the type all sides waged (mostly unsuccessfully) in World Wars I and II. But again, in certain phases a people's war will have that characteristic. It is not an insurgency or a guerrilla war, although those, too, are means of waging revolutionary war. It is not a war of terrorism, although murders, kidnappings, and other violent acts are part of the arsenal of revolutionary war.

Giap's strategy of revolutionary war totally integrated two principal forms of force—armed force and political force, which the North Vietnamese called military *dau tranh* (struggle) and political *dau tranh*. Their combined use created a kind of war unseen before: a single war waged simultaneously on several fronts—not geographical fronts, but programmatical fronts—all conducted by one and the same authority, all carefully meshed. It was a war in which military campaigns were waged for political and diplomatic reasons; economic measures (land reform, for example) were adopted to further political ends; political or diplomatic losses were accepted to forward military campaigns; and psychological campaigns were launched to lower enemy military effectiveness. All actions, political, military, economic, and diplomatic were weighed for their impact on the other elements of *dau tranh* and on the advance towards the final goal—the seizure of state power.

Military *dau tranh* encompasses all forms of military action from the assassination of a government official by a lone terrorist to the employment of armies, navies, and air forces in a massive conventional war campaign. Due to its nature, revolutionary war is a changing war. In theory, military *dau tranh* progresses through three distinct phases of warfare. Since in the first phase the opponents of the revolutionary warrior are stronger, the revolutionaries adopt guerrilla warfare (raids and small attacks) to avoid decisive combat. As the revolutionary military arm increases in strength and achieves rough parity with the state's forces, the revolution enters into the "mobile war" phase, a blend of conventional war and guerrilla actions. Finally, in the third phase, the military arm of the revolution becomes stronger than the government forces and enters into the "offensive" stage, where it uses large conventional forces to do battle with the state forces. Military *dau tranh* culminates, in Giap's strategy, with the "General Counteroffensive" by which the government forces are totally defeated and the State is overthrown. Revolutionary War is by its nature a protracted war. The revolutionary needs time to build his forces. The protracted war erodes the morale and resolution of the revolutionary's enemy.

While in theory there is a steady progression from the first phase to the third, in practice this did not necessarily occur. Due to changing factors in the combat situation, the revolutionary force might find it necessary or desirable to reverse the progression—for example, to move from conventional war back to a form of guerrilla war following a major defeat. Giap's own operations illustrate the progression and retrogression of phases. In 1944 he started by executing guerrilla actions in remote areas of the China/Vietnam border. By 1945 he had amassed a sizable guerrilla force. Thereafter, he transformed the guerrilla force into a conventional force which in 1954 won the battle of Dien Bien Phu by waging a conventional campaign, while conducting guerrilla operations and mobile war elsewhere in Vietnam. In the war against the Americans and South Vietnamese (Indochina War II), the North Vietnamese/Viet Cong force again went from small-scale guerrilla actions in 1957–1960, to conventional operations in the early sixties, to a stand-up conventional war against the United States/RVN forces in 1964–1968, culminating in the defeat of the Communist "General Offensive" launched at Tet in 1968. As a result of that defeat, Giap reversed the theoretical progression back to a form of guerrilla warfare, but one carried out by Regular, commando-type forces. By 1972 Giap had rebuilt his forces and again launched a conventional campaign which was again defeated. After another lull, in late 1974 Giap entered the final "General Offensive" phase by launching a massive conventional campaign of (eventually) twenty-two divisions which overthrew the Thieu government and brought victory to North Vietnam.

Political *dau tranh* encompasses a much broader spectrum of nonmilitary weapons than the term would imply to Westerners. Included in the term political *dau tranh* are not only political and diplomatic weapons, but psychological, ideological, sociological, and economic weapons as well. Political *dau tranh* consists of three separate programs: first, action among the people and troops in Communist-controlled areas; second, action against the enemy soldiers, called "troop proselyting"; and third, action among the enemy people. All of these campaigns employ a mixture of terrorism, subversion, propaganda, diplomacy, disinformation, riots, and uprisings to weaken the enemy's will to resist and to strengthen the revolutionary force's will to victory.

The first arm of political *dau tranh* is called *dan van,* action among the people controlled by the Communists. The main purpose of this program is to organize the masses and develop a hierarchical organization to control and manipulate the people. Douglas Pike believes that the secret of success of *dan van* is the Communists' ability to mobilize the people and use them as a political weapon.[38] Every device of propaganda, including agitation, indoctrination, education, and intimidation, is used to bring the people under Communist control to a heightened commitment to the revolutionary cause. *Dan van* includes an intensive program among the military forces of the revolution, which in the North Vietnamese Army (NVA) was particularly effective.

The second program, *binh van* (action among the enemy military), aims at lowering the effectiveness of the government's forces by getting

the government's soldiers to defect or desert. During Indochina War II
the Communists used 12,000 special cadres in an effort to subvert South
Vietnamese troops.[39] These agents tried to spread demoralizing rumors,
to exploit kinship and friendship, and to reward those who defected or
deserted.

The last program of political *dau tranh* is *dich van* (action among
the enemy people). Its purpose is to spread dissent, disloyalty, and confusion among the enemy populace. Some of the devices used to spread
propaganda are mass media leaflets, posters, cartoons, radio broadcasts,
rumors, even touring shows and plays. "Struggle meetings" in which
specially trained Communist cadre covertly lecture villagers in the government-controlled areas were a common, and effective, means. The cadres
staged mass demonstrations, some taking advantage of real causes, others
exploiting manipulated causes, to show the peasants the power of mass
organization. These *dich van* activities followed a pattern of increasing
militancy. Eventually, the initial dissent was supposed to turn into demonstrations, the demonstrations into "uprisings" (a revolt of the people
in a given area against the government), and the uprisings were to culmi-
nate in the "General Uprising," in which the people arose and overthrew
the government.

The North Vietnamese *dich van* program (action among the enemy)
was changed significantly by the passage of events. Until the spring of
1968 the *dich van* program concentrated exclusively on the people under
the control of the government of South Vietnam. When the Politburo
in Hanoi saw that the Communists' military defeat in the Tet offensive
turned into a psychological victory for them within the United States,
they discerned that their program of *dich van* could be employed effectively against the people of the United States. Hanoi saw something
even beyond that unexpected revelation. It saw that *Indochina War II
could be won in the United States* through the news media, academia,
the antiwar dissenters, and Congress itself. In mid-1968 Hanoi began
an intensive and calculated program within the United States to undermine
American public support for the war. After the signing of the Paris
Agreement in 1973, the North Vietnamese and their American allies
were even more successful in sapping American support for the Thieu
government and in preventing the reentry of American forces into
the war to enforce the postwar settlement which the United States had
guaranteed.

Dich van works best in a "protracted war." Words become weapons, and ambiguities confuse the target people. They see no end to the fighting, no respite from the killing, and no positive gains as the result of battles and campaigns. They begin to question the motives which led to the war and then the truthfulness and competency of the leaders conducting it. Soon they question the morality of the war, and then the war becomes not only unwinnable but immoral as well, providing the justification and excuse for surrender to the enemy.

As both the military and political arms of *dau tranh* theoretically progress through discernable phases, so does the combination of the two. In the early days of a people's war, the revolutionaries place heavy emphasis on political *dau tranh,* not only because the military arm is weak, but because the first requirement of a revolution is a firm political base among the people. As the revolution progresses, the emphasis normally shifts gradually from political *dau tranh* to military *dau tranh.* Again, however, events may cause the emphasis to swing back toward the political. This determination of the weight of effort and resources to be applied to military and political *dau tranh* is the essential problem inherent in Giap's strategy of revolutionary war and through the years generated many violent and critical arguments within Hanoi's Politburo.

This integrated strategy produced by Giap, Ho, and Chinh demanded intense unity of effort and required a new and special kind of leader, one who was a combination soldier, statesman, politician, and psychologist. And in North Vietnam such leaders were found. Ho was one. Le Duan, who took Ho's mantle, made military as well as political decisions for two decades. Truong Chinh, never an active soldier, was both a military theorist and a political leader, and in 1986 he appeared on a platform in Hanoi in the uniform of a North Vietnamese general. Gen. Nguyen Chi Thanh had been a political officer of Thua Thien province in South Vietnam during Indochina War I and was later a military commander in the South. Giap, the general, was also a consummate politician, a former Cabinet officer, and a diplomat who in 1946 negotiated at length with the French.

This duality of outlook and action carried down into the lowest ranks of the North Vietnamese Army and its political infrastructure. The privates of the NVA were indoctrinated constantly in the correct conduct towards the civilian population, in their duty to assist the people, and in the simple measures to be used to propagandize the masses.

The political cadres within the army were the best soldiers of their units and participated in all military decisions. The political cadres outside the army were often not only officials in the political infrastructure, but guerrilla leaders as well.

Giap's preparatory period as a general came to an end in August 1945. He would have a little over a year of essentially civilian duties (as minister of the interior) before he would have to buckle on again the general's sword in combat against the French.

What had his overall preparation for generalship been? In short, not much. Giap had no formal military education, although he had acquired a good amount of book learning about revolution and warfare. He had gained a little combat experience, most of that as a small-unit guerrilla commander. Giap's comparative lack of military experience becomes more apparent when we contrast his military background in 1945 with that of four of his future adversaries—two French generals, de Lattre and Navarre (both much older than Giap), and two Americans, Westmoreland and Abrams (both about Giap's age).

In 1945 Jean de Tassigny de Lattre stood at the crest of his distinguished military career. He had been an outstanding company and field grade officer in World War I. In 1940 he had been one of the few French generals to command a division successfully in the French debacle. He had returned to France in 1944 at the head of the First French Army, the largest French combat force in the war after the French defeat of 1940. He was a contemporary of Montgomery and Patton, the equal of these two superstars, not only in age and rank, but in ability as well.

General Henri Navarre finished World War II as a colonel commanding an armored regiment in the French 5th Armored Division. He was a graduate of St. Cyr and the French Staff College, a recognized intelligence expert, and a brilliant staff officer.

In 1945 General William Childs Westmoreland came out of World War II as a colonel and the chief of staff of the U.S. 9th Infantry Division. He was a West Point graduate (class of 1936) and had acquired vast experience in modern triphibious warfare as a commander and staff officer in the North African and European Theaters. He had already caught the eye of most of the postwar leaders of the American army as a young officer destined for high command.

Finally, there was Gen. Creighton W. Abrams, like Westmoreland a graduate of West Point's class of 1936. He had emerged from World War II as a colonel and its outstanding battlefield commander of armored forces. He had commanded the armored combat command (brigade) which had relieved the paratroopers at Bastogne, and by the end of World War II his battlefield courage and skill had become legendary in the American army.

Compared to these four officers, Giap was a neophyte. In his book *General Giap, Politician and Strategist,* Robert J. O'Neill sums up Giap's expertise this way: "We see Giap in 1945 as an officer with the background of a major, about to commence the tasks of a major general."[40] In fact, O'Neill probably overrates Giap's experience and certainly underrates the task which would confront him. Regardless of the level of Giap's experience in 1945, in 1946 he would be coping with the responsibilities, not of a major general, but of a four-star theater commander. Military command, be it of a company, regiment, or an army, is a constant learning experience, often painful; and Giap would learn—painfully.

Notes—Chapter 1

1. Robert J. O'Neill, *General Giap, Politician and Strategist* (New York: Frederick A. Praeger, 1969), p. 1.
2. Hoang Van Chi, *From Colonialism to Communism: A Case History of North Vietnam* (New York: Frederick A. Praeger, 1964), p. 18.
3. Vo Nguyen Giap, *The Military Art of People's War,* ed. Russell Stetler (New York: Monthly Review Press, 1970), p. 42.
4. Joseph Buttinger, *Vietnam: A Dragon Embattled,* 2 vols. (New York: Frederick A. Praeger, 1967), 1:227.
5. Giap, *Military Art,* p. 42.
6. Ibid.
7. Wilfred G. Burchett, *Vietnam Will Win* (New York: Monthly Review Press, 1970), p. 173.
8. Giap, *Military Art,* p. 40.
9. Oriana Fallaci, *Interview with History* (Milan: Rizzoli, 1974; trans. by John Shepley, Liveright Publishing Corp., 1976), p. 79.
10. Giap, *Military Art,* p. 48.
11. Chi, *Colonialism,* p. 125.
12. Giap, *Military Art,* p. 52.
13. Napoleon Bonaparte, *Maxims* (LXXVIII), collected by the USMA in a pamphlet, *Jomini, Clausewitz, and Schlieffen,* 1951, p. 92.
14. Bernard Montgomery, *Paths of Leadership* (New York: G. P. Putnam, 1961), p. 28.
15. Vo Nguyen Giap, *Banner of People's War, The Party's Military Line* (New York: Frederick A. Praeger, 1970), pp. 3 and 26.
16. Ibid., p. 68.
17. Ibid., *Banner,* p. 6.
18. Ibid., p. 66.
19. Giap, *Military Art,* p. 77.
20. Ibid., p. 74.
21. Ibid., p. 78.
22. David Shub, *Lenin, A Biography* (Baltimore, MD: Penguin Books, 1966), pp. 37–39.
23. Mao Tse-tung, *On the Protracted War,* Eng. trans. (Peking: People's Publishing House, 1960), p. 88.
24. Vo Nguyen Giap, *People's War, People's Army. The Viet Cong Insurrection Manual for Underdeveloped Countries* (New York: Frederick A. Praeger, 1962), p. 68.
25. Mao, *Protracted War,* p. 53.

26. T. E. Lawrence, *Seven Pillars of Wisdom* (New York: Dell Publishing, 1966), p. 200.
27. Ibid., p. 198.
28. Theodore Ayrault Dodge, *Great Captains* (New York: Houghton Mifflin, 1889), p. 213.
29. Ibid.
30. Mao Tse-tung, *Mao Tse-Tung, An Anthology of his Writings*, ed. Anne Freemantle (New York: The New American Library of Literature, 1962), p. 82.
31. Jules Roy, *The Battle of Dien Bien Phu*, trans. by Robert Baldick (New York: Harper & Row, 1965), p. 315.
32. O'Neill, *Giap*, p. 32.
33. Giap, *Military Art*, p. 70.
34. Buttinger, *Dragon Embattled*, 1:299; and O'Neill, *Giap*, p. 35.
35. Giap, *Banner*, p. 47.
36. Douglas Pike, *PAVN: People's Army of Vietnam* (Novato, CA: Presidio Press, 1986), p. 213. Much of what follows is taken from Pike's works on Vietnamese communism.
37. John Shy and Thomas W. Collier, "Revolutionary War" in *Makers of Modern Strategy*, ed. Peter Paret (Princeton, NJ: Princeton University Press, 1968), p. 817.
38. Pike, *PAVN*, pp. 215 and 247.
39. Ibid., p. 244.
40. O'Neill, *Giap*, p. 33.

2 The French Campaign

1946–1947

The distinctive natural characteristics of Vietnam and its neighbors have exerted a profound influence on military operations in all Indochina wars. These natural characteristics (geography, topography, climate, transportation facilities, vegetation, and demography) have had significant impact on such key decisions as when and where to fight, how to fight, and how to supply and support combat operations. They must be understood by anyone seeking to comprehend the "why" of the tactics and strategies of the wars waged for so many years in the Indochina peninsula.

Vietnam is located on the east side of the Indochinese peninsula between 9° and 23° North latitude. Approximately 850 miles long (from north to south), it varies in width from 50 to 350 miles. Its area encompasses about 330,000 square miles. Vietnam's shape is described by Giap as "Stretching like an immense **S** along the edge of the Pacific, it includes Bac Bo or North Vietnam, which with the Red River Delta, is a region rich in agricultural and industrial possibilities; Nam Bo or South Vietnam, a vast alluvial plain furrowed by the arms of the Mekong and especially favorable to agriculture, and Trung Bo, or Central Vietnam, a long narrow belt of land joining them."[1]

Vietnam is bordered on the north by China and on the west by Laos and Cambodia. Vietnam's geographic location gave the North Vietnamese tremendous military advantages. In the early forties, south China provided Giap sanctuary from the French and Japanese. There he fashioned the Communist forces which in 1945 seized temporary control of Vietnam. After 1949 China became a vast "rear area" of logistical support for the Vietminh. Without a friendly China located adjacent to North Vietnam, there would have been little chance for a Vietminh victory against the French, and later against the Americans and South Vietnamese. The location of Laos and Cambodia immediately to the west of Vietnam provided Giap and the North Vietnamese additional advantages. In the French/Vietminh War, the French were forced to defend Laos and Cambodia for political reasons. By threatening Laos, Giap compelled the French to dispatch troops from Vietnam to Laos, thus weakening the garrisons in Vietnam which Giap then attacked. In Indochina War II the geographical location of Laos and Cambodia, plus their inability or unwillingness to deny the North Vietnamese Communists the use of their territory, gave Giap and the North Vietnamese inviolable sanctuaries in which to retreat and a channel from the north through which a vast river of supplies flowed to the North Vietnamese and Viet Cong forces.

⤬   Four of Vietnam's other natural characteristics have military significance. These are the topography, the climate, the vegetation, and the transportation system. The topography of Vietnam presents difficulties for conventional ground operations. Throughout more than half of its territory, Vietnam is a country of hills and heavily forested highlands, ill-suited to human occupancy. The Annamite chain of low mountains runs out of China and continues for two-thirds of the length of Vietnam, a spine along the western edge of the country. The mountains, while not high by American or European criteria, are steep and overgrown with jungle. The narrow, largely impassable roads and trails make good ambush country. Large-scale military operations, particularly with motorized or mechanized equipment, are difficult, and in most areas impossible. In many mountainous areas the *Karst,* tall limestone pinnacles peculiar to the area, contain numerous caves large enough to house storage depots and sizable staffs, and Giap used them as headquarters on several occasions.

Other major topographical features are the deltas formed by the Red River in the north and the Mekong in the south, along with the narrow coastal plains connecting these two great deltas. The two river plains are highly cultivated and among the most densely populated areas in the world. The plains are flat with only the most minor variations of elevation, and they are subject to annual flooding. The predominant military feature of the Red River Delta are the dikes which channel the Red River and its major tributaries. Having been built up through the centuries, the dikes carry the river above the surrounding plain. These dikes constituted a major military vulnerability. Although immense in construction (often over forty feet thick) United States intelligence officers who have studied them believe they could have been breached by ''iron bombs.'' If breached, Hanoi and the populous area surrounding that city would be flooded, forcing a relocation of Hanoi's governmental, military, and industrial establishment.

The Mekong Delta in South Vietnam is a maze of canals, streams, and ditches. During the Southwest Monsoon (mid-May to mid-October) it is almost totally submerged. During this period, mechanized operations are impossible off the roads and difficult on them. During the dry season (mid-October to mid-May) the area becomes hard and trafficable; however, mechanized equipment can move across country only with difficulty due to the numerous ditches and canals. The many streams and canals of the Mekong place a premium on amphibious and water-borne mobility and on helicopter operations. A great deal of the movement in the Mekong area is by small boat and river craft. The United States Navy formed its Riverine Force to control the enemy's use of boats and to provide offensive mobility to United States forces in the Delta. In either the wet or dry seasons, helicopters provided their users both tactical and strategical mobility along the flooded Mekong. Actually, United States Special Force units in the misnamed Plain of Reeds—in the wet season it is a vast lake—built entire camps on oil drum floats, including helicopter landing pads.

Vietnam's climate is subtropical, with high and unpleasant humidity throughout the year. The dominant climatic feature is the alternating flow of the Southwest and Northeast Monsoons. The Southwest Monsoon blows in across the Gulf of Thailand (Siam) starting about mid-May. It brings heavy rains to the Mekong Delta and to those other parts of Vietnam not sheltered behind to the east of the Annamite chain. The Southwest Monsoon crosses Vietnam, swings to the north as it strikes the Gulf of Tonkin and moves into the Red River Delta, making that area subject to its influence. It blows itself out about mid-October. The Northeast Monsoon (far less powerful than the Southwest Monsoon) begins about the middle of September and ends between the middle and end of December. It strikes those areas along the middle coast between Vinh and Nha Trang. The Northeast Monsoon brings not only rain, but drizzle and fog, which the French called *crachin,* or ''spit.''

The monsoons, particularly the Southwest Monsoon, have a predominant impact on all military operations. The Vietminh, and later the Viet Cong and North Vietnamese, preferred to suspend large-scale operations during the Southwest Monsoon. Despite the fact that the weather provided concealment from French or American air power, the difficulty of movements and the debilitating effect of the heavy rain on health and morale persuaded the North Vietnamese that operations during this period should be held to a minimum.

The impact of the monsoons on the operations initiated by the Vietnamese Communists is readily evident. The Vietnamese Communists planned their offensives against both the French and the Americans by the "campaign season" which they called "the winter-spring" season or the period from roughly mid-October to mid-May. A study of the offensives launched by the Vietminh against the French between September 1952 and July 1954, for example, shows that the Vietminh initiated nineteen out of a total of twenty-six attacks during the dry of "winter-spring" season. Of the seven wet season offensives undertaken, four were continuations of dry season attacks which, like Dien Bien Phu, could not be easily broken off.[2] A climatological study of both monsoons shows that there is one period when there is good campaigning weather throughout Vietnam. This is the period from about 1 January to about 15 May. It was during this period that the North Vietnamese Army/ Viet Cong (NVA/VC) launched both the Tet offensive of 1968, the so-called Easter offensive of 1972, and the final offensive of 1975.

The monsoons hampered French and American operations at least as much as they hindered the Vietnamese Communists. The rain and fog closed down offensive air operations, limited aerial observation, made motorized movement on roads difficult, and made off-road movement impossible. The rains and the mud brought to the French and the Americans as well as to their adversaries the same problems of poor health and morale, although to a lesser degree, since the Americans in particular could protect themselves from the elements by adequate housing and special clothing.

The third terrain feature of military significance in Vietnam is its vegetation. About 80 percent of the country is covered by forests varying from dense to moderately open. The forested areas of Vietnam, with their triple-canopied coverage, significantly aided the Vietminh, the Viet Cong and the North Vietnamese. The trees provided concealment from aerial observation of Communist troop concentrations, supply depots, troop movements, and positions. The undergrowth of vines, bamboo, shrubs, and grass made cross-country movement difficult and observation extremely limited—good ambush country. The mangrove swamps southeast of Saigon and on the Cao Mao peninsula at the southern tip of the country are impassable except by small boats, and they offered sanctuary to guerrilla forces for decades.

⋎ The final feature of Vietnam's environment bearing on military operations is its transportation system. Vietnam has several good ports. In South Vietnam there are Saigon, Da Nang, Qui Nhon, and Cam Ranh Bay. The latter, one of the best natural harbors in the world, at one time during World War II sheltered a major portion of the Japanese fleet. In North Vietnam, Haiphong, Hon Gay, and the Cam Pha port complex gave the French adequate port facilities during Indochina War I, and permitted the Russians to pour supplies into Communist North Vietnam during Indochina War II. This dependence of the North Vietnamese on the port of Haiphong, however, constituted a military weakness. While the Chinese supplied the North Vietnamese largely by road and rail, the Russians depended on Haiphong to off-load their logistical support. The closing of the port in 1972 by United States Navy mining operations was a significant factor in obtaining North Vietnamese agreements to the Paris Accords signed that year.

The ground transportation system was, and is, primitive. The Americans improved a few main roads, but otherwise there were no highways worthy of the name. Most of the roads were little better than tracks. Through the years bridges had been demolished, and in the mountains, landslides had covered the roads. Almost all of them had become overgrown and full of deep holes and ruts. The one railroad running from Saigon to Hanoi and thence into China had been built by the French in colonial times. In South Vietnam, despite French and American efforts, the railroad was never able to carry a significant part of the logistical burden, due to maintenance problems and enemy sabotage. In Indochina War II the railroad in North Vietnam was constantly cut by United States air strikes.

In view of the conditions of Vietnam's surface transportation system, almost all long-distance movement of people and a significant part of the logistical support in South Vietnam had to be by air. Both the French and later the Americans built scores of small airfields and several large airports. The Americans developed and perfected heliborne offensive and support operations. Without air transport (both rotary and fixed-wing), United States operations in Vietnam would have been vastly different, and at best, only marginally effective. Without the advantages of air mobility, the peak United States strength figures of 550,000 in 1968–1969 would have been sufficient only to defend American bases and to mount minor, short-range offensives into the inhospitable countryside.

In summary, the natural characteristics of the area of Giap's operations generally favored the defensive (particularly ambush and evasive actions) over the offensive. It conferred advantages on lightly armed, primarily foot infantry or guerrilla forces over heavily mechanized and motorized forces. The terrain, weather, vegetation, and road net limited the tactical application of air power, armor, and motorized forces, but the lack of a good road net gave the advantage in strategic mobility to the Americans with their cargo aircraft and helicopters. Vietnam's geographical location permitted use of Red China as a base of supplies and in some cases a training area, while Laos and Cambodia furnished not only an attack-free sanctuary against the Americans (until 1970), but an overland route and sea access from North Vietnam to their forces in the South.

In addition to looking at the strength of the Vietminh forces in 1947, one must look at their composition and organization, for they vary significantly from the armies of the West. From 1945 until their final victory in 1975, the Vietnamese Communist military machine was divided into three groups of vastly different combat capabilities. During this thirty-year period there were evolutionary changes of sizable dimensions as Communist armed power grew, but these three groupings remained constant.

First, there were the Main Force units. In Indochina War I they were the Regular units of Vietminh forces who fought the French, and in Indochina War II they were the Regulars of the North Vietnamese Army and Viet Cong who battled the Americans and South Vietnamese. These troops did the large-unit fighting. The size, equipment, and organization of the Main Force units varied, from Giap's ill-equipped platoon of 1944 to the division, corps, and ''Front'' size units of 1954–1975, complete with armor, artillery, air units, and a sophisticated antiaircraft system. Regardless of their size or armament, the Main Force units always functioned directly under the commander in chief of the army or a designated Front or area commander. They were well trained, well led, professional, and courageous.

The second grouping of Communist forces were the Regional or Local Forces. These were semiregular, second-line troops recruited from a given province or district. They approximated roughly the unfederalized National Guard units in the United States. The Regional Forces were broken into two groups. First, there were those recruited from, and operating in, a province (roughly equivalent to a United States state). These provincial forces were usually of battalion size, fairly well armed, and well organized. The second category of Regional Forces were those raised within a given district (equivalent to a county) and they operated within that district. These forces were less well armed and organized than the Provincial Forces and had less military capability.

The commander in chief in Hanoi exercised command over the Local Forces through the Interzone, a territorial command which included several provinces. The Interzone dealt not only with military operations, recruiting, and supply, but with political and economic matters as well, including elections, assassinations, propaganda, food, and taxation. In the war against the French, the Vietminh used five Interzones, later called Military Regions (MR's). Four were in North Vietnam, and one, MR V, was in northern South Vietnam. During the war against the Americans, the number of MR's was expanded to ten, the additional ones covering the rest of South Vietnam.

The Regional Forces varied in combat capability. Some, like those around Da Nang, gave a consistently good account of themselves for two decades. Others were ineffectual. They were rifle-grenade-machine gun outfits with little staying power or long-distance mobility. Their main function was to protect an area, to reconnoiter in advance of the Main Force units, and to act as a screen for them. They made small attacks and counterattacks and set up ambushes when enemy troops invaded their area.

The last grouping of forces was the guerrillas (or Popular Forces). These were raised by villages and hamlets. The guerrillas were divided into two subgroups: the *Dan Quan,* which included both sexes and all ages, and the *Dan Quan Du Kich,* which included men from eighteen to forty-five. The *Dan Quan* had no combat capability. The *Du Kich* carried out combat operations. They were poorly armed, without uniforms, working in the paddies by day and occasionally attacking enemy outposts at night. They laid booby traps, "prepared the battlefield" in advance of Main Force units, and acted as intelligence agents and porters for Main and Regional Force units. The guerrillas, too, were controlled and commanded from Hanoi through the Interzone, province, and district chain of command.[3]

A unique feature of the Vietnamese Communist military organization was its recruiting or "promotion" policy. A soldier started his military career as a guerrilla. The guerrillas furnished their most promising men to the Regional Forces. The Regional Forces seasoned the men further, and those that made good were in turn "promoted" to the Main Forces. Thus, the Main Forces received a trained, and often veteran, recruit. This system had obvious merits, but it had serious disadvantages as well. In the event of heavy casualties to either the Regional or Main Force troops, the guerrilla units were drained to fill the two more combat-ready groups. For example, when all three groups took heavy casualties during the Tet offensive of 1968, the draw-down on the guerrilla forces practically destroyed their combat capability.

The size of the Vietminh forces in 1946–1947 is in question, as it was throughout both Indochina War I and later in Indochina War II. Robert J. O'Neill sets the strength of the Vietminh force of 1947 at around 60,000.[4] Bernard B. Fall states it was about 50,000, mostly guerrillas.[5] Buttinger claims that the Vietminh forces were comprised of 60,000 men in Main Force units, with a total strength, including Regional Forces and guerrillas, of 100,000.[6] A reconciliation of these reports indicate that the Vietminh probably had around 50,000 in Main Force units and an undetermined number, probably 30,000 to 50,000, Regional Forces and guerrillas.

In early 1947 the French had approximately 115,000 troops in all of Indochina.[7] They were well armed, supported by armor and air power. Their leaders had been battle tested in World War II, and the soldiers were experienced and professional. In spite of their strengths, the French in Indochina had serious weaknesses. From the start France supported the war in an uncertain and half-hearted manner. In 1946 and 1947 the nation was still recovering from the economical and psychological trauma inflicted by its defeat by the Germans in 1940, and its efforts in Indochina suffered always from their limitations of money, men, and above all, willpower.

⫝ While the Vietminh had numerical superiority in North Vietnam, they too suffered from serious military deficiencies. Their leaders and staffs, from Giap down, were inexperienced and untried, and the men were woefully underequipped. They had no armor, no artillery, no air support, and no logistic or signal communication system worthy of the name. The force was totally untrained in large operations, its largest unit being a battalion of around 1,000 men. On the other hand, the Vietminh had several significant advantages. First, they were fighting in their own country, for their own independence, and they had most of the people on their side. This idea of national freedom and independence, plus a most effective propaganda and indoctrination program, gave the Vietminh a priceless asset—high morale. Second, the physical characteristics of the area, particularly the terrain, weather, vegetation, and road network, favored the defense and guerrilla-type operations of the Vietminh. The Vietminh knew the country and were acclimated to its debilitating conditions. Third, the large size of the area of combat, coupled with the numerical limitations of the French forces, made guerrilla operations difficult to counter. If the French spread out to control the countryside, they subjected themselves to defeat in small detachments. If they concentrated around the key population centers, they surrendered the rural areas to the Vietminh. There was a fourth Vietminh advantage—the location of the Viet Bac (the Vietminh base area) adjacent to China. This factor gave them a priceless sanctuary and logistic base. The Viet Bac/China sanctuary provided a source of arms and equipment, training areas, and above all, defensive locations for the organs of the Vietminh government.

⫝ An examination of the strengths and weaknesses of the adversaries shows that the factor of *time* determined the strategies of both sides. The French had to defeat the Vietminh as quickly as possible, before the French long-range vulnerabilities, political, psychological, and financial, brought them down. On the other hand, the Vietminh had to prolong the war to exploit to the maximum the political and psychological infirmities of the French and to overcome their own initial inferiority of armament and military experience. The French needed a quick victory; the Vietminh needed a protracted war.

Of course, each contender sought to gain his own objective. Although the operational concepts of the French varied from time to time, their aim always was to bring about one big engagement, a "live-or-die" battle in which France's military might would destroy the Main Forces of the Vietminh. This was the underlying French concept from General Valluy's campaign of 1947 to General Navarre's plan for operations in 1953 and 1954.

On the Vietminh side, they sought throughout the early years of 1947 to 1950 to avoid a major engagement, giving them time to build up their Main Force units and maintain this Regular army as a force-in-being. Meanwhile, the Vietminh militia and guerrillas would harass and wear down the French, and if possible, keep them from the regions that were important to the Communists as sources of food, manpower, and other support.

From the start of Indochina War I, the main area of contention was in North Vietnam, principally the Red River Delta and the country north and west of it. There was Hanoi, the capital; there was the agricultural and industrial wealth coveted by both sides; and there was the mass of the population of around six to seven million people. There also were the major concentrations of Vietminh strength and the center of French military power. There in North Vietnam, Indochina War I would be lost and won.

Operations 19 December 1946–31 January 1947

The wars which ravaged Indochina for three decades were all marked by a series of curious and fundamental ambiguities. So it was with the origins of Indochina War I. Even now a dispute smolders as to who started the French/Vietminh War and when it began. The Vietminh claimed that the war started on 20 November 1946, when the French attacked a junk in Haiphong harbor suspected of carrying arms to the Vietminh. Heavy fighting followed. After a cease-fire on 21 November, the French sent an ultimatum to the Vietminh demanding that they get out of Haiphong. On 23 November the Vietminh refused, and the French bombarded the Vietnamese section of Haiphong with tanks, artillery, and warships, "to teach the Vietminh a good lesson" as the French commander in chief Gen. Jean Etienne Valluy told the local French commander over the radio.[8] Vietnamese casualties were heavy. The French say 6,000, the Vietminh claim 20,000. Desultory and unsuccessful negotiations for a cease-fire between the two parties continued well into December. According to the French, the war began on 19 December 1946, when the French demanded that the Vietminh Self Defense Forces in Hanoi be disarmed. The Vietminh reply was to launch a sneak attack on the French at eight o'clock that night in Hanoi, followed by Giap's radio broadcast of a national call to arms at nine-thirty. In either case, Indochina War I had begun.

The truth is that after the breakdown of the Dalat and Fontaine-bleau conferences held in mid-1946 to negotiate a settlement, both sides concluded that the war was inevitable. The French were not prepared to grant the Vietnamese the full independence they wanted, and the Vietminh would settle for nothing less. An armed collision became inevitable.

The fighting in Hanoi which began on 19 December 1946 was fierce, the battle lasting through January 1947. Throughout the rest of Vietnam, conflicts of varying intensity broke out, and a pattern quickly emerged. The French drove the Vietminh from the cities and villages into the mountains and jungles. By the end of March 1947, the French controlled the major cities and their connecting roads as well as the coastal and delta areas of both northern Vietnam (Tonkin) and central Vietnam (Annam). Their control over the cities and towns in southern Vietnam (old French Cochin China), while always tenuous, had already been established.

By the end of January 1947, the Vietminh forces and governmental headquarters had retreated from Hanoi into the Viet Bac, the Vietminh base area north of Hanoi near the China border. Giap knew the country well, as he and Ho had operated there during World War II. This area is made up of extremely rugged hills, with steep valleys abounding with caves. It is subject to the Southwest Monsoon and receives about sixty inches of rain between the months of May and October, making military operations almost impossible during this period. For military uses, roads in the Viet Bac were almost nonexistent. Cart paths and trails were frequent, but even National Route 3, the main road in the area, was a one-lane track with weak bridges, replete with potential ambush sites.

With the French occupying the populated lowlands and with Giap and the Vietminh "holed up" in the Viet Bac redoubt, the stage was set for the second act of Indochina War I.

Operations March 1947—31 December 1947

By early March 1947, the French had cleared Hanoi, Haiphong, Hue, and the other major towns of Vietminh, and they had established tenuous control over the Red River Delta, the coastal plains of Annam, and most of Cochin China. By the time the French had completed their consolidation, only two months remained before the onset of the Southwest Monsoon in mid-May, when military operations would be washed out by the violent rains. The French elected not to attack in the spring of 1947. Thus Giap and the Vietminh gained the period from March until October or November to prepare for the French offensive which would come in the fall of 1947.

In view of the fact that the French wanted a quick victory, their failure to move in March–May of 1947 has confounded observers. The French have never given any reason, but the factors which argued for a delay are apparent. First, there still remained some "tidying up" (Montgomery's well-known phrase) to be done in the cities, the populated lowlands, and along the communications routes joining them. Second, it takes time—much more than the amateur strategist thinks—to reposition troops and to reorient and stock the logistic system to support a new operation. Apparently the French thought that these preparations could not be made and still allow sufficient time for the completion of the offensive before the arrival of the monsoon. The third factor which pushed the French toward the delay was their contempt for the fighting qualities of the Vietminh and their leader, Giap. They even refused to call him *General* Giap, or if they did give him his rank, they did so derisively. The French casually decided that Giap and his forces in the Viet Bac presented no major problem, certainly not one which could not wait until October 1947. This underestimation of Giap and the Vietminh was a major error by General Valluy, the French commander, and he would pay for it.

Gen. Jean Etienne Valluy was the first of the French commanders who attempted to defeat Giap, and he established the pattern of errors which fate decreed that—with one exception—his successors would repeat. Like those who would follow him, he was a competent, highly decorated, and eminently successful general. When Valluy went to Indochina he was forty-six years old, a rising star in the French army, with a distinguished background. In 1917, at the age of eighteen, he joined the French army as a private. After a few months of front-line action in World War I, he won an appointment to St. Cyr, the French military academy. Valluy graduated from St. Cyr in 1918, went back to the trenches, and before the war ended had accumulated a wound stripe and a *Croix de Guerre*. Between World Wars I and II he held routine staff and command jobs, the latter usually with Senegalese or Moroccan troops.

When World War II broke out, Valluy was a major and operations officer of the French XXI Corps. He was taken prisoner in 1940 and repatriated in 1941. By 1944 he had become a brigadier general and chief of staff of de Lattre's First French Army in Europe. In 1945 he took command of the 9th Colonial Infantry Division, where he forged an excellent combat reputation as a hard-driving division commander against stubborn German opposition. Valluy entered the Indochina picture early in 1946 as the commandant of the French troops which went into Tonkin and later into Laos. On 20 February 1947, he was promoted to lieutenant general and made commander in chief of the French troops in Indochina. He was the first French general Giap would defeat.

In the summer of 1947, Valluy had no inkling of the reverses awaiting him. He had a job to do, and he went about it boldly and confidently. There were, as always, complications. Valluy had a major problem— for several reasons he had to win a quick and total victory over the Vietminh in the fall of 1947. First, he was under increasing political pressure from France to show "results" and to win a notable success. Furthermore, he realized that the longer he waited before attacking, the stronger Giap and the Vietminh would become. The main goad for speed, however, lay to the north, because Nationalist China was beginning to crumble. The arrival of the Chinese Communists on Vietnam's northern border would give the Vietminh a "rear base" to use as a sanctuary, a training area, and a logistics stockpile. Valluy had to strike hard and quickly.

Valluy's concept for his offensive, nicknamed Operation LEA, envisioned a combined airborne, amphibious, and overland assault on the Vietminh governmental and military headquarters located in the grubby little Viet Bac village of Bac Kan. With a force of sixteen battalions, Valluy intended to surround Giap's forces. O'Neill says Valluy had 15,000 troops.[9] Buttinger says he had 30,000.[10] One pincer with ten battalions (three infantry, three armored, three artillery, and one engineer

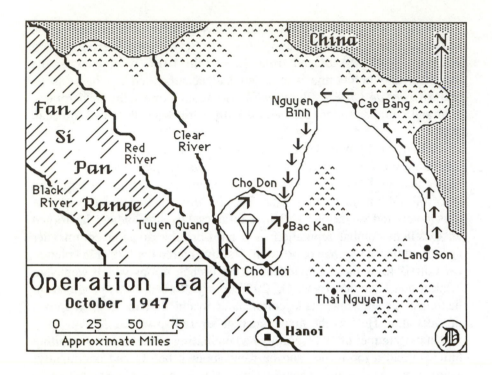

Fan
Si
Pan
Range

Clear
River

Red
River

Black
River

Tuyen Quang

China

N

Nguyen
Binh

Cao Bang

Cho Don

Bac Kan

Cho Moi

Lang Son

Thai Nguyen

Hanoi

Operation Lea

October 1947

0   25   50   75

Approximate Miles

battalion) would move by road from Lang Son to Cao Bang, from there
west to Nguyen Binh, and then south to Bac Kan, the terrain objective
of the entire operation. The plan required the force to travel a road
distance of some 140 miles. The second task force of three infantry
battalions and an artillery battalion would move by naval landing craft
up the Clear River to Tuyen Quang, then up the Song Gam as far as
possible, eventually attacking the Bac Kan area from the west and south.
Two parachute battalions (1,100 men) were to initiate the operation by
dropping directly on Bac Kan, on Cho Don (twelve miles west of Bac
Kan) and on Cho Moi (twenty miles to the south of the principal objective).
The paratroopers would be relieved by the forces moving overland from
the north and southwest.

Operation LEA began on 7 October with the parachute drop on
Bac Kan and vicinity, and just missed the big prize. The airborne assault
surprised Giap and Ho in their headquarters, and the French had them
in their fingertips. In fact, the French captured the letters on Ho's desk.[11]
The two Communist leaders barely had time to jump into a camouflaged

hole nearby while French paratroopers searched the bushes around and over their heads. The lucky escape of Ho and Giap underscores the fact that the destiny of nations—like that of individuals—sometimes turns on nothing more than the accidents of fate. Had the French captured these two men, would Vietnam have been spared thirty years of bloodshed and destruction? Would France and the United States have escaped the divisiveness of national spirit and the trauma of defeat? Unfortunately history never answers these "what-if" questions.

The near success of the paratroopers marked the high point of Valluy's offensive. After that everything went downhill. After Ho and Giap escaped, they rallied the Vietminh troops, and by the next day the Vietminh were battling the airborne troopers on even terms. In another two days the Vietminh had the paratroopers surrounded and fighting for their lives. The French relief columns bogged down early. The northern pincer was delayed by ambushes, blown bridges, felled trees, and demolished roads. The French drive presented a picture of an infantry division restricted by the jungle to a narrow road and consequently forced to fight on a ten-man front. An infantry squad supported by a tank or two led the way, the "cutting edge" of thousands of men. When a few Vietminh shots rang out ahead, the squad deployed off the primitive road and an accompanying tank raked the terrain ahead with machine-gun and cannon fire. Cautiously, the infantry advanced through the jungle toward the Vietminh. If there were no more shots, the French got back on the road and started again, but time—that always precious military commodity—had been lost. Then another few hundred yards or a mile down the track the same scene would be reenacted. Perhaps this time the Vietminh had destroyed a primitive bridge. Now the infantry had to cross the stream, fan out, and secure a bridgehead on the far side. Then, the engineers would come up and put in a bridge. More time lost. So it went, mile after disheartening mile—for 140 miles. Finally, on 13 October, the Vietminh made a determined stand against the northern pincer ten miles north of Bac Kan. On 16 October, after several days of hard fighting, the northern task force broke through to relieve the encircled and battered paratroopers.

The southern pincer, which was moving to the north by way of the rivers, fared no better. Sand bars and other obstructions held up the naval craft. Finally, the troops were off-loaded at Tuyen Quang and began to move toward the objective area on foot. Before they could bring pressure to bear from the south, the Vietminh calmly broke contact with the northern force and escaped to the northwest. On 19 October, as the southern pincers stumbled into the arms of the northern task force moving southward from Bac Kan, Operation LEA came to a fruitless end.

The French initiated two additional operations in 1947. Valluy launched Operation CEINTURE in November against the southern edge of the Viet Bac between Tuyen Quang and Thai Nguyen. The French cleared this limited area of enemy Main Force units and captured large amounts of supplies, but the Vietminh troops evaded battle and infiltrated back into the area after the French departure on 22 December. The last operation of 1947 was undertaken by two battalions of T'ai mountain tribesmen under French officers. This attack cleared the Vietminh out of the Fan Si Pan mountain range lying between the Red and Black Rivers. The T'ais, fighting in their native mountains, had significant advantages over the Vietminh. This time it was the T'ais who knew the country, who were acclimated to it, and who were receiving rapid intelligence from their tribal cousins regarding Vietminh moves and plans. So effective was this operation that the Vietminh stayed out of this area for several years.

The French claimed to have killed 9,500 Vietminh during their three offensives. This casualty figure, like all others of the Indochina wars, is suspect. In view of the primitive medical treatment system of the Vietminh and later the North Vietnamese and the Viet Cong, American intelligence analysts have concluded that the Communist ratio of killed to wounded was somewhere around one to three. Even at this low ratio the French claim of 9,500 killed would mean that the total Vietminh casualties would have been around 25,000 to 30,000, or over half of the Vietminh force. This is difficult to believe. The fighting was simply not that widespread nor that bloody.

When the results of the 1947 French operations are weighed against their intent, it is obvious that the French failed. They did not capture the Vietminh governmental apparatus—although they almost did. They did not bring about a major "live-or-die" battle, and French hope was dashed for a "swift attack and swift victory" over what they thought would be an untrained, poorly armed rabble.

Looked at in hindsight, Valluy's plan for Operation LEA was certainly bold, but it ignored the enemy against whom it would be launched and the natural characteristics of the arena in which it would be carried out. Historically it seems that French generals have an unfortunate penchant—as the Maginot Line demonstrated so eloquently—for beginning to fight a new war in the same way they ended up fighting the old one. So it was with Valluy. His plan was lifted cleanly out of the European Theater of World War II. Its central feature—a paratroop landing to be reinforced by an amphibious operation and a fast-moving overland linkup—evokes nostalgic shades of the Normandy landings and Montgomery's dash for the "Bridge Too Far" at Nijmegen. Valluy's was the wrong plan, applied in the wrong setting, against the wrong enemy. The Vietminh were not the Germans; in their mountainous jungles they were even more formidable than Hitler's legions. More important, the plains and highways of populous, industrialized Europe bore no resemblance to the Viet Bac, where the terrain was rugged, the jungles dense, the road nets primitive and vulnerable to destruction. All of these natural features aided the Vietminh in setting up defenses and ambushes, while they hindered the French, whose plan depended on the speedy relief and reinforcement of the paratroopers. Finally, the area in which Valluy sought to surround Giap's forces was much too large, some 7,500 square miles involving a circular frontage of around 300 miles. There was no way that Valluy could encircle the area closely enough to prevent the escape of the Vietminh when they decided to break contact.

Valluy's greatest miscalculation, however, lay in his underestimation of the Vietminh forces. In September 1947, Valluy confidently predicted that he "could eliminate all organized resistance in three months,"[12] a revelation of his contempt for Giap and the Vietminh. The French foresaw their 1947 offensive in the Viet Bac as rounding up a few thousand untrained, poorly equipped, badly led irregulars of poor or uncertain morale. Instead, the Vietminh met them with some 50,000 Main Force troops, and although the Vietminh revealed deficiencies of equipment and training, the Communists fought bravely and effectively. This underestimation of their enemy would be committed by successive French commanders, a chauvinistic cancer of the intellect which would in time prove terminal.

In the reassuring knowledge of what actually happened, it is easy to censure Valluy's plan as unrealistic. It is more difficult, however, to point out an alternate action Valluy *might* have taken which would have given him a reasonable chance to accomplish his mission—that is, to eliminate all organized Vietminh resistance during the "campaign season" of 1947 (October 1947–May 1948). The limitations of time inherent in Valluy's mission were the source of his dilemma. He had neither the time nor the troop strength to conduct a lengthy series of "clear, hold, and pacify" operations which could have consumed many months or even years. He had to strike boldly in an effort to destroy the Vietminh government and leadership in one surprise pounce. Looked at in this light, Valluy's plan for LEA made a kind of forlorn sense—a "Hail Mary," fifty-yard pass into the end zone by a desperate quarterback in the last moments of a losing game. In truth, the difficulties which the jungles, mountains, and poor roads posed to the French, plus the additional obstacle created by the unexpected strength and combat effectiveness of the Vietminh Main Force units, lead to the conclusion that only one way existed for Valluy to achieve this objective, and that required Giap's cooperation. The only way the French commander could have eliminated the Vietminh Main Force units in 1947 was for Giap to have made an attack on the French in the Tonkin Delta. Giap would not oblige, and thus for Valluy there could be no solution to his problem.

Valluy would not only become the first commander to lose to Giap, but also the first to become the victim of his own national government— a government which declined to define realistic, attainable objectives, refused to provide the needed men and equipment, and embarked on a war lacking the support of its countrymen and the will to persevere to victory. For a generation the same pattern would be repeated, first by the French and then by the Americans.

At least one Frenchman, however, detected the basic French dilemma in Indochina. Before Valluy had been appointed to the Indochina command, General Le Clerc, the celebrated World War II hero and previous commander of French forces in Indochina, refused the combined posts of commander in chief and high commissioner. He based his refusal on the prophetic insight that no French government would give him the 500,000 men that he considered necessary for military success. Beyond that, Le Clerc, even in 1946, was doubtful that the war could be won by military means only. On 30 April 1946, he stated, "The major problem from now on is political."[13] Here is one man, maybe *the* man, who apparently grasped Giap's strategy of revolutionary war.

One of the lessons which can be derived now from both Indochina Wars I and II is that experience taught the contenders little. In this instance, the lesson that the elimination of the Vietminh was beyond the capabilities of the French was rejected in Paris for over five years. The French politicians continued their irresolute, incoherent, and penny-pinching support of military operations in Indochina, while demanding "decisive solutions." In Indochina the generals kept drawing up grandiose plans to achieve such "solutions," while losing battles, territory, and men, consequently becoming increasingly inferior to the growing Vietminh forces.

General Valluy returned to France in 1948 and thereafter held many prestigious positions, several of them with Supreme Headquarters Allied Powers Europe (SHAPE) and with Allied commands in Europe. He got his fourth star in 1955 and soon afterwards retired. Again he was the pattern-setter. Like those who succeeded him, French and American alike, his military career prospered in spite of his reverses in Vietnam— a tacit recognition that he and his successors were more sinned against than sinner.

Valluy's failure was Giap's victory. In his first test as a general, Giap did well. He took two actions before the fighting started in December 1946 which in large measure forestalled a quick French victory. First, beginning in June 1946, he increased the size of his Main Forces from 30,000 to 50–60,000 men.[14] At the same time he built up the Regional Forces and guerrillas. Second, he started in late November, after the serious clashes in Haiphong, to move his Main Force units from Hanoi and the other cities of the Tonkin Delta to the Viet Bac. The combined effect of these two moves was to insure that the French would have to come to Giap in the Viet Bac under conditions favorable to him.

Giap's conduct of the Vietminh defense and evasion, while not brilliant, was sound and effective. The only blemish lay in Giap's inability to foresee the use of French paratroops in an airborne assault on his headquarters and on the seat of the Vietminh government. This tactical error reflected his total inexperience in airborne operations, and he never made the same mistake again. Throughout the wars against the French, and later against the Americans, he was careful to provide his and other key headquarters with antiaircraft gun and missile protection. He dispersed the elements of any major headquarters widely, and he insisted that the major field headquarters be mobile and constantly moving about in its area.

Giap and Ho must have found enormous satisfaction in the professional and heroic way in which the Vietminh troops attacked and savaged the French paratroopers at Bac Kan. In the first fight the Vietminh displayed their high quality. This excellent performance was a tremendous morale booster for the Vietminh and had profound long-range implications for both sides.

Weighing Giap's results against his strategic intention, which was to maintain an effective Vietminh force in being, shows that he accomplished his primary mission. It showed, too, the validity of his developing strategy of revolutionary war, and with a sound strategy, tactical mistakes can be made without incurring disaster. Giap still had much to learn, and he would make other mistakes. But in 1947 he was beginning to learn the general's trade the hard way—on the battlefield, which is the best place.

Notes—Chapter 2

1. Giap, *Military Art*, p. 79.
2. W. Scott Thompson and Donaldson D. Frizzell, eds., *The Lessons of Vietnam* (New York: Crane, Russak & Co., 1977), p. 25.
3. George K. Tanham, *Communist Revolutionary Warfare. The Vietminh in Indochina* (New York: Frederick A. Praeger, 1961), pp. 45–46.
4. O'Neill, *Giap*, p. 53.
5. Bernard B. Fall, *Viet-Nam Witness 1953–66* (New York: Frederick A. Praeger, 1966), p. 13.
6. Buttinger, *Dragon Embattled*, 1:421.
7. O'Neill, *Giap*, p. 53.
8. Philippe Devillers and Jean Lacouture, *End of a War: Indochina, 1954*. trans. by Alexander Lieven and Adam Roberts (New York: Frederick A. Praeger, 1969), p. 11.
9. O'Neill, *Giap*, p. 53.
10. Joseph Buttinger, *The Smaller Dragon. A Political History of Vietnam* (New York: Frederick A. Praeger, 1968), p. 320.
11. Bernard B. Fall, *Street Without Joy* (Harrison, PA: The Stackpole Co., 1967), p. 28.
12. Buttinger, *Dragon Embattled*, 2:1023.
13. Ibid., 2:684; also David Halberstam, *The Best and the Brightest* (Greenwich, CT: Fawcett, 1969), p. 106.
14. Buttinger, *Dragon Embattled*, 1:421.

3 The French Campaign

After Valluy's failure in 1947, the military situation in Vietnam subsided into an uneasy stalemate. In the north the French retired to the Tonkin Delta, but they maintained a string of strong outposts and forts along the Chinese border. The French even held on to Bac Kan in the middle of the Viet Bac until August 1948, when they abandoned it. It had become a useless burden, controlling nothing beyond the range of its guns, and its resupply had become a steady and costly drain of men and equipment.

Giap and his Main Force units once again faded into the jungles and mountains of the Viet Bac. The Vietminh guerrillas harassed the French in the populated areas of the Tonkin Delta and waged an unceasing political campaign of propaganda and terror seeking to gain the support of the people in the French-occupied areas.

In central Vietnam the French held the key towns and little else. In southern Vietnam the French hold was stronger, but even there, their control was tenuous. Valluy had been replaced in 1948 by General Blaizot, who did nothing. But Giap was doing something—something important.

It was during this lull in large-unit combat operations of 1948–1950 that Giap refined the weapon with which he would eventually triumph—the Vietminh Main Force units. The Vietminh troops had fought well in the autumn of 1947 at Bac Kan, but Giap realized correctly that in organization, armament, logistic support, and leadership they were little better than guerrillas. If the Vietminh were to go over to the offensive, their attacking units would have to be strengthened and conventionalized.

57

Fortunately for the Vietminh, Giap had an inherent talent for military organization. His first order of business was to increase the strength of his Main Force units. By the Vietminh system of "promoting" the better soldiers of the Popular and Regional forces, he built his Main Force units from 32 battalions in 1948 to 117 by 1951.[1] Of course, this decimated the Regional and Popular Forces whose number of battalions decreased from 137 to 37. Giap also reorganized the Main Force units. At Bac Kan they had fought in units no larger than battalions. Now he joined three or four of these battalions into regiments whose strength totaled around 2,000 men.

His organizational efforts extended beyond the Main Force units. During this period he established the Integrated Zones, or Military Regions, to give him unity of command over the far-flung and amorphous units of the Regional and Popular Forces. Even more important was Giap's reorganization of the Vietminh General Staff. In 1947 his primitive General Staff concerned itself almost solely with operations, usually guerrilla actions, and with training and military organization. In Western armies these functions are all dealt with by the Operations, or G-3, Section of the General Staff. In 1950, as the size and sophistication of his operations increased, Giap set up a General Staff based on the French (and American) general staff system. There were the four major staff divisions: personnel (G-1), intelligence (G-2), operations (G-3), and logistics (G-4). This staff organization was to last until 1953, when the changing situation and growing Chinese influence brought about another General Staff reorganization.[2]

Logistic support, however, is the fuel which drives the military machine, and no increase in the capabilities of the Main Force units or any staff or command reorganization will bring lasting results without a corresponding improvement in logistic capacity. Here again, Giap had to convert the Vietminh from the "cottage industry" type of support, adequate for guerrilla war, to the more sophisticated logistic systems needed to support large, conventional forces. Of all the tasks facing Giap in 1948–1950, this would be the most formidable—a Goliath of a problem facing a David of resources. The equipment held by the Vietminh in 1948 was not only inadequate, it was a confused mixture of captured French equipment, old Japanese arms, and even some American material parachuted in during World War II. In his entire army, Giap had only a few captured trucks and no parts or mechanics to maintain them.

To overcome this shortage of arms and ammunition, Giap set up factories deep in the vast wilderness of the Viet Bac. At first they turned out only grenades, mines, rifle cartridges, and a few light machine guns. By 1949, however, they were making not only small arms, but even a few 120mm mortars.[3] None of these "factories," however, could produce heavy equipment, and, left to their own resources, the Main Force would have been seriously hobbled by this inadequacy. Only the arrival of the victorious Chinese Communists solved the heavy armament and other complex supply problems of the Vietminh.

The problem of moving the supplies was more amenable to a Vietminh solution—a solution fashioned around "the people," with masses of organized, disciplined coolies acting as porters. This extraordinary feat of logistics has never been clearly comprehended or appreciated by the West. The use of porters continued throughout both Indochina wars, even though from 1953 on the Vietnamese Communists had thousands of trucks. In 1954, at Dien Bien Phu, it was the porters who hand-carried the vast quantities of Vietminh food which allowed Giap to pound the French into surrender. In 1968 it was the porters who carried the supplies of the North Vietnamese and Viet Cong divisions as they stealthily closed in on the major cities of South Vietnam at the time of the Tet offensive. The Vietnamese porterage system was, above all else, an achievement of organization.

Accurate planning figures for load capacities had to be worked out by Giap's staff. Some of these figures were: ". . . 55 lb. of rice or 33–44 lb. of arms and munitions over 15.5 miles of easy country by day, or 12.4 miles by night; 28 lb. of rice or 22–33 lb. of munitions over 9 miles of mountainous country by day, or 7.5 miles by night. A buffalo cart could move 770 lb. over 7.5 miles per day. A horse cart could move 473 lb. over 12.4 miles per day."[4]

Porters had to be conscripted, organized, and fed, on a giant scale. A Vietminh force needed porters at least double the troop strength to carry ammunition, food, and other supplies.[5] Indeed, this ratio of porters to troops is probably on the low side. From a study of available records, the ratio of porters to troops depended on the terrain, weather, and combat conditions, but a figure of four porters to one soldier would seem about right. Not only did the porters have to be recruited, organized, and controlled, they had to be fed, and here the inefficiency of the system was graphically revealed. Hoang, a North Vietnamese who deserted the Vietminh, and who had detailed knowledge of Vietminh logistics, estimated that on a long trip the porters consumed en route 90 percent of the food they carried.[6] But regardless of the system's inefficiencies, it worked.

Giap's expanding Main Force units had not only to be reorganized and supported logistically, they had to be retrained from the guerrilla tactics of "cut-and-run" to the sophisticated operations of a force of combined arms. In this function, the Chinese assumed a large share of the burden. They set up specialist schools in China which trained engineers, signal personnel, and tank troops. The Vietminh desperately needed leaders and staff officers, and the Chinese eagerly grasped the opportunity to train these young men who would someday wear the stars of Vietnamese generals. In Vietnam and in China, noncommissioned officers, company-grade officers, and staff officers were grounded in Chinese tactics and techniques.

Deep in the Viet Bac, the Vietminh trained their own recruits. The military training was by rote, as simple and repetitive as learning the multiplication tables. Emphasis was placed on close-order drill, on camouflage and concealment, and on the use and care of the infantryman's basic weapons, the rifle and bayonet. All of the simple moves and exercises were repeated until they became part of the man. These recruit training methods and subjects differ only in emphasis and detail from the practices of Western armies, but one aspect of Vietminh recruit training differed totally from Western concepts. To the Vietminh, the most critical part of the recruit's training was his political education and motivational indoctrination.

Giap's Political Indoctrination and Education Program (I & E Program) was his most important, if invisible, weapon, and in twenty-five years of combat it never failed him or his cause. From the first, Giap understood clearly that in his battles against the French (and later the Americans) he must overcome his material and numerical inferiority with superior battlefield morale, ideological ardor, and revolutionary zeal. In 1959 he wrote, "Profound awareness of the aims of the Party, boundless loyalty to the cause of the nation and working class, and a spirit of unreserved sacrifice are fundamental questions for the army . . . Therefore, the political work in its ranks is of first importance. *It is the soul of the army.*"[7] (Italics are Giap's) Quoting Lenin, Giap added, ". . . in the final analysis, victory in any war is determined by the willingness of the masses to shed blood on the battlefield."[8]

To describe Giap's I & E Program as an "invisible weapon" overstates its invisibility only slightly. During their wars in Indochina, neither the French nor the Americans ever gained a comprehensive grasp of the methods by which Giap produced the high combat morale and suicidal zeal of his troops. During Indochina War II the most pervasive question among those supreme realists, the American front-line infantrymen, was, "Why are their 'gooks' so much better than our 'gooks'?" I once heard the same question asked (in more urbane language) by Secretary of Defense Clark Clifford and by the Chairman of the United States Joint Chiefs of Staff, Gen. Earle Wheeler. During the war, neither the soldiers nor the two senior defense officials received an adequate answer. Only now are Western analysts beginning to understand how Giap and his colleagues produced the tenacious fighters who gained the respect of both their Western foes.

To build a motivated army, Giap faced an immense task, particularly in the early years of his war against the French. Giap had to build this motivated army from a bunch of illiterate peasants who were shy and suspicious of strangers, particularly of those strangers in authority. Giap's recruits had no sense of time, and since they had played no sports, no sense of team-play or team spirit. Above all, since the typical youth's entire life focus had been centered on his family and hamlet, he had little grasp of Vietnamese nationhood or sense of public duty. Seldom has a leader been asked to forge a weapon from such unpromising material.

But Giap had the tools to do the job—his I & E Program and his political cadres. The I & E Program had been in part inherited from the Chinese Communists and in part developed by the Vietminh. The program consisted of a careful mixture of "brainwashing," paternalism, propaganda, and thought control. Giap insisted that the I & E Program be given first priority, and his troops spent over half of their training time on political and ideological indoctrination.[9] To carry out his I & E Program, Giap called on the political officers (or commissars) and the political cadre, the most dedicated ideologists in each unit. The political officers had the supreme power in the units to which they were assigned. They not only looked after the soldiers' ideological and political training, but their morale, well-being, and even their innermost thoughts.

In addition, the commissars had the authority to override purely military decisions made by the commanders of the unit.[10] Finally, they led the unit in devotion to duty and in their demonstration of revolutionary ardor and Marxist zeal. In short, the political officer, in the words of one Communist defector, ". . . was really the boss of the unit."[11]

Given the human material with which Giap had to work, he had to change the basic pattern of each recruit's life, to refocus the youth's attachment from his family and hamlet to the army and communism. The indoctrination of the recruits had to begin with the mental and emotional baggage which they brought with them, some of which was usable to initiate the program. In the first place, many of the recruits had undergone or heard of some persecution of the Vietnamese by the French; almost all had experienced or knew of exploitation of peasants by rapacious Vietnamese landlords. Secondly, although largely illiterate, the recruits knew from folklore something of the legendary Vietnamese heroes and of Vietnam's centuries-old fight for independence. They were proud to be Vietnamese and contemptuous of and hostile to foreigners. Finally, the young recruit brought with him his sense of family, which made it easy for him to trust other recruits and to share his food and thoughts with them.

Building on these attitudes the political officers began by emphasizing "class consciousness" and by describing the goals of the Vietminh revolution in simple songs, stories, and jokes the new soldiers could understand. Each recruit was made to describe his own personal sufferings at the hands of the landlords or the French, or if he had no such personal experiences, to recount sufferings he had observed or heard of. Skillfully led by the political officers, the recruit began to see a pattern of persecution and abuse. From this beginning, the political officers set forth the goals of the revolution, such as land reform and independence, both of which exercised a tremendous pull on the land-hungry young peasants.

To this ideological dish the cadres added a strong dash of xenophobic patriotism. They reminded the recruits that their Vietnamese ancestors had fought for centuries against invaders and had expelled them all. The political officers not only exploited this native patriotism, but carried it one step further: they preached always that victory in the current war was certain, and that although in the past the recruits had been poor and exploited, now they would win, and with victory, would take a lofty place in the new society. This concept came as a shining revelation to the former peasant who all of his life had passively accepted his role at the bottom of the Vietnamese social ladder.

After this initial indoctrination, the political cadre moved into the second phase—to break down the recruit's attachment to his family and to transfer it to his unit, to the army, and to the revolution itself. The recruits were formed into cells of three men, in effect a three-man "buddy system." The three-man cell became the recruit's military family, people he looked after and who in turn cared for him. As the cell matured and ripened, the three soldiers became close comrades and confidants. Later, under the continued direction of the commissars, the young soldiers began to think of themselves and their company as a "band of brothers," an elite organization able to withstand any hardship and dedicated to the welfare of the common people from which they had sprung. When the soldiers reached this plateau, the recruit's attachment to his own family had been replaced by his attachment to his unit and "the Cause." The political officer had then accomplished the preliminary task of the program.

And preliminary it was, for it only prepared the soldier for the intense ideological indoctrination which would continue throughout his service. Here the other uses of the three-man cell came into play. In addition to giving its members aid and comfort, the cell acted as a prime security device. The cell members met every night to discuss the day's activities, and since the three men shared their innermost secrets among themselves, any hint of ideological backsliding or thoughts of defection or desertion by one soldier would probably be transmitted to his two buddies. They, in turn—each not trusting the other—would inform the political officer, who could then counsel the waverer or take whatever action he thought fit. The three-man cell made defection and desertion difficult. A soldier might discuss plans for the misdeed with a single buddy, but not with two buddies, one of which would surely expose him. Thus, by the use of the three-man cell the Communists extended their security system to the very bottom of the army. One expert describes this method of prevention of defection and desertion as ". . . one of the most effective devised in recent history."[12]

The commissars used two other powerful processes to indoctrinate the soldiers—self-criticism and comrade-criticism. Borrowed again from the Chinese Communists, the procedure took place in company meetings which all had to attend. Each soldier and officer criticized his own actions and those of the other members of the company regardless of rank. After each confession or criticism, a general discussion ensued, in which any person who had been criticized might accept the criticism or attempt to rebut it. Western analysts vary in their opinion of the method's effectiveness as an indoctrination device, and they disagree about the severity of the criticism, particularly of the officers. While the scope of its influence may be questionable, there is no doubt that at the unit level it worked well. First, it gave the soldiers a sense of participation in the unit's decision-making process. They viewed themselves, therefore, not as witless cannon fodder, but as thinking members of a team. Second, it provided a catharsis to the soldiers, permitting them to voice fears and problems without punishment. It provided an outlet for emotions, which if kept bottled up, might lead to desertion or defection. Third, it provided the political officers with a gauge of unit morale, an insight into hidden problems, and gave them some hints about which individuals' revolutionary ardor had begun to flag.

In its final phase, the indoctrination program concentrated on imbuing the soldier with his political role toward the civilian population. Each soldier was trained to be not only a combatant, but a political agent as well. Since the military units frequently lived among the populace, they had many opportunities to help the people and propagandize them. The soldiers not only conducted propaganda classes, but built roads and bridges, and even helped the peasants with planting and harvesting. Thus, Giap's I & E Program produced the desired results. From the most unlikely raw material, it developed a dedicated Communist soldier and a devoted political agent, the lowest practitioner of military and political *dau tranh*. Giap's "invisible weapon" turned out to be the most effective arm in his arsenal.

As Giap built up his Main Force units and the French fiddled while Vietnam burned, 1948 slipped into 1949. French and Vietnamese blood continued to flow, but nothing much came of it. In May 1949, the French government, disturbed by lack of progress, and refusing as always to see that its own incoherence and indecision played the major role in the inadequate performance of its troops in Vietnam, decided to have a prestigious figure go to Indochina and take a "new look" at the situation. That prestigious figure was the chief of the Army General Staff, Gen.

Georges Revers. Revers was an interesting character, an atypical French general. He had not gone to St. Cyr, in fact he was a reserve officer who had risen to a high command position in the French Résistance in World War II. His background and experience, therefore, placed him outside the main stream of the French army. He was as much politician as soldier, and perhaps this was the reason for his selection.

Regardless of the motives which dictated his choice, Revers turned out a clinical diagnosis of the ills of the French position and operations along with the remedies that the French generals and politicians would have to take to correct the situation. His recommendations included: the evacuation of the string of isolated forts and outposts along the Vietnam/China border; the solicitation of more United States military aid; the rapid buildup of a native Vietnamese army; the pacification by this Vietnamese army of the Tonkin Delta before launching another major French offensive against the Viet Bac; and finally, the key proposal that diplomacy and negotiation be given priority over military actions. These recommendations were sound in 1949, and with minor and appropriate changes would have been sound in 1952, 1964–1965, 1967–1968, and in 1972. But it was a Frenchman who said that "The more things change the more they remain the same."

Nothing was ever done to carry out Revers' recommendations. In the first place the validity and potency of the report was destroyed by a peculiar scandal. The report somehow fell into the hands of the Vietminh, who broadcast parts of it over their radio. In Paris the entire plan was found in the possession of a Vietnamese national. A tornado of political charges and countercharges swirled around Revers and his ill-fated report. When the dust and debris finally settled, the French found that among the casualties were a few political underlings, several generals including General Revers himself, and, most unfortunate of all, the prestige of his report. Many French generals alive today believe that the French politicians deliberately "leaked" the report to the Vietminh, thereby effectively sabotaging its influence. The French civilian leaders could not adopt the political recommendations of the report. To do so would have forced them to give the Vietnamese their independence in one form or another. This they could not do, for it would have constituted a clear admission of previous error. Furthermore, if they had granted independence to the Vietnamese, it would have meant the loss of money, raw materials, markets, and prestige which made Indochina valuable to the French government and its influential colonialist supporters. Without these assets Indochina was not worth fighting for.

There were other reasons for not implementing Revers' recommendations. The French leaders in Vietnam, to preserve their image, could not accept the findings and recommendations of the report. Like others before them—and many Frenchmen and Americans to follow—they had been filing glowing reports of the success of the pacification strategy. The acceptance of the findings and recommendations of the Revers' report would be tantamount to an admission of failure, and even worse, a public admission that their overly optimistic reports to Paris were false.

There were reasons—some valid, some muddleheaded—for the French refusal to evacuate the border posts. One was sentimentality. The French staffs wanted to keep a garrison at Cao Bang as a matter of honor, to guard a cemetery containing the bodies of French soldiers. They could not accept the idea of giving up the bodies of their comrades to the Vietminh. There was another subtle factor at work, also. The French staff maintained a frozen silence about evacuation so as not to be accused by the commanders and other staff members of defeatism. Such a charge—vague and difficult to defend against—was a ticket back to France and the end of a military career. Thus the staffs, instead of challenging the concepts of the commanders—a vital function of an effective staff organization—abetted the visions of their commanders and added reasons of their own for holding the forts.

There were some practical objections to giving up the outposts. No officer doubted that there would be many laborious difficulties in evacuating the forts. Vast stores of equipment would have to be abandoned; the retreat would be harassed by ambushes and attacks; and losses of both men and equipment were certain to be heavy. While the evacuation would have been difficult in 1949, it was sure to be catastrophic in 1950.

Last, the malady which had plagued Valluy and which would infect every French commander from Valluy to Navarre at Dien Bien Phu cast its pall over the Revers' recommendations—the chronic underestimation of the Vietminh. The French commanders and staffs reasoned that while the Vietminh had vastly improved their offensive capabilities, Giap and the Vietminh lacked the firepower and technique to besiege and overpower a big garrison. The French held to this illusion in spite of the attack Giap made in April–June 1949 on the small outposts around Lao Cai, one of the large forts on the northern border. What fooled the French was that Giap failed to take the small posts. They did not realize that he had not intended to overrun the outposts; he had attacked them for other reasons. But these attacks, although made in 1949, were in reality part of Giap's 1950 offensive.

So the French, faced with a dilemma which realistically required either that the northern border posts be reinforced or that they be abandoned, did neither. They compromised and elected a course of action that guaranteed disaster—they left the posts as they were.

But the French did take one action—they replaced Blaizot with Gen. Marcel Maurice Carpentier, general de corps d'armée (equivalent to a United States lieutenant general). Lucien Bodard, a French journalist, interviewed Carpentier in 1950 and described him as ". . . full of good will . . . deep-voiced, convincing promises."[13] Carpentier was an "old soldier" and, like Valluy before him and de Lattre, Salan, and Navarre, who would follow him, a good one.

He graduated from St. Cyr in 1914 as a second lieutenant and got into World War I in any war's most dangerous duty, frontline infantry. He barely survived. He was seriously wounded four times and took six additional minor wounds. He was promoted so rapidly that when he "made" captain in March 1915, at age twenty, he was the youngest captain in the French army. He won the Legion of Honor and the Croix de Guerre with five citations, all extolling his personal courage and "remarkable bravery."

When World War II began, Carpentier was a major serving as General Weygand's operations officer in the Levant, and in that position he went with Weygand to North Africa. There in May 1942, as a colonel, he took command of the 7th Moroccan Regiment and led it with dash throughout the Tunisian campaign. He was promoted to brigadier general in July 1943 and became General Juin's chief of staff of the French Expeditionary Corps in Italy. In June of 1944 he became the chief of staff of the First French Army under General de Lattre, and in that position participated in the landing of the First French Army in southern France and its subsequent drive toward the Belfort Gap. In November 1944, as a major general, he took command of the 2d Moroccan Infantry Division and commanded this elite division through the hard fighting of the Belfort Gap, Strasbourg, and the crossing of the lower Rhine river. Judging from the numerous citations which the division earned, he did an excellent job. In 1946 he was promoted to lieutenant general and placed in charge of all French troops in Rabat, and in 1949 he received his orders for Indochina.

Upon his arrival in Saigon in the late summer of 1949, Carpentier saw at once that the strategy Valluy had tried—the set-piece European battle—would not work. Something had to be done, and done quickly. Carpentier had never served in the Far East, and he found himself alone and blind in the labyrinth of Indochina. He needed a guide and almost immediately found one, Gen. Marcel Alessandri. Alessandri was one of a long series of "characters" who drifted around the edges of Indochina before, during, and after World War II, a man who had even gained some measure of fame there. On 9 March 1945, when the Japanese occupiers of Vietnam suddenly turned on the French "hosts" and either murdered or imprisoned most of them, Alessandri, warned of the Japanese treachery, marched his troops from Tonkin (his headquarters) through the jungles of northern Vietnam into Nationalist-held China. He saved most of the French troops that survived the Japanese coup.

Alessandri might have been given the supreme command in Indochina had not several clouds hung over his head. In Paris he was billed as an appointee of Philippe Pétain, little better than a collaborator. In spite of his heroic trek into China—or rather, because of it—there was about him and his feat the unpleasant odor of retreat and defeat, a stench which since 1940 had sickened Frenchmen. What was needed in Indochina in 1949, according to the conventional cant of the Quai D'Orsay, was a "winner," and this meant one of the bright French stars of the recent Allied victory in Europe. Moreover, Alessandri's disposition and appearance cost him favor. He was an ascetic, dried-up, ugly, little Corsican—choleric, distrustful, and testy. He proclaimed loudly and constantly and with dogmatic certainty what ought to be done in Indochina. Worse yet, he never hesitated to force his views on superiors—he was a provincial Charles de Gaulle with a Moses complex.

Within a few days after taking command, Carpentier called Alessandri to Saigon. Alessandri, an old trap-wary wolf, approached the meeting reluctantly. Was Carpentier going to be another "new broom," full of energy, with unrealistic concepts, and enamored visions of a modern-day Cannae? If so, Alessandri had made up his mind to "hand in his belt'' and seek retirement. The conference, however, both surprised and pleased the little Corsican. Far from imposing his views on the veteran, Carpentier went to the other extreme—in effect he abdicated his responsibilities as commander in chief. Carpentier told the astounded Alessandri that he (Carpentier) knew nothing about Indochina, and that he wanted Alessandri to take command in Tonkin with a completely free hand. Alessandri gulped, muttered the required clichés about doing his best, saluted, and jauntily left the room. He had what every commander worthy of his insignia always wants—complete freedom of action. Now he could put his concepts to the test; now he, Alessandri, would save the French Empire in Indochina.

Alessandri had no grandiose visions about how to win the war with one devastating blow. Valluy's failures had convinced him that any concept of driving or enticing the Vietminh into an early Armageddon was a delusion. He saw also that the current French strategy of surrounding the Tonkin Delta—the war's prize and its principal battlefield—was, in his words, ''absurd.''[14] The French held the perimeters of the Delta, but the Vietminh guerrillas and political infrastructure controlled the interior with its millions of people and thousands of tons of rice. Alessandri proposed to change this by occupying the Delta and pacifying it. In so doing he would deny the Vietminh a source of recruits; he would deny them its taxes; and even more important, he would deny them its rice. If this starvation could be prolonged, Alessandri argued, Giap would either have to surrender or come out of the Viet Bac and fight.

Tactically, Alessandri proceeded like a man draining a flooded field. He moved into a small area, built a cofferdam, pumped out the water, and moved to an adjoining area, repeating the process. The French troops would be his dam and local non-Communist Vietnamese would do the pumping out of the Vietminh guerrillas and infrastructure. Alessandri was also the first of a long line of ''pacifiers'' that extended through almost twenty-five years to the American, William Colby.

War is always a two-handed game, however, and the Vietminh responded to Alessandri's pacification initiatives by launching guerrilla warfare in the Delta. Giap described Vietminh tactics this way: ''Our units operated in small pockets with independent companies penetrating deeply into the enemy-controlled zone to launch guerrilla warfare, establish bases, and protect local people's power. It was an extremely hard war generalized in all domains: military, economic, and political. The enemy mopped up; we fought against mopping up. They organized supplementary local Vietnamese troops and installed puppet authorities; we firmly upheld local people's power, overthrew straw men, eliminated traitors and carried out active propaganda. . . . We gradually formed a network of guerrilla bases."[15] Nevertheless, step by step, rice field by rice field, Alessandri expanded his domain as his French troops cleared the area and his Vietnamese allies pacified it. The fighting was at close range—rifle and grenade stuff. Both sides suffered from the mud, heat, and leeches, but on the maps in the French command posts, the blue crayon lines representing French occupation and control pushed steadily outward. For a time, Alessandri's strategy appeared to be working.

In Vietnam the appearance of things, as two generations of soldiers have learned, was almost always deceptive. The Vietminh had not extended themselves in their fight against the French clearing forces. Most of the Vietminh troops were local guerrillas—peasants by day, soldiers by night—and when pressed by the French, they melted into the population, waiting another turn at ambush or local attack. The avoidance of combat by Vietminh guerrillas for a time concealed the first deficiency of Alessandri's concept, which was the inadequate strength of the French forces to execute it in a protracted struggle. The French could clean out an area, but they lacked the troop strength to garrison it and to prevent the guerrillas from infiltrating back into the "cleared" zones and reestablishing clandestine Vietminh governments. While the anti-Communist Vietnamese could and did kill many officials of the Vietminh underground, they had neither the organization, zeal, nor patriotic dedication to eradicate permanently the Communist infrastructure. And if every last root of that infrastructure was not dug up, the Communist weed reappeared in a short time in the French garden of pacification.

Alessandri's concept eventually failed for a second, and an even more fundamental reason: the French made no effort to fight the political war—the war to win the support of the Vietnamese people. To the French, the native masses of the Delta were chattel pawns, inanimate objects, prizes to be fought for and used as soldiers, sources of revenue, and always, as rice producers. The French made no effort to spread their own values and doctrines to the people and areas they conquered, which is understandable, since they had nothing worth propagating. But the Vietminh did. Under Ho and Giap they launched a massive and coordinated campaign to win the affection and support of the Vietnamese in the Tonkin Delta. There was a constant barrage of Vietminh propaganda over the radio and by clandestine leaflets. The Vietminh soldiers were carefully indoctrinated in how to treat the people. Their armed units carried out "army assistance days," when military units helped the villages with rice harvests or flood control. When these benevolent forms of persuasion failed, the Vietminh were equally proficient in the black arts of threats, bribery, kidnapping, and assassination.

Finally, Alessandri's concept foundered in time on one other event— one over which he had no control. This was the victory of the Chinese Communists in mainland China and their arrival at the northern border of Vietnam in 1949. Referring to the Chinese Communist victory, Giap writes, "This great historic event, which altered events in Asia and throughout the world, exerted a considerable influence on the war of liberation of the Vietnamese people. Vietnam was no longer in the grip of enemy encirclement, and was henceforth geographically linked to the socialist bloc."[16] The Chinese Communist victory opened up an avenue by which the Vietminh could eventually receive the supplies and arms that Alessandri was attempting to deny them. The arrival of the Chinese Communists exerted a psychological influence on the French which would, in 1950, be catastrophic. Both Alessandri and Carpentier perceived the need to hold the forts and outposts along the China/Vietnam border to block the flow of Chinese supplies and military units to the aid of the Vietminh. They held this oversimplistic view even though the posts were isolated, vulnerable, and could do little to interfere with the logistic support the Chinese furnished the Vietminh.

In spite of the deficiencies of Alessandri's concept and the leaky nature of his occupation of the Tonkin Delta, for a time his pacification operations did hurt the Vietminh. The vast population of the Delta as a source of recruits for Giap's units almost dried up. The manpower situation became so critical in late 1949 that Ho Chi Minh had to call for a "National Mobilization" in an attempt to man his units. The French occupation of the Delta cut by half the flow of rice to the Vietminh. This blow hit the Vietminh in their most sensitive spot, almost paralyzing the army and government. An adequate supply of rice was not only necessary to avoid starvation, it was the medium of exchange of the Vietminh economy. Troops were paid in rice, and supplies and services were purchased with rice. As Alessandri's embargo increased its hold, rice rations for Vietminh forces were reduced and then reduced again.

In many Vietminh areas and among military units starvation loomed. The rice shortage became so critical that Ho and Giap even began to contemplate the "unthinkable"—a major counteroffensive against Alessandri and the French in the Tonkin Delta to obtain the rice. Both men knew that in 1949 such an attack had little hope of success, so they clenched their teeth and held on throughout 1949 into 1950, when they believed things would get better. But something had happened in 1949 which the French failed to see or understand—the momentum of the war was reversing. With the arrival of the Chinese Communists on Vietnam's northern border, Giap and his newly muscled Main Forces would in 1950 and beyond carry the war to the French. In Indochina there would be other French victories, but there would be no *offensive* French victories.

Notes—Chapter 3

1. O'Neill, *Giap*, p. 66.
2. Tanham, *Warfare*, p. 38.
3. Ibid., p. 68.
4. O'Neill, *Giap*, p. 72.
5. Buttinger, *Dragon Embattled*, 2:753.
6. Chi, *Colonialism*, p. 66.
7. Giap, *Military Art*, p. 111.
8. Giap, *Banner*, p. 97
9. Tanham, *Warfare*, p. 63; and Fall, *Witness*, p. 246.
10. O'Neill, *Giap*, p. 66; and Fall, *Witness*, p. 227.
11. Jon M. Van Dyke, *North Vietnam's Strategy for Survival* (Palo Alto, CA: Pacific Books, 1972), p. 117.
12. Herman Kahn and Gastil Armbruster, *Can We Win in Vietnam* (New York: Frederick A. Praeger, 1968), p. 101.
13. Lucien Bodard, *The Quicksand War: Prelude to Vietnam 1950 to the Present,* trans. by Patrick O'Brian (Boston, MA: Little, Brown & Co., 1967), p. 204.
14. Ibid., p. 206.
15. Giap, *Military Art*, pp. 87–88.
16. Ibid., p. 88.

4 Giap's First Offensive Campaign

1950

As the year 1950 dawned, Giap was ready with a hundred-page plan to win the war. In this analysis, Giap foresaw the war as one of three phases. Phase I (now complete) included the initial retreat and avoidance of decisive combat by the Vietminh. In the second phase, the Chinese Communists would equip and train the Vietminh, permitting them to eliminate the northern border posts one by one. This was the current phase, and to Giap it was the critical one. The real race, as Giap saw things in early 1950, was between the aid furnished to the Vietminh by the Chinese Communists and the American assistance now beginning to flow to the French. In early 1950, Giap believed that the Chinese were winning this race, and he wanted to seize the advantage before the French received massive American materiel help. Phase III, as Giap saw it, would consist of a Vietminh general counteroffensive to be launched sometime in the future to destroy the French forces in Indochina or to drive them from the country.

Giap himself seems to have been of two minds about the timing of the various phases. Both sources who reported on Giap's plan relate that Giap intended to expel the French from Vietnam within six months, that is, by late 1950 or early 1951.[1] On the other hand, Giap must have realized that even with the recent infusion of Chinese aid, his timetable of a few months to achieve final victory was unrealistic. In his plan he speaks of a "war of long duration" and a "long drawn-out

75

war."[2] It would seem that Giap *hoped* for victory in a few months, but was prepared to undergo a protracted struggle of years.

Giap's choice of the border posts as the objectives of his first offensive was strategically sound. In the first place, if successful, his plan would eliminate critical bottlenecks in the vital supply line from Communist China. Second, the elimination of the French posts would permit the Vietminh to expand and clear the "rear base area" not only in the Viet Bac, but into China as well. Third, Giap's attacks would remove, at least theoretically, any threat to his rear when he moved south out of the Viet Bac against the main French positions in the Tonkin Delta.

Beyond the strategic justifications for his choice, Giap wisely weighed the psychological factor. In war it is imperative that a combat unit win its first battle, particularly its first offensive battle. The troops must know beyond doubt that they can defeat their enemy. On this certitude is built battlefield morale, which feeds on victory and is consumed by defeat. Victory was almost assured Giap if he attacked the French border posts. They were vulnerable targets, tethered goats in tiger country, located miles apart, tenuously linked by a wretched road controlled by the Vietminh. No post could come to the aid of another, which meant that Giap could concentrate on them one by one and in any order he chose. Since the only means of French reinforcement would be by the drop of paratroopers, the French could reinforce them only marginally, and even that would be very difficult. Finally, Giap had the initiative. He could dictate not only the time and place of the attacks, but he had no worries about the French upsetting his plans with a counteroffensive or even a meaningful counterattack.

To mount his 1950 offensive, Giap made a final organizational change. Late in 1949 he reorganized his Main Force units into divisions. He had the necessary heavy arms, signal equipment, staff officers, and leaders to move upward to a higher plateau of military sophistication, a combined-arms force built on the divisional structure. In every modern army the division is the basic operational formation, the smallest unit to combine all ground arms, to maintain itself, and to fight independently if need be. In the history of every developing army, the advance into the divisional structure is the move from the minor leagues of warfare into the "majors."

Each of the North Vietnamese divisions, 12,000 men strong, consisted of four infantry regiments, each with three battalions. Each regiment had its headquarters, a small communications unit, and support company of 120mm mortars. The division echelon had its own headquarters, a signal company, and an engineer battalion. By Western standards, the Vietminh divisional organization of 1950, particularly in its lack of organic artillery, was as crude and outmoded as the high button shoes Giap was said to wear. The organization had an unusually high ratio of manpower to firepower, a result of their lack of motor transport. The 120mm mortar company, for example, had only two mortars, but 200 men.[3]

This absence of heavy equipment, however, had advantages. The division could move off roads and fight in the jungle, a capability denied French forces, which were dependent on tanks, trucks, and road-bound supplies. In the final analysis, Giap had adapted his divisional organization to the realities imposed by shortages of technicians in the Vietminh forces and by its lack of heavy equipment. Giap formed five of these divisions and designated them the 304th, 308th, 312th, 316th, and 320th Divisions. Indochinese history of the next twenty-five years would link these divisions with the great battles of all three Indochina Wars, and the 308th Division, the "Iron Division," would come to rank as one of the elite divisions in the military world.

Since the spotlight of 1950 would focus on Giap's attacks on the French border forts, the location, strength, and armament of these posts requires examination. The anchors of this northern line were (from east to west) Lang Son, Cao Bang, and Lao Cai, with a total strength of around 10,000 men. Lao Cai and vicinity boasted a strength of 2,000 to 3,000 men, and was protected by four company-size outposts at Muong Khuong, Pa Kha, Nghia Do and Pho Lu. Cao Bang had as satellite subposts Dong Khe and That Khe, each held by a battalion of the French Foreign Legion. Cao Bang itself housed between two and three infantry battalions plus several hundred odds-and-ends of logistic and administrative personnel. The total strength of Cao Bang and its satellites probably ran around 4,000 men. Lang Son was the main base of the northern perimeter of French posts. Its strength normally ran at about 4,000 men including a high ratio of service support personnel.

The preliminaries of Giap's 1950 offensive began in 1949. As the rainy season of 1949 approached, Giap attacked the French outposts around Lao Cai. The outposts held, but Giap never intended to take

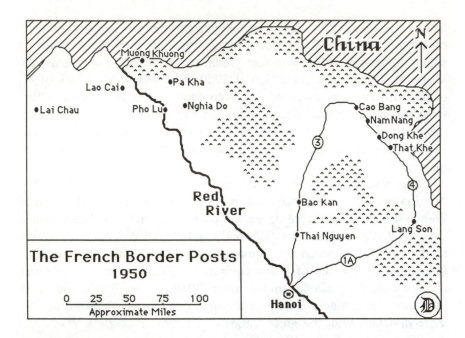

The French Border Posts
1950

them. He attacked them for two other reasons; to train his troops in assault tactics and to determine the reactions of the French to his attacks. Giap's timing was excellent. The onset of the Southwest Monsoon kept French air support grounded and the traditional lull during the period that followed allowed Giap and his staff to analyze the lessons learned and to incorporate them into his plans and training exercises.

Giap's 1950 offensive jumped off in February of that year with attacks against the Lao Cai satellites by the 308th Vietminh Division, the first test by fire for that illustrious unit. Giap designed these attacks, mounted just at the advent of the monsoon, as the first rehearsal for the main offensive, which he would launch at the end of the rainy season around October. For this February attack, Giap selected as his first objective the small post at Pho Lu, a mud and log fort isolated in the midst of a vast rain forest. After pounding the fort with mortars, bazookas, and recoilless rifles, the 308th Division overran the post and the single French company holding it. It was a murderous assault, nine or ten Vietminh battalions (5,000 to 6,000 men) in a human wave against the 150 defenders. The French high command flew in a paratroop company, but it was dropped twenty miles off target. As it moved to the aid of the defenders at Pho Lu, two Vietminh battalions attacked the paratroopers. The fighting was savage; the "paras" were driven slowly backward by the Vietminh coming on in waves. Vastly outnumbered, the paratroopers appeared doomed, but then luck intervened on their behalf. Six French fighter-bombers appeared over the fight, strafing and bombing the Vietminh masses rushing at what remained of the dazed French company. The French paratroops made good their withdrawal, but they had to abandon the bodies of their slain comrades. The French army has always branded such an act callous and dishonorable, and no less a personage than General Carpentier accused the paratroop commander, Lieutenant Planey, of cowardice.

Nghia Do, another Lao Cai satellite, fared better. It, like Pho Lu, was an isolated, half-forgotten, company-sized log fort twenty miles north of the Red River. It was attacked in March by the 308th Division, but it was saved. The French dropped the entire 5th Parachute Battalion plus another paratroop company directly on the post. This airborne reinforcement unsettled the Vietminh, and although the 308th could have taken the post, Giap decided that it was not worth the casualties. He was right, for a few days later the French evacuated the entire garrison.

In April 1950 the 308th Division, its supporting units, and its thousands of supply-carrying coolies trudged from the Lao Cai area back to the Viet Bac. Giap wanted one final test, one last dress rehearsal, before the curtain rose on his main show in the autumn of 1950. He selected Dong Khe, a strongly fortified post held by a French battalion, as his final test. Again he gave the job to the 308th Division, and on 25 May five battalions of the division climbed the hills surrounding the fort and began the mortar and artillery attacks. At the end of the two-day bombardment, the 308th took Dong Khe with a human-wave assault, and on 28 May all French resistance ended.

The Vietminh triumph was short-lived. On the morning of 28 May the weather, which had been foggy and rainy, cleared, and the entire French 3d Colonial Parachute Battalion jumped into a drop zone near the smashed fortress. Giap's troops, busy looting Dong Khe, were surprised by the French airborne assault. The French paratroopers attacked the Vietminh, who now defended the ruins of Dong Khe, and after savage hand-to-hand fighting, the "paras" retook the fort. The Vietminh lost 300 men, two howitzers, three machine guns, and numerous small arms. The French lost the battalion which had originally held Dong Khe (less about one hundred men who escaped the 308th attack) and all its support equipment, but the Vietminh gained experience and confidence. The French had won the first battle at Dong Khe, but in the minds of the soldiers of both sides—where wars are always won or lost first—the Vietminh had triumphed. The soldiers in the field knew that when the dry season came in late September, the forts were doomed. The generals sitting in Hanoi and Saigon did not yet realize it, but the war had changed; the tide of confidence had reversed.

As the Southwest Monsoon of 1950 dripped to its end in late September, Giap was ready for his first counteroffensive. Giap's plan was simple. He would surround Cao Bang and That Khe, drawing the French command's attention to those two forts, but he would seize and hold Dong Khe. His seizure of the latter post would sever the road connection between Cao Bang and That Khe and would force the French to take one of three lines of action, all distasteful, difficult, and probably disastrous. First, the French could attempt to evacuate the garrisons overland. Second, they could take on the backbreaking task of supplying the forts by air and of continuing to do it indefinitely. Third, they could attempt to reinforce the threatened posts.

As later events proved, any attempt at overland evacuation would condemn the French columns to destruction from Vietminh attacks and ambushes. Equally barren of promise was any attempt at air supply of the garrisons. The French air transport force, weak in men and airplanes, was already tottering from exhaustion and overwork. In addition, the mountains and forests surrounding the threatened posts made it easy for Giap to restrict, and probably to shut off, air traffic into the beleaguered garrisons. Certainly, the French would pay a high price for aerial resupply, and the coin would be in the form of trained air crews and scarce transport aircraft. The last option, French reinforcement of the threatened posts, would only compound the disaster. Any reinforcement meant that more troops would be lost in the eventual attempt at evacuation. The aerial resupply force, already strained, would surely collapse if it attempted to support significant reinforcements to the border posts. For the French, this course of action epitomized a classic case of "throwing good money after bad." While this last course of action would have proven futile,

Giap took no chances. To prevent French reinforcements being sent to North Vietnam from southern Vietnam, now largely pacified by the French, Giap ordered Nguyen Binh, the Vietminh commander in the South, to launch a major offensive there.

Nguyen Binh was another of those fascinating and enigmatic characters who flitted in and out of the Indochina Wars. Born in the Red River Delta of North Vietnam in 1904, he, like Giap, Ho, and the others, began his revolutionary career at an early age. His school was the harsh and shadowy world of abortive uprisings and French prisons. But Binh differed from the other Vietnamese Communists. First, he was the only one with formal military training, which he had received at the Whampoa Military Academy under the Nationalist Chinese. The second feature which set Nguyen Binh apart from his colleagues—and they were, and are, with the exception of Giap, a puritanical, sanctimonious bunch—was his all too real humanity. Wine, women, and song were not strangers to Binh, and he appears to have had a lighter side which his subordinates found attractive. Third, Binh did not join the Communist Party until late in his illustrious career, and even then (as will be seen), his manner of joining disquieted the North Vietnamese Politburo.

During his first few years in the South, Binh, the "loner," still a non-Communist and untethered by ties to the North, recorded a series of notable accomplishments. He seems to have been a combination of a resistance fighter against the French and an old-fashioned brigand. Initially, he recruited an army of fifteen battalions, eventually increased to twenty-two regiments. He organized and trained a general staff, long before Giap adopted that staff organization, and he set up a political-economic committee to coordinate his rule in those areas under his control.

Binh's sun was bright and rising, but in 1947 it faded, at least temporarily. A misguided member of one of the innumerable splinter groups in South Vietnam, thinking Binh had grown too close to the Communists, attempted to assassinate him. The attempt failed, but Binh was seriously wounded. His nurse, carefully selected by the Hanoi leadership, was not only a beautiful woman, but a hard-core Communist, and in the best soap opera tradition, she converted the now-vulnerable Binh to communism. As a reward for his new-found orthodoxy, Ho

Chi Minh promoted Binh to major general in January 1948. But as the rewards of orthodoxy came, so did the payments, and Party control over his heretofore largely independent actions tightened quickly.

Binh's revolutionary career peaked in early 1950, and he was promoted to the rank of lieutenant general. By a cleverly planned campaign of propaganda, agitation, staged riots, and above all, brutal murders, he terrified and dominated the chaos to which he and his men had reduced Saigon. Just when it seemed that nothing could stop Binh's seizure of Saigon by subversion and terror, someone did. The man who defeated Binh was a tiny, old, dried-up policeman named Tam, known as the Executioner and the Tiger of Cailay. In a few weeks, Tam destroyed Nguyen Binh's spy network, and, based on the information he got by torturing Binh's former spies, he imprisoned and executed Binh's followers. By mid-1950 Tam had lifted Binh's shadow from Saigon.

But to Ho and Giap, the now-discredited Binh still had some sacrificial value as a strategic distraction. At the monsoon's end he could still attack throughout Cochin China to pin the French troops there while Giap launched his own offensive against the northern border posts. In August–September 1950, as Giap made his final preparations to reduce the border posts, Nguyen Binh launched an all-out attack in the South. Unable to match the French in open warfare, Binh's offensive quickly faltered. His army and the Communist apparatus were cut to pieces and driven deep into the Plain of Reeds, almost into Cambodia. This misdirected offensive in the South cost the Communist forces there dearly. It eventually cost Nguyen Binh his life.

In 1951 Giap ordered Binh to "reconnoiter a fresh line of communications toward Tonkin through Cambodia."[4] It was a death sentence, and all concerned knew it. Giap knew that Binh was seriously ill and probably would not survive the trip through the hellish jungle, and to insure that Binh did not survive, Le Duan had chosen two political officers to accompany Binh. Deep in Cambodia, when capture by some French-led Cambodians appeared imminent, Le Duan's commissars blew Binh's brains out with a United States Army Colt .45. One of the Vietminh officers was captured by the Cambodians, and he told them that the body was that of Lt. Gen. Nguyen Binh, late Vietminh commander in chief in Cochin China. The French officer cut off one of Binh's hands and sent it to Saigon, where the fingerprints were found to be those of Binh. Thus death came to Nguyen Binh in a feverish Cambodian jungle—

alone, sick, betrayed—the price of failure in the world of Giap, Ho, and Le Duan.

Giap's first offensive in the North began on 16 September 1950. Aided by the ground mists characteristic of the late monsoon period, Giap's forces overran Dong Khe (the model for later battles) in sixty hours.

Giap's forces outnumbered the French at least eight to one.[5] The battle began with an artillery duel, the French in the fort, the Vietminh on the heights surrounding it. When the Vietminh mortar and artillery attacks had destroyed the French guns and fortifications, wave after wave of infantry swept in. Finally, there was hand-to-hand fighting in the last redoubts, then silence. This time, when the Vietminh overran the fort, they immediately went into positions from which to repel a paratroop counterattack. There was no pillaging, no confusion on the objective. The airborne counterattack never came, for the French high command now realized the vulnerability of the border posts.

Dong Khe was the first domino along Route 4 to topple, and its fall foretold the demise of the other garrisons. Giap made his plans soundly and carefully, but even he had not foreseen the major assist he would receive from the French commander, Carpentier. Carpentier, too, had a plan for the border posts which he announced on 16 September, the day Giap's counteroffensive jumped off against Dong Khe. Much too late, Carpentier had decided to evacuate the border forts. The plan (Order No.46) provided that Thai Nguyen would be captured as near 1 October as possible and that Cao Bang, one of the key border posts, would be evacuated as soon as Thai Nguyen was captured.[6]

In a war in which the French consistently drew up unrealistic plans, this one stands supreme. The capture of Thai Nguyen was totally unconnected with the evacuation of Cao Bang. Carpentier's plan called for the garrison at Cao Bang to be evacuated not by Route Coloniale 3 (R.C.3), which connected Cao Bang to Thai Nguyen, but by R.C. 4 through Dong Khe. While the capture of Thai Nguyen would contribute nothing militarily to evacuation of Cao Bang, it did have other attractions for Carpentier. It could be taken easily and with little risk, and it had major news media potentialities. If properly handled in the press, its seizure could cover and distort the abandonment of Cao Bang, which for the French was a significant military setback. To Giap, Thai Nguyen was not worth fighting for. It housed only a few Vietminh logistic installations, and these could be quickly moved or abandoned without incurring serious damage.

If the seizure of Thai Nguyen had been the only irrationality of the plan, it might have been forgiven, perhaps even justified, as a press agent's ploy sought at cut-rate prices. The catastrophic deficiency of the plan was not its purposeless seizure of Thai Nguyen, but its concept for evacuating Cao Bang. In Carpentier's plan the successful evacuation of Cao Bang depended on two factors, speed and surprise. Prior to the evacuation, all preparations at Cao Bang were to appear that the French were strengthening the fort for a last-ditch defense, not preparing to flee it. Then, as Carpentier envisioned things, when Giap had been deluded, the garrison at Cao Bang would quickly destroy the remaining stores and hurry down Route 4 to Dong Khe. There it would meet a relieving column coming up from Lang Son. Once the column left Cao Bang, its safety—in Carpentier's concept—depended on speed.

Carpentier's plan, built on fantasy, was doomed from the start. In the first place the plan was fatally outdated. It had been drawn up a year before and depended on Dong Khe being securely in French hands. And yet, before the French tried to put the plan into effect, they knew that Giap held Dong Khe in strength and that the French could not retake it. The second deficiency of the plan was that no French force could move covertly or quickly along Route 4. Giap controlled the road; ambush sites along the track were plentiful and potentially disastrous; and the terrain was so rough that mines, landslides, and blown bridges alone could exact delays of hours, even days.

The plan had other faults. Secrecy, the vital ingredient of Carpentier's plan, was almost certain to be lost before the operation began. Giap's ubiquitous agents would find out about the operation early, and he would know (as he did) more about the plan than did most of the French commanders who tried to execute it. The French command arrangements were vague, and who-commanded-whom never got straightened out. Colonel Le Page, who commanded the Lang Son column, was totally inadequate for the job. He was an artilleryman, a sick man, inexperienced in jungle warfare, confused about his mission, uncertain of his troops, and doubtful of his own abilities. Above all, in the face of Giap's newly muscled Main Force divisions, the French simply did not have the strength to do what the plan prescribed.

Most of the senior French officers were convinced the plan would fail. Alessandri railed against it; he threatened to resign, but he didn't. All knew the plan for what it was—desperation's child—for by September 1950, there was no workable solution to the problem of the forts along R.C. 4. The stupidity and indecision of the French Command in 1949 must, in 1950, be paid for in the blood of the soldiers posted along the road.

In late September, Carpentier attacked Thai Nguyen with the equivalent of about two infantry divisions, copiously supported by tanks, artillery, and fighter-bombers. They met only limited resistance, but had difficulty moving the heavy equipment of the column in the downpour of the unseasonably prolonged monsoon. The French finally took the town in mid-October. It contained little of value, and after sitting in Thai Nguyen for about ten days, the French evacuated it.

The real fighting was being done on Route 4. On 16 September the ill-fated Colonel Le Page and his men, largely North Africans, set out from Lang Son for That Khe, their intermediate stop on the way to Dong Khe, where they were to meet the evacuees from Cao Bang. To preserve the secrecy of the Cao Bang evacuation nobody informed Le Page of his ultimate mission, so he moved northwest toward That Khe hesitantly and blindly. All along the track the Vietminh harassed the French troops by ambushes, mines, booby traps, and road blocks. It became so difficult to move on the road that Le Page had to send his artillery, trucks, and heavy engineering equipment back to Lang Son, causing a significant decrease in the combat effectiveness of his already inadequate forces.

On 19 September, Le Page's force plodded into That Khe, there to be met by what should have been the most welcome of reinforcements, the 1st Foreign Legion Parachute Battalion, which had been dropped into That Khe on 18 September. The 1st Batailon Etranger de Parachutistes (BEP), made up mostly of Germans, had the reputation as the most ferocious French fighting unit in Indochina; they were shock troops, always the spearhead. The 1st BEP should have been an invaluable addition to Le Page's nondescript force, but that was not the way things worked out. The elite "paras" had outspoken disdain for other French soldiers who did not meet their own high professional standards. The Germans, many of them former SS troopers, looked down on and mistrusted the North Africans from Lang Son. The officers of the 1st BEP quickly sensed Le Page's indecision, inexperience, and lack of self-confidence, and this alarmed them. Thus, Le Page's reinforcements, the 1st BEP, which should have strengthened his force, instead weakened it. Nothing is so destructive of fighting morale as a lack of confidence in the commander and a lack of trust in the other units with which one is bound into combat partnership.

Although the French situation was bad when Le Page's troops straggled into That Khe, it rapidly got worse. In the first place, nobody (including Le Page) knew why the force was there or what its final task or objective was to be. Indeed, some staff officer on Alessandri's or Carpentier's staff tacked the nickname "Task Force Bayard" onto Le Page's hodgepodge command. The French, in Indochina War I, consistently came up with ironically descriptive code names for their forces and operations. In code-naming Le Page's group they hit gold, since "Bayard" connotes "blindness and the self-confidence of ignorance." In view of the fact that nobody in Task Force Bayard had any knowledge of its ultimate mission or what lay ahead of it, the nickname appears to have been apt, although there was precious little self-confidence in the force.

The second factor which further reduced the effectiveness and morale were Le Page's orders to conduct a series of small raids and forays radiating out of That Khe. The theory—generally held at very high headquarters—is that these minor operations are necessary to keep the troops busy and their offensive edge honed. Such piddling operations gain nothing, and they get men killed and wounded just as do the big battles. Front-line soldiers of all armies and of all times hate them. But Le Page's raids had a more devastating effect than just causing needless casualties. They widened the "confidence gap" which already existed between the paratroopers and the North Africans. One day a combined force of "paras" and Moroccans were on a sweep, with the paratroopers leading. The Legionnaires surprised a group of Vietminh and cut them up badly, but the rest of the Vietminh unit swung around to the rear of the French force and jolted the Moroccans with a hard counterattack. The Moroccans folded, and the French paratroopers suddenly found themselves hard pressed on all sides. After some tough fighting the Legionnaires got things straightened out, but the skirmish confirmed their distrust of the North Africans.

At last, on 30 September, Le Page got a coded message from Colonel Constans, his commander in Lang Son, telling him *in part* what his

Task Force Bayard was supposed to do. The message ordered Le Page to take his force and recapture Dong Khe, eleven miles away, by 2 October. It gave him no reason for this advance on Dong Khe, continuing to keep him in the dark about what his real mission was. The part of the mission which Le Page received—to take Dong Khe—startled him enough. He immediately sent a message to Constans pointing out the difficulties of the mission, and he made a sound case. He told Constans that he (Le Page) had no intelligence on Dong Khe except that the Vietminh were either there or somewhere up the track in great strength. Due to the ruined condition of Route 4, no artillery or trucks could accompany Bayard's columns, and the drizzle and low clouds precluded air support.

Le Page got his answer quickly—move out for Dong Khe at once.

On the afternoon of 30 September, Le Page issued his marching orders to the four battalion commanders of the three Moroccan battalions and 1st BEP. With the orders issued, he went to confession and took communion, after which he told an old friend, "We shall never come back."[7] The Bayard column totaling 2,500 to 3,500 men set out on the night of 30 September for Dong Khe.[8] Without opposition Le Page and his men arrived on the heights east of Dong Khe at five o'clock on the afternoon of 1 October, where his advance elements received machine-gun and mortar fire from the ruins of the post. Le Page decided to attack the next day by making a double envelopment, one pincer (the Foreign Legion) attacking from the east and the other, the Moroccans, from the west. Frustrated by the limestone peaks, dense jungles, and strong Vietminh counterattacks, both attacks failed.

On the afternoon of 2 October, Le Page at last was told why he and his men had left Lang Son—to meet with the evacuating garrison from Cao Bang and assist its retreat along Route 4 to Lang Son. Since he failed to take Dong Khe, this message, dropped from an airplane, told him to bypass Dong Khe, thrust into the trackless jungle to the west of the ruined fort, and then in a semicircular movement make his way back to Route 4 and meet the Cao Bang garrison at Nam Nang on 3 October.

It was a death sentence for the Le Page force. They were being ordered into a trackless jungle without guides or detailed maps. Everything, even water, had to be carried. Above all, they were surrounded by thousands of Vietminh, who knew the area intimately, and who had

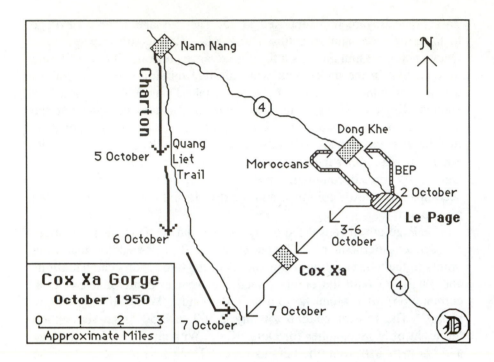

Charton

Nam Nang

4

Dong Khe

Moroccans

BEP

2 October

Le Page

5 October

Quang
Liet
Trail

3–6
October

6 October

Cox Xa Gorge

October 1950

0   1   2   3
Approximate Miles

Cox Xa

7 October

4

7 October

7 October

N

thousands of coolies supporting them. Alessandri, on hearing of the order, wired Carpentier, "Cancel everything. If you carry on it will be a crime."[9] Even this message, threatening and insubordinate, went unheeded.

As Le Page moved off Route 4 into the jungle on 2–3 October, the spotlight shifts to Cao Bang. H-hour and D-day for the garrison's departure was set for midnight of 2–3 October. Carpentier's plan called for the garrison to sneak away, without heavy equipment, and hurry to join Le Page. While this naïve trick would not have worked under any conditions, the commander at Cao Bang, Colonel Charton, a famous fighting Legionnaire, insured its failure in advance. Disobeying his orders, he blew up the ammunition (150 tons of it) and much of the other supplies in one grand, and revealing, explosion. Charton reasoned that the Vietminh knew about the sneak evacuation through their agents anyway. He was right, but he did give the Vietminh the exact time of departure.

The Cao Bang column, 1,600 soldiers, a thousand partisans, and

500 civilians (including the town's prostitutes) got underway, not at midnight 2–3 October as planned, but at noon on 3 October. It was not a speed-march made with light equipment, but a halting, disorganized evacuation with two guns, trucks, the wounded, and a gaggle of straggling women and children.

The first day (3 October) passed without hostile incident for the Cao Bang column. It was the next day which brought the devastating news. First, the column reached Nam Nang, the point where Le Page was to meet it, and found nobody. Then came two radio messages from Lang Son. The first reported that Le Page's column was surrounded in the jungles south of Dong Khe and was being destroyed. The second ordered Charton to move as fast as possible to rescue Le Page. Here was the supreme irony. The plan had prescribed that Le Page would rescue Charton, now the roles had suddenly reversed. Charton was a good soldier, and he took immediate action to comply with the order. He knew he would not get to Le Page by Route 4; he would have to go to him by faint tracks through the jungle. The guns and trucks were blown up and the soldiers' loads lightened. There were many problems, but one was predominant—nobody could find the Quang Liet trail, the only track which would take Charton to Le Page.

Finally, after a long search, Charton's natives found the trace of a trail leading in the right direction. The long column moved off single-file into the dense jungle. Soon the trail evaporated, and the men had to cut their way through the tight, tough vegetation. Forward movement was almost imperceptible, and soon they got lost. Charton pushed on to the south, cutting and slashing, throughout 4–5 October. By the evening of 6 October his column was near the remnants of Le Page's units.

Now back to Le Page and his fate. On 2 October Le Page had received the order to bypass Dong Khe and move to Charton's rescue through the jungle. The Vietminh attacked the column incessantly as soon as it entered the tangle of vegetation and limestone peaks, and the French units were soon broken up and hunted like animals through the jungle. Finally the Vietminh drove the largest group, under Le Page, now desperately ill and barely able to walk, into a deep ravine, called the Cox Xa gorge. Firing from the heights into the ravine, Giap's men mercilessly massacred the French. In desperation, Le Page ordered the Legionnaires to attack at 0300 on the morning of 7 October to link up with Charton's nearby forces. With many casualties and great valor, the Legionnaires broke through the Viet lines, and shortly after dawn they opened a way to Charton's command.

Charton had also been having his problems on that same morning, when the Vietminh for the first time launched a full-scale attack on his column. It started with a battering artillery preparation and followed with human-wave assaults. The French situation deteriorated rapidly, and the Moroccans fled, panic-stricken. The native partisans lost a key hill, and the whole position began to cave in. Charton counterattacked with his Legionnaires, who were partially successful. Charton's group fought on, in spite of his losses and problems.

The destruction of Charton's group was triggered, strangely enough, by the arrival of the survivors from Le Page's command. Le Page's North Africans were so ravaged physically, so terrified and demoralized, that they were subhuman. Their panic and terror passed swiftly to Charton's group, which rapidly fell into a state of chaos. Only the Legionnaires held together as an effective fighting unit, but they were few in number. Thousands of Vietminh began to close in, and soon it was all over. A few escaped, but most were prisoners or dead.

The destruction of the French units near Dong Khe panicked Carpentier and the other senior French commanders. Now their only thought was to get out of the border area. Get out at any cost. That Khe was abandoned on 10 October. Streaming down the road towards Lang Son went the garrison, along with the demoralized survivors from the commands of Charton and Le Page, the civilians of That Khe, and acting as rear guard, the 3d Colonial Paratroop Battalion (3d BPC) which had been dropped at That Khe on 6 October to help gather up the fugitives from the Route 4 disaster. The Vietminh harassed the evacuees almost from the start, breaking up the disorganized mass and then hunting down the fragments. The losses were almost total; the 3d BPC lost all but five men.

But worse would follow. The evacuation of That Khe was followed on 17–18 October by the abandonment of Lang Son, the bastion of the French border position. In contrast to Cao Bang and That Khe, Lang Son was given up before Giap had even threatened it. In addition to the demoralizing effect of the terrible casualties of the Dong Khe jungles, this obvious loss of nerve by the French high command dealt another near-fatal blow to the morale of the French Expeditionary Force. The shame of the premature evacuation was compounded by the loss of tremendous stores of supplies left at Lang Son. Immense amounts of food, clothing, and medical goods were abandoned, but more critical, the French left tons of ammunition, thirteen howitzers, 940 machine guns, 450 vehicles, 4,000 new submachine guns, over 8,000 rifles and thousands of gallons of gasoline.[10] There was enough of everything to supply Giap's army for many months.

By the end of October only the border post of Lao Cai remained in French hands, and Carpentier had decided to evacuate it. Shocked by the disaster at Dong Khe, and paralyzed by the charge that he had prematurely evacuated Lang Son, Carpentier left the delicate decision of when to begin the flight to the commander at Lao Cai, a Colonel Coste. Coste judged well, leaving on 3 November, and after a series of bitter fights managed to bring his column to safety at Lai Chau. Carpentier, congratulating Coste on his successful retreat, made it seem like a victory. It was, of course, another French defeat.

The debacle along the northern rim of Vietnam had been a major defeat. French pride, stupidity, and negligence had cost them 6,000 men out of the 10,000 men holding the border posts, as well as immense amounts of military stores. Bernard Fall dolefully commented that "When the smoke had cleared the French had suffered their greatest colonial defeat since Montcalm had died at Quebec. . . ."[11]

As the year 1950 ended, Giap moved his divisions toward the Tonkin Delta. He positioned one concentration north of Hanoi, another just west of the Delta, and a third, largely guerrillas, south of the Delta. Every sign indicated that Giap was about to launch an all-out offensive against the French position in Tonkin. This threat so demoralized Carpentier that he even drew up plans to abandon all of Vietnam down to the 18th Parallel. But the Vietminh attacks did not come in November, nor did they come in December. Giap's logistic system, built almost entirely on coolies, lacked the capability and flexibility to stock the additional supply points needed to support his new dispositions and his offensive needs. The Vietminh offensive would have to await 1951.

Giap could feel satisfied with his achievements in 1950. He demonstrated the effectiveness of his Main Force units; he seized the initiative; and he demoralized the French command. Beyond that, he had unnerved the French government, which now realized that there was no way to win Indochina War I without a massive effort, and this was politically impossible. As the year 1950 ended, Giap could confidently look forward to mounting an even larger offensive in 1951, an offensive which would drive the French from the Tonkin Delta, perhaps even from Indochina. But unfortunately for Giap, one factor in the "correlation of forces" would be changed early in January 1951. The French in Vietnam would at long last get a leader—Gen. Jean de Lattre de Tassigny, the Douglas MacArthur of the French army.

Notes—Chapter 4

1. Bodard, *Quicksand War*, pp. 246–247; Fall, *Street*, pp. 34–55.
2. Fall, *Street*, p. 34.
3. Tanham, *Warfare*, p. 42.
4. Bodard, *Quicksand War*, p. 197.
5. Edgar O'Ballance, *The Indo-China War 1945–1954: A Study in Guerrilla Warfare* (London: Faber & Faber, 1964), p. 115.
6. Bodard, *Quicksand War*, p. 273.
7. Ibid., p. 278.
8. Bodard says 2,000 plus (p. 278) while O'Ballance reports 3,500 (p. 115).
9. Bodard, *Quicksand War*, p. 282.
10. O'Ballance, *Indo-China War*, p. 118.
11. Fall, *Street*, p. 30.

5 Jean de Lattre de Tassigny

Jean de Lattre de Tassigny was a contemporary of the American general, George S. Patton, and of the Britisher, Bernard Montgomery. There was a remarkable coincidence in the careers of these three men. They were about the same age, and they had graduated from their country's military academies within a two-year span—Montgomery from Sandhurst in 1908, Patton from West Point in 1909, and de Lattre from Saint Cyr in 1910. Each ran into serious trouble as cadets. De Lattre encountered a problem with an instructor and graduated after his class. Montgomery had a severe disciplinary problem, which almost led to his expulsion, and he too spent some extra months as a gentleman-cadet. Patton failed plebe mathematics at West Point and took the ''five-year course'' instead of the normal four-year one. Each was an outstanding athlete at his service academy. All of these officers had brilliant careers in World War I. Each was seriously wounded—de Lattre and Montgomery in the chest, Patton in the thigh—and each received a high decoration for personal valor.

Like the other two, de Lattre was controversial and difficult to serve under or to command. He had an explosive temper, which he made little effort to control. He flew into terrifying rages about the most trivial of matters—a sentry wearing dark glasses, a bearded pilot, a missing star on his personal aircraft. Part of this was put-on, done purely for effect; a part, however, sprang from a sincere irritation at sloppiness and low standards.

He made the lives of his subordinates miserable. He gave them nearly impossible tasks and scant praise if they accomplished them. During World War II he called his corps and division commanders, generals all, to his headquarters at all hours of the day and night, requiring them to drive miles over shell-torn, sometimes icy, roads. He harassed his staff with lengthy conferences and harangues often between midnight and dawn. He fired subordinates with little thought and no remorse and, of course, his staff lived in a constant state of professional terror. And yet, his subordinates not only admired him, they loved him. This man who could be so difficult could also be thoughtful, personable, and when the occasion demanded, charming. He was zealous, dedicated, articulate. He could inspire his subordinates with his enthusiasm and drive to get the job done.

He was no easier to command than to serve. As the commander of the First French Army in World War II he fought constantly with his American superiors. He disobeyed their orders; he appealed over their heads through political channels; and he constantly badgered them for more troops, more supplies, or a more glamorous mission. After World War II he served under Montgomery, first on the Allied Chiefs of Staffs Committee where Montgomery was chairman, and then as commander in chief of the Land Forces, Western Europe, when Montgomery was Eisenhower's deputy. The World War II scenario repeated itself, with constant clashes and bickering between the two. Eventually, they became friends, but the disagreements continued.

De Lattre was born in 1889 to an upper middle-class family in the depths of La Vendée, a remote region of France lying on the Atlantic coast south of the Loire River. After graduation from Saint Cyr, he went into the cavalry, at that time the elite arm of the Western armies. De Lattre began World War I as a troop commander in the 12th Dragoons. Shortly after the war started, he was wounded by shell fragments in the knee. A few weeks later, in a brush with a German cavalry patrol, he killed two of the enemy with his saber, but in turn one of the Uhlans ran him through the chest with a lance. It was a serious wound, and de Lattre barely survived it. For this act he was made a Chevalier of the Legion of Honor. When de Lattre got out of the hospital, the war had moved into the trenches and the cavalry had no usefulness. De Lattre volunteered at once for the infantry.

In late 1914 de Lattre joined the 93rd Regiment of the 21st Infantry

Division as a captain and company commander, where he quickly distinguished himself. He fought with his unit in the bloodiest battle of history, Verdun. He was wounded three more times, and in 1916 took command of his battalion. He commanded the battalion until 1917, when his wounds and the debilitating effects of living in the trenches sent him to the hospital, his life as a frontline infantryman over. De Lattre finished the war as the intelligence officer of the 21st Division, participating in its battles until the end. His record in World War I was superb. He had been promoted from ''Chevalier'' to ''Officer'' of the Legion of Honor. He had been mentioned in dispatches eight times and wounded five times.

Between the wars de Lattre, like his contemporaries Montgomery and Patton, pursued the peacetime activities of the professional army officer. He attended staff colleges and war colleges, commanded battalions and regiments, served in staff positions, and spent time in overseas areas. For de Lattre, peacetime brought a ''small war'' against the Riffs in Morocco. In these desert campaigns de Lattre was wounded twice again. As World War II erupted, all three of these leaders had risen to be major generals and division commanders.

In January 1940, de Lattre took command of the 14th Infantry Division, supposedly one of the best in the French army. In fact, it was in bad shape—demoralized, lax, dominated in ''no-man's land'' by the Germans. By a mixture of personal leadership and ''hell-raising'' he shook the 14th Division into a healthy, happy, and aggressive unit. It was well he did so, for de Lattre and his division were soon to have their mettle tested in the hottest flame of war—a chaotic retreat and an ignominious defeat. On 10 May 1940 the German war machine on the western Front launched its now-famous Blitzkrieg. When the blow fell, the 14th Division was in a rear area behind the lines. On 13 May the division began its movement to the front by train. For the next week the division and its commander operated in a world of chaos. The French army was breaking up. Civilians clogged the roads, and intelligence on both French and German forces was either confused or totally lacking. Signal communications between the division and its higher headquarters as well as with its subordinate units were sporadic, and plans from higher headquarters either arrived late or not at all. By 18 May, in company with other French units, de Lattre temporarily stabilized the situation on his front.

But the respite was short-lived. On 5 June the Germans attacked and by 9 June the 14th Division was heavily engaged. It fought well, but the French division on its left collapsed and exposed de Lattre's flank. Disregarding this threat de Lattre stood firm and fought off three German infantry divisions. Then on the morning of 10 June the French unit on his right flank disintegrated. Retreat was now inevitable.

For the 14th Division, the remainder of the 1940 campaign was a series of withdrawals and rear-guard actions, hounded by Stuka dive-bombers and German tanks. It lost over two-thirds of its strength, but when the hostilities ceased on 24 June, what was left of the 14th Division was intact and under the firm command of de Lattre. It had compiled a remarkable record. While other units and leaders had collapsed, the 14th Division and de Lattre had held firm. For his service in 1940, de Lattre was made a Grand Officer of the Legion of Honor. The citation read, in part, ". . . as a young divisional commander of the first order, who by his courage and skill proved one of the main elements in establishing the defenses of the whole Army. . . ."

After the cessation of hostilities in the summer of 1940, de Lattre's professional career followed a twisting and precarious course. At first the Vichy government gave him command of the troops in the Massif Central, and later command of French forces around Montpellier, an area west of Marseilles near the Mediterranean. Here he disobeyed the orders of his Vichy superiors and tried to resist the German advance of 11 November 1942 into the so-called unoccupied area of France. He was betrayed by two subordinates, and on 9 January 1943, he was tried for treason and for abandoning his post. A military court found him innocent of the first charge, but guilty of the second, and sentenced him to ten years imprisonment in jail at Rion. Aided by his son, Bernard, de Lattre escaped from prison on 3 September 1943, and on 16 October he was evacuated to England by a light airplane which had landed behind the German lines.

In mid-December 1943 he flew to North Africa, and on 20 December he saw General de Gaulle and almost immediately thereafter visited General Giraud, who had admired de Lattre during their previous service together. A day or two later he was given command of a field army, subsequently known as "Army B," later known as the First French Army, and still later as the Army of the Rhine and Danube.

He started on his new job with nothing. He pirated his key staff officers from other French units to the screams of the losing commanders. He got divisions of different origins from North Africa and from Italy, and he had problems in fusing them into a homogeneous whole. De Lattre insisted that there must be one outlook for all—Free French, refugees, natives, or French Regular Army—no looking backward. He set up a training center, a favorite device of his, and paid his usual keen attention to dress, ceremonies, and military courtesy, and he got his army ready for the grand crusade—the liberation of France.

On 16 August 1944, the First French Army landed thirty miles to the east of the fortified city of Toulon on the French Mediterranean coast. It got ashore quickly, and on 18 August de Lattre attacked Toulon, an entrenched camp held by 25,000 Germans. By 21 August the French had reached the outskirts of Toulon, and by 24 August the major part of the city was in French hands, and three days later de Lattre paraded his victorious troops through Toulon.

De Lattre made the major French naval base at Marseilles his next objective even before he completed the capture of Toulon. Here, again, his own "taste for risk" was tested, since the move against Marseilles meant splitting his forces into two segments thirty miles apart, one at Toulon, another aimed at Marseilles, and each engaged with a substantial enemy in a fortified position. Again, the gamble paid off. By 26 August de Lattre was able to bring to Marseilles most of the troops who had taken Toulon. On that date, the battle for Marseilles began in earnest, and on 27 August, although hard fighting continued in some of the positions on the outskirts of Marseilles for several days, the main redoubts within the city had fallen.

Following the capture of the two port cities, de Lattre and his troops with their United States allies sped north against light resistance. The Germans—demoralized, short of fuel, and under constant United States air attack—hastened to the north to keep from being cut off by the deep spearheads of Patton's Third United States Army, which were driving hard from Normandy. On 12 September the Franco-American troops who had landed on the Mediterranean beaches joined those of Patton's army who came into France over the Normandy beachhead, and de Lattre's army, along with the rest of General Devers' United States Sixth Army Group, came under the command of General Eisenhower.

For the rest of the war, de Lattre spent almost as much time and

effort fighting his American allies and superiors as he did fighting the
Germans. In December 1944 he had just entered Alsace when, due to
a serious German threat, General Devers, the American commander of
the Sixth Army Group and his immediate superior, ordered him to withdraw to the Vosges and give up Strasbourg. De Lattre refused to obey
the order, contending that the morale of his army as well as the spirit
of France required that this key Alsatian city be held. The controversy
then boiled over into the political arena with de Gaulle and Churchill
supporting de Lattre. Devers' order was rescinded, but the German threat
in the Vosges was real and dangerous. While de Lattre had won the
political struggle, now he had to win the military battle. He did, but it
required hard fighting by the French plus Devers' diversion of all the
American air power under his command to hold Strasbourg.

From Strasbourg to the end of the war, there was fighting again
with both friend and foe. De Lattre's army fought its way across the
Rhine, around the southern flank of the Black Forest, and took Stuttgart,
although the city was in the American zone of attack. Another "flap"
ensued, and Devers ordered de Lattre to leave Stuttgart, which de Lattre
promptly refused to do. Again, de Gaulle and Eisenhower's headquarters
supported de Lattre, and again Devers had to withdraw his order. In a
few days de Lattre captured Ulm, site of a famous Napoleonic battle,
although it too was in the American zone. This time the patient Devers
erupted in anger. There followed a thunderous scene, and the French
evacuated Ulm. A few days after the end of the war, Devers summed
up in a half-humorous statement this period of de Lattre's career. He
said, referring to his French commander, "For many months we have
fought together—often on the same side!"[1]

The years of 1944 and 1945 saw de Lattre pass his last qualifying
test as a battlefield commander. In World War I he had demonstrated
his ability in the bloody job of a company and battalion commander.
In 1940 he had proved himself as a division commander in the most
difficult circumstances—a rout—and now, finally, he had shown his
capacity as an army commander. By 1945 de Lattre had become France's
premier field commander, and as such, he could look forward to a secure
and comfortable future full of well-earned honors and prestigious positions.

In the spring of 1948 de Lattre was appointed inspector general of
the armed forces. It was not meant to be a post of power, but events

made it one. As the Soviet threat to Western Europe developed in the late forties, the endangered Western European nations began to join together, and de Lattre became the French representative on the Allied Chiefs of Staff Committee under Field Marshall Montgomery. Of course, de Lattre and Montgomery, both egotists, both full of messianic self-confidence, both convinced of the rectitude of their views, clashed at once and continued to squabble throughout their association. But in time a mutual respect grew between them, and while they still often disagreed vociferously, they became firm friends. After de Lattre's death Montgomery referred to him as a "very lovable man," a peculiar and perhaps ironic tribute to one of the most spiky personalities of his time.

In 1948 de Lattre became commander in chief of the land forces of Western Europe. He had arrived at the peak of rank and prestige to which a French officer could aspire. With the formation of NATO, only General Eisenhower and Montgomery, who became Eisenhower's deputy, out-ranked him. Into this comfortable and satisfying scene the final call of duty came in late 1950, just after the French disasters along the China/Vietnam border. The French government asked him to take the combined posts of high commissioner and commander in chief in Indochina. Even de Lattre, with his vaunted "taste for risk," hesitated. He was sixty-one years old, he held the supreme French military position in Europe, and he could see clearly the difficulties and dangers lying in wait, not only in Indochina, but in Paris as well. His hesitation was momentary, and on 13 December 1950 he left Orly Field in Paris for Saigon. France's greatest post-World War II soldier and France's supreme postwar challenge were now joined.

The term "supreme challenge" is no exaggeration. In short order, de Lattre had to revitalize and rally the demoralized French troops in Indochina. They had just seen hundreds of their comrades killed and captured. What made it worse for the French was that these defeats had been inflicted on them by an enemy they still perceived to be inferior by race, training, and military professionalism. The prior French leaders had bungled, intrigued, and grossly mishandled their troops. And finally in December, these same incompetent and fearful leaders had directed that French women and children be evacuated from the Tonkin Delta and that plans be drawn to abandon northern Vietnam.

Into this swamp stepped de Lattre. He seized this demoralized and confused mess and turned it around. De Lattre accomplished this extraordinary task by his usual methods—a combination of charm, personal contact, boundless energy, and explosive anger. He arrived in Saigon on 17 December 1950, and as he descended from the aircraft the band began to play the "Marseillaise," but one of the bandsmen hit an off-note. De Lattre erupted; he called together all those in any way responsible and gave them a tongue-lashing out of all proportion to the trivial offense. When he landed in Hanoi two days later, he relieved the Hanoi area commander within five minutes because he considered the Honor Guard turnout to be sloppy. After the Honor Guard ceremony, de Lattre addressed the assembled officers of all ranks, but it was the junior officers (including his son Bernard) to whom he spoke. He said, "To you Captains and Lieutenants, it is because of you that I have agreed to take on this heavy task. I promise you that from today you will be commanded."[2] The word that a leader had arrived sped by the "barracks telegraph" throughout Indochina. Now there would be no more blunders, no more unnecessary losses, and no more panicky evacuations. French morale began to rise.

But a beaten army cannot be revitalized by talks and tongue-lashings. The causes of its former defeats and demoralization must be removed or changed. One of the first things de Lattre did was to destroy the plans for giving up the Tonkin Delta, nor would the women and children be evacuated. He told them all that the French army would fight, and if necessary, be destroyed in the Delta. He sent immediately for his wife and together they settled in Hanoi. He ruthlessly purged the ranks of the senior officers, sending the incapable back to France. He talked to the troops on every occasion, telling them that they faced heavy fighting without reinforcements or new equipment, but that they would win. De Lattre began a program to strengthen the outposts and defensive positions of the Delta. He integrated the French air force into his planning and saw that it was equipped with a new American device, napalm, a jellied gasoline which ignites on impact. By mid-January 1951, his words and deeds rallied the French forces and they awaited Giap's General Counteroffensive with confidence and resolution. Now, in 1951, Giap would be tested against France's best general.

Notes—Chapter 5

1. Maj. Gen. Guy Salisbury-Jones, *So Great A Glory* (New York: Frederick A. Praeger, 1955), p. 197.
2. Ibid., p. 236.

6 Giap's General Counteroffensive

January 1951–May 1952

By early December 1950, Giap closed his units in around the Tonkin Delta and began the immense job of establishing the logistic bases for his upcoming offensive. At first, he considered mounting a quick attack on the Delta, and boasted that he would put Ho back in Hanoi by the end of December.[1] His probe of the French defenses north of Hanoi, however, brought him a stiff rebuff. French firmness, plus his own difficulties with logistic and troop movements, convinced Giap that he could not pull off a quick and easy victory, so he revised his timetable and settled back to complete his preparations.

The Chinese sent the Vietminh additional mortars, artillery, and antiaircraft guns, and Giap trained his troops in their use. More Regional troops were "promoted" to Main Force status and absorbed into the Regular units. As his preparations neared completion, he had ready sixty-five infantry, twelve artillery, and eight engineer battalions—a complete five-division force. The 308th and 312th Divisions were located to the west of the Delta near Vinh Yen; the 316th Division was north of Haiphong, near the coast; the 320th was in its usual position south of the Delta; and the 304th was in the Viet Bac, initially in reserve. The morale of the Vietminh forces was high. They had just destroyed the French forces along the Vietnam/China border, and they looked forward eagerly to the final battle which would drive the hated colonists from the Tonkin Delta and Hanoi. The time for the long-awaited General Counteroffensive had arrived.

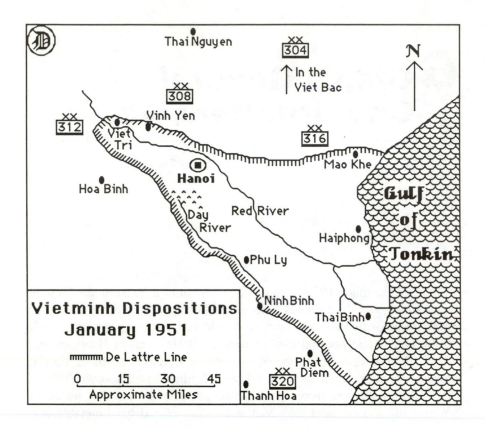

Thai Nguyen

304

In the
Viet Bac

N

308

Vinh Yen

312

Viet
Tri

316

Mao Khe

Hanoi

Hoa Binh

Gulf

Day
River

Red River

of

Haiphong

Tonkin

Phu Ly

**Vietminh Dispositions
January 1951**

Ninh Binh

Thai Binh

mmmmm De Lattre Line

Phat
Diem

0   15   30   45

320

Approximate Miles

Thanh Hoa

To understand what happened in 1951, one must examine the transcendent role which the General Counteroffensive held in Vietminh national strategy. Truong Chinh, one of the Vietminh revolutionary theorists, wrote a book in 1947 called the *Primer for Revolt*. In this book Truong foresaw the French/Vietminh War being fought in three stages. First, the French would be superior in strength, the Vietminh inferior; in the second phase there would be equilibrium of forces; and in the third stage the Vietminh would become the superior force and go over to the General Counteroffensive, called the TTC by the Vietminh (from the acronym formed by the Vietnamese words for the General Counteroffensive, *Ton Tan Cong*). Truong viewed the TTC as the culmination of the war, the last act before the grand finale of victory. Truong Chinh describes this final phase and the conditions bringing it to fruition (the merging again of military and political *dau tranh*) in this passage: "The stage of General Counteroffensive—In this stage the balance of forces having changed in our favor, our strategy is to launch a General Counteroffensive, and the enemy's strategy is to defend and retreat. There are two factors determining our strategy of General Counteroffensive. First, the strength of our army and people, and second the weakening of the enemy and the extreme demoralization of his troops. It may happen that our material forces are even relatively weaker than the enemy's, still, as a result of the special conditions in Indochina, France, in the French colonies and the world over, and the tendency to disintegration in the enemy's morale, we can switch over to the stage of General Counteroffensive.

"For example, as a result of the long war the enemy troops become weary and discouraged, and are tormented by home-sickness. The French economy and finances are exhausted; supplying the army is difficult, the French troops have put up with privations and the French people do not want the war in Vietnam to go on any longer. . . . .

"As for us, although our material resources are not yet adequate, our fighting spirit soars constantly higher. . . .

"During this stage, the enemy surrenders many positions and withdraws to entrench himself in the big cities. . . . As for us, our consistent aim is that the whole country should rise up and go over to the offensive on all fronts. Completely defeat the enemy and achieve true independence and unification . . ."[2]

As the Vietminh leadership examined the situation in 1951, they saw the prerequisites for launching the TTC which Truong Chinh had set forth. In the Tonkin area, Giap's forces were as strong as the French; their morale was better; and he had the initiative and the momentum from his 1950 successes. To Giap, the "objective realities," too, argued for the initiation of the General Counteroffensive.

Finally, there were military, political, and economic imperatives which pushed the Vietminh toward a major offensive. Giap's victories of 1950 had not solved the vital shortage of rice for the Vietminh, and Ho's governmental apparatchiks and his troops were still on short rations. The Vietminh's population control problems continued. They desperately needed more manpower for military and other purposes, and they needed a large number of people to govern if their claim to represent the Vietnamese people was to have credibility. Both problems required the capture of all or a large part of the Tonkin Delta.

The last spur driving the Vietminh to launch an offensive was the old one—time. First, there was the increased pace of United States military aid to the French. This American assistance, estimated to constitute only fifteen percent of the French equipment in 1950 and 1951, was certain to grow greater, and Giap wanted to strike before any additional equipment could significantly increase French capabilities.[3] Then, too, the French were strengthening their defenses and French morale was improving. Finally, any long delay in the attack might tempt the French to seize the initiative and strike Giap in a preemptive attack. Again it was Ho, speaking to his military leaders in a December 1950 critique on the Vietminh victories along the northern border, who summed up Vietminh thoughts on the importance of time. He said, "The enemy is pulling himself in, not to lie still, but actually to leap forward again. He is striving to win time and prepare to hit back. . . . We too must win time in order to make preparations. This is the condition for defeating the opponent. In military affairs time is of prime importance. Time ranges first among the three factors for victory . . . Only by winning time can we secure the factor for defeating the enemy."[4] Ho revealed his definition of "winning time," that is, beating the French to the punch, by the following blunt injunction to the conferees: "It is precisely to win time that this conference should be a short one. . . . The reports must be concise and raise the main and necessary problems. Don't be wordy. This could only waste time and bring no result at all."[5]

To the Vietminh, then, every factor argued for the immediate launching of the General Counteroffensive. Truong's theory was sound; the military situation appeared favorable; the need for rice and people made it imperative; and the necessity to strike quickly made it urgent.

But wise old Ho seems to have had some misgivings about launching the TTC—at least he had them in December 1950. In the address at the critique he warned the senior Vietminh officials, "Let us not . . . underestimate the enemy. We still have to win many more victories before we can switch over to a general counteroffensive."[6] But Ho later apparently changed his mind.

On the French side, de Lattre quickly devised a plan to regain the initiative the French had lost the year before. In effect, his plan was an overdue acceptance of the recommendations made by General Revers in 1949. De Lattre based his strategy on one central concept: he wanted to increase French *offensive* strength to the point where he could seize the initiative from Giap and attack, reasoning that if the French could not mount a significant offensive in North Vietnam against Giap, the war was lost. The French leader planned to increase his offensive strength by two steps. First, he would reduce the number of French troops required for static defensive duties. To do this he would build a fortified line around the perimeter of the Delta; he would step up the pacification program within the area; and he would turn the static defensive duties over to the National Vietnamese Army, under the Vietnamese emperor, Bao Dai. Second, he wanted to obtain increased military aid from the United States. But in early January 1951 this long-range concept was largely academic, and before any of these measures could be implemented, de Lattre had to repulse the first attack of Giap's General Counteroffensive that was rushing at him.

Giap made the initial attack of the TTC on 13 January at Vinh Yen, about twenty-five miles northwest of Hanoi. He called it the "Tran Huong Dao" campaign after the legendary Vietnamese hero who, during

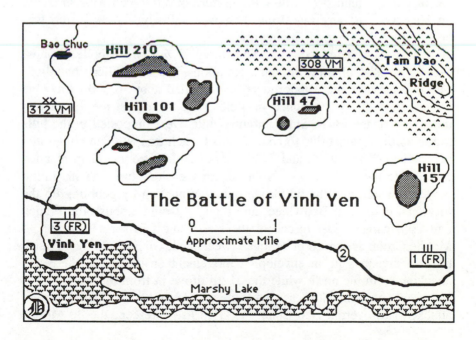

The Battle of Vinh Yen

the 13th century, twice repulsed Mongol invaders. Neither Giap nor any of the other Vietminh leaders have explained why Giap selected Vinh Yen as his initial objective. As a matter of fact, the Vietnamese Communists have never discussed the disastrous campaign of 1951, but their rationale for selecting Vinh Yen as the point at which to break into the Delta can be deduced. The town was a key road junction leading to Hanoi from the northwest and west. The terrain appeared favorable for a Vietminh attack. The Vinh Yen area offered a covered route of approach to the south from the Viet Bac down the Tam Dao Ridge to within ten miles of the town. A series of low hills to the north of the town overlooked it and lay on the Communist line of approach from the Tam Dao towards Vinh Yen. Behind the French position in Vinh Yen ran a marshy lake several miles long and several hundred yards wide—a fatal trap if the French were forced south from the town. Finally, a Vietminh victory at Vinh Yen would cut off the French positions in the Delta to the west of the town and north of the Red River, particularly the critical post at Viet Tri. With a victory at Vinh Yen, perhaps Giap foresaw another hasty and catastrophic evacuation of the more westward French units and forts. There is some evidence, scant though it may be, that Giap planned to follow the seizure of Vinh Yen with an attack on Viet Tri.[7] At any rate Vinh Yen was a likely choice as the first objective of the General Counteroffensive.

The French defended Vinh Yen initially with two Mobile Groups, each composed of three infantry battalions and an artillery battalion. The two Groups plus supporting troops totaled about 6,000 men. One Group, the 3d, was stationed in Vinh Yen, the other, the 1st, a few miles east of the town. Small infantry units were outposted in the hills to the north. Against this force of 6,000 French troops, Giap committed two divisions, the 308th and 312th, about 20,000 troops. Giap planned to separate the Mobile Groups and destroy each in turn. As his initial move he would lure the 3d Group out of Vinh Yen by gobbling up the fifty-man outpost at Bao Chuc, and then he would ambush the French unit as it came to the rescue of the Bao Chuc garrison. With the 3d Mobile Group destroyed or seriously weakened, Giap would then launch his two divisions in an enveloping movement on the town, the 308th attacking from the north while the 312th drove in from the west.

Giap's plan almost succeeded. Late on 13 January the 308th Division attacked and overran Bao Chuc. As Giap had foreseen, the 3d Mobile

Group charged north the next day (14 January) to save the small garrison, and they ran into an ambush set up by the Vietminh 312th Division. The Group was badly hurt. It lost almost all of the Senegalese battalion and a major part of the 8th Algerian Spahis, and by nightfall the 3d Group limped back to Vinh Yen under cover of artillery fire and close air support. By the evening the French had been forced back against the marshy lake and the Vietminh had taken the hills overlooking Vinh Yen from the north. The Vietminh attacks also opened a gap of some three miles between the 3d Group in Vinh Yen and the 1st Group to the east. Giap's operation progressed as planned, and the French situation was grim.

On that same day, de Lattre flew into Vinh Yen in a light plane and took charge of the battle. He immediately ordered the 2d Mobile Group to move from Hanoi to the battle area. He told the commander of the 1st Group to bring extra ammunition for the battered 3d Group and to clear the hills to the east of Vinh Yen. De Lattre also ordered a major airlift of reinforcements into the Tonkin Delta from as far away as South Vietnam. On 15 January, while Giap remained strangely inactive, the 1st Mobile Group moved into the battle, taking Hill 157 in the afternoon. On 16 January the French began their counterattack to retake the hills covering the town. Their assault met only light opposition as the enemy pulled back before them. By mid-afternoon the French had reoccupied Hills 101, 210, and 47.

Suddenly, after a day and a half of inaction, Giap struck. At 1700 hours, 16 January, the entire 308th Division, 10,000 strong, streamed out of the forests of Tam Dao and in an attack reminiscent of Pickett's famous charge, threw themselves at the hastily dug-in French. The attacks went on through the night and into the next day. In the heavy fighting the French lost the hills in the middle of their defensive position, but held on to Hills 210 and 157 which controlled the flanks. The French air force used every plane available, even transports, and poured napalm, bombs, and gunfire with brutal effectiveness into the massed Vietminh attackers. Under the flaming napalm the Vietminh panicked and ran screaming back into the forest from which they had come.

By the morning of 17 January the situation was critical for both sides. De Lattre committed his reserve, the three battalions of Mobile Group 2, hastily constituted as the units arrived from Hanoi, to retake the central hills. The Vietminh launched the 308th Division in a final assault at dawn, but the attack quickly broke down. Again, it was the French fighter-bombers which were decisive. Finally, the 312th Division made a belated attack from the northwest. It, too, failed and the battle ebbed. Shortly after noon the Vietnamese force receded northward into the Tam Dao. The French let them go, too exhausted to pursue. Giap had not only lost his first set-piece battle, he had sacrificed the bulk of his two best divisions—6,000 to 9,000 dead, 500 prisoners, and probably around 6,000 wounded. For Giap and the Vietminh, Vinh Yen spelled disaster.

In typical Communist fashion, Giap quickly (on 23 January) convened a group to analyze the causes of the disaster. In an effort to cover his own mistakes, Giap placed the greater part of the blame on his troops, charging them with lack of aggressiveness and cowardice[8]—a monstrous lie. It was not the Vietminh soldiers who lost the battle of Vinh Yen, it was Giap. First he underestimated the effectiveness of French air support, not only its ability to bring troops into the area, but above all, the casualty-producing power and effect of napalm on the morale of his troops. While other tactical mistakes contributed to his defeat, the French close air support and napalm decided the battle. The French use of napalm should not have surprised Giap, since the French air force had employed this weapon against a Vietminh concentration on 22 December 1950. Second, Giap missed several tactical opportunities. On 14–15 January he had the French forces split, shoved back against the marshy lake, and a full-scale coordinated attack with both the 308th and the 312th Divisions would probably have overrun in turn both of the French mobile groups and Vinh Yen.

Giap's third mistake was to give up the hills north of Vinh Yen on 16 January after having taken them the day before. He should have dug in on these superior defensive positions and bloodied the French as they sought to recapture them. There is no explanation for this lapse from Giap, for he has never commented publicly on this defeat. He probably withdrew his troops from the relatively open hills to the dense cover and concealment of the Tam Dao to protect them from the French air and artillery attacks. But if this retreat to cover was a sound move on the morning of 16 January, then his massed attack that afternoon in the face of the same French close air and artillery support was not only unsound, but suicidal.

Finally, Giap failed to coordinate the actions of his two infantry divisions. He used them together effectively on 13 January when the 308th Division overran Bao Chuc and the 312th conducted the accompanying ambush of Mobile Group 3. His coordination broke down, however, at the crucial moment when the 308th made its all-out assault on 17 January. Here was the moment for the 312th Division to attack too, angling in from the northwest between the French hilltop defenses and Vinh Yen. The inaction of the 312th Division permitted the French to concentrate its air and artillery against the unfortunate 308th Division. Then, belatedly the 312th attacked after the 308th had been so battered it could not help. It was a classic "piecemeal" attack—the kind the service manuals of all armies warn against. It was not the Vietminh troops who should be blamed for the defeat at Vinh Yen, but Giap's unsound judgment and tactical bungling.

The narrowness of de Lattre's victory over Giap at Vinh Yen spurred the French general to accelerate the implementation of his strategic plan to build up the offensive capability of his forces. He began immediately to build a chain of defensive positions around the Delta which became known as the "de Lattre Line." This line ran from the sea north of Haiphong, west to Viet Tri, thence southeast to the sea near Phat Diem. The "Line" consisted mainly of small fortified infantry positions each located so it could support its neighbors. Six hundred of the posts had been completed by mid-summer, 1951, and the remainder, another 600, were finished by the end of the year.

The military worth of this thin line of fortifications is questionable. It ate up manpower, requiring over twenty infantry battalions to man it (over two infantry divisions). It did not prevent the infiltration of Vietminh guerrillas into the Delta, and even sizable Main Force units slipped through it. Gen. Henri Navarre, one of de Lattre's successors, later disparaged it as "a sort of Maginot Line."[9] The line made sense only if eventually the French could man it effectively with Vietnamese troops. This, too, was part of de Lattre's plan, and to bring it about he pressed Bao Dai to speed up the formation and training of the Vietnamese National Army. De Lattre set up a military academy to train Vietnamese officers, and in July 1951 he pressured Bao Dai to introduce conscription. Unfortunately, however, the Vietnamese National Army never attained effectiveness.

In de Lattre's strategy the construction of the "Line" and the formation of the Vietnamese National Army to man it were only steps leading to the final goal—the freeing of most of the French troops for use first as counterattacking troops against Giap's penetrations into the Delta, and finally, as a force to take the offensive against Giap and the Vietminh. Since the Vietnamese National Army remained inadequate, neither de Lattre nor his successors could ever generate the offensive strength the French needed to thwart Giap. This failure was one of the decisive factors in their eventual defeat.

While de Lattre built blockhouses and pressed Bao Dai and the Vietnamese to form a national army, Giap studied his defeat at Vinh Yen and planned his second attempt to penetrate the Tonkin Delta. He shifted his supply bases eastward; he rebuilt the 308th and 312th Divisions; and by late March he was ready to attack again. On the night of 23–24 March, Giap launched the second phase of his previously blunted General Counteroffensive. He chose the small village of Mao Khe, on the northern and eastern end of the French defensive line, as his objective, and named this phase the "Hong Hoa Tham" campaign after a Vietnamese resistance leader who fought the French in the early twentieth century near Mao Khe. In many ways Mao Khe was a good choice. It was only twenty miles north of Haiphong, the northeastern anchor of the French lifeline in the Delta. The loss of Haiphong, or even a serious threat to it, would force the French from the entire Delta. It was also well located for Giap's offensive purposes. There was a covered route from the Viet Bac into the attack positions. It had adequate roads and trails so Giap's porters could support the operation, and it was close to the Viet Bac and China, his source of supply. A small garrison made up of Vietnamese and Africans totaling about 400 men defended Mao Khe, and they should have been easily overrun. There was one disadvantage for Giap at Mao Khe, but this would not become apparent to him until the operation began.

Giap chose the fresh 316th Division to make this attack, and he moved the partially rebuilt 308th and 312th Divisions into the Mao Khe area to support the untried 316th and to exploit any success the latter division might achieve. He ordered the 304th Division (which Giap had moved from the Viet Bac to a position southwest of the Delta) and the 320th Division, south of the Delta, to make diversionary attacks to attract French reserves from the scene of his main attack, or failing to do that, at least to freeze them in place so that they would not intercede at Mao Khe.

Between the initiation of the attack on the night of March 23–24 and 26 March, the Vietminh managed in heavy fighting to drive in all the French outposts except one—a coal mine held by about ninety-five native Tho guerrillas. As at Vinh Yen, the initial state of the battle went well for Giap and the Vietminh. On 26 March Giap deployed the 316th Division for the final assault. Then, the disadvantage of Mao Khe became abruptly and painfully apparent. Three destroyers and two landing craft of the French navy moved up the Da Bac River and opened an intense naval bombardment against the massed troops of the 316th. This gunfire plus a French air attack caused heavy casualties and broke up the attack of the 316th before it could be launched. On 27 March, Giap regrouped the 316th for another attack.

De Lattre had reacted slowly and conservatively to Giap's initial operations against Mao Khe. He was unsure even on 26 March that Giap's effort at Mao Khe might not be a diversion. What troubled de Lattre and delayed his reaction to Mao Khe was his inability to locate the 308th and 312th Vietminh Divisions. He did not know they were supporting the 316th at Mao Khe and had to proceed on the basis that they could reappear, a formidable striking force, somewhere along the northern perimeter at any moment. So on 26 March, de Lattre sent a minimal reinforcement of one paratroop battalion and some artillery batteries to Mao Khe, plus the naval craft. At 0400 hours on 27 March the reformed 316th Division launched a furious attack on the Thos holding the coal mine. The fighting was severe, but the defenses held until dawn, when French aircraft entered the action with bombs and napalm, relieving the pressure. At 1400 hours on 27 March the French paratroop battalion moved from the village of Mao Khe to relieve the unit holding the mine. They quickly came under heavy artillery, mortar, and machine-gun fire and were pinned down for the rest of the day, and only after nightfall could the battalion move back into Mao Khe village.

Twenty-seven March held one final surprise for Giap and his frustrated troops. After dark the Tho guerrillas, who had so valiantly defended the mine against heavy odds, completed a skillful withdrawal around their Vietminh besiegers and made it back to the village. They brought with them not only their wounded, but the Tho families who had lived at the mine with them.

With all the French outposts now driven in, 28 March was to be Giap's day to launch the final assault. At 0200 hours a heavy Vietminh artillery concentration hit Mao Khe village. This was followed by waves of Vietminh, and the fighting in the burning, exploding village was intense. French artillery from nearby brought down close-in protective fire, while the French paratroops and what was left of the original garrison fought the Vietminh hand-to-hand and from house-to-house. A second Vietminh regiment was ordered into Mao Khe to support the initial attack, but it got into an area of prearranged fire by the French artillery and was dispersed. By mid-morning the attackers began to ease their assaults and then withdrew from the village. Giap lost over 3,000 men; he also lost his second set-piece battle to de Lattre, although the Frenchman can claim little credit.

Giap's mistakes at Mao Khe can be catalogued quickly. First, he did not take advantage of de Lattre's hesitation in reinforcing Mao Khe. He should have taken the village before the paratroop battalion arrived. Giap should have foreseen the French naval intervention which broke up his attack. Throughout the whole operation Giap was hesitant, inflexible, and blind to the capabilities of the French navy as he had been blind to the capability of the French air force at Vinh Yen.

Despite the bloody defeats of Vinh Yen and Mao Khe, Giap and the other Vietminh leaders decided to make one more attempt to bring off the General Counteroffensive and to break into the Delta before the monsoon arrived. This time Giap selected the Day River area at the southwestern hinge of the de Lattre Line to make his main effort, calling the operation "Quang Trung," in memory of a legendary Vietnamese hero who defeated the Chinese near Hanoi in 1789. Critics of Giap's 1951 campaigns have universally questioned the wisdom of his launching the Day River offensive after having been so thoroughly defeated at Vinh Yen and Mao Khe. At first glance their doubts would appear valid, but the factors which drove Giap to begin the 1951 campaigns still governed his options. Time, Giap thought, favored the French. They grew stronger with increasing American aid, the Vietminh still needed to increase the population under its control, and above all, their critical need for rice still existed. To Giap and the other Communist leaders the Day River campaign, if successful, would give them control over the Ninh Binh and Nam Ha provinces with their three annual rice crops and their dense population.

Given the political, economic, and military needs which required a third Vietminh offensive, the choice of the Day River line, like its predecessors Vinh Yen and Mao Khe, was a sensible selection. First, an attack along the Day River offered a more limited and more attainable objective than the Vinh Yen and Mao Khe campaigns which had aimed at Hanoi and Haiphong respectively. Operation "Quang Trung" envisioned only occupying the tip of the southern delta, the provinces of Ninh Binh and Nam Ha. If the Vietminh could occupy these two provinces they would control not only a heavily populated, rice-rich area, but they would also strike a blow at their enemies, the Catholics, whose strength in North Vietnam was centered in this area.

To Giap, the Day River area offered tactical advantages. First, there was a good chance of achieving surprise. Both of the prior offensives had been thrown against the northern flank of the de Lattre Line, the area nearest the Viet Bac and the Chinese border, and the heart of Giap's troop concentrations and supply centers. This northern flank was, however, the most logical area for a Vietminh attack. An attack elsewhere, if it could be prepared in secrecy, might surprise the French, who from previous attacks were looking north for the final blow. The terrain along the Day River also lent itself to a Vietminh surprise attack. The western bank (the Vietminh side) of the Day River dominated the eastern bank, which was held by the French. The west side was largely *Karst,* an area of steep limestone cliffs, deep ravines, many caves, and dense vegetation. The attackers could move to their line of departure for the attack undetected through this tangled country. The terrain presented other advantages to Giap. It offered cover and concealment from the French air force, whose napalm had won Vinh Yen, and while the Day River was navigable for light French river and landing craft, the French destroyers, the spoilers of Mao Khe, could not reach this projected battle area. Giap had learned his lessons the painful way, but he had learned them well. The Day River area had one final advantage for Giap. It was the home of the 320th Division, fresh and undefeated. Of equal importance, the area had already been infiltrated by two local Main Force regiments, the 42d Independent Regiment, and the 64th Regiment of the 320th Division. Giap intended these two regiments to add a new element to his third attack.

While Giap's strategic objective was limited, his tactical plan for the Day River campaign was the most imaginative of his 1951 General

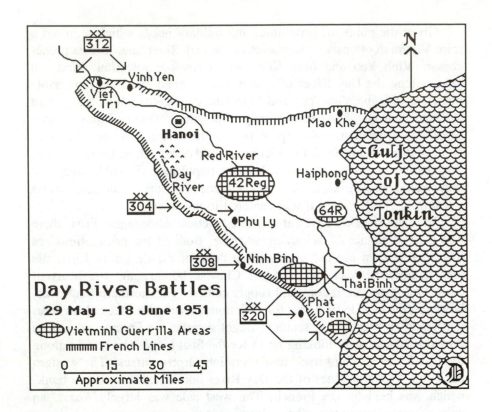

Day River Battles
29 May – 18 June 1951
Vietminh Guerrilla Areas
French Lines
0   15   30   45
Approximate Miles

Counteroffensive. During April, the 312th Division would draw the attention of the French to the Vinh Yen sector and even farther west by appearing to threaten that town and to move into T'ai country west of Vinh Yen. Under the cover of this diversion Giap would move the 308th Division from its position north of the Delta around its western edge to attack positions south of it. In itself this was a monumental task, involving not only the movement of some 10,000 to 15,000 troops, but also at least 40,000 porters. Once in position in the *Karst* country opposite the Day River, the 308th Division and the 304th Division would launch secondary attacks. The 304th would attack Phu Ly, while the 308th assaulted Ninh Binh. When the 304th and 308th attracted French reserves, the main effort of the offensive would then be made farther south and east by the 320th Division. Its goal was to seize the southern corner of the Delta and to join its subordinate regiment, the 64th, near Thai Binh. In the meantime, the 42d Independent Regiment and the

64th Regiment would attack the French behind the de Lattre Line to create havoc in the rear areas and to prevent the movement of French reserves to meet the 320th Division.

The timing of this offensive against the Day River was critical. Giap wanted to initiate it in late April or early May, since this schedule would permit him to make his troop movements and logistic preparations during the dry season. His attack would take place, then, just before the onset of the Southwest Monsoon which normally came in mid-May. If Giap's offensive succeeded, he could use the rains and mists of the monsoon to protect him from French air and surface attacks while he consolidated his gains. If the attack failed, the monsoon would provide cover for the withdrawal of the Vietminh forces.

But in war, rigid and demanding schedules are seldom met, and Giap did not meet this one. He had to move his troops and the army of porters which supported them at night by jungle track to escape notice of the French air force. The movement required detailed staffwork which Giap's inexperienced staff could not provide. The plan depended on procuring rice along the route of march, but this too proved to be overly optimistic. The peasants refused to honor Vietminh requisitions for food, and so rice had to be carried many extra miles. Finally, the monsoon broke earlier than usual that year (in early May), which further delayed movement, so instead of starting the attack in late April, Giap got it off on 29 May.

The location and timing of the offensive surprised de Lattre and the French. They had not expected an attack on the southern side of the Delta, and the *Karst* had effectively hidden the Vietminh troops as they moved to their assault positions. Giap's foresight and planning of the place of the attack had won an initial advantage. An even larger part of the surprise came from the time of the offensive. In this war neither of the adversaries had previously elected to campaign in the wet season. Thus, the delay, while it complicated troop movements and logistic preparations, helped to give Giap one of the key ingredients for success on the battlefield—surprise.

The offensive enjoyed initial success, as had the attacks at Vinh Yen and Mao Khe. The 304th Division crossed the Day River easily near Phu Ly on 29 May and drove in the French outposts. The 308th overran the French positions in and around Ninh Binh and penetrated deeply into the town. In this skirmish the Vietminh killed Lt. Bernard de Lattre, the only child of the commander in chief. On the same day, an ambush set up on the Day River smashed several of the unarmored French river craft chugging to the relief of Ninh Binh. Later on 29–30 May, the Vietminh 320th Division crossed the river and destroyed a string of small French positions south of Ninh Binh. De Lattre reacted vigorously. Within forty-eight hours he dispatched to the battle area three mobile groups, four artillery groups, an armored group, and a paratroop battalion, a force equivalent to about two divisions.

On 1 June the battle began to turn against the Vietminh. Stiff French defenses and the monsoonal mud slowed the Vietminh advances. Since Giap's troops were now in the open rice paddies east of the river, the French air and artillery inflicted heavy casualties. In the zone of advance of the 320th Division, a new obstacle arose—the Catholic militia. These local paramilitary units slowed the 320th until the French could arrive with their overwhelming firepower. The 42d and 64th Regiments failed to prevent French reinforcement. Here again, it was the Catholics who warned the French of ambushes and harassed the Vietminh regiments. Finally, the French river craft units called *dinassauts* by the French (short for Division Navale d'Assaut) had regrouped and returned to the battle area where, with the French air force, they sank the boats and sampans by which Giap tried to supply and reinforce his three divisions east of the river.

By 6 June the French controlled the battle. The Vietminh supply lines across the Day River had been cut, and shortages of food and ammunition at first crippled, and then halted, the Vietminh drive. Giap realized that he had lost this campaign, too, and on 10 June began to withdraw his forces to the west bank of the river. The Day River assault, the final campaign of the General Counteroffensive, ended on 18 June. Vietminh casualties suffered during the Day River campaign have never been disclosed. Most authorities put the figures at around 10,000 of which 1,000 were captured.[10]

The collapse of the Day River operation resulted from two miscalculations by Giap. First, he failed to foresee the effectiveness with which the *dinassauts* would disrupt and destroy his tenuous supply lines across the river. Second, he did not envision that the Catholic militia would slow up his attacking groups on one hand and would nullify the efforts of the 42d and 64th Regiments to prevent French reinforcement on the other. Giap lost the battle for the Day River the same way he lost those at Vinh Yen and Mao Khe—by bad judgment and the inability to appreciate the capabilities of an arm of service (the air force, the navy, the *dinassauts*) with which he had no personal experience.

His disastrous 1951 offensives cost the Vietminh around 20,000 men and the initiative, at least temporarily. De Lattre was too weak to exploit Giap's failures, or Giap might have found himself in dire straits indeed. At any rate, the score of Giap's three offensive campaigns of early 1951 was: de Lattre—three; Giap—nothing.

Those who have analyzed Giap's 1951 campaign censure him not only for launching the TTC in early 1951, but for his tactical handling of the three campaigns as well. While Giap earned their censure, the specific charges upon which his critics have reproached him are largely invalid. They ignore Giap's *real* shortcomings in this offensive, which were much more damaging to his reputation. Of all the military critics who dissected Giap's failures, O'Neill alone blames him for having gone on the offensive at all. It is O'Neill's view that Giap should have availed himself of "the French propensity for the attack," and that Giap should have attempted to lure the French into attacking him on ground of his (Giap's) own choosing.[11] There (a location is not suggested) Giap could have offset most of the advantages held by the French in the Delta. O'Neill's criticism ignores the military and political factors involved. Militarily, Giap would have had to surrender the initiative, the momentum, and the morale factor to de Lattre. He would have given the French time to strengthen their defenses, build up the National Vietnam Army, and obtain more American military aid. Politically and economically, waiting for the French attack would only have worsened the Vietminh's rice shortage and the pernicious effects of their shrunken population base. O'Neill was wrong. Giap *should* have attacked the French in the Delta in early 1951.

The most prevalent criticism of Giap's conduct of the ill-fated General Counteroffensive is that by launching it in the first half of 1951, he did so prematurely. This charge of prematurity goes directly to a fundamental problem facing any revolutionary war strategist. That problem is: what phase of revolutionary war is the insurgency in, and toward which phase is it moving? The answer determines the emphasis of effort between the political and military aspects of the struggle, the correct military strategy, even the military tactics and organization. If the revolutionary war strategist judges correctly the phase of the war, he almost automatically selects the right grand strategy leading to the appropriate military and political strategy and tactics to carry it out. If he is wrong in his judgment of the war's phase, then almost certainly he will adopt improper strategy and tactics, and thus, court defeat.

Giap and Truong Chinh both judged that the military and political situation justified going to Phase III of the General Counteroffensive in 1951. There was some doubt among other members of the Politburo (including Ho himself), but a look at the situation of late 1950 (decision time in the Tonkin Delta) as it appeared to both adversaries justifies Giap's decision to go to the General Counteroffensive. Their common view was that the Vietminh forces would probably overrun the Tonkin Delta in a few days or, at the latest, in a few weeks. Giap thought the French defenses so weak that he almost launched a hasty and ill-prepared attack in December 1950. The French commanders viewed their situation so dismally that they were starting to evacuate French civilians from the Delta and had drawn up plans to give up all of North Vietnam. Both Giap's planned attacks and the French evacuation plans reflected accurately the relative combat effectiveness of the opposing forces.

The two sides were about evenly matched in manpower and material, not considering, of course, the French air force and navy, which had played little part in the war up to December 1950. The factors of morale and leadership, however, weighed the balance in Giap's favor. The battles along Route 4 raised the fighting spirit of the Vietminh to a new high while they depressed the morale of the French. French leadership had been stupid, weak, and irresponsible, while Vietminh leadership had been competent and effective. From his victories along Route 4, Giap possessed two other factors of inestimable military value—the initiative and the momentum. He had a string of victories behind him. He could act—when, where, and how he saw fit. The French could only react, hoping to discover enough of Giap's plans to prevent a fatal surprise. To both sides it seemed that one more Vietminh victory, one more savage blow by Giap, would collapse the French defenses and insure the evacuation of the Delta—or worse—which would surely follow. All of these advantages of morale, initiative, momentum, and leadership would be lost to the Vietminh by delaying the offensive until late 1951. Far from being premature, Giap's initiation of the offensive during the first half of 1951 was fully justified, and he should have been censured had he *not* launched it. Prematurity did not defeat Giap in the first half of 1951; it was Gen. Jean de Lattre de Tassigny and, above all, Giap's own errors of generalship which beat him.

Giap made three blunders which brought about the Vietminh defeats of 1951. His first, and major, mistake sprang from a faulty strategic concept for the conduct of the General Counteroffensive. The geography of the area of operations and the disposition of the adversaries in January 1951 in and around the Tonkin Delta forced Giap to operate on "exterior lines." In layman's language this means that the Vietminh were disposed in a horseshoe-shaped line around the Delta facing *inward*. The French were operating on "interior lines," that is, they were on the inside of the horseshoe facing outward. The open end of the horseshoe was closed by the sea. Analysts who delve into military history itemize some simple, commonsense rules which generally must be followed if an army is to operate successfully on either exterior or interior lines. Since it is Giap's operations which are being critiqued, the rules for the successful conduct of operations on exterior lines will be briefly examined. In the first place, operations on exterior lines normally (although not always) require considerable numerical superiority over the enemy disposed on interior lines. Exterior line operation requires good coordination and communications among the separated, attacking segments. This mode of operation also places a premium on excellent and experienced subordinate commanders, since some improvisation is almost always necessary. *Above all else, a commander operating on exterior lines must prevent his opponent from switching troops back and forth across the interior of the horseshoe to meet the inward thrusts of the exterior attackers. The commander on exterior lines seeks to prevent these shifts by attacking simultaneously all around the perimeter so that the defender cannot take troops from an unthreatened part of the line and reinforce a threatened portion.* It should be noted that Giap had another, and unusual, means of preventing or inhibiting French reinforcement of the perimeter—the Vietminh guerrillas and Regional forces operating behind French lines, within the horseshoe itself.

To be successful on exterior lines, theoretically, Giap should have attacked the French with a simultaneous five-division assault from the perimeter of the horseshoe. The guerrillas and other troops (including Main Force units) operating within the horseshoe would aid the exterior thrusts by harassing and impeding the French reinforcements moving to threatened areas around the interior of the arc. Why did not Giap launch simultaneous attacks from around the perimeter of the de Lattre Line? It was a question of time—the shortage of time—about which Ho admonished his major commanders in December 1950. The longer the delay before launching the Vietminh offensive, the stronger the French grew, the more their morale improved, and the more formidable became the de Lattre Line. For the Vietminh, delaying the offensive would worsen the food and population problem, and would cost Giap the momentum of the Route 4 victories, and possibly the initiative itself.

The key question then becomes, how long would it have taken to mount the five-division simultaneous offensive? The answer lies in a crude analysis of the factor determining the delay—the Vietminh logistical system. It is revealing that it took Giap about two months between his victories on Route 4 and the attack at Vinh Yen to complete his preparations for the latter assault. It took him two and a half months of preparation between Vinh Yen and Mao Khe, and another two months after Mao Khe to set up the Day River offensive. These figures would indicate that it required about one month per attacking Vietminh division to establish and stock the logistic base. A projection of these primitive calculations suggest that a five-division, simultaneous attack could have been readied by mid-April or the first part of May. If Giap had selected a D-day in mid-April, it is probable that he would have had to launch the most distant 320th Division with minimal logistic support. If Giap delayed until mid-April or early May, he risked not only the seizure of the initiative by de Lattre, but the onset of the Southwest Monsoon, which could flood out his counteroffensive. This was the chance Giap had to take, but in war great victories generally come from great risks.

Would a five-division simultaneous offensive have succeeded? Maybe. After all, the outcome of the battles of Vinh Yen, Mao Khe, and the Day River fought individually were very close. Simultaneous attacks coordinated with the guerrilla effort behind the French lines might well have succeeded. It is true that the guerrilla campaign behind French lines in the Day River campaign fizzled out in the Catholic areas of the southern Delta, but such an effort would have been far more successful in the more Communist regions of the northern and western Delta. Surely a five-division simultaneous thrust, even delayed a few months, gave more hope of success than the piecemeal attacks Giap launched. Giap's three individual attacks played into de Lattre's hand, allowing the French to reinforce each threatened area in turn.

Actually, Giap was not only pushed by the lack of time, but he fell prey to that most infectious disease in the Indochina Wars—underestimation of a foe. He underestimated French will, combat capacity, and leadership. His easy victories on Route 4 convinced him that the French were staggering and that one more blow, not even a full one, would knock them out. Giap did not grasp the impact that the hard-driving, magnetic de Lattre made on the French. He was wrong, but not by very much, as the closeness of the three battles demonstrated.

Giap's second major error of the 1951 campaigns was his inability to realize the striking power and decisiveness of the French air force and navy. In each of his three attacks, they turned what might have been a victory into a bloody defeat. It was the French air force whose napalm destroyed Giap's massed assaults at Vinh Yen. It was fire from the destroyers of the French navy which upset his attack at Mao Khe, and the *dinassauts* who slashed his supply lines over the Day River. In each instance, the interventions of these services came to Giap as a surprise. He failed to foresee not only their employment, but their effectiveness. He took no countermeasures, either passive (such as concealment or avoidance) or active (such as antiaircraft machine-gun fire against the aircraft, artillery attacks against the destroyers, or bazooka and artillery strikes against the *dinassauts*). On first examination, the critic is inclined to lay blame for this blind spot on Giap's total inexperience with combined service operations. He had no air force or navy of his own and was totally unschooled in their capabilities and limitations. While his inexperience was no doubt a major contributing factor, there is a recurrence in Giap's campaigns of this fundamental error. He made it first when he failed to foresee the paratroop assaults which almost captured him in 1947 and which surprised him at Dong Khe in May 1950. He would make the same mistake later against the Americans.

Giap's third mistake in the 1951 General Counteroffensive was his inept employment of his troops on the battlefield. Each of the three campaigns produced examples of lack of coordination, inflexibility, and indecisiveness. At Vinh Yen on 16 January when the 308th Division made its all-out attack against the French, the 312th looked on. On 17 January the 312th Division finally attacked after the 308th made its final effort. His withdrawal from the good defensive positions offered by the hills north of Vinh Yen, and then his attack of the same positions after the French secured them is a sign of either indecision or inflexibility. At Mao Khe, Giap failed to take advantage of de Lattre's slowness in reinforcing the threatened position, even though Giap had two divisions (the 308th and the 312th) uncommitted and available. When the naval gunfire broke up the formation for the attack on 26 March, Giap reacted slowly and inflexibly, rescheduling it for the next day, although he had other reserves available which he should have used.

Giap's inflexibility was the major battlefield error in the Day River campaign. He should have held the 320th Division, his main effort, until the 304th and 308th Divisions had drawn French reserves to the north. Actually, he should have held the 320th as a mobile reserve which could exploit any penetration made by the 304th and 308th, or even move it to the north or south of the battle area of these two divisions in a flanking move. As it was, he ended with three divisions attacking abreast and frontally against powerful French defensive forces.

Finally, to Giap's mental mistakes—a faulty strategic concept, failure to appreciate the effectiveness of the French air force and navy, and mismanagement of his troops on the battlefield—must be added a serious deficiency of character. This failing occurred following his defeat at Vinh Yen, when he blamed the Vietminh troops for the disaster, charging them with lack of aggressiveness and cowardice. Military history has seldom recorded a charge so false, or so self-serving. It was as if Gen. Robert E. Lee after Gettysburg branded Pickett's Virginians as cowards. Giap's accusations, while no doubt brought on by his own dire political and military predicament, reveals an ignoble compulsion to protect his own reputation and position at the expense of his troops. Contrast this with Lee's behavior under similar circumstances. As the remnants of Pickett's Division returned to their own lines, Lee met them with tears saying, "It was all my fault." Giap's censure of his troops is an act not only unworthy of a man who aspired to be a "great captain," it is an act unworthy of any man of character. That Giap's troops continued to fight competently and courageously for him is a measure of the effectiveness of the intense indoctrination they received. Few other armies would have done so.

For Giap, the first half of 1951 was a disaster, one of the low points of his career. He failed the tests of a successful general—the capacity to originate a workable plan of offensive operations, the ability to carry it out, and the character to stand firm and uncomplaining under adversity. How he remained in command, even with his political power, is unfathomable. He would not have survived professionally in any other army in the world. But survive he did. Of equal importance, he learned from the bitter lessons of 1951. From these defeats he would develop a new strategy and a surer battlefield touch, and he would fight again. Few commanders in history have been given such an unearned second chance. None have made as much of it.

After the repulse of Giap's attack along the Day River in June 1951, the Southwest Monsoon forced both adversaries to suspend field operations until late September. This pause left the military situation unstable. Giap, who had dictated the type and tempo of operations for the first six months of 1951, had been badly defeated. On the other hand, the victor, de Lattre, had lacked the strength to exploit Giap's defeats. As the end of September approached, Giap and de Lattre were like two duelists armed with pistols awaiting the drop of the starting handkerchief. Who would shoot first?

It was Giap. He attacked the small town of Nghia-Lo, ninety-five miles west of Hanoi and sixty-five miles beyond the western limit of the de Lattre Line. This village was important to de Lattre because it housed the capitol of the T'ai people, who were strong supporters of the French. On the night of 2–3 October, Giap used two regiments of the 312th Division to storm the post defending the town, but in fierce fighting the small garrison beat off the attack. On the next day, General Salan, acting in de Lattre's place while the latter was in Paris, reinforced Nghia-Lo by dropping a French parachute battalion into the defensive positions. This quick reinforcement probably saved the garrison, for that night a second attack by two regiments of the 312th Division was repulsed. On 4 October Salan dropped two more paratroop battalions in and around the besieged post. This second reinforcement, plus heavy French air support, induced Giap to call off the attack and draw back across the Red River. His attempt to seize the initiative had failed. Now it was de Lattre's turn.

While the fight at Nghia-Lo was of minor importance, it did indicate the trend of future events. For Giap, the attack showed that he had learned from his recent defeats. In the first place he had, at least temporarily, given up any idea of head-on attacks against the fortified positions of the de Lattre Line. He would now attempt to entice the French out of their defenses into ground of his own choosing. He would do this by threatening towns, areas, or French allies (such as the T'ais) which de Lattre would have to defend by sending troops to the endangered point. Second, Giap would not persist in bloody attacks unless they held a reasonable promise of success.

De Lattre, in his turn, misread the meaning of Nghia-Lo. The relative ease of the victory convinced him that Vietminh morale and combat effectiveness had faltered, and further, that any French garrison under attack could be successfully reinforced by air. He was wrong on both counts. He correctly recognized, however, that if given a chance, Giap would take the initiative. This meant that de Lattre would either have to seize it by attacking or be forced into a reactive and defensive role. A defensive role was not only dangerous, but to the proud and aggressive Frenchman, it was a personal affront.

Beyond his desire to seize the initiative, other considerations prodded de Lattre to attack. First, an offensive would exploit the high morale of the French forces resulting from their recent victories over the Vietminh. It would also take advantage of what de Lattre perceived to be the failing spirit of his enemy. Second, as always, he needed more troops and equipment from France. To get them he had to show the French National Assembly and the French people that the Expeditionary Force could take the offensive and might eventually win the war. Third, a successful attack was required to obtain additional military aid from the Americans. Many American officials doubted the possibility of a French victory in Indochina and thus hesitated to support her forces there. A solid offensive victory would undercut the doubters in the American camp and obtain the badly needed aid. Finally, Devillers and Lacouture have suggested another reason for de Lattre's going over to the offensive. It is their view that de Lattre knew that there was no hope for a French victory in Indochina and that sooner or later the conflict would have to be settled by negotiations. He wanted France to negotiate from a position of strength, and to gain this position he had to show that the French had not only defensive capabilities, but a significant offensive capacity as well.[12]

Having decided to go on the offensive, de Lattre had to select the objective of his attack. It had to meet three exacting requirements. First, the objective had to have some political, strategic, or operational value to either Giap or to himself. Second, it had to be within supporting distance (not more than twenty-five or thirty miles) from the de Lattre Line. Finally, for psychological reasons, the objective had to be some place in which the French could stay indefinitely once they had captured it.

In late 1951 there were three locations outside the de Lattre Line which fulfilled these requirements (see map p. 106). Thanh Hoa, a large town thirty air miles south of the de Lattre Line, was the center of a region which furnished most of the rice which fed the Vietminh army. The second potential objective was Thai Nguyen, located some twenty-five miles north of the French positions. It was the gateway to the seat of the Vietminh government in the Viet Bac; it housed a major Vietminh supply center and what little industry Ho controlled. Finally, there was Hoa Binh, twenty miles southwest of the de Lattre Line. It was important for two reasons: it was a key link in the Vietminh north-south line of communications, leading from the "bread-basket" in Thanh Hoa to the Viet Bac; and it housed the capitol of the Muong nation, another tribe intensely loyal to the French.

De Lattre chose Hoa Binh. In addition to its importance as a Vietminh communications center and as the capital of the Muongs, other factors made it an attractive objective. First, it was closer to the French lines than either Thanh Hoa or Thai Nguyen. Next, its capture would be a logical extension of the de Lattre Line. Third, the attack on Hoa Binh would be thrusting into territory whose inhabitants, the Muongs, would help the French, in contrast to the residents of both Thanh Hoa and Thai Nguyen, who supported the Vietminh. Finally, an attack on Hoa Binh could be supported by road, river, and air, although each presented serious problems. First, the road running from Xuan Mai to Hoa Binh, Route Coloniale 6, was nothing more than a jungle track. For years the Vietminh had blown up the bridges and cratered the road bed, and the French air force had pulverized what was left. Even worse, the road was bordered by dense jungle, ideal for setting up the murderous ambushes in which the Vietminh specialized. The Black River, the second artery of communications, could be used to resupply troops in Hoa Binh from Trung Ha by small vessels and by *dinassauts,* but here again the jungle came right to the river banks, affording excellent attack sites for the Vietminh groups armed with bazookas and recoilless cannon. Finally,

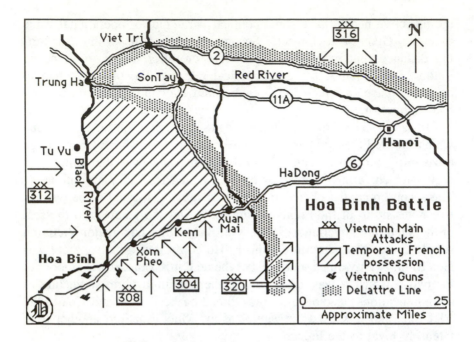

the air strip at Hoa Binh could be interdicted by antiaircraft, mortar, and artillery fire from two hills which dominated the landing field.

De Lattre launched his attack on Hoa Binh on 14 November by dropping three French paratroop battalions on the Hoa Binh airstrip. Against light resistance, the paratroopers quickly occupied the town. On the day of the attack the French began separate operations to clear and use both the Black River and Route Coloniale 6 from the de Lattre Line to Hoa Binh. The land task force, around fifteen battalions, pushed to the west and down Route Coloniale 6 and in two days linked up with the paratroopers in Hoa Binh. The French minimally repaired the road, but the dense undergrowth bordering it remained. The Black River route, too, was opened in two days by some twenty landing craft. Neither of the linkups met coordinated or heavy Vietminh resistance. Like many other French and Vietminh operations, this one started with a deceptive promise of success.

Giap took almost a month to counter de Lattre's attack. First, he had to determine what the French really intended to do. Then, he had to move three divisions into the Hoa Binh area from the north and west. To support them, he had to establish a sizable logistic base to the west of Hoa Binh, always a difficult and time-consuming task for the Vietminh. Finally, he had to develop and transmit his own operational plans. The French took advantage of the delay by establishing a series of small posts on the west bank of the Black River to protect that vital route and by installing a string of defensive garrisons along Route Coloniale 6 from Xuan Mai to Hoa Binh.

Giap planned to thwart the French seizure of Hoa Binh by making his main effort not against the sizable force positioned in the town, but against the transportation routes supplying it—Route Coloniale 6, the Black River, and the Hoa Binh airstrip. Accordingly, he ordered the 312th Division to attack the posts along the west bank of the Black River. The 308th Division would assist the 312th along the river and would put pressure on Hoa Binh itself. The 304th Division would harass the French along Route Coloniale 6 from the south. To draw French reserves from Hoa Binh, the 316th and 320th Divisions would infiltrate the Delta from the north and south respectively, step up guerrilla warfare, and badger French efforts to supply the Hoa Binh garrison.

Giap began his counteraction on 9 December by striking at Tu Vu, one of the posts protecting the convoys on the Black River. Two Vietminh regiments from the 312th Division attacked two Moroccan companies holding the position. The fighting was unusually brutal. The Vietminh used their "human wave" attacks. Regardless of losses, rank after rank of screaming Vietminh charged through the mine fields, over the barbed wire, straight into murderous close-in fire from small arms, tank cannon, and even point-blank artillery. They destroyed the tanks, the artillery, the fortifications, and drove the remnants of the Moroccan companies to a small island in the river. The Vietminh did not follow; they destroyed the post and withdrew at dawn, leaving 400 dead. This Vietminh pattern— attack, destroy, withdraw—continued against the Black River posts for the rest of December. As a result of these attacks, plus stepped-up ambushes along Route Coloniale 6, French losses mounted and morale slumped. To make matters worse, General de Lattre, dying of cancer, had been replaced by General Salan on 20 November.

Early in January 1952 Giap moved into the second phase of his operation. He intensified his attacks against the small posts along the river and increased the pressure against Route Coloniale 6 with the 304th Division. Salan responded by withdrawing all outposts from the west bank of the Black River, in effect giving up this line of communication. To seal the river route for good, on 12 January the Vietminh sprang a huge ambush, sinking six river craft and damaging others.

Coincident with the closing of the Black River, Giap began operations to cut Route Coloniale 6 and to deny the air strip at Hoa Binh to the French. On 8 January, the 304th Division, plus one regiment from the 308th, attacked the string of fortified positions along Route Coloniale 6. The fighting was fierce, and the casualties were heavy on both sides. For example, at Xom Pheo the 88th Regiment of the 308th Division made a night attack against a battalion of the French Foreign Legion. The Vietminh destroyed one company of the French battalion and mauled the others, but the 308th lost over 700 men. By mid-January, however, the Vietminh had closed Route Coloniale 6 between Xuan Mai and Hoa Binh.

During the road-closing operations of the 304th, the 308th began its action to deny the French the use of the air strip at Hoa Binh. Artillery fire from the hills overlooking the air strip, plus unexpectedly dense antiaircraft fire along the landing pattern, destroyed at least six French aircraft. With the road and river routes closed, and with air supply into Hoa Binh becoming increasingly difficult, by mid-January Giap had succeeded in almost strangling the French in Hoa Binh.

Salan decided not only to reopen Route Coloniale 6 from Xuan Mai to Hoa Binh, but also to clear the undergrowth from the roadside. For this job the French used twelve infantry battalions and three artillery groups. Even with this large force, they required eleven days (18–29 January) to clear the twenty-five miles of roads, and each mile had to be purchased with French sweat and blood. By the end of January, Salan realized that the French could not stay in the trap at Hoa Binh. He was losing men needed to counter the guerrilla activities of the 316th and 320th Vietminh Divisions in the Tonkin Delta. The operation had failed, and Salan had now to cut his losses.

Early in February, Salan made the formal decision to withdraw from Hoa Binh, dubbing the retreat Operation AMARANTH. The plan envisioned a three-phase, ''leap-frogging'' operation in which one force would hold open a key terrain obstacle (a pass, for example) while the others withdrew through them. The holding force would then fall back through a second covering force. Finally, the entire force would withdraw through the security forces of the de Lattre Line into safety. To carry out this difficult operation he ordered all French army reserves into the battle, and the French air force was to support the ground forces with a maximum effort.

The withdrawal began at 1900 hours on 22 February. It caught Giap by surprise, and the French garrison at Hoa Binh accompanied by 1,000 Muong civilians got across the Black River without Vietminh interference. Giap struck hard the next morning, and a slashing fight erupted all along Route Coloniale 6. The first blocking position was the hill position at Xom Pheo, where the 88th Regiment of the 308th Division had lost 700 men on 8 January. The Foreign Legionnaires held on there until the Hoa Binh garrison had passed through them. They, in turn, began to retreat along Route Coloniale 6 to Kem Pass, some ten miles toward Xuan Mai. After a running battle, they gained the pass on 23 February and relieved the unit there. The next day the Legionnaires, the last unit, gained the safety of the de Lattre Line at Xuan Mai. It had been a savage fight. The French artillery had fired over 30,000 rounds in support of the 20,000 ground troops, and the French air force had strafed and bombed continuously.

Losses were heavy on both sides. The French lost 5,000 men, and the Vietminh casualties from their "human wave" attacks totaled at least that number. Both sides claimed victory, but it was really Giap who won. It was a significant victory, for the Hoa Binh campaign revealed clearly that the French had little offensive capability outside the Tonkin Delta.

For that redoubtable Frenchman, Gen. Jean de Lattre de Tassigny, it was the last battle. He arrived back in Paris near the end of November 1951 and died of cancer of the prostate on 11 January 1952. He was notified of his promotion to Marshall of France a few hours before his death. To the professional soldier, he will be remembered longest for his feat of leadership in reviving the morale and combat effectiveness of the French Expeditionary Force after the shattering defeats along the Vietnam/Chinese border in 1950. This achievement will be studied for many years in military academies and war colleges of the free world. This controversial man made other valuable contributions to the French cause in Indochina. It was his relentless drive which built the de Lattre Line, and although one of his successors, General Navarre, maligned it, the Line accomplished its purpose—the Vietminh never broke through it. To de Lattre must go also a large part of the credit for organizing and developing the Vietnamese National Army. Unfortunately for France, it never met his expectations. Had it done so, this native force could have unlocked the door to decisive offensive action by the French. It didn't do it, but the failure was not de Lattre's. Finally, "King Jean" was able to attract American support for the war. It was American military aid which armed the Vietnamese National Army and added modern equipment to the French Expeditionary Force. In addition to the material aid, de Lattre was instrumental in drawing to the French cause in Indochina the moral and political support of the United States, an involvement with long-range consequences which neither de Lattre, nor anyone else, could foresee.

In spite of de Lattre's significant accomplishments during his brief tenure of command, he bungled the Hoa Binh campaign and must accept the blame for the failure. Even allowing for all the pressures pushing him to take the offensive—the French and American political requirements, the urge to take the initiative from Giap, the requirement to aid the Muongs, and the need to strengthen the French negotiating position— his decision to seize Hoa Binh was unsound. In retrospect it is obvious that, just as Giap had blundered into de Lattre's strength in the spring of 1951, de Lattre returned the favor that fall. The combination of Giap's three crack divisions, the jungle, and above all, the destroyed roads, narrow river, and enemy-dominated airstrip simply could not be overcome by the force of about two reinforced divisions which de Lattre had available for the Hoa Binh offensive. In the final analysis, de Lattre was beaten by the malady which at some time or other infected all the commanders in Indochina, be they French, American, North or South Vietnamese. He underestimated his enemy.

On the other hand, Giap deserves good marks for his conduct of the Hoa Binh operation. He quickly recognized the vulnerability of the French lines of communication, and he exploited it cleverly and effectively. He avoided set-piece attacks against the defensive position at Hoa Binh, the tactic which cost him so many men in his aborted TTC. Giap showed also that he had learned to negate the effectiveness of the French air force and navy. He nullified the French air superiority by careful use of camouflage and concealment plus antiaircraft guns, and he drove the *dinassauts* from the Black River by close-in ambush and recoilless cannon fire from the jungle-covered banks.

Some analysts have criticized Giap for not having detected the initiation of the French withdrawal from Hoa Binh and for his failure to attack the force at its vulnerable moment as it crossed the Black River. Giap's intelligence failed him. He was operating in the territory of the hostile Muongs, and his normal source of intelligence, the friendly inhabitants, was denied him. There were other reasons for this lapse. The French began the carefully planned operation just after dark on 22 February, and they had crossed the river by sunrise the next day. Beyond the surprise, the Vietminh were always slow to react to a sudden change. Their lack of reliable signal communications, their training (which placed great emphasis on detailed planning and rehearsals), and their cumbersome supply system inhibited swift exploitation of a fleeting enemy vulnerability.

The Hoa Binh campaign concluded large-scale operations in early 1952. The Vietminh continued guerrilla warfare behind the French lines. The French continued counter-guerrilla operations, and by March they were using several mobile groups just to keep their rear-area communications open. Another campaign season in Indochina War I had ended inconclusively, except, of course, for the many thousands of men who had died fighting its battles. For them, the campaign season had been all too conclusive.

Notes—Chapter 6

1. O'Ballance, *Indo-China War,* p. 121.
2. Truong Chinh, *Primer for Revolt: The Communist Takeover in Vietnam* (New York: Frederick A. Praeger, 1963), pp. 152–153.
3. O'Ballance, *Indo-China War,* p. 122.
4. Ho Chi Minh, *On Revolution* (New York: Frederick A. Praeger, 1967), pp. 203–205.
5. Ibid.
6. Ibid.
7. Fall, *Street,* p. 34.
8. O'Neill, *Giap,* p. 90.
9. Henri Navarre, *Agonie de L' Indochine* (Paris: Plon, 1958), p. 22.
10. O'Ballance, *Indo-China War,* p. 138; O'Neill, *Giap,* p. 99 (by indirection).
11. O'Neill, *Giap,* pp. 85–86.
12. Devillers and Lacouture, *End of a War,* p. 30.

7 Winter-Spring Campaign

September 1952–May 1953

In September 1952 the slackening rains of the Southwest Monsoon signaled the beginning of another campaign season in Indochina. To wage the battles of the "winter-spring" campaign of 1952–1953, the Vietminh had about 110,000 to 125,000 men in their Main Force units. Giap had formed them into six infantry divisions (the 325th Division was formed in Annam in late 1951), four independent infantry regiments, and some five or six independent infantry battalions. By 1952 the Chinese had supplied all of these units with ample numbers of machine guns and mortars. To support this infantry force, Giap formed a seventh division, the 351st Heavy Division, composed of two artillery regiments, an engineer regiment, and some light antiaircraft units. The artillery regiments were armed with 120mm mortars and 105mm howitzers; the antiaircraft units had 20mm and 40mm machine guns. Backing up the Main Force units were 60,000 to 75,000 Regional troops of varying quality, and behind them were some 120,000 to 200,000 militia and guerrillas, most of them ill-equipped, untrained, and unorganized.[1]

In mid-1952 the French Expeditionary Force (including the air force and navy contingents) numbered about 90,000 men. There were about 50,000 Frenchmen in this force. The rest were Foreign Legionnaires, North Africans, and French-led Indochinese.[2] These troops were well trained, well equipped, and well led, particularly in the ranks from corporal to lieutenant colonel. The Expeditionary Force was backed up by the Vietnamese National Army of some 100,000 troops. It could provide

137

little help to the French because of lagging recruitment, desertions, a shortage of officers, and a battle between the Americans and Vietnamese on one side against the French on the other over the control of the native units. Thus, in September 1952, a comparison of forces reveals that Giap could muster almost his entire 120,000-man force for offensive purposes, while the French could scrape up, at the most, around 50,000 men for an attack. The remainder were sitting in defensive positions along the de Lattre Line or chasing Communist guerrillas in their own rear areas.

The French had a new commander, Gen. Raoul Salan. Salan is an interesting character, not for what he did in Indochina (which wasn't much), but for his personality and his later role as the leader of a military rebellion against de Gaulle and France. Salan was one of the most highly decorated officers in the post-World War II French army, and among his many medals he wore the Distinguished Service Cross of the United States, given for "extraordinary heroism" while commanding de Lattre's old division, the 14th, in the latter days of World War II. Salan was no neophyte in Indochina. As a young captain he served several years in a remote section of Laos and learned to speak the Laotian language fluently. He returned to Indochina in early 1946 as the commander of French troops in the Far East, departing early in 1947. He returned in 1950 as second-in-command to de Lattre. He became high commissioner and commander in chief of all French forces in Indochina when the stricken de Lattre returned to France.

His nickname in the French army was "*Le Mandarin,*" not only because of his extensive service in the Far East, but because of his love for Oriental artifacts and customs and the air of mystery with which he conducted his affairs. De Gaulle said of him, "there was something slippery and inscrutable in the character of this capable, clever and in some respects, beguiling figure."[3] Regardless of his personal characteristics, in 1952 his operations in Indochina were neither slippery nor inscrutable; actually, they were obvious and confused.

During the rainy months from May to September 1952, Giap concentrated on developing the strategy which would win the war from the French. First, he analyzed the battles and campaigns of the last few years to find the strengths and weaknesses of both contenders. The French strengths were: (1) the defensive power of the de Lattre Line; (2) the reinforcement capability around the perimeter of that line due to the interior position of the French; and (3) the support of the French air force, navy, *dinassauts,* and artillery when distance, terrain, weather, or water permitted. These French capabilities showed Giap what *not* to do—do not attack the fortified French positions along the de Lattre Line.

To develop the positive portion of his strategy he looked for French weaknesses, and they were significant. First, the battle at Hoa Binh had shown that the French Expeditionary Force had little capability to sustain a large ground force at any substantial distance from the de Lattre Line. Its air transport was inadequate, and the poor roads, rough terrain, dense jungles, and bloody ambushes made road or river resupply difficult and costly. Second, for political reasons, France had to defend friendly groups, such as the T'ais and the Muongs, allied religious groups (for example, the Catholics near Nam Dinh), and those portions of the old French Indochinese Empire (Laos) which maintained strong political ties with France. Third, for offensive purposes, the French could marshal fewer men than the Vietminh. Fourth, the French air force was chained to the airfields in the Tonkin Delta, and the farther from the Delta it had to operate, the less support it could give to French ground troops. Giap's strategy, then, called for him to exploit these weaknesses by mounting operations against the T'ais, the Catholics, and Laos, so he could draw the French into areas at a maximum distance from the de Lattre Line. Operations remote from the Tonkin Delta would limit the number of French troops which could be supported, and since the French air force would be operating at a maximum range, severely curtail its support, both tactical and logistical.

To carry out his strategic concept, Giap selected as his first objective for the winter-spring campaign of 1952–1953 the string of posts which the French held along the Fan Si Pan range between the Red and Black rivers and covering the Black River valley itself. Along the ridge there was the principal post of Nghia Lo, the tribal capital of the T'ais and the target of Giap's unsuccessful attack in 1951, plus several small forts garrisoned by French-officered Indochinese. To the southwest of the Black River, the French had a string of stronger posts stretching from Lai Chau in the northwest through Son La, Na San, and finally, to Moc Chau in the southeast. The selection of these objectives was wise. A major attack in this area would threaten not only the T'ai nation, but Laos as well. The French would have to react by moving into a mountain-

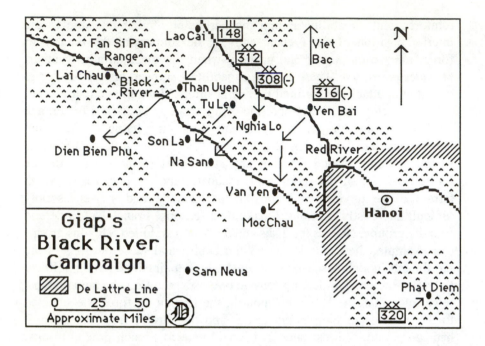

Giap's Black River Campaign

ous jungle, far removed from their bases in the Delta. Every factor favored the Vietminh and worked against the French.

Like most generals, Giap tended to repeat his past successes. In this campaign he went after Nghia Lo as his first objective, thus repeating what he had done in 1950 at Dong Khe. On 11 October he deployed his three assault divisions abreast and crossed the Red River on a forty-mile front north of Yen Bai. In the center was the "Iron Division," the 308th, aimed at Nghia Lo. On its right (west) flank marched the 312th Division with its objective the small post of Gia Hoi, ten miles northwest of Nghia Lo. On the left (east) flank, the 316th Division moved toward Van Yen. The 148th Independent Regiment swung in a wide arc to the north of the main advance, moving on the axis Than Uyen/Dien Bien Phu. The 308th and 316th Divisions each left one regiment on the Red River to protect the crossings and to act as a reserve. The wisdom of this latter detachment would soon become apparent.

The French sensed early in October that Giap was moving, but since the Vietminh had marched at night, they could not determine the direction or strength of his thrust. They found out on 15 October, when a regiment of the 312th Division surrounded the small French garrison at Gia Hoi. Salan realized the danger to the units along the ridge line and on 16 October dropped the 6th Colonial Parachute Battalion into Tu Le, fifteen miles northwest of Gia Hoi and twenty-five miles northwest of Nghia Lo. Its mission—to cover the retreat to the Black River valley. On 17 October at 1700 hours, heavy mortar concentrations began to fall on Nghia Lo. After an intense preparation the Vietminh infantry attacked. In less than one hour the post had been overrun, although sporadic fighting went on all night. The French lost 700 men at Nghia Lo, but more important, they lost the anchor of their ridge-line position. The entire line collapsed. Covered by the paratroopers, each French detachment fled for the safety of the Black River forts. The 6th Colonial Parachute Battalion fought with its accustomed bravery and effectiveness. It bought time, but it could not hold back the overpowering Vietminh, and in the process it was destroyed. By early November Giap's columns had closed on the Black River, but logistic difficulties slowed the advance of the Vietminh divisions toward the posts on the west bank of the stream. It was mid-November before the Vietminh forces arrived at the line Lai Chau/Son La/Na San/Moc Chau. With their supplies exhausted, Giap made one last thrust. He bypassed the fortified French positions and overran the small garrison of Dien Bien Phu.

The French reacted to Giap's successful advance with two counter-measures. First, they reinforced the garrisons at Lai Chau, Na San, and Moc Chau, and second, they launched Operation LORRAINE, a drive against Giap's supply base in the Viet Bac. It was to be a maximum offensive effort using all the mobile forces available, some 30,000 men, consisting of four mobile groups (usually three infantry battalions, one artillery battalion, and supporting troops in each group), a parachute group, plus sizable armor and artillery support, a force of about two divisions.

Operation LORRAINE seemed infallible when plotted in the map room of a high-level command. To the French planners the operation would face Giap with a "no-win" dilemma. If he did not counter the offensive by withdrawing his three divisions from the Black River to protect his Viet Bac bases, the French would not only cut the supply lines to the attacking divisions, but they could seriously damage Giap's entire logistic system. If Giap reacted by bringing his divisions back to defend the Viet Bac, the pressure on the Black River posts and Laos would be relieved. Either way Giap would be the loser. But war is the most unpredictable of human activities, and "infallible" plans often prove all too fallible when they must be carried out bedeviled by the whims of chance and the countermoves of a clever enemy. So it was with the French.

LORRAINE's plan of operations was complicated. One mobile force would cross the Red River near Trung Ha and near its junction with the Black River and move northwest toward Phu Tho. After this force had established a sizable bridgehead, the second column would advance from Viet Tri, linking up with the first group near Phu Tho. Then the combined columns would move swiftly on Phu Doan, a known Vietminh supply center. As this mobile force neared Phu Doan, the parachute group of three battalions would drop across the Clear River from the town. There the parachute contingent would be met by a *dinassaut* force which would ferry the paratroopers across the river, remove casualties,

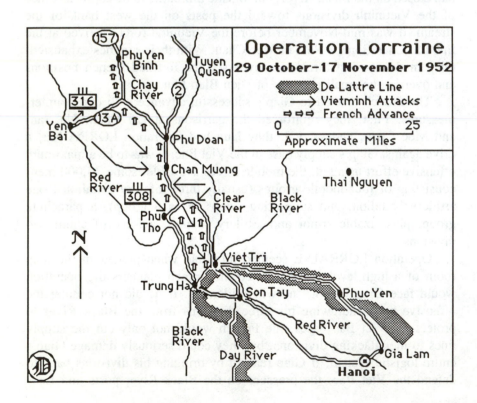

and prevent enemy escape by water. After sacking Phu Doan, the united force would either retire to its starting positions on the de Lattre Line or exploit its success by attacking other targets farther to the west and north.

On 29 October the French began the operation by crossing the Red River near Trung Ha. They moved northwest against light opposition and by 4 November had three sizable bridgeheads on the north bank of the river. On that day the second column jumped off from Viet Tri, advancing along Highway 2 toward Phu Tho. Slowed by poor weather, destroyed roads and bridges, and the delaying actions of the 176th Regiment of the 316th Division (one of the units Giap had left behind when he advanced to the Black River), this second column met heavy going. It was not until 7 November that the two columns reached the meeting point near Phu Tho.

At this juncture Giap had a major decision to make. He perceived the purpose of the French counteroffensive almost immediately, and he knew the French column was big, cumbersome, largely road-bound, and that its size and consequent logistical problems limited the depth of its thrust. Giap calculated that the French could neither reach nor take Thai Nguyen or Yen Bai, both important Vietminh bases, and thus, critical areas. He could afford to lose some supplies from smaller depots without serious damage to the capabilities of his forces, but not from these two areas.[4] Then, too, there were political reasons why Giap wanted to stay in T'ai country. He had to win the T'ai people by one means or another to the Communist side, and he wanted to clear the area as a base for later operations against Laos.[5]

After careful calculations, Giap decided not to overreact to the French threat and to hold to his original campaign plan while meeting Salan's attack with the two reserve regiments he held out of his main offensive. Accordingly, he issued orders to the regimental commanders of the two detached regiments to stop the French advance before it reached either Yen Bai or Thai Nguyen, but how they were to do this was their prerogative. Giap told them bluntly that they would get no further help.[6]

On 9 November the French mobile groups moved out of their junction point, bound for Phu Doan. On the same day the airborne force took off from airfields near Hanoi in C-47's and civilian aircraft, and by 1030 hours the lead parachute elements jumped into the zone across the river from the target. There was no opposition to the jump and the airborne battalions completed their assembly by 1500 hours. At this point, the first boat of the *dinassauts* force beached near the paratroopers and began to ferry them into the undefended objective, Phu Doan. At about 1700 hours, the leading tanks of the ground force arrived. Miraculously, the complex plan worked, although it required the split-second coordination of three services and several separate commands. The total success of the plan astounded even the French, for it violated a cardinal principle of war—simplicity. This principle can sometimes be ignored if one has a professional staff, good commanders, and above all, lots of luck. This day, the French had all three.

The house-to-house search of Phu Doan turned up a moderate amount of booty. The French found 1,400 rifles, 100 submachine guns, twenty-two machine guns, eighty mortars, and 200 tons of ammunition. In the nearby woods, a young French officer found two Soviet trucks and an American jeep. For a start, it was an acceptable prize, but if this was to be the total take, it constituted no justification for a 30,000-man offensive.

Still seeking either to capture a sizable supply depot or to draw Giap away from the Black River, Salan decided to push an exploiting force to the northwest. On 13 November he sent a strong tank-infantry-artillery force of some four or five battalions up Highway 157 towards its junction with Highway 13A. At the same time, he dispatched another force up Highway 2 toward Tuyen Quang with the limited mission of setting up a roadblock some twelve miles from Phu Doan. The exploitation force moving on Highway 157 made excellent progress, overrunning several roadblocks and losing only a few men to hidden enemy snipers.

The decisive moment in Operation LORRAINE came late on the afternoon of 13 November when the leading elements of the task force reached the junction of Highways 157 and 13A, for the latter road led to Yen Bai, one of the two major logistic centers of the Vietminh forces. The French commander sent a mixed battalion of tanks and infantry southwest on Highway 13A to take up a blocking position. The rest of the force continued the march to the northwest. That was the key.

What the French did at Yen Bai road junction was fundamental to the whole operation. If the French were serious in their intent to force Giap to leave the Black River, they had to drive at Yen Bai. If they would not move on Yen Bai, then the operation stood revealed as a mere diversion. So, when the French slid by Yen Bai, they signalled to friend and foe alike that regardless of LORRAINE's original purpose, it had now become a pointless feint.

In war, good reasons can always be found for faint-hearted actions, and Salan had his rationale for bypassing Yen Bai. It would have been hard to capture. It lay some ten to fifteen miles from the junction of Highways 157 and 13A. The country was fairly flat, but the route of approach crossed a natural defensive position, a low ridge line lying between the Chay and Red Rivers. The 176th Regiment of the 316th Division, a Main Force unit of proven capabilities, defended the town and its approaches. Yen Bai could not be taken by a quick grab, and probably could not be taken at all by the French task force on Highway 157. To capture the supply base, Salan would have had to commit a larger force to the Yen Bai area, and that was precisely what he did not want to do. He had to get out of the operation, not get deeper into it.

The simple fact was that Operation LORRAINE had failed. Giap had not pulled back from his Black River position. The French had done no serious damage to the Vietminh logistic system and had scant prospects of doing any. On the contrary, Salan's own logistic capabilities had been strained to the utmost to get the force where it was. Giap had his strength intact and was poised to launch a major offensive. Salan knew that he would need the troops back in the Delta or in the T'ai country to counter Giap's upcoming attack. He could not have them tied up in a bitter fight at Yen Bai.

The next day (14 November) the exploiting force reached Phu Yen Binh, twenty miles northwest of Phu Doan and some fifty miles northwest of the de Lattre Line. This thrust had accomplished nothing. On that same day Salan gave the order to stop all forward movement and to return to the Delta.

The French realized that a retreat is always more dangerous than an advance and hoped to effect their withdrawal with speed. The retirement began on 15 November and progressed well until it reached Chan Muong. This small village lies in a narrow gorge about four kilometers long, set among jungle-covered hills. The terrain gave the Vietminh an ideal site for an ambush, and early on the morning of 17 November the Communists used the Chan Muong gorge for just that purpose. The ambushing unit was the 36th Regiment of the 308th Division, probably the best regiment in the Vietminh Main Force. The regiment was supported by mortars and artillery emplaced in the hills dominating the valley. Some of the artillery had been sited to fire directly onto the road at almost point-blank range.

The leading elements of the French column had almost cleared the southern end of the gorge when the Vietminh sprung the ambush. After destroying some trucks and one tank, thereby blocking the road, the Vietminh infantry closed in on the French soldiers, firing from the trucks and ditches. There was a fierce and bloody melee with submachine guns, rifles, bayonets, knives, and grenades. At first the Communists controlled the fight, inflicting heavy casualties and blowing up many trucks. The French troops rallied, however, and with their air support, which arrived about noon, finally forced the attackers off the road itself. By 1400 hours the French commanders had gotten their troops reorganized and had drawn up a battle plan to clear the valley. At 1530 hours the Legionnaires and the BMI (*Batallion de Marche Indochinois*) attacked to clear the hills on either side of the road. The Legionnaires, who had the easiest hillside (the western side of the road), made rapid progress. It was the BMI—a battlehardened, professional unit made up of Europeans, Cambodians, and Vietnamese—which had the tough job. Time after time the battalion was pinned down by mortar and machine-gun fire as it tried to advance up the slopes to the east of the road. At 1630 hours the word passed down the line of the embattled BMI—fix bayonets! From the underbrush came that chilling sound, the snick of the bayonet being fixed onto the muzzle of the rifle. In a few moments a French bugle rang out, blowing the staccato, urgent notes of the Charge. What was left of the battalion got on their feet and raggedly moved toward the enemy positions—some walking, others running, all firing as they advanced. The Vietminh took one look and faded into the jungle. The ambush was broken. Chan Muong was the major fight of the withdrawal, but the Vietminh harassed and attacked the retreating French until they reached the safety of the de Lattre Line at Viet Tri.

Operation LORRAINE cost the French about 1,200 men—a high price for a few captured weapons. The operation did not come close to disrupting the Vietminh supply system, and it did not draw Giap from the Black River. Giap boldly refused to play his part in the French plan for LORRAINE. He kept the bulk of his three divisions in T'ai country ready to pursue his own aims.

* * *

In mid-November, when it became obvious to all that Operation LORRAINE had floundered, Giap moved into the second phase of his campaign against the Black River posts. In a brief attack in late November the 316th Division captured Moc Chau. On 23 November Giap closed the 308th Division on Na San, confident that a determined attack would take it. To his surprise, the assault, made by one regiment of the 308th, was beaten back with heavy losses. It was a close thing, however. Outposts changed hands several times, and there was heavy fighting in the barbed wire entanglements. Giap pulled back, rubbed his "bloody nose," and wondered what had gone wrong. Deluded by the nearness of victory on 23 November, a week later he attacked with another regiment on the night of 30 November. That attack, too, was repulsed with many casualties. Momentarily Giap forgot the bloody lesson of early 1951 and stubbornly persisted in the attack. The next night, 1–2 December, he threw two regiments (probably what was left of the 308th plus a regiment of the 316th) at Na San. Again the attack was smashed, leaving a thousand dead Vietminh in front of the French defenses. Now, after losing a total of 7,000 men killed and wounded, Giap reeled back from Na San.

Giap was stunned by this defeat. After a string of successes, what had gone wrong? O'Ballance claims that Giap's intelligence failed him.[7] He thought the garrison of Na San contained five understrength battalions, about 2,000 men. Actually, he sent his regiments against ten full-strength, entrenched battalions, with artillery and close air support. Giap's troops never had a chance. Giap forgot that his best source of intelligence was the local inhabitants, who in most areas favored the Vietminh. But when he operated in unfriendly country, as he was doing in the T'ai area surrounding Na San, his intelligence shrank drastically and dangerously.

After Giap's lapse and consequent defeat at Na San, he reverted to his preconceived strategy of drawing the French into distant and difficult areas which for political reasons they had to defend. Early in December he bypassed the strong points of Son La and Na San and moved into Laos, rapidly overrunning the series of weak posts which the French had established along the Laotian/Vietnamese border. As his main objective, Giap aimed at Sam Neua, a key town in northeastern Laos and the capital of the Laotian province of Houa Phan. Although he met little opposition, he stopped short of the objective. His Achilles heel—

logistics—had felled him again. This time it was the work of the recalcitrant T'ais. As always, the Vietminh logistic system depended on thousands of porters. For this purpose Giap imported many lowland Vietnamese into the northwest, but he still had to press the T'ais into service as bearers. The T'ais either vanished before they could be conscripted, or once loaded, threw the loads down as soon as they could safely do so and escaped into the dense jungle. With his supplies dwindling, Giap had no choice but to withdraw back into northwest Vietnam, a move he completed in late December. He was not disappointed at the meager results, and he learned some valuable lessons. There were still four or five more months of campaigning left before the monsoons struck in May, and if he did not go back into Laos in the spring of 1953, he could always return in the fall.

Giap rested and refitted his three assault divisions (the 308th, 312th, and 316th) in T'ai country from December until April, but he gave the French little respite elsewhere. In December 1952, the 320th Division attacked the Catholic center of Phat Diem in the southernmost region of the Tonkin Delta. The French reinforced speedily and beat off the assault (map p. 140). A more serious Vietminh attack materialized in a new area—Central Annam. In January 1953, two independent Main Force regiments, the 84th and 95th, assaulted the post of An Khe as well as the towns of Kontum and Pleiku farther to the west (map p. 206). These attacks showed for the first time that the Vietminh could mount a sizable Main Force threat in Central Vietnam. Even more significant, this was the first of many attempts by the North Vietnamese to sever South Vietnam along Highway 19 and to seize the two towns of Kontum and Pleiku, which dominated the Central Highlands. The attacks were turned back, but only after considerable effort and the commitment of three paratroop battalions. All in all, January to March 1953 was one of those quiet periods in the French/Vietminh War. The Vietminh hacked away at the roads behind the French lines in the Tonkin Delta; the French chased them back and forth and cleared them from areas, only to see the Vietminh seep back in after they departed. Of course, men were killed and wounded, but nothing changed significantly.

As April 1953 approached, Salan and his staff began to hope that Giap would not launch a large-scale operation before the arrival of the monsoon in May. The French needed time to expand and sharpen the

Vietnamese National Army and to recover from the punishment inflicted on the Expeditionary Force in T'ai country and in Operation LORRAINE. But Giap had other plans. He had the initiative, and he intended to use it. In Giap's view, his strategy of enticing the French into distant and difficult areas remained sound. The unsuccessful assault on Na San, however, showed him that to be successful with this strategy, he needed to operate at even greater distances from the Tonkin Delta than the 100–125 miles which separated Na San from the airfield complex around Hanoi. This concept would indicate that he should attack either the French base at Lai Chau, some 200 miles from Hanoi, or launch a full-scale offensive into Laos, even further away. Giap chose Laos.

For Giap, attacking Laos had several advantages. It would help the small and primitive Communist movement in Laos. At the same time, an invasion would further unsettle and demoralize French politicians in Paris as they saw an unpopular and costly war expanding, and worse, expanding into their most loyal Indochinese colony. For Giap, invading Laos was a "low risk" operation. The French forces guarding the country were weak, and they could be reinforced and supported from the Delta only with great difficulty. The arrival of the monsoon in about a month reduced the risk further, for the rains would cover a retreat and limit French counteraction. Also to his advantage, Giap's political and military strategy required no spectacular triumph. He might find an easy victory somewhere, but if he did not find one, he would have accomplished his objectives by demonstrating his capability to invade Laos in force. The French, Laotians, and Vietnamese would remember, not that he failed to win a great battle, but that he seriously threatened Laos. Finally, the incursion would give Giap and his troops valuable experience in the far-ranging, fast-moving warfare in which they had previously not been tried.

While these advantages made the invasion of Laos attractive to Giap, as always there loomed one major problem—Vietminh logistics. Giap remembered the logistic failure which hobbled the attack on the Black River Line of December 1952, and he realized that the success of any Laotian invasion depended on a more effective and dependable supply service. To this end he made three major improvements. In January he began to build a forward base at Moc Chau to cut the distance his porters would have to carry supplies. He contacted the Communists in Laos and had them secretly prestock rice supplies along his projected routes of invasion. Most important, he brought in porters from outside the T'ai area to carry the food and ammunition his three-division force would need in Laos. This time he made certain that his invasion plans would not be foiled by the recalcitrant and slippery T'ais.

Giap's operational concept for the incursion into Laos stressed flexibility. He would advance into the country with the three divisions abreast. The flank divisions would march within supporting distance of the center division and one or all could swing right or left as the situation developed. The 316th Division would move on the left (east) flank from Moc Chau cross-country to Sam Neua. In the center, the 308th Division would leave one regiment to contain the garrison at Na San and advance down the Nam Seng River towards Louang Phrabang, the Royal Capital. On the west flank, the 312th Division would depart from the neighborhood of Dien Bien Phu and march down the Nam Ou River towards Louang Phrabang. Both the 316th Division on the east and the 308th Division in the center could easily move toward the Plain of Jars, which housed Jars Camp, a major French base. Alternatively, one or both of these divisions could bypass the Jars Camp and threaten Vientiane, the administrative capital of Laos.

Giap launched his invasion on 9 April 1953. When it became clear on the next day that the 316th Division was headed for Sam Neua, Salan decided to reinforce the town by air. But Sam Neua had a short airstrip surrounded by hills, and after reflection, Salan decided that the town was indefensible. On 12 April, Salan ordered the garrison to withdraw to Xiangkhoang. The delay cost him the three battalions which had been holding Sam Neua. They departed on foot and in haste the next day, one jump ahead of the 316th Division, and on 14 April the Vietminh caught up with the rear guard, a battalion of French-officered Laotian paratroopers. The paratroopers repelled the first attack, but on 15 April the 316th Division moved up abreast of the retreating column and on 16 April assaulted it throughout its length. The French force fragmented, each bit trying to reach Xiangkhoang. Out of a force of some 2,500, only 235 men made it.

On the west flank, the 312th Division moved out of Dien Bien Phu on 9 April headed for the source of the Nam Ou River and the village of Muong Khoua, which was held by a garrison of around 300 men, mostly Laotians. The Vietminh division arrived there on 11 April and attacked two days later. The French Laotians held, and the Vietminh

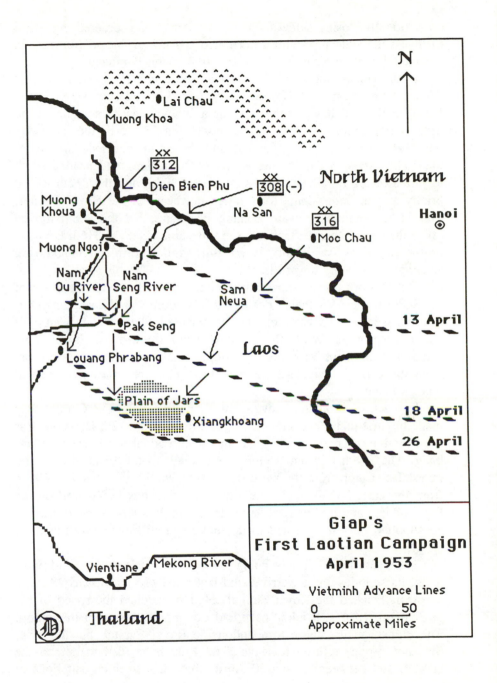

N

Lai Chau
Muong Khoa

XX
312

Dien Bien Phu

XX
308 (-)

North Vietnam

Na San

Muong
Khoua

XX
316

Moc Chau

Hanoi
◉

Muong Ngoi

Nam
Ou River

Nam
Seng River

Sam
Neua

13 April

Pak Seng

Louang Phrabang

Laos

Plain of Jars

18 April

Xiangkhoang

26 April

Giap's
First Laotian Campaign
April 1953

Vientiane   Mekong River

Thailand

▬ ▬ Vietminh Advance Lines

0   50
Approximate Miles

drew off after losing a few men. On 14 April Giap ordered the 312th to invest the little post with a portion of its troops and to continue its advance down the Nam Ou River toward Louang Phrabang.

In the center, the "Iron" Division, the 308th (less one regiment) departed the vicinity of Na San on 9 April, bound southwest toward the Nam Seng Valley. Of the three assault divisions it encountered the lightest opposition—in fact, almost none. On 13 April, the same day the 312th attacked Muong Khoua, and the 316th reached Sam Neua, the 308th Division entered the valley of Nam Seng and headed south toward Louang Phrabang. On 18 April the 308th and the 312th joined briefly at Pak Seng, some forty miles northeast of the Royal Capital. The 312th continued toward Louang Phrabang, but the 308th moved off to the south toward Vientiane. On this same date, the 316th Division on the east flank was twenty-five or thirty miles north of Xiangkhoang and moving steadily toward it.

On 19 April Salan, apparently concerned by the southerly move of the 308th toward Vientiane, decided to abandon Xiangkhoang and shift that garrison of five battalions to the fortified Plain of Jars Camp. It was a wise move. While the 308th Division could easily bypass Jars Camp and drive for Vientiane, its supply lines could be cut by a foray from the camp, a capability denied the French had they remained at Xiangkhoang.

In reaction to Salan's move from Xiangkhoang to Jars Camp, Giap made his first major decision of the campaign. The 312th Division (less the containing force at Muong Khoua) would advance to Louang Phrabang. The 308th Division would move south to the Plain of Jars and invest Jars Camp from the west. The 316th would move on Jars Camp from the east. By 23 April, the Vietminh divisions had closed on the Plain of Jars and by 26 April had surrounded Jars Camp. Now it could be supplied only by air, and to do that required maximum French air effort.

The 312th Division, advancing toward Louang Phrabang, had problems. Its supplies did not arrive, and it got lost, so that it was 28 April before it reached the Royal Capital. Had it matched the speed of the other two divisions, it might have had Louang Phrabang for the taking. The French at first chose to abandon the Royal Capital, but the king, Sisavang Vong, refused to leave. The French decided to defend the capital, and between 28 and 30 April, they flew in three battalions of

Moroccans and Legionnaires plus artillery, barbed wire, and other defensive materiel. By 30 April, the 312th Division surrounded Louang Phrabang, along with the Moroccans, the Legionnaires, and the king of Laos. Thus, by the end of April, Giap had bottled up a large French garrison at Jars Camp, surrounded a sizable force at Louang Phrabang, and isolated a small unit at Muong Khoua. The French were thoroughly outmaneuvered. Giap's control over northern Laos was complete.

But the very speed with which Giap achieved his Laotian triumph brought logistic problems. Again he outran his support. As Giap got deep into Laos he was unable to recruit porters among the Laotians, whose aversion to hard work was exceeded only by their hatred for the Vietnamese. To compound the problem, Giap knew that the Southwest Monsoon would arrive soon. The rains would make logistical support impossible and would endanger the health of his exposed troops. So, on 7 May, the 312th and the 316th Divisions began to move back toward Vietnam, leaving only elements of the 308th Division to keep the French busy, to recruit Laotian guides and agents, and to stockpile rice when they could get it. Another campaign season had ended. In May 1953, Gen. Henri Navarre replaced Gen. Salan, and like Valluy and Carpentier before him, Salan would be given his fourth star for his "accomplishments" in Indochina.

Giap's strategic concept for, and conduct of, the "winter-spring" campaign of 1952–1953 marks his coming of age as a general. He had finally grasped the first principle of strategy—use one's strengths against enemy weaknesses while negating enemy strengths and one's own vulnerabilities. His fundamental concept of drawing the French out of the Tonkin Delta by attacking their allies showed the sophistication and surefootedness of an accomplished strategist. Sophisticated, in that Giap continuously put the French in a dilemma. They had to either defend a local ally or an area at a marked disadvantage to themselves, or let the ally or area fall to the Vietminh without a fight, the strategy of the "indirect approach." Surefooted in his choice of targets and objectives which the French had to defend, and which for political or other reasons they could not let fall without a fight.

In studying the campaign of 1952–1953, one sees a strategic capacity in Giap which had previously been absent. In the first place, there is the ability to see beyond the campaigns of 1952–1953 into those of

1953–1954 and even beyond that. His 1952–1953 operations—the seizure of Nghia Lo, the Black River offensive, the invasion of Laos—were aimed at dominating the T'ais and the Laotians, splitting them from the French, and using their country and people as a base for future operations. From a secure base of operations in northwest Vietnam he could threaten Laos. From this same base he could enlarge the war which had already stretched the inadequate French resources to the breaking point. Both of his invasions of Laos show a patience, a long-range perspective, which were missing in his previous campaigns. Indeed, it is this far-sighted "I can wait" approach of Giap's which most frightened the French and which indirectly brought about their final defeat at Dien Bien Phu.

In the 1952–1953 campaign, Giap demonstrated another strategic subtlety not observed before—the diversionary attacks at Phat Diem and in Annam in December 1952 and January 1953. Giap did not design these attacks to seize and hold the towns which he assaulted. The attacks on Phat Diem and An Khe, launched just before the full-scale invasion of Laos, warned the French that they could not commit all their reserves against Giap's thrust into Laos, and the French got the message. Regardless of the seriousness or magnitude of the Laotian threat, the French had to hold forces out of Laos for a possible attack elsewhere. They committed only thirteen to fifteen battalions to the defense of Laos out of an available mobile force of at least twenty-five to thirty battalions. Of course, their meager support capabilities limited the size of the force the French sent to Laos also. Nevertheless, they dared not denude the Delta, or other critical areas, of reserves.

These diversionary attacks performed another valuable function—they acted as "spoiling attacks." A spoiling attack seeks to force the enemy to react to the "spoiler" so that the enemy cannot act on his own initiative in a much more damaging way. The attacks on Phat Diem and An Khe were successful "spoiling attacks." It is now known that on 30 December 1952, just after that Phat Diem attack and prior to the An Khe offensive, Salan issued Directive No. 40 directing that Dien Bien Phu be reoccupied on 10 January 1953 as the first step of a campaign to regain control of the T'ai country.[8] Giap's An Khe attack "spoiled" the French operation. The troops which would have gone to Dien Bien Phu went instead to Annam.

Finally, Giap's strategy indicates his recognition that by 1952–1953 "the correlation of forces" had shifted significantly in his favor, and that he could successfully pass to the counteroffensive stage—the long awaited phase III of revolutionary warfare. The gauge of battle had swung clearly to Giap and with it that great prize in war, the initiative. The French might make a sortie out of the Delta from time to time, but now, in 1952, they did so at great peril. The French defeat now became a matter of time. In retrospect, it is always easy to see how the gauge of battle has shifted, but in the day-to-day confusion of conducting a campaign, the shift is not always obvious. Giap deserves credit for his grasp of the fundamental realities of the combat situation, a trait which distinguishes a competent theater commander.

But the art of the general encompasses not only the design of a grand scheme, or strategy, it also includes the execution of that strategy, which is a matter of logistics and tactics. One of the marks of a good tactician is that he moves with speed and surprise. Rapidity of movement upsets an opponent's equilibrium and forestalls a coherent reaction. Giap, too, can credit much of his success in this 1952–1953 campaign to this same speed. Throughout the campaign season he moved so swiftly and secretly that he confounded the French command. In October, Salan lost Nghia Lo, the key to the control of the ridge between the Red and Black Rivers, because he moved too late with too little. In late October, the 6th Colonial Parachute Battalion was sacrificed in an effort to slow Giap's rapid advance toward the Black River. In December, Giap met little opposition as he moved into and out of Laos before the French could react. The rapidity of his final invasion of Laos is particularly noteworthy. His regiments averaged ten air miles a day, which means that they walked and ran twenty miles daily on the winding mountainous tracks of Laos. This is an extraordinary feat, particularly when one considers the primitive, cumbersome logistic system, a system based on the feet and backs of 200,000 coolies which supported these rapid advances. It is interesting to note that when the 300-man garrison of Muong Khoua unexpectedly held out against the initial attack of the 312th Division, Giap quickly contained it, and in the best tradition of George Patton, bypassed it with the rest of the division and sped toward Louang Phrabang.

Giap's mobility in the Laotian invasion paid off in the confusion and vacillation which it induced into the French command. They could not get a grasp of the rapidly moving situation, nor could they gain time for a coordinated counteraction. At first, Salan was going to defend Sam Neua and then, belatedly, he abandoned it. He then decided to hold Xiangkhoang, but again gave it up abruptly and moved to Jars Camp. The French at first had no intention of defending Louang Phrabang, but when the king of Laos refused to flee, they held it. The entire Laotian invasion presents an excellent example of how speed of movement can force an opponent into costly mistakes. This was blitzkrieg, Indochinese style, not one executed by thousands of tanks and hundreds of close-support aircraft, but one carried out by thousands of foot soldiers supported by scores of thousands of plodding porters.

Another aspect of the Laotian invasion which shows Giap's competence as a tactician is the flexibility with which he conducted the offensive. The starting positions of his three divisions and the initial objectives of the two flank divisions gave Giap the capability of concentrating the 312th against Louang Phrabang, the 316th against Sam Neua, and the 308th against either the Plain of Jars or Vientiane, depending on the outcome of early battles and the reaction of the French. The "Iron Division," the 308th, was the "swing" division since it could be used not only against the central objectives, but also to reinforce either flank division. Giap did not make up his mind about the employment of the 308th Division until the French moved from Xiangkhoang to Jars Camp on 19 April. In fact it was the threat which the advance of the 308th posed to Vientiane which prompted the French to shift to the Plain of Jars. It was then that Giap completed his tactical combinations. He saw that the 312th Division, less the containing force at Muong Khoua, could handily invest the three French battalions at Louang Phrabang even though the latter were aided by odds and ends of Laotian units. On the other hand, the containment of Jars Camp with its ten to twelve battalions would require more than the 316th Division, and to help the 316th Giap reinforced it with the 308th. The end result saw major French forces in Laos bottled up in two places, Louang Phrabang and Jars Camp, each contained by a superior Vietminh force.

Giap equaled his handling of the Laotian invasion by his performance in defeating Operation LORRAINE. From the start, Giap dominated the French. From his excellent intelligence in the Delta he foresaw that the movement of his three assault divisions toward the Black River might trigger a French sortie into the Viet Bac. To counter this threat, he left two regiments on the Red River with the instruction to prevent the French from getting into Yen Bai and Thai Nguyen, the principal Vietminh supply centers. Thus, when the French embarked on LORRAINE, Giap had two Main Force regiments to contest their advance without having to pull forces from his own offensive toward the Black River. His foremost achievement in countering LORRAINE, however, was his correct assessment of the true French intentions and capabilities. From his intelligence (or from deduction), Giap estimated that the French would not try to break into his critical supply areas, but intended primarily to make a demonstration to draw him back from the Black River. His assessment of French aims in LORRAINE was reinforced by his calculations that French logistic capabilities could support a sizable enemy foray for only a short period of time and to a limited distance from the Delta. Perhaps, reasoned Giap, the French could reach Yen Bai, although this was by no means assured, but they could not support a lengthy, hard-fought battle there. Buttressed, then, by his recognition of the limited nature of French intentions and the thinness of their real capabilities, Giap contemptuously allowed them to run up the road to Phu Yen Binh and back again before he struck at Chan Muong.

In view of Giap's brilliance in sweeping Laos and in defeating Operation LORRAINE, how did he come to make such an irrational and intemperate mistake as his bloody attacks at Na San? It is easy to write off this blunder as an intelligence failure, but this explanation is too pat. An intelligence failure may explain the first attack, the closeness to victory of that first attack may possibly account for the second, but critics offer no explanation for Giap's third and final attack. After having been thrown back with heavy losses in his first two assaults, Giap knew that his original estimate of the strength of the French defenders was much too low, yet he attacked anyway. O'Ballance blames this third attack on Giap's frustration and obstinacy,[9] but this explanation, too, seems overly simplistic. A general who reacted to Operation LORRAINE with monumental coolness, and who calmly withdrew from Laos when he had both Louang Phrabang and Jars Camp surrounded, is not the man to persist in an unsuccessful attack because his "blood was up."

Although Giap has never offered any explanation of his rash attacks on Na San, the true reason for Giap's persistence can be deduced. He badly needed Na San—not the town or the camp, but the countryside surrounding it. He needed it as an area from which to base his coming invasion of Laos, and he needed it to be free of the French. Without

Na San he would have to establish his logistic base for the invasion in the Moc Chau area, which he had captured in late November. But as a base area, Moc Chau was too far to the east, and its location would complicate his already difficult problem of supporting the future Laotian incursion. As events proved, he could base the Laotian invasion from Moc Chau, but the logistic problems he foresaw did arise. Strategically, his desire to take Na San was probably right. Tactically, it was still wrong.

As the monsoonal rains of May 1953 washed out another campaign season in the French/Vietminh War, the French command took a hard look at their situation. As usual, their assessment of the significance of the events of the preceding eight months was partially right, partially wrong. They were right when they saw Giap's most recent campaign as a forerunner of a serious threat to Laos. To counter this threat, they calculated that they had to do two things. First, they had to establish a large base somewhere astride the Vietminh invasion routes to Laos. Second, they had to form, from troops available in Vietnam, a French force which could oppose the Vietminh in mobile warfare on even terms. This meant, as the previous French commanders had seen, an increase in the size and efficiency of the Vietnamese National Army so that it could relieve the French troops of defensive and pacification duties.

The French reached other conclusions from the battles of 1952–1953 which turned out to be fatally wrong. From their experience at Na San, and to a lesser extent at Louang Phrabang and Jars Camp, they concluded that a large fortified camp could be established in enemy territory, supplied by air, and made invulnerable to Vietminh attack. They reasoned further that Giap would attack such a camp, as he had done at Na San, and that if the bait offered Giap were large enough and attractive enough, they could get a great set-piece battle in which Giap would destroy his assault divisions in attacks against the French fortified position. It was this concept of the establishment of a large, fortified, and isolated camp astride the Laotian invasion routes that brought about Dien Bien Phu and the French defeat in Indochina.

From the basis of his accomplishments in the ''winter-spring'' campaign of 1952–1953, Giap could contemplate the immediate past with satisfaction and the future with confidence. His critics could write off his victories in 1950 on Route 4 to French stupidity; they could rightly censure Giap for the defeats he brought on his forces in 1951; they could credit his Hoa Binh victory to French miscalculations and overconfidence, but by 1953, even the French had to recognize Giap as an accomplished general and a dangerous foe. Victory was coming within his grasp. It would require the unwitting help of the French, but that, too, would materialize.

Notes—Chapter 7

1. Buttinger, *Dragon Embattled*, I:759.
2. O'Ballance, *Indo-China War,* note, p. 174.
3. Alistair Horne, *A Savage War of Peace, Algeria 1954–1962* (New York: Viking Press, 1977), p. 180.
4. Fall, *Street,* p. 78.
5. O'Ballance, *Indo-China War,* p. 182.
6. Fall, *Street,* p. 79.
7. O'Ballance, *Indo-China War,* p. 185.
8. O'Neill, *Giap,* p. 122.
9. O'Ballance, *Indo-China War,* p. 185.

8 The Origins of Dien Bien Phu

21 May—20 November 1953

Gen. Henri Navarre, who replaced Gen. Raoul Salan in May 1953, has always seemed an unlikely choice as commander in chief, Indochina. As an enlisted man and young officer, he spent two and a half years in the trenches in World War I, and during the early days of World War II, he was the chief of the German section of the French intelligence organization. He fled France with Weygand in 1940, but in 1942 returned to join the Résistance. After the Allied landings of 1944, he commanded an armored regiment in the French army, and by 1950 he had risen to command the 5th French Armored Division in occupied Germany. When appointed to the Indochina command, he was fifty-five years old and chief of staff, NATO Land Forces, Western Europe.

Navarre had a good military record, but there must have been at least a score of other French generals with better ones. He certainly was not selected for his personality. He was a colorless, icy intellectual, a "loner"—certainly not the leader who could galvanize the hard-bitten Expeditionary Force. Experience in Indochina? None. Ambition? Not for Indochina. Desire for the post? None—he did not want it and accepted it with grave misgivings.

One clue, however, suggests the reason for his selection. The prime minister, René Mayer, hand-picked Navarre for the job. In Germany in 1946, Navarre was the secretary-general to the French commander in chief while Mayer served as the French high commissioner. In 1948, Mayer held the post of mayor of the Algerian city of Constantine, while

161

Navarre commanded a division there. Apparently, Mayer knew and trusted Navarre. To Mayer, Navarre's lack of bravado and his cold intelligence were the very qualities required for the task Mayer had in mind for him—to find or create a way in which the government could negotiate an honorable peace in Indochina. With this vague, uninspiring, but still difficult mission, Navarre went to Vietnam.

On assuming command on 21 May, Navarre published an Order of the Day which ranks as one of the most self-effacing "assumption of command" orders ever issued. He said, "I'm counting on the contacts I shall have with you, particularly with those of you who are fighting in the front line, speedily to remedy my experience."[1] Now there is a stuttering "Charge" sounded on an uncertain trumpet. But there is something in this strange, self-depreciative order which causes the experienced military observer to hesitate before passing judgment on the man. It is *too* unpretentious. Only a general who is supremely arrogant has the self-confidence to introduce himself so humbly. Only a leader who values *only* his own judgment can issue an "assumption" order which eschews the traditional bombast and makes no effort to "inspire the troops."

When they appointed him, Navarre's political masters in Paris instructed him to go to Indochina and assess the military situation. They told him to prepare a plan of operations and to return with it to Paris, including in it a request for any additional troops or resources required to implement it. The government would then approve or disapprove the plan and deny or grant the troops and resources. In compliance with these instructions, Navarre spent his first three weeks in Indochina analyzing the situation. He traveled widely, often at considerable personal risk, and talked with many military and civilian officials.

He found a grim situation. The scales had clearly shifted in favor of the Vietminh in 1952 and early 1953. Senior French commanders and staff officers unanimously expected Giap to launch a major offensive in the fall of 1953 against either Laos or the Tonkin Delta, and Giap had the strength to do it. Around the Delta, the Vietminh had 125,000 Main Force troops organized into seven divisions, six independent regiments, and some independent battalions. Six of these divisions were in the north, one (the 325th) in the Vinh area, and a division equivalent in Annam.[2] In all, Giap had an offensive force the equivalent of eight or nine divisions. Vietminh morale was high, and the Vietminh were well armed and well led. In particular, the Chinese had provided the

Vietminh Main Force units with equipment captured from American and South Korean forces in Korea, superior in quality and quantity to that held by the French troops.

Backing up these Main Force Regulars were some 75,000 Regional troops, and behind the Regional forces stood the militia with an estimated strength of from 150,000 to 350,000 untrained and largely unequipped men, women, and children. These Regional forces and militia played the critical role in the equation of comparative strengths between the two sides. Assisted by three Main Force independent regiments and two Main Force battalions, some of which operated *within* the de Lattre Line, Vietminh irregulars controlled, wholly or partially, 5,000 of the 7,000 villages in the Tonkin Delta. More important, their activities (plus the Main Force threat) tied down more than half of the French Expeditionary Force on static defensive duties in the Tonkin Delta.

Navarre's analysis of the French position reinforced his gloom. The French Expeditionary Force numbered 175,000 ground troops consisting of Frenchmen, Africans, Foreign Legionnaires, and Vietnamese, plus a French naval contingent of 5,000 and an air element of 10,000. The essential problem, as Navarre described it, was that 100,000 of these troops (or the equivalent of four or five divisions) were tied down on defensive and counter-guerrilla duties.[3] For mobile operations either offensive or defensive, Navarre had available only around 75,000 French troops. This force was made up of seven mobile groups and eight parachute battalions, the equivalent of about three divisions. In 1953, the central fact of the Indochina War was that for the conduct of mobile ground operations in the North, the Vietminh held at least a two-to-one advantage over the French.

Such raw statistics, however, can be misleading. Navarre had contingents from the French air force and navy, while Giap had none. Theoretically, at least, these services gave Navarre crucial advantages. The first was that of strategic mobility—the capability to move and support troops at a long distance without dependence on the dangerous and largely destroyed road net. This capacity was limited, however, by the short range of the aircraft and by their inadequate numbers. In addition, the air and sea arms gave Navarre tactical advantages. As they had demonstrated in 1951, both services could strike a heavy combat blow if Giap disposed his troops within their range and without adequate cover or concealment. The campaign of 1952–1953, however, had shown that

Giap had finally grasped not only the capabilities of the sea and air arms, but their limitations as well. Thus, the tactical advantages conferred by French air and naval supremacy proved largely illusory, and the idea of French strategic mobility through airpower turned out to be a particularly disastrous delusion.

The Vietnamese National Army, still in process of formation, numbered some 150,000 troops. It could, however, provide little help to the French. Its most pressing problem was low morale. There was no motivation for the pro-French Vietnamese to fight. While the Vietminh thought they fought for independence, the Vietnamese National Army *knew* they fought only for Bao Dai and the French, and neither inspired them.

But there was more to the war in Indochina than the situation in North Vietnam and the Tonkin Delta. In the "waist" of Vietnam, Annam, the situation gave no cause for French optimism either. The enemy had surfaced there in strength in 1952 with a force of some three independent regiments, and now in 1953 the French held only the large coastal towns of Hue, Da Nang, and Nha Trang. Between these cities, travel by Highway 1 and the railroad was so dangerous that the French used coastal shipping. In southern Vietnam the French fared better. They controlled Saigon and a good part of the countryside, although guerrillas were established in strongholds along the Cambodian border, in the Mekong Delta, and in Quang Nai and Binh Dinh provinces. In Cambodia the situation presented no threat to the French. The local insurgents were poorly organized and equipped, and the Cambodian army, a rag-tag group of 10,000 ill-trained and poorly equipped men, dominated them.

The situation in Laos, particularly northern or upper Laos, was far more serious. The Laotian army of 15,000, while it might keep the Communist Pathet Lao in check, could put up little resistance against a major Vietminh offensive. French garrisons in Laos were small and scattered, and as the campaign of 1952–1953 revealed, incapable of containing, or even impeding, a serious enemy thrust into Laos. Overall, as Navarre saw it, the Tonkin Delta and Upper Laos presented the areas of major Vietminh threats. Annam could be troublesome, but probably not decisive. He could ignore Cochin China and Cambodia.

In addition to the ominous military situation, Navarre found deficiencies and attitudes in the French command in Vietnam which disquieted him. Salan had prepared an operational plan just before Navarre's arrival, but Navarre discovered quickly that the plan had been drawn up without much thought and was prepared largely for presentation to him. Actually, there had been no long-range plan since de Lattre's departure. Everything was conducted on a day-to-day, reactive basis. Combat operations were undertaken only in response to enemy moves or threats. There was no comprehensive plan to develop the organization and build up the equipment of the Expeditionary Force. Finally, Navarre, the intellectual, the cold and professional soldier, was shocked by the "school's out" attitude of Salan and his senior commanders and staff officers. Their tour in Vietnam was over. They were going home, not as victors or heroes, but then, not as clear losers either. To them the important thing was that they were getting out of Indochina with their reputations frayed, but intact. They gave little thought to, or concern for, the problems of their successors.

So, without much help from his staff or senior commanders, Navarre began to devise the plan he would take back to Paris. But he kept running into one snag—what precisely was his mission? The only task his patron, René Mayer, had given him was to create the military conditions in Vietnam which would lead to *"une solution politique honorable."*[4] He knew he had to defend Vietnam, and he assumed he had to defend northern Laos, but he was not sure what his responsibilities were for the latter area.

As a basis for his plan, Navarre set out the military options open to Giap for the campaign season of 1953–1954. Navarre saw Giap's first option to be a full-strength attack on the Tonkin Delta. Navarre evaluated this as a grave threat, but the French were strongest here, and he felt that they could hold Hanoi, Haiphong, and the other key areas of the Delta. Navarre envisioned Giap's second option to be an offensive in Annam and southern Laos. Navarre believed that while menacing, this thrust, too, could be contained. It was a great distance from Giap's center of strength in North Vietnam and the French had significant forces in the area. In Navarre's view, the third course of action Giap might adopt was the invasion of northern Laos and a drive at its two capitals, Louang Phrabang and Vientiane. Navarre calculated that this would be by far the most difficult option to counter. He recognized early that defending upper Laos would be a "delicate problem considering the enemy, the weather, the terrain, the lack of roads, and the distance between his center of power, Hanoi, and northern Laos."[5]

This confusion over the mission, however, had little effect on the operational concept of the now-famous Navarre Plan, which the general took back to Paris. The plan had many fathers—Salan, who hastily drew it up for Navarre's benefit just before the latter's arrival; de Lattre, who faced and tried to solve many of the same problems; and even Revers, whose report of 1948 was still the basis for France's Indochina strategy. But Navarre added some new elements of his own.

Navarre's plan—even viewed in the afterlight of what happened—was sound. It recognized and provided for the Vietminh superiority in northern Vietnam and Laos during the 1953–1954 campaign season, and it took advantage of Vietminh weakness elsewhere. It set forth those actions by the French and their allies which might eventually achieve at least combat equality by 1954–1955, and thus permit Navarre to take the initiative.

The essence of the Navarre Plan was this:

1. Indochina was divided into a northern and southern theater along the 18th parallel.

2. In the northern theater (North Vietnam and northern Laos) the French would assume the strategic defensive during the 1953–1954 campaign season. They would seek to avoid a major battle with the superior forces of the Vietminh during that period. Navarre fully expected that Giap would launch a major offensive in the 1953–1954 season either in northern Laos or against the Tonkin Delta, and his plan recognized that this offensive constituted the greatest danger to the French hold on the country.

3. In view of Giap's superior offensive capabilities during 1953–1954, the plan provided that the French army in Europe would send to Indochina prior to October 1953 twelve infantry battalions, an engineer battalion, and an artillery group (three battalions). This would increase Navarre's mobile ground elements to a total of about five division equivalents. In addition, the naval and air elements would be strengthened.

4. While on the strategic defensive in the north, Navarre would launch a series of raids, sorties, and "spoiling attacks" there, aimed at upsetting Giap's preparations for a major offensive.

5. A major pacification program would be launched in the Tonkin Delta.

6. The formation and training of the Vietnamese National Army would be accelerated.

7. By the fall of 1954, Navarre hoped by these latter two actions to free enough troops of the Expeditionary Force from static duties to form a total of six or seven mobile divisions, a force equal to or slightly superior to the Vietminh offensive force.

8. With this force, Navarre planned to seek a major battle with Giap during the 1954–1955 campaign season. In Navarre's concept, the resulting victory, or at worst, stalemate would enable the French to negotiate an honorable settlement of the war.

9. In the southern theater, where a much more favorable situation existed, the French forces would launch an offensive in Annam and in the Central Highlands (Kontum/Pleiku) during the 1953–1954 season.

This was the plan which Navarre presented in Saigon to his major commanders and key staff officers for their comments and suggestions on 16 June 1953. There was some desultory discussion, but no major changes, and in early July 1953, Navarre left for Paris to present his plan and his request for additional troops.

There is an interesting and little-known facet of the Navarre Plan which involves the United States. In late March 1953, the French premier, René Mayer, called on President Eisenhower, asking for some 400 million to 500 million dollars in increased aid to fight the Vietnam War. In the discussion with the president, who questioned the effectiveness of the French operations in Vietnam, Mayer stated that he would welcome the dispatch of a United States team to Vietnam to evaluate the French plans then being drawn up. The Eisenhower administration accepted the offer, and, in agreement with the French, determined that the American team would arrive in Vietnam sometime in early June.

To head the small team (seven principal members), the JCS selected Lt. Gen. John W. ("Iron Mike") O'Daniel, a highly decorated officer and first-rate division commander in World War II. The Joint Chiefs gave O'Daniel his directive on 10 June 1953, and he and his team set out for Saigon. He was told to forward his report on the French plans within thirty days of his arrival in Indochina. The arrogance and crassness of the Americans in sending the O'Daniel Mission is, even now, almost beyond belief. O'Daniel had visited Indochina briefly in 1952, but had no in-depth knowledge about the culture, the situation, or the contending forces. Yet in one month he was required to file a report which would endorse or condemn the military plans of the Frenchmen who had fought in Indochina for years. The French military in Vietnam, a touchy lot, swallowed their pride, for on the report of the inexperienced Americans hung millions of dollars of military and economic aid.

Actually, the American team arrived too late (14 June) to have any input into Navarre's plan and almost too late even to evaluate it. By 16 June Navarre had not only already drawn up his plan, but had on that date briefed his major commanders and principal staff officers. Navarre planned to get O'Daniel's concurrence, if possible, in his plan, or at least to try to prevent O'Daniel from eviscerating the plan with changes. Yet he had to conciliate O'Daniel and the Americans in order to receive the badly needed increases in military and economic aid. For Navarre, this tricky task meant selling O'Daniel as much of the plan as he would buy, and Navarre would agree orally to any additions or changes O'Daniel wanted, even though the haughty Frenchman had no intention of carrying them out.

O'Daniel's report of 14 July (thirty days after his team had arrived in Saigon) shows how Navarre succeeded in gaining his ends. O'Daniel in general endorsed Navarre's plan, but reported that the French intended to take two actions that he (O'Daniel) had recommended. One was to form the mobile groups and some separate battalions into divisions. This was never done. The second action which O'Daniel reported that Navarre intended to take was to launch a large-scale offensive in Tonkin by 15 September with a force equivalent to three divisions. Again, Navarre had no intention of taking the offensive in Tonkin. His plan states firmly that he wanted to stay on the *defensive* in the Tonkin area, and contains no reference to any major offensive in September.

Navarre's real "scam" is revealed in a touching and naïve comment in O'Daniel's report. The American rather proudly comments, "As evidence of French sincerity in carrying out actions . . . General Navarre and other French officers repeatedly invited me to return in a few months 'to witness the progress we will have made.' "[6] The annals of both Indochinese wars contain no comparable example of American hubris and French duplicity, but the French actions are, at least, understandable. Incidentally, the French got the aid, even though the JCS noted on 28 August that Navarre had failed "to pursue the agreements reached between General O'Daniel and General Navarre."[7]

On 17 July, in Navarre's absence, the French launched the first of his attacks designed to keep Giap off balance and on the defensive.

Navarre called it Operation HIRONDELLE, the Swallow. It was an apt code name since the operation was designed to swoop down on the Vietminh, strike, and fly away. It did just that. On D-day, three parachute battalions dropped on Lang Son on the Vietnam/China border and destroyed over 5,000 tons of equipment and fuel. The paratroopers then quickly made their way to the coast where the French navy picked them up. The operation was well-planned and professionally executed.

Navarre's next blow came on 28 July, with Operation CAMARQUE, the name of a swampy coastal area west of Marseilles. Again, the code name fit. The operation was to take place in Annam, aimed at destroying the Vietminh 95th Regiment, which had dominated Highway 1 and the sandy, salt-covered, barren coastal area between Hue and Quang Tri City. Here was guerrilla fighting at its worst—a hostile population, an enemy who faded away when approached, a land of tunnels, landmines, and booby traps. The French Expeditionary Force in bitter understatement called Highway 1 where it ran through this area, "The Street Without Joy."

The French launched a combined amphibious and land-based assault of thirty battalions (three divisions plus) designed to trap the 95th Regiment between Highway 1 and the sea. This was an overwhelming force to throw at a regiment, and worse, it missed. After several days of desultory fighting, the operation was called off. The French killed 182 Vietnamese Communists and captured 387 prisoners along with minor stores of munitions. Even these meager results must be questioned. In this kind of fighting, nobody knew how many of the killed and captured belonged to the Vietminh 95th Regiment and how many were local Vietminh militia or innocent farmers. At any rate, the 95th Regiment lived not only to fight another day, but to fight for two more decades.

On 8 August, Navarre followed CAMARQUE with the evacuation by air of the fortified camp of Na San. The French skillfully prepared for the withdrawal, always a touchy and dangerous operation. Over the preceding weeks the garrison of Na San was reduced gradually from 12,000 to around 5,000 men. They devised a clever "cover" plan to conceal the evacuation itself. Knowing that the Vietminh Radio Intercept Service monitored radio transmissions from Na San, the garrison commander sent a message asking for additional troops. Thus, when the aircraft arrived at Na San, the Vietminh concluded that the requested reinforcements were arriving. Only too late did they realize that the

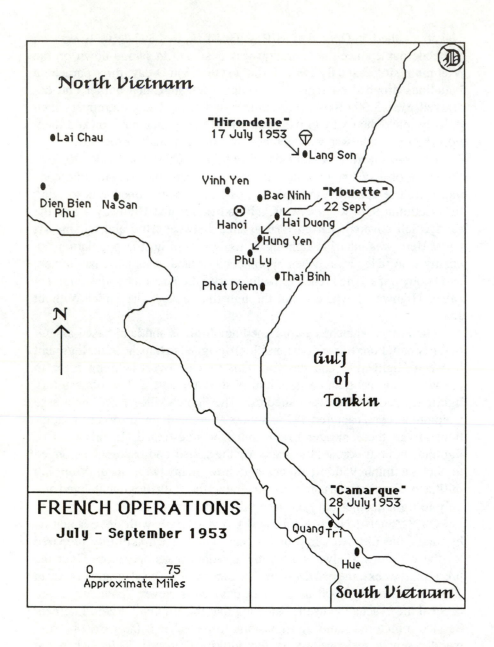

North Vietnam

Lai Chau

"Hirondelle"
17 July 1953
Lang Son

Vinh Yen

Dien Bien
Phu

Na San

Bac Ninh

"Mouette"
22 Sept

Hanoi

Hai Duong

Hung Yen

Phu Ly

Phat Diem

Thai Binh

N

Gulf
of
Tonkin

"Camarque"
28 July 1953

FRENCH OPERATIONS

July – September 1953

0   75
Approximate Miles

Quang Tri

Hue

South Vietnam

garrison was being abandoned. Jules Roy, in his excellent book *The Battle of Dien Bien Phu,* stated that the Vietminh had discovered the evacuation before its completion, but that they could not get the message to Giap due to a faulty radio transmitter. This may have been a factor, but a much more likely explanation is that the Vietminh were never prepared to mount a quick attack in the rainy season. Perhaps the most baneful impact of the successful decampment from Na San was on the mind of Navarre. It convinced him that fortified airheads could not only be held, but could be evacuated without loss. Another spadeful of earth had been dug in a French grave, marked Dien Bien Phu.

In addition to getting the troops out of an exposed position at Na San, there was another reason to bring them into the Delta. In early August the French gained intelligence of Giap's plan for his 1953–1954 offensive. According to Navarre, the Vietminh intended to launch a two-phase offensive to isolate Hanoi and Haiphong. In the first phase, the 320th Division would infiltrate north along the axis Phu Ly/Hung Yen/Hai Duong, joining up with the 42nd Independent Regiment behind the de Lattre Line. There they would disrupt and delay French troop movements. Some weeks later, the 308th and 312th Divisions, supported by the 351st (Heavy) Division, would attack south from the line Vinh Yen/Bac Ninh. In the south portion of the de Lattre Line, the 304th Division and part of the 316th would attack Phat Diem.[8]

Giap's plan thoroughly frightened the French. Navarre ordered all available reserves from Annam and Cochin China into the Delta, and he took immediate action to preempt Giap's offensive. On 22 September 1953 a force of twenty French battalions sought to surround and crush the Vietminh 42nd Independent Regiment. At the same time the French launched another sweep around Thai Binh area to clean out the 64th Independent Regiment and the guerrilla-controlled villages in that area. In both campaigns the Vietminh resisted briefly and then vanished. Navarre then struck at the 320th Division with Operation MOUETTE (Seagull), launched on 14 October. The French occupied Phu Ly/Hung Yen/ Hai Duong, the 320th axis of infiltration, with six mobile groups. The 320th Division put up a stiff fight, but Navarre had now derailed Giap's plan, and on 7 November Navarre ordered the operation abandoned. He claimed that the French had inflicted 3,000 casualties on the 320th, which was probably about right, and that he had put the division out of action for two months, which was wrong.[9]

Navarre could look with satisfaction on his achievements during the first five months of his command. He produced a sound plan. His rainy season operations gave him the initiative, and his operations varied from the successful (Lang Son) to a draw (all others). Compared with the operations of his predecessor, Salan, this looked like success.

After this auspicious start, how did Navarre stumble into the trap of Dien Bien Phu? It is in part an ignoble story—a story of a vacillating and contemptible French government, and of that government's calculated evasion about whether Navarre's mission obliged him to defend northern Laos. It is in part a quixotic story, turning around Navarre's concept of the honor of the French army and of France. It is also a story of military blunders—a misunderstanding among the major French commanders, an unrealistic strategic concept, and an inadequate appreciation of the limiting effects on air support of the distance between Dien Bien Phu and the French air base complex around Hanoi. Finally, there is that fundamental failing which plagued all French commanders in Indochina—a gross underestimation of Giap and the Vietminh.

The disaster of Dien Bien Phu can be traced back to 30 November 1952. On that date, the advancing 316th Vietminh Division threatened the small French garrison holding Dien Bien Phu. The French evacuated the place without a fight. General Salan, in command then, viewed the loss as serious, and on 30 December issued Directive Number 40 to the Tonkin Command, ordering it to retake Dien Bien Phu in a counterattack to be launched on 10 January 1953. The offensive never came off, for the French needed all their troops to counter Giap's threats to Laos and Annam.

Dien Bien Phu, however, continued to preoccupy Salan. He wrote two letters to the minister for the associated states, Jean Letourneau, stressing the strategical importance of Dien Bien Phu. The first letter, dated 28 February 1953, advocated the defense of the T'ai highlands from bases such as Lai Chau, Na San, and eventually Dien Bien Phu.[10] The second letter of 25 May 1953 suggested the possibility of taking Dien Bien Phu as a means of relieving the beleaguered garrison at Na San. Although there was a minimum of communication (or candor) between Salan and Navarre during the brief overlap of their tours in Vietnam, the plan which Salan had prepared just before Navarre's arrival strongly advocated the reoccupation of Dien Bien Phu as a means for defending upper Laos.

During this same period (late May–June 1953), another influence pushed Navarre toward Dien Bien Phu, in the person of Col. Louis Berteil, the commander of Mobile Group 7 at Na San when Navarre visited that fortified airhead in late May. Berteil was a peculiar type—a military theorist, almost a mystic, full of complicated and untried strategic concepts. The two men—both intellectuals, both outside the machismo of the French Expeditionary Force—found quick accord. Navarre was searching for a strategy to defend northern Laos, and Berteil had one, the *herisson* (Hedge Hog) concept, which envisioned establishing a fortified airhead astride a key Vietminh supply line into Laos. In early June, Navarre brought Berteil into his staff as the deputy chief of staff for operations (DCSOPS), the staff officer who formulates and recommends to the commander the tactical and strategical concepts of the command.

Some authors (Fall, O'Neill, Roy) have cast Berteil as the Svengali who mesmerized a pliant Navarre into reoccupying Dien Bien Phu. Experienced military professionals, however, tend to minimize the importance of Berteil's role. The typical DCSOPS is normally a volcano of operational concepts and ideas. Some are good; some are bad. It is the commander who rejects or accepts a concept, usually after it has been thoroughly examined by other staff specialists. There is an old adage in the American army that a commander is his own operations officer, and it is true in the French army as well. If Berteil was able to convince Navarre to establish a fortified airhead at Dien Bien Phu, it was because Navarre wanted to do just that from the beginning.

On 16 June 1953, when Navarre called his senior commanders into Saigon so that they could hear and comment on the plan he would take to Paris, he explained in detail the so-called "Navarre Plan," but he did not mention the *herisson* idea or Dien Bien Phu. It is questionable whether by 16 June Navarre had accepted this, or any other, concept to defend upper Laos. When Navarre had completed his presentation and asked for comments, Maj. Gen. René Cogny, the commander in the Tonkin Delta, expressed reservations about the offensive Navarre envisioned in Annam. Cogny said that this offensive would take troops away from Tonkin, and he needed these forces in the Delta. Instead of the Annam attack, Cogny suggested two other options. First, he recommended that the French concentrate against the enemy forces which had infiltrated into the Delta, and second, he proposed using other mobile forces to harass enemy logistic bases and supply lines in the Western Highlands of North Vietnam and along the Laotian approaches.

During the conference, Cogny mentioned Dien Bien Phu as a base—"a mooring point," he called it, from which the guerrillas and other light forces could operate against Giap's installations and supplies. Cogny's concept envisioned that the base would be lightly held and secured by far-ranging patrols. At the time (16 June 1953), Navarre made no comment regarding Cogny's recommendation to reoccupy Dien Bien Phu, but later Cogny's casual suggestion became one source of a bitter argument between the two. Navarre claimed that it was Cogny who suggested the reoccupation of Dien Bien Phu, while Cogny, admitting as much, countered by asserting that he had visualized the village as a patrol base, not as a fortified airhead capable of withstanding a major siege. This was the first of the "great misunderstandings" which would plague the French at Dien Bien Phu. It was *not* the most important.

While Navarre at the commanders' conference of 16 June had apparently not finally decided to defend Laos, he must have reached a tentative decision to do so somewhere around the end of June or early July. Before he left for Paris on 13 July, he had the staff prepare Operational Directive Number 563. This directive set forth a contingency plan which provided for French reoccupation of Dien Bien Phu *if* Giap threatened to move northwest from North Vietnam into Laos. Since in early July Navarre still had a major reservation about whether his mission required him to defend Laos, he forbade the staff to issue the directive until he had found the answer to this crucial issue in Paris.

This question—whether Navarre was responsible for the defense of northern Laos—was the most critical of the "great misunderstandings." It came to light quickly when Navarre arrived in Paris in mid-July. In his presentation of 17 July to the Chiefs of Staff committee, he discussed at length the difficulties of defending northern Laos. The Chiefs told Navarre that it was their view that his mission did *not* require him to defend Upper Laos. Instead, they suggested that an attempt be made to get the United States and Great Britain to guarantee the territorial integrity of Laos, and to warn Russia and China of the dangers of expanding the war in Vietnam into Laos. One can almost see the haughty Navarre sneer at this fainthearted and unrealistic evasion of responsibility. In his book he disdainfully says of this suggestion by the Chiefs of Staff, "the role of the high military advisors of the Government is to face realities, even if hard, and not to propose easy solutions."[11]

The views of the Chiefs were not binding or final. The ultimate decision had to come from the National Defense Committee, an august body presided over by the president of the Republic and including the premier, the ministers for foreign affairs, the interior, national defense, and the French overseas territories, the secretaries of state for the three armed services, the marshal of France, and the armed forces Chiefs of Staff. On 24 July the committee met, and Navarre promptly confronted it with the question of his responsibility for the defense of northern Laos. The Chiefs of Staff presented their view that Navarre was not required to defend Upper Laos. In the lengthy discussion which followed, some of the participants supported the Chiefs; others took the opposite viewpoint, that for political and diplomatic reasons Laos had to be defended. In the discussion, Navarre frankly stated that he doubted he had the ability to defend northern Laos, and that any such defense might well result in heavy French casualties. After a long and confused debate, no decision regarding Navarre's obligation for defending Laos was reached, although one was vaguely promised. The committee did tell Navarre to take all steps to safeguard the security and the integrity of the Expeditionary Force and to tailor his operations to his means.[12] These instructions were meaningless, for they are implicit command responsibilities, whether explicitly set forth or not.

During the discussion with the committee, Navarre mentioned that he might establish a fortified airhead at Dien Bien Phu as a means of defending northern Laos. The minister of state for the air force, General Corniglion-Moliner, a former air force pilot who in 1946 had flown into Dien Bien Phu, questioned the feasibility of the operation. He told the committee that the valley was dominated by its mountainous rim and that the distance from Hanoi to Dien Bien Phu would seriously limit the air support available over the village. Navarre replied coldly that the minister's criticism was from the airman's viewpoint only, and that he believed that the operation was feasible. There was an uneasy silence around the table, and the subject was dropped.

Consequently, in Paris on 24 July 1953 began the most important controversy which would surround the battle of Dien Bien Phu. Did Navarre have the responsibility to defend Upper Laos, or had he been relieved of it? For years Navarre insisted that the National Defense Committee reached no decision on this key issue during its meeting of 24 July. He further claimed that a decision relieving him of the responsibility to defend Laos was not made until much later—too late to have avoided Dien Bien Phu. On the other hand, Joseph Laniel, the premier, maintained that Navarre's assertions were incorrect, and that Navarre was instructed at the 24 July conference to abandon Laos if necessary. This controversy is central to the issue of who was responsible for the disaster at Dien Bien Phu. If Navarre had actually been given instructions to abandon Laos, then his decision to defend it (Laos) by reoccupying Dien Bien Phu was beyond the scope of his responsibilities, and he had culpably exceeded his authority. On the other hand, if the committee had reached no decision about his obligation for Laos, then Navarre's responsibility for what happened is diffused and mitigated.

On this key issue, the evidence supports Navarre's claim that on 24 July he was given no clear-cut decision regarding his responsibility for Laos. Over the years, when challenged by Navarre, Laniel has never been able to present any written evidence to support his contention that Navarre was instructed to abandon Laos if necessary.[13] The most important reinforcement for Navarre's position comes from Gen. Georges Catroux, the leader of the Commission of Investigation, which in 1955 examined the Dien Bien Phu defeat. Catroux conducted no "whitewash" of Navarre; in his report he criticized Navarre frequently and harshly. Yet Catroux stated that all available evidence convinced him that the directive telling Navarre that he was not responsible for the defense of Upper Laos was drawn up on 13 November 1953. This order was not delivered to Navarre until 4 December, two weeks after he launched the battle of Dien Bien Phu.[14]

The French government acted in an ambiguous and pusillanimous manner. The French leaders must have known that they had not given Navarre a clear, usable answer to his crucial question about his responsibilities for the defense of northern Laos. The truth was that the French government did not intend to defend northern Laos, but for diplomatic and political reasons it could not enunciate such a policy even within its highest council. The committee "leaked" constantly to the French press, and its members knew it. As a matter of fact, within a week an exact account of the committee discussion of 24 July appeared in a Paris newspaper, including Navarre's statement regarding the difficulties of defending northern Laos. For that reason the committee had to avoid giving a straight answer to Navarre's valid and crucial question. The politicians wanted the issue to be fuzzy, and if this meant that Navarre had to be confused or misled in the process, so be it.

Navarre understood the committee's dilemma, anticipated its indecision, and hastened to exploit it. Immediately after the committee adjourned, he radioed Admiral Auboyneau, who acted as commander in chief in Navarre's absence, instructing him to sign and issue Directive Number 563, the plan calling for the reoccupation of Dien Bien Phu. Directive Number 563 was issued on 25 July, Saigon time, less than twenty-four hours after the Committee had adjourned in Paris.

On 22 October 1953, the French and Laotian governments signed the so-called Matignon Treaty, further confusing the issue of France's responsibility to defend Laos. This agreement provided for the independence of Laos and membership in the French Union. The treaty did not contain a clear-cut commitment for France to defend Laos, but such a responsibility was strongly implied by Article 2, which stated: "The Kingdom of Laos freely affirms its membership in the French Union . . . in which all the associates place in common their resources in order to guarantee the defense of the Union as a whole."[15] Navarre believed that the treaty obligated the French government to protect Laos, and that his view of the intent of the treaty was confirmed by the secretary of state for the Associated States, M. Marc Jacquet, and by the commissioner general for Indochina, M. Maurice DeJean.[16] In spite of the treaty, the French government had no intention of defending Laos. The treaty was a charade, a "scrap of paper," but again, nobody told Navarre that.

While the French played their bureaucratic games, Giap readied the Vietminh forces for their role in the oncoming drama. During the summer of 1953, while he intensified guerrilla warfare in the Delta, he devoted his major efforts to increasing the strength and effectiveness of his Main Force units. The 351st (Heavy) Division took on more artillery and heavy mortars. Additional antiaircraft units were formed and trained by the Chinese. He upgraded the armament of the infantry battalions of the divisions by giving them more machine guns, mortars, and submachine guns. Training became more realistic; discipline was tightened; and political indoctrination was intensified. Giap worked particularly hard on expanding his logistic capacity. Roads were improved, and the Chinese provided 600 trucks, most with Chinese drivers. Most important, hundreds of thousands of porters were mobilized.[17] Giap and the Chinese had built a tough, well-equipped, experienced, and dedicated army—a tool awaiting a great task and a master craftsman.

Navarre claims that he preempted Giap's original plan for launching a major offensive against the Tonkin Delta during the campaign season of 1953–1954, and that Giap and Ho changed their plans in late October. While he cites as one reason for this change the fact that his Operation MOUETTE had upset Vietminh plans, Navarre writes that Giap changed his plans mainly for political reasons. According to Navarre, in late October Ho wanted to negotiate and needed a quick and substantial victory to strengthen his bargaining position. Giap did not foresee such a victory in the Delta, but did see the possibilities of a flashy triumph in Laos.[18]

While Navarre claims that the French had firm intelligence about Giap's change of plan, in *his* book, Giap avers that the Vietminh never harbored any intention of making other than minor attacks against the French concentration in the Delta. On this point Giap is probably right. Navarre apparently mistook Giap's small diversionary attacks for a major offensive. In a lengthy exposition of the Vietminh strategy for the 1953–1954 campaign season (which Giap says was developed by the Party Central Committee in early 1953), Giap set forth these four "fundamental principles" (his words) upon which that strategy was based: "First in the liberation war waged by our people the most fundamental strategic principle was to destroy *the enemy effectives and increase our forces*. (Italics are Giap's) . . . All ideas and actions were aimed at reaching the basic goal which was the destruction of enemy effectives.

"Second, we had to strike to win, strike only when success is certain, strike to wipe out the enemy.

"Third, because we wanted to destroy the enemy effectives and to strike only to win . . . our *strategic direction* (Giap's italics) could not allow us to choose other directions than those where the enemy was exposed and relatively weak and where we had many favorable conditions . . . for combats of wholesale destruction.

"Fourth, because our aim was to destroy the enemy effectives, attack the enemy where he was relative weak, and create favorable conditions to destroy him, in the practical military conditions obtaining at that time, whose major feature was the concentration by the enemy of a fairly powerful mobile force in the Bac Bo (Tonkin) delta, *we should not launch large-scale offensives upon that powerful mobile mass* (emphasis added), but seek ways and means to compel him to scatter his forces . . . in various directions, then choose the directions most favorable to us to destroy him."[19]

From these "fundamental principles" of Vietminh strategy, Giap derived his overall concept for 1953–1954. He writes: "To speak more concretely, on the front of the Bac Bo delta, besides the immediate task which was to continue speeding up guerrilla warfare in the enemy rear, we could also use part of our regular forces in minor battles. As for major campaigns, they should be launched in other directions."[20]

Giap then moves from his strategic concept to his operational plan, which was, in his words:

"(a) To use part of our regular forces to launch an offensive in the northwestern direction, destroy the enemy who was still occupying Lai Chau, thus liberating the whole Northwest.

"(b) To propose the Pathet Lao Liberation (Communist) troops to coordinate with the Vietnamese volunteer units in order to launch an offensive in the direction of *Middle* Laos . . . (emphasis added)

"(c) As the enemy's action was not yet clearly seen our immediate tactic was to post an important part of our regular forces at a certain point, completely conceal them, and keep ourselves ready for action. In face of our troops offensive in the northwestern direction, it was possible that the enemy would send his reinforcements there; in this circumstance, we would dispatch more regular forces in that direction to wipe out his effectives. The enemy might also attack deep in some direction of the Viet Bac Base to cut our lines of communication and supply . . . (to) compel our regular forces to withdraw from the northwest. In this case, we would seek ways and means to attract the enemy deep into our rear and then use part of our regular forces to put him out of action.

"(d) In the delta we would speed up guerrilla warfare in the enemy's rear.

"Above was the operational plan worked out for our army on the main battlefield—the Northern battlefield."[21]

The Vietminh had reliable information that during the 1953–1954 campaign season the French intended to launch a major offensive in the South against the Vietminh Fifth Zone, or Military Region V, which was that part of Annam stretching from Da Nang to Nha Trang. Here the Vietminh strategy was not to counter the French attacks, but instead, to launch an offensive of their own against the Western Highlands around Kontum and Pleiku. Giap reckoned that the Vietminh would temporarily lose some territory, but that the French would eventually have to withdraw. Regarding Cochin China, Giap realized his weakness there and prescribed only a continuation of guerrilla warfare. Overall, the strategy was sound, and with it Giap was ready for the campaign season of 1953–1954.

Giap made his first move on 27 October, sending the 316th Vietminh Division out of the Viet Bac toward Lai Chau, one of the gateways to Laos. The French became aware of the move shortly after it began (see map p. 140). The rainy season was over, and Giap's move indicated to Navarre that another major Vietminh offensive against Laos was on the way. This was the contingency for which Directive Number 563 had been drafted, so on 2 November, Navarre's headquarters put out Directive Number 852 ordering Cogny to reoccupy Dien Bien Phu with a force of six paratroop battalions, preferably between 15–20 November, but not later than 1 December.

Cogny protested the order, but then he protested most orders from his superiors. An unusual and controversial character, he was a principal actor in the tragedy of Dien Bien Phu. The first impression one gained of Cogny was of size and strength. He stood six feet four, broad-shouldered and deep-chested. In 1953 he was France's youngest major general, and probably its most highly educated. He held a degree from France's best engineering school, another in political science, and like Giap, a doctorate in jurisprudence. During World War II he had been a Résistance leader; he had been captured and tortured by the Gestapo and had spent some time in Buchenwald. After the war he was a protégé of de Lattre's, and like him, overly fond of the pomp and ceremony with which a general sometimes surrounds himself. Cogny's subordinates liked and admired him, but his superiors disliked him because of his habit of questioning and carping about almost every order they gave him. Cogny, a big man physically, was extremely sensitive emotionally: a sharp word or a rejected suggestion cut him deeply, and when his pride was injured, he struck back fiercely. He was the kind of subordinate who required firm yet tactful handling—a de Lattre could have managed him, Navarre could not.

It should have come as no great surprise to Navarre when Cogny disagreed with his order to retake Dien Bien Phu. The surprise lay in the devious way in which Cogny protested Navarre's directive. On receipt of the order on 2 November, Cogny had his staff draw up a memorandum to Navarre for his (Cogny's) signature setting forth in strong language his objections to the operation. The memorandum opposed the plan on several grounds. First, the memo contended that a force cannot block a road in Indochina, as you might in Europe, by sitting astride it. Second, Dien Bien Phu, once occupied, would suck up vast numbers of troops. Third, any troops put there could be bottled up by Giap with no possibility of large-scale "radiating out" from it to attack Vietminh supply lines and installations. (This last was a curious and belated criticism, since it was Cogny who had proposed Dien Bien Phu as the "mooring point" for this type of "radiating out" operation in northwest Vietnam.) Fourth, the troops which would be committed to Dien Bien Phu were badly needed in the Tonkin Delta. Finally, the memorandum noted that the projected operation would absorb almost all the combat and support aircraft in the northern command.

The memorandum was sound in every criticism of the projected operation. Significantly, the memorandum did not object to the operation because it called for the establishment of a sizable fortified airhead—another Na San. At this stage, apparently neither Cogny nor his staff divined that Navarre might be visualizing a *herisson* instead of a "mooring point." But then Navarre himself probably had not decided at this time exactly what he intended to do at Dien Bien Phu.

In spite of the adverse views of his staff and his own negative opinion of the operation, Cogny did *not* send the memorandum to Navarre. Instead, on 6 November he wrote Navarre an ambiguous letter which seemed to endorse the reoccupation of Dien Bien Phu—after all, Cogny had suggested it—but the letter did state his fears that with the loss of troops to the operation, he might not be able to hold the Delta. In effect Cogny "covered" himself. He did not want to appear to lack aggressiveness, particularly if the operation succeeded. On the other hand, he wanted to escape censure if the operation failed, or if the Vietminh broke into the Tonkin Delta while a significant part of his forces were bottled up in Dien Bien Phu. When his staff officers saw this letter, their lips curled. They recognized it for the "straddle" that it was. Staff officers are always blunter and bolder than their commander. Staffs stand protected behind their commander and do not have to suffer the direct wrath of a superior. The commander has no such safe position; his superior will hold him totally responsible for the correspondence, so it is his career, his future, which he puts at risk when he signs a document. So it was with Cogny.

On 11 November, Cogny's headquarters sent out operational instructions to the army and air force elements which would participate in Operation CASTOR, the airborne assault on Dien Bien Phu. Cogny's order to the paratroop commander, Brigadier General Gilles, emphasized his (Cogny's) understanding of the operation as one to obtain a "mooring point" for guerrillas and other mobile units by instructing Gilles that his defense of the Dien Bien Phu airfield would "exclude any system designed to provide a belt of strongpoints for the airfield."[22] Here is an extraordinary situation. The paratroop assault is nine days off, yet Cogny and Navarre have no common understanding of the purpose of the operation. Worse, neither realizes that there is a vast communication chasm between them.

When Col. Jean Nicot, the commander of the French air transport fleet, received the operational instructions, he immediately protested to Cogny and to Navarre. He stated forcibly and in writing that the air transport force could not maintain a flow of supplies into Dien Bien Phu over an extended period, due to poor weather conditions in the valley and the probability of intense antiaircraft fire over the village. Brigadier General Dechaux, the air force commander in northern Vietnam, supported Nicot. He not only repeated Nicot's objections, but pointed out that the distance of 200 miles from Hanoi (the center of the airfield complex) to Dien Bien Phu would limit to a few minutes the time his fighter aircraft could spend over the target area, and that this minimal support could be furnished only at great cost in fuel, crew fatigue, and engine wear.

In the face of these objections by his air force commanders, Cogny wavered and then reversed his position. Cogny gave Colonel Berteil, who had come to Hanoi to coordinate the details of CASTOR, a letter to Navarre in which for the first time he expressed his clear opposition to the projected operation. Thus, by the evening of 13 November or early on the morning of 14 November, Navarre knew that Cogny (in overall charge of CASTOR) and the air force commanders (who would have to support it) opposed the operation. This opposition Navarre ignored. On 14 November, Navarre issued his final orders for the airborne assault. These orders confirmed previous instructions without clarifying the basic question as to whether he intended Dien Bien Phu to be a "mooring point" or a *herisson*.

Cogny and his air force subordinates had one final chance to air their misgivings about CASTOR. The commissioner-general for Indochina, DeJean, who was visiting Vietnam from Paris, flew with Navarre to Hanoi on 17 November, where they were briefed on the upcoming operation. The briefing for DeJean was a "snow job," describing Operation CASTOR in general and confident terms. But the real confrontation came before the briefing for the civilian commissioner. Navarre and Cogny first met in Cogny's office. This is customary in all armies since it permits the generals to speak much more frankly. In front of subordinates a general is careful not to disparage the views of another general, even though he may be junior in rank.

In this man-to-man conference, Cogny expressed his objections to the operation clearly and firmly. For the first time he produced and read to Navarre his staff's memorandum of 4 November denouncing the operation. The negative views set forth in the memorandum were now his views, Cogny told Navarre. What Navarre said to Cogny is not known, but on either that day (the 17th) or the next, Navarre told an aide in reference to CASTOR that he "didn't manage to find out exactly what General Cogny thought."[23] Navarre has never expanded or explained this peculiar and apparently untrue statement. Either there was such a gulf of communication between the two men that Cogny's objections to CASTOR did not even register with Navarre, or Navarre's ears were closed to objections.

Later that day, in a conference still restricted to military men, Navarre flatly asked Generals Gilles and Dechaux, the ground and air commanders of CASTOR, if they objected to the operation. They said that they did. Gilles, the paratrooper, posed minor objections to the tactics of a single landing on the village in view of late intelligence that showed the 148th Vietminh Regiment in Dien Bien Phu. He wanted to drop in several places surrounding the village and close in on it after landing. Dechaux, the air force commander, repeated his previous objections to the entire concept, based on weather, antiaircraft fire, aircraft maintenance problems, inadequate time-over-target, and attrition of fuel, engines, and airmen. Navarre listened and said little. Finally, he quietly said that he knew the air force could do the job in spite of the problems and concluded the conference by announcing that Operation CASTOR would be carried out on 20 November, three days later.

Here is posed another fundamental question surrounding the battle of Dien Bien Phu—why did Navarre persist in carrying through the operation? Every facet of the planned operation argued against his undertaking it. All his major subordinate commanders—Gilles, Cogny, Dechaux—opposed it. These were men of intelligence, experience, and courage. Like their counterparts in all Western armed services, they would not oppose an operation on superficial or frivolous grounds. The matter is too important, not only to their country and to their troops, but to their own careers. By objecting to a proposed operation they open themselves to charges of lack of aggressiveness—strong grounds upon which to relieve a subordinate commander. For these reasons, the senior commander always gives the objections of his major subordinates the most careful consideration. The overall commander, of course, may persist in an operation against the advice of his subordinates, but he knows that he then bears a double responsibility, and in the event of failure he will surely forfeit his command, his career, and his reputation.

Navarre could have justified the operation, had he been given a clear order from the French government to defend Laos. He could have argued that despite the objections of his commanders, the reoccupation of Dien Bien Phu was the best way to carry out a difficult, perhaps impossible, mission. But Navarre had no clear mission to defend Laos. On the contrary, he had sat in on the deliberations of the National Defense Committee on 24 July and knew the conflicting and indecisive views of his government on France's obligation for the defense of Laos. Finally, Navarre realized, as he told the committee on 24 July and repeated in his book, that there was no easy way to defend Laos. He knew that the operation had enormous disadvantages and hazards, and yet in spite of them he went on with it.

What compelling reasons caused him to continue? There was Navarre's self-confidence and arrogance. He had only contempt for the leaders of the French government who could not make the hard decision. In Navarre's view their refusal to make a decision, in effect, transferred their responsibility and authority to him. If the National Defense Committee would not make the decision, he would. He relished the responsibility and the freedom of action it gave him. Whatever his shortcomings might have been, Navarre never sought shelter behind his superiors. He acted.

Another reason which impelled Navarre to defend Laos was that he thought the war would be lost if he did not do so, and that he alone would be blamed. Navarre wrote that M. Marc Jacquet, the aforementioned secretary of state for the Associated States, told him in mid-November 1953 that he (Jacquet) believed that the loss of northern Laos, particularly Louang Phrabang, would so shock French opinion that the continuation of the war would be impossible.[24] While Navarre does not clearly support this view in his book, he does not dispute it, and he certainly accepted it as a factor in making his decision. Years later Navarre confirmed the strength of this motive in a slightly different way. In a letter written in 1959 to a French newspaper, he said that to let the Vietminh arrive "in force on the Mekong would be equivalent to opening to it the door to central and southern Indochina"[25]—in other words, to losing the war. Navarre again revealed this motive when he said in 1963, "Suppose that I had abandoned Laos on my own initiative and opened to the Vietminh the road to total victory: I would be branded today as the man who betrayed the honor of his country."[26]

Those last four words contain the key. In his mind the honor of the French army and of France itself required him to defend Laos. The French army has always regarded itself as the guardian and custodian of the honor of France. In this role it holds itself above the government, above the politicians, whose motives the army has always mistrusted. In the minds of French army officers, it is the army, the preeminent service, who must insure that France acts always in consonance with their concept of her glory and honor. If the civilians who control the government act dishonorably or cravenly, then it becomes the duty of the French officer corps to usurp civilian authority.

The French army has made heroes of its generals who have defied governmental authority and disobeyed orders to bring victory and honor to France. Charles de Gaulle, in his pre-World War II book *The Edge of the Sword,* wrote: "Those who have done great deeds have often had to take the risk of ignoring the merely routine aspects of discipline. Examples are plentiful: Pelissier at Sebastopol stuffing the Emperor's threatening dispatches into his pocket unopened and reading them only after the action was over; Lanrezac saving his army after Charleroi by breaking off the battle, contrary to orders; Lyautey keeping the whole of Morocco in 1914, in the teeth of instructions issued at a higher level. After the Battle of Jutland and the English failure to take the opportunity offered them of destroying the German fleet, Admiral Fisher, then First Sea Lord, exclaimed in a fury after reading Jellicoe's dispatch: 'He has all Nelson's qualities but one: he doesn't know how to disobey!' ''[27]

After France's fall in 1940, General de Gaulle continued the war in defiance of the legal government headed by Marshall Pétain, and for this action the Vichy government sentenced him to death *in absentia*. In this tradition, would not Navarre, a senior French general, take what he saw as the road of honor, particularly when that road had been left unbarred by the politicians?

Once Navarre decided that he had to defend upper Laos, the crucial question became—how? Navarre thought first of defending Laos by mobile warfare—fighting a war of movement, attacking the enemy columns advancing into Laos. He quickly discarded this concept. He saw correctly that the mountainous jungle and primitive road net would not permit the Expeditionary Force, burdened with trucks, tanks, and other equipment, to move and supply itself. In addition, the French were largely untrained in jungle warfare, and psychologically unfit for combat waged by squads and platoons armed with small arms and mortars only. To support such a mobile war deep in Laos would overextend ground and air supply lines and was obviously infeasible.

As a second option, Navarre considered—and rejected—the establishment of a linear defense to cover Laos. He did not have sufficient troops to man this concept. Besides, the Vietminh would infiltrate the French lines there, as they had in the Delta, and move into Laos anyway. The third option Navarre considered was to defend the Laotian capitals, Louang Phrabang and Vientiane, by placing troops around these towns. He gave up this idea mainly because the distance between the French airfield complex around Hanoi and the Laotian capitals made large-scale air support and aerial resupply operations over an extended period all but impossible. There were tactical reasons also. Louang Phrabang was dominated by the hills which surround it, and both airfields were at such distances from their towns that a single defensive position could not cover both town and airfield.

The fourth course of action available to Navarre was to mount a major diversionary attack into the Viet Bac just as (or just before) Giap moved into Laos. Theoretically, such an offensive would threaten the site of the Vietminh government and the supply lines of the Main Force units and would force Giap to scurry back to the Viet Bac to defend them. But this concept had been tried twice before and had failed both times. Valluy had thrust into the Viet Bac in 1947 and had almost captured Ho and Giap. Even in those days of Vietminh weakness, however, the operation eventually failed. In 1952, Salan had attempted a similar maneuver in Operation LORRAINE. It did little damage to the Vietminh supply arrangements, and it failed to force Giap to turn back from his attacks on the T'ai country. Now in 1953, with the Vietminh stronger than ever, such an operation would require more troops than Navarre had in Vietnam. Also, such a sortie would dangerously uncover the Delta. Navarre, with Cogny's concurrence, discarded this concept.

The rejection of the attack into the Viet Bac left Navarre with only the concept of the fortified airhead, the *herisson*. He characterized it as *"une solution mediocre,"* but, he writes, it was the only one available.[28] In Navarre's concept, the fortified airhead would have two functions. First, he believed it would block one of Giap's key supply routes from China and the Viet Bac into Laos. This view was theoretical nonsense. This was not Europe, but the mountainous jungle of northwestern Vietnam, where the lines of communications are not highways and railroads, but numerous streams and trails. The occupation of one site would not block the flow of either troops or supplies into Laos. Second, Navarre visualized the fortified airhead as a base from which to attack Giap's supply lines and installations in the event Giap sent a division or two toward Louang Phrabang. This part of Navarre's concept, too, lacked validity. During the previous Laotian campaign, Na San posed a similar threat, but Giap brought up sizable forces and sealed off the camp. Once sealed, the French could not "radiate out" from it, and Giap could then either move around it, or mount a major attack against it. Looking at it retrospectively, Navarre's concept of the fortified airhead as a means of defending Upper Laos was not even *"une solution mediocre."*

Once Navarre settled on the *herisson* concept, there remained only the selection of the site. He had already rejected Louang Phrabang and

Vientiane. The choice then came down to Lai Chau or Dien Bien Phu. Navarre vetoed Lai Chau out of hand. The airfield was too short; it was frequently covered with water; it had a history of unusually bad flying weather; and it was in a narrow gorge (the French pilots complained of receiving ground-based antiaircraft fire from *above* their aircraft). This left only Dien Bien Phu.

If Navarre had to defend Laos, and *if* he determined the *herisson* concept to be the only way to do it—two enormous and questionable ifs—then Dien Bien Phu was the best place to set up the fortified airhead. The strategic advantages of its position are attested to by none other than Giap himself. In his book, he wrote: "Dien Bien Phu is a large plain 18 kilometers long and six to eight kilometers wide in the mountain zone of the northwest. It is the biggest and richest of the four plains in this hilly region close to the Vietnam-Laos frontier. It is situated at the junction of important roads running to North—East towards Lai Chau, to the East and South—East towards Tuan Giao, Son La, Na San; to the West toward Louang Phrabang, and to the South towards Sam Neua. In the theatre of operation of Bac Bo (i.e., Tonkin) and Upper Laos, Dien Bien Phu is a strategic position of first importance, capable of becoming an infantry and air base of extreme efficiency in their scheme of aggression in South East Asia."[29]

There were, however, two significant strategic disadvantages to locating a fortified airhead at Dien Bien Phu. First, it could not be reinforced or resupplied by road; and second, it was 295 kilometers (183 miles) from the French airfield complex around Hanoi. This distance placed it at a maximum operating range of the transports and fighters which would have to support it, permitting the fighters to spend only fifteen minutes over Dien Bien Phu and drastically limiting the carrying capacity of the small force of 70 to 100 transport aircraft available. Navarre was well aware of these limitations and accepted them.

Finally, Navarre points out that Dien Bien Phu's location presented strategic problems to the Vietminh as well as to the French. Dien Bien Phu was 200 kilometers from the Delta and 300 kilometers from the points on the Vietnam/China border where supplies from China for the Vietminh entered the country. He speculated that this distance, combined with the Vietminh's lack of trucks, would limit the supplies which Giap could bring to the Dien Bien Phu area, and thus restrict the size of the Vietminh force he could deploy there.[30]

Tactically, Navarre thought the valley would be secure from artillery fire from the surrounding hills. He notes that the valley floor encompassed a large area, sixteen by nineteen kilometers, and the heights from which Vietminh artillery could be brought to bear were ten to twelve kilometers from the airfield. Then, subtly shifting the blame, he writes that *the French artillerymen* told him that the Vietminh gunners would have to move onto the forward slope to fire effectively on the airfield. When the Vietminh took these positions, so said his artillery advisors, they would be exposed to French counterbattery fire or air attack and would be destroyed.[31] Bernard Fall points out that Navarre's assessment was questionable. Actually, the airfield could be brought under direct artillery fire from a hill line only five kilometers from the airfield.[32]

Navarre's motives for defending northern Laos, his rationale for selecting the *herisson* concept as the means, and his reasons for choosing Dien Bien Phu as the place have been examined. But somehow, all these fall short as adequate justification for the decision which would commit thousands of men to a mission which would be certainly dangerous and probably futile. There must have been something more.

There was. The one fundamental calculation which underlaid Navarre's decision, the one reason which to Navarre justified the operation, *was the estimate by his intelligence staff that the operation carried little or no risk*. His experts assured him that the enemy could not support a major force at Dien Bien Phu. He believed them. He wrote that the reoccupation of Dien Bien Phu was ". . . very acceptable against the enemy it was reasonable to think we would have to deal with."[33] Navarre became convinced that it would take Giap several weeks to concentrate even one division at Dien Bien Phu, and that the enemy could not maintain a two-division force for any extended period. Navarre's intelligence officers told him repeatedly that the enemy could not bring large numbers of artillery pieces to bear, and that artillery ammunition capability of the Vietminh would be very limited. This optimistic view had been earlier confirmed by Salan, who in his study of May 1953 had stressed the point that distance, bad roads, and the Vietminh truck shortage would prevent Giap employing artillery or other heavy arms in any significant quantity. To both Salan and Navarre, what had been done at Na San could be done at Dien Bien Phu—a fatal miscalculation.

While events in Vietnam unfolded in the late summer and fall of 1953, another drama was taking place in Paris. In that city on 13 November an important meeting of the National Defense Committee bearing on the battle of Dien Bien Phu took place. Laniel, the premier, supported by the committee, decided to negotiate a settlement with Ho and the Vietminh. The key question before the committee dealt with the timing of the approach to Ho Chi Minh. Should the approach be made now, or would the French negotiating position be stronger at some later date? The preponderance of opinion favored an immediate approach. The recently signed Korean Armistice would free large quantities of Chinese aid to the Vietminh, and Navarre's recent operational successes, Operations HIRONDELLE and MOUETTE, tended to favor the French in immediate negotiations.

The committee decided to send Rear Admiral Cabanier, the secretary of the National Defense Committee, to obtain Navarre's views about the best time to approach Ho. Cabanier was to go to Saigon to get Navarre's opinion in a private conversation. He was thoroughly "briefed," for the problem of "leaks" still prevented any sensitive material being put in writing. The committee made other decisions which Cabanier was to transmit orally to Navarre. The admiral was instructed to tell Navarre that he (Navarre) would get no additional aid from France; that he must tailor his plans to his current resources; and that he must limit himself to containing the enemy. Most significant, however, was the failure of the committee to send any specific instructions regarding Laos or Navarre's responsibility for its defense. On 15 November, Cabanier left Paris for Saigon.

On 19 November, Admiral Cabanier arrived in Saigon and immediately got in touch with Navarre, who was in Hanoi. Cabanier asked Navarre's permission to fly to Hanoi that day to deliver his message. Navarre told Cabanier to stay in Saigon and that he (Navarre) would see him there on the morning of 20 November.

At 0900 hours on 20 November Cabanier met Navarre in his office in Saigon. After a brief exchange of pleasantries, Cabanier put to Navarre the question he came 5,000 miles to ask: from the military viewpoint, would it be better to open negotiations with the Vietminh *now,* or should the French government wait for a more favorable military situation in the future? Navarre showed Cabanier a message informing him that even as they talked the paratroopers were en route to Dien Bien Phu. Navarre then answered the question. It was his view that the situation would be improved by spring, and that negotiations should be delayed until that season. Cabanier had his answer, and the battle of Dien Bien Phu was about to begin.

Notes—Chapter 8

1. Donald Lancaster, *The Emancipation of French Indochina* (London: Oxford University Press, 1961), p. 264.
2. Navarre, *Agonie,* p. 159.
3. Ibid., p. 76.
4. Ibid., p. 72.
5. Ibid., p. 85.
6. Gareth Porter, *Vietnam: The Definitive Documentation of Human Decisions,* 2 vols. (Stanfordville, NY: Earl M. Coleman Enterprises, 1979), I:452–453.
7. Ibid., I:463 (quoting a JCS report to the secretary of defense, 28 August 1953).
8. Navarre, *Agonie,* p. 159.
9. Ibid., p. 161.
10. Bernard B. Fall, *Hell in a Very Small Place: The Siege of Dien Bien Phu* (New York: J. B. Lippincott, 1967), p. 26.
11. Navarre, *Agonie,* p. 86.
12. Fall, *Street,* p. 315.
13. Navarre, *Agonie,* pp. 337–338.
14. Fall, *Hell,* p. 33.
15. Treaty between France and the government of Laos, signed 22 October 1953.
16. Navarre, *Agonie,* p. 339 and 190.
17. Vo Nguyen Giap, *Dien Bien Phu,* (Hanoi: Foreign Languages Publishing House, 1964), p. 63.
18. Navarre, *Agonie,* p. 161.
19. Giap, *Dien Bien Phu,* pp. 57–59.
20. Ibid., p. 51.
21. Ibid., pp. 54–55.
22. Fall, *Hell,* p. 37.
23. Roy, *Battle,* p. 32.
24. Navarre, *Agonie,* p. 190.
25. Fall, *Street,* p. 315. Letter to *Le Figaro,* 25 May 1959.
26. Fall, *Hell,* p. 35.
27. Charles de Gaulle, *The Edge of the Sword* (New York: Criterion Books, 1960), p. 45.
28. Navarre, *Agonie,* pp. 191 and 199.
29. Giap, *Dien Bien Phu,* p. 77.
30. Navarre, *Agonie,* p. 195.
31. Ibid., p. 196.
32. Fall, *Street,* p. 317.
33. Navarre, *Agonie,* p. 196.

9 Dien Bien Phu

Preparations for Battle
20 November 1953–13 March 1954

The airborne assault of Dien Bien Phu began at 1035 hours, 20 November 1953, when the paratroopers of the 6th Bataillon de Parachutistes Coloniaux (6th BPC) leapt into space over Drop Zone (DZ) NATASHA, located 200 meters north of the village. Almost simultaneously, the 2d Battalion, 1st Regiment of Chasseurs Parachutistes (II/1RCP) began their drop on the DZ SIMONE, 600 meters to the south. With the II/1RCP jumped the command element of the task force, the 1st Airborne Battle Group. The mission of the force was to clear Dien Bien Phu and to secure the small dirt airstrip located just north of the village. The two assault battalions were "crack" units of the Expeditionary Force and were led by the two preeminent field-grade commanders in Vietnam, Major Bigeard of the 6th BPC and Major Brechignac of the II/1RCP. The French started the "first team."

It was well that they did, for the enemy reacted to the landing instantly and effectively. Dien Bien Phu was the headquarters of the elite Vietminh 148th Independent Infantry Regiment, a tough, battle-seasoned outfit made up largely of tribal mountaineers. Three of its four battalions were absent from Dien Bien Phu on the day of the French landing. The 910th Battalion was present (which the French knew before the landing), but what they did not know was that a mortar company, an artillery battery from the 351st (Heavy) Division, and an infantry company from the 320th Division were also training there.

These Vietminh units were on a field exercise around the village when the paratroopers jumped. The Vietminh immediately opened fire on the 6th BPC, hitting several paratroopers in the air and pinning down

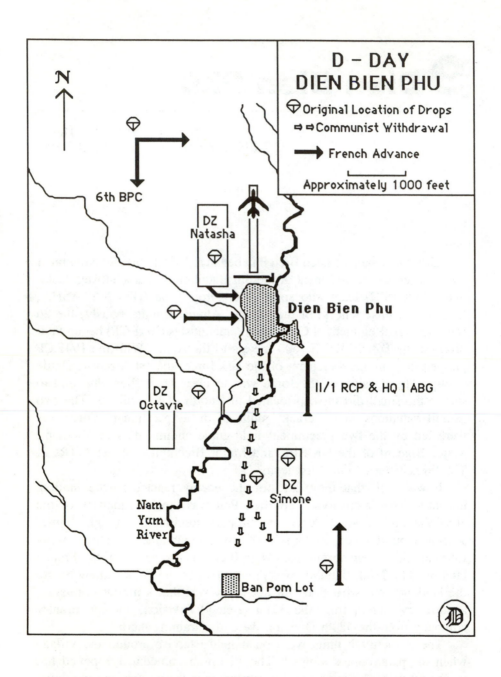

D – DAY
DIEN BIEN PHU

⊖ Original Location of Drops
⇨⇨ Communist Withdrawal
→ French Advance

Approximately 1000 feet

6th BPC

DZ Natasha

Dien Bien Phu

DZ Octavie

II/1 RCP & HQ 1 ABG

DZ Simone

Nam Yum River

Ban Pom Lot

the remainder as they reached the ground. The French situation was further complicated by the inherent disorder of parachute landings. Units were scattered, two of Bigeard's companies landed off-target, and the command radios were smashed in the drop. But the 6th BPC was a veteran outfit and Bigeard slowly got control of his units. At 1215 hours a small French observation airplane appeared. Using it as a radio relay station, Bigeard began to call in air strikes by the B-26's circling overhead. Assisted by the 1st BPC, which had landed on NATASHA in mid-afternoon, the 6th BPC ousted the Vietminh, who withdrew to the south. The II/1RCP was supposed to have come up from DZ SIMONE to block Dien Bien Phu from the south, but the battalion never made it. It, too, had been scattered and had lost its radios. As a result, the Vietminh managed to escape along the brush-lined Nam Yum River. For the French, the first day of operations went well. They accomplished their mission, they carried out the operation with no more than the usual chaos inherent to airborne landings, and they took casualties of only eleven dead and fifty-two wounded. The French captured the files of the 148th Regiment and counted at least ninety Vietminh killed in and around the village.

On D + 1 (21 November), the French dropped the 2d Airborne Battle Group, two more parachute battalions—the 1st Bataillon Etranger de Parachutistes (1st Foreign Legion Parachute Battalion [BEP] and the 8th BPC), an artillery battalion, and the command headquarters for the entire operation under General Gilles. On this same day, the French began to drop heavy equipment on the DZ OCTAVIE, located 300 meters southwest of Dien Bien Phu.

D + 1 was noteworthy for another event—one both curious and controversial. On this date, Cogny held a press conference in Hanoi. He talked of many things—guerrillas, conditions in the Delta, and of course, the paratroop assault on Dien Bien Phu. In connection with the last subject, he made the statement, "If the entrenched camp at Na San had been put on wheels, I would have moved it to Dien Bien Phu five months ago."[1] This is a striking about-face for the man who had argued so vehemently against the operation only a few days before. The peculiarity of this statement is *not* that Cogny now supported the operation. Loyalty to his troops fighting in Dien Bien Phu, as well as loyalty to Navarre, required his enthusiastic endorsement. What is strange, however, is that he now advocated the concept of the fortified airhead at Dien Bien Phu, even though Navarre himself apparently had not yet totally accepted that idea. No other meaning can be put to his linking of Na San to Dien Bien Phu in this statement. Navarre (and others) would recall these remarks with telling effect in the future controversy over the responsibility for the defeat.

On D + 2, 22 November, the sixth and final paratroop battalion of the assault force, the 5th Bataillon de Parachutistes Vietnamiens (5th BPVN), a Vietnamese paratroop battalion, dropped into DZ NATASHA. The paratroopers prepared the airstrip to handle small aircraft, dug light field fortifications, cleared fields of fire, and pushed patrols and outposts to the first ridge lines. So far, so good.

In the last days of November, as the French consolidated their hold on Dien Bien Phu, Giap began his counter moves. Giap expected the French to attack, but he did not foresee the exact time or place (a tribute to tight French security). From security leaks or from other intelligence, he assumed well before the landing that Navarre would attempt to defend Laos. Giap anticipated that his move of the 316th Vietminh Division on 27 October toward the northwest would draw French troops to the area.

Giap speculated that Navarre's reaction in northwest Vietnam would depend on the threat with which Giap confronted him. If the Vietminh threat in the northwest was light, Navarre would hold on to both Dien Bien Phu and Lai Chau. If the threat were increased, Giap foresaw Navarre abandoning Lai Chau and defending Dien Bien Phu. If faced with a maximum threat, Giap thought Navarre would entrench and fight an all-out battle at Dien Bien Phu or attempt to withdraw back to the Delta. As Giap saw the situation, the maximum threat to Dien Bien Phu and Lai Chau should be generated as soon as possible. Accordingly, he ordered the 148th Regiment (which was in the area) and the 316th Division (already en route to the northwest) to attack Lai Chau. At the same time (24 November) he directed the 308th, 312th, and 351st (Heavy) Divisions in the Viet Bac to move by forced marches toward Dien Bien Phu.

French radio intercepts of Giap's marching orders to his divisions informed Cogny immediately that a sizable Vietminh force was moving toward Dien Bien Phu. There were, however, two questions regarding the move. First, was it a move of each entire division, or only portions of each division? Second, when would the divisions (or their portions) arrive at Dien Bien Phu? The latter question could be more easily answered than the former. By simple time-and-space calculations, Cogny's intelligence officers figured that the 316th Division could reach Dien Bien Phu by 6 December, the 308th by 24 December, the 351st by 26 December, and the 312th by 28 December.

There was no way on 25 November, however, to determine whether entire Vietminh divisions were moving or whether only elements of each were on the march. Cogny and his intelligence officers were inclined to think that whole divisions were moving, but Navarre and Berteil believed that only portions of the divisions were involved. Cogny based his estimate on a radio intercept ordering Vietminh engineers to prepare bridge and ferry crossings for 6,000 troops per night over the Red River.[2] Navarre, however, based his opinion on what, to him, was a stronger basis—the enemy could not logistically support four full divisions at Dien Bien Phu, and thus, Giap could not be moving four complete divisions toward that area. As a matter of fact, Navarre and his staff toyed with the idea that the Vietminh messages might be part of a deception plan to conceal either a major Vietminh attack into the Delta, or to tempt Navarre into launching a drive into the Viet Bac where the French troops would be ambushed by those Vietminh divisions which the French thought were bound for Dien Bien Phu.

On 29 November 1953, three events occurred which in considerable measure fashioned the French defeat at Dien Bien Phu. The first was an article which appeared in the Swedish newspaper *Expressen* setting forth a series of answers Ho Chi Minh had given to questions cabled to him by one of its reporters. In his answer, Ho said that he was ready to commence negotiations with the French for an armistice whose basis would be the French government's sincere respect for the genuine independence of Vietnam. The interview stunned the French and the leaders of the rest of the Western democracies, who believed (probably correctly) that time favored the Vietminh.

Navarre, however, held the opposite view. He felt that Ho and Giap knew of his plan, which by late 1954 would produce a French mobile force equal to that of the Vietminh plus a significantly upgraded Vietnamese National Army. Navarre probably overrated the influence of his plans on his adversaries. While the possibility of increased French military effectiveness in 1954 probably influenced Ho and Giap to a limited extent, the major push toward negotiations came from the USSR and Red China. They were becoming increasingly apprehensive about what the new president of the United States, Dwight Eisenhower, might do to resolve the situation in Korea, and wanted to defuse the entire Asiatic confrontation, including the one in Indochina. Regardless of the motives which propelled the Vietminh leader toward the conference table, Ho's announcement introduced a tremendous new factor into the military equation in Indochina. Both antagonists perceived that any settlement reached at the conference table could only reflect battlefield realities, and a major victory by either side would be the prime negotiating tool.

Ho's announcement had one other effect on the military situation— it invalidated the long-range plans of both sides. Since a settlement would probably be reached by mid-1954, neither Navarre nor Giap would profit by husbanding troops or building forces to be used later. To both antagonists, it was a further inducement to go for an all-out victory— particularly for Giap, who had the initiative, and whose dictatorial government would accept large casualty figures without public outcry. Ho's announcement, intentionally or unintentionally, had shoved all the military chips into the center of the Indochinese poker table.

On that same day occurred the second event which helped shape the French disaster. Navarre, accompanied by Cogny, visited the airhead for the first time. Navarre presented the *Croix de Guerre* to some of the paratroopers who had won them for the landing on 20 November. As Navarre toured the busy valley, he liked what he saw. There was room for maneuver, particularly by light tanks which could be flown in in parts and assembled in the valley. Dien Bien Phu could be fought as a ''cavalryman's war''—a series of tank-infantry jabs against Vietminh threats from the foothills. Of course, the surrounding hills *did* dominate the position, but Navarre's artillerymen repeatedly told him that they could quickly neutralize any Vietminh artillery fire from those hills. Besides, as Navarre saw things, Giap lacked the logistic capability to get much artillery or artillery ammunition into Dien Bien Phu. Navarre's predecessor, Salan, and Navarre's staff had reassured him of Giap's lack of logistic capacity, leaving the enemy infantry as the main threat to Dien Bien Phu. As he rode around the camp, he began to think that Dien Bien Phu offered possibilities for something greater than merely blocking a Vietminh advance into Laos. Here might be won a decisive victory using the cavalryman's weapon—the mobile defense.

In the C-47 returning from Dien Bien Phu, Navarre and Cogny made a momentous decision. They talked about who would replace the commander of the assault, Gilles, who had chronic heart trouble. Cogny had promised the paratrooper that he would relieve him as soon as the airborne phase of the operation was over, and that time had now come. Both Cogny and Navarre had in mind as Gilles' replacement Col. Christian de Castries. He was the cavalryman whom Navarre (a cavalryman himself) needed to carry out his concept of the mobile defense at Dien Bien Phu, and Castries was aggressive, brave, dashing, a latter-day Murat. Navarre's choice of Castries to command at Dien Bien Phu, however, completely mismated the man and the ultimate job.

In selecting Castries, Navarre made a critical error in foreseeing what would occur at Dien Bien Phu. He had visualized a free-ranging mobile cavalry fight. What occurred, of course, was a siege—a bloody, cramped, slugging match calling for a Ulysses S. Grant, not a Jeb Stuart. Navarre's past relationship with Castries inclined him to select the man. Castries was Navarre's protégé. He had followed Navarre, two steps behind, up the army promotion ladder. When Navarre had been a lieutenant, Castries had been one of his platoon sergeants. When Navarre was a captain, Castries had been under him as a lieutenant. When Navarre was a colonel commanding a regiment during World War II, Castries had been a major under him. Navarre obviously thought highly of him, and for good reason.

Castries was an anachronism—an 18th-century man transported to the 20th century—an aristocrat, an international-class horseman, a notorious womanizer and gambler, a debonair figure in his red scarf and Spahi kepi. He was a commander of the Legion of Honor, had been wounded three times in combat and mentioned sixteen times in dispatches for bravery. He had graduated from the French army's prestigious War College, and had served two previous tours in Vietnam, where he showed himself to be a talented and aggressive commander of light armor. De Lattre, another cavalryman, under whom Castries served his second Vietnam tour, held him in high regard, impressed by not only his courage and ability, but by his dashing style. Given the right job, and luck, Castries would have acquitted himself well, perhaps brilliantly, on his third tour in Vietnam. But he got the wrong job, and no luck.

The day following Castries' selection, Cogny's headquarters issued Directive Number 739 to the commander of the French forces holding the village. The directive obviously was Cogny's reaction to the French intercept of Giap's radio orders to move four divisions, or elements thereof, toward Dien Bien Phu. Cogny now saw that the village and valley probably would be surrounded and attacked by at least one enemy division, and perhaps by as many as four divisions. From his experience at Na San, Cogny knew that once the enemy divisions invested Dien Bien Phu, the days of "radiating out" of the mooring point were over, and the siege had begun. His directive reflected his acceptance of this grim possibility.

Cogny's directive gave the commander at Dien Bien Phu three missions. First, he was to "guarantee at the very least the full usage of the airfield," and to do this, the order specified that the whole "defensive position of Dien Bien Phu was to be held without any thought of withdrawal." Second, the directive ordered the command to "gather intelligence from as far away as possible," concentrating its efforts toward the east and northeast, the direction of the expected enemy advance. Third, the order instructed the forces at Dien Bien Phu to assist the garrison at Lai Chau in its withdrawal to Dien Bien Phu when so ordered by Cogny's headquarters.[3] The implications of the directive were clear—prepare for another Na San.

Cogny must have cleared the directive, at least in broad outline, with Navarre during the latter's visit to Hanoi and Dien Bien Phu. To Cogny, then, it came as no great surprise when, on 3 December, Navarre issued Personal and Secret Instructions Number 949 (IPS 949). Navarre's order read, in part: "I have decided to accept the battle in the northwest under the following general conditions: (1). The defense . . . shall be centered on Dien Bien Phu which must be held at all costs."[4]

Most authorities who have written about the battle of Dien Bien Phu have described IPS 949 as a major factor in the French defeat. They claim that by this directive Navarre reversed his original concept of avoiding a climactic battle in the north during 1953–1954, and now sought one. This view twists the significance of IPS 949. It constituted no reversal of strategic concept. Navarre thought he *was* avoiding a "climactic battle" at Dien Bien Phu, and he reasoned that Giap could support only about one reinforced division there, making it another Na San, which in the broad sweep of the war had been insignificant. As Navarre saw the situation in late November 1953, he was carrying out this concept. He was avoiding the great, decisive battle in the north, he was defending Laos by his selected means of the *herisson*, and he was preparing for his main offensive effort in MR V, which he would call ATLANTE.

It is significant that nowhere in his book does Navarre mention his IPS 949 of 3 December, apparently thinking it unworthy of special note. He does take notice of the criticism that he undertook Dien Bien Phu to ''smash'' the Vietminh in a set-piece battle. He denies this, but points out that to defeat the enemy is the legitimate preoccupation of any commander. He maintained that he reoccupied Dien Bien Phu and accepted battle there because he deemed it to be the only solution to defend northern Laos, considering the forces available to him.[5]

On 4 December, Navarre received a letter from the National Defense Committee relieving him of any obligation to defend Laos. Like many of the other critical facts relating to the defeat at Dien Bien Phu, this one is beclouded by confusion and controversy. The dispute is largely academic. The key fact is that Operation CASTOR had already been launched when Navarre received the directive, whether he received a copy delivered by Admiral Cabanier on 20 November or a direct letter on 4 December. The central and blunt truth is that the French government was reaping the disaster it had sowed by its ''leakiness'' in handling state secrets and by its self-protective indecision.

But the ''paper war'' was not confined to the French alone. On 6 December, Giap issued an order of the day setting forth the aim of the Party Central Committee in the forthcoming ''Northwest Campaign.'' A translation of this document, made by the United States Army Document Center in Tokyo, follows:

ORDER OF ENCOURAGEMENT TO THE OFFICERS AND MEN AT THE DIEN BIEN PHU FRONT

Comrades,

On orders from the Party Central Committee, Government and President Ho Chi Minh, this winter you will go to the North-West to:
—Destroy the enemy's effectives,
—Win over the population,
—Liberate the regions still held by the enemy.

The enemy is occupying a region of our beloved North-West, scheming to sow division among our compatriots and trample them underfoot, and disturb our rear.

We must repair roads, overcome difficulties and hardships, fight valiantly, endure hunger and cold, go up hill and down dale, cover long distances and carry heavy loads to find the enemy in his refuge to destroy him and liberate our compatriots.

This winter, with the hatred for the imperialists and feudalists we have learnt in the political remolding in the army, with the technical and tactical progresses we have acquired in the recent military remolding, we will certainly strengthen and develop the victory of the North West campaign in winter 1952, and will certainly defeat the enemy.

March forward valiantly.

December 6, 1953

General VO NGUYEN GIAP

It is the usual exhortatory message which some generals, particularly Communists, find irresistible. If the order had any real significance, it was in the clear revelation of the third paragraph that the Vietminh were launching a major effort and in the repeated use of the word "north-west." Giap's reference to the winter campaign of 1952 gave the word "northwest" a double significance, indicating that the Vietminh forces could be bound for Laos as well as for Dien Bien Phu. Note the reference also to the "political and military remolding" of the Vietminh Main Force, signifying the intensive psychological orientation Giap had put his forces through to ready them for the campaign season of 1953–1954. As always, Giap placed first emphasis on the political and psychological indoctrination of his troops.

Two days later, on 8 December, Castries took command of the forces at Dien Bien Phu. The event was overshadowed, however, by another which began on the same day—the evacuation of the garrison at Lai Chau to Dien Bien Phu. Cogny had known from the start of the campaign that Lai Chau, located forty miles north of Dien Bien Phu, could not be held if Giap wanted to take it. Its only ground connection with the outside world was the Pavie Track, a primitive trail to Dien

Bien Phu, usable only by men on foot or by animals. Its airstrip was short, dominated by the surrounding hills, and often flooded.

The trigger which prompted Cogny to evacuate Lai Chau came about in early December when a company from one of the units garrisoning Dien Bien Phu, the 1st BPC, fell into an ambush a few miles north of Dien Bien Phu. After a bloody fight the Vietminh withdrew, leaving behind a few bodies. On one of the dead Vietminh, the French found a document identifying the soldier as a member of the 178th Regiment of the Vietminh 316th Division.

This evidence that the 316th Division had arrived in the Lai Chau/ Dien Bien Phu area convinced Cogny that he had to evacuate Lai Chau at once if he hoped to save the garrison. He ordered the evacuation on 7 December, and it began on the next day. The French air force flew out most of the units stationed at Lai Chau along with some key T'ai civilians, including their ruler, Deo Van Long. T'ai guerrilla units remained behind to destroy the ammunition and other supplies, and then they, too, departed, moving with T'ai civilians on foot towards Dien Bien Phu. The story of their trek toward safety is one of individual courage and group disaster. Of the 2,100 men who left Lai Chau on foot on 9 December, only 185 reached Dien Bien Phu on 22 December. The rest had been killed or captured or had deserted.

On 11 December the French forces in Dien Bien Phu made a major effort to reach and aid the guerrillas withdrawing from Lai Chau. The 2d Airborne Battle Group of three battalions drove to the north from Dien Bien Phu, trying to link up with the T'ai companies which were moving south. The Battle Group not only failed to reach the guerrillas, but was severely mauled and driven back into Dien Bien Phu by the Vietminh.

On 21 December the 2d Airborne Battle Group made another sortie from Dien Bien Phu, this time to the south to link up with a combined French/Laotian force which, on 3 December, had begun moving north from Laos. The French/Laotian force fought a series of small battles in their march to the north and were able to reach the Laotian village of Sop Nao. There they met elements of the 2d Battle Group. The Group had encountered no enemy, but it had run into extreme difficulty in moving through the jungle and over the limestone ridges. After the link-up, both forces returned, laboriously, to their starting points.

Strategically, the link-up proved nothing. It was a public relations ploy—to show that Dien Bien Phu could be used as a "mooring point" for "radiating out." But these sorties actually showed the commanders the exact opposite. They clearly demonstrated the bankruptcy of the concept that Dien Bien Phu could act as a base to harass Giap's supply lines or logistic installations. The enemy was too strong, the jungle too dense, and the limestone cliffs too high. Furthermore, even Navarre saw that for this type of combat the French forces were untrained, ill-equipped, and psychologically unsuited. This left only two alternatives, get out of Dien Bien Phu *quickly* or prepare to withstand a major Vietminh siege there.

It was Navarre, with a rare combination of cold caution and unwarranted optimism, who saw these alternatives. On 29 December, a few days after the link-up at Sop Nao, Navarre ordered Cogny to prepare a contingent plan for a fighting withdrawal from Dien Bien Phu. Cogny, skeptical of the concept, dawdled with the plan and did not submit it to Navarre until 21 January 1954. By then a major enemy force surrounded the garrison, so Cogny made the sensible recommendation that no attempt be made to implement the withdrawal plan. Never serious about the withdrawal plan, Navarre agreed.

But the garrison did little to adopt the alternative—to put in the reinforced fortifications and make the other preparations which would prepare it to withstand a heavy siege. Castries still struggled manfully to carry out his mission of "radiating out" with offensive thrusts, but the Vietminh now limited these to the valley of Dien Bien Phu, and even then, French losses were high. Nevertheless, in late December Navarre was not overly pessimistic about the fate of the garrison at Dien Bien Phu. In a report to Paris, dated 1 January 1954, Navarre pointed out that Giap had brought in heavy artillery, antiaircraft guns, and large amounts of supplies, but he (Navarre) "showed no undue anxiety."[6]

To Navarre, Dien Bien Phu held a subordinate place to the main event, which would be *his* offensive in Annam, Operation ATLANTE, for which he held high expectations. Such an offensive during 1954 had always constituted the key part of the Navarre plan. In Annam, the Vietminh were weaker than they were in North Vietnam, and in this area the climate permitted field operations at a different time of the year than in Tonkin or Cochin China. On 12 December Navarre issued Directive Number 964, which, in part, read, "The essential objective in 1953–54 is the disappearance of the Vietminh zone which spreads from Da Nang to Nha Trang to the Southern Mountain Plateau and the destruction of the military forces of *Lien-Khu* V (MR V). In view of the considerable strategic and political results which one is entitled to expect from the complete execution of that operation, I have decided to *subordinate* to it the conduct of the whole Indochina campaign during the first semester of 1954."[7] (Italics are Navarre's)

The "considerable strategic and political results" which Navarre envisioned were: first, the area contained two and a half million people; second, it was valuable economically for its production of rice and fish; and third, its liberation and transfer to the control of the National Vietnamese government would boost the morale of that government and its people.

While the political results from a successful operation would be significant, Navarre justified the offensive principally on military grounds. MR V contained twelve Vietminh Main Force battalions and five or six effective battalions of Regional Forces, which, with support troops in the area, totaled around 30,000 men. While the armament, training, and organization of the Vietminh troops of MR V lagged behind that of Giap's North Vietnamese divisions, their combat effectiveness was rapidly improving, and Navarre feared that they would constitute a more serious threat later in 1954 and certainly in 1955. Navarre continued his analysis of the strategic threat posed by the enemy troops in MR V by pointing out that their location on "interior lines" and their dispersed supply depots gave them the capability to threaten Da Nang in the north, Nha Trang in the south, or Kontum and Pleiku to the west. To combat this widespread threat, according to Navarre, would require five or six French mobile groups. In his view, this French force could obtain more profitable results in Annam by offensive action than by defensive action in Tonkin.[8]

Tactically, Navarre envisioned Operation ATLANTE as consisting of three phases. The first phase would require thirty battalions and would feature an amphibious landing at Tuy Hoa, where a drive would be launched to the north to clear and hold the coastal area up to Highway 19 from Qui Nhon to An Khe. The objectives and concepts of the second and third phase of Operation ATLANTE are now obscure, but apparently called for the French to attack MR V from Da Nang in the North and

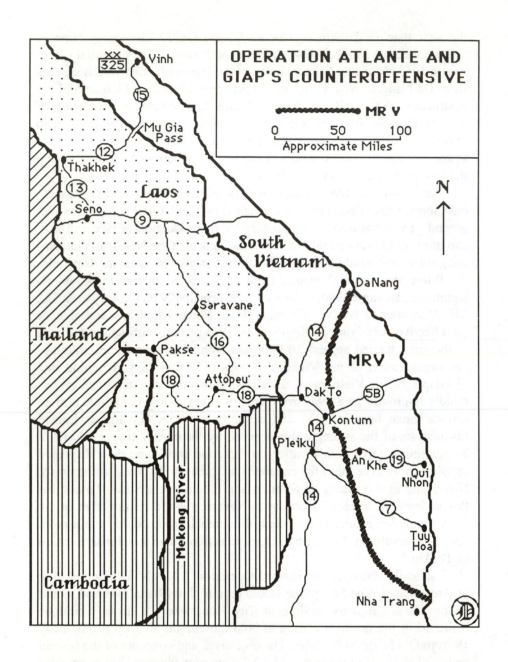

OPERATION ATLANTE AND
GIAP'S COUNTEROFFENSIVE

MR V

0   50   100
Approximate Miles

Vinh

XX
325

15

Mu Gia
Pass

12

Thakhek

13

Laos

Seno

9

South
Vietnam

DaNang

Saravane

14

MRV

16

Pakse

18

Attopeu

18

DakTo

5B

14

Kontum

Pleiku

An Khe

19

Qui
Nhon

Mekong River

14

7

Tuy
Hoa

Cambodia

Thailand

N

Nha Trang

from Kontum/Pleiku in the west. The second phase would require a force of thirty-nine battalions, the third phase fifty-three battalions.

Both Roy and Fall have criticized Navarre for his concept for Operation ATLANTE. They maintain that the area was relatively unimportant, both strategically and politically, and could have been ignored without any great danger or loss. They claim also that the French troops and aerial resupply means could have been better used elsewhere, such as at Dien Bien Phu or in the Tonkin Delta.[9] Navarre rebuts the first criticism (the unimportance of MR V) by pointing out the troubles the Vietminh military forces of the area caused during the period of January–May 1954. He counters the second point (that the troops could have been better used elsewhere) by pointing out that four of the six French mobile groups in Annam were made up of native troops indigenous to Central Vietnam and could not be employed away from their home area.[10] With this, Fall agrees.

This inability to use native South Vietnamese troops outside their home area was an important factor not only in the war between the French and the Vietminh, but later, in the war between the United States and the North Vietnamese/Viet Cong. The families of the South Vietnamese soldiers lived in the barracks with the troops or in nearby villages. A move of the units would leave the families unprotected, without financial and domestic support, and would result in mass desertions, since the soldiers would return to the original garrison area to look after their families. Further, the soldiers came from the area in which they served. They knew the country, they were acclimated to the terrain and weather, and they spoke the native dialect. Above all, they had a personal reason to defend their native area and their families, and little motivation to defend another area.

Concerning the remaining two groups, Navarre grants that the 10th Group, composed of North Africans, could have been used elsewhere. The 100th Group, which had come to Indochina from Korea, had acquired such large numbers of South Vietnamese replacements that it, too, was unemployable outside its home area. Overall, Navarre (probably correctly) maintains that he had to keep two good groups (the 10th and 100th) in the area to stiffen the others. As for the assertion of Fall and Roy that the transport aircraft could have been used elsewhere, Navarre claims that the equipment used in ATLANTE was ''short-legged'' and in such poor mechanical condition that it was unusable at Dien Bien Phu.[11]

The crux of the debate between Fall and Roy on one hand and Navarre on the other lies in the difference in time of their divergent perceptions. Roy and Fall saw Indochina War I in retrospect. They saw Dien Bien Phu, *after the fact,* for the trap and debacle it turned out to be. But Navarre was granted no such retrospective view when he had to make the critical decisions of December 1953. On 12 December he did not see Dien Bien Phu as a monstrous defeat. What he did see was the necessity to maintain the initiative wherever possible. This was what had brought him his minor successes of the summer and early fall. In December he saw also the need to infuse his troops with the offensive spirit. These two factors, the desire to gain the initiative and the perceived need to inculcate the troops with the offensive spirit, were the foundations of his concept and plan for the employment of the Expeditionary Force. Giap had accurately measured his adversary when he wrote, "Navarre had many a time declared that he had to act according to the slogan 'always keep the initiative . . . always on the offensive.' "[12]

While Navarre was deciding in early December to hold Dien Bien Phu and to launch Operation ATLANTE, Giap, too, was active. The 316th Division was harassing the evacuation of the T'ais from Lai Chau, and the other three divisions were hurrying to Dien Bien Phu. The 308th Division, the Vietminh's perennial spearhead, arrived in the Dien Bien Phu area around 23 December, precisely on the date Cogny's intelligence officer had predicted. The 312th Division arrived in late December and early January, accompanied by elements of the 351st (Heavy) Division. The Heavy Division did not get all of its artillery and antiaircraft units into position, however, until the end of January. Finally, the 57th Regiment of the 304th Division began its move from the southern Tonkin Delta to Dien Bien Phu in early January and by forced marches closed there on 23 January. Thus, by the end of January, Giap had concentrated around Dien Bien Phu an army corps of three infantry divisions with supporting artillery and antiaircraft units and, with it, corps-type logistic support units. This smooth and rapid assembly of troops around Dien Bien Phu should have warned Navarre, Cogny, and Castries that Giap and his subordinates had completed their professional education, for the Vietminh troop movements required detailed staff planning. March tables had to be drawn up, bivouac areas had to be selected along the routes, and column security from air and ground attack had to be maintained. The logistic support of these 30,000 to 40,000 troops en route to Dien Bien Phu constituted a prodigious problem. Roads had to be widened and bridges reinforced to take the trucks which the Chinese now poured into the Vietminh supply system. Porters had to be recruited, assembled, organized, cared for, and fed. Above all, the coolies had to be indoctrinated with the patriotic fervor necessary to endure the back-breaking labor, the miserable living conditions, and the possibility of death or mutilation by French bombing.

Giap made one other significant move. Around the end of December he shifted his command post (or battle headquarters) from the Bac Bo to the vicinity of Tuan Giao, some thirty miles northeast of Dien Bien Phu. With four of his best divisions around the fortified village, Giap knew that now his main effort would be made at Dien Bien Phu, and that for the Vietminh, this was the decisive battle of the war.

To understand the developing battle of Dien Bien Phu in the context of the overall war in Indochina, it is necessary to recapitulate the military situation as of 20 December 1953 throughout the entire theater and to review the plans which the two contenders had drawn up since 20 November to adjust to the French landing at Dien Bien Phu.

In the Tonkin Delta, Vietminh guerrilla activities continued unabated. The pressure of Giap's Main Force threat in the Delta had lessened with the transfer of his three best infantry divisions to Dien Bien Phu. The French, too, lost crack units to Dien Bien Phu, but their basic position was secure in the Delta, so much so that Navarre considered French forces there to be his theater reserve. In the southern portion of North Vietnam, around the town of Vinh, Giap concentrated the newly formed 325th Division and reinforced it with one regiment of the 304th Division, which normally occupied a position facing the southern wall of the French defenses of the Tonkin Delta. The reinforced 325th Division was in a position to move north, south, or west as the situation developed. French forces could hold the coastal towns in southern North Vietnam, but little more. In Annam and in the Central Highlands (Vietminh MR V), both sides fielded the equivalent of about two divisions. Navarre planned to launch ATLANTE there and Giap, too, planned attacks in the area. Both knew (or later wrote that they knew) that the other had such plans.[13] In South Vietnam, Vietminh forces were limited largely to guerrillas. These could harass French troops and lines of communications, but had no potential for dangerous attacks.

Operations in northwest Vietnam centered around Dien Bien Phu and constituted the most important front in the theater. In this fortified airhead, the French had built up the original assault force of six battalions to around nine or ten battalions, replacing most of the parachute battalions with infantry battalions. By 20 December the Vietminh had most of two divisions (the 316th and 308th) rapidly nearing the area, and Giap was making a major effort to establish and perfect the complex logistic system needed to support his corps-sized concentration around Dien Bien Phu. Strategically, northern Laos was an appendage to the situation in northwest Vietnam and around Dien Bien Phu. Navarre thought he was defending Upper Laos by holding the critical valley. As for Giap, the Vietminh troops around Dien Bien Phu gave him the flexibility he wanted. He could use them either at Dien Bien Phu or in northern Laos, or if conditions permitted, in both places.

Both believed that the key to success lay in gaining and keeping the initiative. In an article he wrote a decade later (7 May 1964) for *Nhan Dan,* the official North Vietnamese Army newspaper, Giap summarized the strategy of both contenders. In 1964, his foresight strengthened by hindsight, Giap wrote, "Victory in the strategically decisive battles will go to the side whose leadership had seized the initiative. It will go to the force which can force the enemy to fight according to his strategic desires and on an advantageous battlefield of his own choosing."[14]

The plans of the two commanders were simple. Navarre would hold everywhere but in MR V, where he would attack to knock out that Communist stronghold. Giap would go for a major victory at Dien Bien Phu, and at the same time he would step up guerrilla activities throughout Indochina and launch a series of attacks on French strongpoints in Laos and the Central Highlands. These attacks, Giap hoped, would prevent any reinforcement of Dien Bien Phu, inflict heavy casualties on isolated French garrisons, and force Navarre to weaken critical areas (the Tonkin Delta, for example) to counter the threats posed by Giap's peripheral attacks.

A consideration of the prospects of each strategy as they appeared on 20 December exposes further the weakness of the French position. Navarre's offensive against MR V could succeed, but the results on the war in Indochina would be minimal. Giap could lose MR V (an unlikely prospect) and still not lose the war. He would not even be forced to surrender the initiative by having to divert troops from a more important front to save MR V. On the other hand, Navarre could not lose the Tonkin Delta, Dien Bien Phu, large areas of northern or central Laos, or Cochin China without losing the war. A conclusive victory by Giap in any of these areas spelled the finish of the French in Indochina. Giap could win in several places—Navarre in none.

On 20 December Giap made the first move in the execution of *his* plan, twin attacks in middle and southern Laos. On that date, the 101st Regiment of the 325th Division in the Vinh area, reinforced by the 66th Regiment of the 304th Division, moved through the Mu Gai pass and destroyed a number of small French outposts along the Central Vietnamese/Laos border. The 101st Regiment then drove west along Highway 15 toward the town of Thakhek, which the French abandoned on 25–26 December, retreating south to Seno. In the meantime the 66th Regiment had moved south and attacked the French outposts along Highway 9, driving these French forces westward to Seno. On 25 December, Navarre airlifted three parachute battalions from the Tonkin Delta to Seno. The move came none too soon, for on 4–5 January the Vietminh launched an attack on Seno which lasted until 9 January. The French reinforcements managed to beat off the attack, but only after taking heavy casualties. After the unsuccessful assault, the 101st Regiment faded into the limestone hills of Laos, and the 66th began its long march back to rejoin its parent unit, the 304th Division, in the Tonkin Delta.

Keyed to the attack on middle Laos, Giap, on 20 December, mounted an attack by Vietnamese and Pathet Lao forces aimed on southern Laos. After a long march through the mountains, this force defeated a French battalion near Attopeu and captured the town. They then swung north, threatening the key towns of Saravane and Pakse, forcing Navarre to reinforce the latter, a key locality on the Mekong River.

On 20 January Navarre in his turn took the initiative (see map p. 206). He launched Operation ATLANTE, a fifteen-battalion assault from Nha Trang toward the north, assisted by an amphibious landing behind Vietminh lines near Tuy Hoa. The overland force was composed largely of troops of the Vietnamese National Army which had been recently organized and trained. The attackers were to drive north to a line from Qui Nhon to An Khe, clearing out the coastal section of MR V in the process. Giap had anticipated the attack and ordered the Vietminh forces in its path not to give battle, but only to harass and delay the advance. They did this so well that the French attack soon bogged down. The Vietnamese

National troops showed no stomach for a fight and deserted in large numbers—sometimes by whole units. On one occasion, at least, they mutinied, and they looted everything in sight. The dismal performance of the Vietnamese Nationalists was equaled, even surpassed, by the incompetence and corruption of the Vietnamese civilian administrators Navarre brought in to govern the captured territory. Navarre, himself, described the Vietnamese administrators as *"absolute incapables."*[15] In sum, the first phase of Operation ATLANTE failed miserably, and by his criticism of Vietnamese troops and administrators, Navarre admitted it.

Giap was not one to remain passive in this battle for the initiative. On 26 January he struck back in two widely separated areas, the Central Highlands and northern Laos. Taking advantage of Navarre's preoccupation with ATLANTE and the coastal section of MR V, he attacked on that perennial battlefield, the Central Highlands. On 26 January the Vietminh attacked the French posts north of Kontum and by 2 February had taken the key French post of Dak To (a locality continually fought over in all Indochina wars). Navarre rushed Mobile Group 100 to Kontum to hold that important town. The 803d Independent Vietminh Regiment, after taking Dak To, then moved around Kontum and on 5 February attacked Dak Doa, twenty-eight kilometers to the south of Kontum. Although the French took heavy casualties, the troops held the village. On the same day, the 803d blew up all the bridges north of Kontum along Highway 14 as the Vietminh force began encircling Mobile Group 100 in that town.

Navarre wisely decided not to fight for Kontum and on 7 February evacuated the troops, the European civilians, and Vietnamese civil administrators to Pleiku. Mobile Group 100 then dug in around Pleiku while the 803d Regiment followed the Mobile Group to Pleiku and began to harass it there. The Vietminh again attacked Dak Doa on 11 February, and this time, in a bloody, human-wave attack, finally destroyed its 103 defenders. On 20 February the 108th Independent Vietminh Regiment joined the 803d around Pleiku, and both regiments began to press in on Mobile Group 100. On 23 February Mobile Group 100 made a thrust toward Dak Doa, where they found no enemy, but the rear-guard platoon was attacked and almost annihilated by a company of the 108th as it was returning to Pleiku.

To relieve the enemy pressure on Mobile Group 100 around Pleiku, on 1 March, Navarre parachuted Airborne Battle Group 3 with its three battalions into Plei Bon, east of Pleiku along Highway 19. The Battle Group began a fruitless search for either the 803d or the 108th Regiments, and when it failed to find either, the operation was called off.

On the same day that Giap launched his attack on the Central Highlands, he made another diversionary effort—this time into northern Laos. The 308th, the "Iron" Division, plus the 148th Independent Regiment, left Dien Bien Phu and with some Pathet Lao troops, fell on Muong Khoua, where they destroyed the French battalion holding that post (see map p. 151). The Vietminh force pushed rapidly to the south down the Nam Ou Valley toward Louang Phrabang. On 3 February the Vietminh reached Muong Ngoi about ninety miles north of the Laotian capital, and by 8 February its leading elements were only twenty miles from Louang Phrabang. At this point Navarre airlifted five battalions into the capital. The Vietminh halted and gathered the opium crop (as they had done in previous years), providing the government with a valuable commodity for trade with the Chinese Communists. On 23 February the 308th Division and its attachments returned to Dien Bien Phu.

Giap's attacks in Laos and in the Central Highlands forced Navarre to reinforce those areas and thereby to reduce his mobile forces in the Tonkin Delta from forty-four battalions to twenty battalions. Giap took quick advantage of Navarre's dispersion. In late February he attacked hard in the southern and western part of the Delta, "liberating" additional villages and territory. His Main Force units, supported by his guerrillas, frequently cut Highway 5, the critical road between Hanoi and Haiphong, and kept the road severed for days on end.

Giap's concept of operation and its execution between 20 November 1953 and 1 March 1954 had been masterful. He had seized the initiative, he had blunted and neutralized Navarre's offensive, Operation ATLANTE, and he had inflicted significant casualties on the French. He forced Navarre to disperse his mobile reserve to widespread, but secondary, fronts, and most important, he compelled Navarre to expend his scarce air transport force to support these distant fronts instead of building up a logistic reserve at Dien Bien Phu. This was Giap's key to victory at Dien Bien Phu.

Both Giap and Navarre grasped the fundamental point that whoever won the logistic battle at Dien Bien Phu would win the tactical battle.

Both understood that the logistic battle had two separate parts. First, the opponents had to supply their own forces, and second, each had to try to keep his enemy from receiving adequate supplies. This latter battle was particularly critical, and the two antagonists realized it.

The Vietminh logistic system to support Dien Bien Phu depended on two means—trucks and porters. The trucks brought in the artillery, the bulk of the ammunition, and the other heavy supplies. The porters carried in the lighter items, mostly food. These two means of supply won the first part of the logistics battle for the Communist forces, and their victory has been widely and justifiably acclaimed.

The Vietminh truck inventory consisted of around 800 Russian trucks of two-and-one-half-ton capacity plus around 200 American two-and-one-half-ton General Motors trucks either captured by the Vietminh from the French or given the Vietminh by the Chinese, who had taken them from United Nations forces in Korea. Around 350 of these trucks were assigned to NVA Truck Regiment 16, whose mission was to get the supplies from the Chinese entrance points on the Vietnam/China border to the major depot near Dien Bien Phu. The regiment contained nine companies of 100 men and around thirty-five trucks each.[16] Each company operated only on a given segment of the route, with each segment bounded by bridges, passes, or other choke-points likely to be cut by French air attack. If a bridge was down or the pass blocked, the Vietminh hand-carried the equipment around or through the obstacle to the next segment. While the system required several transfers of equipment from the vehicles of one company to those of another, there were always plenty of coolies to make the shifts. The drivers of each company became thoroughly familiar with the road in their segment—so familiar that they could drive the road on a dark night without lights.

The primitive road net, the mountainous terrain, and the thick jungle confined the trucks to one Primary Line of Communications (LOC) and two secondary ones. The primary LOC ran from Nan Kuan Pass (Dong Dang) and Cao Bang on the Vietnam/China border to Tuyen Quang, crossing the Red River at Yen Bai, and from there by Route 13A and 6 to Tuan Giao, the major forward supply base. A secondary LOC ran from Lao Cai down the Red River to Yen Bai, where it joined the primary LOC. Another secondary LOC extended from Ban Nam Coum in the northwest to Lai Chau and then on to Tuan Giao.

Prodigious effort went into the construction, repair, and camouflage

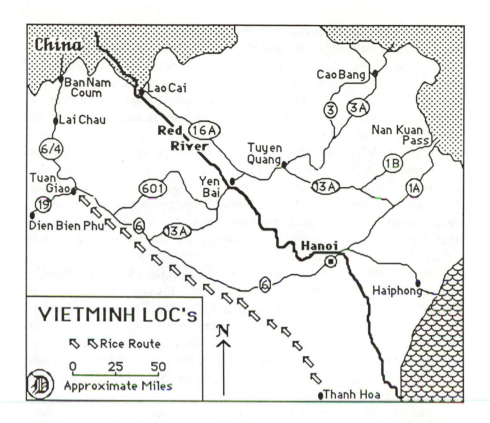

of these truck routes. The thirty-five-mile stretch of road from the major supply dump at Tuan Giao to Dien Bien Phu had to be totally rebuilt. Giap described the original road as a ''mule track (which) crossed an uninterrupted series of hills and valleys with steep gradients and was cut by nearly one hundred big and small streams.''[17] This construction job required the intensive efforts of 10,000 coolies, two Main Force engineer regiments, an infantry regiment, and 7,000 army recruits. Giap paid tribute to the coolies who built the roads and kept them open. He wrote, ''Hundreds of thousands of men and women *dan cong,* not flinching from any difficulty or danger, enthusiastically served the front and contributed over three million workdays.''[18]

Giap organized the road repair service along the same lines as the 16th Truck Regiment—into segments. When the French air force cut the LOC's, the local peasants in each segment, armed with hand tools and determination, immediately began the repairs. They either filled in the craters or built bypasses, and the supplies kept rolling to Dien Bien Phu. As the French LOC interdiction program developed, the Vietminh soon identified the forty points where their enemy would attempt to cut the road. At each cut-point, the Communists stationed a number of *dan cong* to repair the road as soon as it was damaged. In spite of French efforts to impede the repairs by strafing the work groups and by dropping delayed-action bombs, in most cases the roads were back in operation within twenty-four hours. The camouflage effort was equally energetic. On some key parts of the LOC, the coolies interlaced tree branches over the road to form a tunnel, impenetrable to French aerial reconnaissance, either visual or photographic. Navarre himself admitted that the Vietminh camouflage completely thwarted French detection efforts.[19]

Porters have received the major part of the acclaim for Giap's logistic triumph, even though the trucks carried more tonnage to the troops at Dien Bien Phu. The porters carried principally rice, 76 percent of which came from Thanh Hoa province in southern North Vietnam.[20] To move this rice, the Vietminh had to organize another LOC, this one used by the 260,000 porters only. It ran up the Song Ma river valley from Thanh Hoa to Tuan Giao, a straight-line distance of 200 miles and a cross-country length of 350 to 400 miles.

The combination of trucks, porters, animals, and boats accomplished its task. It supplied adequately a combat force of 49,000 at Dien Bien Phu and another 40,000 to 50,000 logistic troops scattered up and down the LOC's. This system provided hundreds of thousands of rounds of small-arms ammunition, thousands of rounds of ammunition for the anti-aircraft guns guarding the valley and the LOC's, and somewhere between 100,000 (French estimate) and 350,000 rounds (Vietminh's estimate) of mortar, rocket, and artillery ammunition. The Vietminh logistic support of the forces at Dien Bien Phu constituted monumental achievement, and as much as any other factor, it won the battle there.

The Vietminh logistic accomplishment becomes even more impressive in view of the fact that the French air arm, both air force and navy, made a maximum effort to throttle the flow of Communist supplies to Dien Bien Phu. The French lost the battle for several reasons. First, the basic concept of air interdiction is invalid. The simple historical truth is that no air interdiction campaign has prevented an enemy from moving adequate supplies to its front-line troops. The Germans moved supplies in World War II, the Koreans and Chinese did it in the Korean War, the Vietminh did it in Indochina War I, and the North Vietnamese did it in Indochina War II.

This is not the failure of airpower alone. In analyzing an air interdiction program, enemy supplies must be looked at as water running through a faucet into a basin. You can never shut off the faucet entirely, but you can reduce it to a trickle or even to drops. Nevertheless, the basin will fill if friendly ground action is not pulling the plug in the basin, that is, if the ground troops are not forcing the enemy to expend large amounts of his supplies. Interdiction is a joint air-ground operation, and this was where the French failed. They permitted the Vietminh to "fill the basin" by not forcing them to use their supplies in combat.

The second reason for the failure of the French air interdiction program was the inadequacy of the forces employed. To interdict the Communist supply lines and to provide close air support to their forces at Dien Bien Phu and elsewhere in northern Vietnam, the French had thirty-two fighters, forty-five fighter-bombers, and between thirty and forty-seven B-26 medium bombers. In addition, they had six C-119 transports equipped for napalm bombing and five privateer navy antisubmarine patrol bombers, each of which could carry two to four tons of bombs deep into enemy territory.[21] Even these meager figures are illusory. The French could keep no more than 75 percent of these combat aircraft operational at one time. Their maintenance force was one-third under-strength, and in the final stages of the war had to be covertly reinforced by United States Air Force mechanics to keep even this small striking force operational.

In addition to an invalid concept and inadequate forces, there was a third reason for the failure of the French interdiction program—the antiaircraft protection the Vietminh gave its LOC's. The principal trunk LOC became a "flak corridor," and almost all of the French aircraft sustained hits when attacking trucks and troops along it, forcing the aircraft to higher attack altitudes and decreasing effectiveness. As early as 26 December 1953, the French had to divert aircraft to flak suppression missions, thus further limiting the force available for their interdiction task.

While one-half of the "battle of logistics" turned around the French aerial efforts to stop the Vietminh ground-based supply system, the other half was the contest between the French air-based supply system versus the ground-based efforts of the Vietminh to choke it. Here again, the French ultimately failed, and they failed for two primary reasons. First, the French had inadequate air transport capability to supply the garrison at Dien Bien Phu. Estimates vary about the size of the French air transport force. A JCS study gives the number supporting Dien Bien Phu to have been forty-three C-119's and twenty-nine C-47's plus a few other transport types.[22] A MACV (Military Assistance Command, Vietnam) study made in 1968 sets the figure at 100 transport aircraft, "some C-119's but mostly C-47's."[23] Tanham, quoting the commander of the French Far East Air Force, General Chassin, states that in March 1954 the French had 124 transports throughout the Indochina Theater.[24] While these figures differ slightly, they indicate that a maximum of seventy-five to one hundred light transports were available to support Dien Bien Phu. A realistic "in-operation" figure would run around sixty to seventy-five aircraft.

The inadequate number of transports constituted only one of the factors which doomed the French aerial supply capability. There was a shortage of airfields from which the transports could operate, and these were located in the Hanoi area at the maximum "reach" of the aircraft. It was almost impossible to construct new airfields closer to Dien Bien Phu. The mountains were too rugged, and they were usually held by the Vietminh. The lowlands were too soft. Every square yard of runway built in the lowlands required a ton of crushed rock, and even that had to be allowed to settle slowly.

Other factors decreased French air transport capacity. The weather varies greatly over Vietnam and is unfavorable for flying much of the year. The French had too few weather stations to make usable weather predictions over an objective or en route to it. Finally, there was a severe navigational deficiency. French maps were unreliable. The heights of peaks were inaccurate, creating a hazard to operational safety. Radio guidance and other navigational aids could not even direct visual flights, much less operations during bad weather or at night.

The second major reason for the French failure to supply adequately the Dien Bien Phu garrison was that Giap recognized early that the Achilles heel of the French position at Dien Bien Phu was its supply, and he gave first priority to impeding the French logistic system. First, Giap attacked the French transport aircraft on the ground. On 6–7 March saboteurs infiltrated the two major French air bases of the Tonkin Delta, Gia Lam and Cat Bi, and destroyed or damaged a total of seventy-eight aircraft, mostly transports. The saboteurs deliberately ignored other aircraft to get at the transports, indicating the importance Giap gave to the French resupply capability. Second, he attacked the airfield at Dien Bien Phu with artillery fire. This cratered the field and destroyed some of the aircraft on it, and by mid-March he had forced the French to deliver supplies by parachute. Even under ideal conditions, delivery of supplies by parachute is wasteful, and Dien Bien Phu presented conditions far from ideal. The concentration of Vietminh antiaircraft artillery around Dien Bien Phu forced the French to parachute supplies from 2,500 feet, then, as the aircraft losses mounted, from 6,000 feet, and finally from 8,500 feet. Of course, supply losses mounted as the height of drop increased with the attendant dispersion. During the battle of Dien Bien Phu (13 March–7 May 1954), the French dropped around 120 tons of supplies per day. The defenders never recovered over 100 tons a day. The Vietminh got the rest, including thousands of rounds of United States 105mm ammunition, which fit their own howitzers and which they promptly used against the airhead.

Excessive dispersion of parachuted supplies was not the only problem. There was the problem of collecting the supplies when they landed within the defensive perimeter. As the Vietminh artillery fire progressively destroyed the few trucks and jeeps which the French had flown into the garrison, collection had to be done largely by hand, an impossible and physically exhausting task. Any semblance of a centralized logistic system at Dien Bien Phu disappeared, and the supplies were used at the various strongpoints on which they fell.

The extent of the French logistic failure can be graphically shown. United States Army logistic experts have calculated that the French garrison at Dien Bien Phu needed a *minimum* of 200 tons a day to maintain its combat effectiveness. It received half this requirement. Giap and the Vietminh clearly won the "battle of logistics" at Dien Bien Phu. The Communists pushed their supplies through the roads and trails in adequate amounts. The French could not accomplish the same task for its garrison. It was this "battle," as much as the one fought in the trenches and on the strongpoints, that decided the fate of Dien Bien Phu and the fate of the French in Indochina.

By 13 March, Giap, with great skill and forethought, completed his preparations for the battle of Dien Bien Phu. He had the French garrison encircled with four Vietminh divisions. He brought to the valley of Dien Bien Phu large numbers of artillery pieces and ample ammunition to feed them. He had prevented Navarre from reinforcing the garrison and from building up reserve levels of supplies in the airhead. His troops were trained in those tactics and techniques which would be needed to destroy the French strongholds—coordination of infantry and artillery, and attack of an entrenched foe. Above all, Giap's troops were thoroughly indoctrinated for their upcoming role. He describes these psychological preparations: ''. . . *Political* work played a great role. (Giap's italics) Taking the Party cells as cores, this work gave officers and men a thorough political education and ideological leadership and imbued them with the great significance of the Dien Bien Phu campaign; it made everyone realize that the success of the campaign, like the success of all revolutionary works, was achieved only through valiant struggles, sacrifices and hardships; it made everyone realize that, to win brilliant success, great efforts should be made, thereby it instilled a great determination to fight and to win into the troops. With regard to the principle of advancing cautiously and striking surely, at first not all the officers and men agreed. Political work did its best to make our troops realize this principle and overcome their tendency to fear fatigue and losses; it gave them and maintained for them the determination to fight unremittingly and as long as possible.''[25]

Giap was ready for the greatest battle of his career—the battle which would make the ex-teacher of history famous.

Notes—Chapter 9

1. Navarre, *Agonie,* p. 198.
2. Fall, *Hell,* p. 41.
3. Ibid., p. 40.
4. Ibid., p. 44.
5. Navarre, *Agonie,* pp. 199–200.
6. Roy, *Battle,* p. 100.
7. Fall, *Hell,* pp. 45–46.
8. Navarre, *Agonie,* pp. 174–177.
9. Roy, *Battle,* p. 76; Fall, *Hell,* p. 46.
10. Navarre, *Agonie,* p. 176.
11. Ibid.
12. Giap, *Dien Bien Phu,* p. 44.
13. Giap, *Dien Bien Phu,* p. 56; Navarre, *Agonie,* pp. 163 and 171–172.
14. Giap, *Nhan Dan,* 7 May 1964, quoted in JCS Study, 31 January 1968.
15. Navarre, *Agonie,* p. 177.
16. Tanham, *Warfare,* p. 71.
17. Giap, *Dien Bien Phu,* p. 100.
18. Ibid., p. 104.
19. Navarre, *Agonie,* p. 208.
20. Chi, *Colonialism,* p. 66.
21. Fall, *Hell,* pp. 130–133.
22. JCS, *Khe Sanh Study,* Annex B., p. 4.
23. MACV, *Study of the Comparisons Between the Battle of Dienbienphu and the Analogous Khe Sanh Situation,* March 1968.
24. Tanham, *Warfare,* pp. 105–106.
25. Giap, *Dien Bien Phu,* pp. 107–108.

10 Dien Bien Phu

The Battle
12 March–7 May 1954

The key to understanding any battle lies in an analysis of the comparative size, armament, disposition, and quality of the opposing forces. On 13 March 1953, around Dien Bien Phu, Giap had 49,000 combat soldiers, plus 10,000 to 15,000 logistical support personnel. The Vietminh combat force was composed of the 308th, the 312th, and the 316th Infantry Divisions, two independent regiments, the 148th and the 57th (the latter from the 304th Division), and the 351st Heavy Division. Counted by infantry battalions (the basic assault unit), Giap had thirty-three battalions—twenty-seven poised to attack the French camp and six disposed to block any French units from Laos which might seek to join the beleaguered garrison. The 351st Heavy Division was made up of the 151st Engineer Regiment, the 237th Heavy Weapons Regiment (82mm mortars), the 45th Artillery Regiment (105mm howitzers), the 675th Artillery Regiment (75mm pack howitzers and 120mm mortars), the 367th Antiaircraft Regiment (heavy machine guns and radar-controlled 37mm antiaircraft guns), and, finally, a Field Rocket Unit, which had Katyusha rocket launchers.[1] To this day the true strength of the Vietminh artillery at Dien Bien Phu remains in doubt. Giap himself has never revealed its numbers and calibers. As a matter of fact he has never even publicly identified the major infantry units which participated in the battle. The table below shows the estimates of the Vietminh artillery made by various United States and French authorities on the battle.

From this chart the soundest conclusion is that at Dien Bien Phu Giap had twenty to twenty-four 105mm howitzers, fifteen to twenty 75mm howitzers, twenty 120mm mortars, at least forty 82mm mortars,

	105mm How's	75mm How's	120mm Mort's	82mm Mort's	37mm AAguns	AAMG's	Katyusha Rocket Launchers
Navarre (p. 218)	20	20			80	100	
US JCS (Annex B, p. 5)	48	48	48		36	80	12–16
MACV (Annex A, p. 7)	24	15	20		24	50+	Unknown
Fall *Hell,* (p. 486)	24	15	20	40	20	50	12–16
Roy (p. 154)	20	18			80	100	

eighty 37mm antiaircraft guns (probably manned by Chicom gunners), 100 antiaircraft machine guns, and twelve to sixteen Katyusha six-tube rocket launchers.

The Vietminh troops were well-armed, thoroughly trained, and capably led. Above all, their morale and determination had been raised by Giap to the highest pitch. For what they had to do, they were as good as any troops twentieth century warfare has seen.

Finally, Giap had a critical terrain advantage. He held the high ground 3,000 to 4,000 meters from the airstrip and 1,500 to 2,000 meters from the French entrenchments. This gave him excellent observation over the French position and permitted his artillery to employ observed fire, using the primitive but effective method of "aiming down the tube." The dense foliage of the hills permitted Giap to conceal and "tunnel in" his artillery and antiaircraft guns and to shift his infantry around the French perimeter without detection.

To oppose Giap's army, the French had 10,800 men in the valley at Dien Bien Phu, but only about 7,000 of these were fighters. The fighters were organized into twelve infantry battalions holding Dien Bien Phu and its satellite strongpoints. Supporting the infantry were two artillery battalions of twenty-four 105mm howitzers, four 122mm mortars, and one battery of four 155mm howitzers, the latter for counterbattery purposes. The French had transported ten light tanks into the airhead in parts and assembled them there on the ground. When the battle started, the French had six fighter aircraft and six observation planes on the Dien Bien Phu strip.[2]

The quality of the French troops varied. Some—the paratroopers, the Legionnaires, and some of the North African units—were first-rate. Others, particularly the T'ai units, were woefully deficient. As the battle wore on, "internal deserters"—those who took no part in the fight and lived in holes near the Nam Yum River—increased. In the end they numbered somewhere between 3,000 to 4,000 men out of a garrison of around 10,000.[3]

In summary, at Dien Bien Phu the Vietminh infantry outnumbered the French by a factor of at least five to one, with a combat effectiveness and morale which surpassed that of the French forces. The Vietminh had the superior artillery, far greater than a comparison of the number of available guns would indicate. The Vietminh accumulated a large store of supplies of all kinds, particularly artillery ammunition, while the French logistic situation, particularly in munitions, was marginal. Finally, the Vietminh held a marked terrain advantage.

The second part of any analysis of a battle looks at the contenders' plans. Giap had a sound and simple concept which he carried out with skill and resolution. It involved a series of phased attacks which would first annihilate the outer defensive posts, then impede and eventually cut off the ability of the French to reinforce and resupply the garrison by air, and finally, smash the main defensive position and the isolated post to the south, called Isabelle. His tactical preparations were careful and far-sighted. He evolved a special tactic to get his troops across the exposed terrain in front of the French positions without incurring heavy losses. It was the historical trench-warfare technique of World War I— communication trenches, saps, firing bays, and dugouts.

Giap thoroughly trained the assaulting infantry and deeply indoctrinated them for their role. The Vietminh assault units were broken into four subgroups. The first manned the heavy supporting weapons (machine guns, mortars, recoilless rifles). Its mission was to furnish close-in fire support to the other groups and, if possible, to knock out key enemy positions such as the command post, the radio dugout, or the heavy weapons emplacements. The second group, called "sappers," were assault engineers or dynamiters. Their task was to blow up the wire entanglements or other obstacles by either "bangalore torpedos," satchel charges, or by tying the charges around their bodies and diving under wire entanglements or alongside the parapets or blockhouses. The sappers were volunteers, actually "suicide-squads," and were honored as such. If they survived, they joined the attack once they finished their job. The third group—the assault infantry or storm troops—moved forward after the first group neutralized the heavy weapons and the sappers breached the defenses. They normally attacked in overwhelming numbers on a narrow front. The fourth group was the reserve. It provided fire support to the assault troops and either exploited the success or covered the withdrawal.

Giap and his subordinate commanders meticulously planned their attacks. In most cases they used sand-table models of the terrain and enemy positions to show the troops what they had to do. In a few instances, they built full-scale replicas of the enemy strongpoint. Each attack was rehearsed many times, and after each rehearsal mistakes were pointed out, and the assaulting troops ran through it again. The political and psychological indoctrination of Vietminh troops played a key role in Giap's military successes. This indoctrination developed a brave, even fanatic, soldier. Few battles in recent history have produced more heroism by both sides than the battle of Dien Bien Phu. While giving the French troops high marks for courage, the experienced soldier can only marvel at, and often be appalled by, the sacrificial bravery which drove the Vietminh infantry in the attack.

Giap's artillery strength and the way he used it constituted an even greater surprise to the French than did the courage and training of his infantry. First, the French believed that Giap would have at Dien Bien Phu only a few 75mm mountain howitzers and some 82mm mortars. Actually, Giap was able to bring to the battle not only more 75's than the French had anticipated, but brought in twenty to twenty-four 105mm howitzers as well, the latter a much more devastating weapon. The French were surprised also by Giap's store of artillery ammunition. They anticipated that the Vietminh could bring to Dien Bien Phu only enough artillery ammunition to support an attack of five or six days duration. In this estimate they made a monumental mistake. Actually, the Vietminh fired *at least* 93,000 artillery rounds during the fifty-five-day battle.[4]

The greatest surprise, however, came in Giap's method of using his artillery. The Vietminh used their artillery as "direct fire" weapons instead of employing them in the "indirect fire" mode. In artillery technique, the difference is substantial. "Direct fire" means that each gun crew makes its own adjustments on a target which it can see by sighting down or along the tube of the piece or by the use of a simple aiming device. The "indirect fire" mode places the guns in four- or six-gun batteries behind a hill or other protection where they cannot see, or be seen by, the target. Their fire is adjusted by forward observers (who can see the target) through a battery fire direction center near the guns. Normally, "indirect fire" is held to be far superior to "direct fire" in that it is more flexible, it offers more protection to the guns and crews, and above all, it permits the quick massing of the fires of a number of guns. "Indirect fire" requires good signal communications and well-trained observers and fire direction personnel. The "indirect fire" mode is used almost exclusively by all Western armies.

Giap knew what he was doing when he used his artillery as "direct fire" weapons. His artillerymen had neither the experience, training, nor the reliable signal communications required to operate in the "indirect fire" mode. If Giap placed his artillery behind the hills surrounding Dien Bien Phu, it could not reach the French position. To have positioned the guns on the forward slope toward the French would have brought the French strongholds into range, but would have exposed the Vietminh guns to the murderous counterbattery fire of the French artillery and to devastating air attack.

Navarre himself describes Giap's employment of his artillery and supporting antiaircraft guns and their effect on the French defenders: "We knew that a large number of artillery and AA gun emplacements had been prepared, but their camouflage had been so perfect that only a small number of them had been located prior to the beginning of the attacks.

"Under the influence of {Communist} Chinese advisers, the Vietminh command had used processes quite different from the Classic methods. The artillery had been dug in by single pieces. . . . They were installed in shell-proof dugouts, and fired point blank from portholes or were pulled out by their crews and pulled back in as soon as counterbattery fire began. This way of using artillery and AA guns was possible only with the expansive ant holes at the disposal of the Vietminh and was to make shambles of all the estimates of our own artillerymen. *It was the major surprise of the battle.*"[5] (Emphasis added)

* * *

In contrast to Giap's innovative and effective planning for his attack on Dien Bien Phu, French planning was unrealistic and dilatory. Castries' plan was simple, because he had little other choice. The essence of this plan was to hold until mid-May when the Southwest Monsoon would flood out all combat in the valley. By the end of January, Castries had lost any capability to carry out serious diversionary or "spoiling" attacks which might upset Giap's plans or punish the encircling forces. From early March on, Castries could only defend in place, hoping to win a defensive battle by a combination of field fortifications, barbed wire entanglements, mine fields, heavy defensive fire, and above all, counterattacks.

To carry out his defensive plan, Castries disposed his forces in the classical pattern of interlocking and mutually supporting positions. The main battle position was centered on the remains of the village of Dien Bien Phu. It was made up of four subpositions and manned by a total of five infantry battalions, a 105mm artillery battalion, and four 155mm howitzers. This central position also housed the two reserve battalions, the 8th BPC and the 1st Foreign Legion Parachute Battalion (1st BEP). Castries earmarked these two battalions plus seven light tanks as his main counterattacking force. The French located three subsidiary positions two or three kilometers to the north, northwest, and northeast of the main defensive area. They called these Anne Marie, Gabrielle, and Beatrice. Each was held by one battalion. Their purpose was to cover the central position and to break up mass attacks against it from the north, which the French correctly thought would be the direction from which Giap would launch his first major assault.

Seven kilometers to the south of the main position, the French located another center of resistance, Isabelle. Here Castries stationed two infantry battalions, two 105mm artillery batteries, and three light tanks. Isabelle's primary purpose was to provide artillery support to the main positions. Secondarily, its troops would constitute another reserve for counterattack purposes. Military analysts have criticized the location of Isabelle, arguing that it put the infantry forces there beyond quick supporting distance of the main position, and that the artillery fire from Isabelle could not reach the enemy attacking the two northern strongpoints of Gabrielle and Beatrice from the north.

The French established two airfields in the valley. The main strip was located within the main defensive position and initially housed a

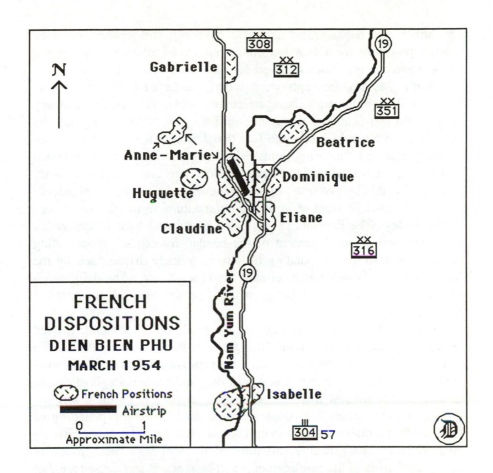

N

Gabrielle

XX
308

XX
312

19

XX
351

Anne-Marie

Beatrice

Dominique

Huguette

Claudine

Eliane

XX
316

Nam Yum River

19

FRENCH
DISPOSITIONS
DIEN BIEN PHU
MARCH 1954

French Positions
Airstrip

0   1
Approximate Mile

Isabelle

III
304 57

permanent air contingent of six Hellcat fighters and six observation aircraft. The airstrip could handle not only its fighters and observation
airplanes, but also C-47's and C-119's, the ''Flying Boxcars.'' A reserve
airstrip was located just north of Isabelle, but was never used.

To defend their strong points, the French relied on classical defensive
concepts and measures. They planned to hit the Vietminh attackers with
mortar and artillery fire as the Communists began their attacks or even
as they were forming for the attacks. The French infantry would remain
in their fortifications protected from the Vietminh artillery fire which
would be supporting Giap's attacking forces. The Vietminh would come
under machine-gun and rifle fire as they attempted to get through the
mine fields and barbed wire in front of the French positions. Finally,

any attack which penetrated and held a French strongpoint would be ejected promptly by a tank-led counterattack by one or more of the crack parachute battalions reserved for that role.

While Castries' concepts were sound, he failed badly in carrying them out. Perhaps the most glaring defensive weakness was the inadequacy of the field fortifications. It was not until the end of December that the French leaders would accept the fact that Dien Bien Phu would not be a lightly fortified "mooring point," but instead, should be a hardened camp which must withstand heavy artillery fire and massive infantry assaults. To this loss of time, other problems and mistakes were added. First, there was a shortage of wood and other natural fortification materials in the valley. The dismantling of every house and barn in the valley furnished only about 5 percent of the needed materials.[6] Woodcutting parties sent into the surrounding hills were quickly driven back by the Vietminh. The French airlift, already stretched to meet the daily needs of the garrison, could not bring in the vast tonnages of construction materials needed.

Without the heavy wooden beams, the steel, and the concrete needed to build adequate fortifications, the garrison had to dig itself into the ground, and hope for the best. Even this primitive method of fortification brought problems. The valley soil was only adhesive enough to permit the digging of shallow trenches and emplacements. Even more serious, the dirt rapidly turned into unmanageable dust under the pounding of the Vietminh artillery. Poor drainage complicated the soil problem. Excessive water caused a further softening of the soil with the consequent collapse of many of the emplacements and bunkers. Water caused another problem—flooding. When the monsoon hit in April, earlier and heavier than usual, parts of all the main position were under water, and Isabelle was almost completely flooded out.

Another weakness of the French positions was the total lack of any camouflage or concealment. The trees in the valley had to be cut to meet construction needs, and the brush disappeared quickly as fuel for the hundreds of cooking fires. The constant moving of men back and forth through the positions wore out the grass. As a result, the French defenses were clearly visible to the Vietminh observers in the surrounding hills, and Giap's men were able to pin-point every artillery and weapon emplacement, every trench, and every barbed wire entanglement. From their visual observations, the Vietminh built detailed models upon which they planned and rehearsed their attacks. Why the French did not use camouflage nets, which are light in weight and easy to transport, has never been explained.

Another French planning deficiency was the inadequacy of the French artillery support. They did not have enough guns in the valley, and by United States standards the French garrison needed three times as much artillery as it positioned at Dien Bien Phu. Fire direction and fire coordination were poor, and on many occasions French artillery fire fell on French troops. French counterbattery fire, for which the four 155mm howitzers had been flown in, was ineffective. These efforts were thwarted not only by Giap's techniques of concealing and "tunneling in" the guns, but by poor French target acquisition and planning. Finally, the French placed their guns in circular pits with no overhead protection. During the battle the French gunners were killed or wounded serving their pieces, and many of the guns themselves were damaged or destroyed by enemy artillery.[7]

The final, and the most important, element in any defensive plan is the counterattack. Sooner or later any defensive position will be breached by a determined attacker. Here the French matched their other inadequacies of planning and execution. It is amazing, in retrospect, that with Navarre, Cogny, and Castries all pinning their primary hopes on counterattacks, so little was done to prepare for them. Few plans were developed; none were rehearsed. General Catroux, who headed the Commission of Inquiry which investigated the battle, blamed Cogny for the failure to have the plans rehearsed other than a "paper" exercise in which no troops were moved. Catroux claims that a rehearsal on the ground would have revealed the deficiencies of the counterattack plans.[8] In March 1968 the Headquarters, United States Military Assistance Command, Vietnam (MACV), then under General Westmoreland, made a detailed study of the battle of Dien Bien Phu to compare it to the one then shaping up at Khe Sanh. The MACV study asserts that the French lack of planning for counterattacks was a prime weakness in the French defensive efforts at Dien Bien Phu. In addition to the lack of rehearsals noted by General Catroux, the MACV analysis points out that no reconnaissance of routes and attack positions was made, and although tanks were to lead the counterattacks, the French carried out no tank-infantry planning or combined training.[9]

There were several reasons for these deficiencies of execution, including the frail fortifications, the lack of camouflage and concealment, the inadequate artillery support, and the poor planning and organization of counterattacks. They reflected first that familiar French fault, underestimation of Giap and the Vietminh. The French leaders were convinced before the initiation of the battle that Giap's artillery fire would be neither heavy nor long-sustained. They believed that the Vietminh had no more than mortars and some 75mm howitzers and that Giap was short of ammunition for even this weak array. And the French expected that what artillery Giap had would be quickly neutralized by French counterbattery fire and air attacks. So—French thinking ran—it was not important if their fortifications were inadequate and makeshift; they could withstand the type of limited artillery bombardments which Giap would throw at them.

From the start of the campaign differences of concept and the lack of a common understanding of the purpose of the operation impeded effective defense planning. It was not until a month after the French airborne assault of 20 November that Navarre and Cogny gave up their idea of Dien Bien Phu as the base from which wide-ranging attack forces would "radiate." Bemused by this unrealistic concept, the French leaders did little concrete planning for a long and hard-fought defensive struggle. Even when the "mooring point" concept vanished under Giap's tightening encirclement, Cogny, particularly, persisted in thinking that the principal defensive tactic would be counterattacks which would sweep back and forth across the valley.

Navarre—at least by early March—had a clearer visualization of the dangers at Dien Bien Phu. On 4 March Navarre suggested that two or three additional battalions be flown into the valley and that Castries establish another defensive position between the main position and Isabelle. Cogny demurred. The garrison was already crowded, he argued, but more important, the Air Transport Command simply could not fly in the supplies for such an additional force. Cogny converted Navarre by assuring him with some intensity that the twelve infantry battalions then at Dien Bien Phu plus their supporting troops would be adequate to win "a great defensive victory" at Dien Bien Phu.

After the defeat at Dien Bien Phu, Cogny's optimistic boast became part of the quarrel between Cogny and Navarre concerning each one's share of the blame. Cogny never denied that he made the statement.

He said that he made it in front of Navarre and Castries to keep up the latter's morale, and that he did not really hold such a view. Jules Roy points out that even if this was Cogny's reason for his bombastic statement, that he failed to tell Navarre his true view of the situation at Dien Bien Phu, even though there was ample opportunity to do so in the airplane which returned the two generals that same day to Hanoi.[10]

Cogny's conduct in this matter must be severely condemned. When he made that statement, Cogny was not talking to an assemblage of enlisted men and junior officers, where Patton-like bravado can be justified as a means of raising the morale of the troops. Cogny was speaking only to his direct superior and to a key subordinate, both senior professionals. Both Navarre and Castries had every right to expect Cogny's statement to be his honest appraisal of the situation. There is an adage in the American army to the effect that "senior officers have no morale," and it is largely true. While senior leaders attempt to raise the morale of the lower ranks, they themselves are almost immune to any artificial stimulation of their own spirit. They want, and expect, that when they are alone with their senior colleagues, each officer will give his true views of the situation, regardless of how forlorn those views might be. Cogny's conduct on 4 March was at best unprofessional, and at worst, dishonorable.

Putting condemnation of Cogny aside, however, an observer wonders why Navarre, Cogny, or Castries did not replace the two T'ai battalions and the eleven companies of the T'ai Mobile Group at Dien Bien Phu with troops more suited to a grueling defensive battle. Navarre listed this failure to replace the T'ai battalions as one of the causes of the defeat.[11]

While the misconceptions and misestimations of Navarre and Cogny in large part brought about the French catastrophe at Dien Bien Phu, Castries must also share the responsibility. From the day of his assumption of command he seems to have been largely passive—a commander molded by events, rather than a molder. The lack of strong fortifications could be laid to other factors (largely shortage of air transport), but Castries should have insured that the positions were camouflaged, that counterattacks were planned and rehearsed, and that Isabelle was moved closer to the main positions. He had no real plan or priorities of effort. One can only conclude that Castries had no appetite for the defense, and no experience or skill in its tactics and techniques. Above all, he had none of the pugnacious resolution that is so necessary in any leader, particularly one charged with the conduct of a desperate defensive siege.

Perhaps the contrast between the preparation and attitude of Giap and his French opponents is capsulized by the location and comforts of their respective command posts from which they would direct the battle. Navarre conducted his battle from a vast, air-conditioned building in Saigon, Cogny from another imposing and comfortable structure in Hanoi, and Castries from a reinforced dugout in Dien Bien Phu in which he dined on a spotless linen tablecloth set with gleaming silver. In contrast, Giap moved his command post to a cave near Tuan Giao sometime in December. From that primitive bombproof chamber he could personally handle the multitude of details which would insure victory. Above all, he was in daily contact with his commanders and his troops, sharing their hardships and inspiring them for the great task which lay ahead. But the differences in command posts represented more than a mere contrast of headquarters. They represented a difference in lifestyles, in cultures, and above all, a difference in dedication, devotion, and the amount of physical discomfort and suffering each contender was willing to suffer for victory.

13–28 March—Phase I

The assault phase (Phase I) of the battle of Dien Bien Phu began at 1700 hours on 13 March 1954. Giap selected the time and date carefully. The hour allowed the Vietminh artillery to fire upon the French positions and emplacements in daylight, and the infantry assault was covered by the darkness of the early evening. Giap chose the night of 13 March because there was a new moon—enough darkness to give concealment, yet enough light to let the Vietminh attackers see what they were doing. This moon phase was what the Americans a decade and a half later would call "a Viet Cong moon." For years almost all of the major Vietminh/Viet Cong/North Vietnamese attacks were started by the light of either a quarter-moon or its counterpart, a three-quarter moon.

The date and hour of Giap's attack was known to the French, who picked it up from radio intercept. The time of the attack, then, came as no surprise, nor did the place. For weeks the French defenders noted that the Vietminh were slowly closing in on both Gabrielle and Beatrice. Their exposed positions, the inadequacy of the artillery support to them from Isabelle, and the difficulty of reaching them by counterattack from the central position told the French that these two positions would be Giap's first objectives.

Giap planned to eliminate Beatrice first. It was a sound selection. Both Beatrice and Gabrielle were held by first-rate units, Beatrice by a battalion of the Foreign Legion and Gabrielle by an Algerian battalion which had distinguished itself in previous battles. But Gabrielle was stronger than Beatrice; it was the only strongpoint which had a second defensive line; and Gabrielle was easier for a counterattacking force from the central position to reach.

To annihilate Beatrice, Giap planned a three-pronged attack using six battalions of the 141st and 219th Regiments of the 312th Division. Each prong, two battalions in strength, would attack a sector held by one French understrength company. The attack would be supported by 105mm and 75mm howitzers and by 82mm and 120mm mortars. Giap planned to begin the artillery attack on Beatrice, Gabrielle, and the artillery emplacements of the central forts at 1600 hours on 13 March. But, as usual in combat, things went wrong. The French discovered the Vietminh assault positions only 200 meters from their defenses on Beatrice, and at 1200 hours they sent a unit to clean them out. This probe triggered the Vietminh artillery attack. Giap's artillery fire was heavy and accurate. The east fortification on Beatrice turned to dust under the pounding; the mortar battery on Gabrielle was smothered; the French artillery emplacements in the main position were hit, where two guns were knocked out and several crews killed or wounded. Giap's preliminary bombardment struck the airfield, where planes, fuel, and munitions began to burn and explode. Here on the airfield the French got another surprise. As the aircraft took off, either to attack the Vietminh or to evacuate the airstrip, they came under accurate fire from concealed 37mm antiaircraft guns which had heretofore been silent. Several French planes were destroyed either on the strip or in the air.

The attacking infantry units of the 312th Division jumped off promptly at 1700 hours and made rapid progress against the dazed Legionnaires on Beatrice. At 1815 hours, Major Pegot, the Legionnaire commander, called on the French artillery to fire on areas just in front of his final line of resistance. At 1830 hours a Vietminh artillery round hit the

French command post on Beatrice and killed Pegot and his entire staff. A few minutes later another artillery shell killed Lieutenant Colonel Gaucher, Pegot's immediate superior and the commander of the northern defensive sector. These two rounds robbed Beatrice of its leaders and of the coordination of fire support which is the heart of a defensive operation. Shortly thereafter the three Legionnaire companies were each fighting their own separate battles. At 2230 hours the 10th Company went under. At 2300 hours the 11th Company sent a radio message that it was fighting around its command bunker. At 0015 hours, 14 March, the 9th Company called for French artillery fire on its own position and went off the air. Casualties were heavy on both sides. One authority says that the French lost 400 out of 500 men who had held Beatrice;[12] another claims 550 were lost out of a garrison of 750.[13] The 312th Division lost 600 men killed and another 1,200 seriously wounded, a substantial part of the attacking force.

At 0730 hours the next morning (14 March), the French attempted a counterattack with tanks and paratroopers from the central position toward Beatrice. Heavy Vietminh fire quickly beat it into the ground. As the paratroopers and tanks were reforming, a badly wounded Legionnaire lieutenant came staggering to them from Beatrice with a message from General Le Trong Tan, the commanding general of the 312th Division. Tan proposed a four-hour truce, so that both sides could pick up their dead and wounded on what was left of Beatrice. After some hesitation, and after getting permission from Saigon, the truce was accepted. Castries postponed the French counterattack on Beatrice, and later, when he had a clearer view of the situation, he abandoned the idea altogether.

Giap's victory on Beatrice galvanized the morale of his troops and depressed that of the French. With his unusual insight into the psychology of his men, Giap realized that the outcome of the first fight for Dien Bien Phu was decisive to the morale of the Vietminh. Giap and his subordinate commanders told their men again and again that they could and would beat the French, but only a victory in the first battle would convince them. Giap himself states that he went to unusual ends to assure that the Vietminh forces were trained and prepared for this first assault.[14] Giap shows here a clear grasp of the combat veteran's old maxim, "always win the first fight."

The day of 14 March 1954 was a busy day for both sides. Giap and the Vietminh were moving their troops and guns into the jump-off positions for an attack on Gabrielle. The Vietminh artillery continued its devastating fire on the airfield, destroying the aircraft which remained, the runway, the control tower, and the radio beacon. Thus, on the second day of the battle the French lost the use of their airstrip. Hereafter supplies and reinforcements would have to be delivered by parachute— the most ineffective delivery method in modern war. The loss of the airfield completed Giap's victory in the "battle of logistics," that vital struggle upon which hung so much of Dien Bien Phu's fate.

On 14 March the French also were busy. They organized and reinforced to meet the assault on Gabrielle which they knew was coming that night. At 1445 hours a wave of Dakotas flew over the garrison, dropping the 5th Vietnamese Parachute Battalion (BPVN) on the old drop zones near the central positions. By some strange quirk the transports escaped the Vietminh antiaircraft fire, but the paratroopers suffered casualties on landing from the enemy artillery fire which blanketed their landing zones. By 1800 hours the 5th BPVN had dug in on Eliane.

At 1700 hours on 14 March, the day following the assault on Beatrice, Giap's artillery began a withering bombardment of Gabrielle and the artillery emplacements in the central position. At 2000 hours two regiments, the 88th and 102d of the Vietminh 308th Division, began their assault on the French holding the northeast and northwest slopes of Gabrielle. The advance was slow and bloody, and by 2200 hours the French had contained it. At 0230, 15 March, the Vietminh artillery ceased firing on Gabrielle, and the Vietminh infantry on the position dug in where they were. The respite was short. At 0330 hours a firestorm of artillery and mortars struck Gabrielle, and the reorganized Vietminh infantry began to move forward again. The two French companies on the north side of Gabrielle had lost all their officers and had taken heavy casualties among the other ranks. Slowly, grudgingly, the remnants of the two northern companies gave ground, moving toward the remaining companies on the crest and southern slope of the outpost.

At 0400 hours a Vietminh artillery round hit the battalion command post, severely wounding the battalion commander, his replacement, and most of their staff. The round also destroyed all the radios connecting the battalion command post with its companies, as well as those communicating with Castries. Gabrielle, like Beatrice on the preceding night, had in one shellburst lost its leadership and its capability to coordinate the fight.

Castries ordered Colonel Langlais, who commanded the paratroop units, but who was now in charge of the reserves as well as the defense of the main positions, to mount a tank-led counterattack to relieve Gabrielle. Langlais chose one company of the Foreign Legion Parachute Battalion (1st BEP) to lead the counterattack supported by the tanks, but then he chose as the major counterattacking force the 5th Vietnamese Parachute Battalion (5th BPVN) which had jumped into the position only the day before. This was a mistake of the first magnitude, and one that doomed the counterattack before it even formed up. The men of the 5th BPVN were exhausted from their activities of the previous day and unfamiliar with the complex barbed wire entanglements of Dien Bien Phu. They were positioned on the southeast side of the central position, which meant that they had to traverse almost the entire main French stronghold to get into their position with the counterattacking force. Finally, and most important, the 5th BPVN had neither the élan nor the experience of either of the other available units, the 1st BEP or the 8th Parachute Assault Battalion (8th BPC). Langlais has never offered an acceptable explanation of this selection. Fall speculates that he wanted to save the paratroopers of his former command from an action which he felt would result in failure and heavy losses.[15]

The counterattack jumped off at 0530 hours. By 0700 it advanced to a ford over a small stream between the central position and Gabrielle. Here the Vietminh hit it with a heavy mortar and artillery concentration, plus the fire of around a battalion of infantry dug in a few hundred meters to the northwest. The tanks and the company from the 1st BEP, both experienced, ran forward through the Vietminh fire zone and suffered only a few casualties. A small part of the 5th BPVN followed and got through, but the main body hit the ground, frozen by fear, and they lay there taking heavy casualties. This paralysis severed the counterattacking force and destroyed any hope of their reaching Gabrielle. The remnants of the Algerian battalion which held Gabrielle managed to join the tanks and the company of the 1st BEP, now themselves stalled under heavy fire south of Gabrielle. Shortly after 0800 hours this dazed conglomerate began an agonizing retreat toward the central position, which it reached about an hour later.

Again, as on Beatrice, losses were heavy on both sides. On Gabrielle and in the abortive counterattack the French lost around 1,000 men. Giap lost somewhere between 1,000 and 2,000 men killed, and probably double that number wounded. Giap paid dearly for Beatrice and Gabrielle.

It is an interesting sidelight that neither Navarre nor Giap devoted much space in their books to these critical battles for Beatrice and Gabrielle. Navarre covers both in about one page of text; Giap in about two pages. Navarre, in an immense oversimplification, blames the fall of both strongpoints on the sudden loss of leadership when the Vietminh artillery rounds hit the French command bunkers.[16] In his turn, Giap completely ignores the early attack on Gabrielle, probably because the French held off the Vietminh. Instead Giap claims that the Vietminh infantry assaults did not begin until 0200 hours—an obvious falsehood, as the heavy early casualties attest.[17]

The fall of Beatrice and Gabrielle left on the northern semicircle of strongpoints only Anne Marie, held by the 3d T'ai Battalion. It fell on 17 March, the victim of political *dau tranh*. Giap had for weeks distributed propaganda leaflets among the T'ai defenders telling them that this was not their fight, and this subversive propaganda, plus the fall of Beatrice and Gabrielle, completed the demoralization of the T'ais. On the night of 15 March the T'ais began to slip away from Anne Marie, and on the morning of 17 March, under the cover of a thick ground fog, the bulk of the 3d T'ai battalion defected to the Vietminh or headed for their families in the mountains. The French and the few T'ais who remained pulled back to the central position and became part of strongpoint Huguette.

An experienced soldier finds it hard to censure the T'ais. They had fought well in the past, even under siege at Na San, but Dien Bien Phu was not their style of fighting. They were not only psychologically undermined by Giap's propaganda, but any remaining will to resist fell to pieces as they watched at close hand a preview of their own destruction in the death agonies of Beatrice and Gabrielle. To remain on Anne Marie, knowing that their time was near, would require the highest order of devotion and discipline, a test which the best of soldiers have failed.

Rather than blame the T'ais, it is Castries, Cogny, and Navarre who must be censured for having the T'ai unit in the valley, and above all, on Anne Marie, a key outpost.

The abandonment of Anne Marie ended Phase I of the battle. For the French it was a bloody calamity; for Giap, it was a costly, but tremendous, success. Giap's strategy in first eliminating the three northern outposts was sound. They were certainly more vulnerable than the central position, and their location permitted Giap to concentrate against each in turn. His order of elimination showed a cool judgment of the defensive potentialities of each. Beatrice was an easier target than Gabrielle, and Anne Marie would fall from within when the other two strongpoints went under. Above all, Giap showed that he had grasped a critical point in the whole campaign—the Vietminh had to win these first fights. They had to demonstrate to themselves—and to the French—that they could take a heavily defended position.

Giap's casualties were very heavy. He lost more men on Gabrielle than he would lose on any other French position throughout the battle. The famed 308th Division would be weak and halting for the rest of the campaign. Even in retrospect, however, there appears to have been no other way to take the positions than by frontal assault—and the price had to be paid in blood.

17–30 March—The Lull

The period of 17–30 March marked a lull in the fighting between Phase I and Phase II of the battle. There were, however, significant developments taking place on both sides. The Vietminh underwent laborious preparations for the upcoming battle for the strongholds on the eastern hills (Eliane and Dominique), which dominated the central position, as well as for Huguette 7 and 6, the strongpoints which protected the western and northwestern side of the airstrip. Giap's troops dug over 100 kilometers of trenches during these twelve days. During this period, the Vietminh encircled the main position, cut Isabelle off from the central stronghold, and made ready to storm Eliane, Dominique and Huguette.

For the French, the period saw not only a brief resurgence of the offensive spirit, but of more importance, a serious crisis of command. The crisis focused on Castries, and the loss of Beatrice, Gabrielle, and Anne Marie brought it to a head. Its infection would spread upward to Cogny and downward to Castries' subordinates in Dien Bien Phu. Its origin was simple. It had become painfully apparent to the senior officers within the encircled garrison—and even to Cogny in Hanoi—that Castries was incompetent to conduct the defense of Dien Bien Phu. Even more critical, after the fall of the northern outposts, he isolated himself in

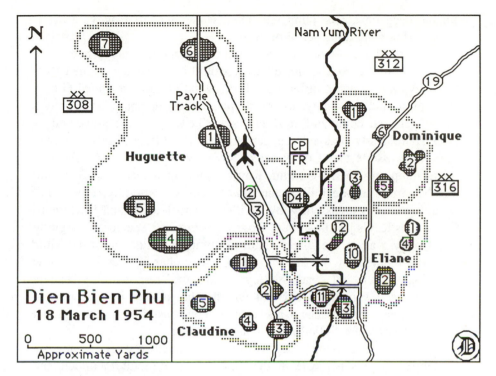

Dien Bien Phu
18 March 1954

0   500   1000
Approximate Yards

his bunker so that he had, in effect, relinquished his command authority.

About noon on 17 March, Cogny tried to land at Dien Bien Phu, but the Vietminh artillery and mortar fire on the airstrip was too heavy, and he had to return to Hanoi. There his conscience and sense of duty began to torment him. He knew, or at least sensed, that Castries could not, or would not, conduct an adequate defense of Dien Bien Phu. For some hours, perhaps for several days, he agonized over whether he should parachute into Dien Bien Phu and take personal command of the garrison. His sense of personal responsibility for Dien Bien Phu told him that he ought to do it, but his cold reason told him that he ought not to. His staff stressed to him that he had larger responsibilities than Dien Bien Phu, and that he could not cast them off to lock himself into an encircled garrison. They reminded him too, that Dien Bien Phu might fall, and if he jumped into the garrison, he would be presenting Giap with a valuable prisoner and hostage. The staff argued that Cogny held the highest military secrets, and as a prisoner he could be exploited for enormous psychological advantage. In the end the staff prevailed, but his decision not to jump into Dien Bien Phu left Cogny, a brave man, with a continuing sense of guilt.

Perhaps the supreme question which Cogny (or any officer in a like situation) had to ask himself was: would his presence at Dien Bien Phu make a significant difference? From what is now known of Giap's strength around the valley, it would appear doubtful that even Cogny's taking personal command at Dien Bien Phu would have prevented or even significantly delayed the garrison's fall. But one never knows. Jules Roy asserts that Cogny acted correctly when he finally decided not to jump into Dien Bien Phu. Roy's argument is that Dien Bien Phu was Navarre's responsibility, and thus Cogny was morally right in not assuming that responsibility by taking personal command.[18] Bernard Fall brands Roy's justification of Cogny's action as "specious," arguing that Cogny was in the direct chain-of-command and was responsible from the moment of the landing on 20 November. It was Fall's view that Cogny could not evade his legal and moral responsibility, except by a protest resignation, and that whether he jumped into Dien Bien Phu or not had no relevance to his command responsibility for the conduct of the defense there.[19] Fall is, of course, correct.

While one can sympathize with Cogny's anguish over his attempt to define his personal role in the battle, it is difficult to understand why he did not take, or recommend to Navarre, the one action which the situation so obviously dictated—the replacement of Castries. Surely, somewhere in Indochina or in the French army there must have been a colonel, brigadier general, or even major general (after all, the force at Dien Bien Phu had reached division size) who could have taken over the command of the garrison and galvanized the defenders. Navarre addressed the question obliquely in his book, but he merely wrote that Castries was the best officer available, and besides, his (Navarre's) command was very short of generals.[20] In reading his half-page account of this critical matter, one senses that Navarre thinks he ought to bring it up, but declines to provide an adequate explanation, since such an explanation would reveal his bad judgment and indifference.

As is invariably the case, Castries' subordinates had to solve the problem their seniors ignored. A vacuum in command, like any other, will be filled. If Castries would not exercise his authority, and if Cogny and Navarre would not replace him, then the senior officers in Dien Bien Phu would have to take over Castries' command functions. Just how this was done, and to what extent Castries was shorn of his command prerogatives, is still confused. Bernard Fall wrote that on 24 March, Lieutenant Colonel Langlais, commander of the central position, and his fellow paratroop commanders, all fully armed, confronted Castries and bluntly told him that he (Castries) would retain the appearance of command, but that Langlais would exercise that prerogative.[21] Castries apparently acquiesced in this arrangement without protest. Thereafter, according to Langlais' testimony before the Catroux Commission, Castries' principal function was to act as the intermediary between Dien Bien Phu and Hanoi.[22]

And yet, to term Castries' function as only a "glorified message center" seems an oversimplification. Apparently, he continued to carry out some of his command functions. On 27 March, three days after Langlais' reported takeover of command, Castries called in Major Bigeard, one of the paratroop battalion commanders, and ordered him to form a task force and with it to clean out some antiaircraft guns menacing the airstrip. When Bigeard asked for more time to prepare the operation, Castries curtly denied him additional time and told him to get on with the job. This does not sound like a "figurehead" commander. On the other hand, if Cogny (in Hanoi) had ordered the attack, then Castries would have acted as he did. Fall notes that Castries continued to exercise some influence on the conduct of the defense.[23] The truth would seem to be that Langlais did take over effective command of Dien Bien Phu, and that Castries became a "commander emeritus" who transmitted messages to Hanoi and offered "advice" about matters in Dien Bien Phu. It is also apparent that as the situation in Dien Bien Phu progressively deteriorated, Castries became more isolated and less influential.

A military professional looks at any command usurpation with profound misgiving. In the military, the authority to command is its most inviolable and buttressed function. To usurp it, even when justified, is not only dangerous (under the wrong circumstances it becomes mutiny), but it agonizes those who must take such drastic action against the failure of a brother officer. Even more disturbing to the usurpers is the knowledge that they are attacking the military hierarchical system, the foundation upon which rests the discipline of any armed force, and upon which all in the system rely for authority. They strike at the very heart of an army.

The lull in the fighting between 17 and 30 March saw not only the usurpation of the French command, but the last French *offensive* operation at Dien Bien Phu. It was born of desperation, bred by the French aircraft losses being inflicted by the Vietminh antiaircraft machine guns located to the west of the central position. The French supply and evacuation system, totally dependent on aircraft, had deteriorated rapidly following the fall of the northern outposts. The airstrip had come under such heavy and accurate artillery and antiaircraft machine-gun fire that it could be used only with great difficulty and danger to evacuate the wounded. Even these mercy flights were terminated on 26 March. The aerial supply system of the French, upon which the very life of the garrison depended, was in an equal crisis. The loss of the use of the airstrip found the French relying on low-level parachute drops for supply, but the Vietminh antiaircraft guns, both the 37mm's and the machine guns, shot down so many transports that this method of delivery became too costly. On 27 March, Colonel Nicot, the air transport commander in Hanoi—the officer who had been so prophetic about Navarre's decision to go into Dien Bien Phu—issued an order ending low-level drops (at 2500 feet) and directing that future deliveries be made at 6500 feet. Even at this altitude aircraft losses were expected to be heavy. So, on that same evening, Castries, perhaps on the urging of Cogny and Nicot, called in Bigeard and ordered him to organize an offensive to be launched the next day to destroy the antiaircraft machine guns around the villages of Ban Ban and Ban Ong Pet, two miles to the west of Dien Bien Phu. Bigeard sat down in Castries' dugout and in six hours mapped out the complex operation employing three paratroop battalions (the 8th Assault, the 6th BPC, and the 1st BEP), a Foreign Legion infantry battalion, a tank squadron, all of the artillery in the central position, plus close air support to be furnished by the French air force. At 0200 hours, 28 March, Bigeard, the task force commander, issued his attack order to his subordinate commanders and the air force liaison officer. In Bigeard's own words, the operation had to be "precise, delicate, and rapid."[24] The Vietminh antiaircraft machine guns were protected by the 36th Regiment of the 308th Division—no easy mark. The pool table terrain over which the operation had to be conducted provided no cover or concealment, yet surprise had to be achieved or the operation would fail and the casualties would be ruinous to the best combat units in the garrison.

Bigeard's plan was simple. Surprise would be gained by the speed of the operation. The troops would go in, destroy the Communist machine guns, and get out before the Vietminh artillery could concentrate its fire on the attackers. The French had discovered the weakness of the Vietminh's "direct fire" artillery—its inflexibility and slowness in shifting and massing firepower—and they planned to exploit this deficiency. The French attack would be preceded by a short but intensive artillery preparation. The paratroopers and the tanks would follow close behind the "rolling barrage," the 8th Assault Battalion would go for Ban Ban, and the 6th BPC for Ban Ong Pet. The two Foreign Legion battalions would be used as reserves. The tanks would accompany the infantry, and the air force would attack the two villages and the hills behind them.

Strangely enough—for as the elder Moltke once said, "The plan is always the first casualty of the battle"—the attack came off almost exactly as Bigeard had designed it. The assault units jumped off at 0600 hours, and by 1530 they were on their way back to the relative safety of their own lines. Seventeen antiaircraft machine guns were captured or destroyed, 350 Vietminh soldiers killed, and ten captured. The prisoners told their captors that the Vietminh had been surprised by the attack of the supposedly demoralized French garrison. The French lost twenty men killed and ninety wounded.

With this attack, the lull between Phase I and Phase II ended.

30 March—30 April—Phase II

In his Phase II battles, Giap's primary objectives were the strongholds on the five small hills to the east of the central position. Using the French designation, these five positions were (from south to north) Eliane 2, Eliane 1, Dominique 2, a small hill between Dominique 1 and 2, and Dominique 1. Giap committed two divisions, the 316th and the 312th, to this attack. Giap also planned a secondary and diversionary attack by the 308th Division, which would go for the positions to the north, northwest, and west of the airstrip, which the French called Huguette 1, 6, and 7.

The French held the five eastern positions with a mixture of Frenchmen, Legionnaires, Vietnamese, Africans, and T'ais, a total of about four understrength battalions. The paratroop units, understrength too, made up the French reserve. The Huguette positions were held by another mixed force of about one small battalion.

Giap's plans for this phase were simple—use the same tactics which had overwhelmed Beatrice and Gabrielle. The Vietminh would start the battle with a tremendous artillery preparation shortly before dark. As darkness fell, the infantry (in which Giap held a five to one superiority over the defenders) and sappers would move in and destroy the French by their sheer weight of numbers and self-sacrifice. As costly as it would certainly be, Giap saw no other way to do it; and it would work, provided the morale and the sacrificial spirit of the Vietminh infantry held up.

At 1700 hours on 30 March, Giap began his Phase II assaults. His preparatory work had been done well. The Vietminh 312th Division got into the defenses of Dominique 1 and Dominique 2 so fast that the defensive artillery fires of the French fell harmlessly behind them. The Algerian unit, which was holding the position, quickly disintegrated and fled to the rear. The troops of Giap's 312th Division captured Dominique 1 by 1830 hours and Dominique 2 by 1900 hours. The situation suddenly became extremely dangerous for the entire French position. If Dominique 3 and 5 fell, the French strongholds east of the river would be outflanked and the undefended general headquarters area in the central position exposed. Dominique 3 was held by a company of Algerians, whose countrymen had so precipitously abandoned Dominique 1 and 2. Would they hold? This question was never answered, for there was another French unit on Dominique 3, a battery of African artillerymen of the 4th Colonial Artillery Regiment, which now entered the fight. With their countrymen fleeing through their position, the artillerymen calmly dropped their 105mm howitzers to minimum elevation, set the fuses on the shells to "fuse zero," and fired the guns as cannons into the screaming Vietminh infantry pouring at them from Dominique 1 and 2. The blasts cleared wide gaps in the ranks of the Vietminh soldiers of the 312th Division. They recoiled in blood and chaos. Then a group of heavy .50 caliber antiaircraft machine guns located near the airfield began to pour a deadly stream of half-inch bullets into the milling Vietminh infantry. They went to ground, then began to flee to the rear to escape the devastating fire. There they ran into a mine field. The attack of the 312th Division was over. In one of those unexpected actions in which combat abounds, the 4th Colonial Artillery Regiment had saved Dien Bien Phu.

The Vietminh 316th Division was more successful against the Moroccans holding Eliane 1. It fell within forty-five minutes of the start of the assault. Eliane 2 had been under heavy artillery and mortar fire since 1700 hours, and shortly after dark elements of the 316th Division launched a mass attack against it. The Communists managed to take about half the position by midnight, as they pushed the French off the hill ahead of them.

While the Vietminh 312th and 316th Divisions were fighting on the east side of the camp, the 308th Division was attacking the woefully exposed position of Huguette 7. A thrust launched shortly after dark succeeded in destroying and capturing the northern bunker. As the Vietminh infantry poured through the gap, it appeared that all of Huguette 7 would be rapidly overrun, but a French sergeant took charge of the remaining defenders and managed to seal the breakthrough. By midnight on 30 March, the French situation was desperate. On the east, Dominique 1 and 2 were lost; Eliane 1, the most critical of the five positions, was in Vietminh hands; most of Eliane 2 had been captured; and a portion of Huguette 7 was held by the 308th Division.

The French leadership had learned some lessons from the fall of Beatrice and Gabrielle, and one of these was that a counterattack, to be successful, had to be launched before the Vietminh could reorganize and reinforce the captured position. Shortly after midnight a mixed force of Foreign Legion paratroopers, Moroccans, and Frenchmen (all of whom had been driven earlier from Eliane 2) began a counterattack, and they succeeded in recapturing half of the position. Just who ordered the counterattack is not clear. It could have been a Lieutenant Lucciani, who commanded the paratroop company which earlier had been pushed off Eliane 2. Perhaps it was ordered by Major Nichols, the commander on Eliane 2, or by Bigeard, on Eliane 4, who never hesitated to insert himself into any battle. At any rate, Bigeard reinforced Lucciani's effort on Eliane 2 with one of his companies from Eliane 4. While the French had temporarily recaptured most of Eliane 2, their overall position on the five eastern hills was grim. They had lost Dominique 1, Dominique 2, and Eliane 1, and these positions, particularly Dominique 2, dominated the French defenses east of the river. Langlais therefore decided to launch a counterattack against Dominique 2 and Eliane 1 on the afternoon of 31 March. The 8th BPC would attack Dominique 2 and the 6th BPC, reinforced by parts of the 5th BPVN, would go for Eliane 1. The counterattack was to be a major effort by just about everybody left in the garrison who could be trusted to fight.

The counterattack jumped off at 1330 hours. After heavy fighting, the 8th BPC retook Dominique 2, and the 6th BPC and the Vietnamese paratroopers had recaptured Eliane 1, but the successes of the French units were short-lived. They were exhausted, the Vietminh were reforming for a counterattack of their own, and no French reinforcements were available.

Bigeard, who was commanding the entire counterattacking force, told the commander of the 8th BPC, shortly after 1500 hours, that no reinforcements were to be had, and to pull back from Dominique 2 if he couldn't hold it with what force he had there. At 1530 hours the 8th BPC began to withdraw from Dominique 2. Since Dominique 2 outflanked Eliane 1, the 6th BPC and the 5th BPVN in turn fell back to Eliane 4. The earlier successes had become failures.

Langlais's original plan provided that the 3d Battalion of the 3d Foreign Legion Regiment and some tanks were to move from Isabelle on the morning of 31 March to reinforce the counterattack set for that afternoon. They never made it. They were hit by the 57th Regiment of the 304th Vietminh Division north of Isabelle and driven back to that stronghold, losing fifteen killed and fifty wounded in the action. This action not only robbed Langlais of his last reinforcements, but signaled to the French that Isabelle was now permanently isolated.

The French knew by 1130 hours on 31 March that the Foreign Legion battalion on Isabelle could not support the counterattacks against Dominique 2 and Eliane 1, yet they persisted in launching them. They persisted because they expected Cogny to send them an airborne battalion which would be parachuted into the camp that day. Better than any other indication, this hope for heaven-borne reinforcements which would arrive at the last moment was a measure of French desperation.

There is a bizarre story about these missing reinforcements. Early on the evening of 30 March, Castries asked Cogny's headquarters to drop another battalion on 31 March. He was turned down, but the answer left some hope that the decision would be changed later that night. But the decision was not changed, and the account of why it was not is to any American officer an incomprehensible story.

The story begins in Saigon on the afternoon of 30 March as Navarre read the messages detailing the French defeat on the five eastern positions. About 1700 hours he decided to fly to Hanoi to assess the situation first-hand with Cogny. He reached Hanoi about 0145 hours, 31 March—

tired, sleepy, and sour-tempered. He was met by Colonel Bastiani, Cogny's chief of staff, who apologized for his general, saying that Cogny was exhausted from the day's events and had gone to bed. Navarre said nothing, got into his car, and was driven to Cogny's headquarters. There the staff briefed him on the situation.[25]

Navarre apparently stayed up most, if not all, of the early morning hours of 31 March. He sent for Cogny about 0400 hours, but Cogny's aide told Navarre's messenger that he was not allowed to awaken Cogny. Receiving this reply, Navarre appears to have taken direct charge of Cogny's headquarters. He and Bastiani worked out a set of detailed instructions for Castries, but unfortunately Navarre made no decision regarding the dispatch of the airborne battalion on alert at Gia Lam airport near Hanoi.

This is Roy's version of the events which occurred in the early morning hours of 31 March. But Roy has always been an apologist for Cogny. Fall, however, has a different, and more discreditable version. He claims that Cogny was not in bed, but had a "social engagement," which prevented his meeting Navarre.[26] At any rate, Cogny did not meet his superior at the plane and did not attend Navarre's briefing. Both are unusual breaches of military courtesy and protocol.

At 0700 hours Navarre again sent for Cogny. Cogny arrived at about 0745 and gave Navarre a briefing on the situation as he (Cogny) had received it the preceding midnight. The trouble was that the situation had changed materially since midnight. It had been significantly bettered by the French counterattacks launched about midnight, and Navarre, who had been in the war room all night, knew it. Much later Navarre told Roy, "I exploded. I bawled him out. And in return he told me to my face what he had been telling others for some time."[27]

This confrontation went well beyond an objective discussion of opposing views on tactics and strategy. It was a name-calling, man-to-man, shouting match beyond any restraint provided by military custom and courtesy. And either during this angry dispute or during one which took place a day or two later, Cogny, white-hot with anger, shouted, "If you weren't a four-star general, I'd slap you across the face."[28]

To an American officer, the conduct of both men during the early morning hours of 31 March is inconceivable. Look at Cogny's actions. First, he did not meet Navarre's airplane when it landed at Hanoi. This is a relatively minor offense against military protocol, but in the American armed forces a junior meets his superior's aircraft when it comes into his command unless operational necessity prevents his doing so. Considering the crisis of 30–31 March at Dien Bien Phu, Cogny had ample excuse for not meeting Navarre, provided, of course, he was busy directing his part of the war. But he was not doing his job; he was either out of his headquarters or in bed. With a significant part of his command about to be overrun at Dien Bien Phu, and with a key decision about logistics and reinforcements to be made, Cogny should have been either in his office or in his war room. Refusing to see and confer with Navarre when the latter came to his headquarters represented more than extreme discourtesy by Cogny toward a superior, it was dereliction of duty.

Cogny's refusal to see Navarre at 0400 hours added a new insult to prior offenses. He had slept for at least three hours, all the sleep he could have reasonably expected to get with an impending disaster looming at Dien Bien Phu. Not only did Navarre need him, but even more important, his command needed him. Cogny's appearance at 0745 hours with an out-of-date situation report was so negligent, so crass, that again, it could only be taken by Navarre as another calculated insult, and further evidence that Cogny had at least temporarily abandoned his command responsibilities.

The final and supreme offense, of course, came in the loud argument and in Cogny's threat of physical attack against his superior. In the American armed forces this conduct would almost certainly lead to a general court-martial, and certainly no officer's career could possibly survive such capricious and affrontive conduct.

There is no explanation for Cogny's actions from either of the principals, nor from the reporting authorities, Fall and Roy. Actually, there are two deductions which may be made. The first, and more charitable, is that Cogny suffered a temporary mental aberration during the night of 30–31 March. For days he had been under crushing mental pressure. He could see that Dien Bien Phu was probably doomed, and while to others he blamed Navarre for the impending defeat, in his heart he blamed himself for the coming disaster. *He* had not objected strongly enough when Navarre proposed the operation; *he,* an artilleryman, had not seen the tremendous effectiveness with which Giap would employ his artillery; *he* had acquiesced in leaving the T'ai battalions in Dien Bien Phu instead of replacing them when he could have done so in early December; *he* had agreed to the selection of Castries as the commander of the camp; and above all, *he* had failed to relieve Castries after the fall of Gabrielle and Beatrice, when it became obvious that Castries had neither the skill nor the resolution to defend the camp. Beneath these self-recriminations there was an even more painful one. Cogny still tortured himself with the thought that he should be in Dien Bien Phu, fighting and, if necessary dying, with his men. On the contrary, he was in Hanoi, safe and comfortable, but largely helpless, while his troops perished in the muddy holocaust of Dien Bien Phu. Cogny, a brave and honorable man, was beginning to doubt his own courage and his own manhood.

The temporary, but severe, depression of a commander in the face of military catastrophe is not unusual. Although it takes various forms, it has struck "great captains" and brilliant generals. Napoleon abandoned his troops in their retreat from Moscow and sat transfixed, mute for days on end, in the coach bearing him back to Paris. That greatest of American generals, Robert E. Lee, just after the repulse of Pickett's charge at Gettysburg, after riding out to meet the returning Virginians, began to ride resolutely toward the area where Union cannon fire was falling among the retiring Confederates. Lee's men, sensing that their leader intended to ride into the shell-swept area, seized his bridle reins and set up the cry, "General Lee to the rear." So possibly Cogny, deeply depressed by his sense of guilt about Dien Bien Phu, temporarily lost his powers of reason.

There is another possible explanation for Cogny's abnormal behavior which does him less credit. That explanation is that he intentionally sought to be relieved. Cogny must have realized on 30 March that Dien Bien Phu would fall, and just as surely he must have grasped that there would be scapegoats. It would be to his advantage to get his story to the public before Navarre could. If he could lure Navarre into relieving him, then he would be free of the official inhibitions which had prevented him from making public his criticism of Navarre. To Cogny there was another advantage to being relieved on 31 March—he would not be held responsible for the final defeat which would be postponed at least several days, and probably several weeks. No officer wants to be relieved of command, but that ignominy would be preferable to being held responsible for the death or capture of 10,000 fellow countrymen.

While Cogny's conduct can be explained either as an aberration or as a shameful desire to sidestep his command responsibility, Navarre's action defies any rational explanation. No general officer in the American army—very few officers of any rank in any army—would have tolerated the series of calculated insults to which Cogny subjected Navarre. Nor would any other French general have borne the insults. Can anyone imagine a de Gaulle or a de Lattre tolerating such conduct from a subordinate? Even if Navarre chose to overlook the personal insults—and he could not and should not have overlooked them—Cogny's obvious dereliction of duty in a crisis dictated that Navarre relieve Cogny on the spot. At 0400 hours on 31 March, when Cogny refused for the second time to appear, Navarre should have told Cogny's aide that when his general awoke he was to inform him that he had been relieved of all duties as of that moment, and that he (Cogny) should leave Hanoi as soon as possible. Navarre should then have informed the staff that he was taking over the Northern Command and that he would act as the commander until he could appoint and install a successor to Cogny.

But Navarre did not take this justifiable and soldierly action. The explanation lies somewhere deep within Navarre's psyche. The only possible explanation of his failure to act is that Navarre did not want Cogny free to assail his conduct of the Indochina campaign, and in particular, the upcoming debacle at Dien Bien Phu. As long as Cogny remained in Indochina, Navarre had some control over him and his statements. Once in Paris, Cogny could command international attention. If this was Navarre's reason for not relieving Cogny, he paid a heavy price in self-respect.

At Dien Bien Phu, the evening of 31 March brought to the officers charged with its defense a deep feeling of hopelessness. Airborne reinforcements had not arrived; they had been forced to give up Dominique 2 and Eliane 1; there were no more reserves; and the ammunition for the artillery and mortar pieces was almost exhausted. The Vietminh were forming for another attack that night, and from a radio intercept the French learned that Giap himself had arrived in the valley to take personal charge of the fighting.[29] Shortly after dark, Langlais told Bigeard over the radio that he had permission to fall back from Eliane 2 and Eliane 4 to the west bank of the river. Bigeard told him, "As long as I have one man alive I won't let go of Eliane. Otherwise Dien Bien Phu is done for."[30]

Giap's assessment of the situation coincided with Bigeard's, and on the night of 31 March he drove two regiments of the 316th Division against Eliane 2. Just as it seemed the French stronghold would be overrun, a few French tanks arrived, and although four were hit and one destroyed, the infantry with their help managed to hold Eliane 2. Eliane 4, under much less enemy pressure, remained in French hands. Huguette 7 saw another Communist attack on the night of 31 March. At 2300 hours the Vietminh shelled the northern portion of the redoubt and attacked that area. The French had already abandoned the northern bunker, and they called in an intense artillery concentration on the attackers. At dawn the French defenders of Huguette 7 counterattacked the surprised and demoralized Vietminh and drove them from the position.

On the morning of 1 April, the French held Eliane 4, one half of Eliane 2, and all of Huguette 7. The morning of 1 April also saw a conference in Hanoi on the vital subject of reinforcements. Both Nicot (the commander of the Air Transport Command) and Colonel Sauvagnac (in charge of paratroop replacements) argued that since the aircraft would have to fly a long leg at low altitude in the face of heavy Communist antiaircraft fire, any attempt to drop an entire airborne battalion would mean a suicidal exposure of both aircraft and paratroopers. On the recommendation of Nicot and Sauvagnac, Cogny finally decided to drop reinforcements at night by single planes flying at irregular intervals. The necessity of the single plane method of reinforcement was confirmed that same night when an attempt was made to drop the 2d Battalion of the 1st Parachute Chasseurs (II/IRPC). Only one company could make the jump. It sustained seven casualties, but murderous antiaircraft fire forced the rest of the battalion to return to Hanoi.

That night saw another attack on Huguette 7 and Eliane 2. By 0400 hours, 2 April, the Vietminh had overrun Huguette 7 except for one bunker. Just as the end appeared inevitable, a French counterattack of 100 men and three tanks hit the Vietminh on Huguette 7 and drove them off the position. But here again, the lack of reinforcements defeated the French. The position's defenses had been destroyed, and no infantry troops were available to hold it against the inevitable Vietminh assault which would come that night. The small French force withdrew during the morning.

Eliane 2 saw another Vietminh attack that night. Giap described the fighting for this position as "the most arduous" of his Phase II operations. He tersely described his attack of 1 April against Eliane 2 with one sentence. "On the night of 1 April, we launched the third attack which degenerated in an arduous tug-of-war."[31] Casualties were heavy on both sides, but each still clung to a piece of Eliane 2.

On the night of 2–3 April, Giap continued his attack against Eliane 2 and probed Huguette 6, as well as Huguette 1. That night saw another small increment of II/IRCP and some artillery replacements dropped at irregular intervals over the position. These additions did not begin to replace the casualties that were incurred that day alone.

The next night Giap again attacked Eliane 2 without significant results, but the main attack came against Huguette 6. The assault on Huguette 6 began immediately after dark and, as usual, initially made good progress. Langlais then committed his reserve—an understrength paratroop company and three tanks. This small force caught the Vietminh attackers by surprise and in the open. Under the fire of the tank's cannons the Communists broke and ran. That night the bulk of the II/IRCP were dropped. Instead of trying to drop the paratroopers in a drop zone, the aircraft simply dumped them all over the camp. There were some jump casualties, but much fewer than expected.

On the morning of 4 April, the newly arrived II/IRCP took up positions on Dominique 3. Shortly after noon, the French on Eliane 2 reported that the Vietminh were pulling back off that position. Giap fails to mention this withdrawal. On the contrary, regarding Eliane 2 he writes, "On April 4 we still disputed every inch of ground with the enemy. . . ."[32] Around Isabelle, the Communists continued to dig themselves closer to the position. During the night, three French tanks sallied forth from Isabelle and shot up the ever-encroaching Vietminh trenches and bunkers.

But the main action of the night of 4–5 April came against Huguette 6, held by ninety Legionnaires. Giap sent the entire 165th Infantry Regiment of the 312th Division against that position. There followed a night of the most confused and—to use Giap's euphemism—"arduous" fighting. In all, the French committed four separate counterattacking forces. The last, under Bigeard, arrived just as the final Vietminh attack began, and, in a furious fight, blunted it. As dawn came, the French artillery and the French fighter-bombers took a ghastly toll of what was left of the 165th caught on the open ground. The French counted 800 bodies on and around Huguette 6, but French casualties, too, were heavy—

200 men—and these, unlike the Vietminh casualties, could not be replaced.

With this fight came a lull in this phase of the battle. Giap paused to evaluate the situation. He had been partially successful in seizing the five strongholds on the eastern side of the river, and he had captured Huguette 7. He had not gained all his Phase II objectives, however, and his casualties were gruesome. About this time (5 April), French radio intercept had picked up a message from Giap to his rear areas ordering them to speed up the flow of thousands of replacements to make up his losses. After he studied the situation, Giap decided to continue to seek his Phase II objectives, but to cut his losses (as much as possible) by placing more emphasis on digging entrenchments to get near and encircle the French defenders.

The next period, 5 April to 1 May, is Giap's stage two of his Phase II, although he does not call it that. The period featured an all-out French attack on Eliane 1, a major Vietminh counterattack on that stronghold, and the fall of Huguette 1 and Huguette 6. During this phase of the battle, French logistic support became increasingly inadequate due to the restriction of the available parachute drop areas, the intensification of Vietminh antiaircraft fire over the camp, and the desperate shortage of trucks and jeeps to pick up and distribute the supplies. Finally, this period saw serious morale problems for the Vietminh.

The attack on Eliane 1 had its origins on 6 April, when Cogny had promised to send another parachute battalion to reinforce the garrison—this time, the 2d Foreign Legion Parachute Battalion (2d BEP). Bigeard, now with the knowledge that he would get replacements, decided to take Eliane 1. This hill position, which the French had given up on 31 March, had been both an unbearable harassment and major threat to Eliane 4. The assault would be preceded by a short and violent artillery preparation (1800 rounds in ten minutes) just before the attack jumped off. The infantry would move forward in small groups, closely following the artillery, bypassing enemy resistance to gain the Vietminh's main battle position. The assault troops would be replaced as soon as they took the objective. Bigeard, without formal military schooling, did not realize it, but he had adopted on a small scale exactly the same offensive tactics, the so-called "Von Hutier tactics," with which the Germans in

World War I had won the battles of Riga and Caporetto and had made stunning advances in the Somme offensive of 1918. In effect, the battle of Dien Bien Phu became a military anachronism. It had reverted forty years to the trench warfare of the Western Front of World War I. The defense featured trenches, dugouts, and mine fields, barbed wire, voluminous artillery and machine-gun fire. The offensive had evolved into sapping, tunneling, short artillery preparations, and attacks by specially selected "storm troops." Tanks were used by the French only in an infantry support role, another World War I characteristic. The heavy casualties of the Passchendaele and Verdun were there too, only in miniature. Only gas warfare was missing.

Bigeard's attack on Eliane 1 began at 0550 hours 10 April. It went largely according to plan, and by 1400 the assault companies were on top of the hill. At 1600 hours Bigeard replaced them with two fresh units. The new companies barely got themselves organized when Giap hit them with a regimental-size counterattack. By 2100 hours the Vietminh were pushing the French off the top of Eliane 1, and Bigeard then threw in all his reserves—Legionnaires, Vietnamese paratroopers—a total of four understrength companies. At the same time Giap committed another battalion. After heavy and confused fighting the Vietminh drew back, leaving 400 bodies on Eliane 1. Another French attack and counterattack had succeeded.

Giap did not wait long to try to take back Eliane 1. On the evening of 12 April, he sent two battalions against the 300 French and Vietnamese paratroopers holding the position. The assaulting force closed quickly with the defenders, and a night of hand-to-hand combat and grenade throwing followed. By dawn, the outnumbered "paras," reinforced during the night by two additional understrength companies, shoved the Vietminh off Eliane 1. Again, losses had been heavy on both sides.

At this juncture, the morale of the Vietminh soldiers broke. The French intercepted Vietminh radio messages which told of units refusing to obey orders, and Communist prisoners said that they were told to advance or be shot by the officers and noncommissioned officers behind them. Giap admitted that he had a serious morale problem. In the turgid euphemisms which Communist leaders always use, Giap wrote, "However, it was precisely at that time that a *rightist and negative tendency* (Giap's italics) appeared among our officers and men, under various forms: fear of casualties, losses, fatigue, difficulties and hardships, under-estimation of the enemy, subjectivism, and self-conceit."[33]

The wonder was that it had not happened before. By 13 April, Giap's overall losses at Dien Bien Phu had reached a total of 16,000 to 19,000 men—6,000 killed, probably 8,000 to 10,000 men seriously wounded, and 2,500 captured. These casualties represented two full combat divisions, or in a more realistic view, the infantry strength (the "cutting edge") of the three Vietminh combat divisions which surrounded Dien Bien Phu.

Other factors attacked the morale of the Vietminh soldiers. They, like the French, had to live in the mud and filth of the trenches, now beginning to be flooded by the monsoon rains. Again like their French enemies, their supply of food was irregular, and they were often hungry. But other than the ghastly losses, the most devastating blow to Vietminh morale was the lack of any effective medical service. Nothing strikes at combat morale like the knowledge that if wounded, the soldier will go uncared for. The Vietminh had *one* surgeon plus six "assistant doctors" to take care of the 50,000 troops around Dien Bien Phu. The medical services themselves were primitive and unsanitary, and the Vietminh doctors fought a constant and losing battle against infection and gangrene. No figures are available, but the losses of men who died from wounds after evacuation must have reached or exceeded those killed on the battle-field.

To combat the sinking morale of his troops, Giap called a conference of the Party political cadres and the political commissars which existed throughout his units. In Giap's words, they planned a "campaign of ideological education and struggle (which) was launched from the Party committees to the cells, from officers to soldiers and in all combat units. This campaign was a great success . . . and one of *the greatest achieve-ments* (Giap's italics) ever scored by this work in the history of struggle of our army."[34]

On 14 April, probably due to his recent losses and the sinking morale of his troops, Giap ordered three battalions (two from the 148th and one from the 176th Regiment of the 316th Division) to return from Laos to Dien Bien Phu. He also directed that a second regiment from the 304th Division, the 9th, move up to reinforce the other regiment from the 304th, the 57th.

While the French and Vietminh battled over Eliane 1 during 10–12 April, another significant, if less dramatic, attack was occurring on the other side of the camp around Huguette 1 and Huguette 6. From the start of this period of the siege, the Vietminh intensified their digging operations so that their trenches encircled and almost isolated both positions. On 11 April the defenders of Huguette 1 attacked the Vietminh entrenchments to destroy the encroaching works. A hot fight ensued. The French artillery on Claudine got into it, and two tanks joined in, but the French could not drive off the Communists. Giap's tourniquet on Huguette 1 and 6 was too tight.

Starting on 14 April the French made several determined efforts to supply Huguette 6 with water and ammunition. The supply force got through during the night of 14–15 April, but it took heavy casualties. Another effort the next night succeeded, but it was badly mauled and could deliver only twenty-five gallons of water. On 16–17 April the French succeeded in reaching Huguette 6 with enough water for the garrison, but the casualties during those last four days convinced Langlais and Castries that the strongpoint had to be abandoned.

At 0200 hours on 18 April, Bigeard made an attack toward Huguette 6 to link up with the French force there and to help it fight its way out of the doomed strongpoint. The attack failed, and at 0730 hours Captain Bizard, the Huguette 6 commander, was told that he could either surrender or attempt to break out. Bizard decided to attempt a breakout at once. At 0800 hours his small force vaulted out of the ruins of Huguette 6, struck the Vietminh by surprise, jumped their trenches, and, with support by mortar fire from the central camp, escaped from Huguette 6 and its Communist besiegers. The escape was a daring, but costly, achievement. Only a few men of the force which had so valiantly held Huguette 6 made it to safety.

With Huguette 6 abandoned, Giap now concentrated on Huguette 1. He followed the same procedure there as he had against Huguette 6—isolation, probes, and constant pressure. The French, predictably, made attempts to break through to the strongpoint with water and ammunition. From 18 April to the night of 21–22 April, there were the same series of breakthrough attempts and bloody fights. Again, as at Huguette 6, the effort became too costly. This time, no breakout. Giap made a major effort at about 0100 hours on 22 April, and by 0230, the Vietminh overran Huguette 1.

The main effect of the fall of Huguette 1 and 6 was to confine even further the space available for parachute drops of men and supplies. Giap had reduced the camp (and thus the drop zone) to about two kilometers on each side. Intense Vietminh antiaircraft fire covered the entire area. In fact, French pilots who had flown in World War II claimed that the ''flak'' was heavier over Dien Bien Phu than it had been over Düsseldorf and the other targets of the Ruhr Valley. Under these conditions, many of the parachuted men and supplies fell into the hands of the Vietminh.

The fall of Huguette 1 and the shrinkage of the drop zone brought Castries, Langlais, and Bigeard together in a council of desperation. Langlais and Bigeard said no to attempting to recapture Huguette 1. The attack would have to be made by the 2d BEP, the last reserve unit in the garrison. Even if the attack were successful, there would be no reinforcements available to hold Huguette 1 against the inevitable Vietminh counterattack. Castries, always sensitive to the requirements for parachute drops of men and supplies, insisted that Huguette 1 be retaken immediately—before 1600 hours that day. Langlais left the planning of the assault to Bigeard, his ''Deputy for Counterattacks.'' Bigeard laid on the air and artillery preparation and briefed the subordinate commanders on the scheme of maneuver, but left the execution of the attack to Major Liesenfelt, the commander of the 2d BEP, the only unit in the attack.

The attack was a miserable failure. The assault companies were quickly pinned down in the open, and they took heavy casualties. The battalion commander failed to react to the situation. By the time Bigeard could regain control, all he could do was pull the battered units back to the central base. The French lost 150 men, killed and wounded, and with them their last reserve. Liesenfelt was relieved of his command.

While the main garrison at Dien Bien Phu was bleeding and shrinking, Isabelle came under increasing Vietminh pressure. To both Giap and Castries, Isabelle was always secondary to the main camp itself. To the French it was an artillery base protected by a small infantry and tank force which could furnish flanking fire to the central garrison. To Giap it was a satellite French position which would fall if and when the main camp fell. He viewed it as a position which had to be isolated to prevent reinforcement of the central garrison and whose artillery fire had to be neutralized as far as possible.

The French garrisoned Isabelle initially with the 3d Battalion of the 3d Foreign Legion Infantry Regiment, the 2d Battalion of the 1st Algerian Rifle Regiment, two 105mm howitzer batteries, and a tank platoon of three light tanks. To this force Langlais disdainfully assigned the remnants of those units which had broken and fled from combat on the central position—the T'ais from Anne Marie and the Algerians from Gabrielle. Isabelle's strength on 30 May totaled around 1,700 men.

Giap entrusted the isolation and neutralization of Isabelle to the 57th Regiment of the 304th Division, reinforced by one battalion of the 176th Regiment, 316th Division, plus an undetermined amount of artillery and heavy mortars, altogether around 3,500 troops. Until 30 March, when Giap launched Phase II of his operation, action around Isabelle had been desultory. There were probes against the position, neutralization fires against Isabelle's artillery, and an increasing number of ambushes and attacks seeking to bar any movement between the main camp and Isabelle.

On 30 March the Vietminh succeeded in isolating Isabelle when they were able to turn back the 3d Battalion, 3d Foreign Legion Regiment, as it attempted to move to the main camp to support the counterattack on Dominique. From that moment until the end of the battle of Dien Bien Phu, Isabelle was on its own. Also on 30 March the Vietminh concentrated a heavy counterbattery fire for the first time on Isabelle's artillery, from batteries which they had moved into position around the stronghold.

The period 4–24 April saw on Isabelle a replica of the fighting at the central camp. There were the same encroaching Vietminh trenches, the same French attacks to clear and destroy them, and the same heavy Communist artillery fire. Isabelle had its own problems which, although similar, were more severe than those of the central position. Isabelle, located in a river-bottom swamp, suffered more from flooding and mud, and being much smaller than the central garrison, lost much more through supplies dropped outside the position. As April ended, the supply situation on Isabelle was critical. The stronghold had exhausted its supply of food and had fired almost all its artillery ammunition.

Enemy artillery fire against Isabelle's bunkers and dug-in gun emplacements increased daily as April neared its end. The trenches of the Vietminh came ever closer, and it was obvious that the final assault on Isabelle would coincide with Giap's major attack on the central position.

As Phase II ended, the finale was about to begin.

1–7 May—Phase III

The finishing blow began on the night of 1 May 1954. By 0200 hours on the morning of 2 May, Eliane 1 and Dominique 3 had fallen, and Eliane 2 was under heavy attack. On the other side of the central camp, the Vietminh pounded Huguette 5 with an hour of intensive artillery fire and then overran it. The French garrison was being squeezed to death. The monsoon and Giap's artillery reduced the inadequate French trenches and bunkers to mud and rubble. Both sides fought in water often waist-deep. The wounded on both sides suffered cruelly from gangrene, lack of care, and from the mud and filth of the field hospitals. Whatever else it may have been, Dien Bien Phu was for both sides an epic of agony and courage.

Eliane 2, where so much of the heaviest combat had taken place throughout the battle, was to be the scene of yet another bloody fight. Early on the evening of 6 May, Giap's best unit, the 102d Regiment of the 308th Division (the Capital Regiment), attacked the pulverized strongpoint, now heavy with the stench of hundreds of decaying bodies. The attack was preceded by an intense concentration of artillery and mortar fire, and by something new—the screech of the Katyushas, the Soviet rockets. The Katyusha is not a particularly lethal weapon. It is inaccurate and depends almost purely on blast alone for effect. Its whine, however, can be unnerving to troops unused to it, and its blast can do serious damage to fortifications already weakened by rain and the constant pounding of artillery.

At about 1900 hours on 6 May, the 102d Regiment, supported by another crack regiment from the 308th, the 88th, went "over the top" toward the summit of Eliane 2. The French artillery was ready, and they hit the exposed Vietminh infantry with a "TOT" ("time on target") concentration in which the various artillery units fire at different times (depending on their distances from the target) so that the rounds all arrive on target at the same moment. The French artillery then repeated the salvo several more times. The artillery forward observer on Eliane 2 called a halt then, so he could see the effect. When the smoke and dust had cleared in the target area, the assault wave had vanished— only several hundred new bodies remained. The French had won the first round, but the fight for Eliane 2 was far from over.

Giap had one more ploy to use against Eliane 2—one borrowed

again from World War I, and even further back, from Petersburg in our own Civil War. He drove a mine shaft under Eliane 2 and loaded it with 3,000 pounds of TNT. The Vietminh touched off the TNT at 2300 hours and its explosion literally blew up Eliane 2. The 102d went in again, but incredibly, the few French left fought on heroically. Further resistance was useless, however, and by 0500 hours the Vietminh had overcome the defenders.

By mid-morning on 7 May, the situation on the main French position was hopeless. Fighting still continued on the west flank near Claudine and on the east bank of the Nam Yum River, but resistance weakened rapidly as white flags began to appear. At 1500 hours Giap ordered an all-out assault by all units toward the center of the camp. By 1730 hours, 7 May 1954, the Vietminh had taken the central camp and its defenders. On Isabelle, the garrison hung on for a few more hours, then tried unsuccessfully to break out of the trap. Their fate, however, is part of another story.

Over the following days, the French troops were rounded up and marched off to prisoner-of-war camps. The battle of Dien Bien Phu was over. For the French defenders, the Greek historian, Thucydides, had fashioned a suitable epitaph centuries earlier when he wrote, "Having done what men could, they suffered what men must." For Giap, it was, in his own words, "A great victory."[35] He had won a battle and a war.

The account of the battle of Dien Bien Phu would be incomplete without reference to three planned operations named after three birds of ill omen—VULTURE, CONDOR, and ALBATROSS. They were operations, born of despair, to save the beleaguered garrison of Dien Bien Phu from Giap and the Vietminh. Those foreboding cover-names conveyed the pessimism in which the French held the three operations. VULTURE impacted most on the United States, and its portents, its "might have beens," echo to this day.

VULTURE began with a visit to Washington on 20 March 1954 by General Ely, the French chief of staff of the armed forces. Ely came begging. He wanted additional aircraft—B-26 bombers, F8F fighters, and C-47 transports. He asked also for assurance that the United States would intervene in Indochina if Communist China came into that war. He got his airplanes, and indirectly, his assurance of United States support in the event of Chinese intervention. Just before his scheduled departure on 25 March, Adm. Arthur Radford, chairman of the United States Joint Chiefs of Staff, asked Ely to stay over one more day. On 26 March Radford proposed to Ely that 75 to 100 American B-29 bombers, based at Clark Air Force Base in the Philippines, strike Giap's troops at Dien Bien Phu on three or four successive nights. The bombers would be escorted by 170 United States Navy fighters aboard two aircraft carriers already in or near the China Sea. Radford told Ely that both governments would, of course, have to approve the plan. There appears to have been some discussion about using three atomic bombs, although reports of how seriously this was considered and by whom are even now vague and contradictory.[36]

Looking back through the corrosive divisiveness brought on by the United States' later involvement in Vietnam, Radford's proposal—extraordinary even in 1954—now seems simply unbelievable. First, there was no assurance that Operation VULTURE would be successful militarily, that is, that the bombing would punish the Vietminh so severely that Giap would be forced to lift the siege. The use of atomic bombs would pose monstrous problems. There would be not only worldwide psychological and political repercussions, but the heat, blast, and radiation effects of atomic bombs would likely strike the French defenders almost as hard as the Vietminh besiegers. The bombs would have to be dropped with pickle-barrel accuracy if they were to destroy the Vietminh attackers without devastating the French garrison as well. This kind of bombing accuracy at night would require that the bombers use SHORAN (short range navigational radar), and there was not one set in all of Indochina. Nor was there any feasible way of planting the three required sets (which would have to be manned by Americans) in the mountains around Dien Bien Phu.

But there was a greater question. Even if the desired accuracy could be attained, would the bombardment either with or without atomic bombs deal Giap's forces around Dien Bien Phu a mortal blow? With accuracy—and luck—the Vietminh infantry could be heavily hit, but Giap's artillery was dug deeply *under* the hills, and it would not sustain vital damage. Enough Vietminh antiaircraft would likely survive so as to continue to deny the French the ability to land and take off from the airstrip. Thus, under the most optimistic forecasts, the French could hope only for a stalemate at Dien Bien Phu. The French would be unable to break through the miles of enemy-infested jungles between the garrison and friendly units in Laos or the Delta, and the Vietminh would be unable to overcome the defenders. A stalemate, however, would be a French victory.

There was an even more fundamental military question—one that appalled the other American chiefs of staff. That question was—what was the United States to do if the air strikes failed to lift the siege? As a nation, would the United States shrug its shoulders and admit that its one-shot intervention effort had failed? Was the United States prepared to follow up the aerial bombardment with more military power, including ground troops? Even Admiral Radford had to admit that the United States Army and Marines might have to be used.

Gen. Matthew B. Ridgway, the United States Army chief of staff, spearheaded the opposition to VULTURE. Ridgway based his position on his solid experience in the recent American effort in Korea. His view was that air and naval power could not win in Indochina any more than they had won in Korea. He reasoned further that the people of the United States would not support the necessary ground effort to insure success. Ridgway's position was compelling, valid, and, as it turned out, eerily prophetic. Gen. Nathan Twining, the air force chief of staff, and Adm. Robert Carney, chief of naval operations, supported Ridgway's opposition to Radford's scheme. They based their opposition not only on Ridgway's fear of a land war on the Asiatic land mass, but for service-oriented reasons as well. The air force—and to a lesser degree, the navy—feared that a failure of the bombing attacks on Giap's troops at Dien Bien Phu would deal the prestige of United States air power a crushing blow in the interservice battles of that era.

As cheerless as were the military prospects of VULTURE, the diplomatic, political, and psychological potentialities were even more dismaying. Would Radford's raid bring the Chinese Communist masses into Indochina? Would Russia join the Chinese, particularly if we were forced to attack China with atomic weapons? Would, then, the United States be starting down the slippery road to World War III? What about allies, or would the United States and France have to "go it alone"? These questions dealt with the very survival of the United States, and nobody could answer them. Then there was the problem of the American people. Would the country support another Asiatic war so soon after it had gratefully untangled itself from Korea? Would public opinion sanction United States intervention to aid the French "colonialists" against the

Vietminh, the "fighters for Vietnamese independence"? Again, these were grave questions, and there were no answers.

Amazingly, with the stakes and risks as high as they were, Admiral Radford found two American supporters, or more accurately, quasi-supporters. They were John Foster Dulles, the old "Brinksman" and "hardliner" against communism, and Vice President Richard Nixon. Dulles did not flinch from Radford's concept of a B-29 operation to relieve Dien Bien Phu, but he wanted more. He proposed a long-range plan which foresaw an international organization of allies which would guarantee Southeast Asia against a Communist takeover. Vice President Nixon, too, endorsed VULTURE, but he was more "hawkish," more candid, and more realistic than even Admiral Radford. He was prepared to advocate the commitment of American ground forces if the bombing attacks failed, while Radford consistently evaded this fundamental and repugnant question.

President Eisenhower, characteristically, had seemed on occasions to support Radford's plan, and at other times to reject it. He instructed Dulles to arrange a meeting with congressional leaders which he, as president, would not attend. This meeting took place on 3 April at the White House, and it was VULTURE's "moment of truth." Those in attendance were Senators Knowland and Milliken (both Republicans), and Democratic Senators Russell, Clements, and Lyndon Baines Johnson. From the House of Representatives came Congressmen Martin, McCormack, and Priest. Dulles, Deputy Secretary of Defense Roger Keyes, and Navy Secretary Anderson represented the State and Defense Departments. Significantly, Admiral Radford was the only military man present.

Radford made a straightforward presentation stressing three points: (1) Southeast Asia and Indochina were important to the national security of the United States; (2) the French were about to collapse in Vietnam and the Communists would take the country; (3) the United States must take a decisive action *now* if it wished to avoid a much more costly commitment later. Radford then outlined in broad terms his recommended plan, Operation VULTURE.

Radford's proposal stunned the legislative leaders; one reporter described them as "bugeyed."[37] Then they began to ask questions. Would such action be outright war? Radford replied that it would. Would the Chinese intervene? Dulles said that he did not know, but that he didn't think they would. Would ground troops be needed? Radford said that he didn't know. Then Senator Clements shot in the first key question: "How many of the other Joint Chiefs of Staff agree with your plan?" None, answered Radford. "How do you account for that," he was asked. Radford replied, "I have spent more time in the Far East than any of them and I understand the situation better."[38] Surprisingly, the legislators allowed Radford to slide by the question with this arrogant (and factually untrue) answer. Lyndon Johnson then fired the next question: What allies would we have who would put sizable forces in Indochina? Had any allies been approached? Dulles replied that none had. After two hours it was obvious that the legislative leaders would not support Radford's plan, at least not without the inclusion of "serious allies." VULTURE had taken a mortal wound, but it would die hard.

This question of allies was to be the principal obstacle to Radford's plan. The British, in the persons of that doughty old warrior, Winston Churchill, and his foreign secretary, Anthony Eden, adamantly opposed United States military action in Indochina. They foresaw Chinese intervention, followed quickly by escalation, Russian intervention, and World War III. The British wanted no move which would endanger the Geneva Conference, scheduled to meet on 26 April, to set up procedures by which peace might be attained in Indochina.

Even the French—who, militarily at least, had the most to gain from Operation VULTURE—vacillated from support for the plan, to opposition to it, and then back to support again. On 4 April they informed the United States government that they welcomed the operation as long as it was massive and immediate. The American reply came the next day, 5 April. The United States could take no action unless a coalition including the British Commonwealth could be formed. Obviously, the congressional views which the legislators expressed on 3 April had stalled VULTURE. Then on 6 April the French suddenly switched and opposed Radford's plan and Dulles' scheme of a coalition to defend Southeast Asia. In their reply to the United States, the French Cabinet stated that French public opinion would no longer support the war. France wanted out of the Indochinese struggle, and the upcoming Geneva Convention looked like the quickest exit. Nothing should be done, such as launching VULTURE, which would endanger a compromise solution at Geneva. Another setback for VULTURE.

On 23 April, however, as the French situation disintegrated at Dien

Bien Phu, the French reversed their position again. In desperation, they asked Secretary Dulles to countermand the United States decision of 5 April and authorize operation VULTURE. Dulles refused, and cited several reasons: congressional approval would have to be obtained and that would take time; the United States military believed that it was now too late for VULTURE to relieve the garrison; and, besides, the fall of Dien Bien Phu did not mean that France must capitulate in Indochina.

But VULTURE still had one last gasp. The French made a final plea for the operation on 24 April. The Americans now decided to authorize the operation, if the British, even symbolically, would join the United States and France. Again, the British refused to go along, and although there were some feeble spasms in its death agony, VULTURE died.

Looking back through the mists which still shroud some aspects of VULTURE, one is impressed by the clarity of vision of Nixon, Dulles, Radford, and Ridgway. For a moment in history, these men glimpsed something of the future. The first three foresaw, dimly perhaps, that American intervention in Indochina was inevitable, and that the country ought to get in early rather than late. But that distinguished old soldier, Matt Ridgway, saw something even beyond intervention, something even more important—he saw that American ground troops would have to be committed in strength in Vietnam, and that meant a major, lengthy, and bloody war on the mainland of Asia.

While VULTURE was futilely flapping its wings between Washington, London, and Paris, CONDOR was trying to walk to the relief of Dien Bien Phu from Laos. If Operation VULTURE was an American improvisation fathered by a sudden concern about Indochina and Southeast Asia, Operation CONDOR was a French delusion born of a guilty conscience and deep despair. Giap, with his keen sense of reality, covered Operation CONDOR in a paragraph of four lines. Navarre's staff had conceived of CONDOR as early as December 1953. It went through several modifications, always downward in strength, as the hard realities of the shortage of transport aircraft bore down on the planners. Eventually, the staff planned to launch four infantry battalions plus a guerrilla force of friendly natives toward Dien Bien Phu from the line of the Nam Ou River, some forty air miles south of the camp. About half-way to the objective, this force would be augmented by an airborne battle group of three or four parachute battalions. In all, the plan foresaw that CONDOR would involve a total force of 5,000 to 6,000 men.

One can only wonder if Navarre and the other French commanders were ever serious about CONDOR. In his book, Navarre candidly sets forth the infeasibility of the eventual plan of operations. To be effective, wrote Navarre, CONDOR would have required from fifteen to twenty battalions, yet no more than seven could have been supported by the available air transport. This small force could not have relieved Dien Bien Phu, continues Navarre, and the most that could have been hoped for was that Giap would be distracted from his attacks on the camp.[39]

When it became apparent on 5 April that the United States would not launch Operation VULTURE, Navarre decided to go ahead with CONDOR. But the lack of air transport blocked the operation. The desperate supply need of Dien Bien Phu ate up every available transport aircraft, and once again Navarre had to postpone the operation. Finally, Navarre decided to send only the infantry and guerrilla elements toward Dien Bien Phu. The paratroop battalions had been fed into Dien Bien Phu as reinforcements, and the availability of air transport to support CONDOR had gotten even scarcer. This infantry and guerrilla force made some progress in their move to the north, but the terrain, the jungle, and the humid heat slowed progress and took casualties. Around 2 May, progress to the north stopped some eighteen miles south of Dien Bien Phu. The force then withdrew to the south and CONDOR, like VULTURE, died.

Of all of the three planned operations, ALBATROSS was the most forlorn, the most unrealistic. ALBATROSS envisioned a French break-out from Dien Bien Phu in three columns—one to the southwest, one to the south, and one to the southeast. Navarre issued planning instructions to Cogny's headquarters on 3 May. The concept met instant and forceful objections from Cogny and his staff. Cogny stated that the French could not get through the ring of Vietminh attackers, and if by some miracle they did escape, they would be hunted down and destroyed in the jungle. Nevertheless, on 4 May Cogny's headquarters passed the directive to Castries, giving him complete authority to choose the time of implementation, if any. Castries thought the plan so demoralizing that he, Langlais, and Bigeard kept it to themselves. Bigeard called it Operation *PERCÉE DE SANG*—Operation Bloodletting.[40] The leaders at Dien Bien Phu knew that the men were too exhausted to survive an assault on the Vietminh encirclement and the march through the jungle which would follow. By the time Castries decided to implement the plan, the Vietminh had overrun the main camp.

On Isabelle, things went somewhat differently. On the night of 7 May the garrison of the southern strongpoint made an attempt to break out to the south. The main body never got out of the valley. However, about seventy men did eventually escape to join the French forces in Laos.

The battle of Dien Bien Phu had ended. The French lost an empire and the Communists gained one. The world had a victorious general and a new military hero—Vo Nguyen Giap.

Notes—Chapter 10

1. Navarre, *Agonie*, p. 128; Fall, *Hell*, Appendix D, p. 486.
2. Navarre, *Agonie*, p. 213; JCS *Study*, p. 4; Fall, *Hell*, Appendix A, pp. 480–481.
3. Fall, *Hell*, p. 453.
4. JCS, *Study*, Annex B., p. 5.
5. Navarre, *Agonie*, pp. 218–219.
6. Fall, *Hell*, p. 89.
7. O'Neill, *Giap*, p. 145.
8. Fall, *Street*, pp. 318–319.
9. MACV, *Study*, p. 5.
10. Roy, *Battle*, pp. 151–152.
11. Navarre, *Agonie*, p. 251.
12. Roy, *Battle*, p. 171.
13. Fall, *Hell*, p. 148.
14. Giap, *Dien Bien Phu*, p. 111.
15. Fall, *Hell*, p. 150.
16. Navarre, *Agonie*, p. 222.
17. Giap, *Dien Bien Phu*, p. 113.
18. Roy, *Battle*, p. 189.
19. Fall, *Hell*, p. 167.
20. Navarre, *Agonie*, p. 205.
21. Fall, *Hell*, p. 117.
22. Roy, *Battle*, p. 195.
23. Fall, *Hell*, pp. 185 and 179.
24. Ibid., p. 186.
25. Roy, *Battle*, p. 206.
26. Fall, *Hell*, p. 204.
27. Roy, *Battle*, p. 207.
28. Ibid., p. 215.
29. Fall, *Hell*, pp. 205–206.
30. Roy, *Battle*, p. 210.
31. Giap, *Dien Bien Phu*, pp. 102–121.
32. Ibid.
33. Ibid., p. 130.
34. Ibid., pp. 131–132.
35. Ibid., p. 136.
36. Roy, *Battle*, pp. 203, 213, 225; Fall, *Hell*, p. 299; Devillers and Lacouture, *End of a War*, pp. 71–99; Richard Nixon, *RN: The Memoirs of Richard Nixon* (New York: Grosset & Dunlap, 1978), p. 150.

37. Fletcher Knebel, "We Nearly Went to War Three Times Last Year," *Look*, 8 February 1955.
38. Chalmers Roberts, "The Day We Didn't Go to War," *The Reporter*, 14 September 1954.
39. Navarre, *Agonie*, p. 247.
40. Fall, *Hell*, p. 399.

11 Dien Bien Phu

A Critique

In their books on the battle of Dien Bien Phu, both Giap and Navarre listed their reasons for Giap's victory and Navarre's defeat. They agreed that the sudden and massive increase in Chinese aid following the suspension of the Korean War fueled Giap's victory. Giap listed two additional basic factors in his success: correct strategy and high Vietminh morale.[1] While this is an oversimplified explanation for a complex success, Giap accurately put his finger on three fundamental factors which brought him victory.

Navarre offers more complicated reasons for his defeat than Giap does for his victory, but then the loser always makes the lengthier explanations. Navarre starts his discussion of the reasons for his defeat by listing the minor ones. This catalogue of ''minor'' causes includes: (1) the separation of the northern outposts and Isabelle from the central garrison; (2) the failure to replace the T'ai battalions; (3) the compartmentation of the central camp which hindered counterattacks; (4) the fragility of the fortifications; (5) the questionable employment of reserves; (6) the failure of counterbattery operations against Giap's artillery; (7) the lack of energy by Cogny; and (8) the poor air-ground coordination.

But, Navarre continues, these were not the real reasons for the fall of Dien Bien Phu. As the *causes profondes* (his words), Navarre put the sudden increase of Chinese aid as the *second* fundamental reason for his defeat. The first was the basic inadequacy of French means, both on the ground and in the air.[2]

As another fundamental reason for his defeat, he states that his intelligence, that is, that produced by his staff within Indochina, was good, however, the intelligence that came from "other organizations" (presumably from the French National Intelligence Agencies) gave him little information regarding Chinese assistance and, above all, the intentions of Giap and the Vietminh high command. He contrasts the inadequacy of his intelligence about the Chinese and Vietminh with the "leaks" from the French government and press which, Navarre contends, kept Giap informed of French plans and operations.

The last "fundamental" reason Navarre gives for his defeat is the decision of the French government to go to the Geneva Conference to find an end to the war. He maintains that this decision, known immediately by Ho and Giap, emboldened Giap to press home his attack at Dien Bien Phu since he (Giap) realized that there would be "no tomorrow" after the battle. This reason has some, but not much, validity. Both sides knew from the start of the Dien Bien Phu operation that there was a strong probability of negotiations. It was a factor each had to consider, and Giap made a sounder analysis of it than did Navarre.

As should be expected, none of Navarre's *causes profondes* can be attributed to his own lack of generalship. Slyly, and by implication, he passes the cold ashes of his defeat to the French government in Paris. It was the French government, implies Navarre, which denied him adequate means to defend Indochina, and whose national intelligence agencies failed to tell him about the decisive increase in Chinese aid and about Giap's plans. It was the French government whose "leaks" revealed his own plans, and finally, by deciding to seek peace at Geneva, undermined his strategy.

Navarre listed some of the reasons for his defeat, but he failed to mention others. For example, Navarre does not list as a cause of his defeat the fact that he failed to relieve Cogny and Castries from their commands when each clearly revealed himself to be inadequate to his responsibilities—Castries by his abdication of his command authority and Cogny by his irresponsible and undisciplined behavior. Decisive, resolute leaders in Dien Bien Phu and Hanoi might have made the difference.

Navarre has glazed over some of the reasons he does list. As an example, he mentions the poor quality of some of the French units at Dien Bien Phu. What he does not relate is that near the end of the fight, 3,000 to 4,000 men out of the 10,000-man garrison had become "internal deserters," the so-called "rats of the Nam Yum" who did not fight, but who did devour the precious nonmilitary supplies, particularly food. Would not another 4,000 brave men have made the difference at Dien Bien Phu? Bigeard, who of all the French leaders comes through as the man with the surest mental grasp of the battle, thinks so. Years later, he said, "If you had given me 10,000 SS troops, we'd have held out."[3] Probably—but this is speculative, too.

What is not speculative is that one of the prime causes of Navarre's defeat is that he lost the "battle of logistics." He could not stifle Giap's supply system, while Giap eventually was able to throttle Navarre's. Most besieged garrisons have been forced to surrender when they ran out of supplies. American history offers Vicksburg and Corregidor as examples, and the French ran out of supplies at Dien Bien Phu. But the loss of the "battle of logistics," while key to Navarre's defeat, is in itself only a symptom of the two fundamental errors which brought defeat to France and to Navarre.

The first of these fundamental causes of defeat Navarre himself hints at—although he misses the real reasons—when he complains in his book about "inadequacy of means." He implies that this "inadequacy" was really beyond his control, beyond his making. This is an evasion. It was not "inadequacy of means"; *it was the failure to adjust his ends (his objectives) to his means*. It was Navarre who by his decision to defend northern Laos drastically expanded his military mission. This expansion of his task stretched his means beyond adequacy, and in so doing he violated the first law of generalship. The renowned British writer B. H. Liddell Hart, probably the foremost of modern theorists on strategy, puts as the first principle of that art: "Adjust your end to your means. The beginning of military wisdom," he writes, "is a sense of what is possible."[4]

Navarre's most basic error was not in overreaching, however. It was his failure to foresee Giap's sudden and massive increase in combat effectiveness which made all of Navarre's calculations of ends and means erroneous. The real fault—and one which he tacitly admits several times in his book—*was his gross underestimation of the Vietminh and Giap*. He notes that French commanders throughout the war had committed this fundamental and deadly error. Navarre correctly calls it "the first of the lessons in the military domain."[5]

Giap himself agreed with Navarre's analysis that underestimation of the Vietminh constituted Navarre's original and greatest error. Giap wrote that Navarre's ". . . . greatest mistake was that with the conception of the bourgeois strategist he could not visualize the immense possibilities of a peoples' army and the entire people who were fighting for independence and peace; it was still more difficult for him to realize the evolution and remarkable progress of our people and our army . . ."[6]

If the first great cause of Navarre's defeat was his underestimation of his enemy, then the second was even more galling to him: Giap simply outgeneraled him.

In retrospect, the battle of Dien Bien Phu and Indochina War I was won around a conference table made from rough boards somewhere in the Viet Bac in the summer of 1953. Around this table sat Ho, Giap, Pham Van Dong, and Truong Chinh. The Vietminh high command arrived at one central conclusion—the war against the French must be won in 1953–1954, for this favorable "correlation of forces" existing in mid-1953 was precarious and time-sensitive. If the French could carry out their plans, this auspicious advantage might not exist in 1954, and almost certainly would not exist in 1955.

Giap went into a lucid analysis of the problem of how to win the war in 1954. First, the planned Vietminh operations had to be confined to northern North Vietnam and to northern Laos, because that was where the bulk of their strength (the assault divisions) was located. Next, the committee considered attacking the French in the Tonkin Delta. But shades of de Lattre and 1951 rose to haunt the Communist high command, and they decided not to attack the French in their stronghold—an obvious and wise decision. As a result of this analysis, Giap decided to place Navarre on the horns of a strategic dilemma. They would threaten northwestern Vietnam and northern Laos and see how Navarre reacted. If he failed to defend these areas, Giap had a cheap, but potent, political and psychological victory. While this victory might not have driven France out of the war—although Navarre and others believed it would—the move would have drastically changed the entire situation in Indochina.

If, on the other hand, Navarre decided to defend northern Laos or northwestern Vietnam, he could do so only at a significant disadvantage to himself due to the harsh terrain, the distances from his center of power (Hanoi), and his lack of strategic mobility. If Navarre elected to attempt to thwart Giap's conquest by attacking his bases in the Viet Bac, Giap still had the advantage of strength and of fighting in difficult terrain which he knew well. To carry out this concept, Giap drew up a simple plan. He would start one division, the 316th, towards Lai Chau and northern Laos. The rest of his divisions would remain in reserve in the Viet Bac, awaiting Navarre's reaction. Giap's strategic concept and operational plan exemplified all those virtues which are extolled in the military academy textbooks and in the staff colleges. It seized the initiative, placing Navarre, regardless of what he did, in a reactive role. It provided for concentration of effort. The plan was flexible; it could be easily adjusted to counter any move by Navarre and to take advantage of any mistakes he made. *It exploited Giap's strengths and Navarre's weaknesses.* In some dim Valhalla, the great Napoleon himself must have saluted his Vietnamese admirer and pupil.

Giap's strategic performance in Phase II (after the French parachute assault of 20 November 1953) rivaled in excellence that of the summer and early fall (Phase I). After the French landing at Dien Bien Phu, Giap quickly massed his forces there. He feared a French move which did not occur to Navarre and Cogny until much later—a French withdrawal from Dien Bien Phu by air. While such a withdrawal would have denied Giap his prey, it would not have upset his strategy. But Giap took no chances. His speedy movements of four divisions to Dien Bien Phu—itself a masterpiece of planning and execution—penned up the French defenders in the desolate valley.

The principal threat Giap foresaw was that Navarre might attack the Vietminh bases and LOC's in the Viet Bac. But there were other problems, although of lesser importance, which Giap had to consider. How could he limit the French concentration at Dien Bien Phu? How could he prevent the French build-up of supplies at Dien Bien Phu during the months before he could attack there? How could he negate Navarre's Operation ATLANTE?

All of these problems could be solved wholly or partially by the Phase II (post 20 November) strategy Giap devised. That strategy called for the Vietminh to launch a series of attacks at wide-flung, vulnerable areas of either political or military importance to the French. These attacks did not have to take the threatened objectives to succeed. All they had to do was to so imperil the objective that Navarre would have to respond by reinforcing the threatened areas. This strategy of diversionary attacks would force Navarre to dissipate any striking force which might be built up in the Tonkin Delta, a force which might be used to attack Giap's bases or LOC's or to reinforce Dien Bien Phu beyond the size which Giap could defeat. Furthermore, the attacks strained Navarre's air transport capability by forcing him to use these scarce assets to move men and supplies to the threatened areas. While the aircraft were expended to fight the fires Giap lit all over Indochina, they could not be used to stockpile supplies at Dien Bien Phu. And since the strength of the French garrison there depended directly on the quantity of supplies which could be delivered, in a second way the attacks held down the size of the defending force to manageable proportions—for Giap, that is.

The problem of neutralizing Operation ATLANTE called for special solutions. It could be only partially solved by Giap's strategy of diversionary attacks throughout Indochina. These attacks would not be enough to prevent Navarre concentrating enough force along the Annam coast (MR V) to launch a large-scale offensive. But as Giap studied the problem, he saw that the threat was greater in appearance than in reality, a "paper tiger" to use Mao's expression. The significant factor in this equation was that there was nothing of vital importance to the Vietminh in MR V, nothing which *had* to be defended. This key dictated Giap's counterplan, which was to withdraw before the French offensive, harassing and delaying it, and counterattacking in Kontum and the Central Highlands. This strategy succeeded.

Operation ATLANTE spotlights Giap's sure grasp of the fundamentals of strategy, contrasted with Navarre's tenuous and superficial understanding of these same principles. For a diversionary attack to be successful— and ATLANTE was in reality diversionary—it had to threaten an objective or objectives vital to the enemy. The enemy *must* defend the objectives against the attack. Giap's wide-flung attacks did just that. The French had to react to them. Navarre's Operation ATLANTE did not. In fact, Navarre aided Giap's scheme, for ATLANTE diverted French troops and French transport aircraft, without threatening Giap and the Vietminh in any critical way. In effect, it forced further French dispersion and further dissipation of French resources, which were the twin objectives Giap sought. Giap condemned ATLANTE as ". . . a strategic mistake . . . he (Navarre) dispersed his main force, a thing to be avoided . . ."[7] It is not often in warfare that a general's mistakes contribute so directly to the success of his opponent's strategy. Had Giap been dictating Navarre's moves, he could not have made a better selection for the Vietminh cause than Operation ATLANTE.

Some historians have condemned Giap's tactics at Dien Bien Phu largely because of the heavy Vietminh casualties he took there. But Giap found himself confronted at Dien Bien Phu with a tactical problem which imposed tremendous restrictions. He had to reduce a besieged position, fortified on all sides. Such a position can be taken in only two ways—starve it out or assault it head on. Giap had not the time to starve the garrison into surrender. The upcoming Geneva Conference had denied him this alternative. Under these circumstances, the criticisms of Giap's tactics are superficial. On the contrary, the longer one examines Giap's tactics at Dien Bien Phu, the better they appear.

First, in a situation which permitted little use of stratagems or imaginative ploys, Giap achieved surprise by the employment and volume of fire of his antiaircraft and artillery. Navarre, himself, paid tribute to the devastating effect of the dug-in deployment and unexpectedly intense firepower of these two arms. Giap's second tactical triumph was his use of the World War I siege tactics and techniques. The laborious digging of miles of trenches permitted his men to get within assaulting range of the French without the prohibitive casualties which attacks across open ground would have brought. His subterranean mining operation against Eliane showed imagination, and with better timing and luck, might have been decisive.

Giap merits praise for the sequence in which he chose to eliminate the northern three French strongpoints. He took out Beatrice first, because Gabrielle was stronger and easier to reach by counterattack from the main position. Then he struck at Gabrielle, as the loss of Beatrice exposed it. Then he moved in on Anne Marie, which the demoralized T'ai's abandoned without a fight after having seen at close hand the fall of the two stronger outposts.

Giap deserves great credit, too, for his action in taking every measure to insure that these first two attacks against Beatrice and Gabrielle brought success. To insure victory, he sent in an overwhelming infantry assault force supported by an intense artillery and mortar preparation. Had his troops been repulsed on Beatrice and Gabrielle, the story of Dien Bien Phu would probably have been different. Combat morale is a delicate plant, attacked constantly by the blights and searing winds of mismanagement and mischance, but nurtured only by the deeply held faith of the troops that they are superior to their foe. High combat morale is hard to maintain at best, but, once a unit is whipped, it takes months to recover its battlefield élan.

Giap's victory at Dien Bien Phu and his defeat of the French in Indochina provide a point in time to evaluate his overall performance as a general in Indochina War I. As a military strategist and tactician, he started as an amateur and finished as a professional. He earned even higher marks as a logistician. His ability to supply his forces around Dien Bien Phu was an achievement of first rank. It was in the field of organization, administration, and motivation that he excelled. In this area he was a genius.

The death-knell for Dien Bien Phu and for the French in Indochina continues to toll through the years. On 27 April 1977, there was a newspaper story and photograph of an ironic meeting in Paris. Bigeard, the French hero of Dien Bien Phu, and Pham Van Dong, the North Vietnamese foreign minister, were invited to a luncheon by the president of France, Valery Giscard d'Estaing. The photograph shows a bald, pudgy Bigeard—now a four-star general and a recent deputy minister of defense—shaking hands with Dong, the latter looking somewhat apprehensive. Bigeard said that the President's invitation "makes me think of all the dead." Later, he stated, "For me, Dien Bien Phu is yesterday. It's as if I were still there." In spirit he is there, and always will be, along with the shades of the other brave men of both sides who fought at Dien Bien Phu.

Notes—Chapter 11

1. Giap, *Dien Bien Phu,* p. 146–147.
2. Navarre, *Agonie,* p. 252.
3. Fall, *Hell,* p. 453.
4. Basil. H. Liddell Hart, *Strategy,* 2d ed. (New York: Frederick A. Praeger, 1967), p. 348.
5. Navarre, *Agonie,* p. 324.
6. Giap, *Dien Bien Phu,* p. 86.
7. Ibid., p. 160.

12 Interbella

The pundits of academia hold that in war there are no victors, only losers. This may be true in some abstruse philosophical sense, but soldiers and statesmen know better. They know that there are always winners and losers, and in Indochina War I the Vietminh won and the French lost. They lost not only a war, but their Asiatic empire with it.

The Vietminh celebrated their victory in Hanoi beginning on 9 October 1954. The French hauled down the Tricolor, and their troops slipped silently out of town. Then in triumph the now-famous Vietminh 308th Division marched in. A huge victory parade was held the next day in a city turned blood-red with the flags and banners of the Vietminh. Neither Giap nor any of the other Communist leaders were there to review the troops or to exhort the population in one of their patented three-hour speeches. Neither Giap nor the others have ever explained this strange absence. Ho must have ordered them to stay away, and how it must have galled the egocentric Giap, a Napoleon deprived of his *Arc de Triomphe*. But Giap was not far behind his victorious troops. He returned to Hanoi on 12 October, late for the victory celebration, but fittingly, ahead of all the other leaders. Giap was the national hero, the conqueror of the French, the triumphant general.

Giap learned, however, as have many other victorious generals before him, that when the bullets and shells stop flying, the problems do not go away, they only change. Giap's new problems came at him quickly and in a massive array. Some were purely military, some partly military, and some wholly political. The first problem facing Ho, Giap, and the other Vietminh leaders was the job of rebuilding North Vietnam. While

283

the meager industrial base in the north had largely escaped the destruction of the fighting, the French and pro-French Vietnamese had dismantled almost all of the industrial machinery there and taken it to South Vietnam. The irrigation system for agriculture, at best marginal, had been badly damaged by the fighting and urgently needed repair. Roads and railroads, particularly around Hanoi and in the Viet Bac area, were almost totally demolished.

The entire nation, under its grim Communist leadership, set about rebuilding North Vietnam as an industrialized, productive, and self-sufficient nation. The army led in this reconstruction effort, building roads, repairing dikes, restoring villages, and harvesting crops. The troops fought floods and helped the peasants in other emergencies. In keeping with the political *dau tranh* of Ho and Giap, the army incessantly propagandized the peasants toward support of the Communist regime and its Marxist ideology.

In 1958 the North Vietnamese leadership extended even further the army's role in the civilian economy. Some Main Force units established and operated collective farms, so that by 1959 there were some forty of these farms in various stages of development. Some units built and worked the factories, while others tunneled and dug coal in the mines. By 1959, Giap's forbearance with this nonmilitary use of the North Vietnamese Army (NVA) exploded. While he publicly supported the policy of using soldiers as laborers, privately he violently disagreed with Le Duan and Truong Chinh (the policy's proponents), maintaining that the first duty of the army in peacetime is military training. Apparently Giap lost this battle, for shortly thereafter his rival, Nguyen Chi Thanh, an ally and protégé of Le Duan, was given four-star rank equal to Giap's. Giap's fight with Thanh was now joined.

But in the fifties other purely military problems claimed Giap's attention. He realized that the struggle for control of Indochina had not ended, and that he must prepare for the future war he believed to be inevitable. Giap recognized that his Main Force units, while victorious over the French, were laced with deficiencies which would prove fatal against a more powerful foe, such as the Americans. First, his officer corps had no knowledge of the broader aspects of the military profession. All had risen from the ranks during combat, and due to the press of war, had been taught only what each needed to know to carry out the responsibilities of his particular rank and position. As a result, combat experience had deeply schooled each officer in the narrow niche of his job, but this harsh teacher had left each one almost totally ignorant of the broader aspects of the military art and science.

Officers' schools provided the obvious solution to this problem. Permanent schools for infantry, artillery, and staff officers were established in and around Hanoi. The instructors of these advanced schools, as they had been in the formative years in the Viet Bac, were Chinese Communist officers. Based on his experiences against the French, Giap insisted that all courses include the employment of air power and the defenses against it. Looking ahead, Giap began to send North Vietnamese pilots to be trained in China. Nor was the sea arm neglected. A naval training school was established at Dong Hai. This small school specialized in coastal defense, since the North Vietnamese navy possessed no ships larger than patrol craft. It was these patrol boats, incidentally, which fired on a United States destroyer in 1964 and launched the United States openly into Indochina War II.

While the new schools helped to overcome the professional deficiencies of the officers, there remained a unit training problem. To overcome what Giap considered a key deficiency, he held small maneuvers and combined-arms exercises. Since most of the North Vietnamese units were infantry, he set up numerous rifle ranges and insisted on a high standard of marksmanship. Artillery ranges were established, and artillery officers were trained in indirect fire methods and in the massing of artillery fire.

In the late fifties, Giap also had to face the massive logistic problem resulting from the mismatched assortment of materiel with which his Main Force units were equipped—a mélange of French, Chinese, Japanese, and American equipment. Giap began to standardize materiel based largely on Chinese equipment. Some Soviet weapons came into the Main Force inventory, such as the P-76 tank (an outdated, very light-weight, amphibious vehicle) and some artillery pieces of 122mm caliber. Giap wrestled, largely unsuccessfully, with the haphazard and cumbersome logistic system which had supported—and handicapped—his Main Forces in the French war. He built permanent depots; he used army troops to reconstruct roads and railroads; he rebuilt the harbors at Haiphong and Hon Gay in the north and Ben Thuy, near Vinh; and he improved the effectiveness of the radio and telegraph system. To support the combat troops, he built up his inventories of trucks, drivers, and maintenance personnel. While progress was made in solving the battlefield support problem, this deficiency would control and curtail North Vietnamese combat operations for years to come.

During the mid-fifties, Giap was forced to do battle with that old hobgoblin which haunts all armies—administration. In the Western armies there is always too much administration, as "Operation Paperchase" in the United States Army stridently attested. But in Giap's army the problem was reversed—there was too little administration. The Main Forces were run with the loose informality of a guerrilla force, and rank, promotion, and salaries had never been formalized. The Main Forces had to be issued uniforms and insignia. These were purchased, but many of the old veterans of the war against the French refused to wear them, even on duty. It seems that in the North Vietnamese Army, as in all others, old ways and old soldiers give ground grudgingly.

Finally, to Giap's military problems were added those of the North Vietnamese Land Reform Program, with its violence, imprisonments, and deaths, which forced Giap to face a soldier's most odious task, shooting his own countrymen. The revolt of the North Vietnamese peasants against the horrors of Trong Chinh's Land Reform Program erupted into violence on 2 November 1956 in Nghe An province. This open rebellion, totally unexpected by Ho and his comrades, shocked the North Vietnamese leadership. Not only had North Vietnamese peasants revolted, but it had happened in Nghe An, Ho's birthplace and for years a bastion of communism. The insurrection spread rapidly throughout the province. Local militia could not contain the uprising, and Ho ordered Giap to suppress it. Giap sent in his nearest Main Force division, the 325th, stationed nearby in Vinh. Giap must have hesitated before committing this particular division. It was composed of soldiers from Nghe An and surrounding provinces, and most of the men were peasants themselves. Perhaps the 325th would go over to the rebel side. But as was the case during the Indochina wars, logistic necessity overrode strategical, tactical, and psychological considerations. The 325th Division could march by foot to the troubled areas, and they could get there quickly. The other Main Force divisions were garrisoned many miles, and many days, away. The rebellion had to be smashed speedily before it could spread. Thus, the 325th once more heard the call of the trumpet, although this time there were some plaintive notes. Regardless of their inner thoughts or sympathies, the 325th Division promptly and bloodily snuffed out the spreading flames of the rebellion. No exact casualty figures are available. Some authorities state that 1,000 peasants were killed and 6,000 deported.[1] The *Pentagon Papers* claims that thousands of lives were lost.[2]

The greatest problem facing not only Giap, but the entire North Vietnamese Politburo, was the question of basic priorities. Was first priority to be given to the economic and social development of North Vietnam, or was it to be given to the "liberation" of South Vietnam and its reunification with the North? But this question was only the outer layer of the real controversy. The fundamental problem underlying all these arguments goes back to the dual nature of the basic North Vietnamese strategy for the conduct of the war, military *dau tranh* and political *dau tranh*. While these arms work in unison, the fundamental question of revolutionary war is: how much effort should be allotted to political *dau tranh* and how much to military *dau tranh?* This question leads to another one: what stage is the revolution in? If it is in the first stage, then revolutionary war theory dictates that the emphasis should be on political *dau tranh* to build the revolutionary base among the masses. If the war is in a later phase, then the priority should be shifted to the military *dau tranh*. Other strategists contend that theory is not always an infallible guide. They hold that sometimes the actual situation dictates that the military *dau tranh* can bring about the revolution, even though the political groundwork is incomplete. This was the real essence of the debate between the "North Vietnam firsters" and the "South Vietnam firsters."

The "North Vietnam firsters," Truong Chinh and Giap (with luke-warm support from Pham Van Dong), saw a significant difference in the stages of the revolution in the North and South. The North had been liberated. The important task was to "build socialism" in the North, principally by developing the economy of that area. The South was faced by the need for a "national, democratic people's" revolution, a revolution in its early stages which must be carried out by native southern-ers. The "South Vietnam firsters," led by Le Duan, Nguyen Chi Thanh, and Le Duc Tho, believed that Truong Chinh's concepts revolving around the different stages of the revolutions in the North and South were largely theoretical and of little practical value. To Le Duan and his supporters, the key task confronting North Vietnam was to unify all of Vietnam under communism. If the economic growth of the North had to be stunted, so be it.

The two varying concepts of North Vietnam's top priority carried over into strategy. The "North Vietnam firsters" favored a protracted struggle in South Vietnam waged by the people of South Vietnam, in which political action and guerrilla warfare would be the dominant tactics. Le Duan and his cohorts wanted to speed the course of the revolution in the South by the use of conventional force—at first using South Vietnamese forces, and later, if necessary, armed units from North Vietnam.

The split in the North Vietnamese leadership reflected not only the leaders' views, but their early lives and duties. Truong Chinh, Giap, and Dong had been born in North Vietnam, and during the war against the French their duties had kept them in North Vietnam. On the other hand, the "South Vietnam firsters" had been born in the South and during Indochina War I had served there. Le Duan had conducted the Vietminh effort in South Vietnam and remained there after the war until about 1957. Le Duc Tho had been Duan's deputy during the war, while Nguyen Chi Thanh had served as Party secretary in Thua Thien province in the northern part of South Vietnam.

This fundamental dispute over priorities and strategy breaks down into several clearly delineated periods. The first of these runs from the signing of the Geneva Agreement in 1954 until January 1959. During this period the views of Truong Chinh and Giap held sway. Ho decided in 1954—with some prodding from Moscow—to emphasize political *dau tranh* in South Vietnam while he strove to build the economy of the North. Ho's rationale for this policy is obvious. First, the government of South Vietnam's Ngo Dinh Diem appeared doomed. Diem had inherited chaos—a mishmash of conflicting political cliques and religious factions, an ineffective and almost nonexistent governmental apparatus, and a farce for a police force and an army. Ho probably saw Diem's government collapsing from its own debility, with the Communists taking over the ruins. There was another factor supporting Ho's 1954 decision to use "peaceful political action." Since many of the former Vietminh soldiers in South Vietnam had been repatriated to the North by the terms of the Geneva Agreement, the military capability of the Communist Party was too weak in the mid-fifties to sustain an armed struggle in the South. At any rate, in 1954 the word went out to the southern Communists to agitate for "personal rights, freedom, and negotiations concerning the general elections in accordance with the stipulations of the Geneva agreements."[3]

While there was some rumbling from the "Southerners," this policy of "peaceful political action" held firm until mid-1957. Then, as the elections mandated by the Geneva Accords failed to materialize, and as Diem began to hunt down the Communist insurgents in the South, a groundswell of criticism from the "South Vietnam firsters" began to rise, with Le Duan leading the chorus. He began to hint that the political struggle "would sometimes have to be backed up with military action."[4] The words of Le Duan gained additional force as Diem moved ever more effectively against the Communists in South Vietnam. In 1957 and 1958, the Communists admitted that Diem had "truly and efficiently destroyed our party."[5] Party documents captured years later reveal that an increasing number of Communists in South Vietnam began to agitate for armed struggle to preserve the movement. In 1957, Ho Chi Minh began to lean towards Le Duan's view of the necessity for an armed struggle in the South. He recalled Le Duan from South Vietnam to Hanoi and shortly thereafter Le Duan replaced Truong Chinh as the second-ranking Politburo member, behind Ho himself.

In 1958 the Politburo began to tilt toward Le Duan and his "South Vietnam firsters." The year was spent in preparing the leadership and the public for a shift of policy. The preparatory work done, the Central Committee decided in January 1959 to launch an armed insurrection in South Vietnam. In May 1959 the Fifteenth Plenum of the Central Committee formally adopted the policy and sent orders to that effect to South Vietnam. Documents captured in 1966 plus recent statements of senior NVA officials indicate that the Communists date North Vietnamese intervention from this date. In July the vanguard of some 4,000 trained regroupees began infiltrating into South Vietnam.[6] In September 1960, North Vietnam publicly announced its support of the insurgency in the South.

Ho Chi Minh's decision to move from "peaceful, political action" to "armed revolution," from emphasis on political *dau tranh* to military *dau tranh,* ignited an argument in the Politburo about how to carry out the new policy. This time the debate centered on whether the armed revolt in South Vietnam should follow the August 1945 model or the concepts and policies which had defeated the French in 1954. The combatants and lineups remained unchanged. Truong Chinh, Giap and the "Northerners" argued that the French experience offered the correct model. This was to be expected since they could point to this scenario, with its emphasis on protracted struggle, political over military action, and guerrilla warfare, as having been successful. Also, the "French model" meant less North Vietnamese involvement. Le Duan and his southern cohorts, on the other hand, stressed the August 1945 model as the correct approach. This concept stressed large-scale military action and a quick solution to the South Vietnamese problem, even if NVA troops had to be used. This concept, with its dangers of United States intervention and the resulting threat to North Vietnam, dismayed the "North Vietnam firsters."

While the debate seems to have been evenly contested, the actions taken by the North Vietnamese in 1959 clearly indicated that Le Duan and his group had won. That year the 559th Transportation Group was formed from NVA units to operate the logistic system by which North Vietnam would support operations in South Vietnam by way of the Laotian Panhandle. In 1959, the South Vietnamese Communists set up a center to train cadres from the men who had regrouped to North Vietnam in 1954, and in 1959 some 4,500 of these men began infiltrating to form the nucleus of the Viet Cong battalions and regiments.

To Giap, Ho's decisions of 1959 and events of the next two years constituted a serious defeat. Although Giap held the positions of minister of defense and commander of the North Vietnamese Army, Ho relieved Giap of control of military operations in the South. Ho entrusted these to a secretariat composed of "Southerners" Le Duan, Nguyen Chi Thanh, and Le Duc Tho. And worse was to follow. In 1959 Giap's old rival, Thanh, now a senior general (Giap's own four-star rank) was in effect given command in the South. Then, in 1960, both Giap and Truong Chinh were demoted in standing by the Third Party Congress. Chinh was replaced as the number two man in the Politburo by Le Duan, while Giap dropped from the fourth slot to the sixth. Giap, defeated and bruised, retired from the Hanoi scene for "medical treatment." Le Duan and his supporters were now firmly in command.

With Ho's decision in 1959 to go to an "armed revolt" supported by North Vietnam, war between the two Vietnams now began in earnest, and in 1960, the Viet Cong and the North Vietnamese were winning it. The Viet Cong held vast areas of the Mekong Delta, the Central Highlands, and the Coastal Plains. In November 1960, a coup almost overthrew Diem. The Viet Cong launched battalion- and regimental-size assaults against ARVN (Army of the Republic of Vietnam) outposts and forts, and in 1961, the situation for Diem worsened as Viet Cong attacks increased in size and effectiveness. By early 1961, Diem's situation had become critical.

The deteriorating situation in South Vietnam in January 1961 fell heavily on the new occupant of the White House, John F. Kennedy. Vietnam, however, was not the only thunderhead blowing toward the president. Other storms crowded the horizon, and these would make Vietnam the ultimate stake in a superpower poker game. The game started just before Kennedy's inauguration, when on 6 January 1961, Nikita Khrushchev proclaimed that "wars of national liberations" were just, and that world communism would support them. Shortly thereafter, Hanoi recognized the National Liberation Front (NLF), a Communist facade in South Vietnam. In April 1961, the fiasco at the Bay of Pigs cost Kennedy a sizable number of his political poker chips. In June 1961, Khrushchev tried a brutal bluff on Kennedy in Vienna, where he belligerently threatened the young president with a blockade of Berlin. To call Khrushchev's bluff, and to show his own resolution, Kennedy looked around for a spot on the globe on which to place his stack of political chips. That spot appeared to be Vietnam. Even in 1961, however, the president recognized Vietnam as a political and diplomatic mine field—intricate, tricky, and dangerous. It posed problems not only with the Communist bloc, but domestically as well, particularly for a president from the Democratic party.

From the beginning of American involvement, its policy towards Vietnam was warped by two powerful myths. Ever since 1949, when the Republicans had branded Harry Truman as "the man who lost China," Democratic hearts quailed at the thought of another defeat in Asia under a Democratic president. Of course, Truman had *not* "lost China." The United States could not lose what it never possessed, and there was no practical action that Truman could have taken in 1949 to prevent China from falling to the Communists. These facts, however, did not reduce the political mileage the Republicans made out of China's "loss" and would make again out of another Asiatic defeat. A Democratic president could not see Vietnam fall to communism without inviting a devastating political attack at home.

The second myth working on the Vietnam problem was the old and oft-repeated warning against fighting a large-scale ground war on the land mass of Asia. People as diverse in outlook and ideology as Dean Acheson and Douglas MacArthur sententiously proclaimed this strategic admonition, although both had led a war (Korea) on the Asiatic mainland. Of course, men as wise and experienced as these two understood that under the right circumstances a war could be fought and won in Asia, but to the garden-variety politician and to the man-on-the-street, this oversimplification was a God-given, infallible truth, and a solid operating principle.

A third factor weighed heavily on any president's response to the deteriorating situation in Vietnam—the potential reaction of the Soviet Union and Red China. While Vietnam was important to Kennedy, in 1961 it was not worth the risk of World War III. Thus, any United States action in Vietnam had to be restrained so as not to provoke the entrance into that conflict of either or both of the great Communist powers.

In effect, these negative influences said to the president: "Don't lose Vietnam, *but* don't get involved in a major ground war in Asia, and don't use any weapons, forces, or strategies (for example—bombing the dikes in North Vietnam or an invasion of North Vietnam) which might pull in Russia or China." These three principles fashioned the trap which for the next decade would confine United States presidents to a policy of short-range, inconclusive measures in Vietnam.

Thus, shackled by these nullifying principles of Asiatic action, early in 1961 Kennedy inched ever so reluctantly into the troubled waters of Vietnam. From the beginning, the key issue was the commitment of United States combat troops. During the early sixties, the United States heaped upon Diem and the South Vietnamese government lavish financial support, hundreds of advisors, increased armaments, and gratuitous advice, but it shied away from sending American combat troops. This issue—the commitment of United States combat troops to Vietnam—came up for the first time when on 20 April 1961, Kennedy appointed an Interagency Task Force to recommend what the United States should do to save South Vietnam. As one of its recommendations, the task force report proposed ". . . a modest commitment of United States ground force units in South Vietnam . . .'' Kennedy ignored this recommendation, but a week later directed that the Defense Department (DOD) and the Joint Chiefs of Staff (JCS) make a study on the advisability of committing United States forces to Vietnam, as well as report on the size and composition of any United States forces destined for Vietnam. The JCS reply, dated 10 May, tossed the ball back to the president, recommending that American troops be sent, "assuming the political decision is to hold Southeast Asia . . .'' Kennedy again took no action on this recommendation other than to direct that the study continue. On 12 May 1961, Vice President Lyndon B. Johnson saw Diem in Saigon. Johnson asked Diem if he would accept United States combat troops. Diem told Johnson that he wanted United States combat forces *only* in the event of an open invasion from the North, but not otherwise.[7]

No war stands still, and throughout the summer of 1961 the Viet Cong continued their accelerated conquest of South Vietnam. Diem's troops pulled back from the countryside, and the effectiveness of his government atrophied there, forcing United States policy makers to face a worsening situation in Vietnam. In August 1961 the president approved (apparently with little thought) a recommendation that the United States support an ARVN troop ceiling of 200,000 men, raised from 170,000.[8] During the summer, as Diem's government and his army continued to deteriorate, the question of committing United States combat troops arose again. The Joint Chiefs of Staff advocated it, as did the United States MAAG Chief in Saigon, Lt. Gen. Lionel McGarr. President Diem suggested that now he would not oppose the entry of United States troops, although just exactly what he did want is not clear.

The truth is that in this summer of 1961, nobody in either Washington or Saigon seems to have thought seriously of using American troops to *fight* the Viet Cong. Rather, conventional thought held that the United States troops, if brought in at all, should be used to train ARVN forces, and perhaps to relieve the South Vietnamese troops of static defense duties, which would free ARVN to go after the Viet Cong. What thought was given to the commitment of American troops stressed that they would show United States determination to prevent a Communist seizure of South Vietnam. Again in June and July, as in May, the issue of committing United States troops arose and then languished in the Pentagon and White House, and once again faded away.

There was a pattern in the handling of this thorny issue. It arose, generally brought up by the Joint Chiefs, and then by bureaucratic hocus-pocus, disappeared before President Kennedy had to make a decision—all, no doubt, with the connivance of the president. The record strongly suggests that the president in 1961 did not want to send United States troops to Vietnam, a hypothesis which would be confirmed later.

But as the leaves began to turn in the fall of 1961, President Kennedy saw that he had to make a positive move to stop the slide of Diem's regime into the Communist chasm. During 1961 organized attacks of ARVN outposts had drastically increased. Assassinations of South Vietnamese officials rose from 239 in 1959 to over 1,400 in 1961.[9] In September 1961, the Viet Cong launched a spectacular regimental-size attack and overran Phuoc Binh, a provincial capital forty miles north of Saigon.[10] Hard-core Communists, regroupees from North Vietnam, appeared in increasing numbers in the South, and Viet Cong strength grew from 5,500 at the beginning of 1961 to over 25,000 by the end of the year.

To meet this growing menace to South Vietnam, Kennedy realized that he needed the best advice available. To give him this counsel, he selected from his quiver of advisers his straightest and keenest arrow, Gen. Maxwell D. Taylor, United States Army (Retired), the president's special military representative. In 1961, Max Taylor was sixty years old. He was a general straight out of Camelot—handsome, youthful in appearance, intellectual, self-confident, and articulate, not only in English but in Korean, Japanese, and two or three Romance languages. His army career had been a distinguished one, encompassing almost every "prestige" job in that service. During World War II, he had commanded the famed 101st Airborne Division when it jumped into Normandy. After World War II, he had been superintendent at West Point; commanding general of the Berlin Command (when it was a world hot-spot); operations officer, Department of the Army General Staff; commanding general, Eighth Army, during the latter days of the Korean War; and, finally, chief of staff of the United States Army from 1955 to 1959.

In spite of his prestigious positions and his well-earned honors and decorations, a peculiar misfortune dogged Max Taylor. He always seemed to miss the "big play." During World War II, he was in the United States when his division, the 101st Airborne, was thrown into Bastogne to stem the German tide in the Battle of the Bulge. It was his deputy, Gen. Tony McAuliffe, who became a national hero with his one-word reply, "Nuts," to the German surrender demand. Immediately after World War II, Taylor occupied the superintendent's chair at West Point, just as Douglas MacArthur had done after World War I. MacArthur had completely modernized the military academy in the early twenties and on this record had later vaulted to the position of army chief of staff. But in his turn, Taylor's imprint on West Point was negligible. I was a graduate of the Class of 1939 and returned to West Point as an instructor in 1952 and could note only the most minimal changes in the cadet curriculum and activities. Taylor took command of the United States Eighth Army in Korea in 1953 after the fighting was largely over. Matt Ridgway was the hero of that war, not Max Taylor.

As chief of staff, United States Army, Taylor is remembered by the army as the man who introduced the green "duty" uniform, and as the "Chief" who unsuccessfully opposed Eisenhower's emasculation of the army in pursuit of the "biggest bang for the buck." Here again, Taylor missed his big chance. It was Lt. Gen. "Jumping Jim" Gavin who became the army's hero when he retired prematurely to protest Eisenhower's policies. As it had been throughout Taylor's career, so it was to be in Vietnam—a good try by a good man, but a near miss. He deserved better.

So, as the situation in Vietnam crumbled, Kennedy called on Taylor to go to Vietnam and to explore what could be done to save Diem and American prestige there. Walt Rostow, a key foreign and defense policy adviser, was to accompany the general, along with the usual coterie of "experts" and "bag-carriers." The Taylor Mission arrived in Saigon on 18 October 1961. By 24 October, Taylor's conclusions and recommendations had begun to jell. His preliminary views (as set forth in a cable to the president on the 24th) were: (1) the political-military situation in South Vietnam was critical; and (2) ARVN military operations against the Viet Cong were ineffective because of lack of intelligence and unclear and unresponsive channels of command. General Taylor stated that he was considering recommending a series of actions to improve ARVN's effectiveness. In addition, *he* raised the sticky issue of introducing United States ground combat forces. He suggested that these American troops be disguised, at least initially, as a flood-relief task force to help the victims of a serious flood in southwestern South Vietnam. Taylor realized the touchiness of this recommendation. In a simultaneous cable to the president, he went into detail about his rationale for introducing United

States forces. Taylor wrote: "My view is that we should put in a task force consisting largely of logistical troops for the purpose of participating in flood relief and at the same time providing a United States military presence in Vietnam. . . . To relate the introduction of these troops to the needs of flood relief . . . gives a specific humanitarian task as the prime reason for the coming of our troops. . . . As the task is a specific one, we can extricate our troops when it is done if we so desire. Alternately, we can phase them into other activities if we wish to remain longer. The strength of the force I have in mind is six to eight thousand troops. . . . In addition to the logistical component it will be necessary to include some combat troops. . . . Any troops coming to Vietnam may expect to take casualties."[11]

A few days later, however, Taylor's focus shifted. In a cable to the president, dated 1 November 1961, Taylor goes into additional detail regarding his concept for the use of the American forces. His original flood-relief mission had faded. He now suggests the possible areas of United States troop employment to be the Western Highlands and the Coastal Plains, neither of which had been ravaged by the floods. But good-soldier Taylor pointed out to his commander in chief the hazards of introducing United States troops. In this haunting and prophetic cable, Taylor set forth these disadvantages to the introduction of United States troops: "(1) the United States strategic reserve will be further weakened for a period of unknown duration; (2) although United States prestige is already engaged in South Vietnam, it will become more so by the sending of troops; (3) if the first contingent is not enough to accomplish the necessary results, it will be difficult to resist the pressure to reinforce . . . there is no limit to our possible commitment; (4) the introduction of United States forces may . . . risk escalation into a major war in Asia." Every one of these predictions came true. Regardless of these drawbacks, Taylor came down firmly on the side of introducing United States ground troops into South Vietnam. He cabled, ". . . the introduction of a United States military Task Force without delay offers definitely more advantages than it creates risks and difficulties. In fact, I do not believe that our program to save South Vietnam will succeed without it."[12] From the vantage point of hindsight, one is amazed that General Taylor walked so blithely past his own farsighted warnings. The answer is suggested in the final sentence above. To Taylor, it was a case of putting in United States troops or giving up Vietnam, and Maxwell Taylor never gave up.

General Taylor's cable and his subsequent report of 3 November offered other recommendations for aiding South Vietnam. Some of the more important were: (1) effect a stepped-up joint United States/South Vietnam effort to improve intelligence gathering; (2) make a joint South Vietnamese/United States survey of each province to provide a common understanding of the insurgency problem and a plan to cope with it; and (3) augment the United States Military Assistance Advisory Group (MAAG) and transform it into "something nearer, but not quite, an operational headquarters in a theater of war."[13] Taylor's most important recommendation was that three squadrons of United States helicopters along with light airplanes be sent to Vietnam to improve ARVN's mobility.

Taylor's recommendations, even the one about sending helicopters, aroused only minimal interest in Washington. They had been foreseen and tentatively approved by the president before Taylor went to Vietnam. It was the recommendation to put United States ground combat troops into Vietnam which raised the collective blood pressure of the administration. Here the old "principles of Asiatic action" again exerted their pressure. Kennedy had to do something to stop South Vietnam's slide into Communist hands, but the possibility of getting into a dangerous land war in Asia terrified him. So, on the issue of introducing United States ground troops into South Vietnam, he procrastinated again. Once more, by bureaucratic subterfuge, he obtained from McNamara and Rusk a joint recommendation that the introduction of United States troops "be studied." This he approved, along with the other more positive recommendations.

One can sympathize with President Kennedy. He, and his advisers, realized even in 1961 that in the troop commitment issue they faced a crucial and far-reaching decision. It was a classic case of the choice among undesirable options, three in this case. Option I—Kennedy could make no additional effort and see Diem and South Vietnam drown in the Communist flood. To let Vietnam go under would invite domestic political disaster in 1964 ("the Democrats lost Vietnam") and would encourage Khrushchev's barely contained impulses toward worldwide confrontation and aggression. The president could go to the other extreme, option II—he could put in United States combat forces. But this was politically risky also and might be the first step toward that mythical ogre, the Asiatic land war. In 1961, the concept of committing United States combat troops to South Vietnam's aid repelled Kennedy. To his confidant, Arthur Schlesinger, the president compared sending United States fighting forces to Vietnam to an alcoholic's first drink. He told Schlesinger that "the troops will march in . . . then we will be told we have to send in more troops. It's like taking a drink, the effect wears off, and you have to take another."[14] Option III, while the most inconclusive, averted the obvious perils on either flank of the problem. That course was to increase the current advisory effort (particularly by sending in two helicopter companies instead of the larger force of three squadrons that Taylor recommended) and hope for the best. This course the president chose.

Years later, the authors of the *Pentagon Papers*—liberals all and Kennedy apologists—stressed the criticality and long-term impact of the president's 1961 decisions. Their judgment, even in retrospect, of the rectitude of Kennedy's actions is ambiguous. They wrote, "It (the record) does not prove that Kennedy behaved soundly in 1961. Many people will think so; but others will argue that the most difficult problem of recent years might have been avoided if the United States had made a hard commitment on the ground in 1961."[15]

While Kennedy kept avoiding the hard decision of 1961—the commitment of United States ground forces—Ho Chi Minh, in spite of the divided counsel *he* received, resolutely pushed on with the "South Vietnam first" strategy of Le Duan and Nguyen Chi Thanh, which he had approved in 1959. And despite their conceptual defeat of 1959 and 1960, Truong Chinh, Giap, and their supporters battled on, too. In April 1961, Chinh wrote an article in which he returned to his basic concept that the North and South constituted two separate phases of revolution and that the people of South Vietnam had to make their own way in their revolution. Also in 1961, Giap published his now-famous *People's War, People's Army*. In this work, Giap relates how he won the war against the French, citing as the guidelines for coping with the current situation in the South the strategy developed by Truong Chinh and himself for the conduct of that war. In particular, Giap cautioned about exalting military operations over political action and warned that an effective military campaign required a long preparatory period. In effect, Giap said that in 1961 what was wanted in South Vietnam was primarily political action backed by military action—an old theme. Le Duan and his group immediately took issue with this view. They maintained that equal emphasis should be placed on political and military operations.

Further along in his book, Giap gave Thanh gratuitous advice about where and how the Communist troops in South Vietnam should be used. He advised Thanh to establish bases in unpopulated and inaccessible areas and to hold the troops in these remote bases until political action in the populated areas made operations profitable there. This concept constituted only another variation of Giap's and Truong Chinh's view of the primacy of political *dau tranh* at the 1961 stage of the revolution in South Vietnam. As was to be expected, Le Duan and Nguyen Chi Thanh summarily rejected Giap's concept, characterizing it as lacking aggressiveness and failing to prepare conditions which would lead to a successful armed uprising. Again, Ho sided with Duan and Thanh, who were clearly in the ascendancy.

The triumph of the "South Vietnam first" clique makes one other action which Ho took in 1961 all the more mystifying—he removed Nguyen Chi Thanh from his post as political commissar of the army and made him the chief of the Agricultural Department of the Central Committee. In an even more demeaning move, Ho stripped Thanh of his four-star rank. Some experts on the politics and personalities of North Vietnam (the noted expert P. J. Honey among them) believe that Thanh was unhorsed by Giap in some arcane political-military struggle. All the evidence, however, points to the contrary. It was Thanh's strategy, not Giap's, which Ho was pursuing in the South, and in March 1961 that strategy was succeeding, not failing. A sounder explanation is that Thanh went underground and had actually taken personal command of the Viet Cong forces (although remaining in Hanoi), and that his demotion and assignment were a fiction to conceal his real duties. This view is further substantiated by Thanh's reinstatement to four-star rank in 1964 when he assumed overt command of all Communist forces in South Vietnam.

Despite Thanh's apparent demotion and despite the misgivings and criticism of Giap and Chinh, Le Duan, supported by Ho, pushed on with the strategy which he and Thanh had conceived, and as 1961 ended,

Communist forces in South Vietnam were moving confidently forward on all fronts.

The year 1962 saw another swing of the pendulum of war in South Vietnam. The increased United States support to the South Vietnamese government and armed forces began to pay dividends. A major factor in the shift of the scales in 1962 was the introduction into the war of the United States helicopter companies approved by President Kennedy in late 1961. The entrance of these United States helicopters introduced more than just American "chopper" crews into the war. They brought a whole new style of warfare to the Vietnamese battlefield. "Airmobility" had arrived, and the Vietnam War would never be the same. Helicopter operations gave ARVN vastly increased mobility and with it the capability to surprise the Viet Cong deep in their base areas. At first the sudden appearance of the helicopters on the battlefield terrorized the Viet Cong, who were killed in large numbers as they attempted to flee the strike area. So effective were these heliborne attacks that the tide of the war reversed itself in early 1962 and for several months ARVN mauled the Viet Cong and shook them severely.

In retrospect, one is amazed that the United States/South Vietnamese heliborne operations succeeded at all. The helicopters were used solely as a means of moving ARVN troops to the battlefield, and the thirty-three choppers (H-21's) were old and unsuited for the role. There were no "gunships" or heavy transport helicopters to support the landings. The effort lacked the essentials of unified command, specially trained personnel, organic firepower, and responsive reconnaissance.[16]

ARVN added greatly to these early problems of airmobility. The ARVN infantry in the helicopters used UHF radios and could not communicate with their supporting South Vietnam fighter aircraft which used VHF equipment. American experts wasted much valuable time training the Vietnamese in such basics as loading, unloading, and safety procedures during flight. In the landing areas, ARVN troops showed great reluctance in jumping from a hovering "chopper." When on the ground, they bunched up, milled around, and delayed the following helicopter waves, causing needless casualties. In addition, the quality of intelligence was inadequate for heliborne operations, and ARVN was too slow to react to it or to enemy raids and attacks.

But with all of these deficiencies, the joint United States/South Vietnamese heliborne operations succeeded, because, once again, a battlefield innovation had caught Giap unprepared. As the French had surprised Giap in Indochina War I by their use of paratroops, napalm, close-air support, and naval vessels, so did the Americans with the use of the helicopter. Again, Giap could not grasp the capabilities and potentialities of weapons and tactics with which he had no personal experience. Even after experiencing the heliborne assaults of the South Vietnamese, Giap and his staff were slow to react. Early in 1962, they published pamphlets supposedly telling their troops how to counter these assaults. One such pamphlet stated with unusual candor, ''. . . the enemy has in some places caused us fairly heavy losses. We must therefore find means of coping with the enemy's helicopter tactics. . .''[17]

Eventually, Giap and his staff developed countermeasures. If surprised, the Viet Cong started shooting back at the helicopters rather than running. They ambushed landings and held themselves in jungle and mountainous areas too remote or too tangled for heliborne operations to be carried out. By early 1963, the Viet Cong had begun to neutralize the primitive helicopter operations, but the tide of the war continued to run for a while toward Diem's shore.

In retrospect, the commitment of the helicopter units and other events of December 1961 and throughout 1962 propelled the United States deeper into Vietnam and Indochina War II. The United States manpower commitment rose from around 900 men in November 1961 to 11,326 by the end of 1962.[18] The United States permitted its advisors and pilots to enter into actual combat with the Viet Cong, and thirty-two Americans died in 1961–1962 as the result of enemy action. The United States Military Assistance and Advisory Group (MAAG) to Vietnam had been redesignated as MACV (Military Assistance Command, Vietnam) and had taken on many operational tasks not performed by its predecessor, the MAAG. By 31 December 1962, the United States committed to Vietnam not only pilots and a significant number of advisors, but also its prestige and the blood of its soldiers. Withdrawal, except with victory, had faded as a United States option.

The new effectiveness of the South Vietnamese armed forces in 1962 soon became apparent to the Communists. Pham Van Dong, in a speech made in early 1963, frankly stated that in 1962, ''. . . the South Vietnamese people underwent great trials.'' Even more far-reaching, Dong remarked that ''. . . by 1962 the revolutionary warfare had not developed correctly and had to be reexamined."[19] This reexamination would produce a momentous result.

The beginning of 1963 saw American officials optimistic about the progress of the war. The South Vietnamese military structure was still plagued by its inherent shortcomings, but with greatly increased United States support, it was making headway in the countryside. Viet Cong incidents (assassinations and kidnappings of government officials) were reduced, the government's control of the rural areas increased, and the Strategic Hamlet Program (an early pacification effort) appeared to prosper.

Unfortunately, this progress concealed a widening crack in the foundation of the South Vietnamese government, which would soon peril the entire structure. That fundamental failing was in the South Vietnamese leadership, particularly in Diem himself. Diem, always the "mandarin"—aloof, suspicious, devious, aristocratic, and egocentric—had never been an effective "chieftain," and the deteriorating situation soon to engulf him would magnify his deficiencies as a wartime leader. To Diem, the war against the Viet Cong was secondary to his own political survival. To maintain his waning popularity, he constantly exhorted his commanders to avoid casualties. Any South Vietnamese commander who took what Diem deemed to be excessive losses would be called into Saigon and roundly "chewed out." Since he controlled all promotions, the watch word, "prudence," spread throughout the South Vietnamese Army.

A recluse, Diem lived in pathological fear of a coup, and he put personal loyalty to himself above all other desired traits in an officer. To forestall an army takeover, he intentionally muddled the command lines so that no one man in any area controlled all the troops in that region. As a result of these policies, the senior officers who were promoted were the prudent, politically-oriented loyalists, not the aggressive fighters against the Viet Cong. The American advisors railed against this pernicious system, but as long as Diem had Washington's backing, it was to no avail.

By mid-1963, a serious crisis had once again developed in South Vietnam. The war had ground to a stalemate and the Strategic Hamlet Program, which had looked so promising in 1962, began to collapse. On top of these setbacks, the "Buddhist Problem" hit Diem and his government. The roots of the Buddhist unrest lie deep in Vietnamese history and culture. There was always an abiding Buddhist resentment against the Vietnamese Catholics, who numbered Diem and most of the other South Vietnamese leaders as devout communicants. There were Viet Cong agitators among Buddhists, and some of the Buddhist leaders were power-hungry. All of these forces combined in 1963 to shake South Vietnam to its already crumbling foundations, as Diem overreacted to the Buddhist crisis and lost what little popular support he had. The army devoted itself to trying to suppress the Buddhists, while the Viet Cong, taking advantage of this diversion, made significant gains in the countryside.

The Buddhist uprising gave Diem his *coup de grace* when, in the fall of 1963, the United States government and President Kennedy secretly abandoned Diem and began to look for a replacement. A coup led by ARVN generals (acquiesced in by the United States government through its ambassador to South Vietnam, Henry Cabot Lodge) unseated Diem on 1 November, and the next day a couple of junior officers murdered Diem and his brother. A few days later President Kennedy, too, was assassinated, and as 1963 ended, President Lyndon Baines Johnson inherited the shambles of United States policy toward Vietnam.

And it was a shambles. Following Diem's assassination, a series of power struggles almost destroyed the reeling government of South Vietnam. Emboldened by these diversions, the Viet Cong made widespread political and military advances across the country, and many of the Strategic Hamlets were overrun. In a memorandum dated 21 December 1963, Secretary of Defense McNamara bleakly told President Johnson, "The situation is very disturbing. Current trends, unless reversed, in the next two–three months, will lead to neutralization at best and more likely to a Communist controlled state."[20] It was not just that the trends were desperate; McNamara sensed something even worse. Nobody in authority, either in the United States or South Vietnam, knew how bad the situation *really* was, because there had been under Diem a great deal of false and overly optimistic reporting. McNamara ended the memo by declaring—in a prize collection of platitudes—that "We should watch the situation very carefully, running scared, hoping for the best, and preparing for more forceful moves. . ."[21]

The criticality of South Vietnam's prospects were appreciated by President Johnson. Two days after President Kennedy's assassination, Johnson had a long talk about Vietnam with Ambassador Lodge, then in Washington. Lodge described the situation to the president in realistic and blunt language. "The picture is bad," Lodge told him. "If Vietnam is to be saved, you, Mr. President, are going to have to do it." Johnson responded instantly. "I am not going to lose Vietnam. I am not going to be the president who saw Southeast Asia go the way China went."[22] There it was again, one of the familiar "principles of Asiatic action."

And so 1963, which for the Americans had looked so promising at the beginning, closed on an unpromising note.

But how had 1963 gone for the Communists? The reexamination of Communist strategy, which, in early 1963, Pham Van Dong had said was needed, followed the same scenario as the conceptual debates which had raged in the Politburo since the fifties. Truong Chinh and Giap maintained that the war in South Vietnam would be long and arduous. They held that South Vietnamese revolution lacked the necessary popular and political support in the South, and that military *dau tranh* there was proceeding at too rapid a pace. Le Duan and Nguyen Chi Thanh responded that a quick victory was possible, that the morale and fighting spirit of ARVN was low, and that the South Vietnamese government was about to cave in.

The disputants, particularly Le Duan and Thanh, introduced a new factor into the debate—the Sino-Soviet split. Khrushchev's line of "peaceful coexistence" toward the United States undercut the plans of Le Duan and Nguyen Chi Thanh to gain a quick military victory in the South. It struck directly at the "revolutionary ardor" of the cadres battling in the South. How could sacrifices be demanded from the Viet Cong when the leader of world communism was counseling detente with the leader of world capitalism? Le Duan and his teammates lined up solidly behind the Chinese, particularly when in May 1963 Liu Shao-Chi, in a speech in Hanoi, said that the struggle taking place between the revisionists (Khrushchev and the Russians) and the Marxist-Leninists (the Chinese) turned on "whether or not the peoples of the world should carry out revolutions."

For the first six months of 1963, old Ho sat on the fence between his own factions and between the Russians and Chinese. As an old Communist, the dispute between the two Red superpowers distressed him. It weakened communism worldwide, and more importantly, it diluted the support and aid the Vietnamese Communists needed from both major powers. Sometime around July 1963, however, Ho made his decision. He sided with Le Duan and Nguyen Chi Thanh, as he had consistently done since 1959. Old Ho was a pragmatist, and while the polemics of the Sino-Soviet rift bothered him, the factor which brought him to Le Duan's support was the Buddhist crisis and Diem's weakening grasp in the South. Ho now saw—along with Le Duan and Thanh—the real possibility of a quick victory as Diem floundered and the United States equivocated over whether to support him.

There was another factor in which Thanh, Le Duan, and Ho put great store—the "unquenchable revolutionary spirit" of the Communist troops in South Vietnam.[23] In spite of the possibility of United States intervention, the "South Vietnam firsters" had convinced themselves that their highly motivated troops in the South could and would win, even if the United States intervened with ground troops. In this they echoed Mao Tse-tung's oft-repeated adage that "man is always the decisive factor, equipment is never decisive." Giap thought otherwise, but once again he was ridden under.

From mid-1963, when Ho sided with Le Duan and Thanh, a steady stream of "anti-revisionist" propaganda appeared in the Hanoi press. "Revisionists," a code-name for the "North Vietnam firsters," had become a dirty word, and the struggle within the Lao Dong party leadership became personal and vicious. The Duan/Thanh faction, now with Ho's blessing, turned up the rhetoric against the "North Vietnam firsters" and the Soviet-supporting "revisionists." By the end of 1963, Duan and company were threatening to purge the Lao Dong party of those elements who did not fully support the war in the South.[24] Giap and Truong Chinh were now clearly forced onto the defensive.

Next, Nguyen Chi Thanh attacked not only Giap, but Giap's wife, as a "revisionist." Years later, a North Vietnamese defector under American interrogation stated that Thanh had charged that Giap's wife, who had gone to Moscow in the early 1960s to study history, had known Khrushchev. Through her, Giap and Khrushchev—so Thanh's charges went—became friendly, and the two men corresponded "very frequently." Thanh maintained that Khrushchev exerted a "particularly strong influence over Giap." Giap of course denied this lethal allegation.

More trouble for Giap followed, brought on by his own arrogance and stupidity. In June or July of 1963, according to another intelligence report, Giap and his wife flew by helicopter from Hanoi to the nearby

Ha Long Bay resort to go swimming. For security reasons, Giap's body-guards cleared all the other bathers from the beach so that Giap and his wife could swim in private. Reports of the incident spread quickly throughout Hanoi, and the people complained that while they could not even buy a bicycle to ride to work, Giap and his wife used a helicopter to go swimming.

According to the intelligence report, Nguyen Chi Thanh, on Ho's order—and how Thanh must have savored this—visited Giap's home and upbraided Giap and his wife, telling the latter, "Giap still has the attitudes of a bourgeois because of you. He does not have the virtues of a revolutionary cadre." The source said he had no knowledge about how Giap reacted to the criticism. But the charge was significant. The "virtues of a revolutionary cadre" was a euphemism for "antirevisionist," and Giap was being labeled as a "revisionist." The fight was now getting really dirty.

With Diem dead and South Vietnam fragmented, with threats of expulsion from the Party hanging over the "North Vietnam firsters," and with Giap under heavy personal attack, the Ninth Plenum of the Central Committee met in late 1963. As might be expected, the plenum developed the familiar, embittered arguments. Ho's support of Le Duan and Thanh, as usual, carried the day. The plenum confirmed that the goal of the revolution was to stage a combined general uprising and general offensive—the culmination of military and political *dau tranh*—which would win complete victory. To achieve this victory, Truong Chinh (who, strangely enough, presented the plenum's recommendations) stated, "The key point at this time is to make outstanding efforts to rapidly strengthen our military forces to change the balance of forces between the enemy and us in South Vietnam. It is time for the North to increase aid to the South; the North must bring into fuller play its role as a revolutionary base for the whole nation."[25]

Ho approved this policy. Stripped of Communist rhetoric, this recommendation meant that the Viet Cong with North Vietnamese support, *but without North Vietnamese military units,* were going to launch an all-out offensive against the South Vietnamese government and its armed forces. On this aggressive note, the year 1963 ended. Truong Chinh and Giap had been routed, and Giap had been personally humiliated, but for Giap, 1964 would be even more distressing.

Notes—Chapter 12

1. O'Neill, *Giap,* p. 168.
2. Senator Mike Gravel, Ed., *The Pentagon Papers,* 5 vols. (Boston, MA: Beacon Press, 1971), I:247.
3. Thomas Latimer, *Hanoi's Leaders and Their South Vietnam Policies, 1954– 68* (Washington, D.C.: Georgetown University: Unpublished Ph.D. thesis, 1972), p. 35.
4. Ibid., p. 41.
5. Ibid., p. 47.
6. Guenter Lewy, *America in Vietnam* (New York: Oxford University Press, 1978), p. 17.
7. Gravel, *Pentagon Papers,* II:2, 48, 49, and 55.
8. Ibid., II:64.
9. Adm. U. S. Grant Sharp and Gen. William C. Westmoreland, *Report on the War in Vietnam* (Washington, D.C.: U.S. Government Printing Office, 1968), p. 77.
10. Lt. Gen. Dave Richard Palmer, *Summons of the Trumpet: U.S.-Vietnam in Perspective* (San Rafael, CA: Presidio Press, 1978), p. 20.
11. Gravel, *Pentagon Papers,* II:87–88.
12. Ibid., II:92.
13. Ibid., II:653.
14. Ibid., II:117.
15. Ibid., II:68.
16. Lt. Gen. John J. Tolson, *Airmobility 1961–1971,* Vietnam Studies (Washington, D.C.: Department of the Army, 1973), p. 28.
17. Ibid., pp. 26–27.
18. Gravel, *Pentagon Papers,* II:438.
19. Latimer, *Hanoi's Leaders,* p. 110.
20. Gravel, *Pentagon Papers,* III:494.
21. Ibid., III:496.
22. Halberstam, *Best and Brightest,* p. 364.
23. Latimer, *Hanoi's Leaders,* pp. 138–139.
24. Ibid., p. 144.
25. Lewy, *America,* pp. 29 and 39; Palmer, *Summons,* p. 48; U.S. Embassy, Saigon, *Viet-Nam Documents and Research Notes,* Doc. #96, July 1971, pp. 15, 29, 40.

1. ...

2. ...

3. ...

4. ...

Senior General Vo Nguyen Giap. Hanoi, December 1972.

Ho Chi Minh

French General Henri-Eugene Navarre, February 1954

French General De Lattre de Tassigny, seated to left of President Truman

Le Duan, seated to the left of Ho

Senior General Nguyen Chi Thanh, commander in chief of the Viet Cong armed forces, 1967.

General William C. Westmoreland, June 1972

General Creighton W. Abrams

Truong Chinh (far right), Hanoi, 1973

General Westmoreland and his staff, at MACV Headquarters, (Gen. Creighton Abrams, 3rd from left; Robert Komer, 2nd on right) Spring 1968

MACV staff, key personnel. Author seated at far right.

Special advisor Le Duc Tho at a press conference in Paris, January 1973. (Radio-photo retransmitted from AP)

Part II

13 The Year of Crisis

The decision of the Ninth Plenum of the Lao Dong party announced in December 1963 to expand North Vietnamese support of the war in the South was quickly followed by a ferocious campaign led by Le Duan and the other Southerners against Giap, Truong Chinh, and the other "revisionists." In February 1964, Le Duc Tho, one of Le Duan's lieutenants, announced a "rectification" program, and an accompanying editorial described the combating of "modern revisionism" as "urgent."[1] On 11 February a radio broadcast from Hanoi stated that an "indoctrination" campaign had been initiated in North Vietnam to bring about "vigorous changes" in the attitudes of some North Vietnamese toward the war in the South. The broadcast did not announce the names of those being indoctrinated; this came from another source.

There is now available a detailed interrogation report of a high-ranking North Vietnamese defector who told his American interrogators that Gen. Nguyen Chi Thanh was named head of a "revisionist" study section of the Lao Dong Central Committee in 1964. According to the informant, the formation of this study committee was the first step in an "antirevisionist" campaign against Giap, Truong Chinh, and three other Communist Party leaders. Following Thanh's investigation, all five were labeled "revisionists" and underwent indoctrination sessions given by Ho Chi Minh himself. Ho's objective, according to the defector, was not to purge the deviants from Party leadership, but to "reorient" them. Giap kept his title of minister of defense, because he was still a national hero, but Thanh was given responsibility for the direction of the war in the South because he was 100 percent "antirevisionist."

The defector confided that Thanh's promotion to commander of the war effort in the South was a blow to Giap's prestige, since the discord between the two men was well known.

Although Giap lost control of the military strategy and tactics, as minister of defense he still held the responsibility for the logistical and administrative support of the Communist forces in South Vietnam. In compliance with Ho's decision to increase support to the Viet Cong, Giap took several actions. First, he made an all-out effort to upgrade their arms and other combat materiel. United States Defense Secretary McNamara, in a gloomy memorandum of 16 March 1964, noted that "Since July 1, 1963 the following items of equipment, not previously encountered in South Vietnam, have been captured from the Viet Cong: Chicom 75mm recoilless rifles, Chicom heavy machine guns, United States .50 caliber heavy machine guns on Chicom mounts. In addition, it is clear that the Viet Cong are using Chinese 90mm rocket launchers and mortars."[2] In a more important move, Giap converted the polyglot Viet Cong collection of small arms to a standard family of weapons using a single caliber. The most important of these new weapons was the AK-47, a Chinese copy of the Soviet assault rifle. Matching 7.62mm machine guns came into the inventory as well as an excellent rocket launcher, the RPG-2, and 57mm and 75mm recoilless rifles.[3]

Giap launched a second program to improve the Viet Cong performance by sending thousands (between 3,000 and 12,000) of Northerners— not "regrouped" Southerners, but native North Vietnamese—to South Vietnam as cadremen. No doubt, Giap would have preferred to continue sending "regrouped" Southerners, but the supply had been exhausted.[4] Throughout the war, the use of North Vietnamese cadres in the South presented problems arising from differences in dialect, outlook, and customs between the two regions. Beneath these differences existed a traditional animosity between the peoples of the two areas. To the North Vietnamese, the Southerners were indolent, easygoing, and slipshod. To the South Vietnamese, the Northerners were blunt, prickly, impatient, and demanding. The problems of the North Vietnamese cadremen in the South can be understood in the context of the regional differences of the United States. Imagine the difficulties which would arise if the government sent a zealous young man (or worse, a woman) from New York's inner city, with a heavy Bronx accent, into Georgia to organize the "redneck" sharecroppers along Tobacco Road.

With the increase in the quality and logistical supportability of the Viet Cong weaponry and with the influx of North Vietnamese cadremen, Giap and Thanh began to organize the Viet Cong forces into larger tactical units. The year 1964 saw the first Viet Cong division, the now-famous 9th Viet Cong Division, based in Tay Ninh province, west of Saigon. This division was formed from the 271st and 272nd Viet Cong Infantry Regiments and some other supporting units. By the end of 1964, the 9th Viet Cong Division was in action against ARVN.[5] In similar actions, Main Force Viet Cong battalions were augmented and made into regiments, and companies were upgraded to battalions. Once the Viet Cong had new weapons and better leaders, Giap began an accelerated training program. This progressed so well that by 10 August, Maxwell Taylor, by then American ambassador to South Vietnam, reported, "In terms of equipment and training, the Viet Cong are better armed and led today than ever in the past."[6]

As the effectiveness of the Viet Cong increased, the chill winds of growing disintegration blew over South Vietnam. On 20 January 1964, the government of "Big Minh," who succeeded the murdered Diem, was itself overthrown by a coup led by Gen. Nguyen Khanh. Here was another blow to the shaky American program to help South Vietnam. Even more telling, the unexpected coup shook United States confidence in its belief that its own officials and intelligence operators knew what was going on there. Senior United States leaders charged with developing a policy for Vietnam could only shake their heads and mutter, "What next?"

The "what next" took the form of vastly increased Viet Cong aggressiveness, not only against ARVN, but against the American advisors as well. During the period 3–6 February, Viet Cong forces struck with a major offensive against the South Vietnamese in Tay Ninh province and in the Mekong Delta. On 3 February, the Viet Cong attacked the American advisory compound at Kontum City. There was no United States reprisal. On 7 February, the Viet Cong exploded a bomb in the Capital–Kinh Do Theatre, when it was known to be occupied only by Americans. Three United States personnel were killed and fifty wounded. Again, the United States refused to retaliate. The United States Joint Chiefs of Staff fumed over these attacks, and on 18 February they repeated a prior proposal for a series of escalatory steps toward North Vietnam including aerial bombardment. Nothing came of it, and the already desperate situation in South Vietnam continued its slide.

Chaos and anarchy grew as the government and army slid deeper toward demoralization and defeat. By mid-March, the sticking point in Vietnam had arrived. ARVN was dispirited and the government ineffective, while the Viet Cong grew bolder and more powerful. The United States had to do something different in either scope or style, or both. The vehicle for this high-level reappraisal was another memo from Secretary McNamara to the president, dated 16 March, reporting on a visit which he and General Taylor, then the chairman, Joint Chiefs of Staff, had made to Vietnam. McNamara told the president bluntly, "The situation has unquestionably been growing worse, at least since September 1963: 1. In terms of government control of the countryside, about 40 percent of the territory is under Viet Cong control or predominant influence. In twenty-two of the forty-three provinces the Viet Cong control 50 percent or more of the land area. 2. Large groups of the population are now showing signs of apathy. 3. In the last ninety days the weakening of the government's position has been particularly noticeable."[7]

In addition to a description of the worsening situation, the memorandum suggested a significant revision of United States objectives in Southeast Asia. Prior to the memo's submission, it had been United States policy to help the South Vietnamese "win their contest against the externally directed and supported Communist conspiracy."[8] McNamara's memo, which the president approved the next day as National Security Action Memorandum (NSAM) 288, enlarged this limited United States objective in two ways. First, NSAM 288 expanded American goals significantly toward South Vietnam. The NSAM stated United States objectives toward South Vietnam to be: "We seek an independent non-Communist South Vietnam. . . . South Vietnam must be free . . . to accept outside assistance as required to maintain its security."[9] The first sentence of the stated objectives would be interpreted for the next five years as the foundation of American policy toward South Vietnam, a policy which called for whatever action appeared necessary to defeat a Communist takeover in South Vietnam. This objective would be the banner around which the "hawks" in the American government would rally when pressed by the "doves" for some deescalatory action or for a retreat from the encompassing goal of "victory." Second, the NSAM expanded United States objectives throughout the Southeast Asia area. It stated, "Unless we can achieve this objective in South Vietnam almost all of Southeast Asia will probably fall under Communist dominance. . . . Thus, purely in terms of foreign policy, the stakes are high."[10] Here, the Johnson administration adopted the "domino theory," an inheritance from the Eisenhower regime.

The memorandum proposed to the president that he direct the appropriate United States government agencies to take twelve actions. Two of these were "to make it clear" that we supported (1) the South Vietnamese, and (2) the Khanh government. Eight dealt with increasing financial or material support for the South Vietnamese. One provided for minor United States tactical overflights, and one called for the preparation of plans for "border control" of the Laotian and Cambodian borders and for "retaliatory" actions against North Vietnam. NSAM 288 carried the full weight of the president and the National Security Council, and it constituted an important milestone on the road to full United States commitment to the survival of South Vietnam.

There has always been something curious about NSAM 288. President Johnson adopted it within twenty-four hours of its formal presentation to him and the National Security Council. He apparently gave it only minimal consideration, in spite of the fact that it drastically expanded United States objectives in Southeast Asia. The NSAM itself had a strange ambivalence. It used strong language in describing the worsened situation and in setting forth enlarged United States objectives toward South Vietnam and Southeast Asia, yet the actions recommended remained limited. In essence, the NSAM called for the United States to increase its help to the Government of South Vietnam (GVN), but to take no direct hand in the fighting. The dichotomy within McNamara's 15 March memorandum to the president can be partially explained by noting a draft memorandum from Assistant Secretary of Defense William P. Bundy to the president, dated 1 March. The broadened objectives of McNamara's memo are a direct lift from Bundy's memo, but where Bundy had logically recommended aggressive action against North Vietnam—a blockade of Haiphong, followed by United States air strikes in the North—McNamara proposes a much more restrained program.[11]

McNamara's memorandum contained one section normally never seen in a report of this nature, a section entitled "Other Actions Considered But Rejected." They were: return of military dependents from Saigon; furnishing a United States combat unit to secure the Saigon area; and the assumption by United States officers of overall command of the entire war effort in South Vietnam. All were dismissed due to the adverse psychological consequences such actions would have on the South Vietnamese. This last "rejected action" (assumption of command by United States officers) catches the eye and the mind. It is a first blossom of one of those hardy perennials which flourishes, is cut down, and then blooms again. The Joint Chiefs had recommended this action as far back as 22 January 1964, and it would be consistently recommended and resolutely rejected throughout the stay of United States advisors and forces in South Vietnam.[12] The rationale for rejection always remained the same—the negative impact on the South Vietnamese. One wonders why unity of command was held to be so vital in World War II and in Korea and yet deemed undesirable—or unattainable—in South Vietnam. Here is one of the truly significant military issues of the war, one hotly debated to this day by military professionals.

After studying NSAM 288, the Joint Chiefs of Staff, as might be expected, judged the actions recommended to be inadequate. In another memo to the president, the Joint Chiefs again recommended direct action against North Vietnam, and Johnson again ignored the recommendation, caught in the continuing conflict in an election year between military reality and political expediency. In retrospect, it is clear that all of the "principles of Asiatic action" were alive and working in March 1964. So while American rhetoric grew hotter, American actions remained lukewarm.

The Viet Cong military campaign, however, did not remain lukewarm. The Viet Cong struck savage blows not only at the South Vietnamese, but at United States troops and facilities as well. In early April, the enemy became so aggressive around Saigon that on 7 April, General Khanh set up a special military zone of defense around the South Vietnamese capital. Less than a week later, the Viet Cong captured Kien Long, a district capital in the Mekong Delta, where they killed 300 South Vietnamese soldiers. On 2 May, a Viet Cong underwater demolition team sank the helicopter-carrying U.S.S. Card, while the ship was at berth in Saigon. The United States did not retaliate. On 4 July, a Viet Cong force of regimental size overran the Special Forces camp at Nam Dong, in northern South Vietnam. Fifty South Vietnamese were killed along with two United States Special Forces men. There was no United States reprisal.

By mid-summer 1964, it was evident that the United States actions prescribed by NSAM 288 were inadequate. But an even more pressing problem than the feebleness of NSAM 288 arose—the instability and ineffectiveness of the Government of South Vietnam. Khanh was no administrator. He overcentralized authority, and he lacked the patience to work at pacification and on the social reforms which represented real progress in South Vietnam. Like Diem, he constantly looked over his shoulder, expecting a coup which would drive him from office or kill him. By summer, Khanh's frustration had driven him to talk to the Americans about a "march to the North," suggesting vaguely some kind of an attack on North Vietnam. As the early summer wore on, Khanh's obsession with an "offensive" increased, as did his bombastic discussions of it. This kind of irrational talk alarmed Khanh's senior American advisors. They knew—and Khanh probably did too—that the Government of South Vietnam and its armed forces were incapable of any kind of successful attack on North Vietnam. Even worse, Khanh's trumpeting about such an attack gave North Vietnam a pretext to counter this absurd talk with an offensive of their own, which in all probability would overrun South Vietnam.

Then, in August 1964, a controversial event occurred which changed the course of this strange war—the Gulf of Tonkin incident. If there is any rational explanation for the attack by the North Vietnamese torpedo boats on the United States destroyers in the China Sea, it lies in the erroneous interrelation by the North Vietnamese of two separate operations, one by the United States, one by South Vietnam. First, there was a program known as Operation Plan (OPLAN) 34A, in which the South Vietnamese, with United States advice and support, conducted a series of minor, largely ineffectual raids against North Vietnamese coastal installations. The United States Navy conducted another operational program called DE SOTO, an operation to detect the North Vietnamese ships which were supporting the Viet Cong in the South, to gain intelligence regarding the characteristics of North Vietnamese radar and other electronic devices, and to acquire information about navigational and hydrographic conditions in the area.

On the night of 30–31 July 1964, the South Vietnamese commando forces from OPLAN 34A raided two small North Vietnamese islands off Vinh. At this time the U.S.S. *Maddox* was 120 to 130 miles away from the islands. It was well in international waters, on its way to carry out a DE SOTO mission, on which it embarked the following night (31 July).

The first day of August was uneventful. At 1630 hours, 2 August, three North Vietnamese torpedo boats attacked the *Maddox*. When the torpedo boats began their high-speed run at the *Maddox*, she was twenty-eight miles off the North Vietnamese coast. The attackers fired torpedos and 12.7mm machine guns at the United States destroyer. The *Maddox* answered with her 5-inch batteries and scored a direct hit on one of the PT boats. At approximately 1730 hours, four F-8E fighters from the U.S.S. *Ticonderoga* joined the fracas. They made several rocket and strafing runs, adding to the damage already inflicted by the *Maddox*. By 1800 hours, when the fighters had to leave, one North Vietnamese patrol boat was dead in the water, and the other two craft, wounded ducks, were fleeing north toward sanctuary in the coves and harbors of North Vietnam. As soon as the fighters departed, the *Maddox* steamed off to the southeast.

There has never been any doubt that North Vietnamese torpedo boats attacked the *Maddox* in international waters, but the controversy regarding this action turns around whether the United States provoked the attacks. Those who argue to the affirmative point out that the North Vietnamese logically would confuse the raids of OPLAN-34A with the DE SOTO mission of the *Maddox*. They maintain that the instructions to the *Maddox* to approach no closer than eight nautical miles to the North Vietnam coast and four miles to the off-shore islands would result in violations of North Vietnam's definition of its coastal waters, believed to be twelve nautical miles. Finally, they cite messages of 1 August from the senior officer aboard the *Maddox*, who stated that he realized that the mission was dangerous, but who did not retire from his provocative course or abort the mission.[13]

Those who hold that the *Maddox*'s actions were *not* provocative argue that the North Vietnamese should not have attacked the ship until they were sure that the *Maddox* had in fact bombarded the islands on 31 July. Adm. U. S. Grant Sharp, Commander in Chief, Pacific (CINC-PAC) at the time, has gone further. He maintains that the North Vietnamese had tracked the *Maddox* by radar from the time it crossed the 17th Parallel (the DMZ) and knew throughout its cruise where it was and what it was.[14] In effect, Sharp claims that the North Vietnamese *knew* the *Maddox* had not engaged in the raids and yet attacked her anyway.

Sharp and others maintain that the orders given to the *Maddox* to stay eight miles from the North Vietnamese shore and four miles from the islands was in keeping with the declaration of the North Vietnamese that their coastal waters extended for five nautical miles, not twelve. Finally, those who think the *Maddox* was attacked without provocation hold that the mission of the *Maddox* (to monitor electronic emissions from North Vietnamese shore installations) was nothing new and had been carried out by both surface craft and aircraft all over the world, and that the U.S.S. *Craig* had patrolled along the North Vietnamese coast on a similar mission some months earlier without incident.

President Johnson, with some grumbling and vague threats, initially decided to accept the incident as a mistake on the part of the North Vietnamese. Of course, this was largely a political decision. He was running for president on a "peace ticket," contrasting his restraint to the bellicose blasts of his Republican opponent, Senator Barry Goldwater. The president, however, in an effort to balance himself between action and restraint, ordered the DE SOTO patrols to continue, reinforcing the *Maddox* with another destroyer, the U.S.S. *Turner Joy*. On 4 August, the *Maddox* and the *Turner Joy* apprehensively returned to their patrol route. The cruise continued without incident until around 1915 hours, when the National Security Agency (NSA), after intercepting a North Vietnamese message, flashed the task force commander, Capt. John Herrick, a warning of a possible enemy PT boat attack. At 2035 hours the ship's radars picked up indications of three high-speed craft some thirty miles from the American vessels, and the crews of both American vessels went to General Quarters. At about 2130 hours, a confused fracas began. The night was dark with an overcast sky which limited visibility. Radarmen reported enemy contacts at various ranges, and the sonarmen reported hearing the approach of some twenty enemy torpedos toward the American ships. The skipper of the *Turner Joy* observed a column of black smoke arising from the water, but when he tried to get a closer look, the smoke had vanished. The pilots of the aircraft called in from the *Ticonderoga* saw no enemy boats or any wakes of such craft.

To this day, no one (other than the North Vietnamese) is sure that on 4–5 August 1964 North Vietnamese craft attacked the two American ships. Intercepts of pertinent North Vietnamese radio communications (not all of which have been declassified) indicated almost certainly that the enemy *decided* to begin a hostile action against the American ships. As related earlier, NSA informed Captain Herrick that an enemy attack was imminent, yet another analyst studying the same message or messages believes that the messages ordered enemy patrol boat commanders to *investigate* the destroyers.[15] This latter interpretation would be confirmed by the original (and probably valid) radar sensings of approaching enemy vessels. After the shooting started, the reports of smoke, torpedo noises, torpedo sightings, radar contacts, and sinkings can be put down to combat hysteria. These crews were not combat veterans, and in the fear and excitement of their first or second battle, particularly under conditions of almost zero visibility, their minds could easily have played strange tricks. Captain Herrick, who *was* a combat veteran, was the first to question the factuality of the North Vietnamese attacks. A few hours after the fracas, he reported to his superiors that the "Entire action leaves many doubts except for apparent attempt to ambush at the beginning."[16] To this day Captain Herrick's simple statement remains the most valid summation of the "second attack" of 4–5 August 1964.

There is an interesting postscript to the Tonkin Gulf incident. The North Vietnamese themselves have indirectly confirmed that they made the second attack. They have established as the North Vietnamese Navy's anniversary, or "tradition day," 5 August, the date of the second attack when, as the North Vietnamese put it, "one of our torpedo squadrons chased the U.S.S. *Maddox* from our coastal waters, our first victory over the U.S. Navy."[17] Douglas Pike pithily states that "If the Gulf of Tonkin incident is a myth invented by the Pentagon, as some revisionist historians claim, the PAVN (People's Army of Vietnam) Navy is now part of the conspiracy."[18]

At noon on 4 August (Washington time is thirteen hours behind Vietnam time), President Johnson convened the National Security Council and decided to launch a retaliatory strike against the North Vietnamese support facilities at Vinh, where the attacking boats were based. A strike of sixty-four sorties was launched from American aircraft carriers at 1100 hours, 5 August (Vietnam time). The pilots reported that fuel oil tanks at Vinh were burning and exploding, with smoke rising to 14,000 feet, and that eight North Vietnamese PT boats had been destroyed and twenty-one damaged. Two United States Navy aircraft were lost. In his book, Adm. U. S. Grant Sharp, in a laconic understatement, wrote, "Generally speaking it was a successful action. . . ."[19]

Neither Ho nor Giap have ever explained what motivated them to launch these attacks. The second attack, if it occurred, was senseless and foolhardy. President Johnson and his senior advisers described the second attack as "obviously deliberate, and planned, and ordered in advance."[20] The only motives this high-level group of United States leaders could see for the second attack was that "North Vietnam was intent either upon making it appear that the United States was a 'paper tiger' or upon provoking the United States."[21] Robert Shaplen, in his book *The Lost Revolution,* speculates that the assaults may have been carried out ". . . for the two-fold purpose of seeing how the United States would react, and how serious the Chinese were in their promises of giving assistance."[22]

The authors of the *Pentagon Papers* put forth, albeit hesitantly, two other possible motives for the attacks. In their discussion of the action they write in one place, "The explanation for the DRV attack on United States ships remains puzzling (perhaps it was simply a way of warning and warding off United States patrols close to North Vietnam borders)."[23] Later they speculate that the attacks had "Perhaps . . . the narrow purpose of prompt retaliation for an embarrassing and well publicized rebuff by a much-maligned enemy. Inexperienced in modern naval operations, DRV leaders may have believed that under cover of darkness it would be possible to even the score or to provide at least a psychological victory by severely damaging a United States ship."[24]

Of all the motives for the attacks, the "paper tiger" thesis advanced by United States leaders appears the most valid explanation. This gains increasing credence when an analysis is taken of the pattern of prior enemy attacks on American personnel and installations combined with the absence of United States retaliation. On 3 February, there was the Viet Cong attack against the American compound at Kontum City. On 7 February, the Viet Cong exploded a bomb in a Saigon theatre known to be patronized only by Americans. On 2 May, the Viet Cong sank the U.S.S. *Card.* On 4 and 6 July, there were attacks on Special Forces camps. The United States refused to retaliate for any of the assaults. American soldiers had been killed and a navy ship sunk without reprisal. The failure of the United States to strike back after the daylight attacks of 2 August on the *Maddox* strengthened the views of the North Vietnamese Politburo that the United States—probably for internal political reasons—would not retaliate. Looked at from the viewpoint of Ho and Giap, the United States richly merited the epithet "paper tiger."

This North Vietnamese view was understandable. In that summer of 1964, the election year, Johnson, "the peace candidate," wanted no crisis over Vietnam. Polls showed that more than two-thirds of the American people paid little or no attention to Vietnam, and Johnson was content with that indifference.[25] So the attacks and the killing of Americans went on, unanswered. But this American apathy raises a haunting question. How might the Vietnam War have gone had the early attacks on United States troops and facilities been answered with force and firmness? If the Vietnam War was a "war of lost opportunities," as many pundits proclaim, then Johnson's failure to respond aggressively to the testing attacks of early 1964 was one such "lost opportunity."

The attacks on the United States destroyers bore Giap's fingerprints, underlining again two of his persistent failings. First, ever since his first "strategic" decision in 1944, where, in Ho's absence, he ordered an ill-timed rebellion, until his premature Phase III general offensive of 1951, Giap's career had been marked by moving strategically too soon and too far. In the Tonkin Gulf, his precipitance did him in again. Giap's second hallmark has been his consistent inability to grasp the capabilities of tactics, weapons, and services with which he had no personal experience. These ranged from the French paratroop attack in 1948 to the introduction by the United States of helicopters in 1963. This time it was naval warfare on the high seas. He had never had any experience with it, and he did not understand it.

One critical and far-reaching result of the North Vietnamese attacks was the Tonkin Gulf Resolution, passed on 10 August by a vote of 416–0 in the United States House of Representatives and by a vote of 88–2 in the Senate (Senators Morse and Stevens against).[26] This resolution gave broad authority to the president to use whatever force was necessary to assist South Vietnam and the other allies of the United States in Southeast Asia. As the burden of the war grew heavier, this resolution, too, would come under heavy fire from critics of the conflict.

But this was a long way into the future, and in 1964, Johnson faced more immediate problems. In South Vietnam, chaos deepened and defeat edged ever closer. The Khanh government, never effective, practically disintegrated. In the fall of 1964, the students took to the streets, the Buddhists demonstrated, the Catholics counterdemonstrated, and the final collapse appeared near. As early as 3 September, Assistant Secretary of Defense (International Security Affairs) McNaughton stated bluntly that "The situation in South Vietnam is deteriorating. . . . The odds are very great that if we do not inject some major new elements—and perhaps even if we do—the situation will continue to deteriorate."[27] In Hawaii, Admiral Sharp, CINCPAC, sent his component commanders a message, dated 25 September, which read in part, "1. The political situation in RVN is now so unstable as to raise some serious questions about our future courses of action. For example, we may find ourselves suddenly faced with an unfriendly government or no government at all."[28]

The North Vietnamese and the Viet Cong stepped up the pressure on the fast-weakening South Vietnamese government and on the United States. On 11 October, three Viet Cong battalions attacked ARVN troops in Tay Ninh province and inflicted heavy casualties on the South Vietnamese units. On 1 November, just before the United States presidential election, the Viet Cong mortared the United States airbase at Bien Hoa, a few miles from Saigon. Four Americans were killed, five B-57 bombers destroyed, and eight other aircraft received major damage. There was a "flap" at the White House and in the Pentagon, but no retaliatory action was taken. The White House spewed forth several reasons for this inaction, which fooled nobody. With the presidential election three days away, Johnson, the "peace candidate," was not going to bomb the North Vietnamese and his chances of a reelection victory. As Lenin once said, "There are no morals in politics; there is only expedience."[29] Also during November, two regiments of Viet Cong mounted their most effective offensive, driving through the heavily populated coastal province of Binh Dinh. By the end of the month, this key province was almost completely in the hands of the Viet Cong.

With the 1964 presidential election overwhelmingly won, Johnson now had to face up to the odds-on probability of a defeat in South Vietnam. His senior advisers, military and civilian alike, urged him to do something—anything—to alter the crumbling situation. The president held numerous futile conferences. In late November he called Ambassador Maxwell Taylor in from Saigon. Taylor's report on the state of affairs in South Vietnam was so dismal that he had to leave the White House by the rear door to avoid revealing to the waiting reporters that (in McNamara's words), "the situation is going to hell."[30] For once McNamara was right.

More trouble followed. On 24 December, the Brink BOQ (Bachelor Officers' Quarters), a run-down hotel in Saigon where junior United States officers were billeted, was bombed and severely damaged by persons officially unknown, although the Viet Cong claimed credit for the attack. Two Americans were killed and thirty-eight were wounded. Ambassador Taylor, Admiral Sharp, and the Joint Chiefs of Staff urged the president to retaliate by an air strike against a North Vietnamese Army barracks in North Vietnam. Again, the president refused to strike back.

Four days later, the Viet Cong for the first time launched a division-sized action. The 9th Viet Cong Division seized the Catholic village of Binh Gia, forty miles east of Saigon. In the ensuing battle, the Viet Cong destroyed the South Vietnamese 33rd Ranger Battalion and the 4th Marine Battalion, both elite ARVN outfits. The Viet Cong capped this victory by an unprecedented display of confidence: instead of fading away after the fight (as had been their prior practice), the Viet Cong troops defiantly held the battlefield for four days before retiring. As the year 1964 ended, both the North Vietnamese Politburo and the leaders of the United States realized that the situation of South Vietnam was not only critical, it was now probably terminal.

The worst was yet to come. Into this "Dark December" of 1964 appeared a dreaded specter—the North Vietnamese Main Force units. In December, MACV received hard intelligence that one NVA Main Force regiment had arrived in the Central Highlands of South Vietnam and that two more regiments were following closely behind. The three regiments, the 101st, 95th, and 32d, meant that the entire 325th NVA Division would shortly concentrate in northwestern South Vietnam. Make no mistake: this decision by the North Vietnamese Politburo to send its regular units into the South was one of the "hinge events" of Indochina War II. It changed the war from a Viet Cong insurrection, supported more or less openly by the Communist North, into an invasion of the sovereign nation of South Vietnam by North Vietnam. It began the change from a guerrilla-counterinsurgency war to a large-unit, conventional war of divisions, corps, air forces, and naval flotillas. The North

Vietnamese invasion, the first move into Phase II of the revolutionary war—with the eventual American reaction to this invasion—expanded vastly the size and scope of the war, for no longer would South Vietnam furnish the sole arena for the conflict. North Vietnam would become an air-to-ground battlefield, and eventually Laos and Cambodia would feel the ravages of war, as the two contenders grappled for each others' flanks throughout Southeast Asia.

The Politburo has, of course, never given any public indication of the nature of its deliberations that reached this momentous decision. It has never even admitted that it had troops in South Vietnam. Some information on the rationale of this decision has leaked out, however, and the major missing ingredients of the North Vietnamese analysis can be deduced.

The first clue to a determination of these "missing ingredients" is to find the time of decision—that is, *when* did the North Vietnamese decide to send their Main Force units to South Vietnam? An analysis of intelligence now available permits a narrowing of the limits of the period in which the North Vietnamese decision was made.

The first and probably the strongest clue is the movement of the leading North Vietnamese infantry regiment toward South Vietnam and its arrival in that country. General Westmoreland, in his official *Report on the War in Vietnam*, states that in December 1964, "reports were received that at least three regular North Vietnamese regiments—the 95th, 32nd, and 101st . . . were moving south for possible commitment in South Vietnam."[31] In his book (written several years after his *Report*), General Westmoreland accelerates the movement of at least the leading regiment. He writes, "There were reports that at least a regiment of the 325th North Vietnamese Division had *been in the Highlands since December 1964*, as later proved to be correct."[32] (Emphasis added) The later time frame is supported by the testimony of Secretary Rusk on 18 February 1966, before the Senate Foreign Relations Committee. Rusk testified, ". . . it was in November, December, January over the turn of the year 1964–65 that North Vietnam moved the 325th Division of the regular North Vietnamese Army from North Vietnam to South Vietnam."[33]

Crude time-and-space calculations show that the move of the leading regiment from Vinh in North Vietnam (the home area of the 325th Division) to the Central Highlands of South Vietnam could have been made in around forty-five days. Thus, the leading regiment probably departed Vinh sometime between mid-October and early November 1964. The decision to move the division predated its departure *by at least a month*. This amount of time would have been necessary to prepare the regiment for the long march and to expand the logistic facilities along the Ho Chi Minh Trail which would have to support it. The decision would have had to be made, then, *prior* to mid-September 1964.

There is another piece in this intelligence puzzle supporting the speculation that the decision was made prior to 1 October 1964. A 1971 intelligence report of the interrogation of a high-level North Vietnamese defector revealed that Nguyen Thi Thanh, Giap's old nemesis, who was to command all North Vietnam Army troops (along with Viet Cong forces) in the South, had disappeared from Hanoi sometime in October 1964—no doubt on his way south armed with the decision to use North Vietnamese Army troops.

Gen. D. R. Palmer in his book, *Summons of the Trumpet,* speculates that the critical decision to send North Vietnamese Main Force units was made "in the late summer of 1964, probably in August."[34] Palmer's speculation is sound. If the time consumed by the arguments and bickering within the Politburo in reaching such a decision is taken into account (two–three weeks?) a date of 15 August—give or take two weeks—is probably accurate.

On or about 15 August 1964, then, Ho, Giap, and the others analyzed the various factors which, in the end, caused them to commit NVA Main Force units into South Vietnam. First, there was the estimate of the situation in South Vietnam. Diem, the glue which had held that fragmented South together—however tenuously—was gone. His successors by coup and countercoup were worse. The military situation for South Vietnam was desperate, and one hard push would topple the South Vietnamese generals and their rootless government. This North Vietnamese view has been explicitly confirmed by Gen. Van Thien Dung, then chief of staff of the North Vietnamese Army. In an article in the *People's Army Daily* written in June 1967, he writes, "In the middle of 1964, . . . the Southern revolution was developing advantageously, and the rebel administration and armed forces were disintegrating markedly."[35] To the North Vietnamese Politburo, the extra push which the North Vietnamese Main Force units could furnish would bring about a "general uprising" and victory.

But in August and September 1964, the situation in South Vietnam was secondary in the calculations of Ho and Giap. It was the United States that held the key to Hanoi's move. As the men of the Politburo pondered and debated America's probable reaction to the entry of North Vietnamese Main Force units into the conflict, they focused—for want of other evidence—on two clues. The first clue was the recent actions of the United States in Southeast Asia. What Hanoi saw encouraged boldness. The United States had accepted a series of attacks on its installations and servicemen, retaliating only for the Tonkin Gulf attacks. Even then, the United States had stressed that its reprisal was "surgical," and had publicly proclaimed the limited and unique nature of that retaliation. The second clue was President Johnson's presidential campaign speeches of 1964. These political bromides completed the Politburo's misunderstanding of United States resolve and intent. Hanoi could draw no other conclusion than that the United States would not enlarge the war. When President Johnson said (as he did on 12 and 29 August 1964) that he would not expand the war by either bombing the North or by "committing a good many American boys to fighting a war that I think ought to be fought by the boys of Asia . . ."[36], he fooled Ho Chi Minh and his compatriots with American election year politics and polemics. Communists seldom understand that American campaign speeches bear no relation to the postelection actions of the victorious candidate. As a result, every indication of American intent available to the North Vietnamese in August–September 1964 showed that the United States would not intervene in force in Vietnam if the North Vietnamese Main Force units invaded South Vietnam.

Reporter P. J. Honey has confirmed that this was the Politburo's view in August–September 1964. In September 1966, Honey wrote that "Pham Van Dong confessed to a recent Western visitor to Hanoi that North Vietnam's Communist leaders had been surprised by the United States decision to commit large numbers of American combat troops to South Vietnam. . . . He implied . . . that Hanoi had miscalculated the reactions of the United States government. . . The complete failure of North Vietnamese leaders to understand American political processes was the underlying reason for the incorrect assessment of future American actions. . ."[37]

Honey's report is corroborated by P. J. McGarvey, whose book *Visions of Victory* discusses in detail Hanoi's strategy and thinking in the Politburo. He wrote, "We do have evidence, however, which indicates that in 1964 the Hanoi leadership believed that the United States would not intervene in the war in the South or mount air attacks against the North."[38] McGarvey does not reveal what this evidence is, but a Lao Dong party document states the "possibility is small" that United States ground troops would intervene.[39]

So, in August or September, the North Vietnamese Politburo saw the situation—confidently albeit erroneously—this way: 1. South Vietnam could be conquered if the North Vietnamese Army was thrown onto the Communist side of the scales; and 2. the United States would accept this invasion without retaliation by air against North Vietnam and without sending its own ground forces into a land war in Asia. It was a tragic miscalculation, and was to cost the lives of hundreds of thousands of men, mostly Vietnamese, from both sides of the 17th Parallel.

The view set forth in the paragraph above about the rationale the North Vietnamese used in committing their Main Force units to the South is held by almost all of the experts who have studied the North Vietnamese and this action. There are other speculations about North Vietnamese motives, however, and they merit attention. The first of these contending theories was contained in a cable General Westmoreland, COMUSMACV, sent Admiral Sharp, CINCPAC, in mid-August, 1964. He told the admiral that he (Westmoreland) thought that although the United States viewed the Tonkin Gulf reprisal bombing as a one-time reaction to a specific provocation, the North Vietnamese would see it as an overt attack and an escalation of the war. In his opinion, the North Vietnamese would respond, and for lack of any other effective means, they would respond by attacks on the ground in South Vietnam. Westmoreland prophesied that the most likely course of North Vietnamese action would be to send in NVA divisions to attack United States air bases at Hue or Da Nang. Westmoreland concluded by saying that he had no intelligence that the North Vietnamese were planning any such invasion.[40]

Another military analyst who repudiates the conventional explanation of North Vietnamese motives for sending its regular troops to South Vietnam is Gen. D. R. Palmer. He admits that "The most commonly accepted theory is that Hanoi saw 1964 as the beginning of the end for Saigon." He challenges this theory on the grounds that if the Communists were winning so decisively in 1964, why switch strategies? "Time,"

Palmer writes, was the "least important factor in his (Ho's) equation of victory."[41]

Palmer's challenge can be countered, however. First, although in the long-range perspective of the war from 1961–1964 the Viet Cong were winning, they had been unable to strike the finishing blow which would destroy the armed forces and government of South Vietnam. Nor did such a Viet Cong capability appear to be in the offing. Yes, the Viet Cong would keep winning, but the war—one draining both North Vietnam and its supporters, Russia and China—would go on and on. And second, what of the United States? Would it stand by in 1966 or 1967 as the North Vietnamese believed it would in 1964–1965, accepting a North Vietnam Main Force invasion? Maybe, but again, maybe not. Finally, time, that most precious and unstable of strategic commodities, is relative to a given situation at a given time. In this case, here was a golden, once-in-a-lifetime opportunity to win the war. No leader could forego such a chance.

Since Palmer rejects the conventional consensus, he advances two other hypotheses to explain North Vietnamese motives. First, he suggests that the reason the North Vietnamese intervened is that they were losing their dominance over the Viet Cong. He then scuttles this thesis by noting that in 1963–1964 the North Vietnamese had increased their control over the Viet Cong, not lessened it or lost it. His second hypothesis, toward which he leans—that in Hanoi's eyes the Viet Cong were not winning the war, they were losing it—is unsound. It is now known that such diverse, but expert, authorities as General Westmoreland and North Vietnamese Gen. Van Tien Dung believed that disaster for the army of South Vietnam was imminent.

So, as the fateful year of 1964 drew to an end, the Communist drive in the south waxed. The United States procrastinated, and South Vietnam slipped ever closer to oblivion. But change is the first order of nature, and these conditions, too, would pass, for waiting impatiently in the wings for 1965 to arrive was a vastly different war.

Notes—Chapter 13

1. Latimer, *Hanoi's Leaders*, p. 163.
2. Gravel, *Pentagon Papers*, (Document #158) III:499.
3. Sharp and Westmoreland, *Report*, p. 88.
4. Lewy, *America*, p. 38.
5. Palmer, *Summons*, p. 52.
6. Gravel, *Pentagon Papers*, III:531.
7. Ibid., III:501.
8. Ibid., III:50.
9. Ibid., III:499–500.
10. Ibid., III:500.
11. Porter, *Vietnam*, 2:240–246.
12. Ibid., 2:237.
13. Senator Wayne Morse, United States Senate, *Congressional Record*, pp. 4691–4697, 29 February 1968.
14. Adm. U.S. Grant Sharp, *Strategy for Defeat—Vietnam in Retrospect* (San Rafael, CA: Presidio Press, 1978), p. 42.
15. "The 'Phantom Battle' that Led to War," *U.S. News and World Report*, 23 July 1984, p. 62.
16. Morse, *Congressional Record*, p. 4695.
17. Pike, *PAVN*, p. 110.
18. Ibid., p. 122.
19. Sharp, *Strategy for Defeat*, p. 44.
20. Gravel, *Pentagon Papers*, III:519.
21. Ibid., III:520.
22. Robert Shaplen, *The Lost Revolution: The U.S. in Vietnam, 1946–1966* (New York: Harper & Row, 1965), p. 269.
23. Gravel, *Pentagon Papers*, III:108.
24. Ibid., III:186.
25. Doris Kearns, *Lyndon Johnson and the American Dream* (New York: Harper & Row, 1976), p. 198.
26. Gravel, *Pentagon Papers*, III:187.
27. Ibid., III:537.
28. Ibid., III:569.
29. George Seldes, *The Great Quotations* (New York: The Pocket Book Edition, 1967), p. 736.
30. Gravel, *Pentagon Papers*, III:248.
31. Sharp and Westmoreland, *Report*, p. 95.
32. William C. Westmoreland, *A Soldier Reports* (Garden City, NY: Doubleday, 1976) p. 152.

33. Theodore Draper, *Abuse of Power* (New York: Viking Press, 1967), p. 74.
34. Palmer, *Summons,* p. 62.
35. Patrick J. McGarvey, *Visions of Victory: Selected Vietnamese Communist Military Writings 1965–1968* (Stanford, CA: Hoover Institute on War, Revolution and Peace, 1969), p. 154.
36. Draper, *Abuse,* p. 67.
37. Wesley R. Fishel, *Anatomy of a Conflict* (Itasca, IL: F. E. Peacock Publishers, 1968), pp. 806–807.
38. McGarvey, *Visions,* p. 32.
39. Porter, *Vietnam,* 2:364.
40. Halberstam, *Best and Brightest,* pp. 655–656.
41. Palmer, *Summons,* p. 64.

14 A War That Nobody Wanted

The year 1965 saw the United States shift from "helping the Vietnamese people help themselves" to fighting a full-scale war on and over the land mass of Asia. Over two decades later, what strikes an observer is not only such a massive reversal of policy, but the suddenness and apparent thoughtlessness with which the United States leaders adopted the new concept. Franz Joseph Strauss, that wise old German, recently stated a generality which is appropriate here. He wrote, "Few wars were started with deliberate intention. Most of them arose from neglecting the lessons of history, from underestimating the risks, and from carelessly crossing the border of the point of no return." Eventually, he declares, ". . . events develop a dynamism of their own and . . . they can no longer be controlled."[1]

The spark which ignited this major United States reversal of policy occurred on 7 February 1965, when the Viet Cong attacked the United States air base at Pleiku in the Western Highlands, inflicting heavy material destruction and some American casualties. But Pleiku was only the spark—a relatively insignificant event—which, like the assassination of the Archduke Ferdinand in Sarajevo in 1914, set in motion consequences far beyond its minor importance. The real factors which brought about the policy reversal were a combination of foreign and domestic pressures urging the president to do something about Vietnam. First, there was that always implacable goad, "the situation" in South Vietnam. The year 1965 began as 1964 had ended—dismally. The Viet Cong attack against Binh Gia by the 9th Viet Cong Division began on 28 December 1964 and ran into 1965, resulting in a significant defeat for the South Vietnamese. At the same time, the first (NVA) Main Force unit went into action at Dak To in the Western Highlands. General Westmoreland, COMUSMACV, was convinced that Giap intended to go into Phase III, the general offensive, in February or March, and that the South Vietnamese government and its armed forces could not withstand it. Almost all the other experts both in and out of the American government agreed with Westmoreland. Politically, the South Vietnamese government was in chaos. In Saigon, the junta of suspicious generals plotted against Khanh and each other, and in the countryside the government surrendered vast areas to the Viet Cong, as the Communist shadow over South Vietnam grew longer and darker. Assistant Secretary of State William P. Bundy summed it up in a memo when he wrote that the Communists ". . . see Vietnam falling into their laps in the fairly near future."[2]

The declining fortunes of South Vietnam prompted the top presidential advisers to the tacit consensus that some pressure on Hanoi had to be applied, probably by air strikes in the North. From the record, it appears that the principals reached this position largely on an individual basis. On 29 October 1964, William P. Bundy, chairman of an Interagency Working Group, recommended ". . . United States air strikes against the DRV, as reprisals for any major or spectacular Viet Cong action in the south . . ."[3] At the end of the year 1964, Ambassador Taylor in Saigon somewhat hesitantly suggested to the State Department and the president "an energetic United States program of reprisal attacks . . . against the DRV."[4] Secretary of State Dean Rusk echoed Taylor's recommendations in a discussion with the president on 6 January 1965. The civilian side of the Defense Department was making similar suggestions to Secretary McNamara, but the most forceful advocates of the policy of air reprisal against North Vietnam were the Joint Chiefs of Staff and Admiral Sharp, CINCPAC. At the end of January, the Joint Chiefs (urged on by Sharp) proposed that the next provocation "be met with a positive, timely, and appropriate response," and appended a memorandum giving a list of targets which had been selected for a reprisal program labeled FLAMING DART.[5]

President Johnson himself was the principal factor in bringing about the policy shift. His resounding election victory over Senator Goldwater cut the self-imposed bonds which had shackled his actions in Vietnam when in the 1964 campaign he had run as "the peace candidate." He could now tackle the Vietnamese problem aggressively. It is significant that on 3 November 1964, immediately following his election, he directed the NSC Interagency Working Group under William Bundy to study alternative courses of action in Vietnam. Then, too, the aforementioned consensus of his key advisers that some action against North Vietnam was vital pushed him towards a more aggressive policy. Johnson, the sure-handed expert in domestic affairs, was much less experienced and confident in handling military and foreign policy. In his uncertainty, he found his advisers' unanimity reassuring.

Johnson's views of the Communist threat, not only in Vietnam, but worldwide, had been molded by the experiences of his generation leading to World War II. In the post-World War II capitals of the Free World, conventional wisdom held that the appeasement of Hitler's early aggression had brought on that war. To Johnson the issue was clear: North Vietnam was waging a war of aggression against its neighbor, and it had to be stopped and stopped soon.

The president was extremely sensitive to the domestic political implications if Vietnam were "lost." Describing the early weeks of 1965, Johnson told biographer Doris Kearns, in 1970, "I knew that if we let Communist aggression succeed in taking over South Vietnam, there would follow in this country an endless national debate—a mean and destructive debate—that would shatter my presidency, kill my administration, and damage our democracy. I knew that Harry Truman and Dean Acheson had lost their effectiveness from the day the Communists took over China."[6] To Johnson, then, the problem was not just losing Vietnam, but the destruction of all his accomplishments as president, including his beloved Great Society program. Finally, there was the essence of Johnson himself. He was one of the last products of the American frontier, a subculture which prized boldness and courage. Lyndon Johnson told Kearns that if he lost Vietnam people would say "that I was a coward. An unmanly man. A man without spine."[7] To this complicated and insecure man, Vietnam had become a test of his very manhood, and he had to meet it.

Then came Pleiku. At 0200 hours on the morning of 7 February (just at the end of Tet) the Viet Cong struck at the United States airfield at Pleiku and at the helicopter base at Camp Holloway, four miles away. By the standards of those days, casualties were heavy. Of the 137 Americans wounded, nine died and seventy-six had to be evacuated. Equipment losses, too, were extensive: sixteen helicopters damaged or destroyed and six fixed-wing aircraft damaged.

Almost immediately, President Johnson ordered a reprisal air attack, using the targets already selected for the FLAMING DART program. The attack, however, was ineffectual. The civilian decision-makers selected the weakest of the options given them of various targets and strike forces, and to make matters worse, only the U.S.S. *Ranger* was in a position to hit the targets. By the time the other two carriers, the *Hancock* and *Coral Sea,* were in position, poor flying weather caused most of their sorties to be aborted. The targets were struck again the next day by United States Navy aircraft, and VNAF aircraft struck the North Vietnamese barracks at Vu Con. In its public announcement, the United States government stressed that the attacks had been "appropriate reprisal action."[8] But something much more than "appropriate reprisal action" was in the wind. On 9 February, Secretary McNamara requested that the Joint Chiefs of Staff submit recommendations for an eight-week air campaign against infiltration-associated targets in the lower portion of North Vietnam.

On 10 February, the Viet Cong attacked the enlisted men's billet at Qui Nhon, killing twenty-three American soldiers and wounding twenty-one others. Again, the president struck back. United States Navy aircraft destroyed the Chanh Hoa barracks in southern North Vietnam while VNAF planes attacked the NVA military compound at Vit Thu Lu. This time the administration made no claim that the United States/ South Vietnamese strikes were associated with direct reprisals. The administration carefully characterized them as a generalized response to "continued acts of aggression by the Viet Cong and the North Vietnamese."[9] Although this key change of rationale was muted in public, it constituted a new course in American policy toward United States participation in the war. Three days later, 13 February 1965, President Johnson ordered a "program of measured and limited air action jointly with the GVN against selected targets in the DRV."[10] This program, nicknamed ROLLING THUNDER, would remain in effect for some three-and-a-half years.

From the start, a good deal of the "thunder" of the ROLLING THUNDER program came from the United States civilian officials and their military counterparts, who differed widely and vociferously about the aims and the conduct of the campaign. The dispute had deep roots. One was doctrinal and philosophical, another generational, a third ideological. Underneath it all there simmered a novel confrontation in American history—a military-civilian contest for the power to formulate not only military strategy, but military tactics as well. The concept and execution of ROLLING THUNDER furnished the battleground, but the real battle revolved around the civilian-produced doctrine of "limited war."

The intrusion of civilians into the field of military strategy dates from the end of World War II. The leaders of the American armed forces came back from their victories in Europe and the Far East proud, idolized—and complacent. In the late forties and fifties, the United States military leaders were not interested in grand strategy or strategic theory, and in this neglect they followed a long American military tradition. Although America had produced first-rate strategists—men like Lee, Mahan, and MacArthur—they were the exceptions. The Americans had won every war since (and including) their own Civil War by an overwhelming combination of superior manpower and weight of materiel, a superiority which minimized the importance of strategy. After World War II, a few officers picked at the subject, but the post-war services produced no strategic thinkers worthy of that title. The advent of the atomic bomb encouraged this delinquency. Here was a weapon so powerful, so new, that it seemed to nullify all of the old laws of strategy (the value of mass, surprise, and the initiative, for example), and while some bold officers wrestled with this new monster, most looked on in confusion and apathy. In the late forties and fifties, the military in effect abdicated its traditional role as the formulators of the country's military strategy.

Into this gap infiltrated the civilian theorists, with backgrounds in one of the physical sciences or in economics. Herman Kahn, of the Hudson Institute, was perhaps preeminent. Other prominent thinkers and writers of the fifties include Bernard Brodie, Robert E. Osgood, Thomas C. Snelling, and Samuel P. Huntington. Among these men, military experience was minimal or totally lacking. However, they viewed this lack as no disadvantage. They believed that the atomic bomb had changed everything about warfare, and therefore, past military experience counted for little. Using the techniques of operations analysis and systems analysis, of statistics, of the theory of games and economic-type modeling, these civilian theorists developed their own strategic concepts. Some had validity; some were bizarre. These theories went largely unchallenged by the military, who considered them to be academic and useless exercises played by a bunch of eggheads. Later, the admirals and generals would rue this casual disregard.

One of the theories developed by the civilians was that of "limited war." They based this concept on two assumptions: first, the United States had to contain communism, which was expanding by means of local or indigenous wars; second, a nuclear war with China or the Soviet Union must be avoided. In the broadest application of the theory, the academic analysts proposed a strategy of *gradualism*, . . . "*not* to apply maximum force toward the military defeat of the adversary; rather it must be to employ force skillfully along a continuous spectrum—from diplomacy, to crises short of war, to an overt clash of arms—in order to exert the desired effect upon the adversary's will."[11] Osgood, in his book *Limited War Revisited,* states, "This principle held an appealing logic for the new breed of United States liberal realists who had discovered the duty of managing power shrewdly in behalf of world order."[12] Inherent in this doctrine was a distrust of the military. The liberal academicians believed that, given an opportunity, the military would dangerously escalate any war in their desire to "win" it. To negate this impulse, the doctrine of limited war stressed that the president must have the means of command and communications to enable him to tailor force to a specific political purpose anywhere in the world.

Until the Korean War, the strategy of limited war languished as nothing more than an interesting theory in the classrooms of academia, in the pages of esoteric magazines, and in the "think tanks" of consultants. The Korean War brought the doctrine into prominence. The Korean War *was* a limited war, and to some, it succeeded in accomplishing its primary purpose of containing Communist aggression. This war highlighted also the basic dispute between military strategists (MacArthur) and the proponents of limited war (Truman, et al). This brought the doctrine into the open, but domestic politics and emotion prevented any rational and studied debate of its merits and faults. In 1961, the Kennedys—liberal, young, trendy, contemptuous of all past theories—ardently embraced the limited war concept. Once in office, President Kennedy set about improving the limited warfare capabilities which Eisenhower had allowed to decay. Kennedy brought into the Departments of

State and Defense a number of young "whiz kids," all adherents to the theory of limited war and world order.

Thus, the fundamental dispute about ROLLING THUNDER between the civilians and the military turned around the aims and philosophy of that program. The civilians, led intellectually by Assistant Secretary of Defense for International Security Affairs (ISA) John T. McNaughton, espoused a program of *gradually* applied pressure through air power on North Vietnam, beginning with carefully selected and generally unremunerative targets. In essence, this philosophy maintained that Hanoi would "get the signal" that the United States was serious about the war in Vietnam, and they would cease supporting the Viet Cong. Its restrained inauguration and philosophy offered President Johnson maximum flexibility, in that the pressure could be increased. Its initial restraint would probably not panic the Soviets or the Chinese into entering the war. Unfortunately, from this policy of gradualism Hanoi received almost precisely the opposite signal from the one the United States wanted to transmit. The signal Hanoi got was that the United States was *not* serious about fighting or ending the war in Vietnam.

The strategy of gradualism suffered from other serious shortcomings. United States air power was committed piecemeal and on limited targets (many unimportant), and some air targets were restricted. Gradualism allowed the North Vietnamese time to build up their air defenses and to build alternate installations. In the final analysis, gradualism forced the United States into a lengthy, indecisive air war of attrition—the very kind which best suited Ho and Giap. A war of attrition takes time—a commodity of which the Vietnamese Communists had plenty, and one of which the United States (although its leaders did not grasp this in 1965) had very little.

Led by General McConnell, the air force chief of staff, and Admiral Sharp, CINCPAC, the military urged the president from the beginning to launch an air campaign which would take advantage of mass and surprise. The attacks would strike at airfields, petroleum storage areas, and industrial facilities throughout North Vietnam. They wanted to hit the North hard and keep on hitting it hard. They argued that this was the way to use air power, and that Hanoi would best get the "message" regarding the seriousness of United States intentions from its own destruction. This bolder, more violent course had hazards, too. There could be some effect on world opinion and on the support for the war in the

United States to see the Americans play the "bully boy" and beat up a small opponent, and a devastating air campaign against North Vietnam might force Russia and China to take an active hand in the war.

The gulf between the president's military and civilian advisers went far beyond a difference of doctrinal opinion as to the employment of United States air power against North Vietnam. Between the two groups existed a generational gap. The military men were of the Depression generation. By heritage, training, and experience, they were hardbitten and tough. The civilians were of the post-World War II generation, by birth used to affluence and by education attracted to innovative ideas. The uniform services had been taught from their plebe years in the service academies that war is violent, and that the best way to employ violence is in an all-out assault against the enemy. Violence is violence, their creed taught, and when you try to ameliorate it, you invariably get into trouble. To the civilians, this kind of theory was overly simplistic and outdated. To them, the Vietnamese War was a limited war, for a limited objective, to be fought with limited means. They believed that the violence of war could be and should be tailored to the objective of the war.

Finally, the gap was ideological, the most unbridgeable of all chasms, except perhaps the gulf of disparate religion. The military were social conservatives, middle-class products of West Point and Annapolis, with the Spartan outlook and ideals of those institutions. They were staunchly anti-Communist, intensely patriotic men, believers in the traditional values of the American system, and in "my country right or wrong." The civilians ranged in ideology from liberals to leftists. They were largely the products of the "enlightened" schooling of the Ivy League universities. In outlook, they were more flexible, less doctrinaire than the military. They, too, were patriots, but not in the same way the generals and admirals were. The civilians could perceive faults in the American system, and they wanted to cure them. They believed not in the realities of a great power conflict, but in an "interdependent world order" in which the use of military force had become outdated.

The gulf was widened by mutual mistrust and contempt. The civilians feared that the military, if not restrained, would lead the country into World War III. The military were afraid that the civilians with their fancy theories would piddle around and lose the Vietnam War. To the civilians, the generals and admirals were "old fogies" and warmongers.

To the military, the civilians were "whiz kids," military neophytes who had "never heard a shot fired in anger." Westmoreland, typical of the military group, disparages them on at least two occasions as "field marshals."[13] Of course, the above characterizations are too hard and fast to include all of the civilians and all of the military. Dean Rusk and Walt Rostow were hawkish to the end, and John McCone, then director of the CIA, supported the military position. Maxwell Taylor, then ambassador in Saigon, came out originally for the graduated response, although he later changed his view.

All of this bitter dispute left one man in the middle—President Lyndon Baines Johnson. Having gotten into the war (no doubt reluctantly), he now sought to hedge his action by siding with the civilians and choosing the weakest options of air attack against North Vietnam. Johnson, unfamiliar with war, saw the bombing in terms of domestic American politics, in which he was an expert. The aircraft, the bombs, the destruction itself were only bargaining tools, and he believed in his politician's heart that Ho Chi Minh would bargain. After all, Johnson had risen to the presidency by exploiting the old maxim that every man has his price, and to Johnson, Ho had his—if he (Johnson) could only find it. Thus, the weak start of ROLLING THUNDER would allow Johnson the maximum flexibility in sounding Ho out.

The dispute over the basic aims and broad philosophy of ROLLING THUNDER had a raucous twin in the day-to-day conduct of the program. The airmen could bomb only relatively minor targets, none north of the 19th Parallel. Attack sorties were stringently limited, and the military were galled not only by the ineffectiveness of the program, but even more so by the target selection system. Johnson, McNamara, and their civilian underlings not only established the philosophy of the program, they decided what targets should be hit, the number of planes to be used, and on occasion, even the type and weight of bombs to be employed. To see Johnson and McNamara huddled over maps and aerial photographs planning air strikes would have been ludicrous, had the consequences not been so serious. As a result of the restrictions and the interference of the "self-appointed air marshals" (Westmoreland's words)[14], ROLLING THUNDER's initial efforts were futile. In a political sense, they were also ineffective. Ho Chi Minh ignored all of the "signals" Johnson was trying to send him.

Nobody knows if the more aggressive program advocated by the military would have brought Ho Chi Minh to the negotiating table in 1965. In 1972, a program of heavy air attacks plus the mining of the port of Haiphong drove the North Vietnamese to negotiations. But the situation in 1972 was different than that of 1965, and so no valid conclusions may be drawn. Lyndon Johnson did draw some conclusions, however. Several years later, he told General Westmoreland that his (Johnson's) "greatest mistake was not to have fired, with the exception of Dean Rusk, the holdovers from the Kennedy administration."[15] The army historian S. L. A. Marshal reports, "In the last month of his life, it is said, LBJ told a confidant: 'I am aware of my main mistake in the war: I would not put enough trust in my military advisers.' "[16] But by 1973 it was too late, and the bad advice of his civilian staff in 1965 exacted a severe price. It was the timidity and ineffectiveness of ROLLING THUNDER which brought in its train another event of even greater moment—the commitment of United States ground combat troops.

Up until the time of the Pleiku attack (7 February 1965) there had been a good deal of talk as far back as 1961 about putting ground combat troops into Vietnam, but no concrete plan for their employment against the Viet Cong had been drawn up. McGeorge Bundy's memorandum to the president on 7 February makes no mention of ground troops, although the staffs of CINCPAC and COMUSMACV had prepared generalized contingency plans for their deployment and use. But then all military staffs do this, and these headquarters would have been derelict had they not done so.

As the FLAMING DART program shifted into ROLLING THUNDER, General Westmoreland became increasingly uneasy about the overall situation in South Vietnam and about the local security of the airfields where the attacking United States Air Force aircraft were based. In particular, Westmoreland was concerned that the North Vietnamese would retaliate against the ROLLING THUNDER program by attacking its principal launching airbase at Da Nang. On 22 February, his deputy, Gen. John Throckmorton, made a detailed inspection of ARVN's ground security arrangements at the Da Nang airbase. Appalled by what he found, he reported to Westmoreland that the base was in grave jeopardy. To secure the base, Throckmorton recommended that a Marine Expeditionary Brigade (MEB) of three infantry battalions plus supporting troops be landed at Da Nang. Westmoreland, with a clearer feel for what the political traffic might bear, cut the request to two marine battalions.

Ambassador Taylor, an old soldier, objected to bringing in the marines. He pointed out that one marine battalion could adequately protect the field from a Viet Cong ground assault, but that at least six battalions would be needed to push the security perimeter out far enough to keep 81mm mortar fire off the field. Taylor then went on to point out that mobile operations against the Viet Cong were bound to be attractive to Westmoreland, but such employment would raise serious problems. He questioned whether United States troops were trained and equipped for such missions, and whether a workable system of United States/GVN command relations could be worked out. In spite of his doubts, Taylor did recommend, however, that one marine battalion be brought in.

There is something incomprehensible about Taylor's antipathy to the entrance of the marines at Da Nang. It was he who as far back as 1961 had recommended bringing the "flood relief" task force of American soldiers into South Vietnam. Even in August of 1964, he advocated landing air defense units and a marine ground combat force at Da Nang. Probably his experiences in late 1964 with an unstable South Vietnamese ally had convinced him that if the United States brought in ground forces, the South Vietnamese would only unload more of the combat burden onto the United States as the situation deteriorated. Nor is an explanation available regarding his comment about the inability of the American soldier to fight a counterinsurgency war in the jungles of Vietnam. The puzzle becomes more baffling when one realizes that the United States ground soldiers did superbly well in Vietnam. Taylor, who as the army chief of staff from 1955 to 1959 had been largely responsible for their training, organization, and equipment, should have recognized their worth. Perhaps he was in a "dovish" period, for at about this same time he joined Johnson's civilian advisers in espousing the air strategy of gradualism.

On 26 February 1965, President Johnson approved the dispatch of two marine battalions to Da Nang. Everyone, from the president on down to Ambassador Taylor and Admiral Sharp, saw these two marine battalions as purely security troops and "as an isolated phenomenon rather than as part of a sequence."[17] The *Pentagon Papers* hints that only General Westmoreland viewed it as the first step in a build-up of

United States ground forces in South Vietnam. In support of this contention, the authors cite some corroborating but weak evidence.[18]

Westmoreland denies this. He wrote, "I saw my call for marines at Da Nang not as a first step in a growing commitment but as what I said at the time it was; a way to secure a vital airfield."[19] The truth seems to lie somewhere between the two contradictions. Quite probably General Westmoreland on 22 February 1965 did view his call for the two marine battalions as purely a means of securing the Da Nang airfield, but by the time the marines landed on 10 March (or a day or two thereafter) his thinking had changed, and so had the viewpoint of the other key American actors, including that of the president.

There were two reasons for this rapid change of viewpoint within the American leadership regarding the commitment of ground troops. First there was, again, "the situation." Although the Viet Cong had been unusually quiet during the latter part of February and early March, Westmoreland, Taylor, and their staffs expected a major enemy offensive later in the year. In Westmoreland's opinion, the Republic of Vietnam Armed Forces (RVNAF) could not long hold the fort in the south. The second factor was the ineffectiveness of the ROLLING THUNDER program. Although the president had approved the program on 13 February, for various reasons the first air attack was not launched against North Vietnam until 2 March. By 8 March, the feebleness of the program became so evident that Ambassador Taylor expressed his sharp annoyance at the delays, the weakness of the attacks, and the targets.[20] Westmoreland, in his turn, could see no results coming from ROLLING THUNDER for at least six months, and before then the government of South Vietnam might well go under. This concern over the early collapse of the Vietnamese military effort in the south was shared by the key actors in Washington, including the president.

On 2 March, President Johnson ordered Gen. Harold K. Johnson, the army chief of staff, to go to Vietnam to determine what could be done in South Vietnam to improve the situation there. In Saigon, General Johnson conferred extensively with General Westmoreland, and Johnson's recommendations on his return to Washington reflected Westmoreland's concepts. Johnson recommended a twenty-one-point program. Among his recommendations were two which would increase the effectiveness of ROLLING THUNDER. He also proposed that one United States Army division be sent to Vietnam to be employed either in the Central

Highlands (Kontum and Pleiku provinces) or around the airfields at Tan Son Nhut (in Saigon) and Bien Hoa, nearby. General Johnson also recommended that additional helicopters and advisors be sent in along with logistical troops.[21] President Johnson, on 6 April, in NSAM 328, approved most of General Johnson's proposals, including those for toughening up ROLLING THUNDER, but he took no action on the recommendations calling for the logistical troops and the army division. The president did, however, approve the insertion of two additional marine battalions and one marine air squadron. Most significantly he "approved a change of mission for all marine battalions . . . to permit their more active use under conditions to be established and approved by the Secretary of Defense in Consultation with the Secretary of State."[22]

This action on the part of the president represented the first major switch in the strategy governing the use of United States ground combat forces. No longer were ground forces to be pinned down on base security missions. Now, Westmoreland could use them aggressively against the Viet Cong. But if the mission of base security was gone, what was the new mission to be? NASM 328 had set forth generalities about "more active use" of the marines, and then under "conditions to be established and approved by the Secretary of Defense in consultation with the Secretary of State."[23] It was Maxwell Taylor who, as ambassador, raised the question about the new United States strategy in Vietnam. On 17 April, he cabled the State Department that we "badly need a clarification of our purposes and objectives."[24]

If Taylor needed guidance, so did all of the other principal United States actors, and that guidance was produced at a high-level conference held in Honolulu on 20 April 1965. McNamara, McNaughton, William Bundy, Taylor, Westmoreland, Gen. "Bus" Wheeler, the chairman of the Joint Chiefs of Staff, and Admiral Sharp, CINCPAC, attended. The strategy which eventuated from this high-level conference was that proposed by Ambassador Taylor, the so-called "enclave" strategy. It foresaw the establishment of United States enclaves around important coastal areas such as Da Nang, Nha Trang, Qui Nhon, Phu Bai (north of Da Nang), and Chu Lai (south of Da Nang). American troops would defend these areas and would be authorized to sally forth not more than fifty miles to assist ARVN troops or to undertake their own counterinsurgency operations. It was a relatively cheap and cautious way to see how United

States troops would perform in active operations against the Viet Cong.

Taylor's enclave strategy reflected his opposition to bringing in United States ground combat forces, and his fears that "white-faced" troops (as he called them) could not successfully meet the Viet Cong in counterinsurgency operations. His strategy would have severely limited the operations of United States ground forces and placed them in coastal areas from which they could easily and rapidly be withdrawn. In Taylor's thinking, *if* the United States *had* to have ground combat troops in Vietnam at all, the enclave strategy was the cheapest and the least risky way to use them. It appealed to President Johnson, who wanted to minimize his commitment of ground troops, and who wanted to experiment prudently with United States forces in an offensive role.

While the president and Ambassador Taylor embraced the enclave strategy, both General Westmoreland and the Joint Chiefs of Staff opposed it. They pointed out that the enclave concept would station American troops in the heavily populated coastal areas, a sure way to arouse the antagonism of the xenophobic Vietnamese. The admirals and generals invoked the memories of the two French commanders, de Lattre and Navarre, who had tried a form of the enclave concept. The French found that they either had to react to Vietminh moves far outside the enclaves or stand by and watch their native allies and their territories be inundated by the Communist flood. Navarre's response to Giap's operations in Laos had brought on Dien Bien Phu—or so many of the American generals argued. While this might have been an oversimplification, there was substance there, too.

The American generals foresaw an even grimmer picture of what the enclave concept would bring. ARVN would not be able to stand up to the Viet Cong in the countryside. Steadily, they would be defeated and driven into the United States enclaves or destroyed and scattered. In time, the United States troops would be surrounded in static defensive positions, subject to artillery fire and to massed attacks by Giap's NVA Main Forces.[25]

The military's fundamental dislike and distrust of the enclave strategy sprang from the defensive nature of the concept, and because it forced the United States forces voluntarily to give up the "offensive" and to surrender the "initiative." This violated the most cherished tenets of the military creed by which the army and marine generals lived. It was an article of faith that (in the words of the army's *Field Manual on*

Operations) "wars can be won only by offensive action." That principle of war, "the offensive," is one of the army's most sacrosanct. The "initiative" is closely linked to the "offensive." The American war colleges teach that only by forcing your will on the enemy and by making him conform to your actions can victory be won. The military history of our Civil War, World War I, World War II, and even the Korean conflict confirms this concept.

The enclave concept, like the base security strategy before it, led a short and barren life. Born in mid-April, it was dead by mid-June, supplanted by another strategy, that of search and destroy. With one minor exception (an operation carried out by the marines fifteen miles south of Chu Lai in August 1965), the enclave concept was never tested. And by this one test, it was a partial success. It would be simple to say that the American generals and admirals killed the enclave concept, but other forces really did it in. First, there was ROLLING THUNDER. Although the president had toughened the program in early April, it still did not strike the critical targets, nor did it strike unimportant targets with a decisive weight of bombs. The proponents of the enclave concept based its validity on the thesis that the enclave strategy would deny the Communists victory in the South while ROLLING THUNDER punished them in the North. When in the late spring it became evident that ROLL-ING THUNDER was not punishing the North Vietnamese and would not bring Ho Chi Minh to negotiations, the key assumption of the enclave strategy collapsed, bringing the concept down with it.

Another factor which gutted the enclave strategy was the old problem of the command and coordination of military operations between the forces of the United States and South Vietnam. Base security was a clear-cut and militarily definable mission, but the fifty-mile offensive area of operations for United States troops, which the enclave strategy contained, brought the United States commanders and troops into the tactical area of operations of the South Vietnamese units. The United States would not give the Vietnamese any authority over American troops; and the Vietnamese, from their experience under the French, would not relinquish command of their units to the United States generals. During the short life of the enclave strategy, this command and coordination problem was never resolved. During the two major battles in May and early June, Ba Gia and Dong Xoai, the ARVN units needed help badly; United States troops were available, yet they were never used.

And even more central to the death of the enclave strategy was the deterioration of the military situation in South Vietnam. By late May, the real question was whether there would be any ARVN left to support. The long-awaited Viet Cong summer offensive had jumped off on 11 May, when more than a regiment of Viet Cong troops attacked Song Be, in Phuoc Long province. The enemy overran the town, causing heavy casualties among United States advisors and the South Vietnamese troops. The enemy held the town overnight and withdrew the next day. Later in May, the Viet Cong struck in Quang Ngai province near the small outpost of Ba Gia. The Viet Cong ambushed and destroyed a battalion of the 51st ARVN Regiment. A battle raged for several days in which ARVN lost a second battalion. Even worse, the ARVN commanders had shown gross tactical ineptitude and rank cowardice. In Saigon, panic arose among the Americans. The nightmare of a speedy and total ARVN collapse appeared to be more than a bad dream. To make matters worse, intelligence agencies picked up in South Vietnam all elements of the 325th NVA Division, and they noted signs that the 304th NVA Division was on the way south, too.

On 7 June 1965, General Westmoreland sent a message to Admiral Sharp, CINCPAC, expressing his consternation over the situation. He pointed out that the Viet Cong were better trained and equipped than ever before, and that they had not yet employed their full strength in the campaign. He condemned ARVN severely. Their desertion rate was inordinately high; battle losses had been greater than expected; and their spirit was wilting. Westmoreland concluded, ''I see no course of action open to us except to reinforce our efforts in South Vietnam with additional United States or Third Country forces as rapidly as practicable. . . Additionally studies must continue and plans developed to deploy even greater forces. . . Ground forces deployed to selected areas along the coast and inland will be used both offensively and defensively. . . I am convinced that United States troops with their energy, mobility, and firepower can successfully take the fight to the Viet Cong. . . The basic purpose of the deployments recommended is to give us a substantial and hard-hitting offensive capability on the ground to convince the Viet Cong they cannot win.''[26]

Three days later, Westmoreland's desperate outlook was confirmed. On 10 June, the Viet Cong struck the Special Forces camp at Dong Xoai with two regiments and inflicted a catastrophic defeat on ARVN in a battle lasting five days. By mid-June, the long-awaited Communist offensive was picking up speed, as the enemy now focused his operations on the Central Highlands of the ARVN II Corps area. On 25 June, a North Vietnamese Main Force regiment took a district headquarters in Kontum province. Other district headquarters came under attack by the NVA Main Force units in the remote Highlands. To General Westmoreland and to the president's advisers in Washington, these attacks signaled the long-awaited Communist offensive aimed at cutting South Vietnam in two along the line of Highway 19, running between Pleiku and Qui Nhon. If this was not the enemy's intent, then another possibility, equally chilling, was that the Viet Cong would carve out an enclave in the Highlands and set up the National Liberation Front (NLF) as a functioning government there.

Eyeing these two potentialities, Westmoreland fired off another cable late in June. He again asked for a speedy deployment of United States and Third Country combat forces and repeated his view that if South Vietnam was to survive, the United States had to have ". . . a substantial and hard-hitting offensive capability . . . with troops that could be maneuvered freely."[27]

Westmoreland's messages of June put the issue squarely to the president. Westmoreland had requested reinforcements on a large scale, and he had made it plain that with them he meant to take the offensive against the enemy. The specter of the long-dreaded ground war in Asia was now real. In mid-June, Ambassador Taylor weighed in with a cable confirming Westmoreland's pessimistic view of the military situation in the South. This cable temporarily broke the back of the Washington opposition to greater United States ground force involvement in Vietnam. By 22 June, General Wheeler cabled Westmoreland that forty-four combat battalions would be phased into South Vietnam as soon as possible. On 26 June, Westmoreland received authority to commit United States troops "when in COMUSMACV's judgment their use is necessary to strengthen the relative position of GVN forces."[28]

The very next day, Westmoreland conducted an offensive operation into War Zone D, northwest of Saigon, using the United States 173rd Airborne Brigade, an Australian battalion, and about five battalions of ARVN infantry. Thus was born the military strategy of search and destroy, a concept much debated and often maligned, which would govern United States ground operations for three years.

This American foray 27 June locked the United States into a ground-force war in Asia. The concept of air base defense of late February 1965 had rapidly evolved into the tactical offensive of June. With the acceptance of the search and destroy concept, the United States was totally committed, and the *Pentagon Papers* paint Westmoreland as the man who took the United States into the large-scale ground war in Asia.[29] Westmoreland, himself, is much more modest. He writes in his book that he merely told his superiors what troops he needed to do his job. Of course, only one man can be held responsible for the large-scale commitment of the United States ground troops to Vietnam. That man is Lyndon Baines Johnson.

Regardless of the part Westmoreland played in involving the United States in a ground war in Vietnam, that war quickly became known among the senior military officers in Vietnam and in the Pentagon as "Westy's War," and rightly so. While he was not responsible for getting the United States into the ground war in Vietnam, he played a major role in developing the strategy and tactics which governed its conduct from 1965 to mid-1968.

Westmoreland's strategy of search and destroy has fueled many smoky fires of controversy. Westmoreland, himself, described it as "an operation to find the enemy and to eliminate his base camps and logistic installations."[30] This definition surprises even the senior United States commanders and staff officers who served with the general in Vietnam from 1964 until his departure in mid-1968. All of them would define search and destroy in a simpler and bloodier fashion: find the enemy and destroy—not his base camps—but the enemy soldiers. In his book, Westmoreland is more candid. He categorically states, "The United States military strategy employed in Vietnam, dictated by political decisions, was essentially that of a war of attrition."[31] In these words, General Westmoreland sums up his strategy as *attrition,* and this is the sword which his critics have used to attack him and his concept.

Westmoreland and his strategy of attrition had supporters as well as attackers. The Joint Chiefs of Staff and CINCPAC wholeheartedly supported Westmoreland's strategy throughout the period from 1965 to mid-1968. Secretary of Defense McNamara and Secretary of State Rusk both backed Westmoreland and his concept, although McNamara's support flagged from mid-1967 until his resignation on 29 February 1968. President Johnson and his national security adviser, Walt W. Rostow, at least tacitly lent their backing to the concept of attrition. And finally, all of the above luminaries either wrote or concurred in a 1966 directive to Westmoreland which officially established attrition of enemy strength as one of his primary missions. This directive, incidentally, was not superseded until August 1969, over a year after Westmoreland left Vietnam.

The principal attackers of the strategy of attrition included Townsend Hoopes, once deputy assistant secretary of defense, Lt. Gen. James Gavin, Sir Robert Thompson, the Britisher who conducted the successful counterinsurgency war against the Malaysian insurgents, and Ambassador Robert W. Komer, the United States pacification chief in Vietnam from 1967 to 1969. Other critics found positions around the periphery of the argument from which to snipe at Westmoreland and his strategy.

Hoopes and Gavin espoused a variation of the enclave strategy. Although the two men differed in conceptual details, both agreed that United States troops should hold populous areas near the coast which could then be pacified. They proposed a cessation of the search and destroy operations, since they offered no permanent protection for the people. Both advocated a halt to the bombing of North Vietnam as a means of bringing Ho Chi Minh to negotiations. The Hoopes/Gavin version of the enclave strategy would have surrendered most of South Vietnam to the enemy. Beyond that, the negotiating record of the North Vietnamese refutes the suggestion that in 1965 a bombing halt would have moved the North to the bargaining table. Significantly, General Gavin, after a visit to Vietnam in 1968, qualified his advocacy of the enclave theory by telling General Westmoreland that the *logistic bases* which Westmoreland had established along the coasts were "exactly the enclaves he (Gavin) had been talking about."[32] Westmoreland correctly brands Gavin's remark as "illogical." There is a total difference between coastal bases built to support offensive operations and coastal enclaves of a purely defensive nature.

Sir Robert Thompson, speaking from his experience as the victor over the insurgents in Malaysia, roundly censured not only Westmoreland and his strategy but all of the United States governmental leaders, civilian and military alike. He condemned United States operations in Vietnam between 1965 and 1969 as lacking a national aim, pursuing a wrong strategy, and lacking control over the three major aspects of the war—defeating the military threat, nation building, and pacification. He would correct these errors of policy and strategy by first placing all three efforts under the control of a "pro-consul," probably an American general. This man would have total authority over all United States agencies in the country. Thompson proposed setting up formal coordinating machinery between the United States and South Vietnam. He would make the military effort an adjunct to the pacification program. Thompson would have clarified the aim of the United States in Vietnam to include not only a precise statement about what we were trying to do there, but some indication as to what the United States was prepared to expend in troop commitments, money, and time.[33] *Time?* Now, there was something new.

Robert Komer, a brilliant and abrasive bureaucrat, generally supports Thompson's criticism of Westmoreland's strategy. Komer, who was involved in policy-making at the Washington and Saigon levels from 1966 to 1969, maintains that the strategy of attrition was wrong because the enemy could control his losses by avoiding combat and by infiltration from the North. Komer agrees with Thompson that the United States made a compartmented approach to the war, and that the lack of any combined United States-Vietnam management system limited the effectiveness of the allied effort. Komer further supports Thompson in his statement that the intelligence effort in Vietnam was targeted at the wrong segment of the enemy organization—the Main Force units—instead of being aimed at the Viet Cong infrastructure. Finally, Komer avers that pacification was never really tried until 1967, and by then the effort was too little and too late.[34]

The Hoopes and Gavins, with their enclave strategies and bombing halts, are easy to shoot down based on prior (and as of 1965, future) experience in Vietnam. The criticism of Thompson and Komer, however, is not disposed of so easily. Westmoreland counters their faultfinding by asking the question: "what alternative was there to a war of attrition?"[35] For political reasons, he was not permitted to invade North Vietnam. He was forbidden to go into Laos, even though he had several detailed plans to cut the Ho Chi Minh Trail by a ground incursion into that country. He could not attack the Communist military headquarters, Central Office South Vietnam (COSVN), and bases in Cambodia which controlled and supported Viet Cong operations in South Vietnam. The United States troops had to be used in South Vietnam, and they had to be used offensively. Over two millennia ago, Sun Tzu prophetically described Westmoreland's plight. The Chinese sage wrote, "To put a rein on an able general while at the same time asking him to suppress a cunning enemy is like tying up the Black Hound of Han and then ordering him to catch elusive hares."[36]

Westmoreland does not discuss the possibility of using United States troops in support of the pacification effort, that is, in clear and hold operations. The reason for this omission can be deduced from other sections of his book and from his official report on the war. To Westmoreland, the greatest threat to the South Vietnamese government came not from the Viet Cong guerrillas and the NFL political infrastructure, but from the Main Force units, both Viet Cong and particularly NVA. He compared the guerrillas to termites gnawing away at the house of the South Vietnamese government. The enemy Main Force units he called "the bully boys" who, Westmoreland claimed, would tear the house down with crowbars if not kept in check. To keep the Main Force units off the population, Westmoreland felt that he had to keep the initiative by seeking them out and attacking them.

Another argument Westmoreland used to buttress the defense of his search and destroy strategy was that enemy Main Force units operated in difficult and unpopulated areas, and the search for them took United States troops out of the highly populated areas, where their presence would cause military, social, and economic problems. Another plus for search and destroy operations was that they were conducted in remote areas, which eased the problem of United States/South Vietnam coordination of effort. In effect, the United States could fight its own ground war unhampered by the necessity to coordinate not only military operations, but civil affairs as well, with the South Vietnamese. The final reason for Westmoreland's selection of his search and destroy strategy was that it left pacification largely to the South Vietnamese government and its troops. To Westmoreland, the South Vietnamese were infinitely more able in handling their own people than the Americans would be, no matter how competent or motivated the latter might be.

It is significant that later, both Komer and Thompson appeared to temper their criticisms of Westmoreland's strategy of attrition. Writing in 1972, Komer advanced the thesis that while the strategy of attrition may have been wrong, *realistically* not much else could have been done. Komer's central point is that bureaucratic constraints and experience forced the United States and South Vietnam agencies to fight the war as they did. As an example, he notes that the United States Army was trained and equipped to fight large enemy units. Instinctively, this is what it did. None of the multitude of United States agencies which operated in South Vietnam was trained or traditionally interested in pacification. As a result, writes Komer, pacification fell through the cracks.

Sir Robert Thompson made an even greater move towards a later acceptance of Westmoreland's strategy. In the mid-seventies, in a seminar with other "experts" on the Vietnam War, he argued that by late 1972 the enemy had been attrited until he "hurt."[37] Other participants noted, however, that conditions were different in 1972 from those which existed in 1965–1968. They were saying that the painful attrition of 1972 had been brought on by the enemy himself in launching the disastrous offensives of 1968 (Tet) and 1972, not by the United States initiatives of 1965–1968. So Thompson's endorsement of the attrition strategy fuzzes into near ambiguity.

Other critics of lesser prestige and experience than Gavin, Hoopes, Komer, and Thompson banged away at Westmoreland's strategy of attrition. One of Westmoreland's former aides, Gen. D. R. Palmer, states categorically that "Attrition is not a strategy. It is, in fact irrefutable proof of the absence of any strategy. A commander who resorts to attrition admits his failure to conceive of an alternative. He rejects warfare as an art. . . He uses blood in lieu of brains. To be sure, political considerations left military commanders no choice other than attrition warfare, but that does not alter the hard truth that the United States was strategically bankrupt in Vietnam in 1966."[38]

It is hard to discern just what Palmer's point is. Apparently he does not blame Westmoreland for his choice of attrition strategy, since he says that Westmoreland had no alternative. Here Palmer is wrong. Westmoreland could have gone the pacification route, as Komer and Thompson advocated. Furthermore, Palmer's unqualified declaration that "attrition is not a strategy" is incomprehensible. Attrition is a strategy, and in the right time and place, it is a good one. The great Clausewitz wrote that if one could not immediately destroy the enemy's armed forces, then one should concentrate on what he calls "wastage" of the enemy (another name for attrition)—making the war more costly to the adversary by laying waste to his territory, increasing the enemy's suffering, and eroding his morale and physical assets. American military history provides classic examples of this "wastage": World Wars I and II were wars of attrition. Grant, Sherman, and Sheridan won the Civil War using the strategy of attrition. In fact, Grant utilized pure search and destroy operations. From 1864 on, he focused on Lee's army, attacking it at every chance, and eventually eroding the Confederate force into impotence and surrender. Sherman, meanwhile, laid waste the "bread basket" of the South, while Sheridan ravaged the Shenandoah Valley of Virginia. Incidentally, Grant and his subordinates were lucky. Grant would have been relieved from command had the television cameras brought the Battle of the Wilderness with its excessive casualties and horror into the Union homes every night at six o'clock, and Sherman and Sheridan would certainly have fallen prey to the liberals' charge of waging an "unjust" and "immoral" war.

The strategy of attrition has been successful in other than conventional wars. The American Indians, a redoubtable guerrilla force, were subjugated by a series of relentless campaigns designed to attrite their strength and means of livelihood. And although it took the American army a century and a half to do the job, they—and the settlers and railroads who followed them—destroyed the Indians as a guerrilla force not by brilliant campaigns, but by grinding attrition.

Other critics, Col. Donaldson D. Frizzell, United States Air Force, a strategic thinker for the Air War College, and Mr. Thomas C. Thayer, a civilian who had worked in McNamara's office during the war, make the oft-repeated charge that the United States could not adequately attrite an enemy who could avoid heavy combat, who had a significant replacement capability, and who was willing to take severe casualties.[39] Neither they nor Palmer suggest any alternative to the search and destroy strategy.

The debate about the proper strategy was further confused by the ideological biases, the personal experiences, and the self-interests of the various proponents. Westmoreland, Sharp, the Joint Chiefs, and the other senior military saw the war as a variation of conventional warfare with which they were familiar. The president, McNamara, Rusk, and company saw it slightly differently, as a war in which conventional forces, both air and ground, could be used to obtain a bargaining position in negotiations. On another side of the argument, Sir Robert Thompson and Ambassador Komer saw the war principally as an insurgency, or at least as a war in which the defeat of the insurgency was the paramount goal. These views reflected Thompson's experience and Komer's self-interest. Thompson had become famous for destroying the insurgency in Malaysia (a *pure* insurgency without intervention by foreign troops). Komer's reputation was tied completely to the success of his pacification program, giving him a one-dimensional view. The attacks on Westmoreland's search and destroy strategy by Hoopes and Gavin sprang from their deep ideological aversion to the Vietnam War and to the deployment of United States forces there. But since American troops were deployed in Vietnam, they espoused the static enclave concept, supporting that strategy by claiming that the war was an insurgency against which the enclave concept made some sense. It was the classic example of the blind men trying to describe an elephant by feeling different parts of the beast—each got a different animal.

The criticisms of the search and destroy strategy by Thompson, Komer, and others, as well as Westmoreland's rebuttal of their charges, have reverberated through the halls of those institutions—the Pentagon, the Washington "think tanks," and academia—which have attempted to mine the Vietnamese experience for the timeless lessons of that conflict. Was Westmoreland's strategy of attrition wrong? Would a pacification strategy of clear and hold operations have worked better? Nobody knows. Komer himself writes that these questions must "remain a historical 'if'."[40]

How could so many intelligent and experienced people hold such widely contradictory views on the proper United States ground strategy? The answer is that the proponents of the various strategies debated the wrong question. The real question was *not* what was the proper strategy to guide the ground war in South Vietnam, but *what kind of war was the United States fighting in Vietnam at any given period*. Clausewitz said it best: "The first, the supreme, the most far-reaching act of judgment that the statesman and the commander have to make is to establish . . . the kind of war on which they are embarking . . . neither mistaking it or trying to turn it into something that is alien to its nature. This is the first of all strategic questions and the most comprehensive."[41] If the "statesman and commander" correctly determine the kind of war they are fighting, they can establish the proper strategy to fight it. To determine the correct United States strategy at any given period, one must focus on the strategy and phases of revolutionary war as waged by the North Vietnamese, for the North Vietnamese held the strategic initiative. This tremendous advantage came about principally due to the restrictions placed on the United States military effort. If the war in

Vietnam was a Phase I insurgency, then one American strategy was correct; if the war has moved into Phase III, a conventional war, then another United States concept was right; if the war was a combination of an insurgency and a conventional war (Phase II), then a third strategy was proper.

With this proviso one must attempt—helped materially by hindsight—to determine what kind of war the United States had to fight at any given period. If this question can be answered, then a proper strategy for a given time can be selected. In the late fifties, when the United States began to get irretrievably involved in Vietnam, the Communists waged an almost pure Phase I insurgency, or, as the distinguished expert on Vietnamese communism, Douglas Pike, called it, the revolutionary guerrilla war.[42] Of course, it was even then controlled by the North Vietnamese Politburo, but it was carried out by native South Vietnamese with considerable freedom from Northern control. The insurgency stressed political *dau tranh,* with military action used principally as an adjunct to political strife. In the early sixties, the war remained in Phase I, an insurgency, drifting always, however, toward the conventional mode.

The insurgency mode of warfare held until mid-1965. By this time, sizable forces of both the NVA Main Forces and United States troops were in South Vietnam. Infantry divisions began to fight enemy divisions. On the American side, Field Forces (corps) made their appearance, and on the Communist side, Fronts (another corps-type formation) came into being. Artillery and air power (on the American side) appeared in quantity, and both sides set up elaborate logistical installations. Nevertheless, the Viet Cong insurgency and its political infrastructure remained strong, with significant capabilities, particularly against Allied pacification efforts. Thus, from 1965 until early 1968, the war had moved into Phase II, a combination of insurgency and conventional war.

This mode lasted until the Tet offensive of 1968, when the war moved into Phase III. From then on, the war was a conventional one. The Viet Cong guerrillas and the VC political infrastructure, the insurgency operators, were virtually destroyed in the Tet offensive. The Communists increasingly filled the gaps in nominal Viet Cong units with NVA replacements. In mid-1968 and until 1972, Giap retrogressed from conventional war to a *form* of guerrilla war, which featured guerrilla-type actions carried out by highly trained North Vietnamese commandos (which the Communists called sappers). Interspersed among these sapper operations were the so-called "high points," attacks around South Vietnam which involved sizable NVA units. This "sapper-high point" type of operation was only a transitory stage leading in 1972 to the Easter offensive, a large-scale attack by modernized, conventional NVA forces.

With an understanding of revolutionary war and its changing phases, one can begin to fit into each Communist phase the proper American counterstrategy for that phase. In Phase I, the pure Communist insurgency period (until around mid-1965), the best strategy would have been to emphasize pacification with its military adjunct, clear and hold operations. It was a passive strategy, one surrendering the initiative to large Communist units, but then prior to 1965 there were few large enemy units in South Vietnam to take advantage of this passivity. It had advantages, too. It was simple, it required no high order of staff work, communications, or weaponry, and it was directed against the real enemy in this phase—the guerrilla and the insurgency's political infrastructure.

It had its problems, too. Clear and hold operations brought the troops into close contact with the population. It required, therefore, that the troops have a high level of discipline and motivation. Indeed, the conduct of the troops themselves was one of the key factors bearing on pacification. Looting, killing, and raping by the soldiers destroys pacification just as surely as the reoccupation of the area by the insurgents. These problems of close military-civilian contact are often compounded by the use of foreign troops.

In a Phase I situation (insurgency), the enclave concept had some advantages, too. It protected the bulk of the people, giving them the long-term security required for the slow process of pacification. For American troops it had the added advantage—as Gen. Maxwell Taylor saw—of garrisoning areas from which they could be expeditiously evacuated by sea or air. The enclave strategy had disadvantages, also. It surrendered a major portion of the country to the insurgents. It completely gave up the initiative, and with the continual drift toward large-unit, conventional war, insured that eventually an enemy attack of major proportions would hit the enclave. It, too, required highly disciplined troops.

Phase II, the combination of insurgency and conventional warfare, is more complex and difficult to deal with strategically. In this phase the United States and its allies had to fight both the insurgent and the conventional opponent. Here a part of the force must carry out the clear and hold-type operations while another part fights off major enemy units in a largely conventional-type war. This is precisely the type of strategy which Westmoreland tried to carry out from June 1965 until 31 January 1968. In his concept, the South Vietnamese would do most of the clear and hold operations while the Americans fought the NVA and Viet Cong Main and Local Force units.

One quarrel between Westmoreland and his critics arose over what portion of the American force should have been employed in clear and hold and what part in search and destroy operations. Those who attack Westmoreland's strategy claim that not enough United States forces were dedicated to clear and hold action. To this nebulous question, "how much is enough," there can be no valid answer.

Finally, in early 1968, the war progressed into Phase III, or the almost pure conventional war. Here occurred the Tet offensive, the siege of Khe Sanh, and the 1972 offensive. Guerrilla warfare by indigenous South Vietnamese Communists had virtually vanished, and the original insurgency had been almost completely overcome. Now the war had become an invasion of one nation by another, each using largely conventional means of warfare.

Now a critic might argue, with some justification, that this discussion of the phases of Indochina War II and of the various strategic options is oversimplified. For example, a critic might point out that after the Tet offensive of 1968 and into 1969, 1970, and 1971, the Communists reverted to small-unit guerrilla-type warfare, and that General Abrams (in command of MACV after mid-1968) correctly emphasized clear and hold operations and intensified pacification efforts. Douglas Pike calls this phase the "Neo-Revolutionary Guerrilla War" period, implying a shift back to an insurgency form of warfare. While he is correct that this phase saw a return to guerrilla *tactics,* the important difference is that the small-unit actions of the enemy were not carried out by local Viet Cong guerrillas (the insurgents), but by alien NVA sappers from Main Force units.

To this complex problem (determining what phase of revolutionary war the enemy is in) is added another complication. Clausewitz's "statesmen and commanders" must determine not only what phase they are countering, and the correct strategy with which to combat it, but they must anticipate future phases projected months and even years ahead. An army trained, equipped, and organized to combat an insurgency will be at a deadly disadvantage in fighting a conventional war. To

transform the counterinsurgency army into a conventional war army requires a long lead time and a great deal of planning and preparation.
Conversely, it takes time and effort to convert a conventional army
into a counterinsurgency army, and Vietnam shows that it may be impossible—but that is another story.

As Westmoreland developed his strategic concepts through the summer and early fall of 1965, a basic question disturbed the United States
military professionals running the war. Put bluntly, that question was:
how would American soldiers do against the veteran NVA Main Force
units in the difficult terrain and weather of South Vietnam? Since the
United States troops had been trained and equipped to fight on the plains
of Europe, could they now "hack it" (to use the old GI expression) in
Vietnam? The answer was soon forthcoming, and it would come, ironically, from the only unit in the American army which traditionally cele-
brates its own massacre—the 7th United States Cavalry. This was the
regiment which had ridden to death and glory in the Valley of the Little
Big Horn under George Armstrong Custer. These modern 7th Cavalrymen
rode helicopters, not horses, but they cherished the regimental history
and sang the old regimental song, "Garry Owen." The 7th was part of
the First United States Cavalry Division (Airmobile), a unique unit,
and by training, equipment, and motivation, the elite division of the
American army.

The stage for this first test was to be the Ia Drang Valley in the
Western Highlands of South Vietnam. The actors were two regiments
of the NVA Main Forces and the 1st Battalion of the 7th Cavalry, later
reinforced by other elements of the 1st Cavalry Division. Both sides
were looking for a fight. The cavalry division wanted to seize the initiative
from the NVA, which had been attacking isolated Special Forces camps
in the area. The NVA commander, Gen. Chu Huy Man, an old friend
of Giap's, wanted to win a victory over the newly arrived American
troops. In the Ia Drang Valley, they collided.

On 14 November, the 1st Cavalry Division threw the first punch
by helicopter-lifting the 1st Battalion, 7th Cavalry into a remote landing
area (named X-Ray) which was in the middle of a suspected NVA base
area in the valley. General Man responded by rushing three NVA battalions
to X-Ray to annihilate the cavalry troopers. By late afternoon, the American position had become desperate. Lt. Col. Harold G. Moore, the

battalion commander, radioed his superior, Col. Thomas W. Brown, the 3rd Brigade commander, for reinforcements. Brown responded immediately by sending in one company from another battalion by helicopter and alerted another whole battalion to reinforce Moore by foot.

As evening fell, senior military professionals from Moore and Brown to Westmoreland must have had some uneasy moments wondering if Custer's last stand with the ill-fated 7th Cavalry might not be reenacted in the valley of the Ia Drang. Here again was the 7th Cavalry surrounded in a lonely valley by a force several times their number, bent on their annihilation. But Moore and Brown were no Custer and Reno. They were cool, professional soldiers—smart, tough, and experienced. And their troopers were not the old, boozy, Civil War veterans of Custer's command. These "Garry Owens" were young, well trained, and brave.

On the morning of 15 November, General Man launched a violent and coordinated three-battalion attack on X-Ray. Here some of the fiercest fighting in American history took place, some of it hand-to-hand, almost all of it within the length of a football field. The United States Army's official account of the action reports graphically the closeness and intensity of the combat. Here is the description of the fight of one platoon: "The North Vietnamese laced the small perimeter with fire so low to the ground that few of Herrick's men were able to employ their intrenching tools to provide themselves cover. Through it all the men returned the fire, taking a heavy toll of the enemy. Sergeant Savage, firing his M16, hit twelve of the enemy himself during the course of the afternoon. In midafternoon Lieutenant Herrick was hit by a bullet which entered his hip, coursed through his body, and went out through his right shoulder. As he lay dying, the lieutenant continued to direct his perimeter defense, and in his last few moments he gave his signal operation instructions book to Staff Sergeant Carl L. Palmer, his platoon sergeant, with orders to burn it if capture seemed imminent. He told Palmer to redistribute the ammunition, call in artillery fire, and at the first opportunity try to make a break for it. Sergeant Palmer, himself already slightly wounded, had no sooner taken command than he too was killed.

"Sergeant Savage, the 3d Squad leader, now took command. Snatching the artilleryman's radio, he began calling in and adjusting artillery fire. Within minutes he had ringed the perimeter with well-placed concentrations, some as close to the position as twenty meters. The fire did much to discourage attempts to overrun the perimeter, but the platoon's position was still precarious. Of the 27 men in the platoon, 8 had been killed and 12 wounded, leaving less than a squad of effectives."[43]

By midmorning the vast firepower available to the American troopers began to take its murderous toll. A total of over 33,000 rounds of 105mm artillery was fired. United States Air Force fighter-bombers furnished constant air support, and even the "big birds," the B-52's, pounded the area with their 500-pound bombs. By the morning of the next day, General Man had had enough. He rounded up what was left of his force and headed for the nearby Cambodian border.

The first major United States/NVA encounter had resulted in a major victory for the Americans. The 1st Cavalry Division lost 79 men killed and 121 wounded. The NVA had 634 known dead, at least the same number of dead dragged away, plus an unknown number of wounded. The two NVA regiments which had tangled with the "Garry Owens" had been destroyed.

Lieutenant Colonel Moore ascribed the victory to "brave soldiers and the M-16 rifle" (with which his troops had been recently equipped).[44] A more objective observer would add that another factor of success was the leadership and expertise of Moore and Brown, both of whom would later become generals. If the strategy of search and destroy had weaknesses, one of them was *not* the skill and valor of the American officers and soldiers who would carry it out.

The North Vietnamese disaster in the Ia Drang Valley intensified and broadened the strategy dispute which had been raging for at least a year between Giap and Nguyen Chi Thanh. The initiation of the ROLLING THUNDER program against North Vietnam and the arrival of American ground troops in Vietnam shocked and confused the North Vietnamese leadership. Ironically, Ho Chi Minh faced the same broad options which President Johnson faced—he could get out of the war and let the Viet Cong go it alone, or he could go on fighting and escalating with NVA troops. But in Ho's mind, there was only the second alternative. Thus, the major strategic decisions of the North Vietnamese revolved around options as to how to carry on the war against the United States.

Now that the United States had joined the ground war, the North Vietnamese saw their overall strategic problem as a three-pronged one.

First, there was the problem of combating United States ground troops in South Vietnam. Then there was the problem of North Vietnam's defense against United States air attacks in the north, the ROLLING THUNDER program. The third prong of the strategic trident turned around Hanoi's fear that the Americans would invade North Vietnam itself.

The North Vietnamese concept of air defense embodied a combination of advanced technology and primitive use of manpower. The Soviet Union furnished the MIG's, missiles, and antiaircraft guns which eventually made the North Vietnamese air defense system formidable indeed. The Soviets furnished technicians, maintenance personnel, and training cadres. The North Vietnamese—xenophobic as always—ignored much of the Soviets' advice, and their "kill-rate" suffered accordingly. Nevertheless, as the war continued, American pilots became increasingly respectful of North Vietnamese air defenses.

The other aspect of the North Vietnamese concept of air defense was more in keeping with the traditional views of Ho and Giap. The core of the concept was that *everybody* in North Vietnam was part of the air defense system. This concept stressed particularly the repair of transportation facilities so that men and materials could continue to move to the southern front. United States intelligence sources estimated that about 100,000 North Vietnamese worked *full-time* on road and railroad repair, and additional hundreds of thousands worked part-time. The system was largely decentralized. Designated groups had responsibility for a given sector and they pre-stocked repair materials along the road or railroad. The American bombs had hardly stopped falling when the crews began to repair the roads. It was primitive and labor-intensive, but it worked.

While the Americans could understand, and professionally appreciate, the North Vietnamese air defense effort, Giap's concern with a United States invasion of North Vietnam would have boggled his American adversaries. The Americans *knew* that the president had placed North Vietnam "off-limits" to ground units except for small intelligence-gathering parties. Giap didn't know that. He reasoned that ROLLING THUNDER and Westmoreland's search and destroy concept would fail and prove so frustrating that a more drastic escalation—an invasion of the North—would have to be mounted. He was right about the frustration inherent in the two American programs, but wrong about President Johnson's resolve and the debilitating influence of the internal politics of the United States on that resolve.

Giap built his anti-invasion strategy again around the "People's War" concept. Simply put, each village, district, and province was organized for defense, and the men, women, and children were expected to fight the invaders to the death. Arms, supplied plentifully by Russia and China, were issued to these "self-defense" militia. Of course, in the event of a United States invasion, Giap's Main Force units would fight the large battles, but his mobilization of the peasants guaranteed a long, bitter, no-front war of attrition. Happily for both Americans and the North Vietnamese, Giap's defensive concept was never tested.

Unlike the unanimity with which the Politburo arrived at solutions to the problems of air defense and defense against invasion of the North, the strategic problem of combating the United States troops in South Vietnam evoked a stormy, high-level controversy between the old adversaries. On one side there was Nguyen Chi Thanh, the commander in the South, and Le Duan, and opposing them were Giap and Truong Chinh. The gist of the debate turned around the tactics and forces to be used in South Vietnam now that the Americans had arrived in strength. Thanh and Le Duan argued for a largely conventional war of Main Force units, while Giap's concept emphasized small-unit and guerrilla tactics while holding the Main Force units in reserve.

Thanh held that the Viet Cong and the NVA units had almost won the war in late 1964 against ARVN, and that the entrance of the Americans called not for retrenchment, but for a continuation of large-scale attacks by which Thanh would keep the initiative and generate psychological momentum against the arriving Americans. In a speech made in 1966, a subordinate of Thanh's said, "We started fighting the United States troops when we were winning . . . this gave us an advantageous combat position."[45] In truth, however, the Communist troops lost the initiative in late 1965, in part due to the heavy casualties of such battles as that in the Ia Drang Valley. It was this battle which brought Giap charging into the conceptual fray.

The dispute between Giap and Thanh turned fundamentally on their widely differing estimates of the combat effectiveness of American ground troops and their supporting air power. Thanh, in a nationally publicized speech, chided Giap (although not by name) for "hastily jumping to the conclusions" that it would require seven to nine Viet Cong or NVA battalions to annihilate one United States battalion. Thanh derides this as "a kind of divination" and remarks pointedly that such "diviners are inclined to take regressive steps."[46] Thanh goes on to state that in his opinion the combat ratio between NVA and United States troops is much more even than Giap's figures would show. This in spite of the obvious fact that the battle of the Ia Drang Valley supported Giap's calculations in that seven to nine NVA battalions were pitted against the 1st Battalion, 7th Cavalry.

If Thanh were correct—that American ground forces could be defeated in set-piece battles involving large, conventional units—then his strategy of attacking United States units made sense. By this means, Thanh could seize the initiative and frustrate Westmoreland's search and destroy strategy. In addition, such attacks would produce heavy American casualties— "the coffins going home"—which would erode support for the war in the United States. On the other side of the argument, Giap built his concept of a "Southern strategy" on the somber premise that NVA and Viet Cong units could not defeat American troops without taking excessive, and unacceptable, casualties. If Giap's basic assumption was correct, the only sensible Communist strategy was to avoid large, Main Force battles and shift to a more elusive, less costly, mode of operation— guerrilla warfare.

Thanh, in his speech, confirms this when he criticizes Giap (again not by name) for the latter's concern about "what phase of the revolution we are in."[47] Obviously, Giap thought that in South Vietnam the Communists were in Phase I (the build-up and guerrilla war phase), while Thanh judged them to be in at least Phase II (the combination of guerrilla and conventional war), moving into Phase III.

Giap based his concept not only on what he saw as the unfavorable disparity of forces, but on an even more fundamental set of factors. First, he believed that Hanoi had to view the war against the Americans as a test of wills, not of military might. The essential element of any such strategy was time. Protract the war, prolong the killing, and sooner or later the United States would give up and agree to conditions acceptable to the Communists. This strategy, Giap reasoned, would be particularly effective against the Americans, the most impatient of peoples, who in 1965 were already beginning to show some of the divisive rents in the national fabric resulting from the war. Conversely, Giap's concept of the protracted guerrilla war made the most of the one factor which the Communists had in greatest abundance—perseverance, the ability to continue the war for "five, ten, or twenty years," to use Giap's words.[48]

Thus, the year 1965 came to a close with a fundamental schism of strategy among the North Vietnamese leaders, and with a growing United States ground and air superiority in the South. It was a watershed year: both North Vietnam and the United States had—almost by accident and certainly by miscalculation—plunged into a war which neither really wanted. As the year 1965 ended, the Americans could look with some satisfaction on their exploits. They had blunted the Communist attempt to subjugate South Vietnam. And while the Americans had not won the war, they had prevented its loss. It was appropriate, then, that *Time Magazine,* on 31 December 1965, named as its "Man of the Year" Gen. William Childs Westmoreland, Commander, United States Military Assistance Command, Vietnam.

Notes—Chapter 14

1. Franz Joseph Strauss, "After Afghanistan," *Policy Review* (Washington, D.C.: The Heritage Foundation), Spring, 1980.
2. Gravel, *Pentagon Papers*, III:293.
3. Ibid., III:678.
4. Ibid., III:295.
5. Ibid., III:297.
6. Kearns, *Johnson*, p. 252.
7. Ibid., p. 253.
8. Gravel, *Pentagon Papers*, III:305.
9. Ibid., III:271.
10. Ibid.
11. Robert E. Osgood, *Limited War Revisited* (Boulder, CO: Westview Press, 1979), p. 10.
12. Ibid.
13. Westmoreland, *Soldier*, pp. 138 and 144.
14. Ibid., p. 144.
15. Ibid.
16. Thompson and Frizzell, *Lessons*, p. 52.
17. Gravel, *Pentagon Papers*, III:390.
18. Ibid.
19. Westmoreland, *Soldier*, p. 148.
20. Gravel, *Pentagon Papers*, III:278.
21. Ibid., III:403–404; and Westmoreland, *Soldier*, p. 153.
22. Gravel, *Pentagon Papers*, III:703.
23. Ibid.
24. Ibid., III:704.
25. Thompson and Frizzell, *Lessons*, p. 60.
26. Gravel, *Pentagon Papers*, III:440.
27. Westmoreland, *Soldier*, p. 169.
28. Gravel, *Pentagon Papers*, III:472.
29. Ibid., III:462 and 470.
30. Thompson and Frizzell, *Lessons*, p. 64.
31. Westmoreland, *Soldier*, p. 185.
32. Ibid., p. 156.
33. Sir Robert Thompson, *No Exit From Vietnam* (New York: David McKay, 1969), pp. 156–163.
34. Robert W. Komer, *Bureaucracy Does Its Thing: Institutional Constraints on U.S.-GVN Performance in Vietnam* (Santa Monica, CA: Rand Corp., 1973), pp. vii–xi.

35. Westmoreland, *Soldier,* p. 185.
36. Sun Tzu, *The Art of War,* trans. by Samuel B. Griffith (New York: Oxford University Press, 1963), p. 84.
37. Thompson and Frizzell, *Lessons,* p. 84.
38. Palmer, *Summons,* p. 117.
39. Thompson and Frizzell, *Lessons,* pp. 73 and 85.
40. Komer, *Bureaucracy,* p. xi.
41. Carl Von Clausewitz, *On War,* Michael Howard and Peter Paret, eds. (Princeton, NJ: Princeton University Press, 1976), pp. 88–89.
42. Douglas Pike, "Vietnam War," *Marxism, Communism, and Western Society, A Comparative Encyclopedia* (Cambridge, MA: The MIT Press), p. 270.
43. John Albright, John A. Cash, and Allan W. Sandstrum, *Seven Fire Fights in Vietnam* (Washington, D.C.: Office of the Chief of Military History, 1970), p. 22.
44. Westmoreland, *Soldier,* p. 191.
45. McGarvey, *Visions,* p. 11.
46. Ibid., p. 68.
47. Ibid.
48. Ibid., p. 40.

15 William Childs Westmoreland

The Inevitable General

To understand America's involvement in Vietnam, one must know something of the principal architects of that involvement. The character and personalities of President Lyndon B. Johnson, Secretary of Defense Robert S. McNamara, and Secretary of State Dean Rusk have been thoroughly dissected and documented. Not nearly as much is known, however, about the military architects of American policy and strategy in the Vietnam War: such men as the chairman of the United States Joint Chiefs of Staff, Gen. Earle G. ("Bus") Wheeler; the commander in chief, Pacific, Adm. Ulysses S. Grant ("Oley") Sharp; and perhaps most important of all, the two United States commanders in Vietnam, Gen. William C. ("Westy") Westmoreland, and his successor, Gen. Creighton W. ("Abe") Abrams.

Of these, General Westmoreland was the key American military actor in the Vietnamese drama. During his commandership, from 1964 to 1968, the United States role in Vietnam evolved from advising the South Vietnamese armed forces into carrying the main burden of combat against the Viet Cong and the NVA. He won the great American-fought battle of the war, the now-famous Tet offensive, and both his supporters and critics have attributed to him, rightly or wrongly, the formulation and execution of the so-called strategy of attrition.

Westmoreland fought Giap for a longer period than did the Frenchman, de Lattre, and during a more critical period than did his successor, Gen. Creighton Abrams. For these reasons, Westmoreland deserves more than the cursory treatment which historians have so far accorded him. The one full-length biography about him, Furguson's *Westmoreland: the Inevitable General*,[1] is noteworthy chiefly for its title, which is not only "catchy," but perceptive. Westmoreland, more than any other officer of his time, was from his West Point days marked by his contemporaries as an "inevitable general." Yet there is something ironic here. Westmoreland did not want to go to West Point—he wanted to go to the naval academy at Annapolis, and when he graduated from the military academy, he did not want to go into the ground army, but into the then army air corps (soon to become the air force) as a pilot. So, while he may have been an "inevitable general" in the army, to some extent he got there by serendipity.

William Childs Westmoreland was born in Saxon, South Carolina, on 26 March 1914, the only son of a wealthy Southern family. In high school he was a good student, a fair athlete, popular, president of his class, and an Eagle Scout. Even in his high school days, Westmoreland was an achiever, reared by his family in the high standards of the Southern aristocracy. In 1932, after one year at the Citadel, he entered the United States Military Academy at West Point. He graduated in 1936, First Captain (the top-ranking cadet officer of the corps), a position held by a long list of distinguished predecessors including Robert E. Lee, John J. Pershing, and Douglas MacArthur. Academically he ranked 112 in a class of 275, and shortly before graduation he was elected by his classmates to be their permanent class vice president. While his family and high school classmates called him "Childs" (his middle name), at the academy he picked up the virile nickname "Westy," which he carries to this day.

West Point molded the man. The academy inculcated in him—as it does in all its graduates—the lodestar of Duty, Honor, Country. Of only slightly less importance, his career at the academy and his life before West Point showed him that he had the stuff of success. In South Carolina he had been an Eagle Scout and president of his high school class. At West Point he was First Captain, did well academically, and was unusually active in extracurricular activities, ranging from theatrical productions to the basketball team, from the staff of the yearbook to teaching Sunday school to the children on the post. Above all, he was liked and respected by his classmates, and they have the surest judgment of a man's worth. West Point gave Westmoreland confidence in himself and his future.

After graduating from the academy, Westmoreland went into the field artillery and was stationed at Ft. Sill, Oklahoma. A few years later he was transferred to Schofield Barracks, Hawaii. He was marked early as an officer of unusual promise, and he had a talent, then and afterwards, for self-promotion. In mid-1941, with World War II just over the horizon, the army ordered Westmoreland to the 9th Infantry Division at Ft. Bragg, North Carolina. He rose, in accelerated wartime promotion, through the officer ranks from first lieutenant to lieutenant colonel and acquired command of an artillery battalion in the division. Early in 1943 he sailed with the division to North Africa.

The 9th Infantry Division saw as much combat in World War II as any division in the army—North Africa, Normandy, the Bulge, and the Remagen bridgehead, among other campaigns—and Westmoreland served with the division throughout. In 1944, with eight years' service, he became the division artillery executive officer and a full colonel. Shortly thereafter he became the division's chief of staff. His World War II record was not just excellent, it was superb.

World War II impacted heavily on Westmoreland. From reading his memoirs, one gathers that he not only had a variety of experiences in the 9th Division, but that he analyzed them deeply. The section of his autobiography on World War II is replete with (what the military call) "Lessons Learned." Most of them deal with the details of leading troops in combat, for example, the value of showing confidence and resolution before the troops, the need to act decisively, and the trauma involved in having to relieve a subordinate. Obviously, he learned also the detailed operations of the infantry division, the army's basic unit of large-scale combat. In World War II, Westmoreland, as usual, impressed some powerful senior officers, people who would further his later career. The most prominent of these were the three "greats" of the army's airborne arm—Generals Matthew Ridgway, Maxwell Taylor, and "Jumping Jim" Gavin. Their friendship and support would be invaluable in Westmoreland's climb to the top.

The most valuable asset Westmoreland gained in World War II, however, was the confidence that comes from solid achievement. He had done exceptionally well in combat, and this is the real test of a soldier and officer, particularly one who seeks to lead men in some future war. The self-confidence which had been his as a youth, as a cadet, and as a young officer was expanded by his World War II service, and with it his belief in his special destiny.

In 1945 the war was over, and Westmoreland, a thirty-one-year-old colonel, brought home the remnants of the 71st Infantry Division. To the dedicated military careerist, peacetime does not mean relaxation. Most military careers are made or broken in peaceful duties, and as a man with his eye on the stars, Westmoreland accelerated his career drive. He transferred to the infantry and qualified as an army parachutist. Shortly thereafter, General Gavin offered him command of a paratroop regiment of the 82nd Airborne Division, then the army's elite unit. After service as a regimental commander, Westmoreland served as the division's chief of staff for three years. These assignments were high-octane fuel for his career engine, and more was shortly to be added.

During Westmoreland's service with the 82nd Airborne, and unbeknownst to him, General Eisenhower, then army chief of staff, ordered his personnel chief to prepare a list of ten (some say twelve, others fifteen) young officers who had shown extraordinary promise during, and immediately after, World War II. The careers of these officers, the future leaders of the army, would be specially molded and monitored. There was no formal selection board. The list was compiled through the "old boy" method, each senior general sending in his list of candidates. For years the names on this super-secret list have been a subject of discussion and debate among senior army officers. Almost all of those who purport to know, claim that this "rocket" list contained, among others, the names of three members of the United States Military Academy Class of 1936. They were: Creighton Abrams, the tank tactician; John Michaelis, who had made a name for himself in the 101st Airborne Division during World War II; and William C. Westmoreland. Westmoreland was now on the "special track."

In 1949, Westmoreland went to the Command and General Staff College (CGSC) at Ft. Leavenworth, Kansas, not as a student, but as an instructor—another high-voltage assignment. Westmoreland had never been a student at this famous institution. He had gone too far up the career ladder during World War II, and the army granted him "constructive credit." While Westmoreland was teaching at Leavenworth, the army chief of staff decided to reestablish the Army War College (AWC), its highest institution of study. Typically, the CGSC was ordered to set up and staff the embryo war college, and in the process, Westmoreland went to the AWC, again as an instructor.

Here appears an aberration in Westmoreland's career pattern. Compared to his top-drawer competitors and colleagues, he was uniquely unschooled by the army's formal educational system. As a student, Westmoreland attended only a week of mess management school for second lieutenants at Ft. Sill and the parachutist school. By contrast, Creighton Abrams, Westmoreland's successor as commander in Vietnam, was a graduate of the CGSC at Leavenworth and the Army War College. Harold K. Johnson, another contemporary of Westmoreland's and his predecessor as chief of staff, United States Army, was a graduate of the Infantry School, the CGSC, and the National War College (now the National Defense University).

In Westmoreland's day, duty as an instructor at the CGSC or the AWC was no substitute for study as a student. At the CGSC, an instructor became an in-depth expert on one small area of military technique. In Westmoreland's case, he specialized in airborne operations. The student, however, studied the entire spectrum of military operations. At the Army War College, an instructor did not instruct. He planned broad course curricula and acted as a "den mother" to the student committees. He was not even permitted to guide the committees, since any advice from the instructor would have been brusquely rejected by the students, who were his contemporaries. Thus, when Westmoreland's detractors present him (as Halberstam did) as the arch example of the "machinely-crammed" officer who did things "by the book," their harpoon is wide of the mark.[2] Westmoreland never "read the book." In 1986, Westmoreland told me that he considered his lack of formal military education to be an advantage in Vietnam. He believes that the Vietnam War was "new and different," and that he, unburdened by the military lore of the past, brought a fresh and innovative approach to it. He may have a point.

On 25 June 1950, everything changed, not only for the United States Army, but for those in it. On that date, the North Korean army invaded South Korea by launching a massive and paralyzing drive to the south. In a few days, the American army, more ill-prepared for combat than at any time in its history, responded. Predictably, Westmoreland wanted a piece of the action, and his job as an instructor at the war college, prestigious enough in peacetime, now became an anchor around his neck. He watched as one of his academy classmates on the "fast track," John (Mike) Michaelis, won the star of a brigadier general in 1950 in Korea for his skill and élan in leading the 27th Infantry Regiment. In the early fifties, if a man wanted stars, he knew that meant Korea, and Westmoreland set out in pursuit.

It took some time, but in mid-1952, with his usual luck, Westmoreland landed the most desirable command a colonel could get in Korea—the 187th Airborne Combat Team, a separate reinforced paratroop regiment (that is, not part of a division) and one which had previously been commanded by a brigadier general. Although Westmoreland commanded the unit for about a year and a half, it saw little action. While in World War II, he had gotten to the party as the plates were being laid; in Korea, he arrived as they were sweeping out the place. He won no combat decorations, but he did acquire something in Korea of immense value—the star of a brigadier general at the youthful age of thirty-eight.

As it must to all army careerists, the Pentagon and duty on the Army general staff finally came to Westmoreland. He became a faceless (and relatively junior) staff officer in the G-1 or personnel division. He did his usual outstanding job and his boss, a three-star general, made Westmoreland the "front man" in testifying before the various congressional committees—a wise selection, since Westmoreland was eminently made to impress congressmen and to stroke their egos.

As his tour in G-1 came to an end, Westmoreland engineered for himself a peculiar assignment—a three-month course in advanced management at Harvard University's Graduate School of Business. In his memoirs, Westmoreland covers this interlude in one brief paragraph, stating that he was able to pick up some ideas about management which he used later in his career. Nevertheless, Harvard represents a diversion from his straight-line drive toward the top of the army pyramid. Perhaps, too, it confirms Westmoreland's mistrust and disdain for the army's conventional wisdom and its educational institutions.

A bigger job in the Pentagon was to follow his three months of civilian schooling. In 1955, when he came back from Harvard, he found himself in one of the most powerful jobs in the army—the secretary of the Army general staff (SGS). Among his predecessors were Bedell Smith (Eisenhower's chief of staff in SHAEF), Robert Eichelberger (of World War II fame), and Maxwell Taylor himself, who had been SGS when Gen. George C. Marshall was chief of staff. Now, Westmoreland held the SGS position to General Taylor as chief of staff.

In the army, the SGS is known as the "chief of staff to the chief of staff." Very little staff work goes in to the "chief" which the SGS does not see and comment on. Very little comes out of the chief's office that does not move over the desk of the SGS. While he is normally a major general (Westmoreland was promoted to that rank while in the job), and the chiefs of the principal staff sections are three-star generals, the latter treat the SGS with deference and respect. The SGS can influence the chief of staff for or against their views and projects. He can delay their papers to the chief, or he can expedite action on them. He can give them valuable clues about the thinking of the chief of staff, or he can leave them groping in the dark. In a position requiring dedication, hard work, discretion, and loyalty, Westmoreland, once more, did a superlative job.

Now his career was in full train, and his next assignment had to be the command of troops, and in 1958 he got it, and a plum at that—the 101st Airborne Division, the choice divisional command available. It was one of the two "ready" divisions; that is, one which would be deployed instantly in case of international trouble. More important, it was the test unit for a new divisional organization and concept of employment—the so-called "pentomic division." Traditionally, military units had been organized in sets of threes: three regiments in a division, three battalions in a regiment, and so on down. Under the new concept, the regiment and battalion would be abolished and five "battle groups" of 1,400 men (larger than a battalion but about half the size of a regiment) would operate directly under the division commander and his staff. While the idea was Maxwell Taylor's, and therefore had the push of his prestige and position as chief of staff, the bulk of the army questioned the workability of the new organization. Taylor wanted someone in command of the test division (the 101st) who would give the concept an honest try. Enter his protégé, Westmoreland, and an honest test it got. Westmoreland tried his best to make the concept work, but the overextended span of command (among many other deficiencies) eventually drowned the concept in a sea of adverse reports. In 1960, as Westmoreland was leaving the division—and after Taylor had retired—Westmoreland quietly recommended that the concept be abandoned. It was. The important thing for Westmoreland, however, was that he had succeeded in his division command, alienating neither Taylor nor the senior opponents of the concept. Westmoreland was now headed straight to the top.

His next assignment was the army's most prestigious one for a major general—the superintendent of the United States Military Academy at West Point. His predecessors read like a Who's Who of the American army—Robert E. Lee, P. G. T. Beauregard, John Schofield (of Civil War fame), Hugh L. Scott (chief of staff from 1914–1917), Douglas MacArthur, and Maxwell Taylor. Westmoreland loved West Point and its top job. On those rare occasions in Saigon when he would momentarily relax, he would turn the talk to West Point and his service there as the "Supe." Although not a man to dwell on past triumphs, it was obvious that he felt he had done a particularly good job at West Point and was proud of it.

There was, however, one sour note in Westy's West Point symphony. At dinner one night in Saigon he began talking about the fortunes of the West Point football team. In 1960, when Westmoreland became superintendent, both President Eisenhower and General MacArthur in separate face-to-face interviews told him that he had to improve the army football team. Such advice—a command, in reality—from West Point's two most distinguished living alumni was not to be taken lightly, particularly since their sentiments reinforced Westmoreland's own view that the public image of the army and West Point demanded a winning football team. After two lackluster seasons, he reached the conclusion that the coach had to go, and he went. After a series of "flaps" involving charges that Westmoreland had stolen coach Paul Dietzel from Louisiana State University, Dietzel became the Army coach. Eventually, the furor over Dietzel's recruitment died, but unfortunately so did Army's football fortunes, and Westmoreland was then stuck with *his* losing coach.

After Westmoreland told the Dietzel story, one of the generals at the table asked if the report were true that Westmoreland could have hired Vince Lombardi as the West Point coach. Westmoreland said, "Yes, but Lombardi was too tough, too obsessed with winning, and he had slapped a cadet while he [Lombardi] had been Red Blaik's assistant. This was not the kind of man I wanted around cadets." Lombardi, of course, went on to become the most famous football coach in the country. Dietzel soon abandoned coaching for a series of positions as director of athletics at various universities. Westmoreland showed no regret at his choice.

Another night at dinner in Saigon, he casually remarked that he had turned down a promotion from major general to lieutenant general while at West Point. This remark jolted the other generals at the table, for a military careerist rejects a promotion about as often as the Pope says Mass in the Shiloh Baptist Church. For a major general to refuse a promotion to three-star rank bespeaks extraordinary selflessness or sublime self-confidence, and probably both. Westmoreland explained this unusual action by saying that he had ongoing programs at West Point which he wanted to finish, and in truth he did compile a notable record of achievement there. He broadened the curriculum by adding elective courses, the first in the academy's history. He persuaded President Kennedy to double the size of the cadet corps to a strength of 4,417, and he planned the necessary expansion of barracks and facilities to accommodate the increase.

West Point has always furnished the superintendent an illustrious backdrop if he chose to use it, and, of course, Westmoreland did. At his invitation, a never-ending line of civilian and military luminaries came to the academy to see West Point and, of course, General Westmoreland. Eisenhower, MacArthur, Vice President Lyndon Johnson, and President John Kennedy were only the most important of the guests who were impressed by the handsome superintendent and his beautiful wife, Kitsy. Indeed, Westmoreland so impressed Kennedy that the president sought to make him chief of staff of the army in 1962, although Westmoreland was only a junior major general.[3] Older heads convinced the young president that the appointment of a young major general would be unwise. Nevertheless, there was little doubt now that Westmoreland was on his way to the top.

On 15 July 1963, Westmoreland took command of the XVIII Airborne Corps, composed of the two airborne divisions, the 82nd and the 101st. The third star of a lieutenant general followed shortly thereafter. Westmoreland tarried only briefly as the corps commander. On 7 January 1964, Gen. "Bus" Wheeler, the army chief of staff, called Westmoreland to Washington to tell him that he was going to Saigon as the deputy to General Harkins, the commander, United States Military Assistance Command, Vietnam (COMUSMACV). That final star at the top of the pile was now assured. On 27 January 1964, Westmoreland, "the inevitable general," landed in Saigon. The role for which he had trained throughout his career—throughout his life, actually—had now arrived.

After four years of service in Vietnam, in July 1968 Westmoreland attained the army's pinnacle, chief of staff, United States Army (CSA). His was a particularly difficult tour. The antiwar sentiment was at its height, and Westmoreland, due to his prior service in Vietnam, became a handy focus of protest. He was burned in effigy several times and once had to leave a Yale lecture hall under heavy escort to prevent bodily harm. Then there were institutional (army) dragons to slay. There was the problem of drugs, unknown to any of his predecessors. He had to plan and try to sell the "volunteer army" concept, and regulate disciplinary matters varying from racial relations to the length of a soldier's hair. The consensus of the army is that Westmoreland tried hard as chief, but that the times and its problems overwhelmed him.

Westmoreland would probably agree with this judgment. Near the end of his tour as chief of staff, I sat on the general staff when he told that body that he thought the army (and thus he) had failed to solve the problems of race and drugs. He admitted, too, that he and the army had failed to sell Congress on the importance of the army and its mission. But then the problems of the army in the early seventies would probably have overcome any of his contemporaries as well. In mid-1972 Westmoreland retired from the army, and Creighton W. Abrams, his West Point classmate, succeeded him as chief of staff, United States Army.

Like Douglas MacArthur and Dwight Eisenhower before him, Westmoreland found that old soldiers not only never die, they don't fade away either. In 1974, shortly after his retirement from the army, he ran for the Republican nomination for governor of his home state of South Carolina, and by that combination of ability and luck which had characterized most of his life, he almost made it. He lost the Republican nomination by a few votes, even though he carried five of the six congressional districts of the state. The Republican candidate became a sure winner when the Democratic nominee, shortly before the election, was declared ineligible. After his venture into politics, he turned to writing and lecturing, publishing in 1976 his memoirs, *A Soldier Reports*.

And then, into this quiet retirement, notoriety struck. On 23 January 1982 the Columbia Broadcasting System (CBS) uncased a ninety-minute "documentary" charging that Gen. William C. Westmoreland, as commander, United States Military Assistance Command, Vietnam (COMUS-MACV) had, in 1967, led a conspiracy to mislead his military superiors (up to and including the president of the United States), as well as the press, the American public, and Congress by reducing enemy strength figures in Vietnam. The "documentary," with the general as its central focus, exploded onto the front pages and TV screens of the country and developed into one of the most publicized controversies of this century. Eventually, Westmoreland sued CBS for libel. The case never went to the jury, for just before the final summations, a settlement between Westmoreland and CBS was reached. The settlement was inconclusive—both adversaries claimed victory—and the charges, claims, and counter-charges rebound to this day. Many magazine articles and several books—Renata Adler's *Reckless Disregard* is the most authoritative—have been written about the charges made in the documentary, and doubtless others will follow.

The complications of this complex issue are extraneous to this book. But, as one of the few individuals who was involved in this controversy from 1967, when it began as one of those arcane, esoteric arguments between the CIA and MACV, up to and through the libel trial itself, I have two points to make. First, General Westmoreland did not commit the offenses with which the CBS program charged him, nor did he do anything illegal, immoral, or dishonorable. Second, even if Westmoreland and his superiors had accepted the inflated CIA enemy strength figures, not one policy, strategy, or tactic would have been changed. In a military sense, the whole controversy was piddling, reminding one of Alexander Pope's ironic note that "mighty contests arise from trivial things."

Behind all the controversy, behind all the fame, what kind of man was, and is, Westmoreland? I find it difficult to write about a former and respected commander, a comrade in times of trial, and a friend of some years. Objectivity is impossible; so let me make it plain at the start, then, that I like and respect "Westy" Westmoreland. I hope, however, that this affection and admiration will not blind me to Westmoreland's shortcomings and faults, which, being only human, he possesses in ordinary measure.

First, his surface qualities. When he went to Vietnam in 1964 he looked and acted like a winner. His unbroken string of successes had convinced him (and most of the senior officers of the army) that he could overcome any obstacle, do any job. He himself was convinced—as he told me in 1984—that he was "lucky," and this is a tremendous booster of self-confidence.

Westmoreland is a handsome man, one of the most handsome of his generation. He is erect, well-built, about six feet tall, with a masculine face and a strong jutting jaw. He moves well, with an alert military bearing and an athletic stride. His looks, his self-confidence, and his ambition made him aggressive and optimistic. He has always sought new ways to accomplish his missions, and he drove himself and others hard. This confidence and aggressiveness were particularly apparent in self-promotion. In fact, Westmoreland throughout his career has been a dedicated career opportunist, rarely missing any chance to forward his own fortunes. Nor is this unique to him; nor is it in any way reprehensible.

He is an aloof man, but one without arrogance or rancor. There is a shell around him which is rarely penetrated, and he lacks some of the human touch. This shell carries over to his physical appearance. On even the hottest of days in Vietnam—and the heat and humidity there could be murderous—he never appeared to perspire. The rest of his party would be standing there with sweat running off us, and Westmoreland would be cool with a crisp uniform. But these traits are only facade, the public view of Westmoreland. Beyond this surface, the question again arises, what kind of a man is William Westmoreland?

Perhaps the best way to examine a general's worth is to use Napoleon's method. One of Bonaparte's favorite notions was that a general needs an equilibrium of character and intellect which he called "squareness." Reflecting at Saint Helena, he dictated to one of his two scribes, "A military leader must possess as much character as intellect. Men who have a great deal of intellect and little character are . . . like a ship whose masts are out of proportion to the ballast. . . . The base must equal the height."[4]

Using Napoleon's figure of speech, William Childs Westmoreland carries in his ship a heavy load of ballast, that is, character. Westmoreland is not ostensibly a religious man. In Vietnam, I never recall him going to church or referring to the Deity. Westmoreland was not one (like George Patton) to circulate irreverent prayers, demanding from the Almighty "good fighting weather." But beneath this exterior exists a Christianity and a moral code of the highest type. The words of the West Point motto, "Duty, Honor, Country," were, and are, his watchwords. His personal life and habits exemplify the Christian virtues. He drinks sparingly; he has never smoked. So seldom does he use even mild profanity or obscenity that when he does use it, his listeners are shocked. Only once—and that was for good cause—have I heard him disparage the motives or personality of another officer. He is always in command of his emotions, handling a dangerous crisis or a personal setback with the same coolness with which he accepted success.

His marriage is an unusually happy one. While the Vietnam War forced him to spend months away from his beloved Kitsy, not the faintest whisper of scandal ever touched him. In the soldier jargon of the Vietnam War, Westmoreland was the straightest of "straight arrows." He was forgiving of well-intentioned errors, but a sexual peccadillo or excessive drinking would bring instant banishment from his command, regardless of the rank of the transgressor.

His sense of personal responsibility and loyalty runs deep and strong. During the Tet offensive, when he came under heavy criticism from the media and politicians for the alleged surprise of the enemy offensive, he accepted the blame without quibble or whimper. Not for Westmoreland were any of the dodges Eisenhower used during the Battle of the Bulge about his "G-2 missing the boat." Even in the most intimate of staff gatherings, never did Westmoreland utter a word of condemnation of his intelligence officer (myself) or seek to pass the buck downward to me. It simply never occurred to him.

On another occasion, he assigned an artillery general to command an infantry brigade, although the officer had had no experience in infantry combat. The general's first fight was a tough one, and he made some serious mistakes. Westmoreland relieved him from the infantry command, but accepted the blame for himself, saying that he (Westmoreland) had committed the original mistake in making the assignment. The general later became the artillery officer for a major command in Vietnam, where he turned in an outstanding job.

There is no question of Westmoreland's personal courage. He is fearless. During the Vietnam War he "choppered" into besieged Con Thien after the local marine commander had asked him not to go there because the artillery and mortar fire on the position was so heavy. Westmoreland thanked the commander and said quietly, "Let's go." I accompanied him into Khe Sanh one day when that stronghold was under heavy fire. As a matter of fact, we got three incoming artillery rounds before we even got off the C-130, which promptly took off after our hasty evacuation. Westmoreland ignored the fire.

And finally, among Westmoreland's virtues there stands—tall and strong—old-fashioned American patriotism. In his book and in several magazine articles, he cited President Kennedy's inaugural address, ". . . ask not what your country can do for you . . ." and Kennedy's pledge that this nation would ". . . bear any burden, meet any hardship, support any friend and oppose any foe to assure the survival and success of liberty." These statements reflect Westmoreland's own credo—a simple, sincere love of country, and what he believes it stands for.

If I have made him sound like an Eagle Scout, so be it. He was an Eagle Scout, that is the title that many of his contemporaries use to describe him, a man of elevated character, but given to some naïveté.

In spite of Westmoreland's lofty character, he has his detractors, even among his peers in the army. What quality did they attack? Turn again to Napoleon's metaphor, the ship. There has never been any question of Westmoreland's ballast—his character. Those who derogate him question the height and breadth of his sails, that is, his intelligence. First off, the sails against which Westmoreland must be measured are wide and high. Westmoreland is no dummy; he is a very intelligent man, but in the positions he has held, just being intelligent may not have been enough. Senior generals, theater commanders, and army chiefs of staff are always held to higher standards than even other generals. To their immediate subordinates (who are generals, too) they must be not only intelligent and wise, they must be brilliant and omniscient. As old "Vinegar Joe" Stilwell in his earthy way used to say, "The higher the monkey climbs up the flagpole the more you see of his ass." And it is true. The problems at four-star level are the greatest, the most complex. Each four-star decision receives intense scrutiny from those above and from those below, and the wrong decisions become eventually quite obvious. It is these towering mental standards which some of his colleagues thought Westmoreland failed to meet.

I have asked several of them why they hold this judgment, and after a lot of indecisive backing-and-filling, these are their detailed indictments. The first criticism is that Westmoreland is uncommonly naïve, more Little Boy Blue than Sir Galahad. Asked for particulars, they cite these examples. In Vietnam, throughout his commandership, he consistently tried to deal honestly with the American reporters and television newsmen. Westmoreland felt that by telling the news media the truth (as he saw it), he could bring the reporters over to his view of the war. He held news conferences at which the newsmen badgered and challenged him, and then later misquoted him. He never could see that the news media opposed the war for ideological and other reasons and could not be converted to his viewpoint. And yet he naïvely persisted in trying.

More recently, several retired officers have criticized Westmoreland's naïveté in going on the CBS program, when he knew that Mike Wallace was to be his interrogator. Wallace is the most lethal "hatchetman" of the talk shows. He is infamous for his inquisitorial style and his ability to distort participants' words and meanings. In his interview for the CBS program, Wallace made Westmoreland look, as one columnist wrote, like the village idiot. As one retired officer put it, "Any fool should have known Wallace and CBS are opposed to everything Westy stands for and were out only to chew him up."

Other detractors say that he lacks judgment. During the siege of Khe Sanh, he tried to bring the aviation units of the United States Marine Corps in Vietnam under the operational control of the air force. While the move made operational sense, it aroused the marines' traditional fear of being shredded among the other services, and the resulting wrangle tore the fragile bonds of unified effort in Vietnam. The envisioned gain in efficiency and coordination was not worth the price in command unity. Incidentally, the JCS stalled on his request until the siege was over and the need for his improvisation had vanished. Then they gave it to him too late for him to use it.

His decisions regarding changes which he made in ushering in the volunteer army have brought further criticisms of his judgment. His decisions to permit soldiers to wear longer hair, to stock beer in the barracks, to abolish reveille, among other changes, came under fire. Westmoreland's detractors claim these changes sent the wrong signals to the whole army. The draftees got the idea that the army was adjusting to them, not vice versa. The older officers and the career noncommissioned officers were confused by the changes and what they saw as an attack on their authority and prestige. For an appreciable period, the army almost came to a halt. It finally got straightened out, largely by going back to the old ways, but some interim damage was done.

His detractors accuse him of other intellectual shortcomings. Some say he fails to see the big picture and becomes too immersed in details, and on some occasions I have observed this fault myself. Others criticize him for his inability to grasp quickly complex issues with which he has no prior experience. Finally—as unusual as this may seem—many see Westmoreland as somewhat dull because he has no sense of humor. This is pure perception, and has nothing to do with a man's intellect, but they may have a point. A sense of humor shows an agile mind and a creative intellect. Abraham Lincoln would often make a point or sum up an argument by a funny story. Westmoreland has a sense of humor which comes through in private, but during his active service, when he presided over briefings and conferences, he was humorless.

These are the main areas in which Westmoreland's critics hold him intellectually deficient for the high positions he held. They have some valid points, but by and large they fail to make a solid case. Yes, Westmoreland is naïve. He is the victim of his own high principles, which make him incapable of perceiving that other men can be disloyal, dishonest, and base. But is this such a serious fault?

As with any other official who has made hundreds of important decisions through the years, anybody can select the wrong ones and emphasize those. Balanced against those imperfections of judgment, one must note that of all the principal American decision-makers on Vietnam, Westmoreland had the soundest, and the most perceptive, view of that war. He saw early that the key to the strategic equation of Vietnam was *time,* that is, that the war had to be brought to a successful conclusion before the patience of the American people wore out. Beyond that, Westmoreland had the clearest concept of how to win the war—by moving from the strategic defensive to the strategic offensive in Laos, Cambodia, or the southern edge of North Vietnam.

Although he has been derided for his alleged statement about "the light at the end of the tunnel," in retrospect, his forecasts were uncannily accurate. He saw the need for Vietnamization long before the word had even been coined. In 1967 he prophesied that United States troops could begin phasing out of Vietnam in 1969—and they did. Again in 1967, he told President Johnson that unless there was a significant increase in United States troop strength in Vietnam that American participation in the war could go on for five more years—and it did.

So, to accuse Westmoreland of being short in the sail is, to use a sports term, a bad call. Nevertheless, that perception did, and does, exist.

Being human, William Childs Westmoreland has his strengths and weaknesses, and I have tried to show them objectively. Nobody knows what his final place in history will be, but I am confident that future historians will be far more generous to Westmoreland than his contemporaries have been.

Regardless of history's verdict, he will always march in the ranks of honorable men. In 1969, as chief of staff, he published a letter to every officer in the army entitled "Integrity." In the final paragraph of that letter, no doubt reflecting on his own career, he wrote, "In this uncertain world our best judgments may prove wrong. But there is only one sure path to honor—unfaltering honesty and sincerity in word and deed."[5] That is Westmoreland.

Notes—Chapter 15

1. Ernest B. Furguson, *Westmoreland: The Inevitable General* (Boston, MA: Little, Brown & Co., 1968).
2. Halberstam, *Best and Brightest*, p. 666.
3. Ibid., p. 678.
4. J. Christopher Herold, *The Mind of Napoleon* (New York: Columbia University Press, 1955), p. 220.
5. William C. Westmoreland, letter to the army, 20 November 1969.

16 "Oley's War," "Westy's War," and "Nobody's War"

In January 1966, General Westmoreland had more on his mind than his award as 1965's Man of the Year. A tough, multifaceted war was brewing, and its lack of progress disquieted Westmoreland and the other American leaders. The four-pronged American strategy for waging that war had been firmed up by early 1966. The first prong was ROLLING THUNDER, the bombing of North Vietnam. In the senior headquarters in Saigon, Honolulu, and the Pentagon, ROLLING THUNDER was called "Oley's War," named for Admiral "Oley" Sharp, CINCPAC. Officially, he directed the air attacks against the North, although President Johnson and Secretary McNamara actually controlled them.

By 1966 it had become obvious that ROLLING THUNDER had failed to achieve its goals. The North Vietnamese were still supporting the insurgency in the South, and that support was strong as ever. The fact that ROLLING THUNDER had been widened, however reluctantly, by the president made this disappointment all the more bitter to Johnson and McNamara. By mid-1965, the northern limit of the attack area was extended from the 19th Parallel to 20°33″. The target list was expanded from barracks, depots, and radar sites to bridges, airfields, and power plants. The number of sorties per week increased from 200 in early 1965 to around 900. Still the bombing campaign failed. It continued to be frustrated by the concept of "gradualism" and by its failure to hurt

the North Vietnamese. The targets painful to Hanoi lay in northern Vietnam, and they were off-limits. In late 1965 and early 1966, Johnson
and McNamara continued their piecemeal expansion of the program,
despite efforts by Admiral Sharp and the Joint Chiefs of Staff to escalate
the operation. Although the target list expanded from 94 to 236 by the
end of 1965, Washington still selected the targets.

Into this unpromising situation stepped McNamara and his civilian
assistants, particularly Assistant Secretary of Defense for International
Security Affairs John McNaughton. In November 1965 they introduced
the concept of a bombing pause. In a memorandum to the president,
Secretary McNamara argued that a pause would serve three purposes.
It would provide Hanoi a chance to give up or slow down the war; it
would create the impression that the United States was sincerely interested
in a negotiated solution; and finally, a lack of response from Hanoi
would justify the United States in not only resuming the bombing program,
but in expanding and intensifying it. President Johnson accepted their
recommendation and ordered a bombing pause to go into effect on 24
December 1965.

The strategy of the pause and its execution were blurred by President
Johnson's indecisiveness and secrecy. The Joint Chiefs, along with Westmoreland and Sharp, thought initially that the pause would be for a
few days only. The word got about quickly, however, that this pause
would be longer than the one in May 1965, which had lasted only a
few days. On 27 December, three days after the president ordered the
pause, Westmoreland fired off a cable to the Joint Chiefs of Staff stating
that he considered the immediate resumption (of the bombing) essential,
". . . and indeed, we should now step up our effort to higher levels."[1]
Henry Cabot Lodge, who replaced Maxwell Taylor as United States
ambassador in Saigon, supported Westmoreland's plea, and Admiral
Sharp added several messages recommending that the bombing be
resumed.[2]

Seen in the clearer afterlight of two decades, the concept of the
bombing pause of December 1965–January 1966 looks, to use Admiral
Sharp's words, like ". . . a retreat from reality."[3] The pause, the brain-
child of McNamara and McNaughton, sought to put military pressure
on Hanoi by *relieving* the pressure already being applied. In the convoluted
thinking of the Pentagon civilians, "less" had somehow become "more."
The idea was to send Ho a message that ROLLING THUNDER was

going to get tough. If so, the message to Hanoi got thoroughly garbled. Well into the pause, the administration attempted to use it as a negotiation lure, but this failed, too.

McNamara and McNaughton were intelligent and patriotic men and must have had their reasons for selling the president on the pause. The foundation of the pause concept rested on both men's antagonism to ROLLING THUNDER. Both considered the political price too high. In the United States, antiwar cries had begun to increase in volume and heat. Abroad, the United States was portrayed as a bully. Beyond that, the calculations of the two "Mc's" were overshadowed by the perceived threat of Chinese intervention if the bombing struck lucrative North Vietnamese targets. The two men did not want to refine ROLLING THUNDER, or intensify it, they wanted to kill it.

McNamara had another reason for his antipathy to ROLLING THUNDER. His systems analysts, the "whiz kids," had convinced him that the program was not cost-effective. Nothing could chill McNamara's enthusiasm for a project as fast as the condemnation, "not cost effective." The cost effectiveness approach to selecting various strategical weapons and forces lay at the heart of McNamara's concept of national defense planning, and in late 1965 and in 1966, the systems analysts were telling McNamara that ROLLING THUNDER was financially a losing proposition. During 1965, they pointed out that their estimate of the damage inflicted on North Vietnam amounted to roughly $70 million, but that it had cost the United States $460 million to inflict that damage. In 1966, the damage and cost figures went from damages of $94 million to a cost to the United States of $1,247 million. Of course, one major cause of the cost ineffectiveness was the target selection system—presided over by McNamara and Johnson.

This oversimplification is typical of systems analysts. Many of the results of military operations cannot be quantified. It is impossible to reduce to dollars and cents such factors as the political costs, the decrease or enhancement of North Vietnamese morale, the diversion of NVA combat troops to repair bombed roads, and the elevation of South Vietnamese spirit by the bombings. McNamara listened to his systems analysts, however, and he became increasingly unsympathetic toward ROLLING THUNDER.

The "whiz kids" versus ROLLING THUNDER was a façade which concealed the real power struggle in the Pentagon. The contest pitted the generals and the admirals, the Joint Chiefs of Staff, and other "hard line" bombing advocates such as "Oley" Sharp and Westmoreland on one side against McNamara, McNaughton, and the OSD civilians on the other. The fight was never over "civilian control over the military." The military were, and are, the most ardent proponents of that concept. The struggle, largely by indirection and innuendo, was for dominance in the field of military operations, heretofore the preserve of the uniformed leaders. Both sides distrusted the motives and experience of the other. An observer, even now, wonders where, in 1965–1966, the real war was actually being fought—in the jungles and skies of Vietnam or in the corridors of the Pentagon.

Seen in the light of this power struggle, the bombing pause was a victory for McNamara, McNaughton, and the "whiz kids." It demonstrated to the uniformed chieftains that the president was supporting a different strategy than that being recommended by the generals and admirals who advocated a decisive, punitive air campaign. The pause was one more indication that the formulation of United States military strategy was passing from the military to the civilians. This struggle for supremacy in developing strategic concepts would continue for several years, and the conduct of ROLLING THUNDER would be one of its principal battle grounds.

As the conceptual war went on in the Pentagon, Hanoi remained adamantly unresponsive to the proffered carrot or the threatened stick. So, either reluctantly or eagerly, the key United States players began planning to resume the attacks. The principal debate centered not on whether to intensify the program, but whether to intensify it gradually or escalate it radically. Admiral Sharp and General Wheeler favored the latter; the OSD civilians, led by McNaughton, argued, predictably, for a measured increase of pressure.

This question of how far and how fast the president would push ROLLING THUNDER came up even during the bombing pause, and with added heat when the president ordered the bombing resumed 31 January 1966. The hackneyed struggle between the concepts of gradualism and decisiveness now centered on North Vietnamese oil and gas (POL) storage facilities. The debate began in late November 1965 and ended late in June 1966. Since the bulk of the POL facilities were located near Hanoi, the civilians in the Department of Defense deemed an attack on them to be escalatory and felt they would cause a widening and deepening of the war. Those in favor of the strikes (the uniformed leaders) argued for a program which would "hurt" the North Vietnamese. Finally, on 22 June 1966, the president approved air strikes on POL facilities, and the execution message went to the field. Seven out of nine POL facilities were struck on 29 June. The strike results were good, but the North Vietnamese had been forewarned and had dispersed their fuel supplies by storing drums of POL in caves, woods, and in populated areas, the latter being off-limits to the bombers. As a result, the attacks were not decisive, and North Vietnam pushed on with its aggression in the South.

Although McNamara had personally recommended to the president that Johnson approve the POL strikes, Admiral Sharp, for one, has questioned McNamara's sincerity. Years later, he still wondered if McNamara had not recommended approval in writing, and then orally taken a negative position in private discussion with the president.[4] Admiral Sharp cites no evidence to support this serious charge of double-dealing. Be this as it may, what is now apparent is that the failure of the POL strikes to cripple North Vietnamese infiltration by mid-year 1966 had completed McNamara's disenchantment with ROLLING THUNDER.

In this atmosphere of intrigue and disenthrallment arose one of the most preposterous concepts of this singular war—an anti-infiltration barrier system to be built across the DMZ and the Laos panhandle. The barrier concept had first been proposed in January 1966 by Roger Fisher of the Harvard Law School to the indefatigable John McNaughton. Fisher's concept (adopted with slight modifications by McNaughton) envisioned an airseeded line of barbed wire, mines, and chemicals laced with seismic, acoustic, and other technical detection devices. It would be located just south of the DMZ and stretch from the China Sea through Laos to the Mekong River on the Thailand border, a distance of about 160 miles. The anti-infiltration barrier would be anchored by manned strongpoints and subject to on-call artillery fire and air attacks.

The concept attracted first McNaughton, and then McNamara, by its pseudoscientific patina. In mid-March, McNamara referred the proposal to the Joint Chiefs for comments, and they in turn sent the concept to CINCPAC for his views. Admiral Sharp, always blunt, blasted the barrier concept, stating, "the project would take seven or eight army or marine divisions to construct and man the line; it would require three or four years to become operational; and it would strain the logistical and construction effort in South Vietnam.''[5] Above all, Admiral Sharp viewed the concept as unrealistic and doomed to failure and, predictably, recommended that it be abandoned. General Westmoreland concurred with CINCPAC. The Joint Chiefs were apparently also cool to the project, but no record can be found of their formal disavowal.

McNamara let the concept languish during the remainder of April and May 1966, as the debate over striking the North Vietnamese POL facilities continued. By mid-June, a high-level group of distinguished scientists, brought together by McNaughton, examined the project. The group, known as the Jason Summer Study, concluded on 30 August 1966 that ROLLING THUNDER was ineffective and that the barrier concept should be tried. This group's recommendation, plus other factors, convinced McNamara. The most significant of these other factors was McNamara's now firm conviction that ROLLING THUNDER had failed. It had not interdicted the South Vietnamese battlefield; it had not decisively reduced North Vietnam's POL supplies; and finally, it had not brought Ho Chi Minh and company one inch closer to the negotiating table. To McNamara, the barrier concept was a weapon to use in his running fight with the generals and admirals. It gave him an antidote to the military's constant exhortations to escalate the bombing of the North. Beyond that, if it worked, the civilians (both in and out of the Defense Department) would have scored a devastating strike against military expertise and supremacy.

In September, McNamara again directed that the barrier concept be staffed with the Joint Chiefs and the field. Again, the Chiefs ducked the issue, and Admiral Sharp violently objected. In spite of the military's lack of enthusiasm, McNamara approved the concept and ordered it into execution. This order brought on a classic struggle between the top military leaders and the top civilians in the defense establishment. The military scorned and belittled the concept, calling it ''McNamara's Line,'' obliquely referring to another ill-fated defense minister, the Frenchman Maginot. The generals tried to change the concept; they tried anything to delay or obstruct it. On the other side, McNamara put behind the project his own considerable resources of prestige, power, and funds. The battle would be long and bitter.

McNamara escalated this battle for supreme power in the Pentagon when he returned from a four-day trip to South Vietnam in October. He sent the president a pessimistic memo about not only ROLLING

THUNDER, but the results of the ground war in South Vietnam as well. In effect, he recommended that the president level off the present ground effort in South Vietnam, stabilize the air attacks against the North at the current intensity, and seek a negotiated settlement through diplomatic channels. Once again, he proposed a barrier across the DMZ and Laos. He went even further, recommending either another bombing pause or a shift from the lucrative targets in the Hanoi/Haiphong area back to the unremunerative ones near the DMZ. From a secretary of defense, these recommendations were chilling. He was telling the president that the war could not be won militarily, and the United States ought to try to negotiate its way out of it.

The truth is that the war in Vietnam had defeated Robert Strange McNamara. He had no sudden revelation that the war was evil and useless, no bolt from the blue. McNamara's will to fight the war had just ebbed away, bit by bit, day by day. There were those in the Pentagon, military and civilians alike, who said he had no stomach for the bloodshed and destruction of war. He could be bold and resolute in the peaceful activities of opposing the military on force structure or weapons procurement, but a real war, with its senseless carnage and wanton devastation, appalled him.

Then, too, increasingly he found himself to be a drum, beaten from both sides by two drummers. The military chiefs wanted to intensify the use of military power against the Communists. His civilian advisers wanted to ease it, and his civilian advisers were becoming increasingly dovish. Daniel Ellsberg, already a defeatist, had joined his OSD staff and had McNamara's ear. Other liberals kept telling him that the war was immoral, and that it was dividing the country. Perhaps the principal reason for McNamara's defection was his sense that the war simply could not be won under the then current restraints, most of which he had built or supported. He reasoned—perhaps—how could a sensible man keep pursuing such an unrealistic goal? To his credit, he went on trying to do his job, but his mind rebelled and his spirit weakened. He would carry on for many months, but with an increasing sense of failure and frustration. Eventually, he would become a man divided within himself: officially, a hawk, personally, a dove. He would be the first high-level casualty of the war, but not the last.

Stunned by the secretary's defeatist memorandum to the president, the Joint Chiefs of Staff now aroused themselves and categorically opposed all the secretary's recommendations. In a memorandum which they pointedly requested that Secretary McNamara pass to the president, they argued against any curtailment or stabilization of the air effort against North Vietnam and against any bombing pause. On the contrary, they advocated a "sharp knock" against key North Vietnamese targets.[6] The power struggle continued through October into November 1966. Belatedly, the Joint Chiefs came down hard against the barrier concept. They contended that the barrier would be extremely costly and probably ineffective, and they returned to their old prescription that the cure for the ailments besetting ROLLING THUNDER was to expand the air effort against the North. As 1966 ended, a wide conceptual chasm had opened between the OSD civilians and the military chiefs. The civilians argued that ROLLING THUNDER cost too much both in money and in international goodwill. In their eyes, ROLLING THUNDER had failed in 1966 and offered no promise of success in 1967. The military, on the other hand, argued that only civilian-imposed restraints on targets and levels of effort had prevented the bombing program from accomplishing its objectives. This despite the fact that the sorties flown against the North had increased from 55,000 in 1965 to 148,000 in 1966. In that same year (1966), 128,000 tons of bombs had been dropped in comparison to the 33,000 tons in 1965, and the target list had been drastically expanded. President Johnson sided with McNamara, McNaughton, and the other civilians, stabilizing the ground and air war at roughly 1966 levels and approving the construction of the anti-infiltration barrier. In 1966, the civilians had won a battle in the Pentagon, but the war was far from over.

While both the military chiefs in the Pentagon and their civilian counterparts viewed the ROLLING THUNDER program as ineffective (although for vastly different reasons), one key man deemed it successful—Gen. William C. Westmoreland, the United States commander in South Vietnam. Westmoreland told McNaughton during a face-to-face conference in October 1966 that he "felt the strikes had definite military value in slowing the southward movement of supplies, diverting North Vietnam manpower and creating great costs to the North."[7] But then Westmoreland was looking for all the help he could get, and while he may have had private doubts about the effectiveness of ROLLING THUNDER, the strikes did help his battles in the South—if only marginally. General Westmoreland had not one battle, but three to fight: first, to contain a growing enemy conventional threat; second, to develop the Republic of Vietnam's Armed Forces (RVNAF); and third, to pacify and protect the peasants in the South Vietnamese countryside. Each was a monumental task.

Countering the growing might of the North Vietnamese Army in South Vietnam would not be easy. The defeat of the North Vietnamese troops in the Ia Drang Valley in November 1965 demonstrated not only the prowess of the American soldier, but Hanoi's intention to meet the United States ground force buildup with a like escalation. In *mid-1965*, the North Vietnamese Army had in South Vietnam a force of only five NVA regiments, but by the *end* of 1965, the enemy had built up to twelve regiments. By the end of 1965, the enemy's combat strength (including NVA Main Forces and VC Main Forces, regional forces, and guerrillas) was estimated at 221,000.[8]

During 1966 both sides increased their forces in South Vietnam. Giap sent fifteen new regiments (five divisions totaling 58,000 men) to the South. As a result of this expanded infiltration, by the end of 1966 the enemy combat force in the South had increased to a total figure of 282,000. The total enemy strength figures just cited do not tally exactly. They take no account of VC recruitment or of casualties inflicted by United States and ARVN troops. Beyond that, during the entire Vietnam War, Communist strength figures were always "soft," due to the inadequacies of intelligence. Even accepting some inaccuracy, however, these enemy strength figures sent a powerful message to General Westmoreland as 1966 wore on: the enemy strength would not be eroded; Giap would match escalation with escalation; and Westmoreland had a long, hard war ahead of him.

To combat the enemy buildup in the South, the United States had to increase *its* commitment of ground troops. At the end of 1965, the United States had 181,000 troops in South Vietnam. By 31 December 1966, 385,000 American servicemen had been committed to the war. They made up five army infantry divisions, two marine divisions, four separate army brigades, and an armored cavalry regiment, plus logistic and other support troops, and a sizable air and naval contingent. The organization of the United States ground forces was a relatively simple problem. Westmoreland placed the III Marine Amphibious Force (III MAF) of two-plus marine divisions in the northernmost part of South Vietnam with its tactical area of operation (TAOR) coinciding with that of the I Corps of the South Vietnamese Army. In a similar fashion, the United States I (EYE) Field Force duplicated the TAOR of the ARVN II Corps in north central South Vietnam, while the United States II Field Force functioned with the ARVN III Corps around the Saigon area. Since there were no United States combat formations in the Mekong Delta (nor were there any NVA combat troops there until much later), no comparable United States headquarters was established with the IV ARVN Corps in that area.

The positioning and organization for combat of the Marine's III MAF and the United States Army's Field Forces, along with their relationship with the ARVN Corps, brought up once again the concept of unity of command in Vietnam. An understanding of this continuing problem requires some definitions and a little history. In American military terminology the term "joint" command applies to a force composed of two or more United States services. It is a purely American command. A "combined" command is one composed of American forces along with one or more foreign allies. Each type of command is staffed by members from the composing forces. The United States' Pacific Command is an example of a joint command. General Eisenhower's World War II command, SHAEF, and the United Nations Command in the Korean War were examples of combined commands.

Unity of command became a military catchword in World War II. Eisenhower in Europe attributed a great deal of his success to this organizational concept. After World War II, he elevated the idea to that military pantheon, the principles of war, ranking it with such other hallowed concepts as mass, surprise, economy of force, etc. Those American army officers who came to their professional maturity following World War II accepted unity of command as an article of faith and as a necessary requirement for successful operations.

While some authorities had recommended a unified U.S./GVN command in Vietnam in 1964, the advent of American combat troops in mid-1965 forced the concept to the fore. In April 1965, Westmoreland proposed the idea of establishing a small, combined U.S./GVN headquarters commanded by a United States general with a Vietnamese deputy, the first step in a concept by which all combat forces in Vietnam (United States, South Vietnamese, and Allies) would come under one headquarters. At first, the South Vietnamese favored the arrangement, but for obscure reasons shortly turned against it. But the concept—so desirable, even necessary, in theory—would turn up again and again, always to be shot down by either the United States or South Vietnam.

From 1965 until mid-1968, the principal objector to any consideration of a combined U.S./GVN combined command was Westmoreland himself. His objections fell into two categories, open and hidden. Publicly he declared that a combined command (under a United States commander, of course) would stifle the growth of SVN leadership and the acceptance of responsibility by South Vietnam. He averred that it would leave the RVNAF incapable of defending themselves when the United States departed Vietnam. He also maintained that such a command would "give credence to the enemy's absurd claim that the United States was no more than a colonial power."[9] Westmoreland finally claimed that the system in use (cooperation) worked well, stating, "At no time did an irreconcilable problem of command or coordination occur."[10] Well, maybe, and again, maybe not.

But it was the hidden reasons which really torpedoed the concept of a combined command. First, if the United States insisted on a combined command for U.S./GVN and other allied forces, it must first clean up its own organizational chart in southeast Asia. This would require the establishment of a single unified United States command to include all United States forces operating in, over, or around Vietnam (both North and South), Laos, Cambodia, and Thailand. A monstrous task this, for in 1965 (and thereafter) the American forces fighting in, over, and around Vietnam exemplified *disunity* of command. CINCPAC commanded the air effort through the Pacific Air Force (PACAF) to the Seventh Air Force in Vietnam, and CINCPAC also commanded the naval effort (including naval air) through the Pacific Fleet (PACFleet) to the Seventh Fleet. Westmoreland got his air and naval support in Vietnam by cooperation and coordination with the commanders involved. The marines in Vietnam had their own air force, which responded to none of the other commands. Strategic Air Command commanded the B-52 bombers, which rendered heavy air support to Westmoreland, while he selected the targets. The CIA conducted military and paramilitary operations in Vietnam and Laos. Even the State Department got into the military war. MACV and Seventh Air Force in Saigon selected air targets in Laos, but the targets could be struck *only* if the United States ambassador to Laos approved each target—and he disapproved many of them.

This gross violation of the concept of unity of command resulted from the incremental nature of the war. The war began with the air attacks against North Vietnam, which at first were, and should have been, conducted by CINCPAC through PACFleet and PACAF. But when United States ground troops entered the war, the conflict changed, and a truly unified Southeast Asia command should have been established. The secretary of defense and the JCS apparently believed that the gain to be had by unifying the command in Southeast Asia was not worth the inevitable interservice hassle and upheaval to bring it about, another example of the indecision and aimlessness of the Washington authorities toward the war.

Even if the problem of American disunity of command could have been solved, there still remained substantial barriers to a workable U.S./ GVN combined command. The first, and perhaps greatest, stumbling block was security of classified information. In a combined headquarters, composed of both United States and South Vietnamese, officers of both nationalities would have to be given highly classified and sensitive information about not only American forces and projected operations, but about the enemy and American intelligence methods and sources. Since the Americans had to assume that Communist agents had made substantial penetrations into the RVNAF, this potential for damage to American operations erected a towering wall against a combined command.

Other practical problems loomed. A substantial language barrier existed. No senior American officer spoke, read, or wrote Vietnamese, and the junior American officers who had Vietnamese language training were far from fluent. Many Vietnamese officers had been trained to speak English, but again their numbers among the relatively senior officers (from where the combined staff officers would be drawn) were inadequate. Then finally there was the problem of the skill and experience level. A few Vietnamese officers, the chairman of the Joint General Staff (JGS), Gen. Cao Van Vien, for example, were English-fluent and graduates of several United States Army schools, including the United States Army's CGSC. General Vien could have done any job on the combined staff, but he was almost unique. Most Vietnamese officers did not have the military education, experience, or sophistication to carry their load on a combined staff. When the skill and experience criteria were combined with the need for English fluency, very few Vietnamese would succeed as combined staff officers.

Looking back over the command system to fight the Vietnam War, an observer is struck by the fact that it worked as well as it did. Coordination and cooperation are not substitutes for unity of command, but they can be made to work. The workability of this type of system depends almost entirely on the personalities of the commanders involved. Sharp, Westmoreland, and Cao Van Vien were experienced, flexible, and broad-gauged men. Each was dedicated to the "whole war" effort, and thus the system of coordination and cooperation worked. With other men of lesser intelligence and dedication, it would have collapsed into an embittered, contentious mess.

This system of voluntary cooperation didn't work well below the MACV/JGS level. The United States Army Field Forces and III MAF routinely ignored the ARVN Corps in whose area they operated, and the ARVN Corps returned the disfavor. In some cases, the Field Force headquarters did not even tell its sister ARVN Corps of a projected major operation. The situation was worse at division level and lower where coordination was for practical purposes nonexistent.

A final word on this complex subject. Many Americans believe that a combined U.S./GVN command would have been worth all the disadvantages and difficulties cited above if it could have accomplished one thing—the replacement of the inept, corrupt, and politicized generals and colonels with which ARVN was afflicted. These Americans have a point, for this was ARVN's primary deficiency. But the question is, could a combined command have gotten deep enough into ARVN's structure, and even more, deep enough into the basic system by which President Thieu held power, to have vitalized ARVN leadership? One doubts it.

While the organization of United States and SVN forces for combat presented a problem, the employment of American ground forces in 1966 posed an even greater one. This question, always controversial, was decided at a high-level conference held in Honolulu in early February 1966. Gathered were President Johnson, McNamara, Rusk, Ambassador Lodge, General Wheeler (chairman, JCS), Admiral Sharp, and General Westmoreland, along with South Vietnamese President Thieu and Premier Ky. The Americans, particularly the president, talked a great deal about pacification and other nonmilitary programs. The Vietnamese, always excellent "gamesmen," assured the Americans that they had already developed pacification plans and other programs of governmental reform.

These were "paper plans" only, and nothing of substance would come from them or the discussions.

General Westmoreland did get something of substance, however. He got a formal memorandum giving him a mission for 1966, and, actually, for future years as well. This document, drafted by John McNaughton and Bill Bundy (the assistant secretary of state for Far Eastern Affairs), was approved by Secretaries McNamara and Rusk. General Wheeler, too, must have sanctioned the directive. The memorandum set forth six goals for the United States effort in South Vietnam:

1. Attrit (sic), by years end, Viet Cong and North Vietnamese forces at a rate as high as their capability to put men into the field.

2. Increase the percentage of VC and NVA base areas denied the VC from 10–20% to 40–50%.

3. Increase the critical (important) roads and railroads open for use from 30 to 50%.

4. Increase the population in secure areas from 50% to 60%.

5. Pacify the four selected high-priority areas, increasing the pacified population by 235,000.

6. Insure the defense of all military bases, political population centers, and food-producing areas now under government control.[11]

Westmoreland, somewhat smugly, wrote years later that, ". . . Nothing about those goals conflicted with the broad outline of how the war was to be fought as I had worked it out . . . senior civilian authorities acting for the president formally directed that I proceed as I had planned."[12] He then dismissed the entire directive, and never again referred to it in his book or in his official report on the war. Westmoreland's neglect of this mission statement is a perplexing action, since in the future he was to spend an enormous amount of time and effort defending the strategy of attrition, for which his critics held him solely responsible. Later, when he and his concept were under attack, he could have waved this directive and placed other prominent defendants in the dock alongside him, some of whom skewered him later for the concept and execution of the very strategy which they had prescribed.

Not only did Westmoreland minimize the significance of this momentous directive, but, by omission, so did other analysts of the war. The *Pentagon Papers* does not mention it; nor does Lewy cite it in his excellent and objective discussion of the strategy of attrition. Gen. D. R. Palmer, a devoted foe of the attrition concept, ignores it. Halberstam, a critic of almost everything about the American side of the war, omits any discussion of the directive. These omissions are mystifying. Here is the directive which established American strategy from 1966 to 1969, and which formally made the strategy of attrition the first-priority objective of the United States in South Vietnam, and yet no historian pays it the slightest attention. Strange, indeed.

The official requirement to "attrit (sic), by years end, Viet Cong and North Vietnamese forces at a rate as high as their capability to put men into the field" would plague Westmoreland with awkward problems. The first of these was the formalization of the now infamous "body count." It has a ghoulish sound, and it was a gruesome business. The directive, however, permitted no other method. To obtain the attrition rate, enemy bodies had to be counted. Only one other facet of the Vietnam War (enemy strength) aroused as much controversy.

The accuracy of the body count was constantly questioned, and rightly so. In many infantry fights, the United States unit could not get into the combat area after the battle to count bodies. There were often civilian casualties, either Viet Cong porters or innocents, who got in the line of fire and ended up as a "body count." There was always the possibility of "double-counting" by two adjacent units. By necessity, there had to be some *estimation* (or guesses) of enemy casualties, and these were seldom underestimated. Beyond these honest errors, there were charges of intentional exaggerations of "body count" by commanders attempting to make their units look good.

Most conscientious commanders tried to make a valid count. For example, they would insist that the enemy weapons captured be matched to the body count. An infantry company commander had better have a powerful explanation for a discrepancy such as a body count of one hundred and a weapons count of five, when a ratio of enemy bodies to weapons ran generally at three to one in that given area of operations. In an effort to improve accuracy of count, there evolved during the war a complex set of ground rules governing the reporting of enemy casualties. Nevertheless, the majority of the senior United States ground commanders who served in Vietnam felt the enemy body count to be exaggerated.[13]

There were, however, other factors which tended to balance the overcounting. First, the VC/NVA went to great efforts to remove their dead from the battlefield. Second, the jungles and swamps often made it impossible to find enemy bodies. Third, the casualties inflicted by air strikes and artillery bombardment deep in the enemy's rear areas were uncountable, and finally, there was no estimate made of nonbattle casualties due to injury and disease.

To this day, no American knows how accurate the United States figures of VC/NVA attrition were. Giap, in one of those asides of history, casually corroborated the United States figures of enemy attrition. In early 1969, the Italian journalist, Oriana Fallaci, interviewed Giap. She told him that the Americans reported that the enemy dead totaled about 500,000 men. Giap without hesitation replied, ". . . the exact number."[14] Actually, United States figures at that time were 435,000.

The first priority objective (to balance enemy input by attrition) posed another major problem for Westmoreland and his staff—the determination of enemy combat strength. Like the body count problem, this one was never resolved during the war. The underlying problem was a dearth of intelligence about the strengths and duties of some elements of the enemy force structure. There was no problem relating to the strengths and duties of enemy Main Forces and Regional Forces. Frequent combat with Allied troops brought the usual flood of prisoners of war and documents revealing details of organization and strength. But the strengths of the other categories of the enemy structure were harder to determine. Guerrillas, part-time soldiers, ununiformed, organized informally into small units, were difficult to count. The Communist political infrastructure was by its nature covert, operating deep underground, difficult to probe. The enemy's logistic support troops, called Administrative Services, worked deep in the enemy rear areas and were seldom in contact with U.S./GVN forces. Finally, there were even more amorphous groups, something called the Self-Defense Forces and Secret Self-Defense Forces. These groups were composed of old men, women, and children whose age, gender, or health kept them from serving with more militant Communist organizations. They were unorganized, without military discipline, armed with a few old weapons. Nobody knew what military jobs they did, if any, nor did anybody have any valid evidence as to their strength. With this "softness" of intelligence, it was possible to produce any number of variations as to enemy strength, depending on what categories were counted and what numbers an intelligence officer assigned to each category as its strength.

So, the first priority objective McNamara and Rusk gave Westmoreland generated two of the hottest controversies of the war. The remaining objectives developed not controversy, but bemusement. They reveal, once again, McNamara's obsession with trying somehow to quantify the American goals in the war. Note the language of these objectives. Westmoreland is to "increase the percentage of VC/NVA base areas denied the Viet Cong from 10–20% to 40–50%. He is to increase critical roads and railroads open for use from 30 to 50%, and to increase population in secure areas from 50 to 60%." These are largely meaningless numbers, a vain effort to gauge progress in a messy and unmeasurable war.

The first objective, enemy attrition, claimed Westmoreland's immediate attention in early 1966. He was now formally charged with attriting the enemy, but not told how to do it. The answer was, of course, to focus on the enemy. Wherever he could find the enemy's Main Force units, or wherever they appeared or threatened to appear, then United States and Allied troops would go there and with superior mobility and firepower kill them. At least, that was the theory. Thus, the enemy Main Force units and their intentions determined where and when Westmoreland would attempt to attrite them.

Westmoreland judged that his opposite number, NVA Sr. Gen. Nguyen Chi Thanh, would move against Saigon and against the heavily populated coastal lowlands running from Binh Dinh province to Hue. In line with this concept, he deployed the United States 1st Infantry Division into the old Michelin plantation at Lai Khe, north of Saigon. The 25th Infantry Division he positioned northwest of the capital city. The incoming 9th Korean Division went into the heavily populated coastal area near Tuy Hoa, while the United States 1st Marine Division took up positions in the coastal lowlands around Da Nang. Westmoreland sent the United States 4th Infantry Division into Pleiku in the Western Highlands to counter an NVA Main Force buildup there.[15] The 1st Cavalry Division (Airmobile) remained in the coastal plains of Binh Dinh. With these deployments, the "fire-brigade" phase of the war (Westmoreland's words) was over. Now he could begin a real war of attrition against enemy Main Force units.

The United States 1st Cavalry Division (Airmobile) launched the first large-scale search and destroy operation in January 1966. Operation MASHER (a name later changed by order of President Johnson, who thought the nickname would excite adverse public reaction) drove back and forth through Binh Dinh province. After six weeks, the 1st Cavalry reported enemy casualties to be 1,342 dead, 633 captured, and numerous "suspects" in custody. MASHER/WHITEWING was succeeded by THAYER/IRVING, another search and destroy operation by the same division in the same area. It finally ended in late October 1966 with about 1,000 enemy dead and another large group of "suspects." The ten months' operation of the 1st Cavalry Division netted some 3,000 enemy dead—roughly ten men per day.

Search and destroy operations took many forms. One involved a carefully planned assault by major American ground elements on a large enemy unit or base area, such as Operations JUNCTION CITY and CEDAR FALLS, which will be covered in the next chapter. Often, however, they began when a United States division received intelligence of an enemy unit, or even just enemy activity, in a given area. Depending on the reported size of the enemy unit, the extent of the area, and the "hardness" of the intelligence, an American platoon, company, or battalion would be assigned to sweep the zone. If the enemy unit was located, the helicopter-borne infantry would land, preceded by a tactical air strike, heliborne machine-gun attacks, and artillery fire. Often, the sweep found nothing, "dry holes," as they were called, because the enemy had vanished into the jungle. Sometimes a few enemy were found and killed; infrequently the assaulting unit got into a real fight, when either the enemy attacked it or the enemy got pinned down. Then followed the technique known as "pile-on." All available American ground units were airlifted into the area to surround and compress the enemy. The bombardment by tactical air and artillery reached a crescendo as the target became better defined. After a thorough pounding by air and artillery, the infantry moved in. Even then, the Viet Cong or NVA unit often got away.

Search and destroy operations, like every other operation in this frustrating war, had serious problems. If the strategy of attrition was to succeed, it had to "find, fix, fight, and finish" (to use an old infantry expression) the enemy's large Main Force units. The "finding" of the VC/NVA units turned out to be an almost impossible task. The enemy's large units hid themselves by small and dispersed groups in the inaccessible hills and canyons of the dense, triple-canopied jungle. These detachments shifted positions almost daily, so that intelligence of their location became outdated and useless within a few hours. In the face of these tactics, the intelligence sources which had seen the United States Army successfully through the other wars of this century proved inadequate. Aerial photography could not penetrate the triple-canopy cover of the jungle. Documents and the interrogation of prisoners of war revealed the location of small units, but by the time American reaction operations could be mounted, the enemy had moved on. The range of foot patrols, and thus their usefulness, was limited by the dense undergrowth of the jungle. Airborne electronic means such as infrared devices and radar were virtually useless.

The United States Army, in an attempt to help solve the problem, developed a novel device to scent out the enemy, called the "people sniffer." Carried in a helicopter flying just above the jungle, this machine indicated by chemical reaction a concentration of human urine on the ground below. Since only enemy troops would be in remote areas and in sufficient concentrations to register, it was thought for a short while that this might be the magic intelligence device. At first some good results were obtained, but the Viet Cong and NVA soon found out about the machine and began to "spoof" it by putting buckets of urine in the trees and then moving somewhere else. This tactic destroyed its usefulness in the jungles, although it continued to be of some value in the open areas of the Mekong Delta.

Beyond the problem of "finding" the enemy lay the problem of "fixing" him. In the sense used here, "fixing" means pinning the enemy in place so that he cannot move away and thus may be destroyed by superior fire power. Historically, this had been the American way of war. Ulysses S. Grant "fixed" Lee at Appomattox. In World War I, the United States and its allies finally pinned the Germans against the Rhine, and in World War II, the enemy ran out of space both in Europe and in Asia.

But again, the Vietnam War was different. Large enemy units operated near the DMZ, Laos, and Cambodia. When United States troops attacked, the enemy merely stepped back over the borders into North Vietnam, Laos, and Cambodia, where American troops could not enter. Even those major enemy units deep within South Vietnam could not be brought to battle. The VC/NVA refused to defend any terrain feature. They would abandon even their base areas under a United States attack, hoping that the Americans would miss most of their concealed supply caches, and knowing that G.I.s would have to leave the area within a few days anyway.

American search and destroy operations were easily avoided. Almost always, VC/NVA troops had ample warnings of coming American operations. United States troop movements took time to plan, and the massive preparations were visible to the hundreds of Vietnamese civilians who did the menial labor on the American bases. The preparatory air strikes and ground attacks often had to be coordinated with the South Vietnamese military and civilian hierarchy, and this structure had been penetrated by Communist agents. Even if the SVN military had not been penetrated, their counterintelligence and security procedures were criminally lax, and their carelessness would have revealed most operations anyway.

Nor were the Americans much better at concealing their future operations from a clever enemy. Both junior and senior officers persisted in "loose talk" on short-range radios and on the long-distance (but easily interceptable) radio-telephones. All American units developed crude "brevity codes" (changed daily), which gave the feeling of security, but which the enemy broke—literally within minutes after American troops began to use them. From all of these intelligence sources, the enemy could piece together most of what he needed to know to evade the United States attacks, except for the exact time and place of the assault. This too many United States commanders gave the enemy, by "prepping" the helicopter landing zones with air and artillery bombardment just before the assault went in. Now the enemy knew all, and like Douglas MacArthur's "old soldier," they just faded away.

Other counterintelligence failures were so blatant as to be farcical. The United States Marines made many amphibious landings (both large and small) up and down the coast in their area of tactical responsibility. These were designed ostensibly to trap or strike enemy units along the coast. Of course, the landings had great training value for the marines' primary role in combat, and this was probably the real reason they were conducted. Regardless of the justification for the operations, the element of surprise was totally lost when twenty-four hours in advance of the landing a big hospital ship hove to on the horizon opposite the assault beach and sat there, immobile, for all on shore to see. Obviously, amphibious operations availed little.

Then there was, and is, the persistent myth that the location of

B-52 drop areas were known in advance by the enemy. This is partially true. In the early days of B-52 operations, international air safety requirements forced the "big birds" to indicate flight paths and times to international air controllers located in Hong Kong. Of course, Communist agents had access to these filings and notified the North Vietnamese, who notified the troops along the B-52 pattern. Later, however, this requirement was bypassed, but throughout the war, Russian "trawlers" remained anchored off Guam (the B-52's primary base) reporting the departure of each strike element. Time-and-space calculations would tell the enemy the time (within rough limits) the B-52's would be over Vietnam, but not where. Nor were the United States Navy and the United States Air Force fighter-bombers any more counterintelligence conscious. Up until mid-May 1967, they attacked Hanoi and vicinity "in clusters over a period of a week or so, always at 2:30 in the afternoon" according to John Colvin, the British consul in Hanoi.

If the United States ground troops could not "find" the enemy or "fix" him, they manifestly could not "fight" or "finish" him. Yet that was what the strategy of attrition required—the ability to inflict unacceptable losses on the enemy—and the United States could never do it. The United States armed forces could kill and maim hundreds of thousands of the VC/NVA soldiers, but they could never reach that mystical level of pain where Ho and Giap would say, "This is unacceptable; this is enough."

While the strategy of attrition had not hurt Hanoi enough to cause them to cease their aggression, it did achieve positive results. It seized and held the tactical initiative in South Vietnam; it disrupted enemy activities; it forced the enemy to resort to constant movement to avoid destruction; and it drove the major enemy units away from the population centers. And while in 1966 it had not attrited enemy strength at a rate as high as enemy capability to put men in the field (the crossover point), American and ARVN operations had inflicted heavy casualties on all elements of the enemy's force. Beyond these accomplishments lay the really significant one—U.S./GVN operations in 1966 and early 1967 convinced Ho, Giap, and the Politburo that the ground war in the South had turned against them, and that some drastically different strategy had to be developed.

But in this multifaceted war of 1966 there were other fronts in the struggle. One of these was pacification, which included a broad effort to win the people to the GVN while trying to reform and strengthen the government and improve its armed forces. By 1966 pacification had compiled a bleak history. In the forties and fifties, the French had failed dismally at winning the support of the Vietnamese people. Later, Diem and his cohorts had done little better. Their *agrovilles* and Strategic Hamlet programs launched in 1962 had shown promise, but eventually came to nought—too ambitious, too revolutionary, and too dislocating for the conservative Vietnamese peasants. In mid-1964, the South Vietnamese government developed the *Hop Tac* (Cooperation) Program, but again the government overreached, and General Westmoreland wrote, "The year 1965 was one of great labor which gave forth a very modest result."[16]

This "very modest result" in the field of pacification resulted not only from the incapacity of the South Vietnamese government to plan and execute a workable program, but also from the hesitant and divided approach by the United States. The United States side of the program was fractured and leaderless. The Agency for International Development (AID), the Central Intelligence Agency (CIA), and the United States Information Agency (USIA) competed openly for resources and scarce South Vietnamese manpower. Each had a chain of command running from the South Vietnamese countryside through Saigon to Washington. No United States agency bore overall responsibility, nor did any have authority over the others.

Other United States deficiencies shackled the pacification program. While the American search and destroy operations kept the enemy Main Force units away from the villages and hamlets, they accomplished little in providing the secure environment which pacification required. The United States failed to build up the police and Popular Forces (small, village-oriented security forces) which could provide local protection against the Viet Cong guerrillas. Finally, that old *bête noire,* the lack of a combined U.S./GVN command, multiplied the failings of the pacification effort. Pacification required close coordination between United States search and destroy strikes, ARVN clear and hold sweeps, local security operations, and psychological warfare. This coordination was impossible under the loose command arrangements in existence.

In late 1965 and early 1966, the failure of ROLLING THUNDER and the inconclusiveness of Westmoreland's search and destroy operations pushed pacification into the limelight. For domestic political reasons,

President Johnson realized that he had to show the American people that he was making progress *somewhere* in this increasingly unpopular war. In spite of major commitments of United States ground troops in the South and a sizable air effort against the North, the American people looked in vain for the proverbial, and often-sought, "light at the end of the tunnel." Now the president, in effect, selected another program which he hoped would show progress—pacification. So, in early 1966, key officials in both Saigon and Washington began mounting the pacification bandwagon, an idea whose time had come. Robert Komer, the consummate bureaucrat, first saw the opportunity and positioned himself in the White House as the president's special assistant for pacification. Not only in this role, but later in 1967–1968 as chief of the pacification program on Westmoreland's staff in Saigon, he would wield the big stick in trying to "win the hearts and minds of the South Vietnamese"— a phrase, incidentally, which he always derided in private.

Another agency which tried to "cut itself a piece of the pacification action" was the staid old United States Army. In July 1965, Gen. Harold K. Johnson, the army's chief of staff, assembled in the Pentagon a group of specially selected young officers, all of whom had had experience as province and district advisors in Vietnam. He told this group to develop an alternative concept to Westmoreland's strategy of attrition. They did, and in March 1966 they brought forth a study called PROVN, an abbreviated name for the Program for the Pacification and Long-Term Development of South Vietnam. PROVN turned out to be a massive document recommending a galaxy of actions, ranging from a revision of national strategy to minor personnel changes within the United States advisor setup in South Vietnam.

Reading PROVN now, an observer is impressed with its insight and candor. It defined "victory" as ". . . bringing the individual Vietnamese, typically a rural peasant, to support willingly the GVN."[17] The paper argued: first, that the then current American military campaigns had little effect on this long-range goal; and second, that action should be concentrated at province, district, and village level; and finally, that top priority be given to pacification. Although PROVN recommended that pacification receive top priority, it did grasp, apparently unwittingly, that in late 1965 and early 1966, Giap's revolutionary war was evolving from an insurgency into a combination insurgency and conventional war. With this concept in mind, PROVN prescribed as one of its "highest priority activities" that "the bulk of United States and Free World Forces and designated RVNAF units be directed against enemy base areas and against lines of communication in South Vietnam, Laos, and Cambodia as required . . ."[18] The study pointed out two major deficiencies in the U.S./GVN effort: the poor and divided management of the program, and that no two United States agencies in South Vietnam viewed American objectives in the same manner.

Realizing the implied censure of existing concepts and agencies in the document, General Johnson restricted its distribution to within the Department of Defense. In the late spring of 1966, briefers from the PROVN staff presented the finding and recommendations of the study to the CINCPAC and MACV staffs. Unfortunately, the briefers were young and arrogant, acting as if they were "Christ come to cleanse the temple." They alienated the senior officers whose approbation and support they needed, and neither CINCPAC headquarters nor MACV were receptive. CINCPAC gave its proxy to MACV, and MACV promptly muffled the study by the old bureaucratic ploy of extolling it, and then suggesting it be reduced to a "conceptual document and forwarded to the National Security Council for study." Exit PROVN.

The study deserved more mature consideration. Its executioner was General Westmoreland, and while he does not even mention PROVN in his memoirs or in his *Official Report on the War,* his reasons for throttling it are obvious. PROVN forthrightly attacked his search and destroy concept, which, correctly or incorrectly, Westmoreland sincerely held to be the right strategy. Beyond that, it proposed taking considerable military authority from him (COMUSMACV) and giving it to the ambassador, who, under PROVN, would become the pro–consul and sole manager for all United States activities in-country, including the military. The study recommended a deeper United States involvement in GVN administrative affairs (which Westmoreland thought unwise) and hinted again at the desirability of a single U.S./GVN combined command (the "hearty perennial"), which to Westmoreland was unnecessary and unattainable. In actuality, the major fault in the study lay in its emphasis on pacification and counterinsurgency. Thus, it was a program to combat a Phase I insurgency when the war had already moved into Phase II (combination insurgency and conventional war) and was headed for Phase III, all-out conventional war.

Perhaps as much as any other reason for Westmoreland's rejection of PROVN was the old factor of "not made here," that is, not produced by himself and his staff in Saigon. He could not embrace the study's concept (that search and destroy operations were unproductive) without admitting that he and his strategy were wrong. This admission would have become doubly painful because his error had been revealed, not by himself and his own staff, but by a group of young officers 13,000 miles away. And while PROVN was dead, it left several residual conceptual benefits. It would rise again as "Son of PROVN" in 1969, and then, under different circumstances and a different commander, would gain support and credence.

PROVN did trigger a spate of other studies on pacification. In April 1966, the United States mission in Saigon set up a "Priorities Task Force" which by the summer had produced another long and useless study. In July, the embassy organized another study group to determine the proper role and mission of all military and paramilitary forces operating within South Vietnam. This so-called Roles and Missions Study Group turned out many helpful recommendations before this paper, too, found itself in that limbo of "being studied further."

Finally, General Westmoreland and the MACV staff saw the light, and they too climbed on the pacification bandwagon. On 26 August 1966, MACV published a "Concept for Military Operations in South Vietnam." The concept, embodied in a long message to CINCPAC and the Joint Chiefs of Staff, emphasized the pacification role along with a progressive strategy of assaulting and destroying enemy base areas. The strange phenomenon about the pacification effort in 1966 was that—like Mark Twain's weather—everybody talked about it but nobody did much about it. The Honolulu Conference of February 1966 was followed by a reorganization of the pacification efforts within the Saigon Mission. Deputy Ambassador Porter was put in direct charge of the civilian agencies working on the program, and he failed miserably. Ambassador Lodge failed to support him, and the agencies used their channels to Washington to bypass him. On 26 November 1966 another reorganization took place. This time the Mission set up an Office of Civil Operations (OCO), bringing the civilian agencies concerned with pacification into one operating section under Porter. Again, the agencies bucked the organization, and Lodge continued his lack of support, and time ran out in Washington for OCO. Thus, in 1966, the torrent of exhortatory words and good intentions about pacification accomplished little or nothing in Vietnam.

Not much more progress was made in the other aspects of pacification: nation-building and the improvement of RVNAF. The United States controlled ROLLING THUNDER and ''Westy's War,'' but not the solution to the problems of the GVN and RVNAF. Any lasting progress in reforming the GVN presented formidable obstacles. The first, and perhaps the greatest, snag was the absence of any concept of nationhood among the South Vietnamese. It had never been a nation, and it had no precepts of national patriotism or sacrifice for the national good. The extended family (including long-dead ancestors) was the only recognized symbol of unity and loyalty in the country. Beyond the family, South Vietnam is a nation of minorities, fragmented by race, religion, language, culture, and region. Each of these fragments viewed the others with attitudes ranging from indifference to hostility. None of them had any loyalty towards a central government. Nepotism and ''cronyism'' thrived. An official took care of his expanded family and his friends, and they in turn protected and supported him. Many Americans tried to displace a Vietnamese official or a general because of his incompetence, only to run into a wall of delays, excuses, and subterfuges. Later the American would learn that the targeted official was a brother or a cousin of the wife of the Vietnamese official who was being pressured to fire him.

Then too, Oriental customs, thought patterns, and ethics consistently confounded the Americans. As in most Oriental lands, corruption and the utilization of public office for personal gain are a way of life. Public officials, including South Vietnamese army officers, traditionally viewed bribery and kickbacks as a part of their legitimate pay, particularly when salaries had always been unrealistically low. So widespread and embedded was this type of corruption that any official who refused to help his family or friends by illicitly using his influence was viewed by other Vietnamese not as patriotic and honorable, but as selfish and irresponsible. The top leaders of the GVN used another ploy. They let their wives hold the family purse strings—or so they said. This took the senior official out of the direct chain of corruption, but insured the same results. Many of these wives became enormously wealthy.

The third factor blocking any real reform of the GVN was the ''mandarin system.'' This Oriental custom provided that officials and officers of the armed forces had to have at least a high school education. This device limited the officeholders to the educated and wealthy elite. A peasant, no matter how brilliant or effective, could not rise to power. As a result, the governments of South Vietnam changed frequently, but the same elite stayed in power—haughty, venal, and incompetent.

One facet of this long war which perplexes the casual observer is why could not the Americans, whose men were dying for South Vietnam and whose taxes were supporting it economically, force the South Vietnamese to do the bidding of the United States. From this perplexity arises the factor of "leverage"—that is, methods by which the Americans could have, and sometimes did, force their will on their Vietnamese partners. Robert W. Komer candidly writes that leverage ". . . was more talked about than practiced."[19] He should know. In all the United States government there was no better or more eager practitioner of leverage against the South Vietnamese than the aggressive and ambitious Bob Komer. But Komer was wise enough to see both sides of the "leverage" coin. The dilemma was that if the United States policy-makers pressed too hard on the weak house-of-cards which was the South Vietnamese government, the whole arrangement would topple. Also, United States leadership was wary of developing a set of South Vietnamese "American toadies," an epithet which would destroy their usefulness among their own people. Finally, there was always the sensing that the South Vietnamese were a proud and sensitive, even xenophobic, people. No long-range good could come from degrading and browbeating their leaders. At any rate, the United States failed in getting the GVN leaders to take the necessary actions to strengthen and reform their government. As Gen. George Patton used to say, "You can't push a piece of spaghetti," and yet that is what the United States tried consistently to do.

If the United States efforts to reform and strengthen the Government of South Vietnam failed, the attempt during 1966 to build up RVNAF was equally futile. Many of the same factors (corruption, family ties, cronyism, the mandarin system) which vitiated American efforts in nation-building blocked success in increasing the military effectiveness of RVNAF. During 1966, the service with the deepest problems was ARVN, the Army of the Republic of Vietnam. With a few exceptions, it performed miserably in combat.

ARVN's fundamental problem was lack of motivation. This morale problem showed itself in 1966 in several ways. First, there was the desertion rate, which by 1966 had reached epidemic proportions. For example, the ARVN 5th Infantry Division near Saigon lost 2,500 men through desertion in the first three months of 1966. The ARVN desertion crisis was worsened by widespread evasion of conscription. Huge numbers of South Vietnamese young men simply did not show up for induction. By the end of 1965, an estimated 232,000 youths had become draft evaders. By mid-1966 the ARVN absentee problem had become so great that Westmoreland forbade the creation of any new ARVN units until the existing ones, vastly understrength, had reached acceptable manning levels.[20]

The most acute manifestation of the problem of ARVN's lack of motivation showed itself in the quality of leadership of the officer corps. The senior officers were preoccupied with politics. They did not know their jobs, nor did they care. In the worst sense of the term, they were "political generals," appointed by the GVN leadership to maintain that leadership in office. The junior officers suffered from inexperience and lack of motivation to perform combat roles. Junior officers came from rich families, and there was never any real attempt to bring up the natural combat leaders from the ranks. None of the officers took care of their troops. In order to eat, the troops looted the civilians they were supposed to be defending. The people hated them for it, and pacification languished.

The United States advisors at division and lower level railed through American channels at the incompetence and lack of professionalism of the South Vietnamese they were advising. Their attempts through American leverage to get the incompetents relieved almost always failed. Nor were the efforts of the top United States military leadership much more productive. I heard General Abrams, the "professional soldier's professional," become almost apoplectic about one South Vietnamese division commander. He would say, his voice rising with every word, "that man is not only the worst general in the South Vietnamese Army, he is the worst general in any army in the world!" It took "Abe," by then COMUSMACV, a couple of years to get the "world's worst general" replaced—and then, he got kicked upstairs.

In 1966 the United States entered the fourth "front" in the American war effort in Vietnam—negotiations, or rather, a serious attempt to get a negotiated end to the war. In 1965, the Johnson administration had made a few inconsequential motions toward negotiating a settlement, but neither side took them seriously. Now, in 1966, the nascent political pressure of the domestic "doves" toward negotiations, and the obvious lack of significant progress in the other three "wars" (ROLLING THUN- DER, attrition, and pacification) focused the administration's efforts on an attempt to end the war by negotiations with North Vietnam.

The first effort of 1966 originated from the bombing halt of 24 December 1965–31 January 1966. Through a contact in Rangoon on 29 December 1965, the United States ambassador to Burma, Henry Byroade, established contact with the North Vietnamese consul general there, Vu Huu Binh. Byroade called Binh's attention to the bombing pause and suggested that perhaps some reciprocation by the North Viet- namese might lead to progress in negotiations.[21] For almost four weeks, the only action from the North Vietnamese was a public statement on 4 January 1966, branding the pause as an American trick. Then silence. President Johnson, pressured by the "hawks" in Congress and the mili- tary, ordered the bombing resumed on 31 January. That very day, as the bombs were falling, Binh contacted Byroade with the Politburo's reply. On the surface the reply offered no grounds for fruitful negotiations. However, the subsequent discussion left the door open for additional contacts. Other unproductive exchanges followed, but by 29 February, both sides had lost interest in the attempt, code-named PINTA.

The Rangoon ploy had not quite disappeared when another possible contact appeared in the person of a Canadian, Chester Rouning, whom the Canadian government had designated its special representative to Saigon and Hanoi. Rouning saw Pham Van Dong in early March 1966 and was treated to a replay of the Byroade/Binh game—an unyielding demand that the bombing cease unconditionally and permanently, softened by a number of ambiguities as to whether the Communists would compro- mise their position. Rouning transmitted a series of ambivalent messages between Washington and Saigon, and in late June this contact, too, died.

Just as the Rouning contact folded, another replaced it, code-named MARIGOLD. This time the contact was tricornered. On 27 June, Lewan- dowski, the Polish member of the International Control Commission (ICC), which supervised the terms of the Geneva Convention, told D'Or- landi, the Italian ambassador to South Vietnam, that he had just come from North Vietnam with a proposed peace offer. D'Orlandi promptly passed this information to Henry Cabot Lodge, the United States ambassador to South Vietnam.[22] Then, United States planes struck North Vietnamese POL facilities near Hanoi in late June, and on 17 July, Ho Chi Minh declared negotiations with the United States impossible.

Toward the end of the year, the climate thawed a little, and for a few weeks progress again seemed possible. Then, the inability of the Johnson administration to coordinate its military and diplomatic actions killed it. On 2 December, American aircraft for the first time struck two NVA facilities near Hanoi, and on 4 and 5 December, these and additional targets near Hanoi were hit. Other targets near Hanoi were struck on 13 and 14 December. The attacks incensed the North Vietnamese, giving them the impression that the United States was using military pressure to force them into negotiations. There then ensued a flurry of explanations, but the Politburo broke off the contact. MARIGOLD was dead. And so, the fourth "war," negotiations, was even less fruitful than the United States' other three "wars."

How, then, had the four-pronged strategy of the Americans fared in 1966? Looked at overall, it accomplished little. On the other hand, it had not lost the war, and the promise of improvement and greater achievement was perceptible in all four major programs. ROLLING THUNDER had been ineffective, but perhaps an extension of the strike area and an expansion of the target list could give it the punch it needed. At least, this was what the generals and admirals were saying. In South Vietnam, Westmoreland's strategy of attrition had not reached the directed "crossover point," nor had it hurt the enemy enough to force Hanoi to back off from the war in the South. Again, perhaps increased efforts in 1967 with augmented ground forces would accomplish its objectives. Pacification during 1966 had been almost a total failure, yet in both Washington and Saigon there was a growing sense of urgency about this program, which promised solid results in 1967. Negotiations had proved fruitless, but both sides had at least made attempts at them, even if halfhearted and inept.

In 1966, while all of the United States "wars" might have shown promise, a major problem appeared—lack of coordination of the war effort at the national level. The direction and execution of ROLLING THUNDER involved multiple agencies and headquarters from the White House, the Pentagon, and CINCPAC, to the operating commands in the field. As a result, the air strikes, sometimes those which had been approved weeks earlier, destroyed not only enemy targets, but United States negotiation efforts as well. The ground campaign in South Vietnam went its own way without regard to its impact on pacification or negotiations, and with little or no coordination with ROLLING THUNDER. Pacification itself was fractured and floundering as United States agencies fought for "turf" and resources. No person or agency pulled the entire effort together or dictated priorities of effort. The deficiency, of course, lay in the White House, reflecting the complex and twisted personality and mentality of President Johnson. Nor would the passage of time improve this situation.

But if, in 1966, U.S./GVN victory cups did not overflow, the war did not look any more promising from Hanoi either. They, too, had their arguments, their skeptics, and their failures. The debate regarding VC/NVA strategy in the conflict in South Vietnam, which had begun with the entrance of United States ground forces in 1965, increased in fury during 1966. Gen. Nguyen Chi Thanh, Giap's old adversary and the field commander in South Vietnam, pressed *his* argument of 1965 that the correct ground strategy was to continue the attacks by the VC/NVA Main Forces against major American units and bases. Giap resolutely held to *his* previous position that such attacks were ineffective and too costly, and that the Communists ought to resort to guerrilla warfare. An analysis of VC/NVA operations in the period November 1965 to May 1966 shows that Thanh's concept won out over Giap's. The NVA continued their basic strategy of enticing American units into uninhabited jungle areas near their remote border sanctuaries and attempting to annihilate them there.

In February 1966, the North Vietnamese added a new and dangerous variation of the "border strategy." They sent two NVA Main Force divisions, the 324B and the 341st, south across the DMZ into the northernmost province of South Vietnam, Quang Tri. At the same time, they moved sizable NVA units from their Laotian bases into the next province to the south, Thua Thien. This crafty move confronted General Westmoreland and the U.S./GVN effort with hazardous and complex problems. The first problem arose from the geography of the area. The two northern provinces of South Vietnam are isolated from the rest of the country by a steep ridge which runs from the Laotian border to the sea, striking the ocean just north of Da Nang. A single road traverses this ridge, through the infamous Hai Van Pass, narrow, winding, easily cut, and vulnerable to ambushes. This problem of poor communications was aggravated by the lack of all-weather ports north of the pass. Logistic support of any sizable U.S./GVN countering force in the two northern provinces would be difficult.

The NVA thrust into Quang Tri-Thua Thien (which the North Vietnamese called the Tri-Thien Front) also exploited the lack of U.S./GVN troop strength in the area. To counter the NVA troops in this area of operation, Westmoreland had available only one South Vietnamese division (whose worth nobody knew) and a single United States Marine Corps battalion. Westmoreland believed that Hanoi's primary intent in sending large NVA units into the two northern provinces was to force the United States and GVN to divert troops from operations in the heavily populated areas, but he saw behind this enemy move a more ominous plot—to seize and isolate this northern area and set up a "liberation" government.[23] For some reason which Westmoreland has never revealed, this fear that the VC/NVA would take over an isolated piece of South Vietnam and establish a governmental seat was a long-standing obsession of his.

The correctness of one part of Westmoreland's analysis—that Hanoi had sent large NVA forces into the Tri-Thien area to divert United States and GVN troops from the tasks of pacification and control of the populated areas—was confirmed in a treatise by Giap himself.[24] Giap's statement may well have been self-serving, since the diversion of United States and GVN troops was all that the establishment of the Tri-Thien Front actually accomplished. Westmoreland skillfully countered the NVA move by shifting United States Marine units from Da Nang into the two northern provinces and in reinforcing the marines with army units, including a 175mm gun battalion with a range of some twenty miles. To insure adequate logistic support, he had the Seabees construct all-weather ports along the shores of the two northern provinces. These moves blunted the NVA thrust into the northern area during early 1966.

On the NVA side, there was an interesting difference in the public utterances of Giap and Thanh on the establishment and operations of the Tri-Thien Front. Giap saw the move as the key strategic decision taken by Hanoi during 1966, but Thanh, in his voluminous writings, ignores it completely. The reason apparently was that this front in South

Vietnam fell under Giap's command, not Thanh's, a command arrangement which made sense. Logistical support, signal communications, and the flow of replacements for the units near the DMZ could all be controlled more easily from North Vietnam than from Thanh's distant headquarters in a remote and primitive area in southern Cambodia. Nevertheless, the command arrangements were another cause of bitterness between the two old rivals, and indicated again that command jealousies—the "not-made-here" syndrome—are not unique to the American army. They are as timeless and as universal as military rank and the hand salute.

The NVA debate over strategy began in earnest after the Southwest Monsoon ended VC/NVA operations in May 1966. Hanoi had lost the initiative to Westmoreland's search and destroy operations. They had only heavy casualties to show for their own broken offensives, which stretched from the Michelin plantation near Saigon to the Tri-Thien Front. During the summer of 1966, the North Vietnamese leadership disappeared from public view, an action which always signaled a high-level conference. Beginning in July 1966, the rhetorical guns began to roar. Thanh was called upon to defend his concept of large-scale, set-piece battles. Arrogantly, he counterattacked—not only in the privacy of the Politburo, but in the Communist newspapers.

In July 1966, in an article published in *Hoc Tap,* the official Communist daily, Thanh virulently attacked Giap and the latter's supporters. He bluntly accused Giap (although not by name) of trying to fight the war in the South in accordance with "old customs." Twice he applied to Giap the term "old-fashioned," and he accused Giap of having ". . . a method of viewing things that is detached from reality." He further chastised Giap by charging, "To repeat exactly what belongs to history in the face of a new reality is adventurism." Not only does he attack Giap as backward-looking, but assailed his (Giap's) concepts as ". . . looking for new factors in the formulas that exist in books, and mechanically copying one's past experiences or the experiences of foreign countries . . . in accordance with a dogmatic tendency."[25]

Translated from the Communist rhetoric, Thanh was saying that Giap had no understanding of the actual situation in the South, and that Giap's criticisms and guerrilla warfare concepts were outdated and bookish. Underneath it all, there was the irritation of the independent commander (Thanh) at those who sat back in high headquarters and criticized the efforts of the commander in the field. This resentment is universal; it disregards time, location, or nationality. As a matter of fact, Thanh's battlefield adversary, Westmoreland, shared it. Westmoreland directed his irritation not at his military superiors, but at the "whiz kids" and the "field marshals" in the State Department who, without experience, were trying to tell him how to run the war. This universal rancor against rear-area critics found its best expression over two millennia ago. A Roman consul who had been selected to conduct the war against the Macedonians, Lucius Aemilius Paulus, blasted this type of armchair critic. Wrote the crusty old Roman, "Generals should receive advice . . . from those who are on the scene of action, who see the terrain, the enemy, the fitness of the occasion, who are sharers in the danger, as it were aboard the same vessel. Thus, if there is anyone who is confident that he can advise me in this campaign, *let him come with me into Macedonia*. I will furnish him his sea-passage, with a horse, a tent, and even travel funds. If anyone is reluctant to do this and prefers the leisure of the city to the hardships of campaigning, let him not steer the ship from on-shore."[26] So Thanh challenged Giap, "come with me into Macedonia."

Thanh's initial salvo was quickly followed by reinforcing fires from an anonymous writer who used the pen name Truong Son (The Long Mountain Range). While Thanh had directed his broadsides at his challengers and detractors, Truong Son fired a "protective barrage" in which he sought to show that Thanh's "big war" concepts had, in fact, been victorious in late 1965 and early 1966, and thus were correct. He constantly cites the great victories which the Communists had won over the United States troops. According to Truong, they had annihilated whole United States battalions, had gained the initiative, and had reduced the "number of five American mobile divisions to three."[27] No evidence was evoked to support these boasts, for they were lies. Actually, the reverse was true. Westmoreland had won the victories, gained the initiative, and had seriously eroded VC/NVA strength.

Truong Son's defense of Thanh had hardly been printed when Giap's supporters fired back. A North Vietnamese military expert, who called himself Vuong Thua Vu, on 10 July 1966, broadcast an analysis of Truong Son's article. He agreed with many of Truong's remarks (particularly the boasts of huge successes), but cooled toward Truong's and Thanh's basic strategy of large-scale, Main Force battles. Instead, Vuong suggested that Truong's concepts should be "developed more profoundly"—in other words, they should be debated.[28] With this rejoinder, the debate disappeared from public view until 7 September 1966, when a new voice made itself heard, and from a new and different direction. The Liberation Radio from within South Vietnam (or more likely, Cambodia) broadcast an article by the anonymous writer, Cuu Long (Mekong River). It is now known that "Cuu Long" was the pen name of Tran Do, a NVA major general and the third-ranking officer in COSVN. His views stressed the worth of the guerrilla and the great gains which could be made by guerrilla warfare. In essence, Cuu Long was on Giap's side of the argument. Cuu quotes a 1966 message from Ho Chi Minh in which Ho stated, "The war may still last ten, twenty years, or longer." Thus, Cuu ends his diatribe by promising that the Viet Cong ". . . will strike repeatedly and five or ten times more vigorously" at American LOC's and rear bases.[29] The next salvo in the debate came from an article from another pseudonymous author, La Ba, which appeared in the official Hanoi press on 4 October 1966. The author expressed Giap's views in an undiluted form. He extolled the virtues of guerrilla warfare, giving it credit even for the Main Force successes.

When the 1966–1967 dry season campaign began in late October 1966, however, it became apparent that Thanh had again won the debate. The concept of large battles by Main Force units had won; the strategy of protracted war featuring guerrilla operation had lost—again. "Cuu Long," or Tran Do, was a bad loser, however, and on 13 November 1966 he attacked Thanh again. Cuu made the point in this broadcast that guerrilla warfare is not just a bunch of loosely organized yokels in black pajamas running around in small groups ambushing trucks and digging punji pits full of poisoned stakes. He claimed that Communist guerrilla warfare had progressed to the point where it could successfully combat major American units, even those supported by air power and armor. He stressed that all forces, including Main Force units, could and should engage in guerrilla warfare. About halfway through his address he gave some gratuitous advice to "the leading and guiding echelons," telling them that ". . . they can avoid erroneous concepts such as the idea of depending on concentrated troops. . ." He charged that "If leadership and organization are more realistic, we will deal blows of strategic significance . . . on the United States troops."[30]

Cuu Long's broadcast brought on a counterattack by Thanh. On 12 December, the Liberation Radio broadcast an anonymous piece which answered Cuu Long, but which did not refer directly to him or his views. It claimed that the war in the South was going well, and that the conventional war and the guerrilla struggle were being coordinated. Giap could not let Thanh's remarks go unchallenged, so on 22 December 1966, Radio Hanoi repeated many of Cuu Long's criticisms of Thanh's strategy. The broadcast listed a number of guerrilla accomplishments ". . . testifying to the boundless potential of guerrilla warfare." With this final fusillade, the debate over the military strategy in South Vietnam—at any rate the public part of it—terminated as the year 1966 rolled to an end. But the basic argument was still there—what phase of revolutionary war were the Communists fighting, and how should they fight it?

In the military one hears often of the "brotherhood of arms," a bond of fellowship which supposedly overarches national loyalties and links those who dedicate their lives to the defense of their respective countries. Most of this is sentimental bombast, heard after a few drinks with officers of allied countries. Sometimes there is something to it, and could Generals Westmoreland and Thanh have seen the other's problems they would have realized that, to paraphrase Kipling, they were "brothers under the skin." Both field commanders, Thanh and Westmoreland, held similar strategic concepts of large-scale, conventional warfare to attrite the enemy. The "other war"—pacification for Westmoreland and guerrilla warfare for Thanh—would be fought by lesser troops. Neither commander nor his strategy was resoundingly successful. Thanh kept losing the Main Force battles (and the initiative). Westmoreland could win battles, but his victories could not be translated into political or strategic progress. The Viet Cong were making little headway with their guerrilla operation, and ARVN could make no progress in pacification. Each commander found himself opposed by a group sitting back in Washington or Hanoi arguing for a change in ground strategy. Washington wanted more emphasis—the main emphasis really—placed on pacification. Hanoi wanted more guerrilla-type warfare. In essence, their detractors wanted to go to small-unit warfare, and the commanders in the field wanted large-unit battles. Both Westmoreland and Thanh resisted their critics, and both debates, as well as negotiations, were at a standoff as 1966 ended.

There were other similarities between Thanh and Westmoreland.

Each commander was faced with difficult logistic problems. Westmoreland had to build ports, a gigantic network of airfields, and bases. Thanh and his aides had to keep open the Ho Chi Minh Trail. Both had to assuage and try to direct their junior partners (ARVN and the Viet Cong) who insisted, with historic Vietnamese contrariness, on resisting advice from their senior partners and going their own way. Both sides were bringing into South Vietnam more and more troops, and both Westmoreland and Thanh foresaw that in 1967, the ground war in South Vietnam would expand both in scope and ferocity. What they may not have sensed was that a critical turning point in the war would occur in 1967.

Notes—Chapter 16

1. Gravel, *Pentagon Papers*, IV:39.
2. Sharp, *Strategy for Defeat*, p. 108.
3. Ibid., p. 106.
4. Ibid., p. 116.
5. Gravel, *Pentagon Papers*, IV:114.
6. Ibid., IV:128.
7. Ibid., IV:130.
8. Sharp and Westmoreland, *Report*, p. 100.
9. Ibid., p. 104.
10. Ibid.
11. Thompson and Frizzell, *Lessons*, p. 10.
12. Westmoreland, *Soldier*, p. 195.
13. Douglas Kinnard, *The War Managers* (Hanover, NH: University Press of New England, 1977), p. 75.
14. Fallaci, *Interview*, p. 82.
15. Sharp and Westmoreland, *Report*, pp. 113–114.
16. Ibid., pp. 230–231.
17. Department of the Army, "A Program for the Pacification and Long-Term Development of South Vietnam (PROVN)" (Washington, D.C.: Department of the Army, March 1966), p. 100.
18. Gravel, *Pentagon Papers*, II:577.
19. Komer, *Bureaucracy*, p. 32.
20. Brig. Gen. James L. Collins, *Development and Training of the South Vietnamese Army, 1950–1972*, Vietnam Studies (Washington, D.C.: Department of the Army, 1975) pp. 56, 61, and 62.
21. Porter, *Vietnam*, II:403 (Quoting an aide-memoire from Byroade to Vu, 29 December 1965).
22. Ibid., II:425 (Quoting a cable from Lodge to Secretary of State Rusk, 29 June 1966).
23. Sharp and Westmoreland, *Report*, p. 116.
24. Vo Nguyen Giap, "The Big Victory, The Great Task," *Nhan Dan* (Hanoi: 14–16 September 1967).
25. Nguyen Chi Thanh, "Ideological Tasks of the Army and People in the South," *Hoc Tap* (Hanoi: July 1966).
26. Livy, *Titus Livius*, Book XLIV:22.
27. Truong Son, "On the 1965–66 Dry Season," *Quan Doi Nhan Dan* (Hanoi: July 1966).
28. McGarvey, *Visions*, p. 82.
29. Cuu Long, Liberation Radio, 7 September 1966.
30. Cuu Long, Liberation Radio, 13 November 1966.

17 The Best of Years and the Worst of Years

1967

For both sides, 1967 was the "best of years and the worst of years." The United States would take long strides toward winning the shooting war in South Vietnam and over North Vietnam, and both sides would realize it. Yes, in 1967, *militarily* speaking, there really was a "light at the end of the tunnel." On the other hand, neither side would recognize that the United States would begin to lose the political and psychological war at home. On the other side, Ho, Giap, and Pham Van Dong would come to the stark realization in 1967 that they were losing the war militarily in both North and South Vietnam. As a result they would decide on a course of action which would hand a military victory to the United States and the South Vietnamese in 1968.

One of the conflict's top leaders would die, and three new American leaders would enter the fray. In retrospect, the year 1967 breaks into three distinct segments, January–April, May–September, and October–December, with the war changing character in each period.

January–April

The ground battle in South Vietnam intensified as both sides augmented their forces. The Americans brought in an additional 100,000 men. The

NVA responded by increasing their strength about the same number, while Viet Cong strength dropped as their recruiting could not keep their ranks filled. The enemy began 1967 with a strength of around 280,000, including Main Forces, Regional Forces, Administrative Forces, irregulars, and political cadre. Of these, approximately 50,000 were NVA. This VC/NVA force contained nine divisional headquarters, thirty-four regimental headquarters, 152 combat battalions, and almost 200 separate companies. The strength of the combined United States, South Vietnamese, and Free World forces (Australia, New Zealand, South Korea, etc.) in January 1967 totaled 1,173,800.

To employ this sizable Allied force, Westmoreland and the chief of the South Vietnamese Joint General Staff, Gen. Cao Van Vien, developed a Combined Campaign Plan for 1967. It contained two significant changes from the strategy which had governed operations in 1966. First, Westmoreland had seen the light—at least in theory—about the need for military support to the pacification program. On 24 April, he told the Associated Press managing editors, "the real objective is the people."[1] The plan provided that the bulk of the ARVN would be used in support of pacification while the United States and Free World Forces (FWF) would "carry the bulk of the offensive effort against the Viet Cong and NVA Main Force units."[2] Westmoreland hastened to add that this did *not* mean an emphasis by United States forces on the enemy Main Forces at the expense of the pacification effort. The plan envisioned that over half of the United States troops would be used in the heavily populated areas against Viet Cong guerrillas.

The second major change of U.S./GVN strategy called for large-scale assault operations which would enter and neutralize the major enemy base areas, such as the "Iron Triangle" and "War Zone C," both just northwest of Saigon, and "War Zone D," northeast of the capital. Westmoreland envisioned a sustained series of attacks against these areas which would cripple the logistic potential of the enemy he described as "the Achilles' heel of the NVA/VC."[3]

The rest of the 1967 ground strategy was a carryover (necessarily) from the concepts by which operations had been conducted in 1966. Near the DMZ, the marines had to meet and defeat two reinforced NVA Main Force divisions operating in that area. The Communist base areas inside South Vietnam along the China Sea reaching from Quang Tri province south to Binh Dinh were to be neutralized. In the Central

Highlands, the plan called for the area to be defended only by light covering forces. When the enemy sallied across the Laotian border in strength, sizable United States forces would be sent to meet and destroy him. The Mekong Delta in southernmost South Vietnam would still remain a VC/ARVN fight.

Westmoreland's strategic concepts for 1967 can best be understood as part of the continuing battle for the "Big I"—the Initiative. Westmoreland sought to gain it by a combination of defensive and offensive operations. He would resort to the strategic defense along the DMZ and along South Vietnam's borders with Laos and Cambodia. This portion of his concept merely accepted what could not be changed. From their border sanctuaries, the enemy could mount sizable attacks along South Vietnam's peripheries which could not be preempted or met until the offensives had moved into South Vietnam. Then the combination of the superior American mobility and firepower would be used to counterattack before the enemy offensive had achieved any significant success—a classic example of mobile defense. Within South Vietnam, however, Westmoreland saw a brighter promise. Here he could call the tune; here he would make the VC/NVA adjust to his initiatives and his attacks. He would go after their base areas, particularly the big base areas.

Like many other aspects of this unusual war, the enemy's concept and use of base areas was foreign to historical American military thought. These base areas were located in large zones protected by mountains, swamps, rivers, and dense vegetation. They housed supply bases, hospitals, headquarters, training centers, rest areas, even small and primitive manufacturing plants. Troops were assembled, trained, and equipped here for future operations. To overcome their logistic deficiencies, the Communists would move supplies from these base areas to a forward site near the objective to be attacked and hide them there in small caches. This movement took place over long periods, and the Communists called the practice "preparing the battlefield." These base areas were vital to the continuation of enemy operations.

As Westmoreland saw the enemy situation, the Communists *had* to fight for their critical base areas. When they attempted to defend them, superior American power would destroy the defenders and the base areas alike. Put another way, the criticality of the base areas to the enemy would "fix" him, and United States firepower would "finish" him. Attacks on the base areas promised other important advantages. By smashing up the enemy's logistic apparatus in the base areas, Westmoreland believed he could forestall future enemy attacks (thereby keeping the initiative), because the Communists could not use them to "prepare the battlefield." Also, attacks against the base areas drove the Main Force units quartered there away from the Viet Cong guerrillas, whom the big units supported.

Given the strategic limitations under which Westmoreland labored—no ground attacks outside South Vietnam—the concept of offensives against the base areas was the logical employment of American mobility and power, at least in theory. Thus, with high hopes and great expectations, on 8 January 1967 Westmoreland launched the equivalent of three United States divisions into the Iron Triangle in an operation called CEDAR FALLS. He followed this thrust on 22 February with another multidivision assault into War Zone C, nicknamed JUNCTION CITY.

As is so often the case, consummation fell short of anticipation. The enemy frustrated the fundamental principle of Westmoreland's base area concept by refusing to stand and fight. The enemy preferred to risk his bases rather than endanger his forces. The official report on CEDAR FALLS and JUNCTION CITY states, "It was a sheer physical impossibility to keep him (the enemy) from slipping away whenever he wished if he were in terrain with which he was familiar—generally the case. The jungle was just too thick and too widespread to keep him from getting away."[4] Not only were the Americans unable to bring the enemy to bay in his base areas, the Viet Cong came back as soon as the United States troops left. They returned to the Iron Triangle two days after the American troops pulled out of Operation CEDAR FALLS. Ten days later the base area was (in the words of the official report), ". . . literally crawling with what appeared to be Viet Cong."[5]

Another shortfall from expectations was the material result of the operations. No big headquarters, depots, or hospitals fell to the American assault troops, although United States troops did seize some small arms and ammunition and enough rice to feed a Viet Cong division for a year. The enemy had long ago scattered his installations and carefully hidden them deep underground. The two big operations cost the enemy around 3,500 killed, but American troops paid a price too, with 354 men killed and 1,913 wounded.

Many analysts have written off the United States assaults into the base area as failures. Such indictments, while perhaps justified in the short-term, fail to consider the long-term effect. These operations *did* seize the initiative from the Communists, and they did abort Viet Cong attacks in support of guerrillas in the populated areas. Most important—as is now known from captured documents—Thanh and Giap both viewed these incursions into the base areas as "disasters." The operations convinced the VC/NVA leadership that they could no longer base Main Force units near populated areas, thus forcing Hanoi into an increased reliance on the border sanctuaries.

Of equal significance, the American forays into the base areas severely punished the Viet Cong guerrillas near the populated areas. They lost Main Force support, and their strength declined as the better-trained guerrillas were "promoted" to make up losses in the Main and Regional Forces. Their sources of arms and ammunition dried up, and their morale began to crack. Giap's strategy—emphasis on guerrilla warfare—had reached a crisis. In January and February, it was Westmoreland's game, and he was winning.

In late March, Giap struck back. With his Main Force units driven out of the interior of South Vietnam, he attempted to gain the initiative by an attack from the peripheries of the country, in this instance from the DMZ. On 29 March, the villages of Cam Lo, Con Thien, and Gio Linh, located on the South Vietnamese side of the DMZ, came under heavy artillery and mortar attack. Gio Linh received over 1,000 rounds during one day, and in any war that is a lot of incoming rounds. On 24 April the marine outpost at Khe Sanh, held by one marine company, was attacked by two NVA Main Force regiments. This first battle of Khe Sanh lasted twelve bloody days. The marines, heavily reinforced, killed 900 NVA soldiers, which means that, counting the wounded, the two North Vietnamese regiments were almost destroyed. The marines lost around 150 dead and 400 wounded.[6]

Westmoreland had for some time been uneasy about the enemy threat from the DMZ. Early in 1967, he directed the MACV staff to develop a contingency plan to move a division-size task force made up of United States Army units from central South Vietnam to replace the marine units in the southern part of I Corps Zone. This would then allow the marines to concentrate their entire strength north of Da Nang and to contest more effectively the enemy thrusts in the two northern provinces and along the DMZ. The violent enemy attacks near the DMZ in late March and early April triggered Westmoreland's plan. Task Force Oregon was activated and began relieving marine units south of Da Nang on 20 April. Westmoreland and the marines had beaten off Giap's springtime grab for the "Big I." True, Giap had made Westmoreland move troops from the South, but they were replaced by American reinforcements now arriving in-country.

While Westmoreland was winning *his* war in the South, the United States was losing another war there—pacification. Despite many ringing declarations from Washington and Saigon about the need to "reach the people," despite bales of ambitious plans and unrealistic reorganizations, the problems which had blighted the pacification program in 1965 and 1966 continued into early 1967. But there *was* one improvement. Westmoreland had promised in the Combined Campaign Plan for 1967 to use half of the United States forces in support of pacification, and he claimed then (and now) that he did so.[7] Others dispute this. Lewy points out that for fiscal year 1968, $14 billion was spent on bombing and ground offensive operations while only $850 million was spent on pacification.[8] Robert Komer, who was more concerned and knowledgeable about the pacification program than any other United States official, also denies Westmoreland's claim.[9] The dispute was, and is, largely semantical. There has always been a confusing overlap between search and destroy, clear and hold, and pacification support. In such a climate, any individual can generate statistics proving his point. Regardless of who won the battle of figures, pacification languished in early 1967.

The real problem was not statistical or semantical, however, it was Westmoreland's order of priorities. In 1966 and early 1967, and for that matter throughout his commandership in Vietnam, Westmoreland viewed pacification as a stepchild. While he pontificated about the importance of pacification, he devoted his energies and interest to operations like CEDAR FALLS and JUNCTION CITY, not to clearing and holding the insignificant hamlets and villages around Saigon. And—as an old military axiom goes—whatever the commander emphasizes gets done well by the staff and subordinate commands. So it was in Vietnam. The MACV staff and the American units emphasized big-unit military operations.

This United States emphasis on military operations at the expense of pacification might not have been harmful had it not created an even more damaging side-effect on ARVN. Taking their cue from their United

States counterpart, the good ARVN commanders wanted some of the "big-unit" war too—not the tedious, unglamorous, piddling operations associated with pacification support. Unfortunately, this support was ARVN's primary job, so mandated by the 1967 Combined Campaign Plan, and dictated by the nature of the situation and force structures of the two allies. If ARVN did not do it, or did not do it well, then pacification would wilt, and in early 1967 it was a wilted and unhealthy plant indeed.

Pacification got a rocket boost on 18 March when General Westmoreland requested around 200,000 more troops. The request stunned President Johnson, Secretary McNamara, and the latter's civilian deputies, who were already disquieted by their pessimistic view of the trend of the war. The request was followed by a conference held on Guam two days later. Presidents Johnson and Thieu attended along with high-level assistants and field commanders. Westmoreland, in an unusual candid and grim briefing, told his high-ranking audience that unless the Viet Cong collapsed (which he did not foresee) or the NVA infiltration halted (also unexpected) the war would go on indefinitely. In 1982, General Westmoreland told me that he did not consider his Guam briefing to be grim, but this view is contradicted by his own book.[10] Westmoreland claimed that he asked for the 200,000 additional troops for use as a force to go into Laos, to cut the Ho Chi Minh Trail, and, by remaining in position there, to keep it cut.

Both the troop request and Westmoreland's forecast caused the president and Secretary McNamara to seek alternatives to a massive increase in United States strength in South Vietnam or to an invasion of Laos. One alternative—indeed, the only one readily at hand—was to put a dynamite charge under pacification. The president did just that. He transferred the responsibility for the pacification program to COMUSMACV, General Westmoreland, and he lit the charge, Robert Komer. It would be about six weeks before Komer arrived in Saigon, but with his arrival, the pacification program was on its way.

The other parts of the pacification program—the improvement of RVNAF and the strengthening of the GVN—made progress, slow though it was, in the first half of 1967. The massive United States military advisory effort finally began to pay off. The small South Vietnamese Navy relieved some United States naval units on coastal patrols, while the South Vietnamese Air Force flew 25 percent of all combat sorties within South Vietnam. ARVN, too, improved, although the fundamental problems of inept leadership, corruption, and an unwieldy command structure remained. The M-16 rifle became available for issue to selected ARVN units in April 1967, and by the year's end most ARVN combat units had them. Schools, ranging from one for adjutant generals (personnel bookkeepers) to a revised General Staff College and National Defense College, were established. Some progress was made to insure that the South Vietnamese soldiers were fed and housed properly, and that their dependents were minimally cared for. As a result of United States and South Vietnamese efforts, the desertion rate, which had reached catastrophic proportions in 1965–1966, dropped in 1967 by thirty-seven percent.

RVNAF's most significant advance came in April 1967 when, at the urging of General Westmoreland, the South Vietnamese government and its Joint General Staff began the massive task of planning for a general mobilization of all manpower and resources to support the war. This planning would pay huge dividends later. Like pacification, the improvement of ARVN was due for a rocket assist in May, with the arrival of the new deputy commander, MACV, Gen. Creighton W. Abrams, to whom Westmoreland gave the responsibility for the improvement of RVNAF.

The principal progress in "nation-building" came in the April–May 1967 period, when the South Vietnamese government decided to hold open and free elections for the offices of president and vice president. The struggle between Thieu and Ky in June 1967 over who would run for what office shook the South Vietnamese leadership to its foundation. In 1963 or 1964, this kind of power struggle would almost certainly have generated an attempt at a *coup d'état*. That it did not do so in 1967 evidenced the growing maturity and sense of responsibility of the GVN leaders. This was progress—of sorts.

As pacification sputtered in early 1967, and as the United States ground war in South Vietnam roared into high gear, "Oley's War," ROLLING THUNDER, limped along as it had in the last months of 1966. The Northeast Monsoon severely hampered air operations in the first quarter of 1967. While some new targets were authorized around the Hanoi/Haiphong area, they had to be coaxed target-by-target out of the "Two Targeteers" in Washington, President Johnson and Secretary McNamara.

While the two men were joined in procrastination over releasing "painful" targets around Hanoi, they viewed ROLLING THUNDER from different perspectives. McNamara, by now a devout "dove," operated on the premise that ROLLING THUNDER had clearly failed. It had not driven Ho to the bargaining table, and its costs exceeded its worth. McNamara wanted to limit strikes to south of 20° North latitude, stabilize the sortie rate, and construct an electronic barrier along the DMZ and into Laos. On the other hand, Johnson was convinced that the bombings were achieving favorable results. As always, however, he worried about enlarging the war. He tormented himself with his deep-rooted fear that an air campaign against North Vietnam which was too aggressive or too destructive would bring the Chinese or Russians into the war. Then, too, the politician in Johnson constantly sought compromise between the "hawks" (largely military) who wanted to expand the bombing program and the "doves" who sought to curtail it. And in the first half of 1967, as in 1966, the "hawks" and "doves" largely stalemated each other over ROLLING THUNDER. What resulted from the stalemate was more of the "creeping gradualism" which had previously doomed the program to impotence. But in the second half of 1967, ROLLING THUNDER, like pacification, was going into a rocket-launched orbit.

The final "war," negotiations, saw a serious attempt to end the war by diplomacy. Since 1964 the United States leadership had felt that somehow negotiations with Hanoi had to be undertaken. Many United States "signals" to Ho were unfurled—bombing halts, messages through third parties, enticing speeches—and although from time to time Hanoi appeared interested, all the approaches soon floundered. But in late 1966, as ROLLING THUNDER faltered and the ground campaign in the South proved indecisive, President Johnson and his top advisers became increasingly attracted to negotiations.

MARIGOLD, which had succumbed in late 1966, was succeeded by another effort at negotiations, this one called SUNFLOWER. In January and February 1967, the United States attempted to work through London to Moscow and thence to Hanoi. There was the usual exchange of vague and confusing messages through intermediaries, and a short bombing pause whose purpose confused not only Hanoi, but the United States military as well. With a final fruitless flurry involving British Prime Minister Wilson and Soviet President Kosygin (who was visiting in London), SUNFLOWER went to seed, the victim, this time, not of lack of United States political/military coordination, but of the inability of either side to communicate with the other.

There were other attempts during 1967 to get talks started between the two major combatants, with sometimes ludicrous results. The governments of Norway, Sweden, and Rumania attempted to act as contacts between the two powers. All failed. Twice more, once in April and again in August 1967, United States bombing attacks put an end to diplomatic approaches. In 1967, negotiations suffered not only from the lack of United States governmental coordination, but from the belief by each belligerent that it could win its desired solution on the battlefield. Not until the events of early 1968 had transpired would each government see the weakness of its respective position and determine to end the war by negotiations.[11]

In late 1966 and early 1967, as MARIGOLD and SUNFLOWER withered and died, so did Hanoi's military prospects. The year began with the timeworn and bitter arguments in the North Vietnamese Politburo over what to do in South Vietnam. Giap, Truong Chinh, and their supporters held firmly to the position that in the South, priority should be given to political *dau tranh* and guerrilla-type warfare. Giap, himself, made this clear in a speech given in early January. His old rivals, Gen. Nguyen Chi Thanh and Le Duan, persisted in their view that the key to victory lay in battles between Communist Main Force units and large American formations. Thanh's spokesman, the artful Truong Son, in a speech published in June 1967, bluntly contended that the task of ". . . annihilating enemy forces had been minimized" and ". . . that it is the foremost task in any war." In an even franker vein, he confessed that the task ". . . is not satisfactorily performed in certain areas."[12]

American operations in early 1967 in South Vietnam, however, quickly made the old quarrel within the Politburo irrelevant. For reasons already set forth, Westmoreland's forays into the base areas and his hardhitting mobile defensive operations along the peripheries of South Vietnam had undermined the foundations on which Giap and Thanh had built their competing strategies. Westmoreland's damaging raids into the base areas, particularly CEDAR FALLS and JUNCTION CITY, had struck a catastrophic blow to Giap's strategy of the protracted, guerrilla war, as it drove the Main Forces away from the guerrillas and deprived them of vital Main Force support. Thanh's concept, too, had suffered severely. Just south of the DMZ, in northern South Vietnam, the North Vietnamese effort to gain the initiative had failed, while farther south, Thanh had completely lost the "Big I," and the basis of *his* strategy.

In early 1967, other unfavorable trends, both in the North and South, convinced the North Vietnamese leadership that the time had arrived for a sweeping reappraisal of their strategy. First, the VC/NVA military position in South Vietnam had deteriorated dangerously. VC/NVA casualties in South Vietnam were mounting rapidly. During 1966, Communist battle deaths had totaled about 5,000 men a month, but during the first six months of 1967 Communist KIA's (Killed in Action) soared. MACV estimated that from January through June 1967 the total enemy losses (casualties, POW's, defectors, nonbattle casualties, and unreported defectors) exceeded 15,000 men per month. Since the Viet Cong could recruit about 3,500 men per month, and NVA infiltration ran to about 7,000 per month, the "crossover point" had been reached, that is, more Communist soldiers were being put out of action than they could recruit in-country or infiltrate from the North.[13]

While a caveat must always be attached to enemy strength and casualty figures, nevertheless, they did provide general indicators that the enemy was "hurting." This judgment is confirmed by a senior Viet Cong prisoner of war who in February 1968 told his interrogators that from September 1967 to January 1968, the Viet Cong forces in the VC/NVA MR V (roughly the area between Saigon and Da Nang) ". . . suffered many heavy reverses and casualties and . . . that heavy infiltration of NVA troops was still not enough to fill gaps."

With Giap's and Thanh's historic disregard for their own casualties, they might have accepted these losses, if some strategic or political advantage accrued. Certainly, no strategic gain had resulted and none was in prospect. Nor did the political vista for Hanoi hold any more promise than the military one. In the South, the Viet Cong had lost control of from 500,000 to 1,000,000 Vietnamese in the last half of 1966 and the first two months of 1967. This population loss reduced the tax and food base of the Viet Cong and made recruiting more difficult, while the GVN gained these people, with consequent political and economic advantage. The evidence which Hanoi saw of nation-building in the South was perhaps even more alarming. The GVN's growing efforts at constitutional government and the relative stability of the Thieu-Ky regime signaled a significant shift in the political winds blowing through South Vietnam. Thus, looking at the military and political scene in the South, Ho, Giap, Thanh, and their comrades saw that a strategy of ''more of the same'' in South Vietnam had to be thoroughly restudied, and probably abandoned.

Giap, however, saw in the military situation of early 1967 an even wider and more ominous threat to the Communist effort in South Vietnam. He believed that the United States forces would shortly invade either North Vietnam, Laos, or Cambodia. Any of these incursions would pose the possibility of a war-losing disaster to the North Vietnamese. For the Communists, the base areas in these three sanctuaries were indispensable. Even with them, the war was being lost; without them, the Communists foresaw terminal defeat.

There were other threats associated with a United States invasion into one or more of the three areas. An invasion of North Vietnam would force Giap to defend his homeland with all available units, relegating the war in the South to a secondary operation. A United States invasion of Laos would cut the Ho Chi Minh Trail, depriving Viet Cong and NVA forces in South Vietnam of supplies and replacements. The criticality of the trail was so great that North Vietnam would be forced to mount a major counteroffensive to break the United States hold on this vital artery, a prospect which appalled Giap. Such a counteroffensive would pit a major North Vietnamese force in a set-piece battle against at least a United States corps of several divisions operating under conditions greatly favoring the Americans. The results, even to the sometimes overly optimistic members of the Politburo, were foreseeable—the destruction of the Communist units hurled into such a desperate counteroffensive. A United States strike into Cambodia lacked the potential for disaster which haunted the Communists' forebodings about North Vietnam and Laos. Such an attack, however, would have severe repercussions on any future enemy operations aimed at the heavily populated areas around Saigon and in the Delta. To Giap and the other Communists in Hanoi, these potential invasions by United States troops had to be forestalled.

The second major factor which influenced Ho and Giap's assessment was posed by the United States air attacks on North Vietnam. Hanoi could take a rosier view of this war than of the one in the South, but it gave the Communists no cause for jubilation. The United States sortie rate over North Vietnam had risen from 2,401 a month in June 1965 to 12,249 in September 1966, and although bad weather inhibited the attacks after October 1966, an average of 8,000 to 9,000 per month continued to batter North Vietnam during the rest of 1966 and into early 1967. Then, on 24 January 1967, the president authorized the United States air arms to attack sixteen critical targets around Hanoi. So, in addition to an increase in attack sorties, the level of target "pain" rose, too, for North Vietnam.

It is now known that early in 1967 the Politburo began to be seriously concerned about the mounting destruction from the air in North Vietnam.[14] Roads, bridges, POL facilities, and North Vietnam's limited amount of heavy industry were being destroyed or badly damaged. By the end of 1966, 9,500 ships or boats, nearly 4,100 trucks, and 2,000 pieces of railroad rolling stock had been damaged or destroyed. And, as is always the case when high explosives are used, there was incidental and unintended bomb damage to homes, schools, office buildings, and other structures near military targets.

The indirect cost of ROLLING THUNDER to the North Vietnamese probably exceeded its purely destructive effects. Admiral Sharp estimated that the United States air assault compelled Hanoi to divert 500,000 to 600,000 civilians to air defense or to repair bomb damage. The bombing caused general economic deterioration and dislocation, with agriculture, particularly, suffering. The effect, as time went on, was cumulative. As 1966 turned into 1967, the people of North Vietnam began to experience shortages of food, clothing, and medicine, and malnutrition appeared. Letters and reports began to come out of North Vietnam telling of deprivation and harsh living conditions. Even more significant, there were growing signs of internal unrest in the North. Politburo members made speeches censuring the lack of zeal among cadres and condemning black market activities and profiteering.[15]

Then, on 27 February 1967, the United States Navy began to mine internal waterways and coastal estuaries in North Vietnam below the 20th Parallel. At the same time, Secretary McNamara announced that more targets would be added to the strike list, and on 10 March, United States fighters struck the Thai Nguyen iron and steel complex for the first time. In April the United States began a persistent air campaign against targets in the outskirts of Hanoi, pounding them day after day in contrast to their past spasmodic raids.

While this increase of intensity concerned Hanoi's leadership, their real worry about ROLLING THUNDER was not what had happened, but what might happen. Just as Giap had predicted a widening of the ground war, Pham Van Dong foresaw a dangerous escalation of the bombing campaign against the North. He feared that the United States intended to attack the dikes along the Red River and its tributaries, and his fears were well-grounded. American military planners *were* studying the possibilities of attacks by "iron bombs" against the dikes, and the potential for massive destruction was tempting. As on many rivers in Asia (the Yellow River in China is a famous example), the dikes on the Red River had been built up through the centuries so that the river actually flows in a man-made canal above the surface of the surrounding countryside. If the dikes were breached during the monsoon or flood period, hundreds of square miles of valuable farm land would be flooded, countless villages and cities inundated, including Hanoi itself, which would be under eleven feet of water. The task of breaching the dikes from the air would be difficult, but possible. Here was another "war-losing" possibility which the North Vietnamese had to forestall.

As the Hanoi leadership pondered the dark situation in South Vietnam and the potentially dangerous one in North Vietnam, a disturbing political factor linking the two halves of the country had to be weighed also. It, too, had a "war-losing" potential, for it involved the control of the National Liberation Front (NLF) in South Vietnam by the Communist Party apparatus in the North. While the basis of this concern even now remains unclear, there is some evidence that the Hanoi leadership feared that the NLF on its own might attempt to reach some agreement with the GVN to settle the struggle in the South. Even if the NLF took no direct action to reach an accommodation with the GVN, the Politburo had to ask itself how resolutely the NLF and the Viet Cong would stand up under the steady deterioration of their military and political position. Again, the possibility of the NLF going its own way, although remote, had to be forestalled. In 1982, a former NLF leader declared that the reason for placing the Viet Cong in the forefront of the Tet offensive was to eliminate the NLF leadership and its fighting forces, leaving the North Vietnamese Politburo supreme.

Finally, Hanoi had to consider the international situation to see how its pressures would move it towards a new course of action. First, there was the Sino-Soviet split, a schism which philosophically and pragmatically distressed Ho and his comrades. North Vietnam depended on both of its big allies. China furnished small arms, food, trucks, and other smaller supplies, as well as highway and railroad maintenance assistance in northeast North Vietnam. Russia gave North Vietnam its antiaircraft guns, missiles, tanks, and other sophisticated military equipment. To make matters more touchy, North Vietnam's two major allies espoused different strategies on how North Vietnam should win the war. China, drawing on its own experience, advocated the "protracted war" approach, emphasizing political *dau tranh* and guerrilla warfare in the South carried out largely by the Viet Cong. The Soviet Union, on the other hand, pushed for a strategy of negotiations, which, implicitly at least, advocated large-scale attacks by NVA Main Force units in the South in an effort to create favorable conditions for bargaining. The North Vietnamese tried to steer a neutral course between its two big allies. In public utterances, Hanoi's leaders constantly stressed their independence from both China and the Soviet Union. The uneasy truce between the two Communist superpowers, however, worried the North Vietnamese, and its influence pushed Ho and his compatriots toward some quick solution to their problem.

But as the Politburo looked farther around the international horizon, for the first time it saw promising prospects. In South Vietnam it saw not a "war-losing," but a "war-winning" possibility. In the eyes of the Politburo the people of South Vietnam were not only ready, but eager to go over to the Communists. The Buddhist struggle campaigns and the series of internecine political intrigues convinced them that the Government of South Vietnam had no popular basis of support, and, if given the chance, the people of the South would overthrow President Thieu and the GVN. They believed also that the South Vietnamese hated their "American oppressors" and would turn on them at the first opportunity. Finally, they had long ago convinced themselves that the South Vietnamese armed forces were badly trained and equipped, that their morale was low, and that they had no motivation to defend the South Vietnamese government.

Finally, Ho and company were encouraged by what they saw in the United States and by the impact of the war on American allies in

Europe and elsewhere. Within the United States they saw no great vulnerabilities, but they did see a growing peace movement and a burgeoning
popular discontent with the Vietnam War and its apparent stalemate.
They considered also that in 1968, the presidential elections would place
the American political system under its usual quadrennial stress. But
the Hanoi leadership didn't put great stock in either the election or the
peace movement to aid their cause. Giap said, ". . . despite a possible
change of presidents the nature of the United States imperialist's aggressive policy will remain the same."[16] Pham Van Dong told the American
reporter David Schoenbrun in 1967 that the North Vietnamese were
". . . grateful for the help of the American peace demonstrators, but,
in the final analysis we know we must count mainly on ourselves."[17]
The Communists could hope that in the election campaign, the war
and its conduct would become a partisan issue, which, in Giap's words,
". . . will make the American people more aware of the errors and
setbacks of the Johnson administration in the aggressive war in
Vietnam."[18]

To the Communist leaders, the stress brought about by the friction
between the United States and its European allies constituted an American
vulnerability. Hanoi correctly noted that virtually all the major allies of
the United States opposed American participation in the war and its
methods of conducting combat operations. The reasons were obvious.
The preoccupation of the American leadership with Vietnam distracted
it from the problems of NATO and the defense of Europe. By 1967,
the Vietnam War had begun to suck up American military resources
which in previous years had gone to the Atlantic Alliance. American
participation in the war gave the left-wing political parties and elements
in Europe a useful rallying point to attack the United States and those
in the European political spectrum who supported it. No politician wants
to be surrogate whipping-boy. Above all, many Europeans—even the
most steadfast supporters of American participation in the war—believed
that the American venture into Southeast Asia constituted a danger, not
only to the United States, but to its allies as well. The wiser ones among
them knew that war is always a "dicey" business, full of miscalculations
and accidents. A United States action—invasion of North Vietnam or
Laos, or the breaching of the dikes, for example—might bring the Chinese
Communists or even the Russians into the war. An accident, such as
the bombing of a Soviet vessel or the overflight and bombing of a Chinese

airfield, might instantly enlarge the war to catastrophic proportions. If the Russians and the United States clashed in Southeast Asia, the conflict could quickly spread to Europe and engulf NATO.

Hanoi's leadership clearly understood this fear and exploited it with veiled threats of Chinese intervention. Giap viewed it as a factor restraining the United States from taking an adventurous course of action which might tilt the war heavily against the Communists. This would be particularly relevant if some dramatic North Vietnamese action goaded a vengeful American leadership toward a bold and destructive counterstroke.

So as Ho and his principal advisers surveyed the military, political, and diplomatic scene, they saw one thing clearly—they were losing the war. They needed a new strategy, so in early 1967, probably March, Ho convened the 13th Plenum of the North Vietnamese Central Committee. These plenums were habitually called at critical points of governmental decision. The 12th Plenum, for example, had been convened in December 1965, when the appearance in South Vietnam of United States troops in strength changed the strategic equation there. To the 13th Plenum, Ho gave the task of studying the entire situation and recommending a course of action. After lengthy deliberation, the 13th Plenum called for a ". . . spontaneous uprising in order to win a decisive victory in the shortest possible time." By contrast, the resolution of the 12th Plenum (1965) had called for ". . . victory within a relatively short period of time."[19] The voice of the 13th Plenum clearly said: no more protracted war, but an all-out drive for victory at one stroke. This was the new strategy—the first step on the way to the Tet offensive.

May–September

For the Vietnamese Communists, the period May–September was one of great plans and furious activity as they prepared for their upcoming offensive. The basic recommendation of the 13th Plenum for a spontaneous uprising to win a quick victory had to be considered by the Politburo, and when approved (as it was), handed on to the various staffs which would have to flesh out the concept for what the North Vietnamese would call *Tong Cong Kich, Tong Khai Nghia,* "General Offensive, General Uprising," shortened by the Communists to "TCK-TKN."[20] The operation would be known in the rest of the world as the Tet offensive.

Ho and the Politburo formally made the decision to launch the offensive probably in early May. The military and Party staffs, both in Hanoi and COSVN (Central Office, South Vietnam), Thanh's headquarters in Cambodia, began the detailed planning to implement this decisive change in strategy. In June the Politburo called most of the North Vietnamese ambassadors to Hanoi, a signal to intelligence agencies all over the world either that a momentous decision had been made, or that one was under final consideration.

July was a critical month for the North Vietnamese leadership, particularly for Giap. On or about 4 July 1967, a deadly accident befell Sr. Gen. Nguyen Chi Thanh in his COSVN headquarters. The official North Vietnamese news release stated that he had suffered a severe heart attack and was flown to Hanoi, where he died on 6 July. High-level North Vietnamese defectors later told United States interrogators that American B-52 bombers hit COSVN headquarters, striking Thanh in the chest with bomb fragments. Regardless of the cause of Thanh's death, it was a fortuitous stroke for Giap. The death of his longtime rival made Giap the supreme military leader in Communist Vietnam, and upon him fell the role of planning and carrying out the upcoming and decisive offensive, TCK-TKN.

Every plan for a military operation is based on either stated or implied assumptions about the factors bearing on the conduct of that operation. Such assumptions generally include suppositions about future enemy strength or action, terrain, weather, one's own forces, and other conditions which the planners foresee as pertinent to the execution of the operation. Giap based his concept for TCK-TKN on four major assumptions. First, ARVN lacked motivation and would desert or defect when struck a hard blow. Second, the GVN had no support among the people of South Vietnam, and if given the opportunity, the people would eagerly rally to the Viet Cong and its puppet government, the National Liberation Front (NLF). Third, the people and armed forces of the GVN despised the Americans and would turn on them. Fourth, the tactical situation at Khe Sanh in 1967–1968 paralleled that of Dien Bien Phu in 1953–1954.

With these assumptions, Giap developed a bold and imaginative concept. In broad outline, his plan had three interdependent parts, and the Communists dubbed it a "three-pronged" offensive—military, political, and what the Communists call troop proselyting—in short, here in one operation was the mating of political *dau tranh* and military *dau tranh* leading to the culminating General Offensive-General Uprising. The military prong would be the most important—the Communists called it the "lever." Giap's lever had three distinct phases, to be carried out over a period of several months.

During Phase I (September–December 1967), Giap planned to mount sizable NVA attacks around the edges of South Vietnam. With this gambit, he hoped to replay the successful strategy which had upset and diluted Navarre's campaign plan prior to Dien Bien Phu. By these border assaults, he aimed to draw United States forces out of the populated areas to the peripheries of the country and to lure Westmoreland into launching operations along South Vietnam's borders. This would make it easier for the Viet Cong to storm the cities (his eventual targets), all located in the interior.

Giap had two other reasons for initiating the peripheral offensives. First, he could train his units in large-scale assaults and from them learn practical lessons about the problems of attacking towns and installations. Second, he would "keep the American coffins going home" as the Communist attacks exacted American casualties. Giap knew he would pay a bloody price for these lessons and for the American dead, but he figured that the gain was worth the cost. Phase I of the military plan for TCK-TKN would also see a NVA force of two or more Main Force divisions move into position around Khe Sanh, an outpost held by one marine regiment, in preparation for later operations.

Phase II of Giap's plan for the military phase of TCK-TKN envisioned a countrywide assault, principally by Viet Cong Main Force units on the South Vietnamese cities, ARVN units, American headquarters, communication centers, and airbases. American ground combat units, in so far as possible, were to be avoided. Giap gave the Viet Cong the role of attacking ARVN and the cities in an effort to convince the South Vietnamese that the attacks were originated by their Southern compatriots. Using Southerners would also permit them to infiltrate into attack positions prior to the offensive, a ploy unattainable by the North Vietnamese, whose accents would give them away. Furthermore, using the Viet Cong in this phase allowed Giap to hold his NVA forces in reserve for use later. Giap believed that these assaults against the cities of South Vietnam would disintegrate the "puppet army," as the Communists called ARVN, and destroy its integrity.

The attacks against ARVN and the cities would be assisted by the second prong of the "three-pronged offensive," troop proselyting. This part of the plan called for massive propaganda campaigns, for subversion operations directed at the ARVN soldiers by family and other pressures, and for devastating military blows to obtain wholesale defections and desertions from ARVN's ranks. The Communist planners foresaw whole ARVN units either melting away, or even better, turning their weapons against the hated Americans.

Then, the plan called for launching the final prong—the political offensive of TCK-TKN. This phase saw the people revolting against the Thieu-Ky government, overthrowing it, and rallying to the red and yellow banners of the Viet Cong and NLF. This final phase would insure the defeat of the United States effort in South Vietnam, leaving the American forces and bases isolated islands in a sea of hostile South Vietnamese people. With no South Vietnamese government to support, with no organized ally to aid, with no mission, and despised by the people they had come to help, the American troops could only retreat to the ports and airbases which they controlled for an ignominious extraction from Vietnam. Phase II of Giap's plan (the attacks on the cities, troop proselyting, and the political offensive to overthrow the GVN) held the key to the success or failure of TCK-TKN. On it the whole plan rested.

Finally, Giap would launch his Phase III attack. This phase foresaw at least a partial success of Phase II (the VC assaults on the cities) in which the ARVN units had been badly hurt and demoralized, and the Americans had become confused and dismayed. Then would follow Phase III, the "grand finale," a large-unit conventional battle between the victory-thrilled North Vietnamese troops and the hapless Americans, plus another Tet-like attack on the cities.

Giap's plan for his Phase III attack, a big set-piece battle, is tied into the enemy's actions at Khe Sanh. The enemy's multidivision siege of that outpost had no discernable connection with Phase II of Giap's plan, the assault on the cities and bases. Unschooled commentators have asserted that Giap besieged Khe Sanh to divert United States forces from his attacks on the cities of South Vietnam. This is obvious nonsense. No general uses two or three reinforced divisions (32,000–40,000 men) to divert four marine battalions (around 6,000 men), certainly not divisions which were badly needed in Quang Tri City and in Hue during the Tet offensive. In addition, Giap paid too costly a "butcher's bill" around

Khe Sanh not to have had some important purpose in mind for the use of this corps-size force. Khe Sanh, then, had to be the set-piece battle of Phase III. This is the only hypothesis which makes any logic out of Giap's dispositions and actions around Khe Sanh.

As complex and ambitious as TCK-TKN was, it constituted only part of an even larger plan. This master plan envisioned defeating the Americans as the French had been beaten by a carefully coordinated campaign of battlefield successes and negotiations. And as in 1954, the key to victory lay in getting negotiations started—or at least, under serious consideration—and then in dealing a stunning military blow. In 1954 it was the victory at Dien Bien Phu just before (or as) serious negotiations got underway. In 1968 it was to be the combined political-military offensive of TCK-TKN. By a combination of "fight-negotiate," the "decisive victory" mandated by the 13th Plenum would have been won. Apparently, not only do old generals tend to repeat their successes of the past, but so do old politicians.

In describing TCK-TKN, it is important to note not only what the plan intended to do, but what the plan did *not* intend to do. Many commentators on the Tet offensive have stated that the real objective of Giap's plan was to strike a devastating blow at the will of the American people to continue the war. True, this was what happened, but there has never been one shred of intelligence indicating that Giap's primary or even secondary objective was to attack the will of the American people. As J-2 MACV before, during, and after the Tet offensive, I studied hundreds of captured documents and POW interrogation reports bearing on the attack and its objectives. Not one of these sources indicated that Giap ever intended the attacks at Tet to destroy the will of the American people to continue the war. My conclusion is confirmed by Sir Robert Thompson, who also made a systematic study of the documents bearing on the Tet offensive. He challenged the theory that the attack was aimed at the will of the American people by asking, "Where, in their documents, did you see it put as number one—'This is going to overthrow President Johnson' or whatever? No, all the way through the one thing they were saying at that time was that there would be a mass uprising in the cities."[21] Indeed, Giap consistently degraded any influence the American peace movement and public opinion within the United States could have on President Johnson's conduct of the war. The best direct evidence of Giap's true intentions came from Nam Dong, alias Can, captured during the Tet offensive. He told his interrogators that TCK-TKN ". . . was neither an ordinary campaign nor one staged with the intention of scoring a propaganda victory. It was a campaign designed to bring about a decisive victory and end the war."[22] Dong's statement is confirmed by Gen. Tran Do, one of the Communist leaders of the Tet attacks. He flatly denied that the attacks were made to achieve a psychological impact in the United States. The objectives were to produce a popular uprising and annihilate United States and ARVN forces. The psychological blow within the United States was (as Tran Do put it) an accidental by-product.[23]

Looked at in hindsight, Giap's plan for TCK-TKN had a few good points. It was bold and imaginative. It incorporated the element of surprise—almost always an essential ingredient of military success. Above all, if the plan had succeeded, it would have accomplished the mission set for it by the 13th Plenum's directive to obtain a "decisive victory in the shortest possible time." But if the virtues of Giap's plan were few, its deficiencies were many. First, the plan violated at least two of the most hallowed principles of war—simplicity and mass. Phase II of Giap's plan—the nationwide attack on the cities by the Viet Cong—violated the principle of simplicity by requiring a degree of coordination impossible for the Communists to achieve with their primitive signal communications and their need for secrecy. In actuality, the coordination of the attacks *did* break down, with damaging results. The second principle Giap violated was that of mass. In Phase II, he scattered his troops over the entire countryside of South Vietnam. Only in Hue and Saigon did he have enough concentration of force to make a significant impact. Had he concentrated his forces against fewer target cities, he might well have achieved far greater results.

The second weakness of Giap's plan was that he failed to understand the strategic mobility of the United States forces in Vietnam and the potentialities of such mobility. Here, again, was Giap's old failing—a blindness to military developments with which he had no personal experience. In 1967 Giap had yet to learn that Westmoreland could oppose his peripheral sallies on the borders of South Vietnam and still get the American forces back into the interior quickly enough to counter any attacks there. Thus, Giap's Phase I attacks along the borders did not draw United States forces permanently from the interior and failed to accomplish any strategic purpose.

The third deficiency of the plan was Giap's refusal to make any provision for the failure of his offensive. Observers have explained away this weakness by pointing out that Giap could not order his subordinates into a "go-for-broke," war-winning offensive and then say, in effect, "now if you fail, do thus and so." But the failure to adopt such routinely prudent measures as establishing withdrawal routes for forces attacking the cities, which Giap refused to do, cost the Communists dearly.

The fourth weakness lay in the strategic concept of the plan. If there is one working principle of war it is that a general should attempt to take advantage of *his strengths* and the *enemy's weaknesses* while negating his own weaknesses and the enemy strengths. Giap's plan reversed this principle. He played to Westmoreland's strengths, firepower and strategic mobility. The plan forced the Communist attackers to go head-on into the vastly greater firepower of the American forces. By attacking many widely separated cities, he allowed Westmoreland to counter him by shifting forces to threatened areas using the superior strategic mobility of the American army.

But the overwhelming weakness of Giap's plan was to base it on assumptions which turned out to be not just invalid, *but dead wrong*. ARVN did *not* defect, desert, or dissolve under the hammer blows of the Communists at Tet. ARVN, as a whole, fought with more courage and effectiveness than it had ever done before or would do again. The people did *not* join the Viet Cong attackers; they did *not* revolt against the Thieu government; and they did *not* turn against the Americans.

There were several reasons the supposedly hardheaded realists in the Politburo were so badly misled regarding the accuracy of their assumptions. First, the long-held ideology of the Hanoi leadership forced those zealots to believe that the people of South Vietnam under the corrupt and dictatorial government of ARVN generals *had* to be dissatisfied and rebellious. In Communist thought, the South Vietnamese people *had* to want freedom—Communist style. That was why North Vietnam was waging this endless war to unify Vietnam under the Red Banner. The Politburo could never admit, even to itself, that its attempt to bring South Vietnam into the Communist fold lacked the highest altruistic motives. Second, the members of the Politburo *had* to believe that the South Vietnamese soldiers lacked motivation to fight, and consequently their morale was fragile. The Communist experiences in South Vietnam in 1964–1965, when they almost won the war over ARVN, confirmed

Hanoi's view of the combat worthlessness of the South Vietnamese Army. Third, the Politburo's long-held ideology told them that the Americans, like the French before them, were oppressors, colonialists, and as such, the South Vietnamese people despised them and sought only to rid themselves of this foreign burden.

The truth was that the members of the Politburo were the victims of their own long-held myths. The Hanoi leadership was, and is, a closed, inbred, mentally incestuous group. By 1967 they had been together for over twenty-five years. There may have been some arguments among them about military concepts and strategy, and there may have been pro-Russian and pro-Chinese cliques, but on such basic ideas as the purity of their ultimate goals and the wickedness of their enemies, there existed a consensus. In essence, what the Politburo wanted to believe had to be true. Like Napoleon and Hitler before them, the North Vietnamese had crossed the bridge of reality and were lost in that seductive, but ultimately destructive, land where fantasy has become fact.

To this fantasy was added an almost mystical faith in the efficacy and power of their concept of the "Great Uprising." To Ho and the others the Great Uprising of August 1945 was a peculiarly Vietnamese phenomenon which in a few days saw the Vietnamese people rise up and sweep the Vietminh to total victory over the Japanese and the French. No thought, apparently, was given to the military, political, and social situation which existed in Vietnam and in the world in 1945, a confluence of forces which made the August Revolution of the Vietminh not only possible, but easy.

Then there was the myth of Dien Bien Phu. There Giap had destroyed the equivalent of only one French division, yet it was touted all over the world as a great victory. The fantasy of Dien Bien Phu that Ho, Giap, and the others had come to believe was that the North Vietnamese soldier was invincible in siege operations. They had beaten the French at Dien Bien Phu, and they would conquer the Americans at Khe Sanh the same way, by digging and persevering, killing and dying. The differences between Dien Bien Phu and Khe Sanh became all too apparent later, but by then this deadly myth had been paid for with the lives of thousands of North Vietnamese soldiers.

So in 1967, dreaming and plotting in their closed world of myths and fantasies, the Hanoi hierarchy dug their own trap as they tried to repeat their past successes. From 1945 they resurrected the August Revolution, the "Great Uprising." From 1954 they reached back for a Dien Bien Phu-type victory. From 1964–1965 they foresaw an easy and decisive triumph over a demoralized and feeble ARVN.

The Politburo received erroneous confirmation of their assumptions—ironically enough—from an outside agency, the American news media, which was almost unanimously anti-American and anti-South Vietnamese. Day after day, American reporters and television commentators belittled the United States effort in Vietnam and trumpeted its failures and shortcomings. They harped on the corrupt and dissolute nature of the Thieu regime and its lack of popular support. American reports constantly derided ARVN and its combat effectiveness. So it was the American newsmen who contributed significantly to the misconceptions which led the Politburo to the monstrous defeat of Tet 1968.

Finally, whether the members of the Politburo believed its assumptions or not—and they did—they had to come up with some kind of a "quick fix" to their strategic problem. In South Vietnam, the Communists could not keep on losing battles, people, and influence. They had to make changes. Beyond that, there existed an even more powerful goad to a quick victory—Ho Chi Minh himself. In 1967 Ho was an old man, and, as is now known, seriously ill. Time was fast running out for "Uncle." For fifty years the unification of Vietnam under communism had been his consuming goal, and he wanted to see it in his lifetime. He couldn't wait for a protracted war strategy or for lengthy negotiations.[24] And the others—Giap, Pham, Truong Chinh, Le Duan—his disciples, who loved and respected Ho in an almost religious sense wanted to give the old man this last present, a "decisive victory in the shortest possible time." So, seduced by a mirage of myths and fantasies, indulgent of the desire of a dying old man to see his life's work consummated, the Politburo decided to implement TCK-TKN.

The supreme irony surrounding TCK-TKN, the now-famous Tet offensive, was that Giap, although acclaimed worldwide as its architect, adamantly and consistently opposed it. His opposition to the concept of TCK-TKN began in the deliberations of the Politburo in its debate over the recommendations submitted to it by the 13th Plenum. As usual, Giap and Truong Chinh on one side, and Le Duan and Nguyen Chi Thanh on the other side, clashed in a head-on battle. To the "South Vietnam firsters" (Thanh and Le Duan), the concept for a quick and decisive victory developed by the 13th Plenum echoed their own strategy of big-unit attacks on United States and ARVN forces and bases. Giap and Truong, the "North Vietnam firsters," fought the concept. It is now known, from an unimpeachable and still-secret source, that Giap argued at length that the all-out offensive would fail, and that it would entail heavy casualties. Giap held obstinately to his theory of the protracted war and for its emphasis on political *dau tranh* and guerrilla-type warfare. Giap fought adamantly during July, August, and September to get the concept abandoned, or somehow greatly modified. On 14 September he published in the Hanoi press his now-famous "The Big Victory, the Great Task," a plea for return to the protracted war of guerrilla-type actions, but all of his efforts to abort or modify the concept of TCK-TKN failed.

Nor did Giap stand alone in his opposition to the concept of TCK-TKN. In September 1967, more than 200 senior Party officials were arrested because of their opposition to the course the war was taking. These included the head of the North Vietnamese Intelligence Service, the director of the country's School of Political Studies, and a deputy chairman of the State Science Committee, himself a member of the Central Committee. In November, the North Vietnamese National Assembly passed a harsh edict making "counterrevolutionary crimes" punishable by death or long prison terms.[25]

History will applaud Giap, not for his concept and planning of the Tet offensive, but for his resolute opposition to it. History will record that it was Vo Nguyen Giap who, at a critical moment in Vietnam's history, possessed that ability to sort fact from fantasy and who, like his hero, Napoleon, exhibited that "ineradicable feeling for reality" which is the foundation of generalship. To paraphrase Churchill's words, it was his finest hour.

While in mid-1967 the North Vietnamese leaders were losing the "shooting war" in both North and South Vietnam, the American leaders began to lose the psychological war in the United States. The concrete evidence of the country's apathy towards the war and its distaste for it surfaced in September 1967, when a public opinion poll showed for the first time that more Americans opposed the war than supported it. At the same time and for the same reason, President Johnson's popularity (as measured by the Gallup Poll) plunged to below 40 percent, a new

low for his term in office. By mid-1967 the American people had percepti-
bly turned against the war.

This national withdrawal of support from "Johnson's War" sprang
from several causes. First, and most important, the American people—
whose history had made them the most impatient of races—decided
that the war was making no progress. And "making no progress" to
Americans is losing, and as Coach Vince Lombardi once said, "losing
is like dying." But the defection of support became serious only when
business and professional men, the middle class, joined the professors,
the intellectuals, and the youth in opposing the war. Thus, to the cry
that "the war was morally wrong" was added the much more destructive
judgment that "it wasn't going anywhere."

There were other reasons why the people turned against the war.
In 1967, Americans began to grasp that United States battlefield casualties
were significantly increasing in Vietnam. The total casualties (killed,
wounded, missing) grew from 2,500 in 1965 to 33,000 in 1966, to
80,000 in 1967.[26] Giap was right, those "coffins going home" exerted
a tremendous influence on middle America. The draft call requirements
began to rise drastically also. Young Americans and their middle-class
parents started to take a personal—and negative—view of the war. In
addition to the killed and wounded and the increased draft call of 1967,
the Vietnam War hit the middle class in the pocketbook. In September
1967, President Johnson proposed a 6 percent surtax which Congress
passed. Now the war was indeed coming home to middle America.
Nor were Johnson's problems with the middle class alone, for the Vietnam
War was aggravating the social revolution at home. Martin Luther King
and other minority leaders criticized the war for absorbing resources
which should have been devoted to the correction of social problems
within the United States, and for excessive casualty rates among minority
soldiers on the battlefield. This last charge was unfounded, but that did
not lessen its bite.

Then, there was President Johnson's lack of wartime leadership and
his inability (or refusal) to explain to the American people why the
young men of the United States were fighting and dying in South Vietnam.
The Gallup Poll of June 1967 showed that half of the Americans interviewed had no idea even why the United States was in Vietnam. Johnson
never made any attempt to rally the American people behind the war.

He feared that the country, if aroused, would demand a radical escalation of the war which might bring in the Red Chinese or the Soviets. Also, the president feared that any heated rhetoric from him would incite the conservatives in Congress to greater support of the war, but at the expense of his Great Society programs.

One might argue that the national will of the American people to bear up under the Vietnam War did not really erode or collapse, as many pundits have frequently asserted. Instead, a theory might be advanced that a solid national will to win the war never existed, principally because the president and the other American leaders never made any real attempt to build that national will. Col. Harry G. Summers, United States Army (Retired), who has written a book on the American strategy for the war in Vietnam, maintains that the cardinal error of President Johnson's conduct of the war was the failure to mobilize the national will of the American people behind the war by a formal declaration of war by Congress.[27] Whether such a declaration of war would have placed the American people solidly behind the Vietnam conflict is questionable. There is no doubt, however, that Johnson's refusal to make any serious effort to "sell" the war to the American people surrendered to the antiwar protestors (whose influence had to this point been minimal) the initiative in the national debate about the objectives, strategy, and morality of the war. Eventually, these activists, coupled with the apathy of the American people, destroyed the foundation of the president's war effort.

Finally, as the nation got deeper into the war, Johnson's own image undermined his ability to sell his view of the war to the people. In war, when things go badly—as Americans began to see them in mid-1967—the people want a war leader, one who can appeal to their sense of patriotism, one who can explain the war to them in simple terms. Instead, the American people saw, rightly or wrongly, not an Abraham Lincoln, not a Franklin Delano Roosevelt, but a combination of Richard Nixon and Warren Harding, an indecisive conniver playing politics in the shadows.

This erosion of public support broadened in the summer of this fateful year of 1967 as the news media, such as *The Richmond Times-Dispatch, The Cleveland Plain Dealer,* and *The Los Angeles Times,* shifted from lukewarm support of the conflict to doubts about the war. On 20 August, an Associated Press survey showed that the ranks of those United States senators supporting the conflict had significantly thinned, and that Johnson's war policies commanded the allegiance of only forty-four senators, against forty who opposed the war. Representatives reacted similarly. On 20 September, *The Christian Science Monitor* reported that of the 205 congressmen interviewed, forty-three said they had recently withdrawn their support of the president's policy in Vietnam. In October 1967, the powerful Luce publications, *Time* and *Life,* defected. On 8 October, the *New York Times* reported that its survey revealed that congressional support for the war was falling.[28] Taking their cue from these giants of the news media, the national television coverage of the war began to change and, to quote the *Pentagon Papers,* ". . . were moving beyond the bounds of its traditional adversary relationship *vis-à-vis* the administration and assuming a leading role in catalyzing the swell of public opposition and questioning about the war."[29] During the summer and fall of 1967, the American people, reading the newspapers and magazines and watching the dirty, bloody war on television, decided that the incomprehensible objectives in Vietnam for which the Americans fought were simply not worth the cost.

This attrition of public support for the Vietnam conflict within the United States had a direct effect on the way the war had to be fought. Huge troop increases, whether needed or not, were to be avoided. They would mean higher draft calls, and if the troop requirements became large enough, at least a partial mobilization of Reserves. This action President Johnson deemed to be political suicide. The declining support of the war from the American people also markedly inhibited the president in his choice of strategies. If the American public would barely tolerate the war in its restrained form of 1967, certainly it would not support an extension of that war into Laos, Cambodia, or North Vietnam, or a drastic escalation of the conflict by bombing the dikes or using atomic munitions. This restraint froze the president into the old concept of "more of the same," a fruitless war of perseverance, whose only hope was that "something would turn up."

The lack of public support for the war and its weakening effect on the conduct of the war carried even down to the foxhole. Commanders, from division to company, went to extreme lengths to avoid American casualties. During my service in Vietnam from 1967 to 1969, I never saw an order at any level, nor heard any oral admonition, directing American commanders to hold down casualties. On the other hand, all senior commanders recognized that they had better have an excellent rationale for unit casualties which exceeded the norm, particularly if the ratio of enemy killed to friendly casualties was low compared to other units in similar type operations.

As a result, the United States Army in Vietnam developed a novel method of fighting. Under this new (and unstated) concept, the United States infantry "found" and "fixed" the enemy, and American firepower "fought" and "finished" him. No more did the infantry use the time-honored tactic of fire-and-maneuver to close with the enemy. Now, the concept was: find the enemy, retire to defensive positions, and let the Air Force, the helicopter gun ships, and the artillery kill him. Many American officers have decried this combat method, impugning to it a wide range of sins varying from bad tactics to lack of courage. Even General Westmoreland, under whose commandership the new method began and matured, condemned the tactic, but only after he had left Vietnam to become chief of staff of the army. And then, he aimed his censure not so much at what had happened in Vietnam as at the misleading effect this method might exercise on the thinking about future wars by officers whose total combat experience had been gained in Vietnam. Westmoreland's balanced criticism of the tactic is probably correct. It is significant that none of the method's detractors have attempted to calculate or defend the increased American casualties which would have resulted if the United States infantry had consistently slugged it out with the enemy at small-arms range in a man-to-man fight.

As failing public support restrained the United States decision-makers from bold military initiatives, it forced them toward other less bellicose concepts. The emphasis on pacification and on negotiations came to the fore in 1967. Pacification had been in the doldrums for years, but now as President Johnson shifted his interest and focus in that direction, he energized the program by sending to Vietnam a new American ambassador, Ellsworth Bunker, and a new chief of the pacification program, Robert Komer, who arrived in Vietnam in late April or early May. Both would play crucial roles in Indochina War II.

If there is such a thing as an American aristocracy to which one gains access not only by birth and style, but by achievement, nobility of character, and service to the country, then Ellsworth Bunker was one of the few American aristocrats. He was born in Yonkers, New York, on 11 May 1894 and graduated from Yale University in 1916.

He became a prominent and very successful business executive (National Sugar Refining Company) and industrialist. Before coming to Saigon, he had served as United States ambassador to India, Italy, and Argentina and had gained President Johnson's special trust by his masterful job as United States special envoy in settling the Dominican crisis in 1966.

In April 1967, President Johnson called on him to take one of the most thankless and demanding jobs in the American government—United States ambassador to Vietnam. He was then seventy-two years old. He was tall, thin, and urbane. He kept himself in excellent physical condition by a daily game of tennis. His manners, his patrician reserve, his age, his intelligence, charm, and illustrious record gave him easy dominion over the generals and senior civilian officials in Saigon. And these were strongminded, assertive men. People like Bob Komer and "Abe" Abrams were no shy flowers, but the ambassador won their loyal support and deep affection. Throughout his tenure, Ambassador Bunker was a patriot and a "hawk," even further, an optimistic "hawk." In 1967, he believed that the United States was winning the war and would win it permanently, and had it been fought his way, he would have been right. The country will long be in his debt for his outstanding service to the nation.

From the beginning of his ambassadorship in South Vietnam, Bunker believed strongly in what he called the "one war" concept. While the president had made the basic decision to place pacification under Westmoreland in March 1967, it was Bunker's strong support of the "one war" concept which greatly eased its execution. In his first pronouncement as ambassador, he stated firmly that he wanted no more talk of a "military war" and a "pacification war." The various activities of the war were to be melded into a single whole, he said, under General Westmoreland. Komer, with the rank of an ambassador and thus four-star leverage, would head the pacification program as a deputy to Westmoreland. Thus, Robert William "Bob" Komer, also known as "Blowtorch" (and by other unprintable names), entered the Saigon arena—and any place Bob Komer entered shortly became an arena.

Vo Nguyen Giap would have respected Bob Komer, for he, like Giap, was no "Mr. Nice Guy." He was abrasive, overbearing, devious, obsequious, conceited, self-centered, touchy about his rank of ambassador and its four-star prerogatives, and devoted only to his own advancement and to the success of his mission of pacification. In spite of his difficult personality (or perhaps because of it), Bob Komer was a "mover and shaker.'' He had tremendous energy, and a razor-sharp mind coupled with a single-minded drive to get the pacification job done. He was the quintessential bureaucrat with the sure knowledge and finesse about how to get things accomplished both within and outside ''the system.'' He used a wide repertoire of subtle threats, sarcastic quips, desk-pounding rages, blatant flattery, ''old-buddy'' charm, and smooth reason—all of which he exercised to gain his bureaucratic or personal ends.

The flavor of Komer's personality is evidenced in a memorandum he wrote President Johnson on 18 March 1967, just prior to the Guam conference, where, it will be recalled, Johnson placed pacification under Westmoreland. Komer wrote, ''You know that you can always count on me, as a good soldier and a firm believer in our Vietnam policy, to do loyally any job you want which will help win in Vietnam as soon as humanly possible.

''This said, I also know that you won't take my candor amiss if I feel somewhat disconcerted and confused about the changed role you now have in mind for me. I had thought you intended to send me as No. 2 to run the whole civil side. The change in plans (which I first read of by accident three days late) seems to downgrade me to No. 3 (or 4 coming after Westy), and dealing only with ''pacification''—a lesser role than Porter himself had.

''I will work closely and amicably with Ellsworth (an old friend) and Gene Locke whatever the arrangements, but I do believe that to do the job you want done (perhaps the toughest in Vietnam) requires the position and tools to do it right. For this, I must depend on you, and I think I've proven that I *can and do produce results*. [Komer's emphasis]

''Walt (Rostow) also tells me that you may put *pacification under the military*. I still frankly believe this the best solution (military security is the key, and the military have most of the assets). However, we're doing well enough already that this is no longer *indispensable*. The big problem is *organization on the GVN side*—not the US side. But if we put pacification under Westy, doesn't this drastically alter the role apparently planned for me?

''Finally, State's Guam agenda is abominably long. Once again, you'd waste all your time listening to GVN and US briefings. To get the forward push you want from this critical meeting, and properly use our secret weapon—Lyndon Johnson, we must slash the agenda to *5–6 critical issues* and focus exclusively on these. Rostow agrees. I hope to give you my list, and also hear your personal instructions for me, on the plane.''[30]

On first meeting Komer, an unknowing observer would be inclined to underrate him. He stood about five feet eight inches, wore thick glasses, smoked a pipe, and with his bow tie looked like an assistant professor of medieval history at one of the Ivy League universities. This laid-back facade, however, concealed not only a flaming ambition, but one of the keenest minds in the United States government. He graduated in 1942 from Harvard *magna cum laude* and Phi Beta Kappa, and served in the army during World War II as a junior officer. Following the war, he worked his way up the governmental ladder from a job in the CIA in 1947, to the National Security Council, to special assistant to the president for pacification (1965–67), and in 1967, President Johnson placed him in charge of the program under General Westmoreland. In this last position he achieved something no one before him had been able to do—he made pacification work.

The secret of his success can be attributed not only to his ability and energy, but to that greatest of all benefactors, good luck. He came to Vietnam to head the pacification program coincident with a vital surge of interest in that strategy beginning at the White House and reaching to Ambassador Bunker and General Westmoreland in Saigon. Even this push would not have insured his success had not the North Vietnamese launched the Tet offensive, using the Viet Cong infrastructure as the vanguard of that abortive attack. During the offensive, the Viet Cong leadership and its political infrastructure were blown away, and its organization never recovered. But it was Komer who was the first to see and exploit this stroke of fortune. He reinstated and expanded the pacification program into the countryside and spurred the South Vietnamese government into (for them) heroic efforts in expanding and stabilizing their control over the people.

Komer viewed the American military leaders in Vietnam and the MACV staff with an ambivalent combination of respect, contempt, and caution. He had respect for their abilities, expertise, and dedication; contempt for their monastic unworldliness and refusal to "wheel and deal" in a typical civilian bureaucratic fashion; and caution in that he regarded each as a potential adversary who might wreck *his* program and, with it, the career of Bob Komer.

To Westmoreland and Abrams he publicly paid the deference due their rank and position, but he carried always a half-concealed dagger that both generals knew he would use—his close association with President Johnson. Indeed, he flouted this connection, papering his office in MACV headquarters with pictures of Johnson and himself in close consultation. Westmoreland viewed Komer with an amused and paternalistic, but reserved and prudent, air. But beneath Westmoreland's dignified paternalism resided a healthy respect for Komer's abilities and for his capacity to make serious trouble for Westmoreland. General Westmoreland conducted his dealings with Komer so as to give the latter no opportunity to blame Westmoreland for the failure of the pacification program. Thus, whatever Komer wanted, Komer got.

Komer's relationship with General Abrams differed from his association with Westmoreland. Komer and Abrams respected each other's intelligence and capacity, but each mistrusted the other. Komer knew early in the Saigon game that Abrams, when he succeeded Westmoreland as COMUSMACV, was not going to give him everything he wanted, and that Abrams was not intimidated by Komer's Washington connections. To the singleminded Komer, this made Abrams a potential enemy. On his side, Abrams recognized Komer's potential to make trouble, but instead of being intimidated by this possibility, Abrams responded contentiously by treating Komer with an often ill-disguised contempt. In the numerous MACV staff conferences the two men often appeared to be mental duelists, each warily circling his adversary, seeking never to give the other an opening. Then a quick clash of steel, some bloodletting, and the circling began again.

As Komer took over the pacification program in Saigon in mid-1967, he saw that he faced one major and immediate problem—the philosophy of the organization of his program. It was Komer who had urged President Johnson in early 1967 to put the pacification effort under General Westmoreland. The hardheaded Komer realized that in Vietnam only the military had the organization, the talented people, the discipline, the communications, and the logistic base to carry out the program he visualized. While he loudly proclaimed the need for unification of the two "wars" under General Westmoreland, he determined early to keep them separate, albeit preserving the facade of unity under military control. He set up a separate chain of command with an organization, CORDS, an acronym for Civil Operations and Revolutionary Development Support, which reached from himself down through the commands to the field.

He created a separate reporting system, and his own intelligence organization. He established separate staffs in MACV and the major subordinate commands. Komer, the veteran of countless bureaucratic battles, took no chance on being preempted by the MACV generals or on being dependent on them for staff support. Komer would later say, ''. . . the only way I ever got pacification off the ground was to have two wars! My war and General Westmoreland's war.''[31] The military, including the MACV staff and the field staff and commands, reacted to Komer's ''two war'' ploy by simply withdrawing from pacification, letting *him* fight *his* war with *his* people.

Westmoreland clearly saw Komer's slide toward the ''two war'' concept, but made no move to stop it. He welcomed Komer's ''two war'' artifice, which allowed him to concentrate himself and his MACV staff on the ''shooting war.'' Perhaps Westmoreland was wrong in not insisting on unification of the big-unit war and pacification. True unity of command should theoretically have furthered both Westmoreland's war and Komer's war—but, again, maybe not. True unification under Westmoreland would probably have drawn Komer's opposition, and might well have doomed the effort.

Once the organizational question was settled, Komer had to develop a firm working concept of how he believed pacification should work. His fundamental idea was that only the Vietnamese themselves could do the job. The Americans had to furnish the resources, the planning, much of the military security, the organization, and above all, the urge, but the effort in the countryside and the towns had to be largely Vietnamese manned and controlled.

Pursuing this cardinal principle, Komer elaborated his concept with two operational strategies. First, the rural population must be given long-term and constant protection from the Viet Cong. Second, the programs had to generate rural support for the Saigon government by meeting the needs of the countryside and thus winning the people to the support of the central government. These principles were not novel to Komer. He admits that they had existed in previous United States and South Vietnamese pacification efforts. What was new was, to use Komer's words, ''. . . the comprehensive nature and massive scale of the effort undertaken.''[32]

Armed with an organization, a working concept, and operating strategies, in the summer of 1967 Komer attacked the pacification problem head-on. But as so often happens, the Augean stable of pacification could not be cleaned overnight, even with a Hercules like "Blowtorch" Komer doing the cleaning. For much of 1967 little progress was made. The CORDS organization of some 6,500 people had to be welded together and made operable—no small task. The GVN were slow in appreciating the new importance of pacification and in managing the vastly augmented United States contribution. And as usual, GVN incompetence and corruption hobbled the program.

Komer planted the seeds of progress in 1967, as he began to inaugurate his ambitious programs. He arranged to have CORDS given responsibility for the support and training of the Popular Forces (PF) and Regional Forces (RF), the paramilitary units directly concerned with rural security. Under Komer's drive their numbers were increased, their weapons upgraded, and their training improved. Komer set up the PHOENIX program, aimed at identifying and eliminating the Viet Cong infrastructure. In theory, it was a reasonable and needed program. Later media charges that PHOENIX sanctioned kidnapping, murder, and torture to accomplish its mission proved (when investigated) to be largely false. The problem with PHOENIX was not its barbarism, but its ineffectiveness. The program required first of all a massive and sophisticated intelligence effort to identify and locate members of the Viet Cong political underground. What Komer erected was a hodgepodge of competing United States and GVN intelligence agencies, manned by incompetent and inexperienced people, tied together in a cooperative effort rather than by unity of command. It never succeeded in identifying and locating the heart of the Viet Cong underground movement.

The program compounded its essential failure with one even worse. In an effort to meet an unrealistic "quota system"—the "body count" syndrome again—the South Vietnamese arrested low-level Viet Cong sympathizers who had joined Communist mass organizations often against their will. The South Vietnamese running the program seized other Vietnamese who had nothing to do with the Viet Cong, but who had run afoul of the GVN police or military. Such practices bred massive corruption. Even if members of the Viet Cong infrastructure were captured, the jails proved inadequate in capacity to hold all the incoming prisoners, most of whom were soon released. In 1970, Komer himself, then out of Vietnam, labeled the PHOENIX program a small, poorly managed, and largely ineffective effort.

The other program Komer initiated in 1967 was the Hamlet Evaluation System (HES). This was another statistical device attempting to measure progress in an unmeasurable and often irrational war. HES required hundreds of advisors to rate thousands of South Vietnamese villages and hamlets against a list of eighteen factors which were then converted into a grade from A (secure) to F (VC-controlled). Such a system obviously had faults. It called for the judgments of many people, often inexperienced, and it required an objectivity about the reporter's own efforts seldom found. In spite of its deficiencies, as a general guide to the progress of pacification, it proved useful.

While in mid-1967 some of Komer's programs worked and some did not, for the first time the pacification program had a dynamic leader with the resources, support, and organization to make real progress eventually in "winning the hearts and minds" of the South Vietnamese people. The program was on its way, and so was Bob Komer.

A postscript—Bob Komer left Vietnam and a going pacification program in 1968 to become the United States ambassador to Turkey. In 1969, after Nixon's election, he went to work for the Rand Corporation as a consultant. In 1977 he returned to government service as a deputy secretary of defense, and he remained there until 1980. He is an unusually gifted man. Walt Rostow, both in his book, *The Diffusion of Power,* and in a conversation with me, stated that in his opinion Komer made one of the most significant identifiable American contributions to the whole effort in Vietnam.[33] I agree. The country has probably not seen the last of Robert W. Komer in a high governmental position— nor should it.

Meanwhile in Washington the corporate "heart and mind" of the United States leadership was being torn apart in mid-1967 by the most ferocious debate of the war. Westmoreland's request of 18 March for 200,000 additional troops provided the fuse which ignited the explosive controversy. The acrimonious arguments came clothed in the same old tattered rags of United States troop levels in South Vietnam and the conduct of the bombing program in North Vietnam. The adversaries, too, were familiar. On one side were McNamara, McNaughton, the "whiz kids," and the liberals both in and out of government. Opposed were the Joint Chiefs, the military commanders, and a few hard-line civilians in the administration and in Congress.

The JCS kicked off the controversy on 20 April 1967 by recommending that General Westmoreland be given the 200,000 men which he had requested in March. The Joint Chiefs also proposed that the Reserves be mobilized and that an extension of the war into Laos, Cambodia, and possibly North Vietnam be undertaken. The JCS went further. They suggested that the ports of North Vietnam be mined, and that the United States make "a solid commitment in manpower and resources to a military victory."[34] While not part of their 20 April recommendation, the Joint Chiefs advocated also a bombing of the "target systems whose destruction would have the most far-reaching effects on North Vietnam's capability to fight."[35] In blunt language, the military were saying, "Let's win this war."

Understandably, this advocacy by the military for a radical escalation of the war horrified McNamara, his civilian subordinates, and allies. In mid-May, after some hand wringing and paper shuffling, the civilians came up with *their* recommendations, which in effect would deescalate the war. First, they would hold the troop total in South Vietnam to the present strength of 470,000, with the possibility of a limited increase of 30,000. Second, they proposed to restrict ROLLING THUNDER to the area between 17° and 20° North latitude, the so-called "funnel area" in the most southern part of North Vietnam.

Then the civilians detonated their most powerful bomb. They sought to justify their recommendation for the deescalation of the war by changing the goals which had led to American intervention in Vietnam in the first place. Now, instead of the national objectives set forth in NSAM 288 ("an independent non-Communist South Vietnam," and "defeat the Viet Cong") McNamara and his civilians would substitute as United States objectives in South Vietnam these much less positive ones: "(1) Our commitment is only to see that the people of South Vietnam are permitted to determine their own future. (2) This commitment ceases if the country ceases to help itself."[36] There followed a good deal more discussion on United States objectives in Vietnam, but what it boiled down to was that the civilians thought that the war was lost and were recommending that the United States accept a compromise solution in Vietnam.

McNamara's desertion of the objectives of NSAM 288 brought the Joint Chiefs and the other senior military officers storming out of their war-rooms. They condemned the proposals of the civilians in detail, proclaiming that these recommendations would prolong the war. The Joint Chiefs saved their most savage fire for the change in United States objectives toward Vietnam. They fulminated that ". . . when viewed collectively, an alarming pattern emerges which suggests a major realignment of United States objectives and intentions in Southeast Asia. . . . The Joint Chiefs of Staff are not aware of any decision to retract the policies and objectives which have been affirmed by responsible officials many times in recent years."[37] The Joint Chiefs concluded by recommending that the civilian-sponsored proposals not be shown the president, that national objectives as set forth in NSAM 288 be maintained, and that their previously announced concepts be approved.

On both sides emotions ran high and bitter. McNamara took the unusual and underhanded step of showing the civilian proposals to the president before the Joint Chiefs had commented on them. In their turn, the Joint Chiefs informed the president—so authoritative sources have it—that they would resign en masse if the president approved McNamara's recommendations. Halberstam, in his book *The Best and the Brightest,* reports that McNaughton told friends that had the civilian proposals prevailed there would have been at least two high-ranking military resignations.[38]

A clear-cut split in policy now confronted the president. For the first time, two widely differing strategical alternatives were offered him. Johnson agonized, fumed, and then waffled. He instructed McNamara, who was shortly to visit Saigon, to compromise the troop-level issue in South Vietnam with Westmoreland. As for ROLLING THUNDER, the Stennis hearings settled that issue. Essentially, both the military and civilians lost this round of their increasingly caustic debate. The president did not choose the Joint Chiefs' "war-winning" strategy, nor did he opt for the deescalation recommended by the civilians. What he did do was to approve "more of the same," on a little greater scale.

Secretary McNamara arrived in Saigon on 6 July 1967, the day that Nguyen Chi Thanh died in Hanoi. The briefings which were presented to him on the following two days had been carefully prepared and rehearsed. Ambassador Bunker, Admiral Sharp, General Westmoreland, the senior air force and navy commanders, and key MACV staff officers briefed. Each presentation carefully reinforced the views which the Joint Chiefs had made known in May. I briefed as the J-2 and then sat through the other briefings. McNamara went out of his way to show his arrogant disinterest in the presentations. During most of the briefings he read or worked on papers spread out before him, and he asked almost no questions of the briefers. His indifference to the presentations left no doubt that McNamara believed that none of the presenters could tell him anything he wanted or needed to hear. And, as is now known, that is exactly how he felt.[39]

The McNamara visit to Saigon produced one solid result—McNamara obtained a resolution of the immediate United States ground force requirements for South Vietnam. On the last night of his visit, McNamara sat down after dinner with Generals Westmoreland and Abrams and in a series of "horse trades" arrived at a troop increase of approximately 45,000 men, bringing the total United States strength in South Vietnam to a total of 525,000. This settled the troop strength controversy.

The fate of ROLLING THUNDER was settled in August 1967 as a result of the pressure exercised by Senator Stennis' hawkish Preparedness Subcommittee of the Senate Armed Service Committee. Beginning on 9 August, the subcommittee heard from a full spectrum of witnesses, ranging from Admiral Sharp, who urged an increase in bombing pressure, to Secretary McNamara, who argued that the limited objectives and the restrained nature of the present air campaign against North Vietnam be maintained. In its report issued on 31 August, the subcommittee came down solidly on the side of the military and against McNamara. It criticized the restraints which the civilians had placed on the bombing program; it castigated the doctrine of "gradualism," and it censured the civilians for consistently overriding the unanimous advice of the military. The subcommittee recommended that the United States ". . . apply the force that is required to see the job through," and concluded that "It is high time, we believe, to allow the military voice to be heard in connection with the tactical details of military operations."[40]

For McNamara this was a stinging defeat. The day following the release of the subcommittee report, President Johnson called an unscheduled press conference to deny that policy differences existed between his military and civilian advisers. It was obvious, however, that this was an attempt to conceal vast and vituperative differences within the administration, at least, about the air strategy against North Vietnam. McNamara had lost the fight and with it the president's confidence. Over the following weeks, the president approved fifty-two of the fifty-seven bombing targets which McNamara had previously declared off-limits. While his final humiliation would be delayed, McNamara's resignation (or dismissal) was now assured, and through it ROLLING THUNDER would at last get a chance to prove itself.

While in late 1967 ROLLING THUNDER might get such a chance, the policy of negotiations would not. Negotiations were plagued by the earlier pattern of poor communications between the adversaries and of mutual inability to recognize the objectives of the opposing side. In June 1967, two Frenchmen, Raymond Aubrac and Herbert Marcovich, contacted Henry Kissinger, who had been their professor of government at Harvard. The two men told Kissinger that Aubrac had a direct contact with Ho Chi Minh. After a series of talks in which the United States State Department got involved, the two men visited Hanoi between 21–26 July, where they saw Ho (now old and ill) and Pham Van Dong. Dong told the men that Hanoi would insist that the main precondition for negotiations would be the unconditional cessation of bombing by the United States. Dong went on to state that the goal of the negotiation would be a coalition government for South Vietnam. In the meantime, negotiation "feelers" were being pursued on a second track. On 1 June 1967, the Norwegian ambassador to Peking, Ole Algard, was contacted by his North Vietnamese counterpart, Ngoc Loan, who told him that the Politburo was interested in negotiating an end to the war with the United States. In an August meeting, Loan, too, insisted on an unconditional cessation of bombing as a precondition to negotiations, and that the ultimate goal had to be coalition government in South Vietnam.

As Washington began to consider these proposals, the Stennis Committee put pressure on the president to enlarge the bombing program, and in response the president released sixteen targets, six within ten miles of Hanoi. One target, the Doumer Bridge, was located near the center of Hanoi. On 11–12 August, United States jets bombed the bridge, dropping two of its spans into the Red River. Then, on 23 August, United States aircraft struck Hanoi in the heaviest raid to date.

These raids incensed the Politburo. To this body, the whole scenario looked like the ones played out earlier in the year—a United States offer of negotiations, then an escalation of the bombings. The North Vietnamese interpreted these tandem actions as an effort to drive them to the bargaining table. Indignant, they backed off again. As was the case earlier in the year, the United States did not consciously use a "squeeze play" to get the North Vietnamese to negotiate. It was the old case of the military hand not knowing what the diplomatic hand was doing. Coordination of the "two wars" at the national level—actually the presidential level—had failed abysmally again.

On 29 September, President Johnson made another negotiating effort around the so-called "San Antonio formula." In a speech in San Antonio, Texas, the president told the world that the United States was prepared to stop the bombing of North Vietnam if the North Vietnamese would not take advantage of this cessation. The North Vietnamese refused the bait, and by mid-October the air campaign against North Vietnam was escalated by authorizing more "painful" targets.

October–December

This escalation of ROLLING THUNDER at the end of September began the final phase of the war in 1967. Almost all of the "painful" targets, many near Hanoi and Haiphong, were released by the president for attack. Airfields around Hanoi were struck and the key port of Cam Pha was attacked. The Doumer Bridge, over which passed war materiel from China, had been repaired after being damaged by the raid of 11 August. An additional attack on 25 October dropped two spans into the river. Again, the North Vietnamese (and Chinese) repaired it, and again on 14 and 18 December, United States aircraft severely damaged the bridge. This time it would not be repaired until mid-April 1968. Other critical bridges near Haiphong and on the roads south were struck.

These attacks were part of a sustained program to impede traffic into Vietnam from China, to isolate Hanoi from its port of Haiphong, and to separate the Hanoi/Haiphong area from the logistic bases to the south. The plan succeeded. By October, as the interdiction program cut Haiphong off from its distribution center, 200,000 tons of supplies from the Soviet Union had piled up on the docks of Haiphong. The fragmentation of the North Vietnamese logistic system was aggravated by the attacks on the vehicles carrying supplies and on the road and railroads being used. Admiral Sharp reported that 5,587 trucks, 2,511 railroad vehicles, and 11,763 ships or boats were destroyed or damaged in 1967. While Russia and China could replace the vehicles, considerable delay and dislocation resulted from the destruction of the rolling stock and transportation systems. To the attacks on North Vietnam's logistic system, for the first time in 1967 the United States added coordinated assaults on the war-making potential of North Vietnam. The strikes made in late 1967 against the power-generating capacity reduced it to 15 percent of its original capability. The Thai Nguyen steel plant and the cement plant at Haiphong were almost totally wrecked, and the bulk of North Vietnam's fixed petroleum storage capacity was destroyed.

Now that ROLLING THUNDER had been upgraded, what had it accomplished? There is no clear-cut answer, even now, for it would seem that "accomplishment," like beauty, is in the eye of the beholder. The civilians maintained their position that the air attacks were designed to achieve limited objectives, and that more positive results could not be expected. Their views were reinforced by another Jason study which, like its predecessor, categorically (and predictably) condemned the bombing as ineffective. In rebuttal, the military cited its statistics and arguments showing ROLLING THUNDER's achievements in impeding North Vietnam's prosecution of the war. The president, who was the decisive audience of one, supported—probably halfheartedly and with considerable misgivings—the military and his National Security Adviser Walt Rostow, an avowed "hawk" and a bombing enthusiast. Their optimistic reports convinced Johnson that progress was being made in the air war over North Vietnam.

This rosy view of the effectiveness of ROLLING THUNDER has recently been confirmed by the memoirs of John Colvin, who was consul-general at the British Mission in Hanoi in 1966 and 1967. He states that the United States had won the air war in the fall of 1967 when its air attacks had shut off the flow of supplies into and through North Vietnam. Colvin maintains that by the fall of 1967, North Vietnam, ". . . was no longer capable of maintaining itself as an economic unit nor of mounting aggressive war against its neighbor." Colvin believes that the key to the fall success of ROLLING THUNDER was its consistency. The assaults allowed the North Vietnamese no time to repair facilities, and their capacity of waging a major war had been broken by continually cutting the rail lines from China and from Haiphong to Hanoi and by attacks on the lesser ports.[41]

While in late 1967 ROLLING THUNDER waxed, and the prospects of a negotiated settlement waned, the other United States "wars" made dilatory progress. The South Vietnamese government held an election and an inauguration, largely free of Viet Cong interference. Komer's pacification program got its feet on the ground and began to move, and Westmoreland continued to grind up any enemy units he could find, fix, and fight.

Nor were the Communists idle. They initiated Phase I of their cherished TCK-TKN, the attacks along the peripheries of South Vietnam to draw Westmoreland's forces away from the heartland and to test their new tactics of mass assaults. The first blow fell on Con Thien, a barren marine outpost on the coast near the DMZ. In September the North Vietnamese subjected the post to heavy and persistent artillery and mortar bombardment and near the end of the month attacked the marines with two NVA battalions. The marines, supported by a powerful spectrum of air power, naval gunfire, and artillery, easily beat off the assault, killing well over 2,000 enemy soldiers. In November, north of the DMZ, Giap began to move two divisions toward Khe Sanh. Around this mountainous outpost there were some patrol clashes and exchanges of artillery and mortar fire. By and large, however, the marines in this remote stronghold, like their enemies in the surrounding hills, waited, sensing that their turn in the limelight would come.

Having been repulsed at Con Thien, Giap struck next at the dirty little town in Phuoc Long province, Song Be, located near the Cambodian border in the III ARVN Corps area. On 27 October, a North Vietnamese Main Forces regiment, the 88th, attacked a South Vietnamese battalion near the village. Reinforced by American air power, the South Vietnamese repulsed the attacks and even pursued the North Vietnamese as they retreated. The Communists lost 134 men killed to thirteen South Vietnamese. Two days later, on 29 October, Giap launched another attack nearby. He selected another provincial capital near the Cambodian border, Loc Ninh. This time the 273d Viet Cong Regiment of the vaunted 9th Viet Cong Division made the assault, and the fighting here exceeded in ferocity that at Song Be. Eventually, American ground troops joined in, inflicting heavy casualties on the Viet Cong. When the Viet Cong made a bayonet charge against an American artillery battalion, the artillerymen loaded their pieces with a charge called "Beehive." Of limited range, this round contains hundreds of small razorsharp fragments, similar to the "grapeshot" of past wars. The "Beehives" left rows of dead Viet Cong as the Communists ran screaming toward the artillery across an airfield runway. The Viet Cong lost 852 men dead.

The final "border battle"—and the most intense—occurred at Dak To in the mountainous areas along the Laotian and Cambodian borders in the II ARVN Corps area. In late October, intelligence picked up the movement of four NVA Main Force regiments into the Dak To region. Westmoreland had one United States battalion from the 4th United States Infantry Division in the area, and he immediately reinforced it with another. By mid-November, as probing by both sides continued, General Abrams—Westmoreland was in Washington—reinforced to a total strength of nine United States battalions and six ARVN battalions and preempted the enemy attack. In the heavy fighting throughout November, the four enemy regiments lost 1,600 men and were virtually destroyed. General Westmoreland described the Dak To fight as ". . . an engagement exceeding in numbers, enemy losses, and ferocity even the Ia Drang Valley Campaign of 1965."[42]

The "border battles" were North Vietnamese failures. Giap paid a bloody price for the tactical lessons which he and his staff learned, the main one being—avoid any direct attacks on American positions. Giap apparently learned it well, for the attacks of the Tet offensive carefully avoided United States combat units, concentrating instead on ARVN forces and United States military headquarters. The employment of the Viet Cong 273d Regiment at Loc Ninh was a mistake. This was a well trained, elite unit of the Viet Cong 9th Division, which should have been held back to spearhead the Tet offensive. The new 273d which had to be formed could not approach the original 273d in effectiveness.

But the principal failure of Giap's diversionary battles was their inability to draw American units and command attention to the peripheries of South Vietnam. The strategic mobility of the Americans permitted them to move to the borders, smash Giap's attacks, and redeploy back to the interior in a mobile reserve posture. Giap himself must have realized the futility of his Phase I attacks. If he did not, his subordinates did. A Communist colonel who defected in 1968 characterized the "border battles" as ". . . useless and bloody."[43] He was right.

The final act in the dramatic and climactic year of 1967 occurred in Hanoi. On the evening of 30 December 1967, North Vietnamese

Foreign Minister Nguyen Duy Trinh put another block in place in the edifice called TCK-TKN, General Offensive-General Uprising. In a speech at the Hanoi City Hall, Trinh said publicly and clearly that after the unconditional cessation of the United States bombing, North Vietnam *would* hold talks with the United States. Previously, the North Vietnamese had insisted that talks *could* begin once the Americans stopped the bombing. These changes in the form of the verb were enough to send Washington scurrying to determine what Hanoi had in mind. The diplomatic card had been played. Now it was up to Giap and the Communist soldiers to put in place the final block of TCK-TKN, and in 1968 they tried to do just that.

Notes—Chapter 17

1. Sharp and Westmoreland, *Report,* p. 131.
2. Ibid.
3. Gravel, *Pentagon Papers,* IV:402.
4. Gen. Bernard William Rogers, *Cedar Falls-Junction City: A Turning Point,* Vietnam Studies (Washington, D.C.: Department of the Army, 1974) p. 157.
5. Ibid., p. 158.
6. Robert B. Asprey, *War in the Shadows,* 2 vols. (New York: Doubleday, 1975), II:1302.
7. Sharp and Westmoreland, *Report,* p. 132.
8. Lewy, *America,* p. 89.
9. Douglas S. Blaufarb, *The Counter-Insurgency Era: U.S. Doctrine and Performance, 1950 to the Present* (New York: The Free Press, 1977), p. 251.
10. Westmoreland, *Soldier,* p. 260.
11. Leslie H. Gelb with Rickhard K. Betts, *The Irony of Vietnam: The System Worked* (Washington, D.C.: Brookings Institution, 1979), p. 167.
12. McGarvey, *Visions,* p. 139.
13. MACV Cable 7928, (21 August 1967), para. 2, p. 1.
14. Wallace J. Thies, *When Governments Collide: Coercion and Diplomacy in the Vietnam Conflict, 1964–1968* (Berkeley, CA: University of California Press, 1980), p. 218.
15. Robert Shaplen, *Time Out of Hand* (New York: Harper & Row, 1969), p. 398–399.
16. McGarvey, *Visions,* p. 222.
17. Van Dyke, *Strategy for Survival,* p. 32.
18. McGarvey, *Visions,* p. 222.
19. Thies, *Governments Collide,* p. 343.
20. Pham Van Son, ed., *The Viet Cong "Tet" Offensive 1968* (Saigon: Printing and Publications Center A.G./Joint General Staff, RVNAF, 1969), p. 46.
21. Thompson and Frizzell, *Lessons,* p. 120.
22. Son, *Tet,* p. 48.
23. Stanley Karnow, *Vietnam: A History: The First Complete Account of Vietnam at War* (New York: Viking Press, 1983), p. 545.
24. Douglas Pike, *War, Peace, and the Viet Cong* (Cambridge, MA: The MIT Press, 1969), p. 142.
25. Don Oberdorfer, *Tet!* (New York: Doubleday & Co., 1971), p. 83.
26. Kearns, *Johnson,* p. 311.

27. Col. Harry S. Summers, *On Strategy: The Vietnam War in Context* (Carlisle Barracks, PA: Strategic Studies Institute, 1981), p. 13.
28. Oberdorfer, *Tet!* pp. 86, 338–339.
29. Gravel, *Pentagon Papers,* IV:386.
30. Robert Komer, memo to President Johnson, (Austin, TX: LBJ Library, Guam Conference File Notes, 18 March 1967).
31. Thompson and Frizzell, *Lessons,* p. 188.
32. Ibid., p. 214.
33. Walt W. Rostow, *The Diffusion of Power: 1957–1972* (New York: Macmillan, 1972), p. 458.
34. Gravel, *Pentagon Papers,* IV:154.
35. Ibid., IV:177.
36. Ibid., IV:175.
37. Ibid., IV:180.
38. Halberstam, *Best and Brightest,* p. 782.
39. Gravel, *Pentagon Papers,* IV:522.
40. Ibid., IV:203–204.
41. George F. Will, "Victory Was at Hand," *The Washington Post,* 10 May 1981, p. B7.
42. Sharp and Westmoreland, *Report,* p. 139.
43. Interrogation of Col. Tran Van Doc by the author, April 1968.

18 The Tet Offensive

1968

If 1967 was the Year of Decision in Vietnam, 1968 was the Year of Culmination. The year 1968 saw:

  a. one of the most decisive battles in American history;

  b. an American military triumph transformed into a political and psychological defeat for the United States;

  c. an American president announce that he would make no effort to continue in office;

  d. the manifest bankruptcy of the ground strategies which both adversaries in Vietnam had been pursuing, and the subsequent adoption of new strategies by both sides;

  e. the demise of ROLLING THUNDER;

  f. the near destruction of the pacification program and its subsequent rebound into increased effectiveness;

  g. the beginning of serious negotiations to end the war.

The trigger for these historical events was Giap's Tet offensive of late January 1968, an event long planned by the Politburo and for a short period expected by the Americans. By the beginning of 1968, both sides had completed their preparations for what each knew would be a large, and probably decisive, battle. The North Vietnamese and the Viet Cong were positioning men and supplies to launch their Great Offensive. In mid-January, specially trained commando units called sappers began to infiltrate into the cities and towns with their weapons concealed under loads of farm products. At the same time, Main and Local Force units began to move toward their objectives, the towns and cities of South Vietnam. On the American side, General Westmoreland, his staff, and his subordinate commanders took up a stance of watchful anticipation. As January drew to an end, Westmoreland curtailed operations by United States troops and repositioned them to counter whatever Giap might try.

Between midnight and 0300 hours, 30 January, Viet Cong forces attacked six cities or towns in the middle section of South Vietnam. The initial success of the attacks varied, but by daylight all Communist forces had been driven from their objectives. No other towns or cities in South Vietnam were attacked on that night as the six attacks were premature. According to prisoners of war, the nationwide attacks had originally been set for the night of 29–30 January, but just before D-day, Giap ordered a twenty-four-hour delay until the night of 30–31 January. Some of the VC attacking units apparently did not receive the change of date, or if they did, could not notify their assault units, already moving into their attack positions. The premature attacks of 29–30 January cost Giap dearly, for he lost much of the key element on which the success of his Great Offensive depended—surprise.

January 30 was a hectic day for the Americans and their Allies. As J-2 MACV (the senior American military intelligence officer in Vietnam), I briefed General Westmoreland at 0700 hours, telling him about the enemy attacks in mid-South Vietnam and forecasting that similar assaults should be expected throughout the rest of South Vietnam that night. Westmoreland promptly agreed. He called his senior commanders, warning them to expect heavy enemy attacks on the cities and headquarters in their areas that night, and placed his entire command (including the air force and navy) under a maximum alert. He went to see President Thieu and persuaded him to order all South Vietnamese military personnel on Tet leave to return at once to their units. Some made it; most, however, did not.

The evening presented an incongruous spectacle in South Vietnam. On one hand the South Vietnamese people, refusing to believe that even the Communists would violate the sanctity of Tet, celebrated with parties and fireworks. The Americans and the RVNAF, on the other hand, furiously prepared for the onslaught which they knew was sure to come that night.

To illustrate, I lived with two other brigadier generals and three enlisted aides in an old French house in downtown Saigon, remote from other American billets and friendly troops. Before leaving MACV headquarters that evening (30 January), the two BG's and I armed ourselves with M-16 rifles, several grenades, and a grenade launcher, in addition to our issued Colt .45 automatics. After we got to the billet, a simple plan to defend the house was drawn up—the generals would defend the front of the house, and the three enlisted aides the back. Nobody had any misconception that six Americans could fight off a determined VC attack of any substantial size. After closing and locking the gate and barring the doors, we went apprehensively to bed. Fortunately, nothing happened.

During the night (30–31 January), Giap launched his countrywide offensive against the cities and towns of South Vietnam. The assaults on most of the cities were soon beaten off, although heavy fighting continued in Saigon for about two weeks and in Hue for almost a month. For Giap and the Communists, the Great Offensive failed with enormous casualties. The Communists lost around 45,000 men of the 84,000 with which they initiated the attacks. While this loss figure must be viewed with the skepticism always reserved for enemy strength and casualty figures, there is no doubt that Communist losses (almost entirely Viet Cong) were disastrous. Not only were Viet Cong losses heavy, but they were concentrated in their political leadership cadres who had surfaced during the attacks. In truth, the Tet offensive for all practical purposes destroyed the Viet Cong.

Not only did Giap's Great Offensive come to grief, but the Great Uprising never "arose." The ARVN troops did not surrender or defect, and the South Vietnamese people refused to join the Viet Cong even in those towns where the VC held temporary sway. On the contrary, the Southerners rallied to the support of the South Vietnamese government.

The Politburo and its southern operating arm, COSVN, recognized immediately that the Great Offensive-Great Uprising had failed. In what is perhaps the most controversial captured document of Indochina War II, COSVN admitted the failure of the offensive only two days after the premature assaults of 29–30 January and on the evening of the major attacks of 31 January. This five-page report bluntly admitted that "We failed to seize a number of primary objectives and to destroy mobile and defensive units of the enemy. We also failed to hold occupied areas. In the political field, we failed to motivate the people to stage uprisings . . . The troop-proselyting activities . . . were not conducted on a broad front. We cannot yet, therefore, achieve total victory in a short period."[1] This last statement is, for the Communists, an unusually stark confession of failure of TCK-TKN, whose objective was to "achieve victory in the shortest possible time."

From the date of the document's capture, about 9 February 1968, there were doubts as to its authenticity revolving around the unusual promptness of its issue. The captured circular stated that the Current Affairs Committee of COSVN had met on the evening of 31 January, had reached its crucial judgment that night that the offensive had failed, and had written and issued the document of 2,500 words the next day, 1 February 1968.

Those who thought the document a fraud argued that there simply was not enough time for the COSVN Committee to have met and acted as quickly as the document purported. In the first place, on the night of 31 January heavy fighting was taking place in many towns and cities of South Vietnam. Nobody knew what the nationwide results were or would be. On the evening of 31 January, even the United States forces with their vastly superior signal communications had only an incomplete picture of the situation countrywide or the details of the encounters in the various towns. If MACV and the other American commands were groping for information on the night of 31 January, then surely the Communists with their inferior communication system could have no better or fuller information of the tangled results of some fifty large and small conflicts. In fact, the Communists had major communications problems, particularly in and around Saigon. Those who considered the document to be bogus pressed their case by noting that for the circular to be authentic, the Current Affairs Committee of COSVN would have had to meet on the night of January 31, reach a momentous judgment at that time, and then write and publish the circular the next day. Again, they argued, high-level staffs and committees do not work that fast, particularly the Communists.

Those who considered the document to be authentic pointed out that while it was produced hastily, the circular had accurately portrayed the failure of Giap's ambitious plans. This group further contended that the Communist defeat at Tet forced COSVN to get out a quick and official explanation of the failure of TCK-TKN, plus some plan for future operations, to prevent a total collapse of Viet Cong morale. The document does contain a list of ten points which would govern the conduct of future operations, although these guidelines are only repetitions of previous instructions. It does stress that the Communists "must fight the enemy continuously and fight a protracted war,"[2] apparently a 180-degree change from the go-for-broke strategy of TCK-TKN, but when scrutinized that passage has little concrete meaning.

There is one credible explanation for the extraordinary speed with which the document was produced and disseminated. Some intelligence officers believe that the circular was prepared in draft form in advance of the offensive by someone in COSVN who suspected that TCK-TKN would fail. Perhaps the unknown author viewed the offensive as Giap did—one throw of the dice destined for failure—and forecast events as they actually occurred. The document's stress on Giap's old theory of the "protracted war" would indicate one of his partisans wrote it. All in all, the document is an enigma, one whose timing is still a mystery, although the intelligence community has generally accepted the document as authentic.

The document had one other aspect of crucial significance. There is not one word in it which states or implies that an objective of TCK-TKN was to strike at the public support of the war in the United States. Like the enemy documents issued before the Tet offensive, this COSVN circular confirms that neither the North Vietnamese Politburo nor the Current Affairs Committee of COSVN aimed their Tet offensive at the domestic support of the war in the United States.

Before discussing the long-range effects of the Tet offensive—and they were many and portentous—scrutiny should be devoted to some of the controversies and questions surrounding American preparation for, and response to, the Tet attacks.

First, and in many ways most important, the perennial question about the Tet offensive which critics ask is: what was the true extent and nature of the surprise to Allied forces? Judgments on this question vary widely. On one extreme we have Gen. D. R. Palmer, who in his book, *Summons of the Trumpet,* states: "A military history textbook, printed in 1969 and used by cadets at West Point in their study of the Vietnam War, says, 'The first thing to say about Giap's Tet offensive is that it was an Allied intelligence failure ranking with Pearl Harbor in 1941 or the Ardennes offensive in 1944. The North Vietnamese gained complete surprise.' The Cadets got the word straight and unvarnished."[3] Palmer, incidentally, neglected to state in his book that he, then an instructor in military history at West Point, wrote the immoderate indictment which he quoted. Beyond that, his inflated rhetoric is wrong. Pearl Harbor and the Battle of the Bulge were total strategic surprises. Each involved an attack by sizable and undiscovered enemy forces, at a time and place unsuspected, and by unforeseen methods and tactics. The enemy attacks at Tet involved tactical surprises of a much less drastic nature.

At the other end of the spectrum from Palmer, a few intelligence officers maintain that there was little or no surprise at Tet. They argue that the premature and bootless attacks in mid-South Vietnam on the night of 29–30 January alerted the Allies to the Communist plans twenty-four hours in advance, and thus the Allies were prepared for the main assault which came the next night. While this argument has factual basis, I, and most other officials who bore some responsibility for ferreting out the enemy's plans at Tet, reject it as simplistic and overly defensive.

Most informed and experienced observers of intelligence activities leading up to the Tet offensive would position themselves somewhere between the two extremes cited above. This group includes President Johnson, Walt Rostow and General Westmoreland. They hold that the enemy failed to gain *strategic* surprise at Tet, since a major enemy offensive had long been forecast to occur around that holiday period. These experts point out—and this differentiates the Tet offensive from the Battle of the Bulge—that no new or unsuspected enemy units participated in the attacks, and that there was a close correlation between United States Order of Battle holdings in a given locale prior to the attacks and the units identified in the attacks in that area.

All of these key officials have admitted, however, that Giap's offensive did gain *tactical* surprise. This judgment is borne out by a report of a high-level group appointed by the president's Foreign Intelligence Advisory Board (PFIAB) who investigated the charge that the American forces and their Allies had been caught by surprise at Tet. A summary of the group's findings regarding the element of enemy surprise follows: "Although warning had thus been provided, the intensity, coordination, and timing of the enemy attack were not fully anticipated. Ambassador Bunker and General Westmoreland attest to this. The most important factor was timing. Few U.S. or GVN officials believed the enemy would attack during Tet, nor did the Vietnamese public. There was a good reason for this: Tet symbolized the solidarity of the Vietnamese people.

"A second major unexpected element was the number of simultaneous attacks mounted. U.S. intelligence had given the enemy a capability of attacking virtually all of the points which he did in fact attack and of mounting coordinated attacks in a number of areas. He was not, however, granted a specific capability for coordinated attacks in all areas at once. More important, the nature of the targets was not anticipated. Washington and Saigon expected attacks on some cities, but they did not expect the offensive to have the cities, the civilian command and control centers, radio stations and police headquarters as primary objectives.

"Nevertheless, Washington and Saigon were, as stated earlier, fully aware that the enemy planned a major offensive, probably coordinated attacks in northern I CTZ, at Dak To in the highlands of II CTZ, and toward Saigon from virtually all sides in III CTZ. As early as 10 January, General Westmoreland had cancelled certain planned operations in northern II CTZ in order to reposition U.S. forces nearer Saigon. In subsequent days he issued a series of warnings to his commanders, and to the U.S. Mission, that the enemy was preparing to attack. Although he had not originally expected attacks during Tet, he recognized the significance of the premature attacks in MR 5 and on 30 January notified all his commanders to expect attacks that night."[4]

As J-2 MACV, I presided over the United States military intelligence operation in Vietnam prior to, during, and after Tet, and I would differ with the investigative group's report only in degree. First, the major element of tactical surprise was not the timing of the assault, but the fact that the enemy attacked so many cities and did so simultaneously. Both General Westmoreland and I confidently expected the enemy offensive to be launched either just before or just after Tet. The fact that the enemy attacked *during* Tet was therefore only a mild surprise. Much more unexpected were the assaults on the many cities and towns. Although United States intelligence had dredged up several reports dealing in exhortative terms with the "Great Uprising," no responsible American or South Vietnamese official believed that the enemy would throw himself at the heart of Allied strength—the cities. The result of such rashness— a devastating enemy defeat—was predictable, and thus, intellectually unacceptable to General Westmoreland and to the other military professionals on his staff. One never attributes folly to his enemy—but then, of such stuff are surprises made.

Giap's coordination of the simultaneous attacks against almost forty towns and cities was also unexpected. The Allies believed that the Communists lacked the staff expertise and signal communications necessary to coordinate so many far-flung attacks. Actually, the Allies were right. The premature attack in mid-South Vietnam (a breakdown of coordination) provided the key tip-off to the waiting Allies.

Years later the Americans discovered the disquieting fact that surprise of any nature might well have been avoided. An official monograph written in 1978 by a South Vietnamese colonel, Hoang Ngoc Lung, who had served for several years as the J-2 JGS, stated, "One week before the general offensive actually took place, the RVN suddenly obtained an unprecedented intelligence windfall in the person of a high-ranking enemy prisoner. He was Nam Dong, political commissar of the enemy MR-6 headquarters (author's note: Military Region 6 encompassed Saigon and the surrounding area), captured in an ambush while he was on his way back from a conference at COSVN. After intensive interrogation lasting several weeks, Nam Dong disclosed that North Vietnam was switching its strategy from protracted warfare to general offensive-general uprising . . . ."[5]

Headquarters MACV never knew of Dong's capture nor did it receive any of the critical intelligence provided by his interrogation. Lung's monograph, however, is ambiguous on two points. First, the phrase ". . . interrogation lasting several weeks . . ." blurs the essential point of whether Dong told his captors about enemy plans for the Tet offensive *before* or *after* the initiation of the attacks. Knowing something of South Vietnamese interrogation methods, my surmise is that the South Vietnamese got from Dong what they wanted *prior* to the initiation of the offensive. The second confusing point is Lung's statement that the "RVN obtained an unprecedented windfall," leaving the reader to guess which of the seventeen SVN intelligence and security agencies captured Dong. Further along in Lung's monograph he states that "Y," presumably Dong, was captured by the Military Security Service, a counterintelligence agency with tentacles throughout South Vietnam, and that this agency failed to disseminate Dong's intelligence even to the J-2 JGS, and since it did not get to J-2 JGS, it did not get to J-2 MACV. Here is another example of the often invisible price the Americans and the South Vietnamese paid for the lack of unity of effort among the intelligence agencies which, of course, only mirrored the disunity at the command level.

General Westmoreland and his staff did not expect an attack on the cities, but expected Giap to concentrate his offensive against the two northern provinces. An analysis of available intelligence, influenced and shaped by an extensive MACV war game conducted in late December 1967 and early January 1968, indicated Giap's best chance of success to be this: launch a series of secondary attacks in the Western Highlands, the Central Coastal areas, and around Saigon to pin Allied forces in those areas and make his main effort in the two northern provinces of Quang Tri and Thua Thien with four or five divisions. Such a strategy had several advantages. It concentrated Giap's available forces rather than dissipating them in small packets countrywide. Such an offensive would have been easy to support logistically from bases in Laos, the DMZ, and North Vietnam. There were attractive objectives available. Khe Sanh, with its deceptive similarity to Dien Bien Phu, would have been much easier to overrun with an early coordinated offensive than when Giap later tried to take it. Hue, the old Imperial capital, was psychologically important to both Vietnams. Finally, when it came time to retreat—as Giap should have anticipated—the North Vietnamese troops would have had a short line of withdrawal to their sanctuaries in Laos, the DMZ, and North Vietnam.

No one knows if such a plan would have worked. Militarily, it could not have fared any worse than did the plan drawn up for the Great Offensive. On the other hand, an offensive concentrated in the two northern provinces would not have contributed much, if anything, to the Great Uprising, the political part of TCK-TKN, and this is probably why the Politburo elected not to adopt it.

After examining the question of whether and to what extent the Allies were surprised, the PFIAB investigative group looked at another mystery, that is, how 84,000 Viet Cong and North Vietnamese troops approached the cities through the rural areas without the South Vietnamese people knowing of the substantial enemy movements and reporting them to Allied authorities. The question addressed itself to the acquisition, reporting, and processing of intelligence. More significantly, however, the question was aimed at the claimed progress of the pacification program (in January 1968, Komer proclaimed 67.3 percent of the population of South Vietnam to be secure), and beyond that to the fundamental loyalties of the South Vietnamese people in the so-called pacified areas.

The investigative group found that the inadequacy of civilian warnings sprang from "The enemy's security measures, his rapid deployments through territory much of which was under his control, and the basic difficulty of rapid communication from country-side to city [which] would have prevented friendly villages from passing warnings in many cases."[6] I agree with the answer furnished by the investigative group as far as it went, but would add that the basic reason for the inadequacy of the warning from the South Vietnamese civilians was that prior to the Tet offensive, the bulk of South Vietnam's peasants had not chosen sides. They viewed the Thieu government with apathy, but they feared and hated the Viet Cong and the North Vietnamese. Above all, they wanted only to be left alone to pursue their centuries-old way of life.

The most common question the senior American officers stationed in Saigon during the Tet offensive have asked is, why didn't the Viet Cong sappers attack the billets of these senior officers as part of their attacks against Saigon? The generals, and many of the colonels, lived by twos or threes in individual houses widely scattered about Saigon. Protection for these billets ranged from an eight-man squad of United States Military Police which guarded General Westmoreland's quarters to a South Vietnamese "watchman" who lethargically hung around the billets of the other generals and colonels. Incidentally, all of these "watchmen" disappeared at sundown on the evening of 30 January, a sure harbinger of a Viet Cong attack against Saigon. A small Viet Cong sapper unit could have killed or captured these senior officers, from Westmoreland on down, with relatively few losses. By so doing, Giap could have gained not only a major propaganda victory, but at the same time could have paralyzed MACV's reaction to the Communist attacks until senior officers from the subordinate commands could have come to Saigon and taken over.

Giap's failure to avail himself of this form of attack is made even more inexplicable by the fact that American intelligence later determined that at the time of the Tet offensive, Viet Cong terrorist groups in Saigon not only knew where every general lived, but how he was "guarded." Was Giap too much of a gentleman, too much a military professional, to use tactics bordering on terrorism? Or was he afraid that such a coup might jar the American people and President Johnson into some violent form of retaliation? Again, nobody knows Giap's reasons for not striking such a paralyzing blow against MACV headquarters, the nerve center of the American war effort in South Vietnam. The generals

themselves have always been thankful for Giap's oversight or gallantry—
as the case may be.

Within the United States, the Tet offensive produced a flash flood
of confusion and dismay, overwhelming all who would attempt to guide
or stem it. The reasons for this depression varied. Some were easily
discernible on the surface of the American scene, some buried deep in
the national psyche. One reason for this sudden national lurch towards
defeatism was the surprise of the Tet offensive. The American people
had for some months been assured by no less authoritative figures than
President Johnson, Ambassador Bunker, and General Westmoreland that
we were winning the war in Vietnam, and that there really was a "light
at the end of the tunnel." (Incidentally, General Westmoreland has declared on several occasions that he only used the phrase "light at the
end of the tunnel" once, and that in a backchannel {private message}
from himself to General Abrams. Even then, he put the phrase in quotation
marks, indicating that it was not his wording. Westmoreland states that
Ambassador Henry Cabot Lodge originated and used the term.) And
these judgments that we were winning the war were correct. In late
1967, the Allies *were* winning the war, and the Communists *were*
losing it.

The press and television contributed also to this aura of American
triumph. Edward J. Epstein reported in 1973 that ". . . in reexamining
the nightly newscasts of this period (1967) the dominant impression is
of continuous American successes and enemy losses."[7] Walter Cronkite
reflected the national mood after the Tet attacks when he exclaimed,
"What the hell is going on. I thought we were winning the war."[8]

This optimistic outlook prevailed despite the fact that in December
1967, key American officials were sounding the alarm that a major
enemy offensive in South Vietnam was coming. On 18 December 1967,
General Wheeler, the chairman, JCS, in a speech before the Detroit
Economic Club warned, ". . . there is still some heavy fighting ahead—
it is entirely possible that there may be a Communist thrust similar to
the desperate effort of the Germans in the Battle of the Bulge in World
War II." This warning was ignored by the news media, and thus the
American people. On 20 December General Westmoreland in Saigon
fired off a message to Washington, forecasting ". . . an intensified

countrywide effort, perhaps a maximum effort, over a relatively short period.''[9] This warning was held closely within the Pentagon and the White House and not disseminated further.

Finally, on 23 December 1967, President Johnson, in Australia to attend memorial services for Prime Minister Holt, who had accidentally drowned, told the Australian Cabinet in a closed meeting that ''We face dark days ahead'' and that he ''. . . foresaw the North Vietnamese using 'kamikaze' tactics in the weeks ahead.''[10] This forewarning never got out of Australia. Thus, while the president knew and accepted Westmoreland's forecast of an imminent major enemy offensive, Johnson made no effort to warn the American people. On the contrary, in his State of the Union message delivered on 17 January 1968, he sidestepped Vietnam with a series of platitudes dealing with the possibility of negotiations. The president later admitted that his failure to tell the people in his State of the Union message that a major enemy offensive was coming in Vietnam was a serious mistake.

So, the American public, blissfully unaware of the approaching Communist attacks, was struck a paralyzing blow by the surprise and intensity of the Tet offensive. Military philosophers have known for centuries that a sudden surprise blow against an enemy flank or rear brings paralysis and panic. Such attacks not only upset an enemy's plans, they cause *psychological dislocation*.[11] It was this same psychological dislocation which struck the American public, its news media, and finally its governing elite. This psychological trauma of the American public was exacerbated by two separate, but connected, failings—the United States news media misreported the Communist offensive as an American defeat, and Lyndon Johnson failed to exercise presidential leadership in the crisis.

First, the failure of the news media. From the start of the Tet offensive, both the press and the television networks hammered on the theme that Tet was an American (and South Vietnamese) disaster. History offers no better example of the truth of the old adage, ''the pen is mightier than the sword''—a maxim, of course, now requiring modernization to add the words, ''and the TV screen.'' Only recently has the media's misreporting of the Tet offensive been spotlighted. Peter Braestrup wrote: ''Rarely had contemporary crisis-journalism turned out, in retrospect, to have veered so widely from reality. Essentially, the dominant themes of the words and film from Vietnam (rebroadcast in commentary, editorials, and much political rhetoric at home) added up to a portrait of defeat for the Allies. Historians, on the contrary, have concluded that the Tet offensive resulted in a severe military-political setback for Hanoi in the South. To have portrayed such a setback for one side as a defeat for the other—in a major crisis abroad—cannot be counted as a triumph for American journalism.''[12] In 1978, on the TV program ''Firing Line,'' chaired by William Buckley, Braestrup said bluntly, ''. . . the Tet offensive in particular, in contrast to other times in the war, was badly covered by the media.''[13] Dr. David Culbert, a history professor at Louisiana State University, who spent three years studying the media's reporting of the Tet offensive, censured the news managers for portraying a ''North Vietnamese military and political disaster as a stunning victory contributing to a psychological victory within the United States.''[14]

Braestrup argues that a factor which contributed to the spurious reporting of the offensive was the media's penchant for substituting ''analysis'' for facts. These ''analyses'' he characterized as ''the hasty reactions of the half-informed'' and as a ''serious lapse of journalistic self-discipline.''[15] In effect, what Braestrup says is that the reporters simply filled in their own ''facts'' when they did not have the true ones. Finally, Braestrup points out that a mind-set quickly developed among reporters and editors that ''Tet was a disaster, not only for the highly-visible 10 percent of the South Vietnamese population caught up in the urban fighting, but actually or imminently, for the allied armies, the pacification effort, the Thieu government.''[16]

While the misrepresentation of the Tet offensive by the print media as an Allied defeat shook the American people, it was the television coverage which shattered public morale and destroyed the support for the war in the United States. Gen. Maxwell Taylor wrote: ''In forming the popular concept of what had happened during the Tet offensive, TV was the dominant factor. The picture of a few flaming Saigon houses, presented by a gloomy-voiced telecaster as an instance of the destruction caused in the capital, created the inevitable impression that this was the way it was in all or most of Saigon. This human tendency to generalize from a single fact to a universal conclusion has always been a prime cause for the distorted views regarding Vietnam and certainly contributed to the pessimism in the United States after the Tet offensive in 1968.''[17]

President Nixon backed up General Taylor's view, stating categorically that television's reporting of the Tet offensive demoralized the home front. Howard K. Smith of the American Broadcasting Company said of the television network's coverage during this period, "Viet Cong casualties were one hundred times ours. But we never told the public that. We just showed pictures day after day of Americans getting hell kicked out of them. That was enough to break America apart."[18]

Braestrup points out in his book that even after the uncertainties surrounding the original attacks had lifted and Giap's defeat was readily ascertainable, the "major media were producing a kind of continuous black fog of their own, a vague conventional 'disaster' image . . . in the case of *Newsweek,* NBC, and CBS . . . the disaster theme seemed to be exploited for its own sake."[19] Walter Cronkite made a hurried tour of Vietnam in late February 1968 and shortly thereafter on national television dolorously called Tet an American defeat, saying on 27 February that "the only rational way out will be to negotiate, not as victors but as an honorable people."[20] President Johnson watching this program lamented to his press secretary, George Christian, "If I've lost Cronkite, I've lost middle America."[21]

There is an interesting epilogue to Cronkite's broadcast of 27 February 1968. During his preparation for the broadcast, Cronkite visited one of the senior American field commanders. After the customary briefings on American and South Vietnamese successes, Cronkite told the general that he would not use any of the material just presented to him. He went further, saying that he had been to Hue and seen the open graves of the South Vietnamese civilians murdered by the NVA troops and that he (Cronkite) had decided to do everything in his power to see that this war was brought to an end—a peculiar and reverse reaction to an enemy atrocity.

Nor has Cronkite, even now, changed his view that the Tet offensive was an American defeat. In an exchange of letters in 1982 with General Westmoreland, he said (in refuting Westmoreland's claim that the Tet offensive was a U.S./RVN military victory), "As for the outcome of the Tet offensive: I guess we just divide on that issue. Of course, it is obvious that we won in the sense that the Communists did not, but the fact that they mounted such an offensive and succeeded in wreaking such destruction seems hardly to indicate a victory on our part."[22]

Edward J. Epstein reported in *TV Guide* that in late 1968, a field producer for NBC suggested ". . . a three-part series showing that Tet had indeed been a decisive military victory for America and that the media had exaggerated greatly the view that it was a defeat for South Vietnam. After some consideration the idea was rejected because '. . . Tet was already established in the public's mind as a defeat, and therefore it was an American defeat.' "[23] In the never-never land of television, fantasy had become reality.

In his book Peter Braestrup confronts the failure of the news media at Tet by asking the rhetorical question, "Why did the media perform so unsatisfactorily?"[24] Both in his book and in his television appearance with Buckley on "Firing Line," what Braestrup seemed to say was that the reporters and news managers who misreported the Tet offensive were to a large extent innocent victims of a set of "unusual circumstances." He makes this point explicitly in his book. There, he writes, "The special circumstances of Tet impacted to a rare degree on modern American journalism's special susceptibilities and limitations. This peculiar conjuncture overwhelmed reporters, commentators, and their superiors alike."[25]

But other experts on the media coverage of the Tet offensive are less charitable to the journalists and commentators who distorted their reports of those attacks. One correspondent with several years' service in Vietnam, Robert Elegant, has scathingly reproached his colleagues for their misleading reports, not only on the Tet offensive, but on the entire war. He wrote, ". . . never before Vietnam had the collective policy of the media—no less stringent term will serve—sought by graphic and unremitting distortion—the victory of the enemies of the correspondents own side."[26]

Elegant believes that the American correspondents in Vietnam went astray because of their enforced isolation. It is Elegant's view that the American newsmen in Vietnam were separated from the Vietnamese by language and cultural barriers, and from the United States military by differing "moralistic attitudes and political prejudices."[27] As a result of this isolation, Elegant contends that "Reporting Vietnam became a closed, self-generating system sustained largely by the acclaim the participants lavished on each other."[28] Then, too, there was the herd instinct. Most correspondents reported the war negatively because the other newsmen covered it that way. As Elegant points out, the reporter who refused to accept and report the negative views of his journalistic brethren risked professional and personal ostracism. Elegant lists other reasons for the news media's misleading coverage of Vietnam. Most correspondents, he asserts, were woefully ignorant of the setting of the conflict and of war in general, particularly guerrilla war. Added to this ignorance was an unwarranted and inordinate sense of their own omniscience. What the correspondents did not see or believe to them did not exist—regardless of obvious evidence to the contrary.

But under these surface reasons for misleading the American people about the Tet offensive ran a deeper stream. Elegant, in answer to his own question, "why was the press . . . so superficial and so biased?" writes, "Chief among many reasons was, I believe, the politicization of correspondents by the constantly intensifying clamor over Vietnam in Europe and America. The press was instinctively 'against the government'—at least reflectively, for Saigon's enemies."[29] At last, Elegant has said it—the media is made up principally of ideological liberals, and so slants the news.

The media, however, is composed not only of reporters, but of a vast network of rewriters, columnists, bureau chiefs, editors, publishers, TV anchors, news executives, producers, and film editors. The correspondents wrote not only for each other, but also to win the approval of their bureau chiefs, editors, and publishers who had hired them and who, if displeased, could fire them. What kind of people are these journalistic elite? A recent poll is revealing. While taken in late 1981, it accurately reflects the ideological preferences and biases which have been in evidence for the last two decades. The study involved interviews with 240 journalists and broadcasters working for the most influential media outlets. These include the *New York Times, Washington Post, Wall Street Journal, Time, Newsweek, U.S. News & World Report,* CBS, NBC, and ABC.

The poll revealed that some 54 percent of leading journalists count themselves as liberals. Only 19 percent describe themselves as right of center. Even greater differences show up when they rate their cohorts. Fifty-six percent say the people they work with are mostly on the left and only eight percent on the right. Overwhelmingly, the media elite vote for Democratic candidates in presidential elections. The big guns of the media come down on the liberal side of a wide range of social and political issues. They show special fondness for welfare capitalism. Some 68 percent believe the government should substantially reduce the income gap between rich and poor. Many top journalists express general discontent with the social order. A substantial minority—28 percent—favor overhauling the entire system through a complete restructuring of its basic institutions. The same proportion take the view that all political systems are repressive because they concentrate power and authority in a few hands.[30]

The television coverage of the Tet offensive revealed the awesome power of that medium to influence national events. On 18 July 1982 Tom Wicker, the columnist, appeared on the television program "The David Brinkley Hour" along with continuing television panelists Brinkley, Sam Donaldson, and George Will. This group, widely variant in ideological outlook, unanimously agreed that it has become impossible for a nation to fight a war if the blood and carnage of the battlefield appears nightly on the country's television screens. George Will cited the Battle of Antietam in the American Civil War as an example, saying, "If the North could have seen that battle in living color, it would have elected McClellan president, and we would be two nations today." Another participant added that "it really gives TV and the other media control over national policy." On 1 August 1982, this same program featured Ben Bradlee, the editor of the *Washington Post*. He agreed that television could sway a nation, and that the British policy adopted in the Falklands' War of not releasing television coverage of the battles probably prevented a softening of British public support for that war. David Brinkley concluded the program by quoting Will's Antietam example presented on 18 July 1982 and added—"That's the way it is."

Alistair Horne, a British military historian, reinforces the points made in the Brinkley program. Discussing the lessons of the Falklands' War he wrote, "Despite the extreme frustration of the pressmen with the Task Force, the British operation was undoubtedly much aided by the rigid clampdown on the news. In marked contrast to Vietnam, there was no live television from the battlefront, and, on the few occasions (such as Bluff Cove) when excessively realistic accounts of the agony of British wounded leaked through, the impact on morale at home was noticeable. I have often reflected that, had there been live TV coverage in World War I, fighting would have been called off some time before the Battle of the Marne, and we would all now be speaking the language of the less squeamish Germans."[31]

I once heard Gen. Maxwell Taylor tell a few senior officers at an informal briefing that he thought the greatest mistake of the Vietnam War was the failure to impose censorship on the news media. In a magazine article written in 1971, General Taylor went further, implying that the news media, coupled with radical intellectuals, exploited the Vietnam War to undermine the confidence of the people in the government and in its established institutions. He viewed these attacks as so damaging to national defense that "The protection of the sources of our power must be included in any adequate concept of what our national security requires today."[32] The implication of Taylor's remarks is that some form of press and TV censorship should be imposed *within* the United States as well as in an overseas combat area. He does not say how such a concept should be carried out, but he may well be looked on as a prophet ahead of his time.

Morton M. Kondracke, the executive editor of *The New Republic,* in 1982 summed up the arguments for censorship over the press and TV reportage. He states, "The lesson of recent wars surely is that nations are well advised, if they can, to make censorship total. The pictures Israel has let through [from Lebanon] have hurt its case, as the footage from Vietnam hurt ours. Britain beat the Argentines and then released the bad news about how. You can be sure that the Soviets will never show what they've done in Afghanistan, and so the world will not scold them for it. The CIA, if it were wise, would equip Afghan rebels with videotape cameras as well as rifles. In the modern world, TV tape is mightier than a cannon."[33]

This awesome power of the news media—plus their bias and irresponsibility in reporting the Vietnam War—has led informed critics of all ideological shades to suggest that some form of censorship be imposed in future conflicts. Nor is this idea of late vintage. In 1965 General Westmoreland seriously considered recommending censorship of the press and television in Vietnam, but he could see no practical way to do it. In his book, Westmoreland relates that in 1972, on a visit to President Johnson's Texas ranch, the former chief executive remarked that "Early in the war he should have imposed press censorship, no matter how complex the problems that might have generated."[34]

And the problems would have been truly complex, starting with a whopper: who would administer media censorship, the Americans or the South Vietnamese? After all, the Americans were titular guests of a sovereign power, the South Vietnamese government, and early in the war the United States government decided that the GVN would either have to conduct censorship activities or at least play a major role in the operation. With that decision the idea died. The GVN had no apparatus, no training or experience, and certainly no stomach for it. Even if the United States had carried out media censorship, serious constitutional, organizational, and operational problems would have confronted the program. To be factual, no one had then, or has now, any concrete concept of how to carry out television censorship. Indeed, the United States Department of Defense is moving the other way, away from any form of media censorship. The Defense Department has disbanded the army Reserve units which were being trained to administer the media censorship program. But the problem—a serious one—remains, and it will be solved. It will be solved by either total media censorship à la Grenada and the Falklands or in some softer form.

The news media's distortion of the Tet offensive as an American defeat and the carping of the war's critics about the immorality of the struggle still might have been overcome in February and early March 1968 had President Johnson exercised forceful leadership. He did *not* go on television a day or two after the offensive started and tell the American people that their forces had suffered some tactical surprises, but that the United States and its South Vietnamese Allies were winning. He did *not* say emphatically that the news media was wrong in reporting Tet as an American defeat and that it was in reality a victory. Johnson made no Rooseveltian "Day of Infamy" speech and made no effort to rally a disoriented, divided, and demoralized nation. Instead, he ordered Westmoreland to go on television in Saigon and tell the people that Giap's offensive was failing. When that proved ineffectual, he ordered Westmoreland's key staff officers (myself included) to explain the war on national television. That effort turned out even worse. At the president's behest, Secretary of State Rusk followed by Secretary McNamara appeared on domestic TV to tell the American people the real story. All to no avail. In a crisis, Americans want to hear from their president, and they want to hear straight talk, positive plans, and some sign of courageous leadership. From Johnson, the people got none of these.

Johnson's lack of leadership at this critical time remains a mystery. Johnson's memoirs ignore the failure. Walt Rostow, Johnson's national security adviser, in his excellent book *The Diffusion of Power,* avoids the matter. Of course, there is always the old shopworn explanation that Johnson did not want to arouse the beast of vengeance in the American people who then would demand that he take some intemperate action which could widen the war. There is, no doubt, some truth in this explanation, but it will not totally suffice. A presidential speech on national television could have informed the country of the true situation of Tet without leading to an escalation of the conflict. There must, therefore, have been other reasons.

Braestrup and others furnish them. It is Braestrup's thesis that Johnson himself was unnerved by the press and television coverage of the war. The president knew from his official sources what was actually going on in Vietnam, but from the newspapers and the TV screen (to which by all reports he was unusually sensitive) he was getting a different and demoralizing story. At best the president was confused, at worst, intimidated.

That this phenomenon (confusion and disorientation resulting from conflicting information from two variant sources) upset and unsettled the president is credible. One has only to listen to the reaction of Harry McPherson, President Johnson's counsel and one of his speechwriters: "I felt that we were being put to it as hard as we ever had. I would talk to Walt Rostow and ask him what had happened. Well, I must say I mistrusted what he said because like millions of other people who had been looking at television, I had the feeling that the country had just about had it. I suppose that from a social-scientist point of view it is particularly interesting that people like me—people who had some responsibility for expressing the presidential point of view—could be so affected by the media, as everyone else was, while downstairs was that enormous panoply of intelligence-gathering devices."[35]

Thus, the greatest casualty of the media's misreporting of Tet was the president himself. Confused, apprehensive, aware that events were fast spinning out of control, Johnson froze. The fleeting moments passed when he might have informed, inspired, and led the country. The president had lost the first two battles of the campaign being waged for the mind and soul of America following the Tet offensive. He had lost the battle of the mind to the news media, and he had forfeited the battle of the soul to his antiwar critics. Another reversal—this one to be administered by one of his most trusted and experienced advisers, Gen. Earle G. Wheeler, the chairman of the Joint Chiefs of Staff—was imminent.

This reversal would originate from the Washington perception that General Westmoreland needed reinforcements as a result of the Tet offensive and the threat at Khe Sanh. From this benign beginning, the "troop request issue'' (as it came to be called) would grow into one of the most devious and damaging episodes in American military history.

One of the principal actors in this bizarre drama of 1968 was Gen. William C. Westmoreland. In 1970 as chief of staff, United States Army, he had the Department of the Army publish what it calls a "White Paper" (a documented staff study) to clarify his role in the affair. In the foreword to this document, Westmoreland pointedly announced that General Wheeler, Admiral Sharp, and Ambassador Bunker (three other prime actors) had seen the paper and indorsed its accuracy. As General Westmoreland explains in the White Paper, the "troop request issue" broke down into three broad chronological and topical phases. The first of these was the problem of limited reinforcements; the second, the consideration of a new strategy for operations in Southeast Asia; and the third, General Wheeler's visit to Saigon and its aftermath.

The first phase, the problem of immediate and limited reinforcements to United States troops in Vietnam, began on 3 February 1968 and ended on 12 February. This phase opened with a message from General Wheeler to General Westmoreland expressing the president's concern about the situation in South Vietnam, particularly around Khe Sanh, and quoted the president as asking, ''. . . is there any reinforcement or help we can give you?''[36] The next day, 4 February, General Westmoreland sent off a generally optimistic message about the combat situation, although he did admit to some uneasiness about the enemy threat in the two northern provinces of South Vietnam. He said nothing about any need for combat reinforcements.

But now the enemy took a hand in the drama. On the night of 5 February, the North Vietnamese attacked Khe Sanh village (close to but unconnected to the marine base of the same name) with a ground assault supported by heavy artillery, rocket, and mortar fire. On 6 February, the North Vietnamese overran the Lang Vei Special Forces camp, five miles southwest of Khe Sanh. There was still heavy fighting at Hue, and the enemy appeared to be moving toward Da Nang airbase. These enemy operations heightened Westmoreland's anxiety about Khe Sanh, the two northern provinces, and the entire I Corps area. On 7 February, he convened a conference at marine headquarters in Da Nang attended by the senior marine and army commanders in the area. There was a lot of interservice bickering and argument, and then General Westmoreland did some old-fashioned "head knocking." By the time the session ended, there were in place not only joint marine-army plans to defend the Da Nang airbase, but plans to rescue any United States or South Vietnamese troops which had survived the Lang Vei attack.

To meet this threat in the northern two provinces, General Westmoreland decided on 8 February to transfer one brigade of the 101st Airborne Division from the Saigon area to northern I Corps, and he informed General Wheeler of his proposed move. This shift perturbed Wheeler, since he felt that Westmoreland was taking a sizable risk in thinning out United States forces around Saigon. General Westmoreland, however, judged the risk to be minimal. While in a strategic sense the move of one brigade (3,000 to 5,000 men) was a minor deployment, the wide differences in the assessment of the risk between Wheeler and Westmoreland emphasized the varying perspectives from which each viewed the combat situation. Even by 8 February, General Westmoreland confidently believed that he had broken the back of Giap's Tet offensive, and that he had little to fear from an enemy resumption of the Communist attacks against the South Vietnamese cities. He saw the next enemy challenge to be a drive against Khe Sanh and the two northern provinces, and Westmoreland wanted to position himself to preempt that thrust if possible, and to blunt it if he could not preempt it. On the other hand, General Wheeler, shaken (like the president) by the gloomy and false reporting of the news media, thought that the enemy remained a serious threat capable of mounting a second wave of attacks against the cities, particularly Saigon.

Seized by these anxieties, on 8 February, General Wheeler sent General Westmoreland an unusually blunt cable saying, "Do you need reinforcements? Our capabilities are limited. We can provide the 82d Airborne Division and about one-half of a Marine Corps Division. . . . The United States Government is not prepared to accept defeat in South Vietnam. In summary, if you need more troops, ask for them."

General Westmoreland replied the same day (8 February), saying that ". . . it was only prudent to plan for the worst contingency" and requested that plans be made by the JCS to deploy the troops mentioned in Wheeler's message. Then he recommended that the 82d Airborne and the marines be put ashore by amphibious landing in the Northern I Corps area in April. *In April?* Westmoreland's recommendation that the deployment of the reinforcing troops be delayed until April stunned the president and his fearful advisers in Washington, who thought that reinforcements were desperately needed now, not two months later. General Wheeler tactfully replied the next day suggesting that it might be desirable to deploy the reinforcing units *before* April. He ended the message by stating, ''. . . my sensing is that the critical phase of the war is upon us, and I do not believe that you should refrain from asking for what you believe is required under the circumstances.''

General Westmoreland's seemingly naïve obduracy in not pleading for immediate reinforcements had a solid basis, revealing again the divergent viewpoints between the president's advisers in Washington and the commander in Saigon. One reason—there was another—General Westmoreland proposed that the reinforcements be delayed until April was that he doubted that he had the logistical capacity in northern I Corps to receive and support them. This sort of practicality meant little to the senior officials in the Pentagon and even less to those in the White House. They wanted not only to help General Westmoreland, whom they perceived to be hard pressed and beleaguered, but they wanted to position themselves so that they could say later, if things went badly, that they had given General Westmoreland every possible support.

At any rate, by 12 February, General Westmoreland began at last to comprehend Wheeler's game plan. On that date he sent a message to Wheeler formally asking that a marine regiment and a brigade of the 82d Airborne Division be deployed immediately to Vietnam. He noted that a major enemy offensive in the two northern provinces would force him to reinforce from other areas and thus face a major risk unless he got the additional troops. The remainder of Westmoreland's message, however, stressed the offensive opportunities the reinforcements would give him rather than the need for them to repulse further attacks.

The first part of General Westmoreland's message describing the risk associated with the enemy threat in the two northern provinces had by now become practically obligatory when asking Washington for reinforcements. It was the latter and optimistic part of the message which was significant. By mid-February, General Westmoreland, his major commanders, and his staff were beginning to appreciate in ever-increasing detail the true extent of the catastrophe which the Tet offensive had wrought upon the enemy, particularly the Viet Cong. To General Westmoreland there were other signs of promise as well. The Thieu government and the people had responded well to the crisis, and ARVN had fought its finest battle. The pacification program, which early in February seemed to lie in ruins, showed signs of a boisterous resurrection as the energetic Bob Komer began to capitalize on the Viet Cong debacle. In Saigon, there was the sweet smell of victory.

The optimistic tenor of Westmoreland's message put the ball back into Washington's court—and into a back corner at that. On 12 February, Walt Rostow convened a meeting at the White House attended by Rusk, McNamara, Helms, Clark Clifford (soon to replace McNamara), Generals Taylor and Wheeler, and himself. This august group now played coy. General Wheeler sent General Westmoreland a message saying that the group interpreted his (Westmoreland's) message requesting the reinforcements as expressing the following thoughts: "You could use additional United States troop units, but you are not expressing a firm demand for them; in sum you do not fear defeat if you are not reinforced." The message went on to note General Westmoreland's concern about the capacity of his logistic system in I Corps and finished with the thought that ". . . additional forces would give you increased capability to regain the initiative and go on the offensive at the proper time." The next day, 13 February, General Westmoreland dutifully replied to Wheeler's message, saying, "I am expressing a firm request for troops, not because I fear defeat if I am not reinforced, but because I do not feel that I can grasp the initiative from the recently reinforced enemy without them."

What is to be made of the Washington message? Neither General Westmoreland's White Paper nor his diary nor any of the perceptive historians (Rostow, Schandler, or Lewy) offer any explanation. General Westmoreland's request for the two reinforcing units (which Wheeler had coaxed from him) was clear enough. True, his optimism in emphasizing *opportunity* over *risk* flew into the face of Washington's gloomy forebodings, but that was not enough to evoke this peculiar message. The key lies in the first sentence of the Washington message and in the words ". . . in sum, you do not fear defeat if you are not reinforced." If General Westmoreland accepted this postulate—and he did—then Washington and the Joint Chiefs in particular were off the hook in not sending the units. And that is precisely what the Joint Chiefs of Staff meant to do.

What had happened is that sometime between 3 February, when General Wheeler had transmitted the president's benevolent query as to what he could do to help General Westmoreland, and 12 February,

"Bus" Wheeler had developed a far-reaching scheme to solve one of the most serious and perplexing problems facing the Joint Chiefs of Staff—the reconstitution of the strategic reserve force in the United States. General Wheeler had every reason to be concerned about the weakened condition of this emergency force. The seizure of the *Pueblo* on 23 January and other incidents in Korea drew his anxious eye to that perennial trouble-spot. There were tensions and troubles in Berlin, and the Middle East was, as usual, worrisome. Behind those foreign problems loomed one much closer to home. With the strategic reserve dissipated, the United States government could not defend itself domestically against a major antiwar demonstration or a large racial incident. Nor were these domestic concerns idle. The antiwar movement was growing stronger and more violent by the day, and a serious racial riot loomed as a constant threat. While the National Guard units of the various states were by law and practice the first line of domestic defense, they were of uneven quality and were largely untrained and ill-equipped to quell massive civil disturbances. No one in the Pentagon had any doubt that if large-scale violence erupted at home, the professionalism and discipline of the regular army would be required to reestablish law and order. The only regular army troops within the continental United States available for use in such a contingency would be the 82d Airborne Division, and it was being torn to pieces to provide troops to Vietnam.

Thus, armed with General Westmoreland's expressed confidence, General Wheeler now thought he saw how to reconstitute the strategic reserve, and he (and the JCS) recommended to McNamara and the president: "a. The decision to deploy reinforcements be deferred at this time. b. Measures be taken to prepare the 82d Airborne Division and 6/9 Marine Division Wing team for deployment to Vietnam. c. . . . . call certain Reserve units to active duty. . . . in addition bring selected Reserve units to full strength and combat readiness."[37]

These recommendations meant that General Westmoreland's reinforcements would be held hostage to a Reserve call-up and reconstitution of the strategic reserve. But the president would have none of this—at least not at this time—and on 12 February he ordered the immediate deployment of the short-term reinforcements to Vietnam. As to the reserve call-up, he instructed General Wheeler (who, of course, advocated it) and McNamara (who opposed it) to study the problem and agree on a recommendation.

While General Westmoreland had stated in his cable to the JCS on 13 February that he ". . . did not fear defeat if I am not reinforced. . . ." the approval of the immediate dispatch of the short-term reinforcements had (as he put it in his diary) "greatly simplified my problems." He went on, "Based on their deployment, the risk factor is considerably reduced. The stakes are high, since we cannot afford psychologically and politically to suffer a setback anywhere in country at this time. We cannot afford to have a United States unit defeated; we cannot have a large ARVN unit defeated; we cannot afford to lose any territory in South Vietnam. Any such setback would have a major impact on the morale at home."[38]

At first glance, Westmoreland's cable of the 13th ("I do not fear defeat if I am not reinforced") appears to conflict with this diary entry. The cable to the Joint Chiefs on 13 February seems to reflect the swashbuckling bravado of a commander who says, "Bring 'em on, I'll whip 'em with what I've got." The diary entry seems to reflect a different sentiment, the doubts and anxieties of a prudent and experienced soldier. On long study, however, the two statements are consistent. The two key words are "defeat" in the cable of 13 February and the word "setback" in his diary entry. By "defeat" General Westmoreland meant a major military disaster—the loss of the two northern provinces, the defeat of a major United States unit, or the destruction of a large segment of ARVN. By "setback" he meant a minor loss of much less magnitude, such as he describes in his diary. In December 1982, General Westmoreland confirmed this interpretation to me.

The president's decision to send the short-term reinforcements to General Westmoreland ended the first phase of the "troop request issue." There was an aftereffect, however, which had a far-reaching, but intangible impact. On 17 February, President Johnson went to Ft. Bragg, North Carolina, to see off the paratroopers of the 82d Airborne whom he had ordered to Vietnam. It was a solemn and moving occasion. The men were military, but grim and unenthusiastic. Most had served one tour in Vietnam, some two or three, and they knew what loomed ahead. The president was troubled and shaken by their demeanor, and he would say in his memoirs that "These visits with brave men were among the most personally painful meetings of my Presidency."[39] Did President Johnson's "personally painful meeting" of 17 February influence his decision of 31 March to renounce the nomination of the Democratic party? There are many who think it did.

Act II in this drama of misunderstanding dealt with the consideration of a new and more offensive strategy for Vietnam. It began in the interchange of cables on 12 February, which has been previously discussed. In the same message in which he requested reinforcements, General Westmoreland stressed the need for the United States to take a new look at its strategy for Vietnam, saying, "If the enemy has changed his strategy we must change ours." In General Wheeler's coy reply of 12 February, he told General Westmoreland that at the White House meeting there had been a considerable discussion about the change in enemy strategy, and "The question arose as to whether or not we too should not change our strategy." On 18 February, General Wheeler sent a message to General Westmoreland telling him that he (Wheeler) was coming to Vietnam to discuss the overall situation, since "the administration must face up to some hard decisions in the near future. . . ." General Westmoreland probably read more into these messages than Wheeler intended, for the cables kindled General Westmoreland's long-held hope and growing belief that the administration was about to adopt a more offensive strategy. There were other signs which encouraged Westmoreland to hope that a new strategy was in the offing. Admiral Sharp, CINCPAC, informed Westmoreland that he saw some signs in Washington that they would "relax the military troop ceiling." Later in February, Admiral Sharp became even more positive, concluding in one message to Westmoreland that "All these facts lead to the conclusion that the 525,000 ceiling cannot stand." When General Westmoreland reviewed a draft section of this manuscript, he noted in the margin that "Congressman Mendel Rivers, chairman of the House Armed Forces Committee, was vocal about a Reserve call-up and more offensive strategy."

While in mid-February 1968 Westmoreland began to believe that his commander in chief was about to opt for the "offensive strategy," he himself had long held that carrying the war into either Laos, Cambodia, or southern North Vietnam was necessary. He believed strongly that only by these offensive methods could the conflict be terminated successfully and within a time frame bearable by the American people. Certainly, it took no Napoleon to see that Communist operations in South Vietnam hung by a thin thread—the Ho Chi Minh Trail. This lifeline had proved surprisingly resistant to air attack, but appeared invitingly vulnerable to a sizable and sustained ground operation. The huge enemy bases in Cambodia and the North Vietnamese forces in the DMZ and in southern North Vietnam were also remunerative targets, and an attack on either would change fundamentally the conceptual framework of the war.

General Westmoreland, typically, acted quickly and boldly on his belief that in late February the United States would turn from the strategic defensive to the strategic offensive. On 8 February he told his staff officers to "get cracking" on plans for various offensive contingencies and what troops he would need to carry them out, assuming that the 525,000 troop ceiling would be lifted. On that same day he sent the cable to Wheeler making the seemingly cavalier statement (already reported) that he wanted the marines and the 82d Airborne Division to come ashore by amphibious landing in April somewhere in or around the DMZ. This request was not as indifferent to the immediate threat as Washington thought. General Westmoreland was not only properly concerned about the area's logistic capacity to support the forces, but he had more ambitious (and undeclared) plans for their use. He wanted to use these crack assault troops not as defensive reinforcing units for northern I Corps, but as an airborne-amphibious force to be launched against North Vietnam, just north of the DMZ. As he pointed out, the weather, to which General Westmoreland was always strategically sensitive, would not permit an amphibious landing in southern North Vietnam before April.

It was in this optimistic and aggressive frame of mind that Westmoreland awaited General Wheeler's visit to Saigon on 23 February. General Westmoreland had developed outline plans for various offensive contingencies and the troop requirements to execute them, and was ready and eager to go over to the strategic offensive. But was General Wheeler? On this question the second act of this ambiguous drama ended, and Act III began.

Even now, it is unclear if General Wheeler still thought on 23 February (the day he arrived in Saigon) that the president would support a change to a more offensive strategy in Vietnam. Schandler, whose book *The Unmaking of a President* is the most authoritative coverage of this twisted affair, believes that General Wheeler had little hope that the president's long-held policy against expanding the war would be altered unless a United States defeat in Vietnam appeared imminent. While Wheeler's views were (and still are) obscure as to the probability of a new strategy evolving from the Tet offensive, he had no doubt that somehow he had to reconstitute the strategic reserve, and, if possible, get General Westmoreland some "insurance" troops. These considerations weighed heavily on "Bus" Wheeler as he stepped off his plane in Saigon to be greeted by his old friend, "Westy" Westmoreland.

The MACV briefing for General Wheeler began immediately after his arrival. Those senior officers assembled in the MACV briefing arena were shocked at General Wheeler's appearance. He was haggard, gray, obviously tired, and most astounding of all, he had acquired a notable "potbelly." He was not the erect, stalwart, alert, and handsome man most of the senior officers remembered from past service with him. He was, as usual, courtly and softspoken, a man vastly admired and liked by the senior officers of the army.

General Westmoreland began the MACV presentations with an overview which was positive and upbeat. I followed with a briefing on the enemy situation. It, too, was encouraging, stressing the difficulties and the heavy casualties the enemy had brought upon himself by launching the Tet offensive. In the lengthy discussions which followed my presentation, General Westmoreland was at his best. Persuasive, articulate, he exuded confidence and showed a firm grasp of the details of the military situation. It became evident early in the briefings, however, that General Wheeler and his party did not appreciate the opportunities provided by the favorable situation. Several times General Wheeler and members of his party apprehensively questioned the MACV briefers about the enemy's capability and intent to launch a second round of attacks against the cities of South Vietnam. The MACV generals dismissed this threat as minor. By the end of the briefing, it was obvious that the efforts of General Westmoreland and his staff had not lightened the gloomy view of the situation which General Wheeler and the Washington contingent had brought with them. These officers, too, were mental and psychological casualties of the news media's gloomy misreporting of the Tet offensive in the United States. General Wheeler would later confirm this saying, "I guess I was influenced by those newspapers I read. Those newspapers colored my thinking; they said it was the worst calamity since Bull Run."[40]

Others have advanced additional reasons for General Wheeler's pessimism. General Westmoreland, in lengthy discussions with me in 1982, attributed Wheeler's pessimism to his poor physical condition. General Westmoreland described General Wheeler as an "exhausted and ill man." General Wheeler's depression was deepened when on the first night of his visit an enemy rocket landed close to his billet, a requisitioned civilian house normally occupied by General Abrams, then commanding MACV Forward in the north. The next day General Westmoreland insisted General Wheeler move into a small sandbagged room in the MACV Operation Center.

John Henry, in an article in *Foreign Policy,* suggests another explanation for General Wheeler's apparent dejection. In a footnote to his excellent article, he cites Wheeler's already quoted remark about the baneful reporting of Tet by the news media, and then Henry raises a question about Wheeler's real estimate of what the danger was in Vietnam. He quotes a remark Wheeler made on 20 February before departing for Saigon which suggested an optimistic view. Wheeler said, "The enemy effort has not been successful. He has not forced General Westmoreland to draw troops from the critical Khe Sanh/DMZ area. He has not succeeded in overrunning and holding a major Vietnamese city. He has not succeeded in achieving a military success which . . . is worth the cost to him."[41] Henry implied that General Wheeler had a sounder and more sanguine appraisal of the situation than his remarks and mien in Saigon would show, but that he adopted a false attitude of gloom to further his own purposes, which would soon become evident.

Regardless of General Wheeler's true estimate of the situation in Vietnam, he and General Westmoreland held a long and productive conference on 24 February. For planning purposes, the two generals decided to examine force requirements for Vietnam to meet a wide spectrum of possible situations. These contingencies varied from the "worst case," which envisioned an ARVN unable to carry out its missions, the collapse of the GVN, the withdrawal of the South Korean forces (deemed a possibility due to the Communist threats in Korea), and the commitment by the North Vietnamese of major additional forces to the South to, on the other end of the spectrum, the "best case," that the added units would give General Westmoreland an offensive capability with which to strike the enemy a damaging and possibly lethal blow—

provided, of course, that the president would approve a shift to the strategic offensive.

As a result of the Wheeler/Westmoreland study of the contingencies, the two men and their staffs developed MACV's force requirements for 1968. In the army's White Paper, General Westmoreland stresses the words "force requirements," using the JCS-approved definition of the term to mean "forces that would be required to accomplish approved military missions." General Westmoreland adds, "In other words the requirements would materialize *only* if the reappraisal of the national policy being conducted in Washington resulted in the approval of new strategic objectives." (emphasis added) Thus, while General Westmoreland understood the force requirements to be of a contingent nature, not an actual request, General Wheeler's understanding of their nature is less clear.

Regardless of this understanding (or lack thereof), the two generals arrived at a list of reinforcements totaling about 206,000 men, divided into three increments. The first increment of 108,000 men was to reach Vietnam by 1 May 1968; the second, 42,000 strong, was to be *ready to deploy* to Vietnam by 1 September; the third, of 55,000, was to be *prepared for deployment* by 1 December. There was, to use General Wheeler's words, a "clear understanding" between General Westmoreland and himself that only the first increment was definitely to go to Vietnam. The latter two increments might be deployed to Vietnam if needed to repel another major Communist offensive or if the president approved the adoption of an offensive strategy. Otherwise, these troops would reconstitute the strategic reserve within the United States. Thus, when General Wheeler departed Saigon on 25 February, he had the list of General Westmoreland's "requirements" for 206,000 additional men. As was soon to become evident, the entire concept of this troop request had been built on the shifting sands of contingent situations, possible strategy changes, ambiguities, and misunderstandings. With such a foundation, confusion was bound to result.

General Wheeler had a challenging job facing him on 25 February—how to "package" the troop request for "sale" to his civilian superiors, the secretary of defense and the president. And "Bus" Wheeler, as a veteran Pentagon bureaucrat, knew that he would have extreme difficulty getting the president and the secretary to approve a 206,000-man augmentation. First, it meant a major call-up of Reserves, not just 200,000, but perhaps even something like 400,000, which was McNamara's estimate. The president had resolutely disapproved all previous recommendations of a Reserve call-up and all suggestions for a major mobilization. Second, General Wheeler had to believe that the president and his principal civilian advisers (except for Walt Rostow) would not approve a widening of the war into North Vietnam, Laos, or Cambodia. Indeed, McNamara wanted to wind the war down, not escalate it; and the president, too, had showed great reluctance to expand the conflict. Third, the Communist threats of early February to Korea, Berlin, and the Middle East had eased. What had appeared then to be a coordinated Communist maneuver against the outposts of the United States' global position appeared, by the end of February, to have been nothing more than a series of coincidences, and these were cooling off. Fourth, General Wheeler knew the president was concerned principally about the aftermath of the Tet offensive and particularly about Khe Sanh. If the chairman reported that General Westmoreland held no fear of a recycled Tet-type attack or of losing Khe Sanh, then the pressure on the president to approve additional forces would subside or vanish. As General Wheeler analyzed the problem, he saw only one way to get the troops he thought General Westmoreland needed and at the same time to reconstitute the strategic reserve—he had to paint a most pessimistic picture of the situation in Vietnam and to portray the 206,000-man augmentation as necessary to avoid defeat there.

General Wheeler and his party left Saigon on 25 February. On 26 February they stopped over in Honolulu to brief Admiral Sharp and to cable Wheeler's report to the president. The report was the bleakest possible evaluation of the battlefield situation in Vietnam. It stated dismally that the initial enemy attacks "had nearly succeeded in a dozen places. . . In short, it was a very near thing."[42] (There was an unconscious irony here in that in his last sentence, General Wheeler was using almost the identical words the Duke of Wellington employed to describe his *victory* at the Battle of Waterloo.) Wheeler continued his gloomy report by noting that the enemy had the will and the capability to recycle the offensive, and that the pacification program had suffered a severe setback. He concluded that if the enemy synchronized his attacks at Khe Sanh, in northern I Corps, in the Highlands, and toward the cities that "MACV will be hard pressed to meet adequately all threats.

Under these circumstances, we must be prepared to accept some reverses.''[43] General Wheeler then went on to describe the three troop increments and to recommend that they be called up and that the first increment of 108,000 be prepared for deployment.

The omissions from General Wheeler's message were as significant as its contents. It mentioned no "best case" contingency; it ignored General Westmoreland's upbeat view of the situation; it neglected to discuss plans for a possible change to an offensive strategy, even though General Wheeler knew that General Westmoreland had linked the "troop requirements" indirectly to such a conceptual shift.

As a further indication of General Wheeler's motives, he did not send General Westmoreland a copy of the cable he sent to the president. Military staff procedures, protocol, and simple courtesy dictated that General Westmoreland should have been made an "information addressee" on Wheeler's cable. After all, General Wheeler is reporting on a conference with General Westmoreland and on matters vital to the latter's command. Since there was no disclaimer in the message stating that it did not reflect General Westmoreland's views, Wheeler implied that the opinions expressed in the cable were General Westmoreland's as well as his. In fact, the *Pentagon Papers* state that the cable contained "the substance of his and General Westmoreland's recommendations."[44] From this failure to send a copy of his message to Westmoreland, one must conclude that General Wheeler consciously distorted the situation in Vietnam, and that he did not want Westmoreland to fire in a cable repudiating Wheeler's gloomy assessment.

Wheeler arrived back in Washington early on the morning of 28 February and went immediately to the White House. Waiting there were President Johnson, Vice President Humphrey, Secretaries Rusk and McNamara, Secretary of Defense-designate Clark Clifford, Deputy Secretary of Defense Paul Nitze, General Taylor, Richard Helms, and Walt Rostow. General Wheeler presented orally the same depressing report that he had already forwarded in his cable. Clark Clifford remembered the briefing this way: "Bus Wheeler's report was so somber, so discouraging, to the point where it was really shocking. And the thrust of his reaction, which he sought to impress upon us, was not only that the recent offensive was a colossal disaster for us, but that another one was on the way. It is not possible to overestimate the degree of concern and even fear that possessed the heads of our government when Wheeler returned. He said we were in an emergency situation—that we were in real peril. The main thrust of this briefing concerned a second wave, and the dire need for 206,000 more forces to meet that emergency. We took Bus very seriously, for it looked as though the war could get away from us if they hit us again. President Johnson was as worried as I have ever seen him.''[45]

The president's already heavy anxiety about the situation in Vietnam deepened when he asked Wheeler the question, ''What are the alternatives?'' and Wheeler told President Johnson that ''. . . if we did not send troops in the numbers suggested that we might have to give up . . . the two northern provinces of South Vietnam.''[46] This judgment implied the strong possibility of a major military disaster in Vietnam, which Wheeler knew the president would not accept. Furthermore, it flew directly in the face of the favorable forecasts General Westmoreland and the MACV staff had repeatedly made to General Wheeler during his visit to Saigon.

General Wheeler's cable and his follow-up briefing shocked the president and his principal advisers. In effect, Wheeler had told the president to bite the bullet—but which bullet? Johnson was not going to give up the two northern provinces and Khe Sanh without doing everything in his power to hold them. He realized that such an enemy success would mean the certain loss of the war at home, even though the friendly forces in the field would survive it. On the other hand, the alternative, a call-up of sizable Reserve forces, would arouse the antiwar voices in Congress and the country to a new crescendo of vituperation. In particular, it would set against him the last bastion of his support, the middle class, whose sons, if not in college, had joined the Reserve (to include the National Guard) to dodge the shooting war in Vietnam.

The available evidence is inconclusive as to which course the president preferred at the end of February. Actually, he wanted neither a disaster in Vietnam nor a mobilization of the Reserves at home. Faced with this dilemma, he temporized as usual. He asked Clark Clifford, an old friend and confidant, to chair a task force to advise him what to do about the 206,000-man request, an action which itself triggered other momentous decisions.

General Wheeler's ploy had its final consequence on 10 March 1968 when the *New York Times* broke a front-page story to the effect that

General Westmoreland had asked for 206,000 more troops. The article strongly implied that Westmoreland needed the troops to stave off defeat. It did not mention the contingency nature of the troop requirement, or Westmoreland's offensive concepts, or the reconstitution of the strategic reserve. The article struck a damaging blow to the administration's claims that the United States had won a great military victory at Tet. The ordinary American had to ask the question: if the United States had achieved such a military triumph, why did Westmoreland need 200,000 more troops in Vietnam to avoid defeat? To say that General Wheeler had been—to use an old cliché—hoisted on his own petard understates the case. Impaled with him were General Westmoreland, the JCS, the administration, and perhaps the last chance to win the war in Vietnam.

What effect did General Wheeler's stratagem have on President Johnson and General Westmoreland, the two officials most directly affected by it? To the president it was another in a the series of hammer blows which were fast shattering his morale and with it his will to continue in the presidency. No conclusive answer is available as to whether the president saw through General Wheeler's ploy. In his memoirs, President Johnson states that ". . . from 28 February to 4 March . . . I had almost been ready to call up a large number of reserves, not for Vietnam alone but to strengthen our overall military position . . ."[47] This remark would indicate that the president realized that the troop request involved not just reinforcements for Vietnam, but the reconstitution of the strategic reserve as well. In 1982 Walt Rostow, the president's closest adviser in national security matters, stated that he was not sure whether President Johnson saw through Wheeler's game.

General Westmoreland has always publicly expressed his views of the "troop request issue" with restraint. He has stated that when he read the 10 March article in the *New York Times* he was "perplexed and puzzled." He told John Henry in an interview given years later that he was "shocked to later learn that my recommendation was portrayed as an urgent request."[48] In their book *The Irony of Vietnam: The System Worked*, Gelb and Betts quote General Westmoreland as saying privately that he had been "conned" by Wheeler.[49] In 1982, I discussed the episode of the "troop request" on several occasions with General Westmoreland and once asked him outright if he had ever said he was "conned" by Wheeler. Westmoreland politely changed the subject. On another occasion he did say that "He was and always has been very sensitive about this issue." This sensitivity was amply demonstrated when in the midst of his battle with CBS Westmoreland issued a number of papers dealing with the CBS controversy and included among them the army's White Paper dealing with the 1968 troop request, although the latter issue was tangential to the CBS dispute.

While he will not admit it, even in private, one cannot talk to General Westmoreland about this matter without gaining the impression that he feels he was used. Nevertheless, in his memoirs and in his public discussions he has consistently excused and rationalized Bus Wheeler's actions. To me he has implied that he believes that Wheeler's judgment was impaired by fatigue and illness, and that Wheeler fell prey to some bad advice from his (Wheeler's) key staff officers. General Westmoreland liked and respected Bus Wheeler, and even beyond that, Westmoreland is a man of forbearance and compassion.

Bus Wheeler remained chairman of the Joint Chiefs of Staff until 1970, when he retired. Both before and after his retirement he freely discussed the troop request episode with any serious historian who interviewed him. He candidly recounted his actions and thoughts, but always stopped short of any admission that he had intentionally misled President Johnson.

An observer, particularly a senior military observer, is ambivalent about judging General Wheeler's role in the troop request incident. There is little doubt that he attempted to mislead the president of the United States and his civilian advisers. His senior colleagues, both military and civilian, men of honor and integrity such as Westmoreland, have never condemned him for his actions in this incident. They realize that he had one of the most difficult jobs in the United States government. He had to try to get the secretary of defense and the president to do what he (Wheeler) thought was best for the country, despite their deep reluctance to do so. His colleagues understood the honorable ends he sought, and further, that he wanted nothing for himself—neither personal gain, nor greater power, nor self-aggrandizement. He sought only to serve his country.

His misuse of his friend and brother-officer, Westmoreland, is less forgivable. But again, it is the old philosophical question of whether the ends justify the means. Bus Wheeler thought they did and continued to think so until his death in 1975 from a heart attack—the result, incidentally, of the long years of intense pressure under which he had labored as the chairman, Joint Chiefs of Staff.

Wheeler's somber briefing of 28 February in which he presented President Johnson with the alternatives of a large-scale Reserve call-up or the possibility of a major defeat in Vietnam caused the president to direct the incoming secretary of defense, Clark Clifford, to convene a group to conduct a complete review of American policy in Vietnam. As chairman of the review group, and as an individual, Clifford would play a pivotal role during that fateful month of March 1968 in turning the United States onto a new course in Vietnam.

By 1968, Clifford had become a legend around Washington. He was reputed to be the most highly paid lawyer in the country, and as a shrewd politician, he had long been a behind-the-scenes adviser to Democratic presidents. While a staunch Democrat, he defied any ideological pigeon-hole as either liberal or conservative. He was one of the "Wise Men," a senior Establishment group which advised President Johnson on the Vietnam War and associated matters. Within this group he was known as a hard-liner on the war, a "hawk."

In the late summer of 1967, the president sent Clifford and Gen. Maxwell Taylor on a tour around Southeast Asia to get the friendly nations there to increase their troop commitments to Vietnam. The trip was unsuccessful. Perhaps of more importance, the reluctance of these countries to increase their troop support in Vietnam, or even to be much concerned about the Communist menace in Southeast Asia, eroded Clifford's confidence in the validity of American policy there.

If in late 1967 Clifford was beginning to have his doubts about the conduct of the war, he concealed them well. In November 1967, when the "Wise Men" met, he, with the others, strongly advised the president to continue the conduct of the war along the lines then being followed. Thus, the president, who had become disenchanted with McNamara's increasingly defeatist views, saw in Clifford, the new secretary of defense, a supporter of his own position on the war. What Johnson did not realize was that Clifford had an ego equal to Johnson's own, that Clifford had no burning desire for high governmental position, and that he wanted nothing from Johnson—and therefore, could not be dominated by the president.

The men with whom Clifford would work most closely within the

Defense Department, the JCS and the top civilians in OSD, also saw Clifford as a hawk. The JCS were elated. They were rid of McNamara, whom they detested, not only for his "whiz kids," his operations analyses, and his omniscient attitude, but because they felt deeply that his tenure had harmed the national defense of the United States. With Clifford's appointment the Joint Chiefs believed that they would find as their civilian superior a man whose views largely coincided with their own. On the other hand, Clifford's appointment disquieted the top civilians in the Defense Department. They had been selected by McNamara, were loyal to him, and had supported McNamara and his attempts to curtail the war. If Clifford were as hawkish as reports indicated, many of the civilians were prepared to resign rather than to repudiate their views on the aims and strategy of the war. This was the man, then, Clark Clifford, to whom Johnson entrusted the review of the overall situation in Vietnam.

It was characteristic of the Vietnam War that even the most routine procedures tended to become enmeshed in contradiction, confusion, and controversy. So it was with the presidential directive to the Clifford Task Force. Clifford and those working with him on the task force claim that they never received a written directive from the president or the White House to make an assessment of the overall situation in Vietnam. The president and Walt Rostow, on the other hand, claim that the president's oral instructions of the morning of 28 February were followed that afternoon by a detailed written directive which called for a broad review of the situation and available strategic options. Clifford, however, has reiterated through the years that he never received any such directive.

With or without a written directive, Clifford convened the task force on the afternoon of the 28th. Present were Secretaries Rusk, McNamara, and Fowler (Treasury), Deputy Secretary of Defense Nitze, Helms of CIA, Rostow, and General Taylor. In the opening briefing, Secretary Fowler made it clear that filling Wheeler's troop request for over 200,000 troops would impact adversely on the country, economically, socially, and politically. The president's beloved "Great Society" would have to be slashed, and foreign aid programs would be almost demolished. Taxes would have to be raised and the stability of the dollar would be threatened. The task force, already troubled by Wheeler's dire report of the morning, sank now into deeper depression. From the discussions which followed Fowler's briefing, it became apparent that certain fundamental questions had to be asked, although such questions may not have been indicated by the president's directive. As Clifford saw the problem, it was not "how could we send troops to Westmoreland, but what is the most intelligent thing for the country."[50]

Clifford's fundamental question established the focus of the review. To obtain answers to this question, Clifford assigned the various participants topics which they were to analyze in written memoranda to provide a basis for the review. The replies were to be in Clifford's hands by 2 March. In addition, he directed General Wheeler to ask Westmoreland nine questions, which were dispatched by cable to Saigon that day. Of the nine, two were key. These were: "1. What military and other objectives are additional forces designed to advance? 2. What specific dangers are their dispatch to SVN designed to avoid, and what specific goals would the increment of force . . . aim to achieve in the next six months? over the next year?"[51] The answers to these and the other seven questions were to be submitted on or before 2 March.

While the participants labored on their various contributions, Clifford began a crash course in national strategy. From the civilians in the Defense Department he received a series of pessimistic reports and briefings. The Systems Analysis (SA) group in OSD was particularly gloomy. It prepared papers dealing with pacification, alternate strategies, and the status of RVNAF. The SA people stressed that the current policies in Vietnam had failed. For example, they dismissed pacification with the words, "the enemy's current offensive appears to have killed the program once and for all."[52] While SA did not quite write off RVNAF, they held little hope that it could become an effective force. In analyzing alternate strategies, the Pentagon civilians painted a bleak picture of American operations in Vietnam. They castigated the search and destroy operations as useless, and gratuitously added that the surprise of the Tet offensive had resulted from the fact that "We judged the enemy's intentions rather than his capabilities because we trusted captured documents too much" and because "we became mesmerized by statistics of known doubtful validity. . ."[53] This last was a most peculiar comment from the agency whose primary job it was to produce statistical analyses of the war. In all of the other papers that SA submitted, the theme was the same—the dismal failure of United States strategy and GVN performance. Hindsight reveals that the SA assessments were almost totally wrong.

The CIA submitted three papers in which it added its voice of doom.

In the first it forecast that "the *least likely* outcome of the recent phase is that the Communist side will expend its resources to such an extent as to be incapable thereafter of preventing steady advances by the United States/GVN."[54] (emphasis added) And this—the "least likely" outcome—was precisely what happened. The second CIA paper prophesied that the Communists would exert widespread military pressure throughout South Vietnam over the succeeding several months. The third capped the agency's forebodings. It warned, "In sum, there is a high risk that both the ARVN and the GVN will be seriously weakened in the next months, and perhaps decisively so."[55] And, like the dire prophesies of the SA, the CIA forecasts proved to be totally erroneous.

At first glance, the fallacious fears of the SA group and the CIA experts confirm the old lesson that prophesy is a risky venture, and one usually calling for a recurring diet of crow. On review, however, a more damning picture emerges. The officials who produced these bleak forecasts should have known better. By the end of February, information and intelligence was available which indicated that the Communists had suffered a major defeat over the last month, that the RVNAF (particularly ARVN) had fought well, and that the pacification program had suffered only a temporary setback, not a death blow. The false prophesies made by the SA group and the CIA resulted not just because they ignored available intelligence, but because their deep-seated liberal and antiwar bias distorted their judgment. They *wanted* to see the bleakest picture, and from it to extrapolate the gloomiest forecast of future events in Vietnam. These "experts" did a major disservice to Clark Clifford, and more importantly, to their country.

In addition to the papers from SA and CIA, three senior officials saw Clifford every morning during this period, and they added *their* doleful analyses of the situation in Vietnam. The first of these officials was Paul Nitze, the deputy secretary of defense, a respected member of the Establishment. Nitze was no mourning dove. He thought the war in Vietnam could be brought to a satisfactory solution, but that such a favorable settlement would destroy United States policy in other parts of the world and was not worth the cost. To support the Vietnam War the United States had denuded its forces in NATO and had virtually dismantled the strategic reserve at home. The conduct of the war was causing increasing problems with United States Allies and within the country itself. While Nitze did not minimize the importance of Vietnam, he felt that furnishing Westmoreland large numbers of troops would only be "reinforcing weakness."

From these vague generalities, however, Nitze derived an essentially defensive strategy for Vietnam. Nitze recommended to Clifford that the United States should cease bombing North Vietnam and set a limit on men and resources to be committed to Vietnam. Nitze suggested that Westmoreland be given a new strategic directive telling him to concentrate on improving the GVN and RVNAF and on protecting the populated areas of Vietnam. He counseled that United States operations along South Vietnam's frontiers and search and destroy attacks should be reduced. Nitze's recommendations brought a cooing in the dovecotes along the Potomac.

The second official who advised Clifford was Assistant Secretary of Defense for Public Affairs Phil G. Goulding. He weighed in with a memorandum to Clifford which, after reviewing five options for the conduct of future operations in Vietnam, came down hard for the one which would deny the troop request and make some unspecified change in strategy. This, Goulding wrote, would be most acceptable to the American people.

Finally, there was Assistant Secretary of Defense for International Security Affairs Paul C. Warnke. He was the leader of the antiwar clique of Pentagon civilians, and the man whom Clifford had charged with the orchestration of the so-called "A to Z" assessment of the Clifford Task Force. Warnke, a bastion of the far left, had long opposed the war for ideological reasons. When a reporter asked him when his doubts about Vietnam had begun, he replied, "At the beginning, in 1961. I could never understand why a smart politician like Jack Kennedy was always against insurgencies when we should obviously have tried to be for them."[56] The fact that almost all the insurgencies of the early sixties were either Communist-inspired or Communist-led made no difference to Paul Warnke. Added to this ideological distaste for the role the United States was playing in Vietnam was an even more fundamental value—a profound repugnance toward the use of military force by the United States. Indeed, he would be labeled by Brian Crozier, the eminent English military analyst, as a "self-avowed pacifist."[57]

To this ideological aversion for the war and to his pacifistic queasiness was added the pragmatic view that the United States could not win the war militarily. To him the Vietnam War was essentially political and the claims of military progress by the United States were irrelevant to the real conflict. It was Warnke who in November 1967 had been instrumental in convincing McNamara of the need for a new strategy of cutting back the bombing, of curtailing United States ground participation in South Vietnam, and of trying to get into negotiations. This was the man, then, who would exercise the greatest influence over Clark Clifford in the latter's development of his evaluation of the situation in Vietnam and in his choice of strategic options.

While Warnke was assembling the various reports and drafting the presidential memorandum which Clifford would present to the president, the new secretary's education in the making of grand strategy continued—this time by the Joint Chiefs of Staff. On either 1 or 2 March, Clifford joined the Chiefs for a discussion of their views of the Vietnamese situation and the strategic options. It would be the most important conference Clifford would hold during this frantic and critical period. The discussion quickly became a question-and-answer session with Clifford asking the questions and the JCS attempting to answer them. When the secretary asked if 206,000 more men would "do the job," the Chiefs could give him no assurance that they would. To Clifford's question that if 206,000 were not enough, how many would be needed, there was no answer. There followed other pointed questions from Clifford regarding the effectiveness of the bombing and the status of RVNAF. None of the answers he received from the JCS satisfied Clifford. Then came the *coup de grace*. Clifford asked, "What is the plan for victory?" The Joint Chiefs responded, "There is no plan." Clifford: "Why not?" The Chiefs: "Because American forces operate under three major restrictions; the president has forbidden them to invade the North, . . . he has forbidden the mining of Haiphong harbor, . . . he has forbidden pursuing the enemy into Laos and Cambodia." When Clifford asked how the United States could then win, the JCS fell back on the old answer that the enemy could not continue to stand the attrition. But the Joint Chiefs would not speculate as to how long it would take to achieve a satisfactory solution by attrition. Finally, none of the Chiefs could see any sign that past or current operations in Vietnam had diminished the enemy's will to fight. If Clark Clifford had not already accepted the truth that the current strategy for Vietnam was hopeless, he did then. From that point forward, he was convinced that the United States had to level off its involvement in Vietnam and work toward disengagement.[58]

At first blush, the performance of the Joint Chiefs in their discussion with Clifford appears not only inept but discreditable. On reconsideration, however, a different perspective appears. In his article in the magazine *Foreign Affairs,* Clifford, intentionally or otherwise, saddled the Chiefs with failing to provide strategic plans aimed at winning the war. This charge will not stand inspection. The JCS had formulated plans to win the war, and so had Admiral Sharp and General Westmoreland. These plans provided for shifting from the strategic defensive to the strategic offensive by executing one or a combination of the following operations: a "right-hook," airborne-amphibious landing just north of the DMZ; cutting the Ho Chi Minh Trail by a corps-sized ground operation into Laos; invading the enemy's sanctuaries in the DMZ, Laos, or Cambodia; and finally, bombing vital targets in Haiphong and Hanoi. All of these plans to seize the strategic offensive had been consistently disapproved in 1966–1967 by Secretary McNamara and the president. Nor were the misgivings of the Joint Chiefs over these vetoes concealed from the president. In a memorandum dated 17 October 1967, the Chiefs told the president essentially what they told Clifford at his early March 1968 discussion—that is, progress, if any, would be slow so long as strategic limitations on offensive military operations continued in effect.

The Joint Chiefs were not the principal culprits. If blame had to be assessed, it lay with the president and his civilian advisers in the State Department and in OSD. It was the civilians who had convinced the president of the feasibility of carrying out a limited war; it was the civilians who had sold him on "gradualism"; and it was the civilians who had, through the president, placed the United States forces on the strategic defensive—a "no-win" concept.

Not that the Joint Chiefs were themselves blameless. Somewhere in 1967 or early 1968, one or more of the Chiefs should have stood up and told the president publicly that what he was doing in Vietnam would not work, and then resigned. It might not have changed American strategy in Vietnam, but the integrity of the Joint Chiefs of Staff—a valuable national commodity—would have been preserved. On 14 April 1981, Congressman Newt Gingrich, speaking as a civilian on civilian-military relations to a number of senior officers, made these remarks: ". . .

we've gotten into a circle where I set the parameters for your advice, you then give me that advice and . . . afterwards . . . discuss how stupid I am. . . . On occasion after occasion, we've done the wrong thing because you're trapped into a model of behavior which you think is essentially necessary, so you then blame me because I don't give you the right tools, the right doctrine, or the right authority, and then I blame you because you didn't deliver. And we end up with a country that is terribly weaker and in terribly greater danger. In a sense, at its most extreme, *I guess I'm saying that the Joint Chiefs have to be more willing to resign over doctrinal failure.* I'll give you the greatest example of that by citing one example from Clausewitz who might well have been writing on the Vietnam War. On page one of the actual document *On War,* he said, 'kind hearted people might, of course, think there was some ingenious way to disarm or defeat an enemy without too much bloodshed, and might imagine this is the true goal of the art of war. Pleasant as it sounds, it is a fallacy that must be exposed. War is such a dangerous business that the mistakes which come from kindness are the very worst.' Does anything more than that sentence need to be said about what happened in Vietnam? And how many cases can you find me of senior officers who said that explicitly and openly? We designed a war we were going to lose, and we managed to lose it the way we designed it, and nothing unusual happened'' (emphasis added).

Many officers in the armed forces have asked the same questions Congressman Gingrich has raised. Where were the resignations from their senior military leaders? They, too, have received no answers.

Regardless of who should be blamed for the failure of American strategy in Vietnam, in early March 1968 it was clear that the past concepts of gradualism and attrition were bankrupt. To fill the strategic gap which now yawned before Clifford, the OSD civilians, smelling victory, in solid rank behind Warnke pressed forward with their solution. On 1 March they presented to Clifford the first draft of his memorandum to the president. As might be expected, it presented a bleak picture of the situation in Vietnam and forecast a dismal future. The draft memorandum foresaw increasing Communist gains in the rural areas of South Vietnam as ARVN hunkered down around the towns and cities, and that the GVN would be ''unlikely to rise to the challenge.'' The paper stated bluntly that the current United States strategy in South Vietnam, even if implemented by a troop increase of 200,000 men, would see "no early end to the conflict, nor any success in attriting the enemy or eroding Hanoi's will to fight." The draft memo prophesied that within the United States the effects of continuing the present policy in Vietnam would be equally distressing. Reserves would have to be mobilized, casualties would soar, and taxes would have to be increased. The memo forecast "growing disaffection accompanied . . . by increased defiance of the draft and growing unrest in the cities . . . (with) great risks of provoking a domestic crisis of unprecedented proportions."[59] Strong language this.

Finally, the draft memorandum came to the key point. It stated, "We can obtain our objective only if the GVN begins to take the steps necessary to gain the confidence of the people and to provide effective leadership. ARVN must also be turned into an effective fighting force. Our military presence in South Vietnam should be designed to buy the time during which ARVN and the GVN can develop an effective capability. In order to do this, we must deny the enemy access to the populated areas of the country."[60] The memo then outlined the area to be held to the east and south of what it called the "demographic frontier," a line running down South Vietnam along the Annamite chain, thence west to about Loc Ninh. It was the old enclave strategy reborn and enlarged.

The draft appalled Walt Rostow and General Wheeler, Rostow at the pessimistic tone of the memo and Wheeler at its proposed strategy. At a meeting with Clifford and the Pentagon civilians, Wheeler vigorously attacked the "demographic frontier" concept on two points. First, the proposed strategy would mean increased fighting in, or close to, population centers, and hence, would result in increased civilian casualties. Second, by adopting a policy of passive defense, we would allow the enemy an increased capability of massing near population centers, especially north of Saigon. Wheeler did not use the argument many thought even more powerful—the "demographic frontier" strategy meant giving up vast areas of western South Vietnam to the enemy, thus providing the Communists with the opportunity to establish a government in South Vietnam and to claim sovereignty over a substantial part of the country.

The next day, 2 March, Warnke counterattacked Wheeler's two objections to his proposed concept. In answer to Wheeler's first objection that the demographic frontier strategy would lead to increased civilian casualties, Warnke claimed that if the enemy wanted to fight in populated centers that no United States strategy could stop him. Warnke's proposed strategy, he argued, might even reduce civilian casualties if the United States forces could attack enemy troops before the Communists attacked the cities. To counter Wheeler's second objection that the proposed strategy of static defense would allow the enemy to mass near population centers, Warnke denied that this concept advocated a posture of static defense. On the contrary, he wrote, "One of the primary missions of United States forces would be to operate in the area [beyond the demographic frontier], remain highly mobile, and carry out attacks against suspected enemy base camps."[61]

When both of Warnke's replies are linked, he seemed to say that United States forces should carry on about as they had operated in the past, except that the American troops would be withdrawn from the DMZ, the Western Highlands, and from the United States bases which supported activities in those areas. While Warnke and the other civilian strategists did not recognize it, they had proposed the same strategic concept which the French general, Navarre, had employed in 1953–1954. This strategy had contributed to the defeat at Dien Bien Phu and the withdrawal of the French forces from Vietnam.

On 2 March, General Wheeler again attacked Warnke's concepts. By now he had Westmoreland's reply to his cable of 29 February which he could use in his attack. Westmoreland's response to Wheeler's first question—what military and other objectives were the additional forces designed to advance—dutifully paid deference to purely defensive and pacification requirements for the troops. Westmoreland did, however, state again his concept of going on to contingency operations if required. The term "contingency operations" was a euphemism for attacks into and north of the DMZ, for raids into Cambodia, and for cutting the Ho Chi Minh Trail in Laos by ground forces. Wheeler's second question to Westmoreland had asked, "What specific dangers are the dispatch [of the troops] designed to avoid, and what specific goals would the increment of force aim to achieve?" Westmoreland's answer was vague and amounted to little more than a statement that he would continue his present strategy, only with more force.

Westmoreland's answer to either question could not have been of much help to Wheeler in his battle with Warnke. Nevertheless, he (Wheeler) did manage to stalemate Warnke, requiring the draft presidential memorandum to be almost totally rewritten. Where Clifford had originally found Warnke's draft "quite persuasive," he felt that the memorandum to the president should not be too dramatic, but should indicate doubts and *suggest* future changes. The second draft of the memorandum, produced on 3 March, differed markedly in tone from the initial memorandum. Gone was any discussion of grand strategy.[62] The memorandum recommended that: 1. Westmoreland be sent immediate reinforcements of about 22,000 men and three tactical fighter squadrons; 2. Early approval be given to a Reserve call-up to meet the balance of the Wheeler request and to restore the strategic reserve; 3. The decision as to whether to meet the Westmoreland troop request in full be reserved, based on a further and continuing reexamination of the situation; 4. No new peace initiative be undertaken; 5. An urgent effort be made to improve and modernize the RVNAF as well as to pressure the leaders of the GVN to improve their political performance; 6. A general decision on bombing policy in North Vietnam be made; and 7. A study, to be initiated immediately, of possible new political and strategic guidance for United States operations in Vietnam.

The memorandum was a compromise. No new strategy was proposed, and all but two of the other actions were subject to "further study." One of these solid recommendations dealt with the 245,000-man Reserve call-up. Like a wolf quietly sitting among a flock of sheep, it looks eerie among the rest of the rather innocuous recommendations. Nor was there any great debate on it in the document. Tab C of the memo justified it briefly as necessary to provide Westmoreland more troops, if needed, or to reconstitute the strategic reserve. And yet, most of the prior discussions and drafts leading to the presidential memorandum dealt with actions which Westmoreland could take with either the forces already available or with only token strength increases. The "demographic frontier" strategy was based on the premise that Westmoreland would receive little or no increase in strength.

Furthermore, this Reserve call-up breached the custom which had grown up around all previous troop requests, which was to furnish what could be made available without mobilizing the Reserves or without disruption of the political and economic life of the country. Of all the people who have written about the Clifford Task Force, only Townsend Hoopes, in his book *The Limits of Intervention,* comments specifically on the radical departure represented by the Reserve call-up. He was struck not so much by the incongruity of it when compared with past troop requests, but by "its failure to gauge the horrendous political implications of its basic recommendation that the military manpower request be met."[63]

The second solid recommendation had even more far-reaching implications than did the Reserve call-up. This recommendation dealt with the need to augment and modernize RVNAF. That proposal, coupled with the one to initiate a study on new political and strategic guidance for Vietnam, carried the seeds of a whole new United States approach to the Vietnam problem. In essence, the national policy which General Westmoreland described as "hurting the enemy until he came to the conference table" had now not only been challenged, but had been found wanting. And found wanting with it was Westmoreland's implementing strategy, that of attrition, the mission which had remained unchanged since it had been assigned to him on 8 February 1966 by Secretary McNamara.

One of the policy questions the Clifford Task Force considered was the future of ROLLING THUNDER, the bombing campaign against North Vietnam. As the presidential memorandum revealed, the Clifford group could arrive at no firm recommendation as to the future of this always controversial program. The Pentagon civilians wanted to stabilize or curtail the bombing campaign, while the Joint Chiefs wanted to expand it. But the Tet offensive significantly changed the old battle over ROLLING THUNDER between the military and the civilians. Those enemy ground attacks had demonstrated beyond any doubt that the interdiction part of the air campaign had not prevented the North Vietnamese from achieving a substantial build-up of men and materiel in South Vietnam. The other reason consistently given by its advocates for continuing or expanding ROLLING THUNDER—to break Hanoi's will to continue the fight—had also been invalidated. "Gradualism" and the unavailability of targets had killed the program.

The Clifford memorandum gave the president two conflicting views regarding the future of ROLLING THUNDER and its related naval programs. The JCS urged the reduction of the Hanoi/Haiphong restricted perimeters, extension of SEA DRAGON naval activities against enemy coastal water traffic from 20° North to the Chinese border, authority to use sea-based surface-to-air missiles against North Vietnamese MIGs, and the closing of the port of Haiphong through mining or by other means. As was to be expected, the Pentagon civilians, led by Warnke, opposed all of these JCS recommendations. There was the usual civilian handwringing about the probable adverse reaction of key third nations, mainly Britain. Warnke emphasized the dangers of a confrontation with the Soviets inherent in mining Haiphong. He did, however, recommend an increase in the bombing of North Vietnam, but within the existing restrictions.

Since no more than four good flying days per month over North Vietnam could be anticipated before May, none of the recommendations regarding ROLLING THUNDER either by the JCS or the civilians would make any quick difference in the effectiveness of the air campaign. But the weather factor, which in the calculations of both the JCS and the Pentagon civilians had been relatively insignificant, now suddenly became critical. It became critical not in a military sense, but in a diplomatic one.

One of the aspects of the Clifford memorandum which troubled President Johnson was its recommendation that no new peace initiative be undertaken. During the discussion of the memorandum on 4 March with Rusk, Clifford, Rostow, and others, the president deplored this negative approach to possible negotiations. Dean Rusk suggested that the United States could suspend most of the bombing of the North for the next couple of months (the bad flying weather) without much military risk, and that such a step might lead Hanoi to consider negotiations. The president jumped at Rusk's suggestion, telling him, "Really get on your horses on that."[64]

The next day, 5 March, Rusk produced for the president a proposal to suspend bombing operations north of the 20th Parallel, which ran some 200 miles north of the DMZ. As noted, it was based largely on the fact that bad weather over North Vietnam severely limited air operations in March, April, and early May. So in a military sense little was being sacrificed. Rusk saw four other advantages to his proposal. First, it could be made without conditions. If the North Vietnamese reacted favorably, well and good. If they did not react, the bombings could be resumed. The second advantage, as Rusk saw it, was that the bombing could be restarted if the North Vietnamese launched a major operation against Khe Sanh or the cities of South Vietnam. Third, Rusk saw the bombing suspension as making a dovish gesture toward the antiwar factions among the intelligentsia, the news media, and Congress in an attempt to dilute the growing virulence of their opposition to the war.

Assistant Secretary of State William Bundy remembers the bombing suspension as being proposed for "its utility in temporarily placating American public opinion."[65] Finally, Rusk was convinced that the North Vietnamese would spurn the offer and that the president and the other hard-liners could use that rejection to escalate the war. This was the view of Clark Clifford and his dovish Pentagon civilians. In Clifford's opinion, the offer ". . . did not constitute a good faith effort to get negotiations started." Its rejection by the North Vietnamese "would be the basis for launching a more effective and far-reaching attack against North Vietnam."[66]

Like other key events of this hectic period, Rusk's suggestion to suspend air bombardment of North Vietnam—in reality, a cynical throw-away—would produce unforeseen results.

The new policy proposals contained in Clifford's presidential memo-randum and Rusk's proposal for a bombing halt faced the president with an Armageddon between the hawks and the doves. On one side were the hawks—Rostow, Rusk, Max Taylor, the JCS, and the field commanders, Sharp and Westmoreland. They believed that the war should be escalated, either on the ground or in the air, or both. They might support a suspension of the bombing north of the 20th Parallel, but only as a means to escalate ROLLING THUNDER if and when the North Vietnamese rejected the ploy. They felt that at Tet the United States and the South Vietnamese had won a major victory in South Vietnam, and that this triumph should be followed up by an offensive into the DMZ, North Vietnam, Laos, or Cambodia.

Opposing the hawks were the doves, now led by the new secretary of defense, Clark Clifford. They argued that the United States could not win the war militarily, because the ground war was stalemated and would remain so if the United States forces were limited to South Vietnam. Of course, they resolutely opposed any expansion of the war into the countries bordering South Vietnam. Finally, they considered ROLLING THUNDER to be a confirmed failure. Their proposed strategy had three parts: the United States and Free World forces pulled back to guard population concentrations; the air war against North Vietnam halted; and the burden of fighting transferred as soon as possible to the South Vietnamese.

Each side, particularly the Clifford clique, sought influential allies in this decisive struggle. Clifford was able to recruit Senator Fulbright and Senator Henry Jackson of Washington. Two one-time hawks, Senators Richard Russell of Georgia and Stennis of Mississippi, joined Clifford's forces in opposing a Reserve call-up. While Clifford knew that congressional support for his position would be helpful, he feared that he might lose the battle in the White House. Accordingly, he cast about for an ally in that labyrinth of intrigue. He soon found one, Harry McPherson, one of the president's speech writers and special counsels. He was the same man who had earlier confessed that although he had access to the official reports on the Tet offensive, he had chosen to believe the misreports emanating from the news media.

Although Clifford had recruited significant reinforcements, by mid-March he was, nevertheless, losing the battle for the president's mind. But the doves, now aroused, were winging to his rescue. On 12 March, Senator Eugene McCarthy, a whimsical poet turned quixotic politician, ran against the president in the New Hampshire primary as a "peace candidate" and did surprisingly well. The election was nationally trumpeted as a repudiation of the president's Vietnam policies. As is not unusual, the media's hasty reading of the results of the New Hampshire election was wrong. Later analysis revealed that McCarthy's support came not so much from the antiwar faction as from those who thought the president ought to take a *harder* line in Vietnam. The analysis was not available until much later, however, and its initial impact buffeted the president's already shaky approach to the war.

On 15 March, Arthur Goldberg, another dove and the United States ambassador to the United Nations, sent Dean Rusk a memorandum which Rusk promptly transmitted to the president. Goldberg's memorandum advised the president to "stop all aerial and naval bombardment of North Vietnam for the limited time necessary to determine whether Hanoi will negotiate in good faith."[67] On 18 March, Chester Bowles, the American ambassador to India submitted a similar proposal. The president rejected both on the grounds that a total halt of air and naval action against North Vietnam would endanger American troops fighting near the DMZ. Again, these two proposals served to weaken the president's resolve to continue his past policies in Vietnam.

About this same time, another blow fell upon the president's determination to stay his course in Vietnam. Its originator was Dean Acheson, a noted anti-Communist and a former secretary of state under President Truman. In late February, President Johnson asked Acheson for his advice on American policy in Vietnam. Acheson told the president that he wanted to interview officials of his own choosing to get the facts. After a number of interviews with second- and third-level officials, Acheson told Johnson that he was being "led down the garden path" by the JCS and that the war in Vietnam could no longer be won. Acheson recommended that the strategy of the ground war be changed, that the bombing of the North be stopped or greatly curtailed, and that the war be brought to a close. The president was impressed.

While the advice of Goldberg, Bowles, and Acheson no doubt gave the president grounds for serious reflection, he initially responded to their counsel with belligerence. On 17 and 18 March he made two tough speeches on the war. Basically, he reaffirmed his Vietnam policies, portraying himself as a man following a middle course between escalation and surrender. For the first time he publicly questioned the patriotism of those Americans who opposed his war policies.

In spite of the bellicose nature of the president's mid-March speeches, Clifford perceived that Johnson's stance on the war was softening. Now Clifford resolved to mount a major offensive to gain control of the president's mind, and his attacking force would be the Senior Advisory Group, known around Washington as the "Wise Men." Wise or not, they were certainly a prestigious group: Dean Acheson, George Ball, McGeorge Bundy, Douglas Dillon, Cyrus Vance, Arthur Dean, John J. McCloy, General Omar Bradley, General Matthew Ridgway, General Maxwell Taylor, Robert Murphy, Henry Cabot Lodge, Abe Fortas, and Arthur Goldberg. All were men of proven patriotism with a wide range of experience in political and military affairs.

At Clifford's request, the president agreed to meet with the Wise Men after they had been briefed on the situation in Vietnam and had consulted among themselves. The principal briefings were given by Philip C. Habib, representing the State Department, Maj. Gen. William E. DePuy of the JCS, and George Carver from the CIA. Some of the Wise Men who heard the briefings have recorded their opinions of them. Maxwell Taylor heard them as "temperate and thoughtful presentations."[68] Rusk thought the picture the briefers presented was slightly tilted toward the pessimistic side. Rostow, who also attended the briefings, judged them to be mediocre, but not misleading or unduly depressing.

After the briefings, the discussions continued on into the evening.

It soon became apparent that the resolute support on Vietnam which the group had given the president in November 1967 had been blown away by the Tet offensive. The group met with the president over lunch the next day, where they delivered their verdict. Although the group was split, the majority favored any action which would lessen the American commitment in Vietnam. The president brought in Generals Wheeler and Abrams, the latter just back from Vietnam. They gave a factual and favorable report on the situation there. All to no avail; the Wise Men, troubled more by perceived domestic difficulties than by the military situation in Vietnam, refused to budge from their pessimistic assessment.

The president was shocked at their consensus—not only shocked, but angry. As he left the meeting he made the remark, "somebody has poisoned the well."[69] His irate eye fell quickly upon the briefers. He had them called back to the White House where they gave him the briefings they had given the Wise Men. After listening to their presentations, he absolved *them* of "poisoning the well."

The man who had "poisoned the well" was, of course, Clark Clifford. There are knowledgeable officials who maintain that Clifford had "prepped" some of the Wise Men before they gathered at the White House. If he had not "prepped" them, he at least knew how most of them viewed the situation in Vietnam. Clifford's use of the Wise Men to serve his dovish ends was a consummate stroke by a master of intrigue, and it—more than anything else—convinced the president that he had to revise his policies on Vietnam.

In a slightly blasphemous vein, what happened was that Johnson had fired a doubting Thomas (McNamara) only to replace him with a Judas. Indeed, this is Clifford's characterization of his own role during March 1968. He would later recall, "The irony was that he (Johnson) chose me to replace McNamara because he wanted a good staunch stalwart supporter of his policy in the Pentagon. Then this Judas appeared!"[70] For this role during the decisive month of March 1968, the president never forgave Clifford. Nor did Lyndon Johnson forgive the Wise Men. Shortly before his death he told an aide at the LBJ Library in Austin, Texas, that (to use his earthy language) "he had been 'screwed' by a lot of people—the press, the Congress, even his own staff, 'but the big-name foreign policy types did a royal job on me.' "[71]

Notes—Chapter 18

1. McGarvey, *Visions,* pp. 252–256.
2. Ibid., p. 254.
3. Palmer, *Summons,* p. 179; and David Richard Palmer, *Readings in Current Military History* (West Point, NY: Department of Military Art, USMA, 1969).
4. President's Foreign Intelligence Advisory Board, *Intelligence Warning of the Tet Offensive in South Vietnam* (Washington, D.C.: April 11, 1968), p. 4.
5. Hoang Ngoc Lung, *General Offensives of 1968–69,* Indochina Monographs (Washington, D.C.: U.S. Army Center of Military History, 1978), pp. 21–22.
6. President's FIA Board, *Intelligence Warning,* p. 8.
7. Edward Jay Epstein, "Vietnam: What Happened vs. What We Saw: We Lose Our Innocence," *TV Guide,* 6 October 1973, p. 13-F.
8. Oberdorfer, *Tet!,* p. 158.
9. Westmoreland to Wheeler and Sharp, Cable, MAC 12397, 20 December 1967.
10. Lyndon Baines Johnson, *The Vantage Point, Perspectives of the Presidency 1963–1969* (New York: Rinehart and Winston, 1971), p. 379.
11. Liddell Hart, *Strategy,* p. 340.
12. Peter Braestrup, *The Big Story,* 2 vols. (Boulder, CO: Westview Press, 1977), I:705.
13. PBS, *Firing Line,* 24 March 1978, Transcript p. 11.
14. Dr. David Culbert, "Television's Vietnam, The Impact of Visual Images," (TV Documentary as reported in *The Monitor,* McAllen, TX, 20 March 1981).
15. Braestrup, *Big Story,* 1:713–714.
16. Ibid., 1:715.
17. Gen. Maxwell Taylor, *Swords and Plowshares* (New York: W. W. Norton, 1972), p. 384.
18. Epstein, *TV Guide,* p. 13-F.
19. Braestrup, *Big Story,* 1:706.
20. Epstein, *TV Guide,* p. 13-F.
21. Culbert, *The Monitor.*
22. Walter Cronkite, letter to Gen. W. C. Westmoreland, 15 June 1982.
23. Epstein, *TV Guide,* p. 14-F.
24. Braestrup, *Big Story,* 1:705.
25. Ibid.

26. Robert Elegant, "Looking Back At Vietnam: How To Lose A War," *Encounter*, August 1981, p. 89.
27. Ibid., p. 74.
28. Ibid., p. 75.
29. Ibid., p. 84.
30. S. Robert Lichter and Stanley Rothman, "Where the Media Elite Stand," in *Public Opinion*, reproduced in *The American Spectator*, April 1982, p. 36.
31. Alistair Horne, "A British Historian's Meditations," *National Review*, 23 July 1982, p. 888.
32. Gen. Maxwell D. Taylor, "New Concept of Security," *Ordnance*, July–August 1971, p. 31.
33. Morton M. Kondracke, Viewpoint, "Reagan Diplomacy and the Rehabilitation of the PLO," *Wall Street Journal*, 22 July 1982, p. 19.
34. Westmoreland, *Soldier*, p. 470.
35. Stephen Rosen, "After Vietnam: What the Pentagon Has Learned," *The American Spectator*, October 1979, p. 10.
36. Paul L. Miles, hist., U.S. Department of the Army, Office of the Chief of Staff, Untitled Staff Study ("White Paper"), 9 November 1970. (Department of the Army Staff Study, 1970) The cables quoted in this chapter are from the "White Paper" unless otherwise noted.
37. Gravel, *Pentagon Papers*, IV:541–542.
38. Westmoreland, *Diary*, 17 February 1968.
39. Johnson, *Vantage Point*, p. 387.
40. John B. Henry, "February 1968," *Foreign Policy*, #4, Fall 1971, p. 15.
41. Henry, *Foreign Policy*, p. 15.
42. Gravel, *Pentagon Papers*, IV:547.
43. Ibid.
44. Ibid., IV:239.
45. Henry, *Foreign Policy*, p. 23.
46. Johnson, *Vantage Point*, p. 391.
47. Ibid., p. 406.
48. Henry, *Foreign Policy*, p. 20.
49. Gelb and Betts, *Irony*, p. 173.
50. Herbert Y. Schandler, *The Unmaking of a President: Lyndon Johnson and Vietnam* (Princeton, NJ: Princeton University Press, 1977), p. 141.
51. Cable JCS 02430, United States Department of Defense, Office of the Joint Chiefs of Staff, 29 February 1968.
52. Gravel, *Pentagon Papers*, IV:556.
53. Ibid., IV:557.

54. Ibid., IV:551.
55. Ibid., IV:552.
56. Halberstam, *Best and Brightest,* p. 792.
57. Brian Crozier, *National Review,* Fall 1982, p. 24.
58. Clark Clifford, ''A Vietnam Reappraisal—The Personal History of One Man's View and How It Evolved,'' *Foreign Affairs,* July 1969.
59. Gravel, *Pentagon Papers,* IV:562–564.
60. Ibid.
61. Ibid., IV:568.
62. Ibid., IV:573.
63. Townsend Hoopes, *The Limits of Intervention* (New York: David McKay, 1969), p. 179.
64. Johnson, *Vantage Point,* p. 399.
65. Schandler, *The Unmaking,* p. 251.
66. Ibid., p. 241.
67. Johnson, *Vantage Point,* p. 408.
68. Taylor, *Swords,* p. 390.
69. Schandler, *The Unmaking,* p. 264.
70. Marvin Kalb and Elie Able, *Roots of Involvement, The U.S. In Asia 1784–1971* (New York: W. W. Norton, 1971), p. 229.
71. Roger Morris, *Uncertain Greatness: Henry Kissinger and American Foreign Policy* (New York: Harper & Row, 1977), p. 45.

19 Decision, Dissent, and Defection

1968

As the month of March ebbed, decision-time arrived for President Johnson. The war policies, premises, and strategies which had governed the Vietnam War since 1966 were demolished by the Tet offensive and the powder train of events which it ignited. The debris from the explosion had come back to earth, and the wreckage was all too evident to the White House.

The Tet offensive and its aftermath starkly revealed the strategic vacuum in which United States policy had been operating since 1966. The problem was *not* that the United States was pursuing the wrong strategy in Vietnam; the problem was that it was pursuing *no* strategy. The Joint Chiefs had admitted this to Clifford in one of his "educational" sessions with them in early March. Military strategy—that is, the use of armed forces to achieve a national objective—must spring from a political objective, and the civilian leadership must articulate that political objective. From it, the military leaders are supposed to devise the strategic objectives of the war or campaign. These are transmitted to the theater commander who in turn sets his own strategic and operational objectives.

In March 1968, a new and integrated strategy had to be devised. It had to cover ground operations in South Vietnam, the air attack against the North, and negotiations with the North Vietnamese. Unless this new strategy was to suffer the deficiencies and ultimate failure of the old, it had to be based on an attainable, articulated objective. To determine this objective, the entire situation in Vietnam, changed as it had been

529

by the Tet offensive, had to be analyzed. This analysis had to consider the combat situation in and over Vietnam, the diplomatic and military factors worldwide, and the political and psychological climate within the United States. Indeed, it was the domestic scene which dominated the other considerations, and the controlling event within the domestic scenario was Johnson's refusal to call up the Reserves. This purely political decision pulled all military policies in its wake, and ruled out any significant troop increases for Vietnam. This in turn precluded strategic offensive operations against the enemy in Laos, Cambodia, the DMZ, or North Vietnam.

By forsaking the strategic offensive, the president tied the United States to the strategic defensive, which could take three forms. First, the United States could continue its past policy, strategically on the defensive, tactically on the offensive—in short, Westmoreland's search and destroy operations. But this option represented more of the same policy which the country, rightly or wrongly, now condemned as a result of the Tet offensive. The second option was the Warnke proposal— withdrawal to the "demographic frontier" and defense of the population centers. This concept, however, had been dealt a mortal blow by General Wheeler's condemnation of it in the discussion leading to Clifford's presidential memorandum. What remained was a third policy, now coming to the fore, a policy which came to be known later as Vietnamization— providing maximum assistance to strengthen South Vietnamese forces and intensifying pacification. This double-barreled policy had as its ultimate purpose the phasing out of American forces and the turning over of the war to the South Vietnamese.

The central thrust of the new strategy, then, would concentrate on improving ARVN's capabilities and strengthening the government of South Vietnam's control over the population so that they could eventually oppose the Communists alone. American forces would provide the shield behind which this enhancement would take place, and they would be withdrawn when the RVNAF and the GVN could defend themselves. The air strategy would support the ground strategy. Bombing would be restricted to that area of North Vietnam south of the 20° North latitude in direct support of the ground combat in South Vietnam. This unilateral scaling down of the air campaign in the North provided also the third facet of the new strategy—a move towards negotiations. For the first time in the war, the United States government had devised a strategy which was coherent, integrated, and above all, attainable.

The new strategy was a United States strategy. The Government of South Vietnam was not consulted about the basic concept and was consulted only marginally about the implementing details. Gen. Cao Van Vien, the chief of the South Vietnamese Joint General Staff (General Wheeler's counterpart), years later wrote about President Johnson's 1968 decision: "Many questions arising from Vietnamization remained unanswered, which ushered the GVN into complete darkness as to true United States motives. Was the United States bent on tucking the tail and violating its commitments as President Johnson had once vowed never to do? Was the United States initiating a new strategy to preserve United States honor and still protect South Vietnam? Was the United States using Vietnamization . . . to disengage itself from the war with honor and leave South Vietnam to its own fate? . . . South Vietnam only learned about the policy through piecemeal statements by the United States officials involved."[1]

There was good reason for not consulting the Government of South Vietnam. The new concept of Vietnamization was essentially a "cut and run" strategy, designed by and for the United States. Vietnamization was dictated not so much by the increased potential of the South Vietnamese as shown at Tet (although this was a welcome and surprising development), but by the collapse of the will to support the war among the decision-making elite in the United States. American policymakers approved and supported the policy of Vietnamization without any assurance that it would leave South Vietnam capable of defending itself. To the American leadership this was not its primary purpose.

In fact, in early 1968, any cold-blooded analysis of the capacity of the South Vietnamese to carry out their part of Vietnamization would have argued against its adoption. True, the GVN, the RVNAF, particularly ARVN, and the South Vietnamese people had responded effectively to the Tet offensive. Even here, however, a cynic might have noted that their heroics sprang not from some new surge of patriotism so much as from the "back-to-the-wall" courage of the cornered. The fundamental weaknesses of the government and its armed forces remained unchanged.

The predominant weakness of the South Vietnamese armed forces have been pinpointed by Douglas S. Blaufarb in his book, *The Counter-*

Insurgency Era. He points out that Thieu maintained himself in power in South Vietnam only by a system of "purchased support." Thieu could retain power only by holding the allegiance of the top military leaders. These men were chosen for their political loyalty, not their soldierly competence, a practice guaranteeing corruption and incompetence. Combat merit goes unrewarded; the soldiers go uncared for; and the demands of the martial spirit—Duty, Honor, Country—go unanswered.[2] Such an army may improve superficially as foreign equipment and training are lavished on it, but such improvement is deceptive, for the foundation of the force remains rotten. To tear down such a structure and rebuild it requires years of effort and these years were not likely to be available. But in late March 1968, no such thoughts impeded the United States policymakers in their rush to Vietnamization. Such thought may have been one of the reasons, however, which caused the more knowledgeable and realistic among the United States elite to keep the total implications of the policy from their Vietnamese allies.

Not only were the South Vietnamese denied knowledge of the new policy but, amazingly, so were many key American officials. The president, after days of consultations, briefings, analysis, and soul-searching made one of the most crucial decisions of the war, and it received practically no dissemination. No new directives were issued to the JCS and the military commanders concerned. Nobody told Westmoreland that his primary mission *now* was to improve the RVNAF as quickly as possible. As one of the key staff officers in MACV, I can testify that MACV was given no directive or even any intimation of any shift in strategic priorities. Indeed, no new mission was given officially to MACV until June 1969, when the Nixon administration issued a revised "mission statement." This directive ordered MACV to provide maximum assistance to the GVN in building up their forces, to support pacification, and to reduce the flow of supplies to the enemy.

Two factors produced this peculiar silence on the part of the administration. First, the principal actors did not believe that they had made a major policy change. President Johnson saw it as a continuation of past policies, with the difference being merely a change in tactics. General Wheeler, Secretary Rusk, and Walt Rostow all viewed the decision of later March 1968 primarily as a means to rally public support behind the war, which would go on much as before. Even Paul Warnke, the "dove's dove," felt that in late March the president had not changed any of his past policy objectives.

There was a second reason why nobody disseminated the policy change. Such an announcement would constitute an admission that the past policies had been inadequate and wrong. It is interesting to note that the very officials (the president, Wheeler, Rusk, and Rostow) who judged that the presidential decisions of late March represented no major change of policy were themselves the architects of the past strategy. This point is reinforced by Senator Eugene McCarthy, whose surprise showing at the New Hampshire polls had shocked the nation. Years later he said that one of the reasons President Johnson refused to run in 1968 was that "he would have had to admit that the war policy was wrong. . ."[3] Clark Clifford stands in contrast to the president, Wheeler, Rusk and Rostow. His hands were unstained by past policies, and he was the official who kept insisting publicly that the war *had* entered a new and different era.

In a way President Johnson and the senior officials were right—the new decisions did not represent a major policy shift. A look at the three decisions which Johnson made lends support to this view. First, there was the bombing cut-back to the 20th Parallel. In view of the adverse weather factor, the president and the others viewed this cut-back as a bagatelle tossed to Hanoi to which the Americans expected no response. Second, the dispatch of a few thousand more troops—far less than the military had asked for—had a long and consistent history. Nothing new here. Third, the transfer of more responsibility for the war to the South Vietnamese had precedent too. In November 1967, General Westmoreland told a press conference in Washington that he believed it possible that in two years the United States could begin turning the burden of the war over to the RVNAF and begin phasing out the American commitment. Thus, looked at in one way, there was little "new" in the policies.

But in another and more fundamental way, the president and his chief advisers deceived themselves when they reasoned that Johnson's decision represented "more of the same." There *had* been a major change of policy. The military strategy governing the conduct of the war *had* been basically changed. The strategy of attrition was out; the punishment of the North by strategic air attacks was out; out went the rock-bottom strategy of punishing the Communists until they either negotiated or gave up their aggression in the South. Also, the president's decision of March 1968 marked the demise of the open-ended commitment of United States forces to Vietnam. Nobody in authority proclaimed this policy, but those in the know, military and civilian alike, realized that March 1968 represented the apex of American troop commitment to Vietnam. Third, the decisions represented the first steps toward the disengagement of the United States from Vietnam. It was plain, for those who wanted to see it, that the American governing elite were now prepared to accept the defeat of the United States in Southeast Asia. What had been the United States policy of getting a settlement with honor had now become peace at any price.

In spite of the president's insistence that nothing had changed, there was one public presidential action which did indicate that something new and different might be afoot. On 22 March, President Johnson announced that in June 1968, General Westmoreland would be relieved as COMUSMACV to become the army chief of staff, and General Abrams would replace him in Vietnam. Of course, the news media, still keening its spurious message that Tet had been a military defeat for the United States, seized on this transfer to charge that "Westy had been kicked upstairs." Nothing could be less factual. The president believed that General Westmoreland had done an excellent job in Vietnam. The president admired General Westmoreland as a soldier and liked him as a man. On several occasions Westmoreland had gone "that extra mile" for the president, and Johnson, who placed a high value on loyalty, was not a man to forget such efforts.

In a personal letter dated 22 December 1967 (over a month before the Tet offensive), General Wheeler told Westmoreland that "you are the obvious candidate for Chief of Staff Army (CSA)," and he went on to assure Westmoreland that he would become the CSA either in mid-1968 when the incumbent, Gen. H. K. Johnson retired, or a year or two later if General Johnson stayed on. The letter continues by discussing various positions Westmoreland might occupy while standing in the line of succession.[4] The letter leaves no doubt that President Johnson had already selected Westmoreland to be CSA. The only question was when he was to succeed to that position.

It is the timing of the president's announcement of Westmoreland's reassignment that is puzzling. The president must have surmised that the news media would draw the wrong conclusions about his reasons for the reassignment. The president's timing becomes even more puzzling when it is realized that the president thought he had made no basic change of war policy in Vietnam, or at least would admit to no such change. Yet, by announcing Westmoreland's reassignment in late March, he opened himself to the charge that he was repudiating his past policies, which, more than anyone else except the president, Westmoreland personified.

Extensive research has uncovered no convincing reason for the timing for the president's announcement. Westmoreland states in his personal diary that the president made the announcement well in advance to avoid "The situation that developed during the delayed announcement of the new commandant of the Marine Corps," referring apparently to the internecine rivalry which had shaken the marine corps in 1966 when the selection of the new commandant was delayed for several months. As authority for this statement he cites a letter he received from the president, dated 23 March 1968.

Walt Rostow told me that he could only speculate as to the timing of the president's announcement. He confirmed that the president thought highly of Westmoreland and that Johnson had no desire to disparage Westmoreland's accomplishments in Vietnam or to embarrass him. Rostow conjectures that by 22 March, the president had at least tentatively decided that on 31 March he was going to announce that he would not seek reelection. While the president would retain the normal power of nomination until the end of this term, any key designation, like Westmoreland's, would be viewed, and possibly attacked, as a "lame duck" appointment.

Regardless of the reasons which impelled the president to announce Westmoreland's reassignment on 22 March, the country would shortly have not only a new commander in Vietnam, but a new strategy to fight the war there as well.

President Johnson made one more decision as the month of March 1968 came to a climactic end. On 31 March he announced in a national telecast, "I shall not seek, and I will not accept, the nomination of my party for another term as your president." His announcement stunned the nation and raised questions about the motives for this renunciation that abound to this day. No one, then or now, is sure of the real reasons for Johnson's refusal to seek the presidency in 1968.

In his memoirs, President Johnson gives two primary reasons underlying his decision. First, he feared for his health. He had been stricken by a serious heart attack in 1955 and had undergone two operations while in the White House. He was tired, and he doubted his capacity to endure four more years of the presidency. Johnson had a special fear of incurring a paralytic stroke; in fact, he had recurring nightmares of lying paralyzed in the White House, powerless and helpless, while the government disintegrated around him.

The second reason President Johnson gives for his renunciation of the nomination is that he thought that some extraordinary act on his part was necessary to convince the North Vietnamese to take seriously his offer of negotiations. His political hari-kari, he believed, would show Hanoi that his bid for negotiations was sincere and unmotivated by any hope of domestic political gain. In effect, in the president's mind, he was sacrificing himself politically to find peace in Vietnam.

As strange as it may seem, President Johnson is not the best authority on his motives for not running in 1968. The historians now at the LBJ Library in Austin, Texas, are men who admire Johnson and who are in his debt. These men have warned me repeatedly, however, that on any subject LBJ was inclined to make numerous statements, many of them contradictory. In the afterlight of events, he was not above selecting the account which best served his purpose. So what President Johnson said and wrote about his motives for refusing to seek the presidency in 1968 may not be the whole story.

Yet there is evidence which confirms some of what he said and wrote about his reasons for not reseeking the presidency. LBJ told General Westmoreland in November 1967 that he was worried about his health, that he was weary, and that he wanted out. Westmoreland believed then (and believes now) that the president, by that November conversation, had already firmly decided not to run in 1968. If Westmoreland's surmise is right, then the turbulent events of January, February, and March 1968 did not bring about President Johnson's decision to renounce the presidency. He had made up his mind before these events occurred. Incidentally, Walt Rostow told me that, in his opinion, the only person who could have convinced President Johnson to run for reelection was Westmoreland. Rostow believes that if Westmoreland had convinced President Johnson that LBJ's renunciation of the nomination would have lowered the morale of the troops in Vietnam, the president would have run.

The second reason given by the president for refusing to run—his political self-immolation to convince Hanoi of the sincerity of his overtures toward negotiation—rings more tinnily. He had no plan to bring on negotiations with North Vietnam until Rusk suggested an approach in early March. Even then, Johnson was unconvinced that his bombing halt and diplomatic approaches to Hanoi would bring North Vietnam to the conference table. Viewed in this light, his declared renunciation as a means to further negotiations with Hanoi appears to be an afterthought, a lofty justification for a decision he had already tentatively made for other (and less high-minded) reasons.

There are those who hold that Johnson's withdrawal from the presidential race sprang from motives other than the concern for his own health and his desire to bring Hanoi to the negotiating table. These people point out that, while Westmoreland may have felt that Johnson was earnest in his statement to him in November 1967, other actions tended to discount Johnson's sincerity. In his memoirs, Johnson wrote that he had intended to announce his renunciation of the nomination in his State of the Union message delivered in January 1968. He found when he got to the Capitol, however, that "he had forgot to bring it along."[5] This is not the conduct of a man who was resolved to make the most important announcement of his life. Rather, it is, at best, the action of a man toying with the decision. Walt Rostow, in his book, relates the several hints Johnson dropped in 1967 about not running in 1968, but he and the others did not believe him.[6] Finally, President Johnson himself lends corroboration that the decision he announced to Westmoreland in November 1967 was not final. In his memoirs he writes that the final decision not to seek the presidency in 1968 was made at 9:01 P.M., 31 March 1968, when he sat down to address the nation on television.[7] Lady Bird Johnson confirms the last-minute nature of LBJ's decision, stating that it was not made until the afternoon of 31 March. Therefore, if we are to believe Johnson, his wife, and those close to him, the decision not to seek reelection was made finally, not in November 1967, or before, but on 31 March 1968. And if one accepts this proposition, then one must also grant that factors other than Johnson's health may have come into play in the making of his historical decision.

There are two schools of thought about what these factors were and their relative weight with President Johnson. There is one group who believe that domestic politics lay at the root of Johnson's decision. The second group argue that the war in Vietnam was the underlying cause. Those who believe that domestic politics caused LBJ to give up the presidency cite his own oft-repeated remark about "political capital." Johnson held the belief that every president came into the White House with a given amount of "political capital," that is, the power to get things done in government. In Johnson's thesis, this "capital" was steadily dissipated by getting things done until by or near the end of a president's term he had little or no "capital" left. Nor could this "political capital" be replenished by reelection. Johnson felt that by 1968 he had exhausted his "political capital." He believed that his post-1968 presidency would not only be more difficult, but that he would accomplish less than he had in his first term.

Then there was the mounting evidence of the failure of his Great Society programs. Johnson, in spite of his great political insight and sophistication, believed that the passage of social legislation automatically brought about social betterment. Now in 1968 it was becoming obvious that the Great Society was bringing about, not social change, but only the appearance of social change. The Great Society programs were not being fully funded, for the Vietnam War was sucking up those dollars to pay for bullets, bandages, and bombs. Instead of improving the plights of the minorities and the poor, the Great Society programs were harming them. The underprivileged expected massive help, and when it never materialized, their frustration brought on disillusion and bitterness. The white middle class, too, was fooled by Johnson's rhetoric. They thought the president was giving everything to the underclasses, and they resented it. Both the middle class and the underclass turned on Johnson. The Great Society, from which he had such great expectations and for which he had expended so much "political capital," had not only failed, it had backfired on him.

Everybody blamed him, Johnson, for their troubles and broken dreams. Joe Califano, who was close to Johnson during this period, believes that Johnson realized that he had divided the country, not only over the war, but over civil rights and the Great Society. Even worse, LBJ had lost faith in himself to bring the country together. Lady Bird Johnson reinforces Califano's view. In her memoirs she wrote that uppermost in Johnson's mind was the thought, "I do not believe I can unite this country!"[8]

The New Hampshire primary, in which Eugene McCarthy gained 42 percent of the vote, told Johnson that the people had lost faith in him and in his leadership. The candidacy of McCarthy did not really worry him. The president felt that he could easily beat McCarthy, but what did concern LBJ was that in the political jungle lurked a more dangerous rival, who, sensing Johnson's weakness, would now attack. That rival, Robert Kennedy, backed by the money and prestige of the Family, would be difficult to beat. At the very best, Johnson now had to look forward to a bloody and bruising battle for the Democratic nomination. On 16 March 1968, when Robert Kennedy announced his candidacy, the president's forebodings were realized. Thus, taken as a whole, Johnson could only view the domestic political scene as unpromising, even ominous. He had lost the trust and confidence of the people. He presided uneasily over a tormented country torn with riots and demonstrations, and he faced a formidable political challenger. Even if he won the nomination and election, in his view, he could look forward only to a weakened incumbency, his "political capital" spent.

If the arguments from the political scene against his candidacy were forceful, the arguments made by the Vietnam War were at least as strong. Regardless of how one viewed the war, in March 1968, it was unpopular and growing more so every day. The original antiwar protestors—the hippies, leftists, and far-out liberals—had been joined by much of Congress, the news media, the Establishment, and many of the middle class. To compound the problem, all of the discontent did not lie on the antiwar side. As the true results of the New Hampshire election showed, there was a substantial segment of the American people who were dissatisfied with Johnson's conduct of the war because they wanted it carried on with *more* force, not less.

The war itself had turned into a no-win proposition. He could not escalate the war and win it militarily, and yet he could not just walk away from it. The liberals and Democrats would not stand for the former, and the conservatives and Republicans would castigate him for the latter. In his own words, he had "a bear by the tail." He couldn't whip it, and he couldn't let go. He just had to suffer.[9] It was not just the no-win aspect of the war which disturbed him, but the prospect that he and the United States were losing control of the war. By stressing Vietnamization and negotiations, he was passing the initiative in the war to the South Vietnamese and the North Vietnamese—to Thieu and Ho. He was giving them control of the war, and this was anathema to Johnson.

Beyond all of these aspects there loomed before Johnson the specter of failure. Although he denied it, Johnson knew he had made a significant change in his war policies in March 1968. He had to admit to himself that his previous strategy—if his prior policies could be dignified by that word—had failed. ROLLING THUNDER and Westmoreland's search and destroy operations had not brought Hanoi to the conference table. Beyond that, he had never devised or articulated the basic political objective of the war—and that was his failure, and his alone. He, the president, had failed in the one war-time job he must do. Instead of winning his war, he knew he could very well lose it. At last the storm-troopers of reality had breached the walls of that last bastion of fantasy, the White House. And when they did, Johnson ran up the white flag.

In North Vietnam, as in the United States and South Vietnam, the Tet offensive produced momentous and far-reaching results. The failure of the Great Uprising-Great Offensive (TCK-TKN) propelled the Politburo into another fundamental reexamination of Communist strategy for South Vietnam. Over the next days, as the reports from the various cities and towns of South Vietnam came in, Giap and his comrades realized that they had fashioned a battlefield failure of monstrous proportions. Not only had casualties been heavy, but even more disheartening, the Viet Cong leadership had been almost completely destroyed. The concept behind TCK-TKN had proven bankrupt, and now, as the beaten Communist units ran for cover, a new strategy had to be designed.

The first try at redrafting a new strategy—obviously a hasty improvisation—appeared in the aforementioned COSVN circular which appeared on 1 February 1968. After admitting the failure of the Tet offensive, the circular shifted its ground and claimed that the TCK-TKN was not designed to achieve total victory in the shortest possible time, but was ". . . a prolonged strategic offensive that includes many military campaigns and local uprisings." The circular went on to counsel that the Communists must "permanently strengthen our will to fight the enemy continuously and to fight a protracted war." The tactics implementing the new concept were also prescribed. Units were instructed to "use artillery, mortars, and sappers to attack the enemy'' and were cautioned against using Main Force units in an attack.[10]

A Viet Cong captain captured in Da Nang on 5 February 1968 expanded on the subject of these tactics. He said that he had attended a briefing on the Tet attacks on 22 January in which the plan for the uprising and offensive were set forth. He related that the Communist briefer told his group that if the initial attacks against the cities failed that the VC/NVA forces would pull back, encircle the towns, and from these positions hit the cities with heavy rocket attacks. Whether the Communists had any such preconceived plan is doubtful. At any rate, after their initial repulse in the cities, the VC/NVA forces were too weak to hold encircling positions around most of the towns anyway.

This improvised strategy held sway until March 1968 when COSVN, in the Sixth Conference of its Central Committee, promulgated the so-called Sixth Resolution governing future strategy for South Vietnam. With typical Communist disregard for truth, the Sixth Resolution claimed (in its words) ''great and unprecedented success in all fields.'' After three pages of vague and distorted descriptions of these ''successes,'' the resolution got to the heart of the problem—the failures and deficiencies of the Communist forces in the Tet offensive. The document frankly admitted that at Tet, no part of the three-pronged offensive had worked. The armed forces, the ''lever,'' had failed to ''create favorable conditions'' in the towns. The troop-proselyting prong had ''failed to precipitate a military revolt,'' and the uprising prong had not motivated ''the masses to join in violent armed uprising.'' Then came a long series of generalized instructions as to needed improvements, followed by another call to ''step up the three-pronged offensive.'' In other words, so the Sixth Resolution proclaimed, the plan for the Tet offensive was sound; only its execution was faulty. Now, it told the Communist troops, try again.[11]

The effect of the Sixth Resolution on the Communist soldiers, particularly the Viet Cong, was predictable. They knew that a repeat of the Tet debacle was suicidal madness and wanted no part of it. Defections, particularly among Viet Cong officers, increased. Col. Tran Van Dac, a long-time Viet Cong political officer with responsibilities equivalent to those of a major general, turned himself in to United States troops on 19 April. His defection was followed shortly by that of Lt. Col. Phan Viet Dung, commander of the elite 165th VC Regiment. I interrogated both Communist officers. They had viewed the war as hopeless for some time, but it was the Sixth Resolution which had acted as the catalyst for their defection. Both saw the resolution as totally unrealistic, a prescription which could only lead to failure and another bloodbath. The defection of these two senior leaders was accompanied by those of many lower-ranking officers, most of whom said they deserted because they believed that the Communists could not win the war and that they did not want to squander the lives of their soldiers in another hopeless Tet-type attack.

There was another factor adding to the despair of these Communist veterans. As seasoned campaigners, they knew that the most futile operation in the military art is to repeat a failed attack with the same or smaller forces. The attacker has lost the critical element of surprise. The morale of his forces is low, while the spirit of the defenders is high. To achieve success some new factor has to be added, or the attacking forces must be reinforced. In the forthcoming attack, as prescribed by the Sixth Resolution, neither was to be done. To replace the gruesome losses of Tet, the North Vietnamese had rushed 80,000 to 90,000 replacements down the Ho Chi Minh Trail between 1 January and 5 May 1968. The quality of the new troops, however, was low. In October 1967 (before the offensive), 82 percent of the enemy prisoners revealed that they had had more than six months service. By May 1968, however, only 40 percent had that much service and 50 percent had less than three months service, including infiltration time. So the Communist commanders now had to try to accomplish what they had failed to do at Tet, but with no surprise and with raw recruits. These experienced soldiers saw where that would lead, and they acted with their feet.

The repeat of the Tet offensive as directed by the Sixth Resolution took place in May. This series of attacks, known around MACV headquarters as "mini-Tet," was a pallid copy of the original Tet offensive. The American and South Vietnamese intelligence services had gained almost complete knowledge of the details of the enemy's offensive plans. A COSVN directive of 10 June 1968 admitted that ". . . our second phase was launched under conditions where the enemy had been warned and had strengthened his defenses." As a result of this intelligence, the attacks on Hue and in the I Corps area, as well as those in the Western Highlands, were preempted. The attack on Saigon launched on 7 May did manage to penetrate the city; however, the Communist

Main Force units engaged there were quickly destroyed or driven into the countryside. Small guerrilla bands did infiltrate into the Cholon area of Saigon where they fought suicidally until killed by South Vietnamese police and soldiers. By 13 May, the fighting in Saigon was largely over.

While Giap and his staff were planning the "mini-Tet" attacks, the Politburo, and particularly Truong Chinh, were busy taking a longer and more judicious look at Communist strategy for the South. Coincident with the failure of the May attacks, Truong Chinh, acting probably as spokesman for the "North Vietnam firsters," announced a new strategy for South Vietnam. On 5 May, Truong reported on the details of his revised concept to the Politburo. As usual, it met with opposition generating "several sessions of heated debate," in the words of Radio Hanoi.[12]

While the Viet Cong and the NVA troops were getting slaughtered in the "mini-Tet," Truong was saying that what had to be done was exactly the opposite to what the Communist military was then doing in the South. In essence, Truong said that the Tet offensive was a failure and that the Communists must return to a lower level of warfare—back to protracted and guerrilla war. He emphasized the possibility of a negotiated settlement and insisted that primary reliance should be placed on political means rather than military. It is significant that while Truong presented his report on 5 May to the Politburo, it was not made public until August. One reason for the long delay between Truong's original presentation and the public announcement was that the report aroused strong opposition from Le Duan and the Southern clique. Another reason for the delay was that the Politburo could hardly condemn the concept which had led to the Tet offensive and to "mini-Tet" while the soldiers were trying to carry out the latter.

In detail, Truong set forth a fundamental change in Communist strategy. His key points were three in number. First, the Tet offensive was ill-conceived. The assumptions upon which it was based had been wrong, particularly the assumption of a South Vietnamese populace ready to revolt. In fact, said Truong, the southern Communists had not built the political base from which an uprising could occur. Second, the disaster suffered by the Communist forces in the Tet offensive had shifted the "correlation of forces" in favor of the Americans and their South Vietnamese allies. By Leninist theory, such a negative shift required a corresponding move from the offensive to the defensive, from Tet-type attacks to protracted war, and from reliance on military means to reliance on political action and negotiation. "At times," Truong wrote in his report, "under certain circumstances, we must shift to the defensive to gain time, dishearten the enemy, and build up our forces to prepare for a new offensive."[13] The third major point of Truong's thesis went back to his long-standing disputes with Le Duan and the Southern clique. Truong expounded once more his concept that the Politburo must have two separate policies, one for North Vietnam, and one for South Vietnam. In North Vietnam the Communists should attempt to build a better life under socialism, while in the South the NLF and the Viet Cong should continue their attempts at liberation.[14]

Truong's treatise was a resounding victory for the "North Vietnam firsters." Even though Truong had the endorsement of the Politburo, Le Duan and his cohorts publicly opposed Truong's concepts. In October and again in early January 1969, articles appeared in official Communist newspapers challenging Truong's view that the Tet offensive had been a disaster and that follow-on offensive plans should be abandoned.

Regardless of the opposition of the Southern clique, it became evident after the May offensive that Truong's concepts had been adopted. There were no more large-scale Main Force attacks in the latter half of 1968. From May, the Communist assaults consisted almost entirely of standoff mortar and rocket attacks. August brought a spasmodic enemy effort referred to as "mini-mini-Tet," but Allied intelligence had it "cold," and United States preemptive strikes killed it before it could be launched.

Shortly after the abortive August offensive, COSVN, echoing Truong Chinh's new policy, in September issued Directive No. 8. As always, it claimed glorious battlefield successes, but also candidly stated that all three of the offensives, Tet, May, and August, had failed. Directive No. 8 emphasized the value of the "protracted war" policy, but without explaining in detail what the term meant. The only clue was the use of phrases such as "fight for a long time" and "engage in a protracted war with transitional phases."[15] At any rate the vision of victory in one major offensive had been abandoned.

In South Vietnam, as in North Vietnam and in the United States, the Tet offensive produced profound changes. The Tet offensive caught the South Vietnamese, like their American counterparts, in varying degrees of surprise. In Pleiku, for example, the South Vietnamese had captured Communist plans for an assault on Pleiku City, and with the United States 4th Infantry Division, had preempted the attack. In Ban Me Thuot, on the basis of local intelligence, the commander of the 23rd ARVN Division cancelled all Tet leaves prior to the offensive and put his troops on maximum alert. The 5th ARVN Division, near Saigon, reacted similarly to indications of a major attack in their area of responsibility. By and large, however, the South Vietnamese and RVNAF leaders either did not foresee the scope of the enemy's offensive, or if they had some inkling of the attack, chose to disbelieve the reports. The South Vietnamese, like the Americans, could not believe the enemy would adopt a strategy guaranteeing his own disaster. Beyond that, the Southerners could not conceive that any Vietnamese, even the Communists, would violate their most sacred holiday, Tet.

Once the South Vietnamese recovered from the shock of the enemy offensive, they fought well. Since the Communists had concentrated their attacks against South Vietnamese units and installations, ARVN and its sister services bore the heaviest combat load. ARVN had to fight principally in the cities, a type of warfare for which their training and experience had not equipped them. Nevertheless, even in this strange environment, they did a professional job.

They fought not only well, but in many cases, heroically. As an expedient to assemble enough forces to clear the enemy from Saigon and to set the example for the entire RVNAF, Gen. Cao Van Vien, the chief of the Joint General Staff (JGS), decided to use all staff and service personnel of the JGS as combat troops (with the exception of a few key staff elements). The general himself took personal command of these forces. Several battalions were thus activated overnight, and it was an impressive sight to see colonels and majors acting as platoon leaders while company grade officers carried rifles as privates. In Saigon, as well as in other cities throughout South Vietnam, big crowds of servicemen on Tet leave reported to the Saigon garrison headquarters, eager to get back to their units. Because of the lack of transportation, the JGS authorized all sector headquarters to employ these servicemen for immediate combat duties. The National Police Force, condescendingly called the "White Mice" by the Americans because of their white uniforms, threw the crack Viet Cong C-10 Sapper Battalion out of Saigon after numerous citywide street corner and alley battles. During February and March, the South Vietnamese lost about 5,000 men killed and 15,000 wounded, indicating the intensity of the fighting. The professionalism and steadfastness of ARVN during the Tet offensive surprised not only the enemy, but the Americans and themselves as well.

Not only did ARVN rise to unexpected heights, the people of South Vietnam responded to the Tet onslaughts with unforeseen courage and tenacity. Like a cold wind, the Tet offensive woke the South Vietnamese people from their lethargy. The initial bewilderment and terror gradually gave way to anger and self-assurance. To the city-dwellers, the war had exploded into their heretofore secure habitat, bringing them face to face with an enemy whom they had only heard about. Nevertheless, the urban people kept their faith in the Thieu government and its troops. Among the Communist prisoners of war, 90 percent said that they received no aid from the population, and only 2 percent reported unsolicited assistance.[16]

In the cities, the South Vietnamese rushed about to stay away from crossfire, but they did not panic. As their homes turned into battle positions behind which the intruders entrenched themselves, the urban population suddenly became conscious of their duties to defend not only themselves, but their nation. They could do this only by taking up weapons and joining in the fighting. Thus, the idea of a self-defense force took shape and became stronger as the South Vietnamese people not only refused to join the Communists, but fought against them.

The patriotic zeal unleashed in the South by the Tet offensive continued throughout the year. In June 1968, the National Assembly passed a far-reaching draft and mobilization law. The JGS estimated that the new law would produce about 268,000 additional soldiers by December 1968. What the JGS did not expect was that three months ahead of schedule nearly 90 percent of that quota had been met. The popular response to mobilization was unprecedented, and it overwhelmed the RVNAF processing and training facilities. By September, 240,000 draftees had beaten the deadline by volunteering or reporting to draft centers ahead of time. Among them, 161,000 were volunteers who enlisted in combat arms or service branches of their choice. Most remarkable was the fact that about half of that manpower consisted of urban youths, again an unprecedented record. The surge of volunteers and draftees was such that basic training had to be reduced from twelve to eight weeks. As a result of the mobilization law, 6 percent of the South Vietnamese population had become combatants in one way or another.

It was as if some fifteen million Americans had suddenly joined the colors.

In the cities across South Vietnam, especially in Saigon, the urban people beyond the draft age displayed a similar enthusiasm in organizing themselves for defense. Given their previous indifference to the war, this demonstration of patriotic fervor seemed incredible. Without being told or asked, they set up self-defense committees, organized fund drives to purchase barrier materiel, fenced off their own blocks with barbed wire, and took up guard duties at the only entrance gate to each block. At night, they became particularly vigilant, screening people coming in or going out, letting in only those people who lived in the block, and reporting all strangers to the police. In Saigon, the people were not satisfied to organize passively for defense. They wanted guns. And after some initial hesitation, the GVN gave them guns. The movement spread to other cities and villages, and thus, the People's Self-Defense movement came into being.

In terms of internal politics, the RVN also gained a resounding victory. The South Vietnamese people, with the enemy at their doorsteps, had made a clear-cut, political decision. They had unwaveringly opted for South Vietnamese government and against the Communists. Never before had the rapport between the people and the armed forces and the people and the government been so close. With Tet, the GVN had won a major battle for the hearts and minds of the South Vietnamese.

The Tet offensive and President Johnson's decisions produced by that attack had altered the strategy of the ground campaign in South Vietnam ("Westy's War") and had emasculated ROLLING THUNDER ("Oley's War"). As the first reports of the Tet fighting poured into MACV, the American operation which seemed most badly hurt was pacification. The estimates of the damage varied. The optimists stated that the program had been set back months or years, while the pessimists dolefully pronounced it dead forever. Of course, Tet dealt pacification a heavy blow. On 24 January 1968, one week before the Tet offensive, CORDS Hamlet Evaluation System showed that about 67 percent of the South Vietnamese villages and hamlets were "relatively secure." By the end of February the figure had declined to 60 percent.[17] Actually, the drop probably was much greater immediately after the onset of the enemy offensive. The South Vietnamese security forces evacuated the countryside to defend the towns, or they were bottled up fighting for their lives in their own villages. During the most severe fighting, thirty-six of the fifty-one ARVN battalions in direct support of pacification were shifted to the cities, and 480 of the 5,000 militia posts guarding the hamlets were overrun.[18]

But as the attacking Communist troops were killed or driven off, the momentum began to shift. Bob Komer was the first to perceive that for pacification the Tet offensive presented a great opportunity. As the Viet Cong casualties mounted, and as the VC political infrastructure surfaced, only to be destroyed, Komer began to push his CORDS people, the South Vietnamese officials, and the security troops back into the rural areas. By the end of February, eighteen of the ARVN battalions had returned to their pacification job. By the end of June 1968, the figure of "relatively secure" villages had risen to 63 percent. For the rest of 1968, the resurgent pacification program made spectacular progress against the Viet Cong, who, depleted in strength and low of morale, could not resist the CORDS and ARVN counteroffensive. By the end of 1968 the count of villages "relatively secure" reached 76 percent, with glittering prospects for continued success.[19]

The prospect for the negotiating prong also brightened. President Johnson's announcement in his speech of 31 March that United States bombing would be restrained to the southern part of the North Vietnamese panhandle (south of 20° North latitude) brought a prompt and unexpected reply from Hanoi. The Johnson administration had anticipated that the North Vietnamese would either ignore the American ploy or would condemn it with their usual venom. Instead the Politburo snapped at the bait. On 3 April, Hanoi made a public broadcast which, after bitterly criticizing the motives and actions of the United States, declared "its readiness to send its representative to make contact with a United States representative . . . so that talks could begin."[20] Hanoi's quick response had led some observers to believe that the Politburo was readying a negotiations proposal of its own when Johnson's proposal was tossed at them.

Again, it appeared that this most promising of openings to negotiations would be unwittingly blasted by the military. On 1 April, United States fighters struck Thanh Hoa, a key logistic and transfer point, just south of the 20th Parallel. This had been the original restraining line imposed by the president, but in his speech of 31 March, he had confused his audience by seeming to have set the line farther to the south. Fulbright and the other congressional doves promptly detonated, charging Johnson with bad faith and a desire to torpedo negotiations. Johnson, frightened by the effect this storm might have on the North Vietnamese, on 3 April lowered the restraining line to 19° North latitude. Round one of the negotiations went to the North Vietnamese by default.

From 3 April until 10 May 1968, the two parties tried to arrive at a mutually agreeable site for the parley. The United States proposed Geneva; the NVN ignored the proposal. Hanoi insisted on Phnom Penh, Cambodia; Washington demurred, saying that they had no embassy there. Next the Politburo nominated Warsaw; the administration refused this offer stating that to hold negotiations in a Communist capital would, in President Johnson's words, "stack the deck against us."[21] Finally, on 3 May the North Vietnamese proposed that the meetings be held in Paris and that representatives of both parties meet there on 10 May or a few days later. The North Vietnamese had shown an acute feel for the limit of Johnson's patience. Three days before Hanoi's proposal of Paris the president had held a lengthy discussion about resuming the bombing north of 19° North latitude and promised to decide the issue in a few days.

The period from 10 May until later October 1968 was marked by what was to become Hanoi's standard negotiating tactics—an obstinate unwillingness to get to "serious" negotiations, concealed in the usual Communist barrage of virulent propaganda and outlandish charges against the United States. The United States delegation stoically suffered the Communist abuse and tried doggedly to get the North Vietnamese down to business. The Americans offered to stop all bombing in North Vietnam if the enemy would agree to certain "understandings." These understandings, unwritten and unpublicized, were: 1. The NVN must accept the GVN as a party to the negotiations. 2. The NVN must refrain from ground and rocket attacks on the major cities of South Vietnam. 3. The NVN must not send troops across the DMZ or fire artillery from it. 4. The NVN would permit unarmed aerial reconnaissance over North Vietnam by United States forces. 5. Serious negotiations would immediately follow the bombing halt. The United States negotiators made it clear that any violation of these understandings would trigger a renewed air offensive against North Vietnam.[22]

Throughout the late summer and into the fall of 1968, the North Vietnamese delegation in typical Communist fashion haggled over each of the understandings. Just when it appeared that no progress was possible, presidential politics in the United States propelled all parties, the United States, North Vietnam, and South Vietnam, toward a terminal position. President Johnson and the Democrats wanted a complete bombing halt and the beginning of serious negotiations to help the uphill, but fast-closing, presidential campaign of Hubert Humphrey against Richard Nixon. The North Vietnamese, now alive to the nuances of United States domestic politics, also wanted a Humphrey victory, believing they could get better terms from the liberal Humphrey than from the anti-Communist Nixon. On the other hand, the South Vietnamese wanted a Nixon triumph, thinking that he would be more supportive of their position than Humphrey. While Nixon and the Republicans could not oppose a bombing halt and the opening of serious negotiations, they were well aware of the disadvantageous effect such a development would have on their campaign.

Johnson, after consulting the Cabinet, congressional leaders, the Joint Chiefs, Ambassador Bunker, and General Abrams (now in command in Saigon), announced on 31 October the cessation of bombing of all North Vietnam. As was to be expected, the South Vietnamese tried at the last minute to snag the whole procedure and, having failed, then refused to go along. Averill Harriman, the chief of the United States negotiating team, would later claim that the Republicans had counseled President Thieu to wait until after the election.[23] President Johnson himself made the same accusation.[24]

"Serious" negotiations, which were supposed to begin immediately after the bombing halt, predictably stalled. The negotiators did not get to the plenary sessions until 25 January 1969 and then nothing of consequence occurred—not then, not for months, and not for three-and-a-half years. Further, the North Vietnamese promptly violated the other "understandings" as well. They used the DMZ, they fired rockets into South Vietnamese cities, and they fired on unarmed American reconnaissance aircraft over North Vietnam.

Thus, round two went overwhelmingly to the Communists. They had lifted the bombing from North Vietnam at no cost to themselves. Later, the principal architects of the 31 October decision would themselves question its wisdom. Rostow, in a contrite defense of that decision, would later write, "Whether a longer perspective will judge Johnson's October 31 decision wise or unwise is moot. It can be recorded that at the time Johnson and his advisers judged it to be, in Abrams' phrase, 'the right thing to do.' "[25] Johnson himself questioned the soundness of his decision when he wrote, "Did I make a mistake in stopping most of the bombing of the North on October 31?"[26] Later, in December 1969, Johnson told President Nixon that "all the bombing pauses were a mistake."[27] The validity and motivation of Johnson's decision become even more doubtful when one considers that, on 29 October, the president directed General Abrams to make a maximum offensive effort in South Vietnam and to urge ARVN to do the same. In effect, the president, in a paradoxical action, pushed his ground force forward with one hand while pulling back his air arm with the other. History will probably judge that Johnson erred by stopping the bombing on 31 October, but the mistake itself will be less condemned than its blatantly political motivation.

More drivel has been written and televised about the siege of Khe Sanh than about any other episode of Indochina War II. First there was what Braestrup called the "Dien Bien Phu syndrome."[28] Reporters, both print and television, went to great lengths to report the similarities between the two tactical situations, and either directly or by inference forecast that Khe Sanh was doomed. Of course there *were* similarities. The NVA surrounded both garrisons with superior numbers. The enemy held the ground around the bases from which he could pour artillery and mortar fire on the French and American positions, and both garrisons depended entirely on air for resupply.

The differences between the two situations, usually overlooked by the pundits of the news media, outweighed the similarities. The two factors which had finally proved fatal to the French at Dien Bien Phu were Giap's superior artillery and mortar firepower and his ability to cut the aerial supply line into the garrison. Giap never had the firepower advantage at Khe Sanh, nor anything close to it. The Americans' combined air power and external artillery fire gave Westmoreland a tremendous predominance in destructive capacity. While Giap theoretically had the capacity to sever, or at least severely inhibit, air resupply to Khe Sanh, he never did so.

The second Khe Sanh myth circulated by the news media alleged, with no factual basis, that Giap viewed Khe Sanh as a strategic diversion to cover his attacks against the cities at Tet. A comparison of the numbers involved on both sides at Khe Sanh attests to the fallacy of this fable. Giap committed two divisions, the 304th and 325C, directly to the siege of Khe Sanh, a strength with supporting troops of around 20,000 to 25,000 men. In addition, Giap held two more NVA divisions, the 320th and part of the 324th, another 12,000 to 15,000 men, within supporting distance of the marine outpost (about twelve miles away). The marine garrison of four Marine battalions, reinforced by the 37th ARVN Ranger battalion, totaled only 6,000 men. In effect, then, Giap's alleged diversion consisted of some 32,000 to 40,000 NVA troops (and good ones at that) tying down 6,000 marines and ARVN Rangers. If Khe Sanh was an NVA diversion, military history provides few examples of one more expensive.

Ah, but the newsroom and ivory-towered generals counter, these figures are simplistically misleading. They contend that from 20,000 to 45,000 other United States troops were tied down in reserve, supporting Khe Sanh. This is nonsense. The American troops in northern I Corps Zone were not in support of Khe Sanh, nor were they tied down in reserve. These troops were fighting along the DMZ and in the populated coastal plains.

The news agencies immortalized a third myth—that the fighting at Khe Sanh was fiercer and the American casualties heavier than in any other battle of Indochina War II. Actually, the fighting at Khe Sanh was lighter than at Hue, Saigon, and several other points in Vietnam during the Tet offensive. The American casualties at Khe Sanh totaled 205 KIA and 852 wounded, a daily average of three killed and twelve wounded, much less than the losses suffered by units of comparable size in normal combat operations.

Finally, the news media hammered on its most cherished fable—the doom of Khe Sanh. Walter Cronkite in his lugubrious analysis on 27 February 1968—the one President Johnson said cost him middle America—forecast that "Khe Sanh could well fall, with terrible loss in American lives, prestige, and morale."[29] Other reporters and telecasters echoed this prestigious voice of doom. The truth was that Khe Sanh was never in danger of falling, nor did any officer in authority from marine Col. David E. Lownds, the Khe Sanh commander, to Westmoreland ever hold any such thoughts.

Now that the myths about Khe Sanh have been disposed of, a factual examination of the NVA siege of the marine combat base can be made. There were two reasons why the marines were in this isolated outpost. The post at Khe Sanh served as a patrol base from which to control Highway 9, which leads from Laos into Quang Tri province. True, Highway 9 was only a broken-up track, and the enemy could just walk around the base, but the detour did complicate his logistic operations. The second reason the marines were in Khe Sanh was that Westmoreland wanted it as a potential base, in fact, the only available base, from which he could mount a corps-size operation into Laos to cut the Ho Chi Minh Trail around the critical choke-point of Tchepone. Not only did it sit on Highway 9, which could be repaired for use as an American supply road, but Khe Sanh had an airstrip capable of handling C-123's and C-130's, the logistical workhorses of the sky.

Why, some critics ask, didn't Westmoreland pull the marines out of Khe Sanh, a vulnerable base, when he saw the NVA divisions heading for it? First, of course, there were Westmoreland's original reasons for putting the marines into Khe Sanh, that is, its usefulness as a base to control Highway 9 and as a platform for future offensive operations into Laos. Second, neither Westmoreland nor Lieutenant General Cushman, the marine commander in South Vietnam, ever believed that the North Vietnamese could overrun the marines at Khe Sanh. Further, Westmoreland saw Khe Sanh as an opportunity to use to the optimum his greatest asset—his tremendous firepower. The area was isolated and uninhabited. There were no RVN activities in the area requiring coordination with RVN officials. Here was the place to use his firepower against Giap's weakness—the need to mass his troops to overrun the base. Lastly, Westmoreland wanted to fight the enemy at Khe Sanh where the situation favored him rather than in the populated coastal areas where conditions negated the Allied firepower advantage.

Knowing Westmoreland's reasons for holding Khe Sanh, what were Giap's reasons for wanting it? Only one credible reason exists. Giap meant Khe Sanh to be Phase III, the culmination of the Great Offensive-Great Uprising. A brief review of the assumptions of Giap's ambitious plan for his offensive shows the place Khe Sanh was to play in it. In Phase I of the plan (late fall 1967), United States forces were to be drawn into the peripheries of South Vietnam by a series of attacks along the borders of the country. Giap's Phase II (the Tet offensive) foresaw the attacks on the cities which would bring about the disintegration of ARVN and the rallying of the South Vietnamese people to the Viet Cong banners. This sudden shift of allegiance would overthrow the Thieu government and isolate the American forces in their bases. By this time, according to Giap's plan, the United States troops would be confused, hemmed in, and demoralized, thereby setting the stage for Giap's final blow. Then would come Phase III. Giap would overwhelm Khe Sanh with two, three, or four NVA divisions, ending the war with a stunning military victory.

The battle of Khe Sanh actually began in *late* November 1967. During that period, United States intelligence started to receive reports that several NVA divisions in North Vietnam were beginning to move south *within North Vietnam*. By late December it had become apparent to United States intelligence agencies that two of these divisions, the 325C and the 304th, were headed for the Khe Sanh area. One other NVA division, the 320th, and one regiment of the 324th division were moving to within easy supporting distance of the NVA troops at Khe Sanh.

The first actual contact around Khe Sanh took place on the night of 2 January when a marine patrol contacted a North Vietnamese patrol near one of Khe Sanh's outposts. The marines killed five of the six-man patrol. They turned out to be an NVA regimental commander and his staff on preliminary reconnaissance of the marine positions. By 20 January, intelligence officers in MACV and in General Cushman's head-quarters at the III Marine Amphibious Force (III MAF) knew that Giap had closed two NVA divisions (304 and 325C) in the vicinity of Khe Sanh. On that same day, marine Col. Kenneth Houghton (later major general), then G-2, III MAF, and I visited Khe Sanh and talked to the commander there, Col. David E. Lownds, USMC, and a few of his staff. At first, Colonel Lownds, although aware of the intelligence, did not believe that two NVA divisions had already encircled Khe Sanh. He believed that there were enemy troops "out there," but in no great strength. As Houghton and I started to fly out of Khe Sanh, there occurred some unusual activity at the end of the runway, and word came back that an NVA officer deserter had surrendered to a marine outpost. He told his interrogators that he belonged to the 325C Division and that they were going to attack the marine outposts on Hills 881N and 861, and the combat base itself, that night. The NVA deserter told the marines

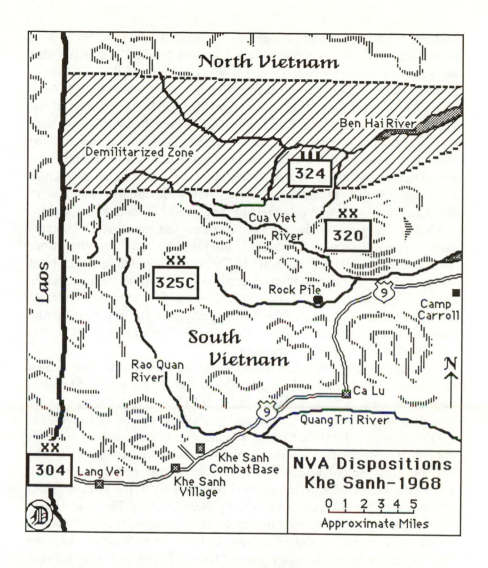

North Vietnam

Ben Hai River

Demilitarized Zone

324

Cua Viet
River

320

325C

Rock Pile

9

Camp
Carroll

Laos

South
Vietnam

Rao Quan
River

N

Ca Lu

9

Quang Tri River

304   Lang Vei

Khe Sanh
Combat Base

Khe Sanh
Village

**NVA Dispositions
Khe Sanh-1968**

0 1 2 3 4 5

Approximate Miles

that not only was his division, the 325C, around Khe Sanh, but that
the 304th NVA Division was there too. On receipt of this information,
Lownds turned to Houghton and myself (we had debarked from the
aircraft), and asked, "Any suggestions?" Houghton and I looked around
at the tents, fuel ammunition dumps, and command post—all above
ground and unprotected—and, as one man, said, "Start digging."

I returned to Saigon late that afternoon (20 January) and briefed

General Westmoreland and his deputy, General Abrams, on my visit to Khe Sanh. Part of the report detailed Lownds' initial skepticism that he was surrounded by two NVA divisions, in spite of the fact that he and his marine superiors held the intelligence upon which both MACV and III MAF had known the enemy was there. The description of the unprotected installations at Khe Sanh and the general lack of preparation to withstand heavy concentrations of artillery and mortar fire agitated General Westmoreland. Finally, he turned to Abrams and heatedly said something to the effect that he (Westmoreland) had lost confidence in Cushman's ability to handle the increasingly threatening situation in his (Cushman's) area. Westmoreland concluded his remarks by saying, "Abe, you're going to have to go up there and take over." Abrams said, "Yeah, I guess you're right," his response most unenthusiastic. Thus was confirmed the concept of MACV Forward, which, under General Abrams, controlled United States operations in the two northern provinces from 13 February to 10 March 1968. General Westmoreland notes in his diary under 20 January (the date I briefed him on my visit to Khe Sanh), "I finally decided to establish MACV Forward at Hue/Phu Bai and put General Abrams in command."

Actually, faulty command arrangements in the marines' tactical area of responsibility (which coincided with the ARVN I Corps area) played at least as large a role in the crisis as did Cushman's competence or lack thereof, and this faulty command setup must be laid on Westmoreland's doorstep. The III MAF area was the largest and the most complex combat area in South Vietnam. In the two northern provinces (Quang Tri and Thua Thien) a full-scale conventional war between American and North Vietnamese divisions was being fought. In the three southern provinces of the marines' area (Quang Nam, Quang Tin, and Quang Ngai) the most virulent form of the combination of insurgency and conventional war in Vietnam was underway. In fact, the bulk of the Vietnam War lay in the marines' diverse area. United States and Allied forces in the III MAF area outnumbered their enemy by a ratio of only about three to one, in contrast to the Army Field Force areas further south where the ratio ran about six or seven to one. In 1967 the marine area had yielded about half the enemy killed and in turn suffered nearly half of the friendly KIA's.

To complicate matters, a spur of the Annamite chain cut the northern area off from the southern area just north of Da Nang. The only ground route over the spur ran through the infamous Hai Van Pass, the scene of scores of demolitions and ambushes going back to the French/Vietminh war. As a further complication, Cushman commanded not just marines, but two army divisions, and one army infantry brigade plus assorted support troops from all the services, and had to advise the ARVN corps commander as well as coordinate operations with him.

What was needed was at least one, and perhaps two, corps headquarters between III MAF (to be elevated to army-level command) and the marine and army divisions in the field. One such headquarters would handle the conventional war in the north and the other the unconventional war in the south. Westmoreland should have anticipated the need for this alteration since at least mid-1967. Now with the crunch on him, his only solution was to superimpose Abrams over Cushman—in effect to supplant Cushman with Abrams in the two northern provinces.

Westmoreland revealed his lack of confidence in Cushman by his selection of his four-star classmate, Abrams, to command MACV Forward, which was actually a corps headquarters, a three-star command. If Westmoreland had had great confidence in Cushman, he would have placed MACV Forward under a two-star or three-star U.S. Army or Marine Corps general who was junior, and thus subordinate, to Cushman. Several outstanding U.S. Army and Marine Corps generals were available in Vietnam and could have done the job. Several more, thoroughly qualified for the position, were in the United States and could have been flown into Vietnam within twenty-four hours. But Westmoreland availed himself of none of the officers junior to Cushman because such an arrangement would have left Cushman in overall command, and that Westmoreland would not accept.

General Westmoreland's establishment of MACV Forward with authority over General Cushman and the marines in the two northern provinces raised a storm of protest within the marine corps and a flurry of hostile and speculative comment by the news media. Westmoreland promptly held a press conference in which he denied that he had lost confidence in Cushman and for that reason had placed Abrams over him. Westmoreland privately condemned the press, writing in his diary under 23 January, "The conduct of the press is another example of their tendency to . . . create confusion in the ranks, embarrass the command or do anything possible to fragment the essential integrity of the command." The truth was that the news media and the marines were close to the mark. Westmoreland, however, avers to this day that he did not "lose confidence" in Cushman, but adds, candidly, that he was "dissatisfied" with Cushman's efforts during Tet.

One must assume that to Westmoreland dissatisfaction did not amount to loss of confidence. Beyond that, Westmoreland desired to protect and succor Cushman, a decent and honorable man, a conscientious officer, but one who was struggling to command the most far-flung, difficult, and complex area in South Vietnam. Above Westmoreland's consideration for Cushman, he realized he had to fight a major battle against Giap, and he certainly did not want a concurrent one with the United States Marine Corps. The controversy swirled around for three or four weeks, and then when Westmoreland replaced MACV Forward with an army corps which he placed *under* Cushman's command, the matter died.

True to the predictions of the NVA deserter on 20 January, the enemy struck Khe Sanh and its outposts at 0530, 21 January. The Communist troops hammered the marine positions with rocket, artillery, mortar, and small-arms fire. The ammunition depot and the fuel supplies blew up. There was a fierce fight on Hill 861 which the marines finally cleared with heavy casualties on both sides. On that same day, an NVA battalion overran Khe Sanh village, which was about two miles from the base.

On 21 January, General Westmoreland ordered Operation NIAGARA to be executed. This operation, which had been in the planning and reconnaissance stage since early January, envisioned that Khe Sanh would be defended not only by the marine garrison, but by a mighty waterfall of firepower composed of B-52's, tactical air, artillery, and mortars. This awesome striking power would be targeted by an expanded intelligence effort utilizing all intelligence collection devices, including the newly arrived acoustic and seismic sensors.

One aspect of Operation NIAGARA kicked over another hornet's nest between Westmoreland and the marines. To coordinate the tactical air operations around Khe Sanh and in the DMZ, General Westmoreland designated a "single manager" (his words) to control all tactical aircraft operating in the Khe Sanh area, including those of the air force, the marines, and on occasion, the navy. He appointed as his single manager his deputy for air, Gen. William W. Momyer, USAF, CG Seventh Air Force. With this appointment, the marine corps, from Khe Sanh to the Pentagon—to use their salty expression—"went through the overhead."

The commandant of the marine corps, General Chapman, sought to get the Joint Chiefs of Staff to overturn Westmoreland's decision. Chapman charged that the arrangement violated marine corps doctrine and interservice agreements. The army and navy Chiefs, fearful of losing control over their own aviation assets, supported the marines. The row soon grew bitter and emotional, fueled by the marines' historic phobia of being taken over by another service. General Westmoreland, normally the most unemotional of men, reacted in kind to the marine attacks. He "backchanneled" General Wheeler that if the JCS intended to reverse his decision, he wanted to appear personally before them to explain his problems of air control and his solution to these problems. Westmoreland felt so strongly over this issue that he later wrote that this was the only occasion "that arose during my service in Vietnam to prompt me to consider resigning."[30] Whether as a result of this threat, or for other reasons, Westmoreland's arrangement prevailed. Although Westmoreland's concept was to be implemented on 10 March, it did not become effective until 1 April, long after the threat to Khe Sanh had vanished.

On Khe Sanh combat base, Colonel Lownds neither knew nor cared about the dispute between the generals over control of marine air power. He needed help, and on 22 January, General Cushman ordered the 1st Battalion, 9th Marines, to Khe Sanh, where Lownds had them establish positions southwest of the base. On 27 January, the ARVN 37th Ranger Battalion reported to Khe Sanh and was positioned along the eastern edge of the defense perimeter. On 5 February, an enemy battalion attacked Hill 861A in concert with heavy shelling of the combat base. The NVA unit penetrated the defensive perimeter of the marine outpost on 861A, but the marines counterattacked and drove the Communists out of the position, killing over 100 of them.

On 7 February, the Special Forces camp at Lang Vei, five miles southwest of Khe Sanh, was destroyed by an NVA battalion using Russian PT-76 light tanks, the first enemy use of armor in South Vietnam. On 8 February, a combat outpost of the 1st Battalion, 9th Marines, southwest of Khe Sanh, was partially overrun by an NVA battalion. Marine counterattacks, supported by heavy artillery fire, restored the position and killed 150 NVA soldiers. Giap's plan for the reduction of the marine combat base was now evident. The 325C Division would drive in the marine outposts to the north of the base and attack the camp from the north and west. The 304th Division would attack along the axis of Lang Vei/

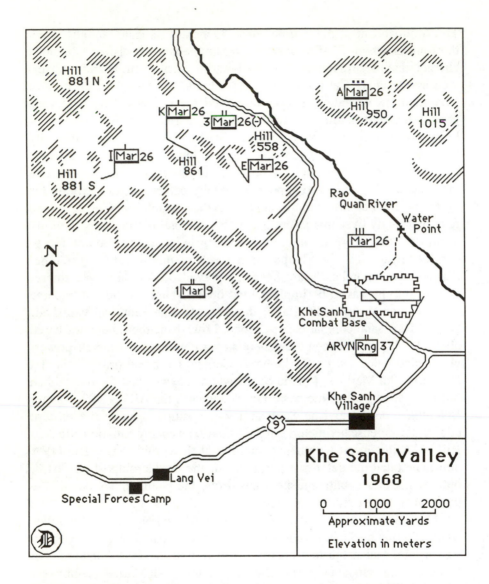

Hill
881 N

K Mar 26
3 Mar 26 (-)

A Mar 26
Hill
950

Hill
1015

I Mar 26

Hill
861

Hill
558

E Mar 26

Hill
881 S

Rao
Quan River

Water
Point

Mar 26

N

1 Mar 9

Khe Sanh
Combat Base

ARVN Rng 37

Khe Sanh
Village

9

**Khe Sanh Valley
1968**

0   1000   2000

Approximate Yards

Elevation in meters

Lang Vei

Special Forces Camp

Khe Sanh village and then make a final assault on the base from the south and the east.

But something went wrong with the plan. Around 10 February, Giap began to withdraw NVA units from the Khe Sanh area and from other portions of the DMZ to reinforce his beleaguered troops at Hue. Two battalions of the 29th Regiment of the NVA 325C Division and the entire 24th Regiment of the NVA 304th Division were moved from Khe Sanh to Hue, a total of five battalions.[31] From 8 to 22 February, the NVA continued their pressure on Khe Sanh combat base using artillery, mortars, machine guns, and snipers, but there were no major ground assaults. On 23 February, Khe Sanh combat base received the record number of incoming rounds for a single day—1,307. Colonel Lownds believed that a major NVA ground assault was imminent, and he was right.

During the early evening hours of 29 February, the acoustic and seismic sensors along Highway 9 indicated a major troop movement by the NVA 304th Division toward the combat base from the east. Immediately the fire support control center called for maximum fire against the area. The resulting United States firepower was in truth a NIAGARA of explosives and steel as artillery, radar-equipped fighters, and B-52 bombers struck at the NVA attackers. At 2130 on 29 February, a battalion of the NVA 304th Division assaulted the area held by the ARVN 37th Ranger Battalion. Hit by the concentrated American firepower, the attack was smashed before it got to the defensive wire. A second attempt by another NVA battalion at 2330 was similarly destroyed. A final attack launched at 0315, 1 March, met the same fate. This regimental-size attack was the largest ground assault of the Khe Sanh siege.

This NVA attack on the night of 29 February–1 March marked the turning point of the siege. Although the NVA troops continued to harass the marines, the enemy never again mounted a sizable attack against the base or its outposts. On 6 March, the NVA began to withdraw from Khe Sanh, and on 10 March, the enemy stopped repairing their trenches.[32] From then on it was the marines and the ARVN Rangers who were making forays into the NVA positions. By 11 March, the enemy units were all in movement away from Khe Sanh, and although some enemy artillery and mortar fire would harass the base until 30 March, the siege of Khe Sanh ended in effect in early March.

On 1 April, Operation PEGASUS, a combined relief force of marines and troopers of the 1st U.S. Air Cavalry Division, began operations toward Khe Sanh. By 8 April the relieving force contacted the Khe Sanh defenders, and shortly thereafter Colonel Lownds and his 6,000 marines and ARVN Rangers left the base. The siege was lifted; the marines' ordeal was over.

*   *   *

The siege of Khe Sanh is unique not only because the news media put out so much misinformation about it, but because it is *the* battle of Indochina War II which most perplexes those who study it. Peter Braestrup, in his book *The Big Story* (an excellent coverage of the battle of Khe Sanh), first noted the peculiar inconsistencies in Giap's conduct of the battle. He points out that Giap brought to the Khe Sanh area too many troops just to isolate the combat base, and yet he never made a serious effort to take it. Braestrup speculates that the tremendous United States firepower at Khe Sanh and the tenacity of the marines convinced Giap that he did not want to risk enough troops to "overwhelm Khe Sanh by sheer force, heedless of losses."[33] Braestrup notes also that Giap never attempted to mass 37 mm or .50 caliber antiaircraft machine guns off the Khe Sanh runway, which would have imperiled the aerial resupply of the combat base. Braestrup concluded that "the enemy's performance at Khe Sanh remains a mystery."[34]

A reexamination of the facts partially raises this pall of mystery, but in other respects only deepens it. Here is the key information bearing on Giap's intentions at Khe Sanh:

1. In December 1967 and early January 1968, Giap sent to the Khe Sanh area three NVA divisions (the 304th, 325C, and 320th) and one regiment of a fourth division, the 324th, which acted in a supply and support role to the other three. The 304th and 325C Divisions had tanks with them and were supported by two artillery regiments, the 68th and 164th. This force was too strong to be a diversion at Khe Sanh, too strong even if Giap intended only to isolate the combat base. As of 20 January, Giap obviously intended to overrun Khe Sanh and its marine defenders.

2. Enemy actions from 21 January to around 10 February support this hypothesis. During that period, he made five battalion-size assaults against the outposts covering the base to include Lang Vei and Khe Sanh village. This is precisely the action of a besieger who hopes to take the high ground commanding the combat base and to sever the ground lines of communication into it. Indeed, one can find the exact counterpart of these operations at Dien Bien Phu. There was one difference, however. At Dien Bien Phu, the French outposts fell; at Khe Sanh only the outposts of Lang Vei and Khe Sanh village were overrun, and neither was critical to the defense of the base.

3. There is an intriguing series of intelligence reports which indirectly

support the theory that Giap intended a culminating offensive at Khe Sanh. Shortly after the Communist attacks on the South Vietnamese cities of 30 January 1968, a major enemy headquarters set up shop in the limestone caves of the DMZ just northwest of Khe Sanh. Aerial photographs revealed intense vehicular activity in the area and even showed a bank of radio antennas near the cave entrance, and shortly thereafter, prisoners of war reported the presence of a large headquarters in the cave complex. The more senior POW's told their interrogators that Giap himself was directing operations from the cave. Starting in early February, the Seventh United States Air Force bombed the headquarters complex repeatedly. On one occasion, falling rocks and debris sealed the entrance, but the Communists quickly reopened it. Finally, as the battle for Khe Sanh turned against the Communists, the activity of the headquarters lessened. Then, while the headquarters remained in its subterranean location for many weeks, its importance faded into insignificance.

Was Giap himself directing operations from the cave headquarters? Only he and a few other Communists know. O'Neill, who relates the story in his book, doubts it. He writes that "On the face of things it seems most unlikely that a commander in chief would absent himself from the only headquarters (Hanoi) from which he could control the whole of his army's activities."[35] He goes on to say, however, that if Khe Sanh had been a North Vietnamese victory, that Giap's immediate control of operations from the DMZ might have become public knowledge. While O'Neill's point that Giap had to be in a headquarters from which he could direct the whole campaign has obvious validity, two pieces of intelligence suggest that in fact Giap *was* in the cave headquarters. First, at Dien Bien Phu, Giap *did* set up his headquarters near that battlefield and personally directed operations from a forward command post there. He did not stay in Hanoi in 1954, although important and delicate military operations were then in progress throughout the whole of Vietnam. There is a second, and perhaps more relevant, piece of evidence indicating Giap's presence near Khe Sanh. An intelligence report reveals that Giap was not seen in Hanoi between 2 September 1967 and 5 February 1968. While these dates may be skewed, Giap was absent from Hanoi for a significant period while the cave headquarters was in operation. The best guess is that Giap was in the cave and that he planned a Phase III battle at Khe Sanh.

4. Between 8 February, when the NVA attacked the outposts of the 9th Marines, and about 10 February, when Giap began to send troops from Khe Sanh to Hue, something caused Giap to change his mind about overrunning the combat base. Only speculations are available. The most common of these holds that Giap intended Khe Sanh to be the climactic battle of his campaign, which was to follow the successful execution of his Phase II (the attack on the cities). Giap realized in early February, however, that Phase II had failed abjectly. The necessary foundation for his climactic Phase III battle, therefore, had failed to materialize, so he changed his mind about overrunning Khe Sanh.

Allied with the above speculation is the one which hypothesizes that what really forced Giap to change his mind about Khe Sanh was the resolute defense of the marines and particularly the immense and destructive firepower generated by Westmoreland's Operation NIAGARA. Those who advance this theory speculate that Giap realized that he had at Khe Sanh an unsolvable dilemma. The tenacity of the marines had shown him that he would have to mass his troops to overrun the combat base. And yet, if he massed his troops, he exposed them to almost certain destruction by the massive American firepower. In short, barring an unlikely fluke, Giap could not take Khe Sanh, even if he was willing to pay dearly for it. Once Giap reached his decision, he looked for another place to use the troops he had positioned at Khe Sanh, and he chose Hue, the only place in South Vietnam where he had any success in Phase II.

There is a final hypothesis to account for Giap's change of intentions at Khe Sanh. While it is bizarre and highly speculative, many believe that it was the real reason Giap backed off. First, a short history of a little known event in the Tet offensive: Shortly after Khe Sanh was invested, Westmoreland organized at MACV a secret staff group to consider the use of small atomic munitions around Khe Sanh. In his memoirs, Westmoreland gave his rationale for his consideration of such employment: "Because the region around Khe Sanh was virtually uninhabited, civilian casualties would be minimal. If Washington officials were so intent on 'sending a message' to Hanoi, surely small tactical nuclear weapons would be a way to tell Hanoi something, just as two atomic bombs had spoken convincingly to Japanese officials during World War II and the threat of atomic bombs induced the North Koreans to accept meaningful negotiations."[36]

During early February, the president himself gave some thought to the use of atomic munitions in Vietnam. He asked General Wheeler if he (the president) was going to have to make any decision on this desperate measure. Wheeler assured him that he would not have to do so, but at the president's request Wheeler asked Westmoreland the question. To the consternation of both Wheeler and the president, Westmoreland replied that nuclear weapons or chemical agents *might* have to be employed at Khe Sanh.

While the possible employment of atomic bombs or shells disturbed President Johnson, it panicked the doves both in and out of the government. True to fashion, they promptly leaked it to the press, which on 9 February (note that date) featured the story that Westmoreland had asked permission to use atomic munitions at Khe Sanh.[37] The press reports and the furor in Congress forced the president to tell Wheeler to instruct Westmoreland to cease such planning immediately.

At the time (and long afterward), both Westmoreland's nuclear initiative and the Washington reaction to it looked like a typical case of overkill. But to Giap it must have appeared as something much more ominous. From his struggle at Dien Bien Phu he remembered Operation VULTURE, the plan proposed by Admiral Radford to have American aircraft relieve the French garrison by dropping atomic bombs on Giap's encircling forces. Giap must have reasoned that if the Americans were proposing the use of atomic bombs in 1954 to break his encirclement of the French, they would be much more likely to use them in 1968 to save their own troops.

In this speculation Giap was probably right. The loss of Khe Sanh and its 6,000-man garrison would have sparked within the United States a political and psychological explosion of massive proportions. President Johnson knew this, and for this reason in early 1968 the fate of Khe Sanh became and remained his primary concern. He had relief maps made of the area, and rumor has it that he forced the individual members of the JCS to sign statements that Khe Sanh could be held. If the fall of the marine base became imminent, Johnson could not stand by and see it happen. Something would have to be done, and that might include drastic measures—even, *in extremis,* the use of atomic weapons. What had been clear to Westmoreland was clear to Giap. The situation at Khe Sanh was almost ideal for the employment of nuclear weapons. The area was remote and, in February 1968, free of noncombatants.

American intelligence had consistently pinpointed the location of the NVA troops, and if Giap massed for an assault, he provided the United States forces with an ideal atomic target.

The more far-reaching implication of even the possibility of American use of atomic munitions at Khe Sanh frightened the North Vietnamese Politburo. Certainly, the American employment of atomic munitions presaged the advent of a totally different war. Would the Americans restrict their use to South Vietnam? Would they "nuke" the dikes along the Red River, or the vast Communist base areas in unpopulated Cambodia, or the choke-points along the Ho Chi Minh Trail? If the United States adopted such a drastic step as the use of atomic munitions at Khe Sanh, would they not undertake a less drastic step—an invasion of North Vietnam, or Laos, or Cambodia?

And finally, the possibility that the United States would use atomic weapons must have thoroughly alarmed the Russians and the Chinese. Could these Communist giants stand idly by while the United States battered their small ally with nuclear weapons? But their entrance into the Vietnam War, either directly or indirectly, would almost surely bring on World War III. For what? A small marine garrison of 6,000 men, whose obliteration would decide nothing, not even in the Vietnam War. The risk of a vast escalation of that conflict into a nuclear war, even if that was a remote possibility, was not worth it. And so, about 10–12 February, the preliminary assaults to drive in the outposts ceased; and the cessation of these necessary preliminary attacks indicated that Giap's determination to overrun Khe Sanh had crumbled—the victim of marine resolution, NIAGARA firepower, or Westmoreland's aborted nuclear study.

Giap indirectly confirmed these speculations in his interview with Oriana Fallaci. She asked him, "Am I mistaken, General, or did you already try a second Dien Bien Phu at Khe Sanh." Giap answered, "Oh no, Khe Sanh didn't try to be, nor could it have been, a Dien Bien Phu. Khe Sanh wasn't that important to us. Or it was only to the extent that it was important to the Americans—in fact at Khe Sanh their prestige was at stake."[38] The words "important" and "prestige" are the significant words in Giap's answer, the clue that he thought the Americans would stop at nothing to save Khe Sanh and their national pride and prestige.

While the above analysis may clarify some of the mystery surrounding

Giap's shifting intentions at Khe Sanh, his motives behind other strange NVA actions remain enigmas. After Giap's decision of 10–12 February not to overrun Khe Sanh, he continued to waste men and materiel in purposeless operations. On 23 February, the base received a record number of incoming mortar and artillery rounds—1,307. On 29 February–1 March, the NVA launched their largest attack of the siege, a regimental assault on the perimeter held by the ARVN 37th Ranger Battalion, which was smashed by B-52, tactical air, and artillery strikes. The mortar and artillery attack of 23 February can be explained as an attempt to exploit the lugubrious media coverage of Khe Sanh. By that date the Politburo could see that their Great Offensive-Great Uprising had failed in Vietnam, but had achieved an unexpected psychological success in the United States. So for a few hundred mortar and artillery rounds, the enemy kept the American media prophets of gloom-and-doom in business. On the other hand, the NVA firepower demonstration may have been nothing more than a logistical solution to their ammunition problem. They knew they were going to withdraw; they didn't want to leave the ammunition, yet they could not move it. The solution—shoot it up.

The purpose of the regimental attack of 29 February–1 March is more difficult to fathom. The purpose was not to take the combat base. One NVA regiment (the attacking force) could not do that. One reason for the attack might have been that the NVA felt that the assault would increase the distorted and depressed media coverage that Khe Sanh's demise was imminent. On 27 February, Walter Cronkite had prophesied Khe Sanh's fall to the American people. But to sacrifice a regiment to news media "hype" makes no sense. Was the choice to attack the ARVN unit a clue? No doubt Giap thought the ARVN Rangers would be an easier target than the United States Marines, but not much easier, for the ARVN Rangers were an elite unit, no pushovers. Perhaps Giap's attack on the rangers had some political motivation. A successful penetration of the ranger perimeter would have embarrassed both the South Vietnamese and the Americans.

The most valid explanation of this useless and bloody attack is a strictly military one: Giap used the attack on the rangers to cover his disengagement and withdrawal from Khe Sanh which began in early March. This is one of the standard tactical methods to cover a withdrawal. But under the circumstances existing in Khe Sanh in early March, there would appear to have been no reason to use this tactic. So the purpose of Giap's regimental attack against the ARVN Rangers remains one of Khe Sanh's mysteries.

There are other enigmas which eclipse this one, however. The first of these riddles arises from Giap's shift of troops from the Khe Sanh area to Hue on or about 10–12 February. He moved five battalions, almost one-third of the infantry strength investing the Khe Sanh combat base. But why only five battalions? If by 10 February he had decided not to overrun the marines at Khe Sanh, why not send at least one NVA division from Khe Sanh to Hue? In mid-February, one more NVA division would have made the task of the Americans and South Vietnamese at Hue far more difficult and costly. Indeed, General Abrams, from his vantage point at MACV Forward (near the DMZ), told Braestrup in January 1969 that if the NVA had shifted one whole division to Hue in early February 1968, "we would still be fighting there."[39] So Giap kept too many troops at Khe Sanh just to threaten it, and too few to overrun it. At the same time he sent too few troops to Hue to influence the battle there. The mystery remains.

The last mystery of Khe Sanh revolves around Giap's refusal to strike at the greatest vulnerability of the combat base—its water supply. And this enigma provides not one mystery, but two. Westmoreland, Maj. Gen. Rathvon McC. Tompkins, the commanding general, 3d Marine Division, whose troops occupied Khe Sanh, and Sir Robert Thompson (the British counterinsurgency expert) all state that the marines depended for water on the small Rao Quan River which rose in the NVA-held hills north of the combat base, and that the marine water-point was beyond the marines' defensive perimeter.[40] Since the enemy did control the water supply of the marine base, why didn't the NVA shut it off by contamination or by other means? The simplest explanation—and probably the most valid—is that neither Giap nor the local NVA commander ever realized the vulnerability of the marines' water supply. Stranger oversights have happened in war. General Tompkins tends to support this explanation.

If the NVA *did* realize the tenuous nature of the marines' water supply, why didn't they shut it off? Benevolence on the part of the NVA for the marines can be ruled out. It is within the Rules of Land Warfare to poison the stream. The Geneva Protocol of 1925, which the North Vietnamese ratified in 1957, permits the chemical pollution of a stream, provided the stream is used only by military personnel. Since the Bru tribesmen (the only local inhabitants) evacuated the Khe Sanh area early in the siege, the stream served no civilians and could have been poisoned. If the NVA knew about the vulnerability of the marines' water supply, they deliberately refused to shut it off. Why would Giap and the NVA forego such a critical advantage?

Linked to the water mystery is another perplexity about the NVA's conduct of operations at Khe Sanh. That mystery is, why did not the enemy try harder to shut down or severely restrict the American aerial resupply operations which sustained Khe Sanh? Braestrup noted that the NVA made no effort to mass .50 caliber machine guns off the runway, or to use 37 mm antiaircraft against the aerial approach routes (as they later did in the A-Shau valley).[41] If Giap had shut off the water supply, thereby forcing the marines to fly water into the garrison, and if he had concurrently taken action to drastically limit aerial resupply operations, the situation of the marine combat base would have been precarious. General Tompkins is quoted by Pisor (in his book about Khe Sanh) as saying that the marines could not have kept the base supplied if they had been forced to fly in water;[42] however, in a letter to me, General Tompkins stated that he believed then (and now) that the marines could have been supplied adequately by air (including water).

At the very least, a combination of shutting off the water supply and restricting incoming aerial flights would have made the logistic support of the garrison difficult and costly. At the worst, it would have forced Westmoreland and the marine commanders to launch a premature and bloody relief expedition to extricate the garrison at Khe Sanh. No consideration would have been given to any attempt to evacuate the marines at Khe Sanh by air or overland after the siege began, since any such effort would have resulted in heavy marine casualties. A single reinforced marine regiment cannot fight its way on foot through two or three NVA divisions when the latter have the initiative, superior numbers, and every terrain advantage. An air evacuation could probably have lifted out half of the garrison, but the half which remained behind would have been sacrificed.

When one couples Giap's refusal to take advantage of the vulnerability of the marines' water supply with his reluctance to make an all-out attack on the aerial resupply system, an observer is forced to the conclusion, again, that somewhere around 10 February Giap decided that he did not want to take Khe Sanh. The reason for this decision is the key mystery of Khe Sanh from the NVA side.

The final mystery of Khe Sanh lies on the American side. With the base's water supply so vulnerable, why did the American command elect to hold Khe Sanh? Westmoreland's strategic rationale for holding Khe Sanh has been given earlier in this chapter, but the exposed nature of the marines' water supply puts the question in a different light. I raised this question with General Westmoreland and he said that he did not know about the vulnerable nature of the marines' water supply at Khe Sanh until the NVA divisions had surrounded the base, and then he thinks he learned of it from his scientific adviser at MACV, not from the marines. By the time he knew about the vulnerability of Khe Sanh's water supply, evacuation of the garrison by air or overland was impossible.

Westmoreland's statement only raises other questions. Why didn't General Cushman, General Tompkins, or even Colonel Lownds tell Westmoreland about the hazards of Khe Sanh's water supply? General Tompkins wrote me that he knew as early as November 1967 that the base's water supply point lay 500 yards north of the outer defensive perimeter. He states also that he never informed General Westmoreland, Cushman, or Abrams about the location of the water-point. From his letter one gains the impression that General Tompkins considered that the location of the base's water-point constituted no major vulnerability. He wrote, "Had the water-point been occupied by the enemy, we would have had to drive him out and extend our position to include it." Actually, the water supply problem at Khe Sanh was bigger than the vulnerability of the water supply point. If the enemy contaminated the stream or diverted it, control of the location of the water point would have been meaningless. In the final analysis, however, General Tompkins was right—the marines' water supply constituted no major vulnerability.

But the water supply problem at Khe Sanh deserves at least a footnote in history because it casts a shadow over Westmoreland's handling of the situation there. If one overlooks the water supply problem, Westmoreland's determination to hold Khe Sanh with one marine regiment, thereby pinning down two or three NVA divisions, was a superb tactical decision. His employment and coordination of United States air and artillery firepower to hold a fortress whose garrison is vastly outnumbered by its besiegers was innovative and masterful. Khe Sanh has always appeared to be Westmoreland's finest tactical hour. Now one must ask if Westmoreland's success at Khe Sanh resulted from his own tactical brilliance, or from Giap's oversight or lack of imagination.

In reality, then, Khe Sanh, long billed as the epic battle of Indochina War II, was a bad act in a drama of errors. The news media overplayed it and misreported it; Giap thoroughly mishandled the entire operation; and Westmoreland won a colossal gamble, not so much by his own brilliance as by Giap's ineptitude and vacillation. In war, as in life itself, it is often better to be lucky than skillful. The god of war, however, smiles on those who make the fewest errors, and at Khe Sanh, Westmoreland erred far less than Giap.

In June 1968 General Westmoreland left Vietnam to become chief of staff of the army, and Gen. Creighton W. Abrams replaced him as COMUSMACV. Almost immediately the news media began to push the story that Abrams was abandoning Westmoreland's large-unit search and destroy tactics in favor of security operations by smaller forces. This was untrue. Abrams made no abrupt and voluntary change of operational strategy. As Bob Komer said later, "I was there when General Abrams took over . . . there was no change in strategy whatsoever. . . . The myth of a change in strategy is a figment of the media imagination."[43] I was J-2, MACV when General Abrams took over and can confirm what Komer said. I talked daily with Abe about the enemy situation and every Saturday conducted the Weekly Intelligence Estimate Update (WIEU), a gathering which Abrams used (as Westmoreland had before him) to discuss operations with his principal commanders and staff. In 1968, Abrams never spoke of any new strategy nor did he ever voice any dissatisfaction with large-unit search and destroy operations.

What did happen in mid-1968 was that the war itself changed. The Tet offensive and its follow-up in May virtually destroyed the Viet Cong and severely damaged the NVA units. By mid-1968, Truong Chinh had secured Politburo approval for his concept of returning to guerrilla-type small-unit action, and in accordance with Truong's concept the Communists scaled down their operations. Abrams reacted to the enemy operations with increased small-unit patrols and raids of his own, but he kept maximum pressure on the VC and NVA in his own war of attrition. In fact, Abrams would have welcomed a large-unit battle, but in the latter half of 1968 Giap would not oblige him. It was not Abrams who changed the American strategy for the ground war, but Giap and Truong Chinh. Abrams was no pallid imitator of Westmoreland and certainly no dupe that Giap could exploit. Abrams was a man of eminent good sense, courage, and character. Giap would test Abrams' steel as he had that of Generals de Tassigny and Westmoreland, and General Abrams would join the other two as the trio of great commanders against whom Giap tilted.

Notes—Chapter 19

1. Gen. Cao Van Vien and Lt. Gen. Dong Van Khuyen, *Reflections on the Vietnam War*, Indochina Monographs (Washington, D.C.: U.S. Army Center of Military History, 1980), p. 91.
2. Blaufarb, *Counter-Insurgency,* pp. 303–305.
3. Michael Charlton and Anthony Moncrieff, *Many Reasons Why, The American Involvement in Vietnam* (New York: Hill and Wang, 1978), p. 166.
4. Wheeler, personal letter to Westmoreland, 22 December 1967.
5. Johnson, *Vantage Point,* p. 430.
6. Rostow, *Diffusion,* p. 521.
7. Johnson, *Vantage Point,* p. 424.
8. Lady Bird Johnson, *A White House Diary* (New York: Dell Publishing, 1970), pp. 702 and 708.
9. George Reedy, *Lyndon B. Johnson, A Memoir* (New York: Andrews and McMeel, 1982), p. 149.
10. McGarvey, *Visions,* pp. 253–255.
11. "The Sixth Resolution," Viet-Nam Documents and Research Notes No. 38 (Saigon: United States Embassy, July 1968).
12. Latimer, *Hanoi's Leaders,* p. 322.
13. Ibid., p. 335.
14. Ibid., p. 336.
15. "Elaboration of Eighth Resolution," COSVN. Viet-Nam Documents and Research Notes No. 67 (Saigon: United States Embassy, September 1968).
16. Douglas Pike, "Giap Offensive Aims at War's End by Midyear," *Washington Post,* 25 February 1968.
17. Sharp and Westmoreland, *Report,* p. 235.
18. Robert Komer, Saigon News Conference, 18 April 1968.
19. Collins, *Development,* p. 86.
20. Johnson, *Vantage Point,* p. 495.
21. Ibid., p. 502.
22. Ibid., pp. 504, 516, 519.
23. Lewy, *America,* p. 389.
24. Johnson, *Vantage Point,* pp. 517–518.
25. Rostow, *Diffusion,* p. 524.
26. Johnson, *Vantage Point,* p. 531.
27. Nixon, *Memoirs,* p. 431.
28. Braestrup, *Big Story,* IV:344.
29. Walter Cronkite, "Who, What, When, Where, Why: Report from Vietnam," CBS Television, 27 February 1968.
30. Westmoreland, *Soldier,* p. 418.

31. Lt. Gen. Willard Pearson, *The War in the Northern Provinces 1966–1968*, Vietnam Studies (Washington, D.C.: Department of the Army, 1975), p. 72.
32. Robert Pisor, *The End of the Line: The Siege of Khe Sanh* (New York: W. W. Norton, 1982), p. 235.
33. Braestrup, *Big Story*, I:351.
34. Ibid.
35. O'Neill, *Giap*, pp. 195–196.
36. Westmoreland, *Soldier*, p. 411.
37. Pisor, *End of Line*, p. 174.
38. Fallaci, *Interview*, p. 85.
39. Braestrup, *Big Story*, I:351.
40. Westmoreland, *Soldier*, p. 421.; Maj. Gen. Rathvon McC. Tompkins, U.S.M.C. (Ret.), personal letter to author, 22 April 1983; Thompson, *No Exit*, p. 69.
41. Braestrup, *Big Story*, I:350.
42. Pisor, *End of Line*, p. 226.
43. Thompson and Frizzell, *Lessons*, p. 79.

20 General Creighton W. Abrams

One of a Kind

Gen. Creighton W. Abrams died on 4 September 1974 while holding the office of chief of staff, United States Army, the first officer to die in that position. The mighty hastened to lay their laudatory wreaths around Abe's bier. President Ford's offering—a modest one—praised Abrams as a rare combination—a man of action who was also a first-class administrator. Abrams' successor, Gen. Fred C. Weyand, went further, describing Abrams as "one of a kind," and Secretary of Defense Schlesinger topped them all when he acclaimed Abrams as "an authentic national hero." Now the cynic would say that such paeans are the usual building blocks of eulogies, but in Abe's case the cynic would be wrong. I don't know whether Abrams was "an authentic national hero," because, as Abe used to say, the term evaporates when you look closely at it, but he was without doubt one of a kind.

He had three unique attributes that justified this description of him. First, there was his superb record in both war and peace. Second, he had a clear mind, a store of common sense, and that very rare quality—wisdom. Last, he had a dynamic and volatile personality. All of these combined to make Abrams one of the army's most "unforgettable characters."

Abrams' renown—and that is the correct term—came to him in France in 1944. Although Abrams had served in the horse cavalry after his graduation from West Point in 1936 and later in the 1st and 4th Armored Divisions, fame did not touch him until he became the com-

575

mander of a tank battalion in the 4th Armored Division. Gen. George S. Patton, somewhere in France, supposedly dropped a chance remark about him to a group of newspapermen. Georgie is alleged to have said, "I'm supposed to be the best tank commander in the army, but I have a peer—Abe Abrams." In Saigon one night I asked Abrams if he believed that Patton had actually said that. Abrams said, "Well, he never said it to me, and I doubt he ever said it to anybody. That's not the way Patton was."

If Patton didn't make the remark—and it appears doubtful that he did—the reporter who invented it deserves credit for keenness of judgment, if not for truthfulness. For with or without Patton's endorsement, Abrams was the best battlefield commander of tanks in the World War II army. He came out of the war with probably the best combat record of any young American officer in that conflict. He led the breakout from Normandy which drove the Germans back to the Moselle River, and he commanded the tank-infantry force which relieved the surrounded paratroopers at Bastogne during the Battle of the Bulge. Near the end of the war he drove his combat command through the German lines to the Rhine River. During this push, his force destroyed more than 300 German vehicles, 75 artillery pieces, 75 antitank guns, and 15 tanks, consequently destroying the enemy command and communication apparatus on a broad front. For his exploits in World War II Abrams won *two* Distinguished Service Crosses (for extraordinary heroism), *two* Silver Stars (for gallantry in action), *two* Legions of Merit (for achievement in a position of great responsibility), plus a hatful of other United States and foreign decorations. Since decorations are the coin of the military realm, Abrams came out of World War II hearing distantly, but clearly, the ruffles and flourishes of the Generals' March.

His peacetime service added to his brilliant war record. After the war Abrams became the director of tactics at the Armored School, followed by attendance as a student at the Command and General Staff College at Ft. Leavenworth, Kansas. Then he did another tour in Europe followed in 1953 by a year as a student at the Army War College. In 1954 he went to Korea, where he served successively as chief of staff I Corps, X Corps, and IX Corps. In 1956 Abrams was promoted to brigadier general, one of the first of his class to reach star rank, although his classmates Michaelis and Westmoreland had attained that rank before he did.

The years 1956 to 1963 saw Abrams in a constant oscillation between command of ever larger armored units in Germany and duty on the army staff in the Pentagon. In 1962, Abrams, now major general in charge of the army's Civil Affairs Branch, picked up one of those assignments which can make or break an officer's career. The army careerists call these touchy tasks "bomb disposal jobs." If the officer defuses the "bomb," that is, gets the job done well, promotions and prestigious assignments follow rapidly. On the other hand, if the "bomb" goes off in the officer's hands, his career is blown into small pieces. Abrams' bomb disposal job came when he was placed in command of federal forces assembled to deal with serious unrest on the campus of the University of Mississippi due to the efforts of James Meredith, a black, to enroll at the university. Later in 1963 he held a similar job near troubled Birmingham, Alabama. In both places his good sense and coolness impressed President Kennedy, his brother Bobby, and Cyrus Vance, then the secretary of the army. Vance described Abrams as "unflappable" and called his work in this explosive arena, "a tremendous performance." With civilian backing such as this, Abrams was promoted to lieutenant general in August 1963. On 4 September 1964 he was promoted to full general and became vice chief of staff (second-in-command) of the army. In May 1967 he became deputy COMUSMACV to Westmoreland and in June 1968 he became COMUSMACV. In 1972 he followed his classmate, Westmoreland, into the position of army chief of staff.

Abrams' combat record alone would have won him the respect of the army, but it was his intelligence and wisdom which commanded its admiration. He had probably the best mind in the army during his prime (1960–1974). The often expressed consensus that "Abe is the smartest officer in the army" was held almost unanimously even by his senior colleagues and competitors. He had that rare quality, common sense, the knack of going straight to the heart of the problem, and insisting on a simple and workable solution. Woe to the briefer who gave Abrams some involuted theory or complex statistical mish-mash. If Abrams was in a jovial mood, he would get to the point of the briefing by a series of probing questions. If he was in a bad mood, he would break off the briefing and tell the staff principal to get "that 'damn' thing in some intelligible shape," a stinging indictment his principal staff officers sought to avoid at all costs.

Abrams was not a man to rush headlong into a critical decision. He would discuss all aspects of it with his key assistants, and then he would wrestle with the problem, turning it around and looking at all sides, trying to foresee all the consequences. In November 1968, some major North Vietnamese units withdrew from south of the DMZ to North Vietnam. At the same time American intelligence detected an enemy buildup west of Saigon. As Abrams' J-2, I not only briefed him on the enemy moves, but participated in many discussions with operational and logistic officers as Abrams grappled with the decision as to whether to move the 1st Air Cavalry Division from near the DMZ to the Saigon area. Painstakingly, he went over the facts, speculating on probable consequences, and playing the devil's advocate against the move of the division. After a couple of days and numerous discussions, he ordered the division to move. As things turned out, the decision was correct.

General Abrams was more than just a smart man. One of his colleagues described him thusly: "He wasn't an intellectual, but he was bright and wise. He found the wise thing to do and did it."[1] Abrams had a penchant for turning relatively trivial questions into profound discussions of basic principles. In a congressional hearing a senator once asked him why the United States needed sixteen (or some such number) divisions. Abrams countered, very respectfully, by asking the rhetorical question, "Why do we need an army at all?" He then went on to develop the reasons the country needed an effective fighting arm on the ground and from there got to the justification for the needed number of divisions.

He had a self-deprecatory wit which could deflect the questions of a hostile congressman or reporter. Testifying on another occasion before a congressional committee, one of the congressmen asked Abrams why the army's "tail" was so much bigger than its "teeth." This, of course, is the oft-asked question about why so much of the army's strength is in its support echelon and so little in its direct combat force of doughboys and tankers. Abrams hesitated for a moment—he could "milk" a scene like Jack Benny—and said deferentially, "Congressman, I don't know much about this tooth and tail thing, except one fact—nobody wants to be in the tooth part." This candor and touch of humor disarmed the questioner so that Abrams was able then to explain the reasons for the army's support-to-combat ratio.

Abrams' handling of the news media demonstrated his intuitive grasp of the essentials of a problem. As Westmoreland's deputy, he had watched the news media consistently, and often villainously, savage Westmoreland. The more Westmoreland tried to cooperate with the reporters the more they attacked his policies and his veracity. By the time Abrams had assumed command of MACV, he had decided that any attempt at cooperation with the Saigon news media was futile. One of his first orders as COMUSMACV was: no press conferences. And during his five years in Vietnam he never held one. He would, however, talk on the record and informally with one or two reporters. Strangely enough, his blunt candor and sly humor caused most of them—against their will and prejudices—to admire him and to believe what he told them. On Abrams' death, one of these reporters wrote a laudatory article about him entitled "General Abrams Deserves a Better War."[2]

While the army respected Abrams for his combat record and intelligence, it loved him for his volatile and ebullient personality. One of Abe's classmates described him as "a man of a thousand moods, each running headlong behind the last," and in any of his moods Abrams was a technicolored production of lights, colors, movement, and sound. His rages were tempests, full of thunder and lightning. He could be vicious, his sarcasm—fortunately rare—was cold and venomous, destructive to the recipient and painful even to the bystander. His praise was fervid and fulsome, and his geniality warm and captivating.

In a two-hour conference, I have seen Abe's initial mood of joviality turn to haughty disdain, then to sullen truculence, to a table-pounding rage, and finally, to a quiet and businesslike discussion of the problem at hand. In informal surroundings his moods would vary even further. He could be the most relaxed of all senior commanders. He loved to tell stories, laughing uproariously at some ludicrous tale which he told on himself. He could be modest, self-deprecatory, even humble. He was sentimental, and his stories of old soldiers and gallant deeds of long ago would bring tears to his eyes. Yet just as suddenly he could turn morosely silent, or scathingly sarcastic, or loudly belligerent. And, then, a few minutes later his mood would mellow again.

No doubt many of these emotional shifts, particularly his famous temper tantrums, were playacting designed to impress his audience with the importance of what he was shouting about. But often, Abrams would lose control of the act, and the mood took over the man. He forgot he was acting and as his subordinates would say later, "Ole'

Abe got carried away again.'' Abrams in full flight of temper was a memorable sight. No Giap-like "Volcano Under the Snow" was Abrams. He was Mt. Vesuvius, there for all to see. His arms would wave, he would pound the table, he would shout, and his face would turn a fiery red. And strangely, the officers listening to these tirades—even those against whom he railed—were not offended or hurt. The audience enjoyed them as one would enjoy a good play. Above all, the tantrums revealed a man who was human, a man deviled by the frustrations of MACV, a man to whom an unprofessional performance brought pain and irritation. Of course, the tantrums were always followed by a quiet spell, or by a humorous quip, or by some expression of deep wisdom. Leadership is an incomprehensible quality, and Abrams had it. And so, in spite of his volatility—or maybe because of it—things got done, and done well, and the men loved him while doing them.

Abrams came from no great military family as did Douglas MacArthur and George Patton, nor did he spring from the southern aristocracy as did his classmate, Westmoreland. Abrams was born into a middle-class New England family on 16 September 1914, to a father who was a repairman with the Boston and Albany Railroad. Abrams had a normal American boyhood in a small village near Springfield, Massachusetts. In high school he excelled scholastically and was captain of the football team. Not much there that would hint at future greatness.

Like many another youth, his life was to change sharply when, in 1932, after graduating from high school, he entered West Point. The Abrams' saga began at the military academy. By the accounts of his classmates (1936), as a cadet Abrams was a free spirit and something of a prankster. As a plebe he caught more than his share of hazing, and as an upperclassman gave out more. Having been in the Class of 1939, I can personally attest to the latter. Even as a cadet he became known for the loud voice and the mercurial changes of mood which characterized his later life.

Abe's prowess—or rather lack of it—on the Army football team became the centerpiece of the Abrams' legend at West Point. While he was an excellent high school football player (some said All-State), as a plebe he could do no better than to make the sixth team. Not that Abrams lacked athletic ability; it was that his classmates on the plebe team were bigger and more experienced than he. Most of them had played at least one or two years of college football, and some had played three years. West Point's peculiar eligibility rules of those days ignored previous playing experience in other colleges or universities. It was common in the early and mid-thirties for Army to field a plebe team composed largely of All-Americans and All-Conference players. Red Smith, a long-time sports writer for New York newspapers, once wrote that the Army varsity of that era could hold its own against any college team in the country, but was likely to get beat badly every Tuesday when they scrimmaged the plebes. Of course, most of these plebe gridiron stars had majored in their prior college in Physical Education 1411 and Football Theory 404 and were ill-equipped to contend with the quadratic equations and irregular French verbs which the mandatory curriculum of the academy threw at them. By the end of the first semester most of the "jocks" had fallen prey to the high academic standards of West Point and were on their way back to their college gridirons and phys ed classes.

Abe's lack of success on the gridiron as a plebe failed to discourage his efforts to make the "A" squad as an upperclassman. Handicapped by lack of experience and size (the 1936 West Point yearbook, *Howitzer*, described him as [about 5 feet nine inches and 175 pounds] the smallest lineman on the team) he attempted to win his major "A" not so much by brawn and ability as by a combative spirit and a loud mouth. The 1936 *Howitzer* chronicles Abrams in this passage:

Creighton Wm. Abrams
Agaway, Mass., (13th Dist)

Abrams was never a star, never a regular, but he can point with justifiable pride to his undisputed title of the loudest, happiest "fightingest" man on the squad. He was not immovable on defense, but could drive an opponent frantic with verbal onslaughts . . . he was not a polished blocker, but what he lacked in finesse he supplemented with fight. Indeed a team of Abrams might conceivably prove a champion.[3]

More in recognition of Abrams' "fight" than for his playing ability, the army coaches awarded Abrams his "A" in his senior year. What is important here is not Abe's mediocrity on the football field, but his combativeness and determination. These qualities not only won him the respect and admiration of his classmates, but indicated traits of character of a future leader.

On 12 June 1936, Abrams graduated from West Point, standing 184 out of a class of 275. His academic record was mediocre; he had risen to the rank of cadet lieutenant, but that was no great honor. His extracurricular activities (including athletics) had shown no unusual promise. Yet, his classmates all say—aided by the clear light of hindsight—that as a cadet there was something special about Abrams. Maybe it was his loud mouth, or his ebullience, or his persistence in trying to make the Army team. Maybe it was his "fight," but there was about him an unusual quality. Maybe even at the academy, Abrams was "one of a kind."

Beneath all the bluster and volatility, behind the superb record and the keen intellect, there was the man. Abrams had character, the ballast Napoleon wanted in his symbolic ship in which he weighed his generals. It did not show plainly as did Westmoreland's, but then Westmoreland projected an unusual combination of moral cleanliness and of West Point, with its emphasis on Duty, Honor, Country. Outwardly, Abrams showed none of these traits, but they were there.

Falsehood in any form appalled him. I once had to tell him that I was convinced that a senior CIA official had knowingly distorted a crucial report that he had given to his superiors, including the president. Abrams looked at me aghast, asking, "Are you saying the man lied?" I told him that was my opinion and gave him the evidence. Again, a silence, and then he said slowly, "That's a terrible thing, my God, that's almost treason."

There was other evidence of his high moral and ethical standards. His resounding battle with United States officialdom over his attempt to bring to justice some of the Green Berets, who allegedly murdered a double agent, reflected his strongly held principles of what he believed to be right and wrong. Then there was the case of the unauthorized bombings in Cambodia. Some of Abrams' detractors—and, like all dynamic men, he had them—pointed out that the bombings of Cambodia in 1969 happened while Abe was commanding MACV. Later, in hearings held in 1972 before the Senate Armed Services Committee, these same people raised the question of Abrams' complicity in concealing them. The committee concluded, in the words of its chairman, Senator John

C. Stennis, that, "no testimony put a hand on General Abrams or put a speck on him."[4]

Abrams' personal life, like that of Westmoreland, was blameless. He was a devoted family man, and no hint of personal misconduct ever touched him. And like Westmoreland, he was quick to banish any officer whose conduct failed to meet the highest professional and moral standards. Abrams might have been known to the troops as "Old Scruffy" because his uniforms were wrinkled and loose-fitting, but there was nothing loose or wrinkled about his character. His integrity was as starched and West Point perfect as Westmoreland's.

Abrams was a very complex man. Trying to understand his complexities could be even more baffling because his public image was so at odds with the real man himself. The news media portrayed Abrams as a stocky, hard-driving, taciturn, bourbon-drinking, cigar-chomping general, slouching about in a wrinkled uniform which never seemed to fit—a modern Ulysses S. Grant. And Abrams never tried to rebut this view; in fact, he enjoyed it and passively encouraged it. Some of the troops called him—behind his back, of course—"The Old Sergeant," and he savored that title, too. The net result, however, depicted Abrams as some kind of "salt-of-the-earth" type, who only liked cigars, six-packs, and John Wayne movies.

Such a perception was grossly distorted. Abrams was no man of common or proletarian tastes. On the contrary, he loved classical music, particularly Mozart, and he had the tastes of a gourmet for fine food and drink. In Saigon an invitation to dine with Abe was always eagerly accepted. One knew not only that the food, wine, and liquor would be superb, but that Abrams was the most genial of hosts and a first-rate conversationalist. He loved good company, a few drinks, and funny stories, of which he had a full store.

Abrams read widely, concentrating on history and philosophy. He studied these works, and once startled a staff meeting by stating something to the effect that, "We always have to operate on less than perfect knowledge and be satisfied with probabilities, not certainties." It was relevant to the problem under discussion and the conferees were about to give Abrams credit for another piece of wisdom when he admitted that he had gained the idea from *The Lessons of History,* by Will and Ariel Durant.

Abrams had another, and peculiar, side. This commonsensical, well-read, sophisticated man harbored some of the longest lasting, strangest, and most unusual prejudices. For one, he hated halfbacks, football halfbacks, that is. I suppose as a third- or fourth-string guard he somehow came to harbor a profound aversion to the men carrying, catching, or passing the ball who got the limelight. But Abrams hated *all* halfbacks, not just those from Notre Dame or Navy; he hated Army halfbacks too. I have heard him, drink in hand, disclaim loudly and at length that "those damn halfbacks get all the credit, but the real game is played down in the mud and dirt of the trenches," meaning by the interior linemen. He could become particularly vitriolic about a famous All-American Army halfback of the mid-thirties. Nor was this unusual narrow-mindedness a passing fancy. Not long before his death, Abrams once described Gen. John Ryan, a distinguished airman, chief of staff of the air force, and a colleague of Abe's on the Joint Chiefs of Staff as "nothing but an old halfback." This was true. Ryan, as a sophomore, had played halfback on the Army team where Abrams as a senior had barely won his letter. No doubt there was a good deal of his usual exaggeration, but beneath the hyperbole, Abrams was serious. The unusual thing about this warp was not that he held it, but that he held it for so long.

Abrams held another unusual, and more serious, bias: he disliked paratroopers. Not that he discriminated against airborne officers for promotion or position, but when they left his command, he almost invariably replaced them with non-airborne "types." Perhaps he associated paratroopers with halfbacks, both "glamour boys" who got the headlines while the "straight-leg" infantry, armor, and artillery did the heavy fighting. There was another theory circulated in the army that Abrams had watched the so-called "airborne clique" run the army from the immediate postwar years until the early seventies and had not liked what he saw and had vowed to change things when his turn came.

I know he was convinced for the most pragmatic reasons that landing troops by parachute was the most ineffective and wasteful way to introduce troops into battle. One of the most famous rages of his Vietnam service came one Saturday morning at the weekly strategy conference when the J-3 reported that United States aircraft had dropped an ARVN airborne battalion by parachute into an objective area. He castigated those present who bore any responsibility for authorizing the operation, and, as was often the case, took a verbal lick at some of us who had nothing to do with it. As usual, however, after the blast his good sense came through. Abe's point was that the United States and its Allies had over 2,000 helicopters in Vietnam. "Why," he demanded, "not use the easy and efficient way to get the troops into the area (i.e., by helicopter) instead of the hard and inefficient method by parachute?"

The reverse of Abrams' aversion to paratroopers was his predilection for officers of his own branch of the army, the armor. He was particularly fond of the officers in the armor branch who had begun their service, as Abrams had, with the horse cavalry. Since the horse cavalry trotted off into the dust of history in the early forties, by the seventies retirement and death had drastically thinned the ranks of those officers still on active duty who had served with the horses. As "old Abe" would say to those of us who had so served, "There's just a few of us left now." Then he would often go into a story of a horse he had ridden or an old cavalry soldier he had known. Abrams loved the horse cavalry, because, I suspect, it reminded him (as it did the rest of us) of those carefree days of our youth when polo games, horse shows, and hunt breakfasts occupied us, rather than the later days of high rank filled with "teeth-and-tail" disputes, congressional hearings, and that annual bloody encounter, the battle of the budget.

No account of Abrams' life would be complete without some mention of his family life. Like Westmoreland, he was a loving husband, and the father of six children. Abrams married Julia Harvey on 30 August 1936, shortly after graduation, and as a new second lieutenant took his bride to Ft. Bliss, Texas. Abrams met "Julie," as she was known throughout the army, on a blind date when he was a sophomore at West Point, and she an undergraduate at Vassar College, located a few miles up the Hudson at Poughkeepsie. It was a "love match," to use the old army expression, and it lasted until Abe's death in 1974.

Well, that was Abrams—at least as I saw him. He had character, and wisdom, and a volatile humanity. He had his faults, too, of course. He could be vicious without cause to subordinates, and he could and did hold grudges. But he was a Mt. Everest. The army, for reasons which are always obscure and incoherent, loved him and admired him. Maybe Fred Weyand, who probably knew Abrams best, said it all when he called Abrams one of a kind.

Notes—Chapter 20

1. George C. Wilson, quoting Maj. Gen. DeWitt C. Smith, Jr., "Creighton Abrams: From Agawam to Chief of Staff," *Washington Post,* 5 September 1974, Section D, p. 4.
2. Kevin P. Buckley, "General Abrams Deserves a Better War," *The New York Times Magazine,* 5 October 1969.
3. United States Military Academy, *Howitzer* (West Point, NY: 1936) p. 285.
4. Wilson quoting John Stennis, *Washington Post,* 5 September 1972, Section D, p. 5.

21 Nixon's War

Peace With Honor
1969

On 20 January 1969, Richard Milhous Nixon took the oath of the office as president of the United States. "Johnson's War" had now become "Nixon's War," and it became his task, aided by his national security adviser, Dr. Henry Kissinger, to lead the country out of the war which he had inherited. During his presidential campaign, Nixon had repeatedly stated that he had a plan to end the war. This was political hyperbole, for Nixon had only a vague, generalized approach to getting out of the war which combined the ideas of weakening the enemy, strengthening the RVNAF, and beginning United States troop withdrawals. The first *concrete* plan for the conduct of the war was devised after the Nixon administration had been in office some four months.

Henry Kissinger, on the other hand, did have—maybe not a plan—but at least a firm concept as to how to deal with the Vietnam War. The outline of Kissinger's plan appeared in January 1969 (although written earlier) as an article in *Foreign Affairs* magazine. The main points of Kissinger's article were:[1]

1. The strategy of attrition was futile and incapable of producing victory.
2. Further increase of United States troop strength in Vietnam would, at best, be limited.
3. The war, inevitably, had to be ended by a diplomatic solution.

4. The diplomatic solution (negotiations) had to progress on three tiers.
   a. Between the United States and Hanoi regarding a cease-fire and mutual troop withdrawal.
   b. Between the Thieu government and the Viet Cong's National Liberation Front (NLF) regarding the political settlement.
   c. In a third forum, an international conference to work out guarantees and safeguards for the agreements arrived at.
5. The United States must give the GVN increasing responsibility for the conduct of the war.
6. During negotiations the United States should act so as to:
   a. Reduce United States casualties
   b. Protect the SVN population
   c. Strengthen RVNAF
   d. Broaden the base of the GVN

Kissinger's article thus provided clear guidelines for a future policy for Vietnam, but no concrete plan.

The first move to develop a solid concept for waging the Vietnam War occurred on Inauguration Day, 20 January 1969, when Kissinger dispatched a voluminous questionnaire on the status and conduct of the war to the governmental agencies and military headquarters charged with responsibility for its conduct. As one of the key staff officers in MACV, I can report that the questionnaire (of twenty-eight major questions and fifty minor ones) boggled us. Some of the questions were inappropriate for our level; others required detailed answers. Some were highly controversial, and many invited subjective opinions. Finally, the accompanying directive ordered MACV (and all the other agencies) to forward their replies direct to Kissinger's office in the White House without going through normal military channels or coordinating the answers with other agencies.

The answers to Kissinger's questionnaire fell into two general classes. In the optimistic class, MACV, CINCPAC, the JCS, and the United States Embassy, Saigon, held sanguine views about the potential of the RVNAF, the diminished capability of the enemy, and the progress of the pacification program. The pessimistic group (CIA, State, and the civilians in the Defense Department) argued that all progress in Vietnam was illusory, pointing out particularly the flawed Vietnamese leadership in Saigon and in the military hierarchy. The differences, however, were largely ones of degree. Nobody believed that the war could be won in the foreseeable future, and even MACV and the embassy in Saigon doubted the RVNAF's long-range capability to defend the country against *both* the VC and NVA without United States combat support.[2] Furthermore, neither of the American agencies in Saigon held high hopes for the GVN's ability to win the hearts and minds of the South Vietnamese people in the near future.

The answers to Kissinger's questionnaire became the basis for National Security Study Memorandum (NSSM)-1. Cleverly, it revealed the differences of viewpoint as to the status and future of the war. For example, NSSM-1 pointedly surfaced the continuing disagreements between MACV and the CIA regarding enemy strength in South Vietnam and the importance of Sihanoukville and Cambodia as a Communist supply route. The document used these disputes as examples showing that the agencies could not even agree on basic facts, let alone interpretations of those facts. Of course, that was the prime purpose of NSSM-1—to accentuate and exploit the lack of consensus about the current status of the war and how to fight it.[3] These differences could be used by Kissinger to neutralize one agency with another. Obviously, some of the agencies were wrong, but which ones? The only answer was to ignore them all, which is precisely what Kissinger and Nixon had intended to do from the start of the exercise. One of the fundamentals on which these two agreed was that foreign and military policy could not be conducted by the bureaucracy, but had to be directed from the White House.

The first requirement for the development of a new policy for Vietnam—who would design it—had been settled. Before any policy could be devised, however, the Hanoi Politburo took a hand in the game— they hit the new Nixon administration with a "sucker punch." So, on 22 February 1969, before the Nixon administration could even absorb the answers to the massive questionnaire of NSSM-1, Giap launched countrywide attacks throughout South Vietnam.

To understand the genesis of these attacks, one must now move to "the other side of the hill" and look at the situation in January and February 1969 from the Politburo's perspective. As a result of the military disasters which 1968 had visited on the Communists, the NVN Politburo decided in the late months of that year that something had to be done. The force structure and morale of the Communist forces, particularly the VC, were in tatters. The U.S./SVN pacification program was making significant inroads into Communist controlled areas. Their last two attacks in 1968, May and August, had fizzled out almost before they began. Something new had to be found, and it was Truong Chinh who found it—refound it actually. The new strategy was "back to protracted war"; the new tactics—guerrilla warfare with a twist—the use of highly trained, suicidal commandos, or sappers. So, from August until the end of 1968, the war subsided into a number of small-unit clashes, raids, and stand-off shellings.

But as 1968 ended, things weren't *all* bad for the Politburo. On 31 October 1968, President Johnson had canceled the bombing campaign against North Vietnam, which allowed them freer access to South Vietnam. Negotiations had started, and these could be used to some political and psychological advantage, and it was apparent to Ho, Giap, Le Duan, and the others that the United States would not pursue the war to a military victory. Beyond that, they discovered that the people of the United States were extremely vulnerable to their *dich van* program (action among the enemy people) for in 1968 another, and increasingly powerful, front had been opened in the war—antiwar dissent within the United States.

In early 1969, something else happened in the United States which to the Politburo required Communist action, the inauguration of Richard Nixon as president. The Politburo knew Nixon as a dedicated anti-Communist, but that label didn't tell the North Vietnamese much. And so, they decided to test Nixon by launching a minor offensive. Such an offensive had other attractions as well. By producing American casualties, it would incite the antiwar movement within the United States to new heights. It might aid negotiations, although that was doubtful. An offensive would probably force Nixon to show at least part of his hand, to reveal by his reaction how he and his administration planned to conduct the war.

Accordingly, on 31 January 1969, COSVN issued Directive No. 71 ordering that an offensive be undertaken on 22 February 1969. In contrast to the enemy offensives of 1968, the directive prescribed that the primary target would be United States forces and installations, with secondary priority going to destruction of lines of communication and attacks against the snowballing pacification program. Strikes against South Vietnamese troops and bases were of low priority. To achieve its goals the offensive had to have *some* impact, and while it was no all-out attack, as at Tet of 1968, it did surpass in intensity the feeble efforts of May and August of 1968. The enemy, largely Main and Local Forces with a heavy NVA flavor, attacked over 125 targets with small-scale sapper attacks and shelled 400 others. There were two attacks by regimental-size units and sixteen battalion-size assaults. All were easily repulsed. Allied intelligence had watched the attack as it was being planned and had accurately forecast the details of its execution. While United States casualties rose (1,140 Americans killed in three weeks of fighting), there was no halt in the pacification program, nor was there any other visible damage to the United States and Allied war effort. The enemy gained little militarily by the offensive except, of course, media and dissident attention, which advanced his *dich van* program within the United States.

Giap and his comrades did not foresee, however, one result of the failure of the Communist offensive—the morale of their VC troops and cadre, already shaky, plunged to a new low. During the first week of the attacks, over a thousand defectors surrendered to Allied authorities, and this rate remained constant over the following weeks. By 1 July 1969, 20,000 enemy personnel had defected, 2,000 more than for the entire year of 1968.[4]

The Politburo failed to foresee another result of the 22 February offensive—it infuriated Richard Nixon. Obsessed by some kind of mystic machismo, he wanted to strike back, to punish Hanoi for its attempt to humiliate him and for breaking a set of vague "agreements" (never formally ratified, or even put into writing) by which Hanoi "agreed" in return for the bombing halt to abstain from certain aggressive actions, including just the type of attacks they launched in February 1969.

Nixon's problem was not *whether* to retaliate, but *how* to retaliate. One readily available option would be to resume the bombing of North Vietnam, but the disadvantages of this course outweighed the doubtful advantages. The bombing (as perceived at that time) had not worked well when practiced before, and besides, any resumption of the air attacks on North Vietnam would bring out the antiwar dissenters in full and vociferous force. In addition, a resumption of the bombing might well scuttle the negotiations in Paris, with resultant political and diplomatic problems for Nixon.

Nor did the situation on the ground in South Vietnam offer any usable options for retaliatory action. If the enemy refused to come out and fight in large numbers, there was no way General Abrams could punish him. An American offensive into Laos, Cambodia, or the DMZ would appear as an excessive reaction to the relatively minor enemy attacks of February 1969. The antiwar legions would surely seize on such American operations as an unjustified extension of the war. Realistically, such incursions require significant lead times, and before they could be mounted, the delay would dilute the retaliatory aspect.

In the face of these unattractive alternatives, opportunity, in the guise of a Viet Cong defector, entered the picture. For years the J-2 section of MACV had assembled intelligence on the location and operation of COSVN, the headquarters which conducted the Communist operations in much of South Vietnam. Some of the data was sound, some unsound, but eventually a fairly clear picture emerged of COSVN's command relationships, its territorial responsibility, its leaders, and its operating procedures. From electronic intelligence, particularly radio direction finding, MACV determined the general area in Cambodia from which COSVN operated, but MACV was never able to pinpoint the *exact* location of the principal elements of COSVN headquarters.

In late January 1969, a Viet Cong defector turned himself in to an American unit, stating (among other things) that he had been in the COSVN headquarters area a few days before his defection and could provide details of COSVN's location. The defector was quickly evacuated to Saigon for high-level interrogation. His reports checked well with intelligence already in MACV's hands on COSVN. Nevertheless, I, as J-2, approached this possible intelligence bonanza with considerable skepticism. To ingratiate themselves with their captors, defectors frequently claim to know much more than they actually do. All of the intelligence agencies operating in Vietnam had at one time or another been "burned" by glib, but ignorant, defectors. Since we worked closely with the CIA officers in Saigon, I turned the defector over to them for separate interrogation. The CIA officials reached the same conclusion I had—that the defector was *probably* telling the truth, but that they too viewed the intelligence on COSVN furnished by the defector with some mistrust. Finally, I asked CIA to give the defector a polygraph test on his COSVN information, but only if the man would volunteer to take it. The defector agreed, and he passed the lie-detector test in good shape. I had, then, to accept the fact that we had a valuable source.

The J-2 Section, MACV, put together a briefing on COSVN's location and its detailed layout for General Abrams. He "bought off" on the briefing and on 9 February had me prepare a backchannel message from him to General Wheeler, chairman of the JCS, telling Wheeler that we had reliable intelligence as to COSVN's location just across the Cambodian border and requesting authority to attack COSVN with B-52 bombers.

Nothing happened to Abrams' request for a few days, and then a hurried call came from the JCS to MACV, directing General Abrams to send briefers to Washington to present MACV's intelligence on COSVN's location. This was done and by 18 February the briefing team (two majors) had briefed the JCS, Secretary of Defense Melvin Laird, and Dr. Kissinger. With this briefing, a retaliatory option was born—an air strike against COSVN in Cambodia.

This option offered several attractions. It would punish the North Vietnamese who had numerous logistical base areas and headquarters in Cambodia. It would inflict no damage or casualties on the Cambodian people who had been evicted long ago from the border areas by the North Vietnamese. The bombing might be done secretly without arousing the fury of the doves at home. Since the North Vietnamese had never admitted that they had troops or installations in Cambodia (or Vietnam), they might accept the bombing in silence. Prince Sihanouk, the ruler of Cambodia, had already lost control of the border areas of his country to the North Vietnamese, and had told Ambassador Bowles that he would not object to American action against those Communist base areas and units in Cambodia. Finally, the extension of American operations outside South Vietnam was a forceful hint to Hanoi that the United States might not continue to fight the war in shackles, and that the new administration would not be bound by the restraints which had so hampered Lyndon Johnson.

But then, as always, there were disadvantages. Bombing attacks against Cambodia might wreck any hope of progress in negotiations. But the main drawback, however, would be the adverse reaction of the American antiwar dissidents and most members of the international community when knowledge of the bombing became public—if it did. As a result of the enemy's 22 February attacks, therefore, the president on

23 February ordered that Base Area 353 in Cambodia (which was thought to contain COSVN) be struck from the air.

Then began one of those minuets which often surrounded critical Nixon decisions. Kissinger (and other counselors) persuaded the president to rescind his bombing order. Then followed some pushing and pulling among the presidential advisers, and on 9 March the president once again passed the order to bomb, and shortly thereafter again canceled the order. Finally, on 15 March, after the enemy had struck Saigon with five rockets—another direct violation of the ''understandings''—Nixon ordered an immediate strike on Cambodia. Again, this order evoked frantic arguments and appeals among his advisers. This time the president set his jaw, and on 18 March, Base Area 353 was blasted by B-52's. The bomb damage assessment reported many secondary explosions. The area was hit again in April, and from April to August other base areas (all, like 353, within five miles of the Cambodia/Vietnam border) were attacked. The covert strikes continued until May, 1970 when they were made openly in support of United States/RVNAF ground operations in Cambodia.

Like so many other questions related to the Vietnam War, one doesn't know if the strike of 18 March 1969 on Base Area 353 struck COSVN headquarters as well as a supply area. Some evidence indicates that the attack did strike COSVN. Henry Kissinger, in his book *White House Years,* states that ''Communist leaders in Phnom Penh eight years later also confirmed that the deserter's information had been right on that score.''[5] Truong Nhu Tang, onetime minister of justice in the NLF, stated in his book that COSVN was located in Base Area 353, and that ''American intelligence had located COSVN rather precisely.'' In his book, Tang writes that the personnel of COSVN moved out of Base Area 353 to positions deeper in Cambodia on 19 March, that is, *one day after* the first B-52 attack on COSVN's location.[6]

My personal experience tends to confirm Kissinger's statement. As part of the intelligence collection plan to evaluate the results of the bombing, I had a helicopter-borne patrol from the Studies and Observation Group (SOG) go into the area immediately after the last bombs had fallen. I had hoped to pick up a dazed prisoner or two to determine exactly what the B-52's had hit. As the patrol approached the target they could see secondary explosions and clouds of dust about the area, but there were no dazed POW's to be snapped up. On the contrary, the patrol met heavy ground fire from alert security troops which inflicted casualties on the Americans and damaged the helicopter. The patrol leader described their reception: "like somebody had kicked over a hornet's nest." This is precisely the defensive reaction one would expect from elite troops guarding a high-level headquarters complex.

Following the first attack on Base Area 353, Nixon and those other Americans who knew of the attack awaited a protest from either Sihanouk or the North Vietnamese, or both. Neither protested. The administration had no reason to publicize the raid, and several reasons to conceal it, particularly to avert the dovish outcry which was sure to follow any public announcement. To conceal the subsequent attacks, a dual reporting system was established. This device proved futile, and in May 1969, the story of the attacks broke in the *New York Times,* followed eventually by the condemnations from the antiwar dissenters, who, of course, overlooked the fact that Americans were being killed in substantial numbers by troops who used those Cambodian base areas as sanctuaries.

Beginning in March 1969, both sides strove to develop a strategy and the tactics to carry it out. Here the North Vietnamese Politburo had the easier task. Faced with serious VC morale problems, and aware of the limitations of Nixon's options due to dissent and discord within the United States, the Communists returned to small-scale, economy-of-force warfare. COSVN's Directive No. 55, issued in April, stated in effect, "Never again, and under no circumstances are we going to risk our entire military force for just an offensive. On the contrary, we should endeavor to preserve our military potential for further campaigns."[7] For the Communists this strategy would accomplish several purposes. It would hold down their own casualties, and thus, shore up a crumbling morale. It would provide time to rebuild the VC guerrilla force and the VC political infrastructure, both of which had been seriously damaged by the Tet offensive, pacification gains, defections, and faltering morale. Finally, a lull would convince President Nixon and the antiwar dissenters that the war could, and would, go on interminably at this low level.

Nevertheless, pressure had to be kept on President Nixon, so the Communists had to break the lull following the abortive 22 February attacks with another offensive effort. On 11–12 May, they made a sporadic flurry, initiating 212 shellings around South Vietnam. Most of these efforts were insignificant, and only a few were followed by infantry attacks, none exceeding battalion in size. The whole effort evaporated by the end of the second day.

Starting in March, Nixon and Kissinger continued *their* search for a national policy on the war. In March, Nixon for the first time publicly proclaimed his criteria for the unilateral withdrawal of American forces. These were: the ability of SVN to defend itself, the progress of negotiations, and the level of enemy activity. In a major speech delivered on 14 May, he abandoned the old demand that NVA troops leave South Vietnam six months before United States withdrawal and adopted the Kissinger formula, calling for mutually phased withdrawals of United States and NVA troops, an international body to supervise any agreements, and a proposal of supervised elections hinting at a political solution. The North Vietnamese ignored Nixon's proposals, and Thieu actively objected to some of them, asking for a face-to-face meeting with Nixon.

Under the surface, however, another facet of United States policy was working its way to the top—Vietnamization. Once Nixon had decided on unilateral withdrawal of American troops, then the South Vietnamese forces had to be strengthened to defend themselves, or the United States withdrawals would be seen as nothing more than an unconcealed retreat and the ignominious desertion of a weak ally. The first indication of a new and firm United States policy came on 8 June 1969 from Midway Island, where Nixon met Thieu, as the latter had requested. By now the new United States policy toward Vietnam had been formulated, and it consisted of four parts: United States troop withdrawals, Vietnamization, pacification, and negotiations. Simply put, the policy proposed a theoretical balance between United States withdrawals and the strengthening of the GVN and RVNAF by Vietnamization and pacification with negotiations as the vehicle of United States disengagement. Nixon activated the policy when he announced at Midway that with Thieu's concurrence, he was directing the immediate withdrawal of 25,000 United States troops. Actually, as Nixon himself admits, this statement "involved some diplomatic exaggeration" since both Thieu and General Abrams objected to the withdrawal.

As a result of this formulation of a firm policy toward Vietnam, in early July the White House through the Pentagon sent Abrams a new mission statement, replacing the one given General Westmoreland in 1966. Gone were the brave old words about winning the war and attriting the enemy. Abrams was told to give first priority to Vietnamization, to support pacification, and to reduce the flow of supplies to the enemy. This directive, to become effective 15 August, brought Abrams' mission into line with national policy. As Henry Kissinger notes, "We were clearly on our way out of Vietnam by negotiation if possible, by unilateral withdrawal if necessary."[8] A remarkably candid statement.

During June and July there was a lull in enemy-initiated operations throughout South Vietnam. Nixon and Kissinger, always optimistic in those early days, sought to capitalize on any hidden meaning in this inaction. On 15 July, Nixon wrote a letter to Ho Chi Minh attempting to get the negotiations, then in a deep freeze, into forward movement. Nothing happened for over a month.

In the meantime, President Nixon had flown to Guam for the splash-down of Apollo XI, the first moon vehicle. There, in an informal press conference, he casually enunciated what came to be known as the Nixon Doctrine. Briefly, the Nixon Doctrine stated that in the future the United States would furnish to other nations fighting aggression, military and economic assistance, but would not send American troops. As is often the case, the doctrine got misinterpreted as meaning that United States troops would be withdrawn from Asia and all other parts of the world. Senate Majority Leader Mike Mansfield so interpreted it. So probably did Ho Chi Minh.

While President Nixon and Kissinger had been formulating national policy for the war, the Politburo issued a document which established *their* strategy. In July 1969, COSVN issued Resolution No. 9. This document, copied after a companion piece published by the North Vietnamese Politburo, formalized for the Viet Cong Hanoi's decision to retrograde to a form of guerrilla warfare, stressing attacks by small units of highly trained and motivated sappers. In compliance with this directive, there were a series of sapper attacks against United States and SVN personnel and facilities during July and August. The attacks killed a few people, mostly civilians, and wounded many more. Their impact on the military situation was negligible, but they did grab the headlines and encouraged the antiwar dissidents within the United States.

Ho's real reply to Nixon's conciliatory letter of 15 July came on 12 August, when the Communists attacked over 100 towns and cities in South Vietnam. Ho's formal reply to Nixon's letter, dated 25 August, was strident and insulting. Taken in conjunction with the attacks, Ho had taken the peace pipe Nixon had offered him, hit him with it, and then put the hot tobacco in Nixon's hand as well. And so the month of August 1969 ended with both sides equipped with firm policies and strategies for fighting the war. Peace was certainly no nearer, and as the Nixon administration saw things, it had receded significantly. The attacks and Ho's insulting reply to Nixon's letter had affronted Nixon, and once more he decided to teach the North Vietnamese a lesson.

In early September, under Kissinger's guidance, Gen. Alexander Haig (at that time a Kissinger assistant) began to plan another retaliatory blow, to be known as DUCK HOOK. As it evolved, DUCK HOOK went beyond retaliation. It proposed mining Haiphong, instituting a naval blockade, resuming the bombing in North Vietnam (intensified by striking population centers, military targets, and key roads and bridges), and even considered what had previously been sacrosanct—bombing the dikes on the Red River with iron bombs, and the use of the "nuclear option."[9] In September, Kissinger presented the plan to Nixon, Laird, and a few other key advisers. The predictable wrangle ensued with Laird and the others waving the red flag of public reaction to such an expansion of the war. Nixon, impressed with Laird's arguments, swallowed his anger and ordered the plan put on indefinite hold, another victim of a growing force in America—antiwar dissent.

In 1969, presidential decisions were made increasingly with one eye on Vietnam and one on the antiwar movement in the United States. As time went on, the domestic dissidence became dominant. Indeed, analyses of the situation in Vietnam and elsewhere in the world determined what the United States *ought* to do in Vietnam, but the push of the antiwar dissenters within the United States determined what the United States *could* do. Nixon ordered the bombing of Cambodia partially because it might be kept secret. Nixon suspended DUCK HOOK mostly because of his fear of the arousal of the antiwar dissenters. The major facets of the Nixon policy toward Vietnam—Vietnamization, United States troop withdrawals, and negotiations—were dictated, not primarily by the situation and requirements in Vietnam, but by the need to assuage the antiwar dissidents in the United States, and the dissidents knew it. Every administration retreat, every withdrawal, only whetted their appetites for more withdrawals and retreats. The dissidents sought not some reasonable and honorable way for the United States to get out of the war in Vietnam;

they wanted nothing less than a total and cowardly American retreat from Vietnam, the abandonment of the Thieu government, and the public surrender of Vietnam to the Communists.

As the summer ended and the college students returned to class, dissidence grew. On 14 October, Pham Van Dong sent a message to the dissenters urging them on and congratulating those who planned to appear in the first big antiwar demonstration the next day, 15 October. On this day, some 250,000 people came to Washington for the so-called October 15 Moratorium. Since the dissidents had much more ambitious plans for another moratorium scheduled for 15 November, Nixon realized that he had to respond. Most of his advisers, Rogers, Laird, and even Kissinger, urged that he emphasize his desire for peace and avoid, as far as possible, a confrontation with the "peaceniks." This advice Nixon rejected. In a major speech of 3 November, he proclaimed that the United States intended to keep its commitment to South Vietnam and emphasized that his policy would not be influenced by street demonstrations. For the first time, he enunciated his policy—the strategy of Vietnamization, troop withdrawals, and negotiations, pointing out that Vietnamization offered a way out of the war independent of both North and South Vietnam. Finally, in a master stroke, he went over the vociferous dissenters and appealed to the "great silent majority" of the American people for support.

The response was dramatic. The "silent majority" spoke, and in thousands of telephone calls, letters, and telegrams, they supported the president and his Vietnam policy. Estimates of the impact of the president's 3 November speech varied. Most ventured the opinion that the administration had gained some breathing room domestically for the first time in its tenure. Others opined that Nixon had scored a triumph, but that for policy purposes, the battle for the hearts and minds of the American people between the administration and the dissenters was a stalemate. Yet in spite of the stalemate, or more correctly, because of it, the United States had at last a conscious, articulated policy to end the war in Vietnam.

While the 12 August sapper attacks and standoff shellings angered Nixon, they failed to satisfy the Communists. They knew the attack, or "high point" as they called it, had failed. In a report on the August offensive dated 30 October 1969, COSVN stated, "In sum, the Autumn

Campaign has not met the planned results. . . . our victories were limited, and the enemy . . . has fulfilled his most pressing require-ments . . ."[10] Apparently the discouraging results of the August offensive triggered another COSVN resolution, Resolution No. 14, issued 30 Octo-ber 1969, the same date as the report cited above. Resolution No. 14 did not replace Resolution No. 9; it supplemented it, reemphasizing and explaining again the rationale behind the return to small-unit warfare. Resolution No. 14 was an unusually candid assessment. It admitted that the August Campaign was a failure, that the effort to increase guerrilla strength had not succeeded, and that the US/SVN pacification effort was making significant, and to the Communists, damaging progress. In the Resolution No. 14, COSVN, as usual, placed the primary blame for the failure of the new concept of sapper warfare on its subordinate leaders, stating, ". . . the principal cause of the shortcomings . . . was the fact that we did not . . . clearly see the strategic importance of guerrilla warfare in the General Offensive and Uprising. . ."[11] The directive then goes on to declare categorically that "the only way to cope with an enemy who has a large number of troops and war facilities is to wage guerrilla warfare. . ." The directive says that guerrilla warfare will wear down the enemy, stretch him thin, erode his morale, collapse his organization, and prepare the way for large-scale offensive operations.

In addition to the deficiencies of leadership, the directive blamed the failure of the guerrilla warfare concept on the inability to expand that mode of combat. Too much reliance, said COSVN, was placed on "consolidated" forces (apparently meaning large Main and Local Forces), and there was inadequate coordination between guerrillas and Main and Local Forces. The solution to these problems, according to the directive, was to improve coordination between guerrillas and Local Forces, includ-ing breaking down the larger Main and Local Force units into company-size sapper packets to aid the guerrillas. Finally, the Party leadership must be indoctrinated and instructed in the importance and techniques of guerrilla warfare.[12]

Resolution No. 14 worsened one of the most critical problems it sought to solve—Communist morale. The "old soldiers" in the Commu-nist units, particularly the Viet Cong, did not swallow the line promulgated by the Politburo and echoed by COSVN in Resolution Nos. 9 and 14. They were all too aware of the battlefield realities, too cognizant of the failure of all Communist offensives in 1968 and 1969. They reasoned that this new concept was not going to solve their problems, and further, that the failure of the offensives had forced the Communist leadership to retrogress from conventional to guerrilla warfare. Middle-level cadre listened to SVN and American broadcasts avidly for some clue that the Paris peace talks might end the war. And with this defeatism, the doubters lost their appetite for continued hardship and battle. Morale sagged still lower and defections mounted.

As a result of COSVN Resolution Nos. 9 and 14, in the latter part of 1969, particularly after the August high point, activity by enemy units battalion-size or larger ceased. There was an increase in raids and shelling by small enemy units, but for the first time in three years, Giap had no plans for another large-scale offensive. As 1969 ended, the watchwords from Hanoi were *guerrilla warfare,* to hold down Communist casualties, and *patience,* to wait until the United States withdrew its troops. These were the Politburo's counteraction to President Nixon's announced war policy, which by the end of 1969 was becoming—in his oft-used phrase—"perfectly clear." That policy was a "four track" program of Vietnamization, negotiations, pacification, and United States troop withdrawal.

Vietnamization was a unilateral American policy designed to serve the national interests of the United States, and the United States only. In the highest councils of the American government there was the hope—generally forlorn—that the policy might also prepare South Vietnamese to defend themselves against both the Viet Cong and the North Vietnamese. This facet, however, was distinctly secondary to the American imperative of getting out of the Vietnam War with some honor—or at least, what would pass for honor.

Although President Johnson had begun a form of Vietnamization in March of 1968, the Nixon administration delayed until mid-1969 before adopting the concept as the centerpiece of its new strategy for Vietnam. The formal policy of Vietnamization had many titular fathers. Presidents Johnson and Nixon, Generals Westmoreland and Abrams, Secretary Clifford, and National Security Advisers Rostow and Kissinger could—and some did—claim parenthood. The man who is usually given primary credit for the concept in its final form, however, is Nixon's secretary of defense, Melvin Laird. Laird returned from a trip to Vietnam in March 1969 with a glowing report about the increasing capabilities of the RVNAF, and these views shortly matured into Laird's concept of "Vietnamization." Laird could not sell the idea to Nixon, however, until after Nixon's speech of 14 May had drawn negative reactions from both Saigon and Hanoi. So in late May, Nixon, searching for another gambit to move the Vietnam war off stalemate, embraced Laird's concept of Vietnamization and in effect made it the central theme of his emerging strategy.

Melvin Laird was a "total politician." Politics was his profession, his hobby, and he was good at it. He had served several terms in the United States House of Representatives and had become an expert in national defense matters, particularly the workings of the defense budget. Whatever might have been his thoughts about the war prior to assuming the office of secretary of defense, he soon evidenced a dovish trend. Practical politician Laird had no feelings of guilt regarding the war, none of the muddled sympathy for the Vietnamese Communists which infected the liberals, the media, and some members of Congress. In 1969, Laird saw the war pragmatically as a losing proposition, one that was likely to pull down all who were closely associated with it, including Melvin Laird. And so, to Laird, Vietnamization offered a way to get the United States, the Republican party, Richard Nixon, and most important, Melvin Laird, out of the Vietnamese quagmire. Whether it would work or not was secondary. It was an exit. By early June 1969, Nixon had accepted the concept and was ready to spring it on the people most intimately connected with it—the South Vietnamese people and their president, Nguyen Van Thieu.

The timing of the official launching of Vietnamization, mid-1969, was propitious. The Communist military disasters of 1968 and early 1969 had ravaged the strength and morale of the Viet Cong guerrillas and the VC political infrastructure. Giap and Truong Chinh had at last forced their strategic views on the Politburo, stressing small-unit, casualty-saving actions interspersed with lulls in the fighting, giving the South Vietnamese a needed respite. The United States forces within South Vietnam, too, had subtly changed their tactics by mid-1969. There were no more big search and destroy operations, no more plans to counter large enemy offensives. Now the American strategy sought to push pacification and to counter the enemy's small-unit actions with similar-sized counteractions. In effect, this meant that General Abrams and his principal assistants could now concentrate their attention on helping the RVNAF to modernize and improve.

Among the South Vietnamese themselves, the time was also advantageous for Vietnamization. As a result of the Tet offensive, the military had gained self-confidence, and its prestige among its fellow citizens reached an all-time high. The South Vietnamese people themselves had been galvanized by the Tet attacks into various forms of self-defense and had rallied, by and large, to the Thieu government. The sudden burst of patriotic zeal which had resulted in the massive mobilization provided the manpower needed to expand the RVNAF. Vietnamization officially became a controlling part of the United States policy toward Vietnam on 8 June 1969, when President Nixon met President Thieu on Midway Island. Here, the Siamese twins of United States policy, Vietnamization and United States troop withdrawal, made their appearance.

From the beginning, a confusing ambiguity surrounded the concept of Vietnamization. The United States did not issue an overall plan or controlling timetable. The project was never formalized by a treaty or joint agreement. MACV had only a generalized notion of the scheme and never issued a plan. In their turn, the South Vietnamese gave out *no instructions whatsoever* about what the program consisted of or how it was to be carried out.

There was a fundamental reason for this ambiguity. Any realistic American plan for Vietnamization had to depend on two major factors—United States troop withdrawals and enemy pressure—and both were unpredictable. The enemy and his plans were, of course, subject to no control or even prophesy by the United States. The rate of United States troop withdrawals depended on the enemy's actions, on South Vietnamese progress, on the status of negotiations, and most heavily, on domestic political pressure. So, Vietnamization, like the troop withdrawal program, became an extemporaneous exercise moving sometimes too slowly, more often too fast.

The South Vietnamese had *their* problems with the concept of Vietnamization. The South Vietnamese from Thieu on down hated the term. They never used it, for to them it implied that they had *not* been fighting a war for their own survival. Gen. Cao Van Vien, the chairman of the South Vietnamese Joint General Staff (their JCS), wrote years later, "Why Vietnamization? . . . Why make it sound that only United States forces were fighting the Vietnam War? The amount of blood shed by the South Vietnamese was many times greater than that of (the) gallant United States troops. . . . The use of Vietnamization as a term deeply hurt the people and the armed forces of the RVN. We feel it unwittingly admitted the United States error in strategy and the failure of United States military efforts. . . ."[13]

Beyond the name, the South Vietnamese reasoned that Vietnamization was an American device developed primarily to solve American domestic problems. They elected to view it as an acceleration of the modernization programs which had been going on since 1965. Thus, the South Vietnamese viewed Vietnamization as nothing more than a fancy title devised for consumption in the United States. In 1969, the South Vietnamese missed the vital point that Vietnamization was more than modernization and expansion of RVNAF; it was a strategy which would clear the way for United States withdrawal, leaving the South Vietnamese to defend themselves against both the Viet Cong and the NVA regardless of their capacity to do so. This somber concept they never grasped—at least, not until it was too late. The South Vietnamese were convinced almost to the end that the United States would support them in whatever way was necessary until they could clearly go it alone.

While neither the Americans nor the South Vietnamese drew up detailed plans for Vietnamization, they did have an unspoken agreement on the general phasing of the concept. In the first phase, the United States would turn over to ARVN the responsibility for ground combat against the Viet Cong and NVA, while the United States would continue to provide air and naval support. The second phase foresaw an expansion of RVNAF's strength in air, naval, artillery, and other supporting arms necessary to allow South Vietnam to defend itself. In the final phase, the American presence would be limited to an advisory role, and eventually, even this assistance would be phased out as the South Vietnamese reached self-sufficiency.[14] Actually, there was nothing new about this phasing. This same broad concept of RVNAF improvement had been bruited about with variations since 1967.

The most important step in implementing Phase I of Vietnamization was the reorganization and expansion of the force structure of ARVN. The South Vietnamese Regional Forces (RF) and Popular Forces (PF), both of whom had given an unexpectedly good account of themselves in the Tet offensive, were to be vastly expanded. It was hoped that this would free some of the ARVN infantry divisions from static security duties for either offensive operations or as mobile reserves. This was a new development. To increase further the offensive capabilities of ARVN, the divisions received additional artillery battalions, the corps got some corps artillery units, ARVN acquired some 500 more helicopters, and there was a concomitant increase in armored cavalry, signal, engineer, medical, and other support units. Concurrently with the expansion and modification of the ARVN, the Vietnamese navy and the Vietnamese air force were to be expanded and modernized to take over the role envisioned for them in Phase II. Since their modernization depended on complex equipment and long-term training, the planners foresaw their development lagging.

The concept, plan, and phasing of Vietnamization, although ambiguous and tenuous, revealed the monstrous problems which stalked Vietnamization. First, there was the training problem. It shouldn't have existed—after all, the United States had been training the South Vietnamese since 1954—but it did exist, and it was critical. The concept of Vietnamization required trained people, not only to use the equipment, but to store, maintain, issue, and repair it. It required skilled leaders who could direct and motivate the troops; and it required clerks, cooks, nurses, and all the other supporting skills which go into making up a modern armed force. Some training, of course, was underway, but the new requirements imposed by Vietnamization dwarfed the previous effort and highlighted the deficiencies.

Training installations and equipment were grossly inadequate. The understrength cadres of officers and noncommissioned officers manning the training installations, being the cast-offs from the combat units, lacked the skills, leadership, and motivation to do the job. Some training, particularly for the navy and air force, required a knowledge of English and perhaps even a tour of duty in the United States, both time-consuming. Finally, training within and by the ARVN units themselves was almost nonexistent. Most of the unit's time (and this was particularly true of the ARVN infantry divisions) was consumed by static defensive operations, and when they could break away from that duty, the requirements for rest, refitting, and maintenance took higher priority.

MACV tried to improvise a way around this last training obstacle. General Abrams established a program of pairing off ARVN units with American units, both army and marine. Abrams believed that imitation was the best form of training, and that with close battlefield association the South Vietnamese would absorb some of the aggressiveness and techniques of the Americans. This was nothing new. The marines had practiced the concept at platoon level since 1965, and army and ARVN units had paired off intermittently from 1966. General Abrams' program was more extensive, but otherwise it was more of the same; and it suffered from the same faults as its predecessors—no master plan, no centralized direction, and vague objectives.

Abrams used another training device—the concept of Mobile Advisory Teams. These teams, each consisting of from three to ten Americans, were the principal tool for the training of the RF and PF, who were scattered in small units around the country. The teams accomplished a great deal, but the monstrous nature of the requirement eventually swamped them. The final training program, which, like the others, had been around for some time, was Operation BUDDY. This program began in 1968, pairing American and South Vietnamese ground logistical units for on-the-job training in maintenance and repair of the complex equipment that ARVN was receiving. Again, it worked well where tried, but suffered from lack of centralized control and direction. These basic training deficiencies consistently limited the effectiveness of Vietnamization.

Another major factor which curtailed any realistic prospect of the success of Vietnamization was the territorial and static nature of ARVN's organization and disposition. With the exception of the airborne and marine divisions, each ARVN infantry division was located in its "home area." It statically defended its area; it recruited from the area; and it received draftees from the area. The families of the soldiers tended to congregate around the military camps in hovels, and often the dependents accompanied the soldiers into the field. As a result of the static defensive requirements of an area and the peculiar living conditions of the personnel, ARVN infantry divisions were for practical purposes immobile—unavailable for offensive operations or counterattack. The JGS tried to overcome this problem by assigning security requirements in an area to the RF and PF, but they were never successful in freeing the infantry divisions to become effective mobile forces.

Even worse, the congregation of the families around the division's cantonment guaranteed disaster in the event of a major enemy attack on the division position. In an effort to get out of the combat zone, families would clog any avenues of retreat. Soldiers would desert their units to assist their families to safety. These chaotic conditions would inevitably turn what should have been an orderly withdrawal into a rout.[15] Thus, the backbone of ARVN, the infantry division, was an illusion. In reality they were, with a few exceptions, a motley crew of Home Guards posing as a strike force, one of the fantasies upon which the United States built its concept of Vietnamization.

These deficiencies of the RVNAF, as debilitating as they were, faded when compared to other South Vietnamese shortcomings. Successful Vietnamization required an almost total restructuring of the South Vietnamese society, government, and armed forces, for these flaws prevented the South Vietnamese from achieving the goal of Vietnamization.

All of these intractable problems facing Vietnamization had one aspect in common—each would require for solution an extended period of time, years, maybe even decades. And adequate time was unavailable. South Vietnam was caught between the United States schedule for troop withdrawal (which would march to the drum of American politics without much relation to the progress of Vietnamization), and the North Vietnamese timetable for aggression. Each of these factors guaranteed inadequate time for Vietnamization to succeed, and without adequate time, Vietnamization can be seen in its true light—an American self-serving illusion.

Although President Johnson had called a bombing halt on 31 October 1968, supposedly to try to get negotiations started, nothing happened until just before President Nixon's inauguration on 20 January 1969. On that date, the negotiators arrived at an agreement as to the shape of the negotiation table. Even this trivial step would loom large compared to the progress of the following months.

The first plenary session took place on 25 January 1969. The chief of the United States delegation, Henry Cabot Lodge, tabled the innocuous proposal that the neutrality of the DMZ be renewed. The leader of the Hanoi delegation, Xuan Thuy, refused to even discuss the American proposal and preemptively demanded that the United States halt its war of aggression against Vietnam. On this rebuff the conference deadlocked. The Americans wanted to talk about the military situation, while the North Vietnamese wanted to negotiate the political future of South Vietnam.[16] Nor was this deadlock temporary; in fact, no real progress was made for the remainder of the year.

Not that Nixon and Kissinger didn't try to advance negotiations. In

retrospect, they might have tried too hard. Even before Nixon's inauguration he sent a secret message to Ho Chi Minh through a French contact,
Jean Sainteny, who was a friend of Kissinger's and who knew Ho.
The message expressed the new administration's desire to move to meaningful negotiations. The North Vietnamese response spurned the conciliatory advances and restated its two demands: withdraw *all* American
forces, and replace the Thieu government.

Then, in March and April, Kissinger devised what President Nixon
referred to as the "Vance ploy." Kissinger's concept was to send Cyrus
Vance, a well-known and respected Establishment figure, to the Russians
with the subtle message that their help in ending the Vietnam War would
be reciprocated by a new American willingness to enter into negotiations
regarding the Middle East, economic relations, and disarmament talks.
Kissinger transmitted this message and Vance's availability to the Soviet
ambassador in Washington, Anatoly Dobrynin. Dobrynin appeared interested in Kissinger's proposal, but nothing was heard from the Soviets
for many months, and then they casually dismissed the idea.

In June 1969, Kissinger made another effort to get negotiations moving. He again contacted his French friend, Jean Sainteny, who suggested
that Nixon send a personal letter to Ho which he would carry to Hanoi.
Nothing came of this idea. Hanoi would not even give Sainteny a visa.
Nixon's letter was given to Hanoi's representative in Paris for delivery
to Ho.

Kissinger made another effort in August, meeting in Paris with Xuan
Thuy. After fawning over Thuy for a few minutes, Kissinger stated
that the president wanted serious negotiations and was prepared to be
flexible, but that if by 1 November no progress had been made, the
United States "would have to consider steps of grave consequence."[17]
The Communists responded at great length, but the answer boiled down
to the same old two points—unilateral United States withdrawal and
replacement of the Thieu government. Two days later came the Communist attacks of 12 August. Finally, on 25 August, Ho Chi Minh, now
at death's door, answered Nixon's letter of 15 July. The letter was
insulting in tone and content and iron hard on Hanoi's two demands.

Negotiations were stalemated in 1969 for numerous reasons. The
North Vietnamese wanted not compromise, but victory; and they thought
they might get it. They saw the United States as weakened by antiwar
dissent and uncertainty of purpose. The United States troop withdrawals

sent them a signal of eventual United States unilateral departure. The Politburo had at last realized the power of the dissident minority within the United States to sway American policy toward settlement and surrender, disguised or undisguised, and they set out to exploit it. With this growing "Viet Cong Front" in the United States, all Hanoi had to do was to wait things out, and, by a military operation now and then, keep the American coffins coming home. Anyway, that's the way Hanoi saw it.

The United States could not move negotiations forward either. The doves had achieved a *de facto* veto over any escalation of the war or any significant military pressure on the Communists. Without this military pressure—the only kind of pressure the Communists would respect— no progress in settling the war was possible. Stripped of the option of using adequate military force, the United States had to face the North Vietnamese demands of unilateral United States withdrawal and the destruction of the Thieu government. The first, in time and under the right circumstances, could be accepted. Hanoi's second demand—the dismantling of the GVN—the United States refused to accept. As Henry Kissinger wrote, "Our refusal to overthrow an allied government remained the single and crucial issue that deadlocked all negotiations until 8 October 1972, when Hanoi withdrew their demand."[18]

In 1969, the pacification program continued the remarkable gains made in 1968, when the Tet offensive seriously damaged the Viet Cong guerrillas and its political infrastructure. Although well-concealed in American rhetoric, intensified support of pacification (in its broadest sense) was a part of the loudly proclaimed Vietnamization program—at least that's the way the South Vietnamese saw it. Major General Hinh wrote, "the Vietnamization program, however, was not confined to strengthening the Armed Forces; it was also designed to help South Vietnam institute political stability and social reforms and resolve its economic problems."[19]

The pacification program in 1969 got help from both its friends and foes. General Abrams made pacification "the number one strategy for the war."[20] His new strategy, as set forth in the MACV Objective Plan for 1969, listed as his two primary objectives (1) expanded areas of secure environment; and (2) solidified basis for the GVN and its people to continue developing meaningful institutions and an environment for economic growth and social change. In his command overview of the MACV Objective Plan, Abrams stated, "the key strategic thrust is to provide meaningful, continuing security for the Vietnamese people."[21]

The enemy, too, in 1969, albeit unwillingly, accelerated pacification. The Communist Main Force units had been forced from South Vietnam into sanctuaries in Laos, Cambodia, the DMZ, or North Vietnam. Their absence from South Vietnam withdrew the moral, physical, logistical, and combat support from the Communist guerrillas. The guerrillas and political infrastructure in turn had serious problems of their own making. The Tet offensive of 1968 had depleted their ranks, particularly their leaders. They were unable to recoup their losses by recruitment of South Vietnamese. The vacancies within their ranks, then, had to be filled by NVA soldiers, a practice which brought on crippling problems of language, ideology, and sectionalism. Finally, the defeats of 1968 and the shifting of strategies demoralized the guerrillas and infrastructure alike.

In 1969, for the first time, President Thieu gave his personal support to pacification. He took a personal part in the decision-making process, presiding over the Central Pacification and Development Council, the agency coordinating pacification activities. He appeared in the villages and training camps, stressing the priority he gave pacification. Finally, Thieu personally set the objectives for the 1969 GVN Pacification Plan, called by the Vietnamese the Special Campaign.

This Special Campaign aimed to retake the hamlets lost to the enemy and to expand territory under GVN control. This departed from the 1968 effort, which had concentrated on populated areas and urban centers. The broad objectives of the campaign were to expand territory under GVN control, destroy the VC infrastructure, and arm the People's Self Defense Forces (PSDF). The plan concentrated its efforts on the villages.[22] This concept aimed at giving the villagers control over their local affairs. Village elections were pressed, so that by the end of 1969 many of the villages in Vietnam had elected their own councils which in turn elected the village chief. In April, Thieu gave the councils control over their own local security forces, and in an unprecedented move, the village councils were given control over village development funds. Finally, a special training center for village officials was established, and some 17,000 leaders passed through the school.[23]

One of the other objectives of the Special Campaign was the organization and arming of the PSDF. This concept of local defense forces had been around for some years, but it was the Tet offensive of 1968 which gave it exuberant life. In 1969, the program gained momentum when over three million people (one million over the objective) volunteered for duties, and they were armed with 399,000 weapons (1,000 short of the objective). The people organized themselves into squads and platoons and received rudimentary military training. The program rallied the masses behind the Thieu government and contributed vastly to local security.

"Blowtorch" Bob Komer left Vietnam in November 1968, to be succeeded by William E. Colby, a senior CIA official who had been associated with Vietnam over many years. In appearance, Colby was the most deceptive of men. Slight, quiet, shy, he looked and acted like Mr. Peepers of the sixties' television fame. Nothing could be more misleading. In World War II, while in OSS, he had made several parachute jumps behind German lines to coordinate operations with the French underground. For these feats he received the Silver Star Medal. His Mr. Peepers exterior concealed a keen mind and a steely resolve to get the job done. Unlike Komer, Colby was a team player and a delight to work with.

This combination of factors produced almost unbelievable results. By the end of 1969, 90 percent of the villages and hamlets of South Vietnam were rated as secure or relatively secure; five million more people lived in government-controlled secure areas than in 1967; and 92 percent of the population lived in secure or relatively secure areas. The number of Viet Cong defectors, both troops and infrastructure, reached 47,000 as compared to 18,000 for 1968. These gains in population control further reduced the capabilities and effectiveness of the VC and VC infrastructure as they lost people and thus recruits, taxes, and resources.

Another result of the pacification drive of 1969 was the clearing of the roads. For the first time in years, transportation could move safely about the countryside. This progress, in turn, meant a significant improvement in the South Vietnamese economy. Rice production increased to 5,115,000 metric tons in 1969, and the markets in the towns and villages sported not only rice, but vegetables, poultry, and livestock as well.[24]

But, as was the inevitable case in the Vietnam War, progress in pacification brought problems, and highlighted deficiencies as well. The PHOENIX program still faltered, hampered by the old ills of unrealistic quotas, inadequate jails, corruption, and conniving officials, but in some areas it hurt the VC infrastructure. While the statistics of pacification looked impressive, there were, as always, doubts as to their validity. The Hamlet Evaluation System (HES), by which pacification gains and losses were gauged, depended on the word of the village and hamlet chiefs, for unfortunately, the district and province official had no means of verification. Other statistics, such as VC defectors, and the results of the PHOENIX program, were even more suspect. Finally, while reform had penetrated to the village level, it had made no headway at district, province, or national level. At these levels, the same old crowd played the same old games with the same old unsatisfactory and undemocratic results.

Nevertheless, pacification had made remarkable progress in 1969, and as the year ended, more progress in the seventies appeared clearly in the offing. Even the enemy agreed with this evaluation. In COSVN's *A Preliminary Report on the 1969 Autumn Campaign,* they wrote, "In sum, the Autumn campaign has not met planned results . . . the enemy . . . has nevertheless fulfilled his most pressing requirements, *particularly those of his rural pacification program* . . ."[25] (emphasis added).

As 1968 faded into history, ground combat in South Vietnam lessened significantly. The NVA and VC, trying to recover their numerical strength and morale, had opted for Truong Chinh's shift from all-out offensives to "protracted war"—whatever the latter meant. General Abrams, on the other hand, sought a big battle. President Johnson had ordered him on 31 October to apply maximum pressure on the enemy, and this Abe tried to do. But Giap, who controlled the timing and size of the battles, would not oblige him as 1968 slipped into 1969, and Johnson's War became Nixon's War. The change of administrations brought no immediate changes of a major nature to the combat situation in South Vietnam. In fact, Nixon's policy in the early days of his administration approximated Johnson's—weaken the enemy, modernize the RVNAF, and then begin withdrawing United States troops. Nevertheless, here and there combat action (and the resulting controversies) heated up.

On 20 January (Inauguration Day), the 3d Marine Division launched an attack against Enemy Base Area 611, which straddled the Laotian/Vietnamese border some fifty miles south of the DMZ. The operation dragged on uneventfully for about two weeks and then got hot—at least in one aspect—when United States Marines entered Laos by intent, and on the sole responsibility of one marine colonel. After destroying large stocks of supplies, they were quickly snatched back without great public outcry, but a previous policy barrier had been quietly, almost clandestinely, overridden.

Thwarted by the enemy's refusal to fight in large units, General Abrams, in the spring of 1969, had to change his tactics to meet Giap's. Abrams broke his divisions into small platoon- and company-sized task forces who concentrated on extensive patrolling and night operations. These tactics were designed to preempt the Communists by keeping the enemy off balance and by disrupting and destroying his logistic arrangements. Abrams called this tactic "getting into his (the enemy's) system."

The Politburo's return to "protracted war" brought a more fundamental change in MACV's concepts. With the intensity and size of the fighting diminished, Abrams could now devote more of his strength and effort towards pacification and Vietnamization, and he was ready for this basic shift. Shortly after he took command of MACV in June 1968, he assembled a group of young officers in Saigon who had served on the army staff in the Pentagon in 1966 and had developed the ill-fated PROVN study. This concept, which was never adopted, stressed pacification and nation-building as the strategy to win the war. Abrams, who in 1966 had been vice chief of staff of the army, had originally approved the study, and in 1969 thought the concept more valid than it might have been in 1966. Beginning in late 1968, the task force updated and expanded the PROVN concept. Abrams closely followed their efforts, approving and modifying the concepts as they developed. At last, in early 1969, the young officers gave a briefing on the new concept to the assembled senior staff officers and commanders of American ground units in Vietnam.

The briefing crashed in flames. Abrams did not tell the assembled generals that he had in effect already approved the concept. By his opening words and actions, Abrams gave the false impression that the purpose of the briefing was for him to make a decision on the concept *after* he had heard the briefing, and the candid comments of his senior commanders and staff officers. While not intending to, Abrams had created an ambush, and senior officers, like all mortals, dislike being hit from the blind side. Then, the briefers, knowing they had Abrams' approval, made the same mistake they had made with the original PROVN briefing in 1966—they superciliously talked down to their seniors. The bulk of the comments of the senior officers were virulently negative. Abrams, now angry, got into the discussion forcefully—and Abe could be very forceful—revealing for the first time his true position. That stifled further dissent, but it left the generals unhappy and unconvinced, and "Son of PROVN"—like its father—began under a needless handicap.

It has become conventional wisdom to claim that the new concept suffered severely because Abrams' senior commanders refused to support it. This is nonsense. In many cases the general officers in Vietnam agreed with Abrams' strategy and carried it out with dedication. Even those who disagreed with the concept dutifully, if unenthusiastically, gave it their full support. Abrams himself would accept no less, and he had the power of enforcement. Every general in Vietnam knew that Abrams held the power of life or death over his career, and they knew further that Abe would not hesitate to use that power.

The "Son of PROVN" became the official strategy in March 1969 with the adoption of the MACV objectives plan for that year. In brief, the plan established the prime objective of the American and South Vietnamese forces to be population security and support to pacification. Thus, Ambassador Bunker's "one war concept" of 1967 became, two years later, the official doctrine. General Vien later joined Abrams in support of the concept, and the Combined (U.S./SVN) Strategic Objective Plan confirmed it as the joint strategy.

Abrams' new strategy did not prevent heavy and violent contact between American and North Vietnamese units. On 10 May, three battalions of the 101st Airborne Division launched a heliborne operation into the A Shau Valley to clean up Enemy Base Area 611, which had been rebuilt by the NVA after the marine assault of January–February 1969. On 11 May, one of the battalions bumped into a sizable enemy force entrenched on Ap Bia Hill (Hill 937), which was to become infamous as "Hamburger Hill." Casualties soared on both sides. Three more airborne battalions were committed before the crest of the position was overrun. The enemy suffered 610 KIA's while the Americans had 56 dead.

The battle catapulted the doves into shrill flight. Congress and the news media decried the battle as a waste of America's young men and criticized it as overly aggressive and as demonstrating a lack of any definable strategy. The criticism stung the Nixon administration. It needed support at home. It needed a breathing space to get its policies straightened out, and so word quietly went out from Washington to Abrams to hold down American casualties. The strategy of search and destroy was officially dead. Not only were American troops leaving South Vietnam, but the offensive spirit was leaving the American army. So, for different reasons, both sides let the war wind down in the latter part of 1969 to sporadic and small-unit actions.

For the United States, 1969 produced one unexpected and pernicious harvest—the *beginning* of the demoralization of the American ground forces in Vietnam. Historically, an army (and in this general term the marine ground units in Vietnam are included) becomes demoralized either by a devastating defeat (the Italians at Caporetto in World War I), or by huge and purposeless casualties (the French army in World War I at Verdun), by unbearable living conditions (the French army under Napoleon in its retreat from Moscow), or by obviously corrupt or incompetent leadership (the Russians on the Eastern Front in World War I). Yet there is an "X" factor, an unknown, which rebuts the above, which makes armies rise above disaster, or heavy casualties, or debilitating living conditions, or incompetent leadership. American military history is replete with such examples. In the Civil War, the Union Army suffered a series of devastating defeats in the East without crumbling. The monstrous casualties incurred by both sides in the Civil War, at Antietam, Shiloh, Gettysburg, and the Battle of the Wilderness, left morale and discipline of both the Blue and Gray untouched. Valley Forge was a classic case of unbearable living conditions, yet the fledgling American army came out of that winter stronger in spirit and effectiveness than it had entered it. And finally, the Union Army survived and grew in stature under the leadership of such incompetents as Burnside, Pope, and Hooker.

But the demoralization of the American ground units in Vietnam could be attributed to none of the causes generally accepted as destructive of the spirit of a military force. American troops were never defeated; their casualties (looked at historically) were light; they lived in conditions which previous American armies would have thought sinfully luxurious; and their leaders, at least at the top, were competent professionals.

There was a combination of events and factors that caused this breakdown of morale and discipline. Nixon's policies—as wise and effective as they may have been for his primary purposes—struck a heavy blow at soldier morale. Vietnamization, troop withdrawals, and emphasis on peace through negotiations meant to the American soldier in Vietnam that the United States in 1969 was openly engaged in a no-win war. More than that, these activities created the false hope that the war would shortly be over, or at least that the war would end soon for the individual by early withdrawal. Why fight, why get killed or wounded in a war, the soldier asked himself, which might soon be ended by withdrawal or peace? Who wants to be the last man killed in this war, became an oft-repeated catchphrase. And in a combat situation, when a soldier's will to fight falters, his morale soon follows.

Dissent on the domestic front also sapped soldier morale in Vietnam. The soldiers in Vietnam resented the lack of support at home for their efforts and sacrifices. The "grunts" held the college protesters and other antiwar dissenters in contempt and hatred, a loathing deepened by difference in outlook, values, and class. Antiwar dissidence caused the soldiers to mistrust the competence and integrity of their leaders, to question their mission in Vietnam and to doubt the value of their sacrifices there—all subtly sapping of morale. The hammering of the antiwar dissenters on the immorality of the war not only caused many soldiers to doubt the rectitude of their efforts, but in some cases to conceive that what they were doing in Vietnam was dishonorable. It furnished a ready-made pretext for those who did not want to fight by giving them an excuse to shirk their combat duties as immoral.

Some of the morale problems the servicemen brought with them to Vietnam. Racial tension and strife strained an already baneful state of morale, dividing and shredding unit cohesiveness. A growing sense of permissiveness, along with a lowering of respect for authority—both characteristic of the sixties—undermined discipline. The soldiers brought with them to Vietnam the drug culture of the young, a vice made worse by the ease with which drugs could be obtained in Vietnam. For the first time in American military history, drugs became a weapon of warfare wielded by an unscrupulous enemy. Brian Crozier, a respected British military commentator, wrote, ". . . the late Chinese premier, Chou En-lai, once boasted to Colonel Nassar of Egypt that China with North Vietnamese participation, had used drugs on a large scale to undermine the morale and efficiency of United States forces during the Vietnam

War.''[26] An unusual wrinkle in the Communists' ''troop proselyting'' program.

Conditions of service in Vietnam also compounded the problems of morale and discipline. For the ground combat units there were the harsh physical hardships and stresses of combat: mud, leeches, snakes, booby traps, mines, death, fatigue, fear, loss of friends, irregular hours, poor food or no food, torrential rain, and humid heat. Over an extended period, these drain a man physically and psychologically. In the rear areas (an indefinite description in this war) conditions were less dangerous and debilitating, but in many cases, not much better. Even in Saigon the personnel were exposed to random rocket attacks, and life in the big headquarters had its own hardships—long hours, poor billets, and bad food.

The peculiar battlefield situation in Vietnam in 1969 contributed its own influence to lowered American morale. The enemy refused contact, and evaded American search parties. Frustration set in as the Allied units redoubled their efforts to get at the elusive enemy. Still, United States casualties continued, produced mostly by the ubiquitous mines and booby traps. So American soldiers were being injured and killed by a seemingly invisible, but ever-present, enemy. Soon Vietnamese civilians, who could be seen, became suspects, and in such angry frustration My Lai occurred. The decrease in the intensity of combat produced inaction, boredom, and lethargy in many American units. Boredom and inaction are breeding grounds for lowered morale and discipline, and with lowered morale, increased problems with drugs, alcohol, civilian relations, and discipline.

A system of military justice which provided for a prompt trial, and where appropriate, swift punishment, might have contained these disciplinary problems. No such system existed in Vietnam. The case load was staggering. Key witnesses either rotated back to the United States or were unavailable due to death or operational requirements. The military lawyers themselves frequently rotated before their cases came to trial. Many offenses were committed in isolated combat areas, and getting the accused, the witnesses, and the court together required Herculean coordination. Frequently, offenses involved Vietnamese witnesses who were difficult to locate and interrogate. Finally, the mass of paperwork required to protect the rights of the accused had to pass laboriously up and down the chain of command.[27] While one sympathizes with the overworked military lawyers, it must be admitted that, in the words of one army report, military justice "was neither swift nor certain and transgressors have been comparatively free to repeat their acts with impunity."[28]

Underlying and aggravating all the other factors lowering morale was inadequate leadership where it was most important, at the noncommissioned officer and junior officer level, where the leaders come in daily contact with the enlisted men—in soldier jargon, "where the rubber meets the road." In the rapidly expanded army and marine corps, men became sergeants and lieutenants who were inadequate in character, intelligence, experience, and motivation. It is always thus in a democracy, but in Vietnam the failure of leadership at the small-unit level was particularly devastating. Vietnam was largely a series of unrelated small-unit actions and patrols, performed, usually perforce, without supervision by more senior officers. Also, leadership suffered from the yearly rotation, which in practice became a six-month rotation for officers in the combat units as they moved from command to staff.

In 1969, the question which harried the senior officers in Vietnam was not if morale and discipline had declined—they accepted that—but how much had it declined? How bad was the situation? Nobody knew for sure then, and nobody knows now. Many offenses went unreported; many that were reported resulted in no disciplinary action. Nevertheless, the available statistics paint a picture of a deteriorating status of morale and discipline. Offenses within the army in Vietnam (and the marine corps had similar statistics) leading to either a court-martial or nonjudicial punishment rose 13 percent in 1969 over 1968, although there was a smaller troop strength in Vietnam in 1969 than in 1968. Drug use, too, climbed, although the figures are unreliable. "Fraggings," the murder of officers and noncommissioned officers by their men, appeared in 1969. In that year a total of 126 incidents was recorded, with 37 deaths. "Insubordination, Mutiny and Other Acts Involving Willful Refusal to Perform a Lawful Order"—a most serious military offense—increased to 128 in 1969, compared to 94 in 1968. Desertions and AWOL's (Absent Without Leave) showed a similar increase. The most prevalent form of low morale and lack of discipline never appeared in the statistics—what the "grunts" called "search and evade." In its simplest form, this consisted of going on a patrol or search operation and intentionally not finding any enemy. Either the patrol just sat down shortly after leaving the patrol base, or it searched an area known to be free of the enemy. The patrol leader returned with a false report of his route and a negative report of enemy contact.

Sifting through the available figures and talking to junior officers and enlisted men, an observer gets the impression (and that is about all it is possible to get) that morale and discipline began to slump in 1969, but that overall the deterioration was minor. But the hairline crack in the army's facade of morale and discipline which appeared in 1969 would become a visible fissure in 1970 and a yawning crevice in 1971.

Notes—Chapter 21

1. Henry Kissinger, "The Vietnam Negotiations," *Foreign Affairs,* January 1969.
2. Samuel Lipsman, Edward Doyle, and the eds. *The Vietnam Experience: Fighting for Time* (Boston, MA: Boston Publishing Co., 1983), pp. 28–29.
3. Karnow, *Vietnam, A History,* p. 589.
4. Lung, *General Offensives,* p. 118. (Note: Lung's figure of three times the 1968 figure is in error. The accepted figure for 1968 is 18,000.)
5. Henry B. Kissinger, *The White House Years* (Boston: Little, Brown & Co., 1979), p. 241.
6. Truong Nhu Tang, *A Vietcong Memoir—An Inside Account of the Vietnam War and Its Aftermath* (New York: Harcourt Brace Jovanovich, 1985), p. 169.
7. Lung, *General Offensives,* p. 118.
8. Kissinger, *White House Years,* pp. 272, 267–277.
9. "A Nation Coming into Its Own," *Time,* Vol. 126, no. 4, 29 July 1985, p. 53.
10. "A Preliminary Report on Activities During the 1969 Autumn Campaign, 30 October 1969" Vietnam Documents and Research Notes No. 82 (Saigon: United States Embassy, August 1979), p. 15.
11. "COSVN Resolution No. 14, (30 October 1969)" Vietnam Documents and Research Notes No. 81 (Saigon: United States Embassy, July 1970), p. 12.
12. Ibid., p. 8.
13. Vien and Khuyen, *Reflections,* p. 91.
14. Nguyen Duy Hinh, *Vietnamization and Cease-Fire,* Indochina Monographs (Washington, D.C.: U.S. Army Center of Military History, 1983), pp. 16–17.
15. Tran Van Don, *Our Endless War: Inside Vietnam* (San Rafael, CA: Presidio Press, 1978), p. 231.
16. Louis A. Fanning, *Betrayal in Vietnam* (New Rochelle, NY: Arlington House, Publishers, 1976), p. 24.
17. Kissinger, *White House Years,* p. 280.
18. Ibid., p. 282.
19. Hinh, *Vietnamization,* p. 18.
20. Lipsman and Doyle, *Fighting for Time,* p. 76.
21. MACV, "One War: MACV Command Overview 1968–1972," (Washington, D.C.: U.S. Army Center of Military History, Undated), p. 15.

22. Tran Dinh Tho, *Pacification,* Indochina Monographs (Washington, D.C.: U.S. Army Center of Military History, 1980), p. 24.
23. Senate Committee on Foreign Relations, *Hearings on Cords,* pp. 709 and 714.
24. Sir Robert Thompson, *Peace is Not at Hand* (New York: David McKay, 1974), p. 67.
25. COSVN, Document No. 82, p. 3.
26. Brian Crozier, "Terror, New Style," *National Review,* 9 August 1985, p. 24.
27. Maj. Gen. George S. Prugh, *Law at War: Vietnam 1964–1973,* (Washington, D.C.: Department of the Army, 1974), pp. 100–102.
28. MACCORDS-PSG, "Anti-American Demonstrations in Qui Nhon," 18 April 1971, p. 18 CMH (quoted in Lewy, *America,* p. 160.)

22 The Cambodian Raids of 1970

In early 1970, neither of the antagonists had come up with new policies or strategies. In North Vietnam, the Giap/Truong clique had gained almost complete policy dominance over the Le Duan/Le Duc Tho group. The North Vietnamese continued their strategy of "protracted warfare," featuring small-scale attacks by sappers, standoff shellings, and a futile opposition to pacification, whose gains caused them great concern. For the Politburo, the watchword in 1970 was, as in 1969, patience—let the United States complete its withdrawal before shifting to the offensive, an offensive which Giap, even in 1970, began to plan.

Morale, particularly among what was left of the Viet Cong, remained a serious problem. The Allied pacification programs continued to make tremendous progress, depriving the Viet Cong of recruits, taxes, and food. Captured documents detailed stories of Viet Cong troops who were hungry, ragged, and despondent. True insurgency-type operations by the Viet Cong nearly disappeared, and the burden of the war was now carried almost entirely by the NVA. Thus, the small sapper operations, which Giap called guerrilla warfare, were, in fact, small conventional warfare attacks, carried out not by indigenous insurgents, but by NVA troops alien to the South Vietnamese population. In the very early months of 1970, all the Communists could do was "hang in there," and wait out Nixon and the United States.

Nor in early 1970 did Nixon, Kissinger, and company produce any new policies or strategies. They followed the same four "tracks"—

623

Vietnamization, pacification, troop withdrawal, and negotiations—which they had trod in 1969. The results improved, particularly in pacification. And thus, 1970, like 1969, might have passed relatively quietly had not an event—unforeseen by either antagonist—abruptly changed the shape of the war. That event was the overthrow of the Cambodian chief of state, Prince Norodom Sihanouk.

Among the characters and bona fide eccentrics who peopled the Indochina wars, Sihanouk stands out. He was a king who elected to lead Cambodia as a commoner. He was a so-so painter, a fair jazz saxophonist, and an untalented thespian who directed, acted in, and produced his own bad movies. In foreign affairs he attempted to walk the icy tightrope between China and North Vietnam on one side and the United States on the other. He let the Communists establish large base areas in his country and granted them the use of the port of Sihanouk-ville, from which they supplied the southern half of their forces in South Vietnam. Then, turning in the other direction, he encouraged the United States to bomb the North Vietnamese base areas with the proviso that the Americans keep the attacks secret.

But as the sixties rolled into the seventies, Sihanouk aligned himself closer to the Chinese, and thus indirectly with the North Vietnamese. The United States cut off its economic aid to Cambodia and the pinch began to be felt throughout the country. In addition, the North Vietnamese began to expand their operations from the border area of Cambodia toward the interior. In early 1970, Cambodian sentiment began to turn against Sihanouk. Then, in an act of cavalier stupidity, on 10 March 1970, Sihanouk left Cambodia to take his annual "liver cure" in France. Coups and countercoups suddenly flourished, and on 18 March, the Cambodian National Assembly, led by the prime minister, Lon Nol, voted unanimously to oust Sihanouk from power.

Lon Nol struck quickly against the Communists in Cambodia—too quickly perhaps. He closed the port of Sihanoukville to the Communists and fatuously proclaimed his intention of ousting the Communists from their base areas on the Cambodian/Vietnamese border. Lon Nol's mani-festo galvanized the North Vietnamese into preventive action. From their base areas in eastern Cambodia, the Communists, 40,000 to 60,000 strong, undertook a vigorous drive to the west. The weak Cambodian forces could not stand against them, and soon the VC/NVA were threaten-ing the Cambodian capital, Phnom Penh. It soon became evident that without outside aid, Lon Nol and his pro-Western government would go down the drain with ominous consequences for the United States and the GVN. If Cambodia fell into Communist hands, the port of Sihanoukville would be reopened and *all* Cambodia would become a major base area outflanking United States and Allied forces in South Vietnam.

As March became April, Lon Nol's situation continued to worsen, and by mid-April it became evident that the United States would have to assist him, or suffer a major setback. Melvin Laird, secretary of state, William Rogers, and the other dovish "pragmatists" in the administration recommended no aid to Cambodia, or such inadequate aid as to be meaningless. And again the tug-of-war between Nixon, Kissinger, and the military on one hand versus his civilian advisers on the other began to play itself out. Meetings occurred, papers were shuffled, and nothing of consequence happened—except the NVA continued its successful offensive toward central Cambodia.

By 22 April, Nixon and his advisers realized that the United States had to intervene in Cambodia decisively or see the war change dramatically for the worse. At a meeting of the National Security Council held that day, Nixon decided that the South Vietnamese should attack the sanctuaries in the "Parrot's Beak" with United States air support, which was to be limited to "demonstrated necessity." He withheld the more critical decision about United States ground force participation. After several more days of debate and procrastination, Nixon made the decision that American ground troops would assault the other principal base area complex on the Cambodia/Vietnam border, the so-called "Fish Hook." The decisive factor which brought about the use of American troops was General Abrams' unequivocal statement that he could not insure the success of any raid into Cambodia unless American troops were used.[1] And so, early in the morning on 28 April, Nixon made his final decision that the South Vietnamese troops would attack the "Parrot's Beak" on 29 April, while United States troops would assault the "Fish Hook" on 1 May.

It is difficult, even now, to discern Nixon's precise objectives for the Cambodian raid. Some of his aims are self-evident; others, the broader ones, blurred and confused. Obviously, the operation sought, by attacking Communist base areas near the Vietnamese/Cambodian border, to relieve the enemy pressure on Lon Nol's ragtag army, to destroy the supplies in the base areas (and troops who might defend them), and to capture

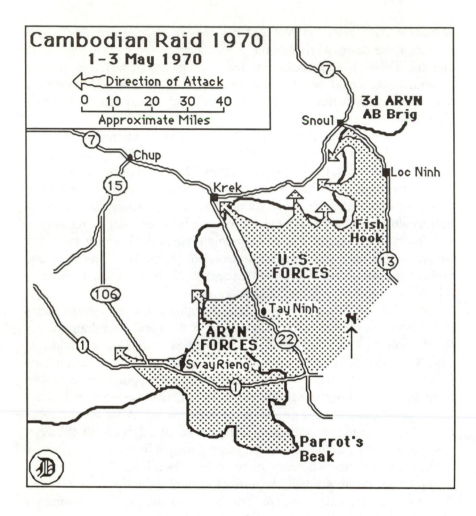

the elusive COSVN headquarters, reputed (incorrectly) to be in the "Fish Hook." Beyond those military goals lay the political and psychological ones. The attacks would notify the North Vietnamese (and the Communist world) that Nixon was not playing by the old rules, and that they now faced a more ruthless and determined foe. The raid might break the stalemate at the negotiating table and certainly would buy time to pursue Nixon's twin policies of United States withdrawal and Vietnamization. In addition, a successful campaign would demonstrate to the people of South Vietnam and the United States the progress of Vietnamization.

The configuration of both the "Fish Hook" and the "Parrot's Beak" invited an enveloping attack, not only on the ground, but in the case of the "Fish Hook," through the air as well. The United States scheme of maneuver for the "Fish Hook" operation called for an American armored drive from the south, coupled with an attack from the east by elements of the 1st United States Air Cavalry Division, supported by another attack by the 3d ARVN Airborne Brigade from the north, and a heliborne envelopment by 1st Cavalry troops into the enemy's rear. The attacking force totaled around 15,000 men. On D-day (1 May), preceded by a B-52 attack, fighter-bomber sorties, and heavy artillery preparation, the tanks moved north and the infantry units began to move west and south. The great battle was on, except—there was no great battle. The enemy fled to the west leaving the Americans and the South Vietnamese their supplies and base areas.

The operation in the "Parrot's Beak" was a copy of that in the "Fish Hook." Three ARVN task forces (totaling 8,700 men), each composed of three infantry battalions and an armored cavalry battalion (some 75 fighting vehicles), enveloped Base Areas 706 and 367, in the tip of the "Parrot's Beak." Once these had been cleaned out, one of the task forces turned west for the key town of Svay Rieng and north to envelop another base area (354). There were some sharp encounters the first two days, but after that the enemy faded off to the west.

By 3 May, the fighting had ended and the drudgery began. Vast amounts of captured equipment had to be evacuated or destroyed and supply bunkers, hospitals, classrooms, and barracks had to be razed or burned. The quantity of captured or destroyed enemy equipment impressed even the Americans. The Allies captured: 23,000 individual weapons, enough to equip 74 full-strength NVA battalions; 2,500 crew-served weapons, 25 battalions' worth; 16,700,000 rounds of small-arms ammunition, the amount the Communists expended in one year; 14 million pounds of rice; 143,000 rounds of mortar, rocket, and recoilless rifle ammunition, and about 200,000 rounds of antiaircraft ammunition. The twin operations cost the Communists about 11,000 dead and 2,500 captured. The Allies lost 976 dead (338 Americans) and 4,534 (1,525 Americans) wounded. The American forces evacuated Cambodia on 30 June, although South Vietnamese forces remained there for an additional period.

From the American and South Vietnamese viewpoint, the Cambodian raid was quite successful militarily. Allied operations did relieve the pressure on Lon Nol and his government and gave them time to build their forces. The border base areas were razed and stripped, and vast quantities of enemy military equipment and food were captured. The Americans and South Vietnamese killed or captured some 13,000 enemy troops, although, as usual, these figures were probably high. The assaulting forces failed to locate COSVN, which, as is now known, fled the "Fish Hook" area on 19 March and moved west and north across the Mekong River.[2] Analysis by Sir Robert Thompson, the British counterinsurgency expert, convinced him that the invasion plus the loss of the port of Sihanoukville set the NVA offensive timetable back "at least a year, probably eighteen months, and possibly two years."[3] Henry Kissinger believed that it gained the United States about fifteen months, and this time was critical.[4] As for the more obscure objectives of the invasion, it did not advance negotiations, but then nobody had much hope that it would. It lessened the dangers to United States withdrawal, eased the progress of Vietnamization, and it had showcased ARVN as an improving and maturing combat force. The raid seized the initiative from the North Vietnamese and strategically unbalanced them.

And while certainly not one of Nixon's objectives, it brought antiwar dissenters, apathetic since Nixon's speech of 3 November 1969, to a new high. The campuses erupted in demonstrations and violence as the students burned thirty ROTC buildings across the nation. At Kent State, Ohio National Guardsmen fired into a crowd of attacking students, killing four and wounding ten; two more students died in a riot at Jackson State in Mississippi. In twenty-one universities across the country, the National Guard had to be called out to put down disturbances.

Nor was the dissent limited to students. On 8 May 1970, about 100,000 people staged a demonstration in Washington, D.C., which threatened to disrupt the government. So serious was the threat that the regular army troops were called out. They handled the potentially explosive situation without injury. On 24 June, the Senate, now in full flight from the dissenters, repealed the Tonkin Gulf Resolution, the one that Senator Morse in 1964 had called a "functional equivalent of a declaration of war." The administration finessed the repeal by sponsoring it, and then contended that for the conduct of military operations in Vietnam it relied on the constitutional authority of the president as commander in chief and not the resolution. On 30 June, the Senate passed the Cooper-Church Amendment barring funds for the support of United States combat operations in Cambodia without congressional approval. The House rejected the amendment on 9 July, and it was dropped.[5] The House of Representatives also mounted the dovish merry-go-round. Liberal and leftist members tried to excel each other in proposing amendments to cut off funds for combat operations in Vietnam, or to mandate total and unilateral withdrawals by an unrealistic date, or to tie the president's hands in some way in his prosecution of the war. With the Cambodian invasion, dissent had become the prime factor in not only Nixon's decisions on how to fight (or not to fight) the war, but in those of Hanoi as well. Hanoi's *dich van* program (action among the enemy people) was working well in the United States. Here was, now, the primary battlefield of the war.

The Cambodian raid not only struck the Communists a stunning blow by destroying their stores and bases in Cambodia, but it gave a boost to Nixon's twin policies of Vietnamization and United States withdrawal. In his book *The Real War,* Nixon states that his principal purpose in going into Cambodia was "to undercut the invasion of that country so that Vietnamization and plans for the withdrawal of American troops could continue. . ."[6] This is, of course, an after-the-fact rationalization. The primary reason Nixon went into Cambodia was to sustain Lon Nol and his forces, but since in the long run this motive turned out badly, for history he had to give a more plausible reason. Regardless of Nixon's motivations, he rightly grasped the fact that any operation which gained time for United States withdrawal and Vietnamization was vital. In April 1970, before the Cambodian raid, he had pledged to withdraw 150,000 American troops during the next year. This would denude South Vietnam of American combat troops, and if Communist forces remained strong in the Cambodian base areas, by mid-1971 they would seriously threaten United States and South Vietnamese forces in the ARVN III Corps area (around Saigon), an area which had produced more American casualties in 1969 than any other sector of South Vietnam. In retrospect, it would appear that if Nixon had not gone into Cambodia to help Lon Nol, that he would have had to manufacture some pretext to do it sometime in 1970 to protect his dwindling forces.

Vietnamization, too, needed time and help. By and large, the South Vietnamese troops had done a good job in the Cambodian raid, so good, in fact, that in some units American advisors were pulled out and not replaced. Overall, the operation had shown that Vietnamization was progressing and was possibly even an attainable goal. On the other hand, to the skeptics, both American and South Vietnamese, the operation exposed critical deficiencies in ARVN which portended future trouble. The fighting had not been fierce, for the NVA and Viet Cong troops had evacuated their base areas, largely without much effort to defend them. The ARVN III Corps commander who conducted the operation into the "Parrot's Beak," Lt. Gen. Do Cao Tri, had used mostly elite ARVN troops, the rangers, the armored cavalry squadrons, and the airborne units. He also bypassed the politicized infantry division commanders by organizing task forces under colonels and lieutenant colonels, even when forced to use infantry division troops. This action revealed once more the incapacity of the ARVN infantry division, the so-called foundation of the South Vietnamese Army. The operation disclosed serious tactical weaknesses. Fire support from ARVN artillery units was practically nonexistent. The South Vietnamese had to use American artillery support, which had not been positioned to provide maximum help, and even then the South Vietnamese had trouble adjusting the fire on target. As a result of their artillery deficiencies, ARVN commanders depended heavily on United States tactical air strikes—so heavily, in fact, that United States observers wondered if they could have succeeded without them.

Finally, ARVN armor succumbed to every tanker's old bugaboo, field maintenance. Most armchair Pattons do not realize that armored thrusts are often stopped, not by enemy mines and antitank guns, but by poor radio communications, traffic jams, and faulty logistics, particularly inadequate gasoline resupply and lack of field maintenance. The ARVN armored drive did not go far enough to tax radio communications heavily, nor did they have enough tanks to generate a paralyzing traffic tie-up. They did, however, fall prey to gasoline shortages and inadequate field maintenance. Many tanks and armored personnel carriers broke down and could not be repaired in the battle area due principally to lack of spare parts. The problem compounded itself when usable vehicles had to tow the "cripples," cutting down on mobility and, in time, wearing out the towing vehicle.[7]

So, while in Cambodia the South Vietnamese put on a creditable performance, to be true, under almost ideal conditions, the fundamental defects of the ARVN system—the lack of leadership both civil and

military, the static nature of the infantry divisions, the shortage of technicians, the politicization of ARVN, the lack of discipline, and the convoluted command system—remained. These could be corrected only with
time, and time was, as before and after, what winning or losing the
war turned on.

While Nixon desperately fought for time to further Vietnamization
and his troop withdrawal program, time worked *against* the morale and
discipline of United States ground forces in Vietnam. In a continuation
of the trends observed in 1969, discipline and morale among American
ground units in Vietnam slid lower in 1970. The troop withdrawal program, Vietnamization, attempted negotiations, and domestic antiwar dissidence convinced the ''grunt'' that he was in a no-win war, and that his
major concern was to survive it. He could desert or go AWOL, and in
increasing numbers he did. Drug use increased as an easier way out of
the boredom and infrequent danger of Vietnam. In 1970, 65,000 men
were on drugs in Vietnam. In 1969 there were 8,440 ''drug busts'' in
Vietnam for an incidence rate of .0157. In 1970 drug arrests totaled
11,058, or an incidence rate of .0273, and for the first time extensive
use of hard drugs appeared. ''Fragging'' incidents increased threefold
in 1970 over 1969, and incidents of insubordination, mutiny, and willful
refusal to obey an order rose from a rate of .28 per 1,000 strength in
1969 to .32 in 1970. All available statistics, plus the appearance of the
bearded, dirty soldiers slackly going about their duties, convinced the
senior officers that in 1970 the morale and discipline in the ground
forces was slowly being destroyed, but the nadir had not yet been reached.
That would come in 1971.

Negotiations, the Nixon administration's fourth ''war'' or track, continued to flounder in 1970, victimized by the lack of real bargaining
tools on the American side, and a rigidity of North Vietnamese goals
and tactics. They thought they could get what they wanted by waiting
out the United States. Negotiations had been stalemated throughout 1969,
and this deadlock persisted into early 1970. As January unrolled, Henry
Kissinger thought he saw an opportunity to reopen profitable negotiations.
In his view the United States occupied a stronger negotiating position
than at any time during the Nixon administration. In Vietnam the war
was going well for the United States, and at home Nixon's speech of 3
November 1969 had temporarily dampened antiwar dissent. The Polit-

buro, too, sought a return to negotiations. They knew the domestic pressures under which Nixon and Kissinger labored, so they were interested in seeing any new American offers. The North Vietnamese were also unsure of Nixon and what he might do. Particularly, they feared that their continued stonewalling in Paris would provoke Nixon into resuming the bombing of the North. And so for various reasons both sides agreed to meet in Paris—secretly.

The concealment of the meetings appealed to both the American and the North Vietnamese chief negotiators, Kissinger and Le Duc Tho. For Kissinger, the hidden meetings gave him a flexibility denied by public negotiations. They freed him from the negative machinations of the American bureaucracy, particularly Rogers and Laird, and it kept Thieu off his back (although the latter was kept informed after the fact). For Kissinger, the secret parleys would prevent the North Vietnamese from making their usual propaganda ploys which would only incite the American doves. Le Duc Tho also saw some advantage in secret meetings. The NVN Politburo was having trouble with its puppet, the NLF, and they wanted the Viet Cong kept out of negotiations.

The first meeting took place in a lower-middle-class apartment in a Paris suburb on 21 February 1970. Later meetings occurred on 16 March and 4 April. At these conferences, Kissinger tried several approaches dealing with the issue of mutual withdrawal of United States and NVA troops. The North Vietnamese rigidly rejected each approach, holding out for complete, unilateral withdrawal of American forces and the dismantlement of Thieu's government. As it had done before, and would do again, the Nixon administration refused Hanoi's demands, and this phase of negotiations collapsed. They were doomed from the start. Hanoi, emboldened by antiwar dissent in the United States and in Congress and by the inevitability of the United States troop withdrawal program, saw no need to negotiate for what, as they saw it, would be surrendered to them in time.

But Nixon and Kissinger, harried always by the dissenters, in the riotous aftermath of the Cambodian raid, realized they had to make another attempt at negotiations to keep the protesters at bay. On 1 July, as the last Americans left Cambodia, Nixon appointed David Bruce, a distinguished diplomat, to head the formal negotiating team in Paris. Henry Cabot Lodge, Bruce's predecessor, had resigned because of illness some months previously, and Nixon had refused to appoint a successor, to show his disapproval of the negotiating deadlock. Bruce's appointment, therefore, was the first American move in another approach to negotiations.

But Bruce's appointment meant little unless he and the Nixon administration had some negotiating offer to put on the table. After searching around for a gambit, Kissinger and Nixon came up with an approach (which had been left over from Lyndon Johnson's time) called a "cease-fire-in-place." It meant that the North Vietnamese troops would not have to withdraw, but only to stop fighting and stand fast. Nixon made the proposal in a speech on 7 October, and Bruce put the offer on the negotiating table in Paris on 8 October.

Almost immediately the administration and the news media garbled the meaning of the proposal. Behind their hands the administration hinted to the Soviets and Poles that the "cease-fire-in-place" did not require an eventual, mutual withdrawal, that is, that the NVA troops could remain in South Vietnam after United States withdrawal. Publicly, Nixon and Kissinger implied, and even stated precisely, the opposite—that the proposal did require a mutual withdrawal.

The American doubletalk made no difference, however. Even before many of the "clarifications" had been issued, the North Vietnamese rejected the proposal. As before, they saw no reason to negotiate. Antiwar dissent would give them eventually what they wanted without having to trade anything for it.

Pacification, the neglected ugly duckling of the early and mid-sixties, in 1970 blossomed into Nixon's full-blown swan, the huge success of an otherwise drab year. The flight of the NVA and Viet Cong Main Force units from the South Vietnam border deep into Cambodia deprived the Local Forces and guerrillas of their support and permitted a tremendous expansion in pacification. The guerrillas were demoralized and frequently reduced to obtaining recruits by "forced induction," kidnapping to be exact. During 1970 the guerrillas could mount aggressive counterpacification operations in only eleven provinces, while in the other thirty-three they could do almost nothing. In many areas the guerrillas could carry out only terrorist attacks (assassination, kidnappings, etc.) and even these declined. In 1968 there had been 32,362 such attacks, in 1969, 27,790, and in 1970, only 22,700.[8] The guerrilla decline, coupled with other U.S./GVN programs, and helped most of all by Thieu's continued personal emphasis on pacification, resulted in significant achievements in that "war." The Hamlet Evaluation Survey for June of 1970 showed that 91 percent of the hamlets in South Vietnam were "secure" or "relatively secure," 7.2 percent were "contested," and only 1.4 percent were Viet Cong controlled. The main gains had come in the rural areas, where the "secure" and "relatively secure" areas gained 19 percentage points.

Several U.S./SVN programs related to pacification began to pay off. The Regional Forces (RF) and Popular Forces (PF) were expanded, better armed, and integrated into ARVN, giving them a significant capability against the Viet Cong guerrillas. The People's Self Defense Forces (PSDF) were also expanded, and by the end of 1970 had grown into a force of 1,397,000 members with almost 500,000 arms of various types, protecting some 95 percent of the South Vietnamese villages and hamlets.[9] Of course, both the RF/PF and the PSDF had deficiencies, including an acute shortage of able leaders and in some cases a decrease in morale and motivation.

United States authorities pushed one program hard—to give increased authority and responsibility to the villagers for the management of their own affairs. Each village elected its council and was given control of their own defense forces. Most important, the village councils could decide how to spend the funds allotted to them. As with all advances in Vietnam, this village independence brought problems, as the villagers now came into opposition to the appointed district and province officials who resented the villagers' newly found authority and attempted to thwart it.

Other programs materially advanced the prosperity and well-being of the villagers. Agricultural programs increased the annual rice yield from 5.1 million tons to 5.5 million, a new post-World War II high. Animal husbandry programs increased livestock production. Tractors were issued to the villages, pumps and irrigation systems were built, and a new strain of "miracle" rice introduced. Government troops opened roads and canals that the Viet Cong had sealed for years, allowing a movement of goods and agricultural products about the countryside and to and from the villages to the cities. For the first time in a decade, one could drive safely from the DMZ to the southern tip of South Vietnam. As the Viet Cong threat lessened, the Government of South Vietnam attacked the refugee program. In 1970, the number of internal refugees decreased from 1.5 million to around 250,000. Most of the progress resulted from the movement of the refugees back to their homes, not, as previously, a movement from their homes to secure urban areas.

The most significant advance came in Thieu's Land Reform Program. Land reform ("land to the tiller") had been tried by the Diem regime, but without success. Thieu put his prestige and support into the program and got a land reform bill passed by the legislature. Each peasant got three hectares (8.22 acres) of land, and no landowner could own more than fifteen hectares, and then only if he and his family cultivated it. The GVN gave the task of redistribution to the village councils, thereby strengthening their authority. In 1970 the village councils redistributed 210,371 hectares of land.

But with all these gains in pacification, the loyalty of the bulk of the South Vietnamese peasants remained neutral between the GVN and the Viet Cong. The hold of the Viet Cong had been broken, but loyalty to the GVN had not replaced it. The villagers liked their new authority, but with typical peasant skepticism realized its limitations, and they were right. The same corrupt and incompetent civilian officials remained at district level and above. The military officers remained politicized, and the soldiers undisciplined and piratical. While things changed at the village level, at upper levels they did not, and short of a respite of many years, could not.

Nevertheless, the pacification program in its narrowest sense—the neutralization of the Viet Cong infrastructure in the countryside—was virtually completed by the end of 1970. It would hold firm, with minor shifts due to the combat situation, until the end of the GVN in 1975. Pacification in its broadest sense—to include the reform of the GVN and RVNAF—would never be won, but its narrow victory would constitute one of the resounding successes of Indochina War II.

Notes—Chapter 22

1. Marvin Kalb and Bernard Kalb, *Kissinger* (Boston: Little, Brown & Co., 1974), pp. 160–161.
2. Tang, *Vietcong Memoir,* p. 177.
3. Thompson, *Peace,* p. 77.
4. Kissinger, *White House Years,* p. 986.
5. John S. Bowman, ed., *The Vietnam War, An Almanac* (New York: World Almanac Publications, 1985), p. 261.
6. Richard M. Nixon, *The Real War* (New York: Warner Books, 1980), p. 109.
7. Brig. Gen. Tran Dinh Tho, *The Cambodian Incursion,* Indochina Monographs (Washington, D.C.: U.S. Army Center of Military History, 1983), p. 180.
8. Tho, *Pacification,* p. 170.
9. Ibid., p. 154.

23 The Raid Too Far

Lam Son 719
1971

All wars are continuous scenarios in which operations are related to what went before. And so it was with Lam Son 719. Named after the village of Lam Son, the birthplace of Le Loi, a Vietnamese national hero of antiquity, it was the most important combat action of the year, and it epitomized and focused the strategies of both sides. For the United States and South Vietnam, the ARVN offensive, designed to cut the Ho Chi Minh Trail and to occupy and destroy the base areas in southern Laos, bought time for continued Vietnamization and United States troop withdrawals. For North Vietnam, the South Vietnamese attacks struck directly at its greatest vulnerability: logistic support of its forces in the South.

The concept of this offensive sprang from the successful U.S./GVN incursion of May 1970 into the Cambodian base areas. Lon Nol's closing of the port of Sihanoukville and the destruction of the Cambodian base areas dealt the North Vietnamese a staggering blow, severely damaging the logistic support of the large Communist forces in central and southern South Vietnam. More importantly, the Ho Chi Minh Trail became the sole artery of support from North Vietnam through Laos to the NVA forces in South Vietnam. On the continued use of this network depended the capacity of the North Vietnamese to carry on the war.

The criticality of the trail was not lost on the Americans or the South Vietnamese. Both had long held plans to cut the trail, but neither had done so—the United States from political restrictions, the South Vietnamese from military incapacity. Now, in 1971, after the U.S./ARVN success in Cambodia, American planners saw that the situation might

637

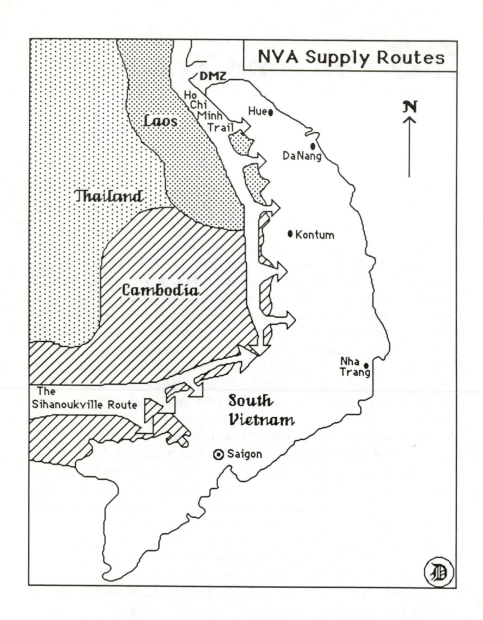

permit ARVN (with United States air and artillery support) to strike the trail at a critical point and deal the North Vietnamese a devastating blow. The ground assault force would have to be solely ARVN because the Cooper-Church Amendment, passed after the Cambodian incursion, forbade American ground troops from entering Cambodia or Laos.

The North Vietnamese, too, saw the vulnerability of their total dependence on the Ho Chi Minh Trail. The Cambodian raid also warned them that the United States had changed the rules of the game and that incursions into Laos, the DMZ, or even into southern North Vietnam might well follow. Accordingly, in October 1970, Giap established the 70B Corps to exercise operational control over the 304th, 308th, and 320th NVA Divisions, located in and around Laos, the DMZ, and southern North Vietnam. With the formation of the 70B Corps, Giap issued instructions that the corps make preparations to counter an ARVN offensive along Route 9, the road leading from Khe Sanh to Tchepone, the center of NVA logistic activity in Laos. Beginning in October 1970, the Communists prepared defensive positions and ambush sites in the area, preregistered their artillery on potential helicopter landing sites, and shifted a substantial part of their supplies to other areas. The NVA made similar preparations to repel an attack into the DMZ or southern North Vietnam. And so, as the Northeast Monsoon began to wane in January 1971, the North Vietnamese were ready.

The parenthood of Lam Son 719 remains ambiguous. Certainly, there was no rush after the controversial event to claim credit for the operation. In spite of the obvious fact that three ARVN divisions participated in the operation, the South Vietnamese brazenly denied responsibility, later saying, "The Cambodian foray in 1970 and the Laos operation to Tchepone in 1971 came into being only because MACV originated them, promoted them, and supported them."[1] While this statement is true as far as it went, Gen. Cao Van Vien, the Chairman of the South Vietnamese Joint General Staff (JGS), and President Thieu both eagerly agreed to the raid into Laos when General Abrams presented it to them. In fact, General Vien had been proposing a similar operation since 1965. Nobody on the United States side compelled the South Vietnamese to launch the operation. No American had that kind of power. But then a rigid adherence to truth has never been a Vietnamese characteristic, either North or South.

The architect of the operation on the American side is also debatable.

Henry Kissinger wrote in his memoirs that he originally wanted to send ARVN back into Cambodia, a repeat of the 1970 raid. He sent Alexander Haig, his military assistant, to Vietnam to discuss that possibility with Abrams. General Abrams proposed a much bolder operation—a relatively small ARVN attack into Cambodia, and a major multidivision offensive by ARVN (with United States air and helicopter support) into Laos to cut the Ho Chi Minh Trail. Later, Kissinger, who adopted Abrams' concept, passed the blame to Abrams for having misled him about the operation's prospects of success. There is an irony here savored by military men dealing with civilians. The civilians want to "play soldier," making strategic and sometimes tactical decisions, but they don't want to play by the rules the soldiers must play by—in victory the decision maker gets the acclaim, in defeat he gets the blame. His is the ultimate responsibility, and if he loses, he cannot blame his staff, even though they misled him. On Kissinger's behalf, however, it should be noted that not only did he approve the operation, but so did the theater commander, CINCPAC, (by then Admiral McCain), the Joint Chiefs of Staff, and Secretary of Defense Melvin Laird.

If any agency should have challenged the operation's concept and chances of success, it was the United States Joint Chiefs of Staff. They didn't do so, and the main reason they didn't was their long-standing tradition of supporting the field commander, right or wrong. There were other reasons. The Joint Staff, which serves the Joint Chiefs of Staff, is a multiservice, overmanned bureaucracy, rife with service rivalries and deeply mired in a labyrinth of tedious and time-consuming procedures. The Joint Chiefs themselves, overworked and engrossed with individual service problems, were, and are, prone to agree with the simplest solution, which in this case was to support the operation.

There was another reason why the Joint Chiefs approved the operation. In the numerous conferences with civilian authorities, the chairman of the Joint Chiefs of Staff speaks—often without prior consultation—for the rest of the Chiefs. This is particularly true when time is short. In December 1970 and January 1971, the chairman of the Joint Chiefs of Staff was Adm. Thomas Moorer, United States Navy, a distinguished navy airman, but one who had never served in Vietnam. He understood little of the complexities of ground operations and virtually nothing about the peculiarities of infantry fighting in Indochina. Unable to challenge the operation, he had to support it. The one man who could have told the Joint Chiefs about the difficulties and dangers posed by the operation was General Westmoreland, then the army chief of staff and thus a member of the Joint Chiefs. He has told me on several occasions (as late as 1987) that he was *not* consulted about the operation until after it had been launched. Admiral Moorer and Secretary Laird have rebutted Westmoreland, claiming that he *was* consulted prior to the operation and that he concurred in it.[2]

The man who made the final decision to launch Lam Son 719 was Richard Nixon. On 23 December 1970, the president approved the Laos operation in principle, subject to final review. So when Abrams proposed the operation to General Vien in early January 1971, he spoke for the president of the United States. Nixon finally approved the operation in detail on 18 January 1971. It was a bold decision, but one that Nixon would apparently prefer to gloss over. In his memoirs he devotes just one page to the entire operation.

And yet from the national viewpoint of Nixon and Kissinger, Lam Son 719 made strategic sense. In the broad perspective the United States had begun a strategic withdrawal (retreat, actually) from Vietnam in 1969. And the best way to carry out any strategic withdrawal is by switching over on occasion to the *tactical* offensive. Hitler's Ardennes Counteroffensive of 1944 is a classic example. In the same way, the Cambodian raid of 1970 and Lam Son 719 in 1971 coupled with the violent American counteraction to the North Vietnamese Easter offensive of 1972 and the Christmas bombing of 1972 were tactical blows to upset the North Vietnamese and, by taking the initiative, to throw the pursuer off balance.

And so, concerning the American parentage of the concept of Lam Son 719, there is Abrams, who proposed the operation to Kissinger, who approved it. Kissinger passed it through the Joint Chiefs and the secretary of defense, who approved it; and they all passed it to the president, who ordered it carried out. Everybody except Abrams has, in one way or another, ducked responsibility for the concept and the results of the operation. Abrams, who died three years later on active duty—and thus to some extent muzzled—never gave his side of the affair.

As an immediate purpose, the offensive sought to destroy the logistic installations and supplies in Base Areas 604 and 611 in Laos. The destruction of logistic support in these areas would preempt any NVA offensive

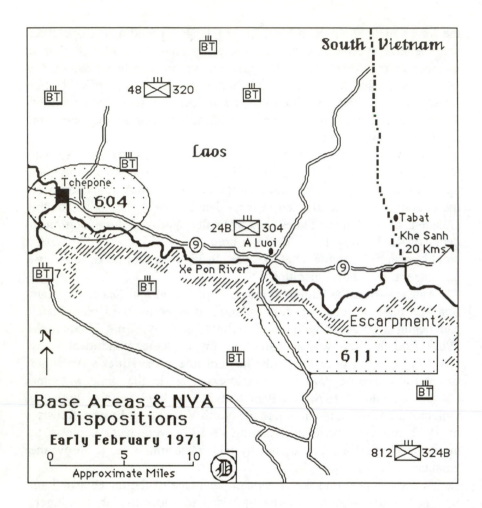

Base Areas & NVA
Dispositions
Early February 1971

0   5   10
Approximate Miles

in South Vietnam. A success in Base Areas 604 and 611, coupled with the destruction wrought on the Communists in 1970 by the Cambodian raid, would buy at least a year free from major NVA offensives, a year of precious time, and the buying of time was the crucial long-range object. In addition to these objectives, Kissinger thought that an offensive into Laos in 1971, following the Cambodian raid of 1970, might convince Hanoi to negotiate.

To strike at the NVA base areas in Laos, Abrams proposed a bold and risky plan of four phases. In Phase I (to start on 30 January) United States troops along the DMZ would clear the area to the Vietnam/Laos border and reactivate Khe Sanh as a base of operations. In Phase II ARVN would launch a three-pronged assault from South Vietnam astride Highway 9 to Tchepone. The central column, consisting of the ARVN Airborne Division reinforced by the 1st Armored Brigade, would attack down Highway 9 by heliborne assault and ground movement to A Luoi. From there, the airborne division would air assault into Tchepone while the armored brigade attacked overland. The South Vietnamese 1st Infantry Division (the only ARVN infantry division worthy of the name) less the 2d Regiment which remained on the DMZ, would advance on a parallel axis to the south of Highway 9, protecting the south flank of the central column. A ranger group would establish a fire base at Tabat and protect the north flank of the airborne division. A Vietnamese marine brigade would be in reserve around Khe Sanh.

After capturing Tchepone, Phase III foresaw the razing of Base Area 604. In Phase IV the ARVN force would move southeast from Base Area 604 to Base Area 611, destroy it, and then make its way back into South Vietnam. The ARVN offensive into Laos was scheduled to begin on 8 February with a duration of ninety days, when the Southwest Monsoon would terminate both tactical and logistic operations. The ARVN force would be commanded by Lt. Gen. Hoang Xuan Lam, the ARVN I Corps commander. On the United States side, Lt. Gen. James W. Sutherland, CG U.S. XXIV Corps, would support the ARVN operation by helicopter, air strikes, and artillery fire from South Vietnam. The Laotian incursion would be accompanied by a minor ARVN operation into Cambodia.

Two factors made Lam Son 719 unique. First, the Cooper-Church Amendment precluded United States ground troops from entering Laos or Cambodia. Second, and more critical, American advisors, artillery forward observers, and air controllers could not accompany the ARVN ground units into Laos either. This made U.S./ARVN coordination difficult and would denigrate support by aircraft of all types.

In February the Northeast Monsoon is just blowing out; nevertheless, weather for low-level air operations would be marginal, permitting them to operate, generally, only between 1000 to 1500 hours. The low clouds plus the hilly terrain would channel helicopter and low-level air operations along a few corridors in which enemy antiaircraft units could concentrate. The terrain was dominated by Highway 9 (a broken-up track) and the Xe Pon River, which ran south of, and parallel to, the highway. To the south of the highway and river ran a sheer escarpment leading to mountainous terrain. The entire area was rugged, covered with dense undergrowth, and along the river, by double-canopy jungle.

While the terrain and weather promised difficulties, so, too, did the enemy. Enemy forces in the area of operations were estimated at three NVA infantry regiments, all Main Force and battle tested. In addition there were eight *binh trams,* NVA logistical units, with some marginal ground combat capability, but who had recently been reinforced by around twenty antiaircraft battalions manning a total of from 170 to 200 pieces of 23 mm to 100 mm in caliber. In all, in the projected area there were 22,000 enemy troops (7,000 combat, 10,000 *binh trams,* and 5,000 Communist Pathet Lao soldiers).

To the U.S./ARVN planners, the enemy's capacity to reinforce the area should have been a matter of great concern. Intelligence officers estimated that within two weeks eight NVA Main Force infantry regiments supported by artillery units could move into the objective area. Thus, within a few days the ARVN assault troops (a scant three divisions) *could* find themselves fighting at least four enemy divisions, with possibly more on the way from North Vietnam. To make the picture darker, both the ARVN and American commands knew from agent reports that the enemy was alert and expecting an assault into Laos or the DMZ.

Yet as D-day approached, both the ARVN and United States commanders and staffs were confident of success. In his *After-Action Report,* Col. Arthur W. Pence, the senior advisor to the ARVN Airborne Division, wrote, ''It was apparent at this time that United States Intelligence felt that the operation would be lightly opposed and that a two-day preparation of the area prior to D-Day by tactical air would effectively neutralize the enemy antiaircraft capability, although the enemy was credited with having 170 to 200 antiaircraft weapons of mixed caliber in the operational area. The tank threat was considered minimal and the reinforcement capability was listed as fourteen days for two divisions from north of the DMZ.''

Lam Son 719 suffered a serious setback before it started. The North Vietnamese discovered the details of the operation from press leaks and from agents within ARVN. Tactical surprise, then, was totally lost. Nevertheless, the offensive began at 0001 hours, 30 January, when United States forces began their operations to clear South Vietnam north of

Highway 9 to the border, to repair Highway 9 within Vietnam, and to rehabilitate the runway at Khe Sanh. By 5 February the Americans had finished their tasks and taken over the security of the ARVN assembly areas in Vietnam near the border.

On 6 and 7 February the operation received another blow. The weather turned bad and the preparatory American air strikes, which were supposed to neutralize the NVA antiaircraft guns, had to be canceled. At 0700 hours, 8 February, the ARVN part of Lam Son 719 jumped off. On that day the lead echelon of the central column on Highway 9 (elements of the 1st Airborne Division and the 1st Armored Brigade) pushed nine kilometers into Laos. The two ARVN forces on the flank made equally good progress, all against sporadic enemy resistance. Giap and the local commander, the CG of the NVA 70B Corps, were holding back until they were sure that Lam Son 719 was the real thing and not a feint to conceal a main attack elsewhere. On 9 February, in bad weather, the armored-airborne column advanced another two kilometers toward its first objective, A Luoi. On this same date the CG, 70B Corps, started the 308th ("Iron") Division from its assembly area around the DMZ toward Highway 9 in Laos. On 10 February the ARVN airborne division "choppered" a battalion into A Luoi against light resistance. Late in the afternoon the armored column moving east on Highway 9 linked up with the airborne troopers in the objective area at A Luoi. So far, so good.

Then on 11 February the inexplicable happened. The ARVN force in Laos froze where it was. They pushed out short-range patrols, which reported increased contacts, while the ARVN fire bases themselves began to get substantial enemy pressure. General Lam, the ARVN corps commander, issued no orders, nor did his subordinate commanders issue any. The operation just stopped for no discernible reason. Abrams, back in Saigon, was stunned and furious. As an experienced tank commander, he knew that success in this type of operation depends on speed and movement, both necessary to keep the enemy off balance. And this was particularly true of the North Vietnamese, who reacted slowly to changes on the battlefield, but who excelled at slow-paced, "set-piece" slugging matches. Abrams went to see Vien, imploring him to get the ARVN troops moving. Abe ranted at Sutherland, who was powerless to achieve any forward movement either. On 16 February, Abrams and Vien flew up to see Sutherland and Lam. At this meeting the decision was made to move the 1st ARVN Division west along the southern escarpment to establish fire support bases from which to support a renewed airborne-armored push westward on Highway 9.

Meanwhile, enemy ground attacks supported by heavy artillery fire constantly increased. The NVA air defense capability, too, had grown menacingly. On 18 February, the 308th Division was identified in action on the northern flank. The 2d NVA Division appeared on the west of the ARVN advance and the 24B Regiment of the 304th Division showed up along Highway 9. Even more ominous, the ARVN force began to sight enemy tanks, and a POW stated that there was an NVA tank regiment in the area.

The sudden breakdown of the ARVN offensive on 11 February at first mystified Abrams and the other Americans. Later, they found that President Thieu had taken a hand in the game. On 12 February, he told Lam and his division commanders to be cautious in moving west and to cancel the operation once the ARVN force had taken 3,000 casualties. Such an order stifles boldness, the one ingredient which might have successfully concluded the mission and have curtailed ARVN losses. Actually, Thieu's order guaranteed that ARVN would lose the initiative and take heavy casualties as the troops hunkered down in their fire bases to await the onslaught by the ever-increasing forces of the enemy.

While Thieu's covert order undermined the offensive—as well as his American supporters—it made some sense in the occult world of South Vietnamese politics. The airborne division, the 1st Armored Brigade, and the marines were not only the total ARVN general reserve, but they were also Thieu's "palace guard," his anticoup defense. Their destruction would expose Thieu to dangers from his internal enemies. Also, a national election was scheduled for the fall. Heavy casualty figures would not provide a popular platform for Thieu to run on. So, on Thieu's order, from 11 to 19 February the invading ARVN force sat while the NVA concentrated its divisions against it.

On 19 February, Thieu held another meeting with Lam and his division commanders. Lam briefed Thieu on the growing dangers of the situation, particularly from Tchepone and on the north flank, where the rangers were under heavy attack by the 308th NVA Division supported effectively by T-34 and T-54 tanks. Thieu told Lam ". . . to take his time and . . . expand search activities toward the southwest."[3] In other words continue to do little or nothing.

With this kind of directive, the situation continued to deteriorate. By the last week of February, the NVA had elements of four divisions (ten regiments) in the operational area, plus tanks and artillery, and they were attacking. A fire base on the north flank was lost and the 39th Ranger Battalion overrun and virtually wiped out. Another fire base, held by a battalion of the airborne division, was overrun and an ARVN brigade commander captured. Large-caliber artillery fire from NVA guns increased markedly, and the now intense antiaircraft fire made heliborne movement in the area costly and dangerous. The NVA units stepped up their combined tank-infantry assaults, and single tanks

used as mobile gun platforms took an increasing toll. Truck convoys on Highway 9 came under frequent NVA attacks and this ground LOC, the only one, was in jeopardy.

In the midst of this approaching debacle, Thieu struck again. On 28 February he ordered the airborne division to be replaced in the attack by the marine division which had joined its one brigade near Khe Sanh. The folly of this decision stunned even the South Vietnamese. While the airborne division had taken losses, it was still in good shape. The marine division had never fought as a division and was an unknown quantity. Worst of all, the relief of one division by another in the face of a strong and aggressive enemy is an extremely ticklish and hazardous undertaking.

With these misgivings, Lam, the embattled and incompetent corps commander, flew that afternoon (28 February) to Saigon to propose an alternate plan to President Thieu. The 1st ARVN Infantry Division (to be reinforced with its 2d Regiment from the DMZ) would assault by helicopter into Tchepone. The airborne division would protect the north flank, and the marine division would deploy behind the 1st Division. Thieu approved Lam's plan and the next day (1 March) informed General Abrams and Ambassador Bunker of his new concept.

Thieu's decision of 28 February completed the collapse of the original concept of Lam Son 719. The original plan (to deal the enemy a telling blow by *occupying* and destroying his logistical bases in southern Laos) was now replaced by a meaningless public relations ploy to get ARVN troops into Tchepone (by now a deserted village of little military value), which ARVN would hold only momentarily. In a conference with Thieu and his generals, Abrams and Bunker concurred in Thieu's change of plans. They could do nothing else, particularly when some of the South Vietnamese conferees assailed Abrams about what they saw as the inadequate support the Americans were giving Lam Son 719. Abrams hotly defended his troops and their efforts. But then bad news always rubs thin the veneer of an alliance, and so it was here.

From 3 to 6 March, elements of the 1st ARVN Division executed a series of airborne assaults to the west along the southern escarpment. On 6 March, after a heavy pounding of the area by B-52's and fighter-bombers, two infantry battalions from the 2d Regiment of the ARVN 1st Division were lifted by 120 Huey helicopters from Khe Sanh to LZ HOPE four kilometers north of Tchepone, a distance of 65 kilometers.

Only one helicopter was hit, and it landed in the objective area. On 7 March, elements of the 1st Division entered Tchepone, and on 8 March they began to withdraw to the south towards the fire bases on the escarpment. The movement into Tchepone ended the offensive phase of the operation.

Now would come the difficult phase—the withdrawal under heavy enemy pressure. On 9 March, General Lam flew again to Saigon to present to Thieu his reasons for withdrawing from Laos and his plan for doing so. Basically, each of his columns would be extracted by helicopter, starting with those in the west, leapfrogging to fire bases to the east. The 1st Division, the most exposed, would leave first, then the airborne division, and last, the marines. General Abrams, who attended the meeting, opposed the withdrawal and suggested that the ARVN 2d Infantry Division, then in Quang Ngai province, be used to reinforce the troops in Laos so that the original mission might be carried out. Thieu sneeringly suggested that a United States division should accompany them. This was, of course, contrary to the Cooper-Church Amendment, and this insult killed Abrams' suggestion.

The withdrawal was an agonizing affair. The NVA units concentrated heavy antiaircraft fire on the evacuation helicopters, attacked the fire bases, and ambushed the retreating ARVN troops. Losses on both sides ran high as B-52's and American fighter-bombers covered the withdrawal with a maximum effort. The television cameras immortalized this phase of the operation by showing panicky ARVN soldiers hanging on to the skids of United States helicopters in an effort to flee the enemy. By 25 March, the ARVN troops had returned to Vietnam.

A look at the enemy situation is required to understand what happened. When ARVN launched the offensive on 8 February with 17,000 men, they were opposed by three NVA infantry regiments, and eight *binh trams,* plus other odds and ends in the area of operations, totaling around 22,000. When the withdrawal phase terminated (around 23 March), the enemy situation had grown to four infantry divisions (12 regiments), a reinforced regiment of tanks, supported by several battalions of light and medium artillery, a substantial (and deadly) antiaircraft capability—in all, a modern, conventional force of at least 40,000 men, pursuing around 7,000 to 8,000 demoralized South Vietnamese.

The results of Lam Son 719 were, as usual in this war, obscure and controversial. Both the South and North Vietnamese claimed victory—the South because they had reached Tchepone, the final objective, and the North because they had ejected the South Vietnamese ignominiously from Laos. The statistics were also ambiguous. The official U.S. XXIV Corps *After-Action Report* showed enemy KIA at 19,360.[4] If the ratio of KIA to permanently disabled of .35 is applied, the permanent NVA losses totaled around 26,000 men. It is probably valid to say that the NVA lost around 20,000 men, or about half the participating force. The greater amount of the killing was done by United States B-52's and fighter-bomber strikes. One cannot read South Vietnamese reports on the operation without being amazed by the detailed evidence from ARVN sources of the recurring effectiveness of these air strikes in inflicting materiel damage and human casualties. The XXIV Corps report revealed that the cumulative American and South Vietnamese casualties for Lam Son 719 totaled 9,065—1,402 Americans (215 KIA), 7,683 South Vietnamese (1,764 KIA). The American news media which covered the operation challenged this figure. *Newsweek* speculated in its issue of 5 April 1971 that ARVN's casualties alone had reached 9,775, with a KIA figure of 3,800.

Equipment losses were heavy on both sides. ARVN lost 211 trucks, 87 combat vehicles, 54 tanks, 96 pieces of artillery, and all of the combat engineer machinery (bulldozers, graders, etc.) which accompanied the units. The materiel losses of the NVA force were even greater: 2,001 trucks (422 confirmed by ground troops), 106 tanks (88 verified), 13 artillery pieces, 170,346 tons of ammunition (20,000 tons verified) and 1,250 tons of rice. Further testimony to the ferocity of the combat in Laos could be found in the damage to the United States helicopter fleet and the expenditure of artillery ammunition. The United States lost 108 helicopters destroyed and 618 damaged, while the Americans and ARVN fired over 500,000 rounds of artillery.

Those are the best statistics available, but they tell little about the results of the operation. The operation did disrupt activities along the Ho Chi Minh Trail for a few weeks. It forced the enemy to expend men and material that might have been used offensively in 1971 or 1972. Kissinger, at least, believes that the attrition inflicted in Cambodia in 1970 and Laos in 1971 might have given the U.S./GVN side the thin winning edge in 1972. Nixon in his oblique way supports him. Lam Son 719 *might* have caused the NVN to postpone their massive attack from 1971 to 1972, although the evidence suggests that Giap had always planned the offensive for 1972. Regardless of any gains the United States and GVN might have made, the price was a steep one.

To determine objectively whether Lam Son 719 was a success or failure, one has only to weigh the results against the original mission. The mission of Lam Son 719 was to seize and hold Base Areas 604 and 611 *for ninety days* and to destroy the supplies and installations in those base areas. Lam Son 719 did not accomplish this mission. The ARVN troops stayed in Laos about forty-five days, most of the time in either a static or retrograde mode. Base Area 604 was "mucked up" (to use the British expression), but neither the base area nor most of the supplies were destroyed. Base Area 611 was scarcely touched. In fact, the Ho Chi Minh Trail was in full operation a week after ARVN's withdrawal.

On the other hand, sometimes a military failure can be a success in other ways. For example, the enemy's 1968 Tet offensive was a military catastrophe for him, but a Communist public relations victory in the United States. But not Lam Son 719. In the United States, the media portrayed it as a debacle. President Nixon described it as a "psychological defeat" in both the United States and South Vietnam, and the South Vietnamese saw it the same way.[5] The South Vietnamese people were shocked by the heavy casualties of Lam Son 719. An even greater shock was the fact that in its withdrawal, ARVN had to leave substantial numbers of dead and wounded. As one South Vietnamese officer put it, "This came as a horrendous trauma to those unlucky families who in their traditional devotion to the cult of the dead and their attachment to the living, were condemned to live in perpetual sorrow and doubt. . . . Vietnamese sentiment would never forget."[6] The operation produced on the South Vietnamese troops who participated in it an equally dismal effect. Those troops wondered if the results justified the casualties, and although Thieu might have proclaimed the offensive a success, the ARVN troops themselves believed they had been defeated. Success or failure of a military operation is really determined in the hearts and minds of the soldiers who fought in it. These are the supreme realists, and the South Vietnamese soldier knew he had been beaten.

Not only had Lam Son 719 been defeated, but the operation revealed the inherent and incurable flaws of the RVNAF, which doomed any realistic hopes of successful Vietnamization. First, Lam Son 719 showed again the painful inadequacies of ARVN's politicized leadership. Lieutenant General Lam, who commanded the operation, could not control two of his three major subordinates, the commanders of the airborne and marine divisions, who, too, were lieutenant generals. The airborne commander, Lt. Gen. Dong, did about as he pleased. The marine commander, Lt. Gen. Khang, delegated his command authority to a subordinate colonel and, in effect, boycotted the entire campaign, in spite of the fact that his marines were hard put to avoid annihilation in the last stages of the operation.

President Thieu's own actions epitomized ARVN's incompetent leadership. Although he attached the airborne and marine divisions to Lam's command, he refused to intervene on Lam's behalf when the latter's efforts were subverted by the insubordination of these subordinate commanders. The reason was obvious. Thieu depended on these two units, particularly the airborne division, as his palace guard, his primary anticoup force.

Nor was this oversight Thieu's only dereliction. At first he enthusiastically agreed to the operation, and then he "chickened out" when the going got tough and the military and political price became apparent. He interfered at critical points during the offensive, always to the detriment of the operation. His decision of 12 February to suspend the operation's forward movement not only doomed Lam Son 719, but placed his troops in a vulnerable and dangerous situation. Later on, to protect his airborne division, he tried to substitute the marine division for them—a totally unrealistic solution—and then, he transferred the spearhead role of the airborne division to the 1st Infantry Division. His decision to send two battalions of the 1st Division to Tchepone was a public relations spectacular, an operation which placed those troops in jeopardy for no military purpose.

One might quarrel, too, with Thieu's refusal in early March to commit the ARVN 2d Infantry Division in an effort to sustain the operation. In the light of what happened, however, it was probably a wise decision. The 2d Division was inferior to any of the units already committed to the offensive, and one more division would probably not have contributed much more than an increase in ARVN casualties. In fact, this might have been *the one* intelligent decision Thieu made.

Lam, the unfortunate and inept corps commander, was totally beyond his depth. He was a military administrator, in effect, the governor of a huge chunk of South Vietnam. He had no experience in large-unit, conventional operations, let alone one as complex and as difficult as Lam Son 719. He tried to conduct the operation from a command post at Dong Ha, some thirty-seven miles from the Vietnam/Laos border and about sixty miles from Tchepone. His staff and major commanders were as inadequate as he was, with the exception of the commander of the 1st Infantry Division. One ARVN lieutenant bitterly summed up the shortcomings of his superiors when he told a United States Marine that ". . . the Americans are using us [troops] as training aids for the senior staff."[7]

In addition to the deficiencies of South Vietnamese leadership, Lam Son 719 exposed again the incurable flaws of ARVN. The static "home-guard" nature of so-called infantry divisions evidenced itself. The JGS judged that the 3d Infantry Division in the northern part of South Vietnam was inadequate for mobile operations, and Thieu canceled the use of the next nearest division, the 2d, for that and other reasons.[8] Since the infantry divisions (with the exception of the 1st Infantry Division) could not meet the requirements of mobile warfare, the entire general reserve consisted of the airborne and marine divisions. Lam Son 719 demonstrated all too clearly that this reserve was totally inadequate, not only in quantity, but in quality as well.

Finally, Lam Son 719 disclosed a glaring lack of professionalism by the ARVN units. ARVN had for years relied too heavily on their American advisors and felt apprehensive without them. This was particularly true in obtaining and adjusting tactical air strikes and artillery fire and in bringing in helicopters. In Lam Son 719 the ARVN officers had to do these complicated jobs by themselves, and in an operation stressing air mobility and firepower, this aspect was critical. A few units did well; most poorly.

Other deficiencies quickly showed up. The units had devoted little time to combined tank-infantry training and coordination. The tanks fought alone, and the infantry fought alone, and both suffered. Reporting by subordinate units was slipshod and sometimes nonexistent. A South Vietnamese general and historian described it as "deplorable." Since the corps and division commanders or their staffs rarely visited the front lines, the operation drifted along without information, intelligence, or control. Communications security was equally bad. The ARVN units sent orders and reports in clear text, not attempting even the most primitive coding procedures. All armies (the American army among them) suffer to some degree from this fault, but in Lam Son 719 the ARVN failings were disastrous, indicative of basic deficiencies in training and discipline.

ARVN troops had picked up other unfortunate traits from their American models. They relied too much on helicopters, using them when foot movement would have been easier, faster, and safer. When they made contact with the enemy, they sat down and called for air or artillery support instead of maneuvering and attacking. As General Abrams once said, "I don't know if ARVN is going to copy any of our good points, but they sure as Hell will copy all the bad ones," and he was right.

Lam Son 719 demonstrated that, while Vietnamization had made progress, the South Vietnamese government and its armed forces had deep flaws which made final success of the concept years, probably decades, away. Above all, the operation showed ARVN's complete dependence on the United States forces. Without United States support, there would have been no Lam Son 719.

Nor did the South Vietnamese have sole option on deficiencies of planning and execution in Lam Son 719. The Americans, too, made mistakes. First, at American insistence, the planning and preparation for the operation was conducted too hastily and was too closely held. The participating ARVN units had no time to undergo special training for the exercise and little time to prepare for it. As a result, the troops went in "cold" and in many cases with the wrong, or no, equipment. The planning was held so closely that ARVN agencies which could have made an input were unaware of the operation. At the JGS level, the J-2, the intelligence officer, was not told about Lam Son 719, and his intelligence data and expertise went unconsulted. The same intense secrecy inhibited United States support preparations as well.

Then the Americans and the South Vietnamese fumbled the command post (CP) problem, a vital factor where an operation depends on close cooperation and coordination. The main ARVN I Corps CP was at Dong Ha, while the United States XXIV Corps CP was at Quang Tri City, about eight miles away. There were inadequately staffed, separate forward CP's at Khe Sanh, but not until three weeks *after* ARVN troops crossed the border was a functioning combined U.S./ARVN CP established at Khe Sanh.

Finally, there was a serious interservice dispute between the United

States XXIV Corps and the United States Seventh Air Force over the concept of air support for the operation. Seventh Air Force believed that the NVA antiaircraft fire in the area would take a heavy toll of the vulnerable helicopters, and that the only way the choppers could survive would be to use large quantities of fighter strikes to soften up the areas before the helicopters went in. XXIV Corps, on the other hand, thought that Seventh Air Force had exaggerated the NVA antiaircraft menace and that helicopters could not only land troops and supplies in the area, but could furnish close air support by helicopter gun ships as well.

Another planning issue between the American services erupted regarding the command arrangements for the operation. Seventh Air Force maintained that the air assault and air support operation should be under a single commander, CG, Seventh Air Force. The air force pointed out that in all previous wars the air commander had controlled air assault operations until a firm terrestrial linkup with advancing ground troops had been made. The army believed that bringing an air force commander into the battle would unduly complicate an already complex and shaky command relationship with the South Vietnamese, and so they spurned the air force request. Who was right and who was wrong is argued to this day, but it did produce, at least in the view of the air force, "inadequate tactical air support."[9] And the weight of the evidence tends to support the air force view. So the Americans embarked on *their* support mission with inadequate planning, deficient coordination with ARVN, and major service differences over the concept and execution of the operation.

At the bottom of all these deficiencies of planning and execution (both American and South Vietnamese alike) lay that old bugaboo, lack of unity of command. Nobody really took charge of the operation; and nobody really coordinated it. As a result, the operation drifted along, blown about by the winds of Thieu's political needs and eventually smashed on the rocks by the storm generated by Thieu's pernicious orders and directives.

In studying Lam Son 719, one gets a feeling of *déjà vu,* a rerun of an old movie of the French generals Valluy and Carpentier and their strategic and tactical concepts of the late forties and early fifties. There was the same old operational concept of an airborne-armor thrust lifted from the European Theater of World War II. There was the same old careless disregard for the effects of terrain, weather, and the road net on the operation. There was the same cavalier underestimation of the enemy and his capabilities to frustrate the operation. And, finally, there was the same false sense of the superiority of one's own troops and resources.

The longer one ponders the operation, the more one wonders how its architects thought it could possibly succeed. First, the planners should have known that the natural characteristics in the area would impede the operation. The terrain was rugged with few areas suited for fire bases or helicopter landing zones. A road net did not exist. Highway 9 was a single-lane, dirt track susceptible to demolitions and ambushes, dominated by the ridges on both sides of it. The road ran through difficult terrain which prevented off-road and cross-country movement. Tanks could be employed, at best, one abreast and the destruction of a vehicle on the road stalled the entire column. The weather was sure to restrict both helicopter and close air support operations, and on these the success of the operation depended.

To the U.S./ARVN planners, the enemy situation and his capabilities should have been even more intimidating than the area's adverse natural characteristics. They knew (and published) that the enemy had a reinforcement capability which could position a total of at least eleven or twelve first-class NVA Main Force regiments in the area of operations by D + 14, in addition to the *binh trams* and other troops in the area. The planners knew also that Giap had recently moved in some twenty additional antiaircraft battalions with both light (7.6 mm and 12.7 mm machine guns) and medium (23 mm to 100 mm) guns. The Allied intelligence sections and the planners underestimated the tank threat and the NVA artillery capability, although previous operations in the Khe Sanh area and along the DMZ should have warned them to expect heavy concentrations of enemy artillery.

To attack this menacing combination of natural characteristics and enemy forces, the planners committed one understrength ARVN infantry division, the 1st (which had left one regiment along the DMZ), one understrength airborne division, three ranger battalions, some light armor, with a marine brigade as reserve. None of these units had extensive experience in fighting as divisions; none had been trained in combined tank-infantry maneuvers or in any other offensive operations against a first-class foe. The ARVN units were going into Laos without their

American advisors, which, at the least, was bound to bring on problems of coordination of artillery and close-air support.

The American planners should have recognized other debilitating deficiencies which were certain to hamper the operation. The coordination between United States and ARVN units presented monstrous problems of a psychological, linguistical, military, and cultural nature. The shortcomings of the South Vietnamese leadership from Thieu on down were well known. Neither Lam nor his major commanders and staffs were up to the job (again, with the exception of the 1st Division staff). Finally, the operation had no room for error or for contingencies. There was no reserve other than those committed to the operation. There could be no reinforcement or relief.

Yet in spite of what was known about the terrain, weather, and lack of roads in the area, in spite of what was known about the enemy and the deficiencies of ARVN, and in spite of having lost both strategical and tactical surprise, the planners thrust ARVN troops into the maw of a superior enemy force. Not only that, but they gave the ARVN troops the mission to attack the most sensitive area (to the enemy) in the theater, one he would *have* to fight for. Nor was this the full measure of the planner's vagaries. The architects envisioned that this force, without significant relief or reinforcement, would reach Tchepone in three days, and would stay in the objective area at least ninety days.[10] Kissinger is restrained when in describing the plan he writes, "Its chief drawback, as events showed, was that it in no way accorded with Vietnamese realities."[11]

The one question which overwhelms all others is why did Gen. Creighton Abrams, he of the fiery histrionics and icy calculation, not only approve the operation, but push it on the South Vietnamese and his American superiors? The question is given added force by Abrams' unique qualifications to assess just such an operation. First, he was an intelligent and wise man, a cautious weigher of chances, an experienced soldier, and an armor expert. Beyond these general attributes he knew as much about the nature of Indochina War II as any man in the United States. For the first year of his tour he spent almost all of his time with the South Vietnamese and ARVN, and if anybody knew its limitations, it was Creighton Abrams. He knew the Machiavellian Thieu, the incompetent Lam, and the other ARVN actors. He knew the condition, morale, and training of the ARVN units.

Nor was Abrams single-faceted. He was always deeply interested in intelligence and the enemy. He spent hours talking to his intelligence officers and specialists, competent men all, and he thought often and deeply about the enemy situation. So in this area, too, Abrams was immensely qualified to judge enemy reaction and capabilities and their impact on the operation. Finally, he had spent almost four long years of fifteen-hour days in Vietnam. Nothing should have misled him or surprised him. And yet in the words of the South Vietnamese, he and MACV "originated, promoted, and supported" the operation.[12]

Abrams never gave his reasons for advocating the operation, and thus, some speculation is necessary. In the first place, what appears to be irrational in an operation *looked at in the after-light* is often hidden in the fog which precedes that operation. In Lam Son 719, the operation looked vastly different in early February than it did on completion in late March. The planners' expectations just prior to D-day are revealed by this item in an *After-Action Report* already quoted: "It was apparent at this time that United States intelligence felt that the operation would be lightly opposed."[13] That is one clue; and historically Abrams and his intelligence officers had a point. The Communists had *never* before in Indochina War II resolutely defended their base areas. They had given them up rather than defend them in operations called CEDAR FALLS and JUNCTION CITY and in the Cambodian raid. So, based on these precedents, Abrams and the intelligence people had some ground for thinking that the enemy would give up Base Areas 604 and 611, too.

Of course, this estimate was wrong—the operations cited above and Lam Son 719 were vastly different. The other enemy base areas, while important, were not vital. Enemy operations, at a reduced tempo to be sure, would go on, and the areas could in time be restocked. But this did not apply to the base areas in Laos. They were critical, absolutely vital, to Communist operations in South Vietnam. The Ho Chi Minh Trail was in 1971 the *only* means of supplying the entire enemy force in South Vietnam, southern Laos, and Cambodia. If ARVN could cut the trail and keep it cut for three months (until the rainy season arrived when movement became difficult), they would deal a devastating blow to all Communist operations in South Vietnam. In addition, time, in

1971 the key factor in the war, would not permit the enemy to reopen, restock, and resupply the NVA units who would launch the already planned major offensive of 1972. The effect on North Vietnam of a ninety-day stoppage along the Ho Chi Minh Trail would be catastrophic. The North Vietnamese had to oppose Lam Son 719 with every resource they could bring to bear.

And so maybe Abrams thought that Lam Son 719 might be lightly opposed, and maybe he didn't. And if he didn't, there were to "Old Abe" other justifications for the operation. First, there was that factor, time. It was even more vital to the United States and Abrams than it was to Giap and the North Vietnamese. Abrams needed time to upgrade Vietnamization and to keep the enemy off-balance while American combat troops continued their withdrawal. To buy time required a strike at some area critical to North Vietnamese offensive preparations. Neither South Vietnam nor Cambodia were critical. There was nothing much in South Vietnam and Cambodia had been pretty well cleaned out in 1970. Besides, Cambodia was now the end of the line. Destruction there would only inhibit operations around Saigon and south thereof. But Laos was critical. Here, time, in a huge chunk, might be bought.

Abrams, the pragmatist, must have had another thought. That was, if the operation doesn't fully succeed, the North Vietnamese are still going to lose men and supplies, they're going to lose the initiative, and they may get set back not the hoped-for year or two, but six months. But that's time and it was precious. Maybe ARVN gets hurt, but they gain tremendously in experience, and in the final analysis, perhaps thinks Abe, better a half success, or even a partial failure, than doing nothing. Clausewitz probably said it best. He wrote, " . . . we should always try, in time of war, to have the probability of victory on our side. But this is not always possible. Often we must act against this probability, should there be nothing better to do. . . . Therefore, even when the likelihood of success is against us, we must not think of our undertaking as unreasonable or impossible; for it is always reasonable if we do not know of anything better to do, and if we make the best use of the few means at our disposal."[14]

On 7 April, shortly after ARVN's forced withdrawal from Laos, President Nixon, in a television broadcast to the nation, proclaimed,

"Tonight I can report that Vietnamization has succeeded"—an Orwellian untruth of boggling proportions. Lam Son 719 had demonstrated exactly the opposite, that Vietnamization had not succeeded. To be sure, it had made progress, but the offensive proved beyond doubt that ARVN still suffered from grave deficiencies.

As a result of Lam Son 719, in June 1971, MACV began efforts to overcome those weaknesses which were curable. Command post exercises for ARVN units were initiated to teach air-ground coordination and combined infantry-tank operations. At General Abrams' urging, General Vien appointed a committee to develop a combined arms doctrine suitable to the Vietnam environment. The committee produced the *Combined Arms Doctrinal Manual,* which was approved late in 1971. General Abrams advised his field elements and advisers that the manual was forthcoming, and directed them to give "dynamic support to the early introduction of the new mode of tactics."[15]

Realizing that in Lam Son 719 the North Vietnamese T-54 medium tanks had outgunned the ARVN M-41 light tank, MACV equipped one South Vietnamese tank battalion with the heavier United States M-48's. Similarly, one ARVN artillery battalion received the 175mm self-propelled guns to combat the Russian 130mm guns in the hands of the NVA. But these upgrades were grossly inadequate. All ARVN tank battalions should have been given the M-48, and several of the artillery battalions should have received the lethal 175mm gun. The episodes regarding the M-48 tanks and the 175mm guns revealed one of the significant weaknesses of Vietnamization. Throughout the life of this policy, the upgrading of the RVNAF came about in reaction to a prior modernization in the weapons or tactics of the NVA. Therefore, the NVA were always at least one step ahead of the RVNAF. Vietnamization was a running story of "too little, too late."

Nor were all the deficiencies revealed by Lam Son 719 confined to the South Vietnamese ground forces. Years later, General Hinh, analyzing Lam Son 719, stated, "The 1st Air Division, Vietnam Air Force, did not play a significant role in providing close air support for I Corps forces. Its participation and contributions were rather modest even by RVNAF standards."[16] Actually, the South Vietnamese Air Force had no role in Lam Son 719. Its absence highlights the tremendous gap between *conceiving* an operational air force and *having* one. The training, equipment, and maintenance problems necessary to improve both the

South Vietnamese Air Force and Navy had been discussed, but they made even ARVN's difficulties pale by comparison.

Pacification, which the South Vietnamese had come to consider a facet of Vietnamization, continued the great gains it had made in 1969 and 1970. By the end of 1971, the Hamlet Evaluation System showed that 97 percent of the villages and hamlets of South Vietnam were either totally secure or relatively secure.[17] As usual, the naysayers disputed not only the accuracy of the figures, but their implications. Pacification officials in the field noted that, even if the figures were correct, they represented the control and suppression of the enemy, and not the allegiance of the people to the South Vietnamese government. Nor, according to its detractors, did the HES accurately reflect growing war weariness in both civilians and military, which in turn generated tactical accommodations between the two sides and inaction against the Viet Cong. Nevertheless, when compared with the other "tracks" the United States was following to end the war (Vietnamization, troop withdrawals, and negotiations), pacification was the big winner in 1971.

The two phenomena which in 1969–1972 undermined American efforts in Vietnam—demoralization of the military and antiwar dissidence—continued apace. Again, no one knows to what depths the morale and discipline of the ground forces in Vietnam sank in 1971. Every indication, however, shows that the depth of the plunge in the army's spirit exceeded those of the years of 1969 and 1970, and those years were wretched enough. The number of general and special court-martials (those trying serious offenses) in Vietnam in 1971 was 26 percent greater per capita than in 1969 and 38 percent greater than those of 1970. In 1971, "fragging" incidents (generally attacks against officers and noncommissioned officers) ran at 1.75 per 1,000 strength compared to .35 for 1969 and .91 for 1970. The year 1971 saw an increase in the most serious military offenses—insubordination, mutiny, and refusal to perform a lawful order. The conviction rate for these crimes per 1,000 soldiers for 1969 was 0.28, for 1970 it was 0.32, and for 1971 0.44. Desertion and absent without leave rates also showed an increase.

While military discipline and morale showed a constantly worsening trend, the major problem in 1971 in Vietnam was drugs. In the army, the number of offenders involved with hard drugs, mostly heroin, increased from 1,146 in 1970 to 7,026 in 1971—almost seven-fold. This vast growth of hard drug usage was even more disturbing when one considers that the mid-year troop strengths had decreased from 404,000 in 1970 to 225,000 in 1971. In effect, hard drug use per capita was fifteen times higher in 1971 than in 1970.

But accurate statistics can mislead, and those cited above must be interpreted. Beginning in 1970 and intensifying in 1971, the services shifted their approach to drug usage. Initially, drug usage was viewed as a criminal offense, but in late 1970 and throughout 1971, military authorities came to see drug users not as criminals, but as sick people requiring treatment. Soldiers on drugs were encouraged to take advantage of amnesty offers, detoxification centers, and drug counseling programs. So, while in 1969 and 1970 soldiers tried to hide a drug problem, in 1971 they confessed their dependency to obtain punishment-free treatment. Even with this caveat, the evidence shows that the drug problem in the United States Army in Vietnam had reached epidemic proportions.

Nor was the drug problem in 1971 confined to the army alone. Marine commanders believed that 30 percent to 50 percent of their men had some involvement with drugs.[18] The marine corps continued to treat drug abuse as a criminal offense, but the last marine commander in Vietnam, Maj. Gen. Alan J. Armstrong, contravened official policy and in effect established a system of treatment with immunity. The drug problem in all services in Vietnam became so serious that it came to the president's attention. On 18 June 1971, the secretary of defense sent a message to all services informing them of a presidential directive that the drug problem be given urgent and immediate attention.

Military derelictions were not confined to drug abuse and offenses by individuals against the United States Code of Military Justice. Units, both large and small, were derelict also. The "search and evade" missions continued to increase. Laxness became the order of the day. In the Americal Division—a "hard luck outfit" if there ever was one—fifty NVA sappers overran a fire base held by 250 Americans, killing thirty and wounding eighty-two. General Westmoreland, who reviewed the case, called it ". . . a clear case of dereliction of duty—of soldiers becoming lax in their defense and officers failing to take corrective action."[19] The secretary of the army took disciplinary action against two generals and four other officers in the division.

The causes of the collapsing morale and discipline of the ground forces in Vietnam have been discussed. Antiwar dissension, idleness, boredom, drugs, racial tension, Vietnamization, troop withdrawal, the permissiveness of the sixties, the long inconclusive war, and failures of leadership all played their part. What had been a minor decline of spirit in 1969 had become, by 1971—to use a term much bruited about then and later—a "crisis in command." On 19 July 1971, Lt. Gen. W. J. McCaffrey, then CG, United States Army, Vietnam, published a report on the morale and discipline of the army troops in Vietnam, in which he admitted that "discipline within the command as a whole had eroded to a serious, but not critical degree. . . ."[20] Another view was submitted by a retired career marine officer and analyst, Robert D. Heinl, when in an article in the *Detroit News* in June 1971 he wrote, "By every conceivable indicator, our Army that now remains in Vietnam is in a stage of approaching collapse, with individual units avoiding or having refused combat, murdering their officers and noncommissioned officers, drug-ridden, and dispirited where not near-mutinous."[21] The truth probably lay somewhere between McCaffrey's judgment of "serious but not critical" and Heinl's "approaching collapse."

It is easy to exaggerate this collapse of morale and discipline in Vietnam. The many well-led army and marine units carried on in the historically high standards of those services. Army units within the United States continued to do their jobs. By 1971 the vaunted United States Army, Europe, which had been gutted by constant levies for Vietnam, began to regain its professionalism. The American armed services have a massive momentum. From time to time they may stagger, but in the words of the army song, they keep "rolling along." With the advent of the volunteer army and the withdrawal of the American troops from an unpopular and unwinnable war, the armed forces were, once again, on the road upwards.

The demoralization of the ground forces in Vietnam was accompanied by growing antiwar dissidence at home. Lam Son 719 once again brought out the antiwar dissidents in full force, and their ranks were growing rapidly. The liberals, leftists, and draft-dodging students were joined by two new groups. The first, a coalition of blacks and Hispanics, opposed the war not only on moral grounds, but because it diverted huge sums from the Great Society programs. The second group was a loose coalition of liberal Vietnam veterans opposed to the war. These groups constituted what social scientist John Mueller called "Believers." "Believers" supported or opposed the war regardless of national policy. "Followers," the other category, will "react like hawks if the president is pursuing a forceful or war-like policy, like doves if he is reducing war or seeking negotiation."[22] Thus, Nixon, by stressing Vietnamization, troop withdrawal, and negotiations, turned more and more of the "followers" into doves. In turn, each United States troop withdrawal or backward step only increased their appetite for more. As a result of the disastrous television coverage of Lam Son 719 and the growing disgust with the inconclusive struggle, popular support for the war dropped to an all-time low in April 1971.

The Democrats in Congress were quick to exploit this growing antiwar sentiment. In late March 1971, House Democrats approved a resolution calling for the termination of the United States involvement in Indochina by 1 January 1973. The action then shifted to the Senate. Senator McGovern proposed to the Senate Foreign Relations Committee a bill which would have the Americans out of Indochina by 31 December 1971. Fulbright, the committee chairman, held widely publicized hearings featuring those who favored the bill calling for unilateral withdrawal. The McGovern measure eventually appeared in slightly modified form as an amendment to the military conscription bill. On 16 June, the Senate defeated the amendment.

But the doves fought on. On 22 June, the Senate approved the Mansfield Amendment, which declared that it was United States policy that all American troops were to be withdrawn from Vietnam within nine months after the approval of the extension of the draft. The wording was later changed in conference from "nine months from passage" to "earliest practicable date."[23]

While the Democrats in Congress sought to undermine the president's war policies and negotiating options, the antiwar activists took to the streets. On 24 April, the leaders organized two massive demonstrations— one in San Francisco which drew 150,000 people and one in Washington of 200,000. The Vietnam Veterans Against the War (VVAW) made their appearance in the Washington demonstration along with Coretta King (Martin Luther King's widow) and an associated group of leftists such as Abner Mikva and Bella Abzug. Thousands of protesters marched in other American cities demanding an end to the war and a unilateral withdrawal of all American troops from Vietnam.

The big demonstration, however, was scheduled for 2 May in Washington, where the protesters had vowed they would "shut down the government.'' On 1 May, however, the government forces seized the initiative and routed 10,000 demonstrators from their campsite along the Potomac River. The demonstrators regrouped the next day and on 3 May began their campaign of blocking roads and ''trashing'' Washington. The police cracked down and eventually some 12,000 protesters were arrested and held in the practice football field of the Washington Redskins. Most of the detainees were freed, but the back of the demonstration had been broken. Nevertheless, antiwar dissent remained a powerful and influential force throughout 1971.

Lam Son 719 impacted indirectly on negotiations. Negotiations between the United States and North Vietnam had lain dead in the water since October 1970. Now with Lam Son 719 completed, Henry Kissinger hoped that the time might be ripe to resume attempts at settling the war by diplomatic means. He reasoned that North Vietnam might prefer to negotiate rather than face the prospect of sporadic forays into its base areas. Beyond that hope, the growing pressure of the antiwar dissidents and the efforts of Congress to legislate a total United States withdrawal in some destructive time frame impelled the administration toward an effort at negotiations, as forlorn as the prospects appeared.

The president fired the preparatory barrage of rhetoric by giving a series of speeches in April 1971 which stressed continued United States troop withdrawals and repeated the negotiating offer of October 1970. The United States negotiating offensive jumped off on 31 May 1971, when Kissinger met secretly with the North Vietnamese chief negotiator, Le Duc Tho, in Paris. The secrecy of not only the contacts, but the negotiations themselves, would later give the administration severe problems with Congress and the news media.

At the 31 May meeting, Kissinger made several proposals which he thought the North Vietnamese would find tempting. He repeated the proposal made on 8 October 1970, that the United States no longer required NVA troops to withdraw from South Vietnam. This offer was the critical bait with which Kissinger hoped to hook the wily North Vietnamese. And in this judgment he was sound, for, as is now known, this concession, plus United States withdrawal, constituted the indispensable prerequisite of the Communist negotiating position. Kissinger proposed also that all PW's be exchanged immediately, and indicated that the United States was prepared to set a deadline for the withdrawal of its forces. He offered a cease-fire in place when the United States withdrawals began, and that there would be no further infiltration of outside forces into South Vietnam, Laos, or Cambodia.

To Kissinger's surprise and dismay, Le Duc Tho turned down the United States' proposals. To the suspicious North Vietnamese, the proposal did not *guarantee* that NVA troops could remain in South Vietnam.[24] Further, they rejected the timing implicit in Kissinger's offer, since United States withdrawal would take place after the POW exchange and the cease-fire had taken place, thus depriving the North Vietnamese of two powerful negotiating tools.[25] Above all, the North Vietnamese rejected Kissinger's proposals because they contained no offer regarding the political future of South Vietnam, or to put it more bluntly, the dismantlement of the Thieu government by the United States. The North Vietnamese, however, did show a new attitude, one implying that real negotiations might now make some progress.

At Hanoi's request, another meeting between Kissinger and Le Duc Tho was set for 26 June. At this secret session the North Vietnamese tabled their counterproposals, nine in number. For the first time the North Vietnamese showed a serious intent to negotiate. Kissinger judged that seven of the proposals could be satisfactorily negotiated. He drew the line, however, at Hanoi's demand for reparations and for the United States to "stop supporting Thieu-Ky-Khiem so that a new administration could be set up in Saigon."[26] The latter—the political future of South Vietnam—was the point which had impaled all previous attempts at a settlement. Nevertheless, compared to former negotiations, the North Vietnamese proposals represented substantial progress.

On 1 July, as Kissinger prepared to begin bargaining on Hanoi's nine points, he got "blindsided." Madame Nguyen Thi Binh, the foreign minister of the Provisional Revolutionary Government (PRG), *publicly* issued a seven-point peace plan of her own. While parallel to the North Vietnamese nine-point proposal, it varied from it in several substantial ways and ran directly contrary to Le Duc Tho's proposal to link POW exchange directly with troop withdrawals. Kissinger, stunned, asked Le Duc Tho if *his* proposals were still valid. Tho replied that they were. Kissinger's immediate reaction to Madame Binh's proposals was that they constituted a device to put pressure on the United States to negotiate on Le Duc Tho's terms. In short, the Communists wanted to negotiate in secret, while appealing in public to the antiwar sentiment within the United States.[27]

Recently, however, information has come to light which throws some doubt on this theory of a Communist conspiracy. In his book, the then minister of justice of the PRG, Truong Nhu Tang, now living in exile, tells in detail of a continued series of bitter policy disputes between the North Vietnamese and the South Vietnamese of the PRG.[28] It is possible that the PRG took a hand in the game without the prior knowledge or approval of the North Vietnamese. At any rate, Madame Binh's plan worked. Congress and the news media, ignorant of the secret Kissinger/Tho negotiations, charged that the administration's failure to reply to the Binh proposals showed again its adamant refusal to negotiate seriously. It was here that the administration (unable to expose the duplicitous nature of the Binh proposals) paid heavily for its penchant for secret negotiations.

Unabashed, the North Vietnamese continued to show their aroused interest in real (and secret) negotiations. Kissinger met with Tho on 12 July, and after an exchange of recriminations about the two Communist proposals, got down to serious business. When North Vietnam's nine points were placed alongside the seven-point proposal of the United States, it became obvious that agreement on all but two points was reachable. Kissinger judged that the reparations demand might be satisfactorily compromised. After all, both Presidents Nixon and Johnson had publicly proclaimed that they would contribute to a fund to rehabilitate Indochina, including North Vietnam. The difficulty lay not in the substance of the proposal but in its form. The final point, the dismantlement of the Thieu government, was to the United States, nonnegotiable. On this note the session broke up, after, however, the participants agreed to meet again on 26 July.

At the 26 July meeting, the negotiators made further progress on all points except the future of the Thieu government. On this point, once again, the negotiations floundered. There was another session on 16 August in Paris, but this vital issue remained unresolved. At the urgings of the North Vietnamese, another meeting was held on 13 September. After a short two-hour session without progress, this one broke up. Thus ended a series of negotiations which could not reconcile the views of the parties as to the political future of South Vietnam. On this issue the gap in perceptions was enormous. The North Vietnamese were convinced that sooner or later the United States would trade the Thieu government for peace. This, however, was the one thing that Nixon would not do. Kissinger, on the other hand, believed that this point, like the others, could be negotiated into some solution short of dismantling the Thieu government. The series which culminated on 13 September showed how wrong both parties were, at least in 1971.

There was one more negotiating spasm in 1971, one last attempt by Kissinger to compromise the sticky point of the future of the Thieu government. He proposed "that a new presidential election be held within six months after the signing of a final agreement. The election would be run by an electoral commission, including Communists, under international supervision. One month before the election, Thieu would resign and his function would be assumed by the president of the South Vietnamese Senate."[29] The offer was transmitted in writing to the North Vietnamese in Paris. After agreeing to a meeting date of 20 November, the North Vietnamese on 17 November canceled the session without commenting on the new United States proposal. Thus, negotiations in 1971, while on occasion seeming to hold promise, in the end failed.

Nobody knows for sure what made the North Vietnamese so intractable. One school of thought holds that the whole North Vietnamese scenario of negotiations in 1971 was a classic example of "talking while preparing to fight," a camouflage to cover preparations for the 1972 offensive. Tang, the PRG minister of justice, confirms this, writing, "Meanwhile in Paris Le Duc Tho was treating Henry Kissinger to a brilliant display of 'talking and fighting,' using the negotiations to cover as long as possible the next real move in the war, the upcoming dry season campaign in the South."[30] In the same passage he describes the North Vietnamese insistence on the removal of Thieu as a North Vietnamese "ploy," designed only to prolong negotiations as a cover for the preparation of the offensive.

Another school believes that the North Vietnamese wanted to negotiate sincerely, but that a combination of factors drove them into an uncompromising stance. Kissinger believes that the divisions within the United States encouraged the Communists to hold out for Thieu's ouster, in effect, for United States capitulation. Military reasons also dictated that the North Vietnamese should hold out. The NVA were in dire straits in South Vietnam, almost moribund, and pacification was making huge strides, forcing the Communists to negotiate from a position of weakness, a stance they feared and abhorred. Above all, however, Le Duan and company wanted one more throw of the military dice. Lam Son 719 had convinced them that they could defeat the South Vietnamese on the battlefield, even if ARVN had American air support. Thus they might gain all by a major offensive in the spring of 1972.

And as 1971 drew to a close, this major NVA offensive loomed closer. As early as late December 1970 and January 1971, the NVN Politburo had convened the 19th Plenary Session of the Lao Dong Party, a meeting of the Central Committee which always indicated that major policy decisions were in the offing. This one was no different. The Party issued announcements once again that the war had priority over economic development. This pronouncement suggests that the old argument between the "North Vietnam firsters" and the "South Vietnam firsters" was being refought, but no concrete evidence is available.

The 19th Plenum had reached the momentous decision to launch an all-out, conventional invasion of South Vietnam in 1972 to win the war militarily. Shortly after the conclusion of the Plenum, Le Duan departed for Moscow to obtain the conventional weapons which the offensive would require. Beginning in the spring of 1971, trucks, T-54 tanks, SAM missiles, MIG 21's, 130mm guns, 130mm mortars, the heat-seeking, shoulder-fired SA7 antiaircraft missile, plus spare parts, ammunition, and POL poured into North Vietnam and began to make its way south down the Ho Chi Minh Trail.

So, late in 1971, as negotiations collapsed, NVA units and heavy equipment began to move into place just north of the DMZ. General Abrams and the Joint Chiefs wanted to bomb the concentrations, but Nixon demurred. Finally, when the North Vietnamese refused to even meet Kissinger on 20 November and then shelled Saigon a few days later (another violation of the "unwritten agreements"), Nixon ordered that bombing raids be reinstituted south of the 20th Parallel to impede the Communist build-up just north of the DMZ. He limited the period of the attacks from 26 to 30 December when the college campuses were clear of students. In this connection, one must note that by now the antiwar dissidents were influencing not only governmental policy and strategy, but battlefield tactics and timing as well. Nixon's ploy availed him little; the domestic outcry was, in Nixon's words, "immediate and intense."[31] There were the usual shrill charges that Nixon was "widening the war'' and trying to ''win a military victory,'' which would have been ludicrous had they not so emasculated American policy. The people who were about to ''widen the war'' and drive for a military victory were not Nixon and Kissinger, but Le Duan, Giap, and fourteen NVA divisions ''revving'' up their tank engines, just across South Vietnam's borders.

Notes—Chapter 23

1. Col. Hoang Ngoc Lung, *Strategy and Tactics,* Indochina Monographs (Washington, D.C.: U.S. Army Center of Military History, 1980), p. 73.
2. Kissinger, *White House Years,* p. 1005.
3. Maj. Gen. Nguyen Duy Hinh, *Lam Son 719,* Indochina Monographs (Washington, D.C.: U.S. Army Center of Military History, 1979), p. 79.
4. U.S. XXIV Corps, *After-Action Report, Lam Son 719,* 1 April 1971, p. 90.
5. Nixon, *Memoirs,* p. 499.
6. Hinh, *Lam Son 719,* p. 140.
7. Ibid.
8. David Fulghum, Terrence Maitland, et al. *The Vietnam Experience. South Vietnam on Trial Mid 1970 to 1972* (Boston, MA: Boston Publishing Co., 1984), p. 91.
9. Gen. William W. Momyer, *USAF Air Power in Three Wars (WWII, Korea, Vietnam)* (Washington, D.C.: U.S. Government Printing Office, 1978), pp. 321–324.
10. Message, MACV to CJCS and CINCPAC, DTG 14 1435Z February 1971.
11. Kissinger, *White House Years,* p. 992.
12. Lung, *Strategy and Tactics,* p. 40.
13. U.S. XXIV Corps, *After-Action Report,* p. 2.
14. Clausewitz, *Principles of War,* pp. 12–13.
15. Collins, *Development,* pp. 109–110.
16. Hinh, *Lam Son 719,* p. 155.
17. Tho, *Pacification,* p. 165; Hinh, *Vietnamization,* p. 83.
18. Lt. Col. Charles R. Shrader, ed. *Proceedings of the 1982 International Military History Symposium, "The Impact of Unsuccessful Military Campaigns on Military Institutions, 1860–1980"* A submission by Mr. Jack Shulimson and Maj. Edward F. Wells, U.S.M.C. "First In; First Out: The Marine Experience in Vietnam, 1965–1971" (Washington, D.C.: U.S. Army Center of Military History, 1984), p. 286.
19. Westmoreland, *Soldier,* p. 447.
20. Lewy, *America,* p. 154 (Quoting a memo from CG USARV to army commanders, 19 July 1971, pp. 1–2).
21. Lewy, *America,* p. 154.
22. John Mueller, "A Summary of Public Opinion and the Vietnam War." *Vietnam as History* (Washington, D.C.: University Press of America, 1984), Appendix 1.
23. Fanning, *Betrayal,* pp. 85–86.

24. Seymour M. Hersh, *The Price of Power, Kissinger in the Nixon White House* (New York: Summit Books, 1983), pp. 428–429.
25. Tad Szulc, *The Illusion of Peace, Foreign Policy in the Nixon Years* (New York: Viking Press, 1978), p. 392.
26. Kissinger, *White House Years*, p. 1023.
27. Kalb and Kalb, *Kissinger*, p. 181.
28. Tang, *Vietcong Memoir*, pp. 186–200.
29. Kissinger, *White House Years*, p. 1039.
30. Tang, *Vietcong Memoir*, p. 194.
31. Nixon, *Memoirs*, p. 584.

24 Totus Porcus

The Whole Hog
1972

On 30 March 1972, Hanoi launched the so-called Easter offensive, a massive invasion by conventional forces in an effort to win the war militarily. The North Vietnamese employed about 125,000 men in fourteen divisions and twenty-six separate regiments, supported by hundreds of tanks and artillery pieces. This force amounted to some twenty divisions (more divisions, incidentally, than George Patton ever commanded in World War II). To man this offensive, Giap used every NVA division and separate regiment in both North and South Vietnam, every NVA combat unit in Laos except the 316th NVA Division and four independent infantry regiments.[1] In contrast to the Tet offensive, the Viet Cong played almost no role in the Easter offensive.

The decision to try once again to win the war by military means was reached by the 19th Plenum which convened in Hanoi in December 1970 and continued into early 1971. The military and political situation as seen by the Politburo gives an insight into the rationale for the invasion. The North Vietnamese saw the military situation as bad at the end of 1970 and likely to get worse. The Cambodian raid had severely damaged the logistic apparatus supporting Communist troops in the southern half of South Vietnam. Vietnamization was making progress. The pacification program had achieved massive gains in the South Vietnamese countryside, and the Viet Cong and its political infrastructure were demoralized and impotent.

On the other hand, the Politburo saw some favorable factors. Antiwar dissent within the United States increasingly hamstrung President Nixon in his conduct of the war. He was being forced to withdraw American troops without regard to the tactical situation in South Vietnam, and by 1972 the United States ground combat elements would be out of the South. A resounding NVA military victory would humiliate Nixon, destroy his war policies, and perhaps defeat his bid for reelection in November. After all, according to the conventional wisdom of the Politburo, if President Johnson had been toppled by a Communist military *defeat,* even a partial victory would ravage President Nixon's prospects for reelection.

The South Vietnamese offensive of 1971 into Laos, Lam Son 719, also contributed to the NVA decision to undertake a large-scale conventional offensive. In its later stages—the South Vietnamese retreat and panic—the offensive had revealed ARVN's vulnerability to tanks and heavy artillery fire along with its deep deficiencies in leadership and training. Lam Son 719 had also demonstrated that while United States air power could inflict serious damage on the NVA, it could not by itself win a battle that ARVN would not fight. The North Vietnamese thought victory would be theirs, even if the United States intervened from the air.

Once having decided to mount an offensive, the next decision which the 19th Plenum had to make was the one on major timing—that is, should the invasion be launched in 1972 or in 1973? And, of course, in this fractious group, an argument ensued. Those who promoted 1973 as the year to invade made a simple case. They argued that by 1973 the United States would be totally out of Vietnam, and in all probability would not return. These proponents argued further that victory was much more assured in 1973 than in 1972. Why not wait for the sure thing? The majority of the Plenum rejected this cautious counsel and contended that 1972 had to be the year. Their arguments stressed the effect of an invasion on the United States presidential elections and on Nixon's prestige. They contended that Vietnamization was moving forward and that pacification was progressing in great leaps. This progress, taken in conjunction with the obvious decline of VC morale and effectiveness, worried the Northerners. They were not sure that the Viet Cong could hold out another year, or how strong RVNAF and the GVN would become. The proponents of 1972 had additional arguments. Since the United States still had forces in Vietnam in 1972, a victory in 1972 over the South Vietnamese would be interpreted, both in the United States and abroad, as an American military defeat. On the other hand, in 1973 the United States would be out of Vietnam, and the NVA could claim no such victory over American forces.

Beyond that there was, as always, the personal equation. The members of the Politburo averaged sixty years of age. They were hard-core Communist revolutionaries, and they had fought almost their entire lives. They wanted not some mealy, half-loaf of triumph handed them on the tray of negotiations. They wanted to end the war with a military victory—as soon as possible, and that meant 1972.

The Politburo's decision of 1970–1971 to launch a major invasion in 1972 had to be a tentative one, for its actual execution depended on several factors. The first, of course, would be the inevitable changes which would occur in the military and political situation between early 1971 and D-day, 1972. For example, the United States Congress might well legislate all American forces precipitously out of Vietnam. Also there was always the possibility of a coup upsetting Thieu and his government. But the Russians held the decisive key to the fate of the invasion. A large conventional offensive by NVA Main Force units would require the Russians to furnish the North Vietnamese hundreds of T-34 and T-54 tanks, scores of the long-range 130mm guns, and several kinds of advanced antiaircraft missiles, plus thousands of tons of spare parts, ammunition, oil, and gasoline. Without this kind of prodigious support, no massive NVA offensive would be possible. Accordingly, in the early spring of 1971, Le Duan made an extended visit to Moscow. There he presented his shopping list and gained not only Russian support for his adventure, but the hardware and consumables to carry it out. Shortly after his return, the Politburo made a second and confirming decision to undertake the invasion. In June or July 1971, the orders went out in Party Resolution #13. While the offensive could still be canceled, it was now well on the tracks.

Throughout 1971, the NVA made massive preparations to prepare their troops and logistic support for the upcoming offensive. They called the offensive "Nguyen Hue," after a Vietnamese emperor and national hero who in 1789 moved his troops hundreds of miles through the jungles of Central Vietnam to North Vietnam, where he surprised the invading Chinese and destroyed their army. By December 1971, the NVA troops in Laos were recalled, augmented with replacements, and reequipped.

The decision to launch the invasion was now firm. In fact, the 20th Plenum, which convened that same month, formally approved the initiation of the invasion. The dice were thrown.

And this was no small-stake game, for the Politburo's objectives were extremely ambitious. The best evidence of Hanoi's objectives for the invasion is contained in an unnumbered COSVN Resolution of December 1971, the period when the 20th Plenum made the binding decision to launch the offensive. This resolution called for "tilting the balance of forces through the use of main force warfare and political initiative."[2] Stripped of Communist double-talk, the Politburo wanted first to win the war militarily by defeating the South Vietnamese forces. And second, failing in the first objective of military victory, the NVN sought to gain bargaining leverage in the negotiations which would surely follow the offensive. Giap and his comrades hoped that the invasion, even if it did not end the war, would result in gaining territory, reversing pacification and Vietnamization, raising Viet Cong morale, disrupting the South Vietnamese economy, discrediting Thieu, and spurring antiwar dissidence in the United States. Truong Nhu Tang, onetime minister of justice in the PRG, wrote that this last objective (spurring antiwar dissidence in the United States) was a major objective of the offensive.[3] Whether this is true or not—and the Vietnamese Communists had a habit of after the fact justification for battlefield failures—it perhaps provides an example of a military action taken at least in part for its impact on the political *dau tranh*.

Giap took these broad military and political objectives and turned them into an operational plan. His plan envisioned three major attacks to be launched more or less simultaneously. On the northern front, he planned to send two NVA divisions, the 308th and 304th, plus three separate infantry regiments, all reinforced by some 200 tanks and several regiments of artillery, across the DMZ aimed at the provincial capital of Quang Tri province, Quang Tri City. A third division, the NVA 324B Division, would slice in from the west to take, or threaten to take, Hue, the old Imperial capital. The eventual objective of this northern offensive was not only to take Quang Tri City and Hue, but to expel all South Vietnamese troops and authorities from the two northern provinces of South Vietnam. If this attack succeeded, it would extend the border of North Vietnam far to the south and threaten Da Nang, the second city of South Vietnam.

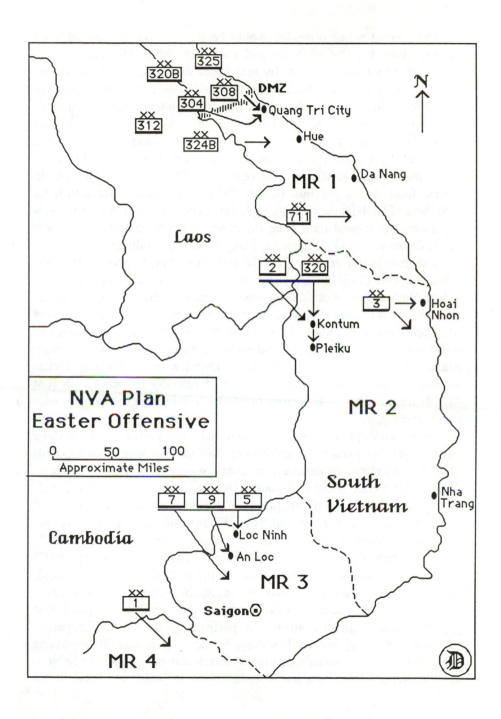

The second major offensive would be initiated on the central front by two divisions, the NVA 2d and the NVA 320th Divisions, again supported by a tank regiment. Its first major objective was Kontum, its second objective Pleiku, both key towns and communication centers in the Central Highlands. Linked with this major attack was a secondary attack to be made by the 3d Division in the coastal province of Binh Dinh. This secondary effort would pin the ARVN troops along the coast and thereby prevent their reinforcing the South Vietnamese forces in the Kontum/Pleiku area. The final objective of these two attacks on the central front was a juncture of the NVA forces from Kontum/Pleiku with those of Binh Dinh, thus cutting South Vietnam in two along Highway 19, a major east-west road from the coast to the Highlands. The NVA 711th Division would threaten Da Nang from the southwest.

The third major offensive, on the southern front, targeted three divisions, the Viet Cong 5th, 7th, and 9th Divisions, with about 200 tanks, at Loc Ninh and An Loc, the provincial capital of Binh Long province. (The three Viet Cong divisions were VC in name only. They had long since become almost totally NVA.) From An Loc, the NVA, if successful, could roll down Highway 13 and threaten Saigon itself. A secondary attack would be made by the NVA 1st Division in the Mekong Delta. Its mission was to seize territory and rice, and by its actions prevent ARVN from moving forces from the Delta to reinforce the troops under attack elsewhere.

Giap's concept was, as usual, bold and imaginative. In these three major attacks he planned a hard-hitting, fast-moving war of tanks, artillery, and infantry, modernized in every way except for air support. Each of his major attacks, if successful, had a war-winning potential. The capture by the northern prong of the two northern provinces of South Vietnam (Quang Tri and Thua Thien) plus Quang Tri City and Hue would demoralize the South Vietnamese, and, if desired, would provide a capital for a Provisional Revolutionary Government (PRG) on South Vietnamese soil. The attacks on the central front, if successful, would cut South Vietnam in two. Again, such a success, always feared by the South Vietnamese, would unnerve the country and place that part of South Vietnam north of the partition in the gravest jeopardy. The southern prong aimed at Loc Ninh/An Loc offered equally promising prospects. Not only would a successful attack seriously endanger Saigon, but the North Vietnamese had detailed plans to install the PRG in An

Loc. Any one of these successes would have had severe repercussions on the morale and staying power of the South Vietnamese people and government. The effect on negotiations of even one NVA victory would be ruinous to the U.S./GVN side. The successful culmination of two or all three of the attacks would have ended the war on North Vietnamese terms—a military victory.

Giap's broad plan for the invasion once again shows Giap's unfortunate penchant for operations on exterior lines. In his defense one may argue that geography, terrain, the disposition of forces, and his logistical support system left him no other choice. Nevertheless, as I have discussed earlier, operations on exterior lines pose heavy burdens on the attacker, requiring a high degree of coordination, good communications, aggressive and flexible subordinates, and above all, *the absolute need to keep the pressure on all points of the periphery of the operation at all times.* This, of course, is necessary to prevent the enemy, operating on interior lines, from moving forces from one part of the periphery to a more threatened spot. On this factor usually turns the success or failure of operations on exterior lines.

Before the invasion could be launched, Giap (and the Politburo) had to make one additional, and critical, decision—the exact time to launch the offensive. Weather, as it always did in Vietnam, exercised a major influence on this decision. Those areas of Vietnam subject to the Southwest Monsoon, generally the lower two-thirds of South Vietnam, could expect dry weather from mid-October until the end of May. Those regions subject to the Northeast Monsoon, Quang Tri and Hue, would be dry from about the first of February to the first of September. Looking at both of these differing climatological areas revealed that the only period of good weather nationwide would be between 1 February and 31 May.

If the campaign started too late it could run well into the wet season, when torrential rains would impede movement and make NVA resupply impossible. Other considerations argued for an early start. After Giap and his commanders had completed their preparation, further delay served only to dissipate the assembled supplies and to erode morale of the troops who would make the assault, and any long delay exposed the troops and supplies to destructive United States air attacks in their assembly areas. On the other side of the ledger, a later starting date would maximize the potential influence of the offensive on Nixon's reelection campaign. After weighing the competing timing requirements, Giap decided to begin the offensive on 30 March, Good Friday. With that decision the biggest military offensive since the Chinese intervention in the Korean War was ready to blast off.

As 1972 dawned, both the Americans and the South Vietnamese knew a major NVA offensive impended. Nor was it difficult for the Allied intelligence officers to pick the general areas of the assaults. The difficulty came in predicting the starting time of the overall invasion and the timing of the individual attacks in relation to each other. Allied intelligence failed to forecast the time of initiation, which, embarrassingly, caught both General Abrams and Ambassador Bunker outside Vietnam visiting their families. Allied intelligence had a final problem—determining the direction and weights of the component attacks in each major offensive. Here the intelligence effort again failed, misjudging the direction and weight of two of the three major offensives. Nevertheless, ARVN was psychologically ready for the major attack coming at them.

The Northern Front

ARVN's total troop strength in the two northern provinces of South Vietnam, Quang Tri and Thua Thieu, totaled 25,000 men. The principal combat units were the 3d ARVN Infantry Division, stationed just south of the DMZ, and the 1st ARVN Infantry Division, protecting Hue against an NVA attack from the west and northwest. In addition to its organic units, the 3d Division exercised operational control over two marine brigades from the general reserve, the 147th and the 258th, plus some cavalry squadrons and other odds and ends.

The 3d ARVN Division, activated in October 1971, would bear the brunt of the initial attack. It was formed from the combat-tested 2d Infantry Regiment (from the 1st ARVN Division) and from some Local Force units in the area which were upgraded and designated the 56th and 57th Infantry Regiments. South Vietnamese Gen. Ngo Quang Truong, who had the closest view of the ensuing battle, states that the 56th and 57th Regiments were veterans of combat along the DMZ and "were expected to perform better than any others in that environment."[4] Other writers have pointed out, however, that the two regiments had to be filled out by recaptured deserters and jailbirds, and that they were officered by cast-offs and incompetents.[5] Even Truong acknowledges that the 3d Division was short of logistic support units, lacked some artillery and signal equipment, and that its troops had not completed their training. The division commander, Brig. Gen. Vu Van Giai, was a competent and dedicated professional, who would be tested under the most arduous conditions.

Armchair generals have asked why the South Vietnamese JGS put the 3d Division, probably the weakest of all ARVN divisions, into the DMZ area and then leave them there when the coming offensive became obvious. The answer lies first in the static, defensive, and provincial role of the ARVN divisions, plus the immobility forced on them by *de facto* attachment of the soldiers' families to the division itself. A shift of a division from one area to another was a major undertaking, requiring in one case seven months to complete. Even then, the transported soldiers performed badly in a strange country against an unfamiliar enemy. The second reason that the 3d Division held the DMZ lay in the erroneous assumption by the incompetent I Corps commander, Lt. Gen. Hoang Xuan Lam (he of Lam Son 719 ignominy), as well as by the JGS, that the major attack in Quang Tri province would come from the *west* and *northwest* and not over the DMZ. The brunt then would be borne principally by the marines stationed in western Quang Tri rather than the less competent 3d ARVN Division along the DMZ. Farther south, the 1st ARVN Infantry Division, the best division in the South Vietnamese Army, protected Hue.

North of the DMZ lurked the famous NVA 308th "Iron" Division, the 304th NVA Division, three separate infantry regiments from the B-5 Front, two tank regiments, and five artillery regiments, armed with the long-range 130mm gun with a range of 27,000 meters, some 10,000 meters beyond the range of all ARVN artillery except its one battalion of 175mm guns. Behind these assault forces along the DMZ stood the 325th NVA Division and the 320B NVA Division, and in Laos, immediately available, the 312th NVA Division. In Thua Thieu province, facing Hue from the west, there was the 324B NVA Division. This powerful force was commanded by the B-5 Front, an NVA corps headquarters located in the DMZ.

The NVA attack, which jumped off at noon on 30 March behind a massive artillery preparation, caught the 3d ARVN Division interchanging

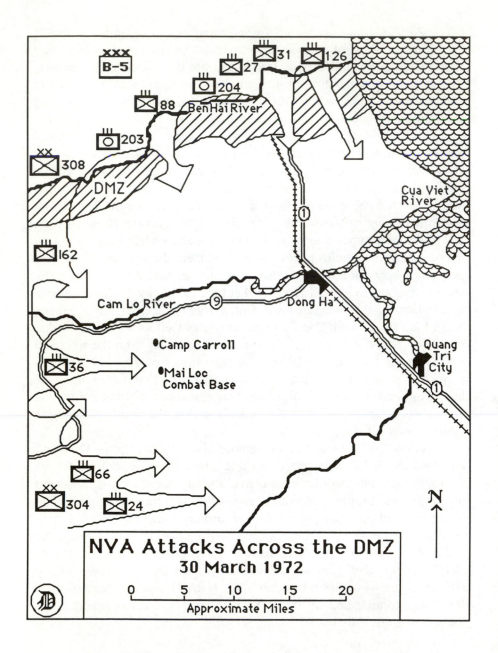

NVA Attacks Across the DMZ
30 March 1972

regiments between positions, and therefore particularly vulnerable. Obviously the timing and the scope of the attack surprised the ill-fated 3d ARVN Division and the incompetents at I ARVN Corps. There followed a good deal of confused fighting, but by 1 April the entire 3d ARVN Division began to fall back to the south, while the west flank (held by the marine brigades) withdrew to the east. On 1 April, the division commander, General Giai, ordered a new line set up on the Cua Viet and Cam Lo Rivers, bending south at Camp Carroll, an old United States Marine fire support base. Giai himself actively supervised the occupation of the positions and stiffened morale. But on 2 April, the next day, all collapsed. The 57th Regiment (3d Division) holding the key sector astride Highway 1, seeing the refugees (including their own families) pouring through their lines from the north, panicked and joined the refugees in their flight to the south. Giai flew to the scene, stopped the rout, and returned the men to their units, but the unit's morale had been badly damaged. On this day worse was to come. The 56th Regiment of the 3d ARVN Division, battered, demoralized, and virtually surrounded at Camp Carroll, surrendered en masse to the enemy along with 22 artillery pieces and other valuable equipment. The South Vietnamese Marines at Mai Loc, now threatened with encirclement from the north, pulled back to the east. There the battered 147th Marine Brigade was relieved by the fresh 369th Marine Brigade.

The NVA troops continued their attacks on 3 April, and after heavy losses, succeeded in compressing the ARVN defensive perimeter by 8 April, but could not break through the South Vietnamese line. After a final abortive attack on 9 April, the NVA withdrew to regroup and resupply, temporarily taking the pressure off the 3d ARVN Division and the northern flank. This terminated Phase I of the Quang Tri offensive.

Meanwhile, the 1st ARVN Division was being tested in the hills west of Hue by the 324B NVA Division, reinforced by one regiment of the 304th Division. The NVA attack jumped off around 1 April and by mid-April had put intense pressure on defensive positions in western Thua Thien. By late April, the situation was critical, and on 28 April several ARVN defensive positions and firebases had been lost. The ARVN situation in the two northern provinces looked bleak, and worse was to come.

Back to Quang Tri, where, during the lull in the fighting from 9–

22 April, the 3d ARVN Division was reinforced by three ranger groups of three battalions each and the recently reconstituted 1st Armored Brigade, which had been virtually destroyed in 1971 in the abortive Lam Son 719. Emboldened by these reinforcements, General Lam—incredible as it seems—now ordered a counteroffensive over the objections of his field commanders. In the face of the superior NVA strength, Lam's dream-world counterattack went nowhere. Worse than its failure, it reduced ARVN's strength and demoralized the "attacking" troops, which in fact never left their foxholes and bunkers. Lam, of course, did not know this because he *never* visited the front lines.

Lam's incompetence now became the critical element in the battle for Quang Tri. First, he saddled General Giai, the 3d Division commander, with an impossible span of control. In late April, Giai commanded his own two regiments, two marine brigades, four ranger groups, one armored brigade, plus the odds and ends of regional and local forces—a total of nine brigades, containing twenty-three battalions, and all of this with grossly inadequate signal communications. To complicate matters, the marine division headquarters and the ranger command headquarters had been left out of the chain of command, but they continued to hold administrative control over their units, thus causing additional confusion. To complete the fiasco, Lam frequently issued orders directly to the regiments, groups, and brigades without telling Giai. In quick order, confusion, distrust, and insubordination destroyed the ARVN command and control on the northern front.

The enemy resumed his attack on 23 April, reinforcing his troops with the 325th Division. Aided by a stupid blunder by Lam and the commander of the 1st Armored Brigade, the NVA troops succeeded by 29 April in compressing the demoralized ARVN soldiers into a small perimeter around Quang Tri City. On 1 May, mass panic and confusion set in among the ARVN troops, who precipitously abandoned Quang Tri City to the NVA. The soldiers, their families, and other refugees fled pell-mell to the south. The NVA tanks and artillery fired into this tangled mass, which resulted in an estimated 20,000 civilian deaths. Phase II of the Quang Tri campaign was over. The attention now shifted to Hue and Thua Thieu provinces.

Alarmed by the fall of Quang Tri province and the city itself, and fearing that Hue and even Da Nang would follow, on 2 May Thieu

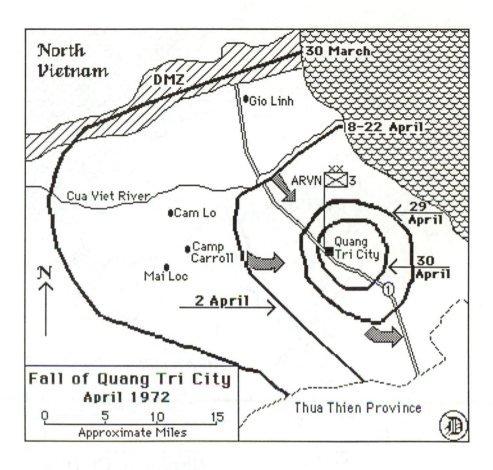

Fall of Quang Tri City
April 1972

0   5   10   15

Approximate Miles

took a long overdue action—he fired Lam. In his place he appointed
South Vietnam's finest combat soldier, Maj. Gen. Ngo Quang Truong,
CG of IV ARVN Corps and formerly CG, 1st ARVN Infantry Division.
For once Thieu picked the right man. Thoroughly professional, completely
dedicated, apolitical, experienced as a battalion, regimental, and division
commander, Truong could have commanded a division or corps in any
army in the world. He arrived in Hue that same afternoon (2 May)
with a small staff and immediately took charge. He issued orders that
deserters and looters would be summarily shot, and he shot a few. He
organized the others into units. He straightened out the tangled command
and control mess that Lam had left him and drew up a simple plan to
defend Hue. The marine division under a new commander—and this

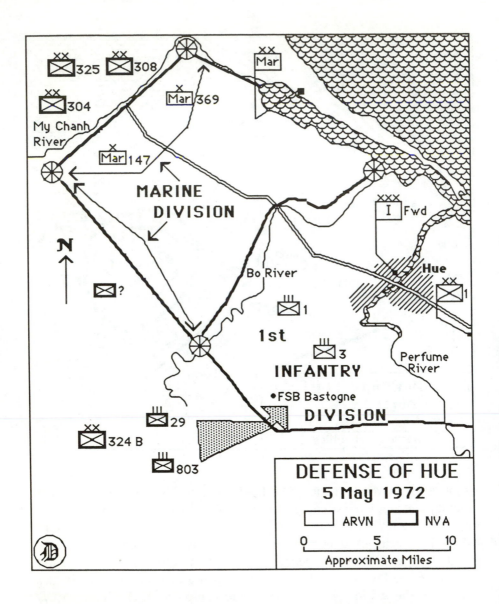

DEFENSE OF HUE
5 May 1972

was another tremendous gain—defended Hue on the north and northwest, while the 1st Division held off the enemy to the west. The 3d ARVN Division had ceased to exist. Arrangements were made for a defense in depth and for a Fire Support Coordination Center (FSCC) to coordinate all United States and South Vietnam firepower and air support. One man, Truong, saved Hue and probably the government of South Vietnam with it.

By 7 May, the ARVN dispositions were in place and Truong initiated a sustained offensive by fire conducted on a large scale. On 8 May, Thieu sent him the 2d Airborne Brigade from the Central Highlands. Truong got the 3d Airborne Brigade on 22 May, and shortly afterward the airborne division headquarters. With this elite group (the three best divisions in ARVN) Hue was not only saved, but Truong began a counterattack to regain the territory in Quang Tri that was lost earlier. There was a flare-up of fighting on 15 May when the 1st Division took back Bastogne, the key fire support base in the west, and again on 21 May when the NVA counterattacked the marines in the north. The marine line held, and with the arrival of the final airborne brigade, the 1st, at the end of May, Truong had the counteroffensive force he needed.

Truong's all-out counteroffensive began on 28 June, with two divisions, the marine division and the airborne division, attacking north, and the 1st ARVN division driving to the west. The NVA B-5 Front threw six divisions (304th, 308th, 324B, 325th, 320B, and the 312th from Laos) into its defenses. The fighting, featuring heavy attacks by United States tactical air and B-52's, ground on through the summer, and on 16 September Truong's troops retook Quang Tri City.

A footnote on the ill-fated 3d Division and its commander, General Giai. The luckless General Giai was relieved of command of the 3d Division at the same time General Lam was sacked. The division was later reconstituted, refitted, and retrained under a new commander. In July it was committed southwest of Da Nang to stave off the attack of the 711th NVA Division toward that city. It performed well, and in 1973 was selected as one of the best divisions in ARVN. At Thieu's order, Giai was tried by general court-martial for "desertion in the face of the enemy" and sentenced to five years in prison.[6] He was there when the NVA overran the country in 1975. They took him from an ARVN prison and put him in a "reeducation camp," an undeserved fate for a good soldier.

It is instructive to stand back from the details of the campaign on the northern front and to try to discern any pattern to the NVA operations. Two points stand out. First, the Communist campaign followed a pattern of a few days of attacks, followed by a lull of about the same length of time in which the NVA forces regrouped, reinforced, and resupplied. Thus, the Quang Tri offensive saw the NVA attack from 30 March to 3 April, then a lull until 9 April, another attack (beaten off by ARVN), another lull until 18 April, another attack (repulsed), another lull, then from 23 April–2 May, the attack which took Quang Tri City. Then there was another lull—and the game was blown for the NVA. On the Hue front, the fighting between the 1st ARVN Infantry Division and the 324B NVA Division took on a more continuous pattern, but there was the same interspersion of attacks and lulls which characterized the fighting in Quang Tri.

The second point which strikes an observer is the direct connection between the flying weather and the progress of the NVA offensives. When the flying weather was bad, and the United States tactical aircraft and United States Army helicopter gunships could not support the ARVN units, the NVA divisions advanced. Of course, B-52's operated regardless of weather, but on the northern front they were hampered initially by ARVN's poor targeting procedures and by the disorder and confusion inherent in the ARVN retreats, which required large areas to be designated as "no-fire" zones. Naval gunfire from United States ships standing offshore played a significant role. They had an all-weather capability and could fire with lethal accuracy anywhere east of Highway 1. Nevertheless, weather and NVA progress bore a discernible relationship.

The Central Front

Unlike the northern front, which opened at Quang Tri with an attempted— and very nearly successful—NVA "haymaker," the NVA campaign on the central front opened with a gentle shove. But first, as always, the Order of Battle. For this battle the NVA fielded three divisions in the central area, two (the 320th and 2d) in the Kontum area and the 3d NVA Division in Binh Dinh province along the coast. The two divisions aimed at Kontum were supported by a tank regiment plus several artillery regiments. The overall command in the area rested with B-3 Front, a corps-type headquarters which was located in the Tri-Border area.

Opposing this NVA force, ARVN had in the Kontum area two infantry regiments from the 22d ARVN Infantry Division, two armored cavalry squadrons, plus the 2d Airborne Brigade. During the first week in March

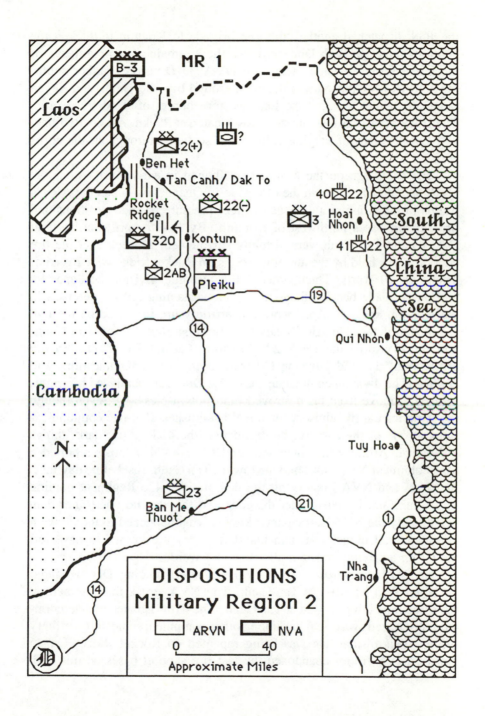

DISPOSITIONS
Military Region 2

ARVN   NVA

0   40
Approximate Miles

the JGS dispatched another airborne brigade to Kontum to thicken the defenses there. In Binh Dinh province there remained two regiments of the 22d ARVN Division facing the NVA 3d Division. Farther south, the 23d ARVN Division was stationed around Ban Me Thuot, and eleven ranger battalions covered the long western border of II ARVN Corps. The II ARVN Corps headquarters was located at Pleiku. ARVN Regional and Local Forces of varying value were scattered throughout the corps area.

The campaign on the central front began in early April—after the NVA had already initiated the offensive in Quang Tri—when the ARVN troops in the Kontum area began to feel pressure on their positions and fire support bases northwest of Kontum. By 14–15 April, the bases at Dak To and Tan Canh were virtually surrounded. A week later the fire support bases held by the airborne troops on Rocket Ridge were overrun. Then, on 20 April, Thieu ordered the airborne division headquarters and one brigade back to Saigon, further weakening ARVN defenses in the Kontum area. As April wore on, artillery fire increased on the two regiments of the 22d ARVN Division holding Dak To and Tan Canh, and on 23 April, the NVA 2d Division attacked Tan Canh. Enemy artillery hit the 22d Division CP, destroying all communications and control. The division commander, Col. Le Duc Dat, paralyzed by fright, refused to move from his destroyed (and now useless) CP, even though the American army advisory team had established alternate communications at one of the subordinate regiments (the 42d). After dark, things got worse. Artillery fire increased, and the ARVN outposts reported a long column of NVA tanks moving toward Tan Canh. Just before daylight, the tanks and NVA infantry hit the demoralized 42d Regiment holding Tan Canh, and it fled in utter disorder. To this day no one (other than presumably the NVA participants) knows what happened to the division commander, Colonel Dat, and his staff. They are known to have left the CP in a driving rain, but after that, no word.

The 47th Regiment (22d ARVN Division) holding Dak To fared no better than its sister at Tan Canh. The NVA struck this regiment at the same time it hit the 42d at Tan Canh. The 47th, isolated and demoralized, just oozed away, leaving among other equipment some thirty artillery pieces. This dismal tale was being repeated on Rocket Ridge. On 25 April, ARVN troops abandoned the last fire support bases on this high ground. And on 4 May, Kontum was open to enemy attack. The preliminaries were over. The main event on the central front was about to begin.

Into this dismal picture a secondary threat surfaced in the coastal province of Binh Dinh, a perennial hotbed of Communist activity. There, the 3d NVA Division and local Viet Cong forces cut Highway 1 at the infamous Bong Son Pass (Hoai Nhon) and isolated the three northern districts of the province. The attacks spread north and southwest along Highway 1, engulfing two district towns. The two ARVN regiments in Binh Dinh, the 40th and 41st of the ill-fated 22d ARVN Division, abandoned their bases. Most of Binh Dinh was now in the hands of the enemy. The ultimate threat posed by the NVA on the central front—the bisection of South Vietnam—was now attainable. But first, the NVA had to take Kontum and link up with the 3d NVA Division in Binh Dinh. Kontum was the crux.

From the end of April until the middle of May, the NVA forces targeted on Kontum pushed south against light resistance. This pause allowed Thieu and the JGS to make two changes which saved Kontum. First, Thieu relieved the II ARVN Corps commander, Gen. Ngo Dzu, another of Thieu's political generals, who had collapsed mentally under the impending threat. Thieu replaced him with Maj. Gen. Nguyen Van Toan, an armor officer and a competent professional. The second change was made by II Corps headquarters—actually, by the senior United States advisor, the legendary John Paul Vann. The 23d ARVN Division in Ban Me Thuot was ordered to send its headquarters and one infantry regiment to Kontum. And with this move there appeared another ARVN hero of the Easter offensive, Col. Ly Tong Ba, commander of the 23d ARVN Infantry Division.

When Ba took command in Kontum, he could anticipate, at best, a bloody defense of the town—at worst, a calamitous defeat. The victorious enemy were closing on him from the north and had already cut Highway 14 between Kontum and Pleiku, thus isolating him. His own troops were disheartened and jittery. He, too, had the same problems of command and control that had doomed Giai at Quang Tri. Ba commanded only his one regiment, but he exercised operational control over three ranger groups, an airborne brigade, and a motley collection of territorial forces. These troops were all looking over their shoulders at their own senior headquarters for support and direction. To make matters worse, on 28 April President Thieu ordered the 2d Airborne Brigade, the best troops in the area, back to Saigon.

Ba's command and control situation was relieved measurably, however, by bringing in the other two regiments of his division, the 44th and 45th, to replace two ranger groups. Ba now had clear control of Kontum's defense, and in early May, as ARVN units gave ground to the north of Kontum, that defense would be tested. Ba was ready. He visited all units on the front, he drew up and rehearsed counterattack plans, he trained his troops in the use of the LAW (Light Antitank Weapon) and convinced his men that they could hold Kontum.

The first NVA attack on Kontum came on 14 May. Five NVA infantry regiments converged on the city. But the attack had been "tipped off," and United States helicopter gunships, ARVN artillery, and tactical air broke it up. The NVA units persisted. They attacked again that night and achieved a breakthrough in the northern arc of Kontum's defenses which they began to widen and exploit. Things were now desperate for Ba. Kontum was cut off, its defenses penetrated. The only hope left now were two pre-planned B-52 strikes. At the last moment ARVN troops in the target area were withdrawn, and on the prescribed minute the bombs hit the attackers. As of that moment, the assaulting units ceased to exist. The next morning revealed a carnage of several hundred NVA bodies and smashed equipment. Round One went to Ba and the thunderbolts of the B-52's.

From 15 May until 25 May, the enemy resupplied and refurbished his troops and pushed in probes, seeking to find the weak spots in the town's defenses. Several of these probes, made in strength, penetrated the defenses, but all were soon ejected. Ba, too, was active. He tightened up Kontum's defenses by decreasing his perimeter, and thus got one regiment into reserve, and he established better coordination of the vast firepower available to him.

The enemy made his final and decisive effort to take Kontum on 25 May. His supplies and forces would not sustain another try, and the Southwest Monsoon was imminent. The NVA attack began at midnight and by dawn had made serious penetrations on the southeastern and northern perimeters of Kontum. Heavy NVA artillery fire fell on the town with lethal accuracy. The next day (26 May) the attack continued with renewed intensity. That night another NVA penetration was barely beaten off with the help of a B-52 strike. An NVA assault launched at daylight on 27 May got well into the town, where the enemy troops dug in and repulsed all of Ba's efforts to eject them.

By the night of 28 May, the situation was critical for both sides. Hourly B-52 strikes were attriting both NVA manpower and supplies, and the ARVN troops were weary and undersupplied. The tide of battle had shifted, however. The 23d Division, urged on by Ba, began the house-to-house fighting to clear the town, and by 30 May the defense was assured. On that date, President Thieu flew into Kontum and pinned the star of a brigadier general on Ly Tong Ba. There would be more fighting, more mopping up, in the Kontum area, but the NVA offensive there had failed.

Meanwhile, in Binh Dinh, the reconstituted 22d Division in July took back the three district towns lost to the NVA in April and May and reopened Highway 1. This recovery ended the campaign. The NVA offensive on the central front had failed.

Looking at Giap's campaign on the central front, again in outline, an observer sees once more a picture of attack, lull, attack, lull. Of course, this is the antithesis of the constant pressure required by operations on exterior lines. The other observation—which was not so clearly seen on the northern front—is Giap's concentration (obsession actually) on a terrain objective, in this case, Kontum. There were other operational options available in the area, and yet he hammered away relentlessly at the enemy's strongest point, which gave devastating opportunities to the United States Air Force. Finally, there was the pivotal role played again by American air power. Without it, Kontum, like Hue—and with them Indochina War II—would have been lost.

The Southern Front

While the NVA invasion on the northern front began with an attempted knockout punch, and the offensive on the central front with a jostle, the Communist attacks on the southern front began with a right hand feint. In the III ARVN Corps area (the area and provinces between the Central Highlands and the Mekong Delta) the South Vietnamese stationed three infantry divisions, the 5th, 18th, and 25th, and three ranger groups. The 25th Division operated in the west northwest zone of the corps area centered in the key province of Tay Ninh. The 5th Division covered the northern provinces of Binh Long, Phuoc Long, and Binh Duong. The 18th Division was stationed in the eastern zone, operating in the provinces Bien Hoa, Phuoc Tuy, and Binh Tuy. In addition to the field forces, there was the usual collection of South Vietnamese Regional and Local forces of varying quality.

On the other side were three famous "old" Viet Cong divisions (now almost completely NVA), the 5th, 7th, and 9th, supported by a tank regiment and several artillery regiments. The divisions had been driven out of South Vietnam and for some months had occupied base areas (BA's) in Cambodia, the 5th in BA 712, the 9th in BA 711, and the 7th in BA 714. There were also in the projected area of operations Viet Cong local forces and guerrillas, but they were weak and demoralized and played no significant role in the operation. The area fell under the operational control of the B-2 Front, commanded by Lt. Gen. Tran Van Tra, strangely enough, a southerner.

As was the case on the other fronts, there was no doubt in early 1972 that a major NVA offensive in the III Corps area impended. The question was: when and where? In spite of a significant captured document and the statement of an NVA defector, both indicating that Binh Long province was the Communist objective, ARVN III Corps headquarters persisted in thinking the upcoming enemy offensive would drive through, and at, Tay Ninh province. Regardless of this perception, the Corps did move a two-battalion task force (TF 52) from the 18th ARVN Division east of Saigon and station it along Highway 13 between Loc Ninh and An Loc.

The offensive on the southern front began on the early morning of 2 April. The 24th NVA Separate Infantry Regiment (not part of any division) attacked a fire support base near the Cambodian border and, spearheaded by tanks, overran it quickly. This prompted the III Corps commander, Lt. Gen. Nguyen Van Minh, to order the abandonment of all the small fire support bases along the border. In the retrograde movement, one of the garrisons got ambushed north of Tay Ninh City by the famous old 271st VC Regiment from the 9th VC Division, which wiped out the ARVN unit. Instead of exploiting its victory, the 271st VC Regiment disappeared, which was strange, but its job had been done, for it and the 24th were only decoys. The main thrust on the southern front would see three reinforced divisions driving against Loc

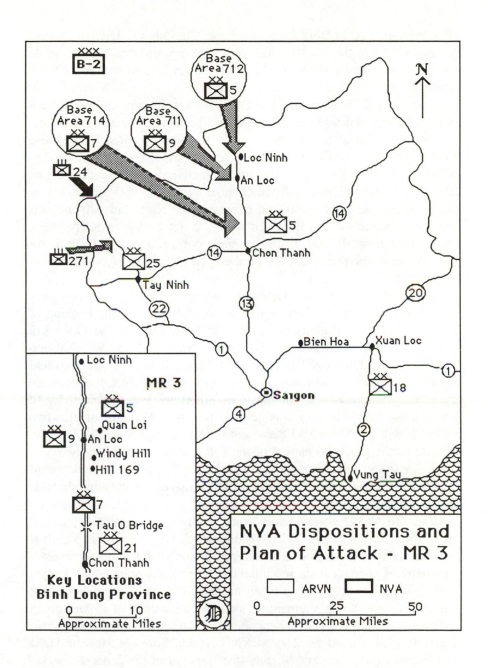

B-2

Base Area 712

5

Base Area 714

7

Base Area 711

9

24

Loc Ninh

An Loc

14

271

25

5

Tay Ninh

Chon Thanh

14

22

13

1

Bien Hoa

Xuan Loc

20

1

18

Saigon

4

2

Vung Tau

NVA Dispositions and Plan of Attack - MR 3

ARVN   NVA

0   25   50
Approximate Miles

MR 3

Loc Ninh

5

Quan Loi

9   An Loc

Windy Hill

Hill 169

7

Tau O Bridge

21

Chon Thanh

Key Locations
Binh Long Province

0   10
Approximate Miles

Ninh and An Loc in Binh Long province. The 5th VC Division would go for Loc Ninh; the 9th Division would attempt to take An Loc; while the 7th would block Highway 13 south of An Loc to prevent ARVN reinforcement.

The 5th VC Division attacked Loc Ninh on 4 April, and by 5 April heavy artillery and tank fire were hitting the town. The defenders beat off an attack that afternoon, due largely to intense United States close air support. On 6 April another NVA attack, this one supported by 25–30 tanks, overran the town. The first objective of the B-2 Front, Loc Ninh, had fallen. The two-battalion task force (TF 52) which before the invasion had been positioned between Loc Ninh and An Loc was ordered to withdraw. As it moved south, it got hit by an NVA attack and then an ambush, and, badly battered, got a few people back to An Loc. An Loc, the prime bastion on the road to Saigon, was now under serious threat.

On 7 April, the 5th VC Division, encouraged by its relatively easy victory at Loc Ninh, pushed south towards An Loc. On the evening of 7 April, the forward elements of the 5th Division took the Quan Loi airfield, three kilometers east of An Loc. Since the 7th VC Division had already cut Highway 13 south of An Loc, the capture of the airfield isolated the town. In addition, the high ground at Quan Loi dominated the city and offered the Communists excellent observation and fields of fire into An Loc. The city was held by one ARVN regiment plus two ranger battalions which had been sent to An Loc on 5 April. An Loc, the site of the proposed capital of the PRG, now besieged by two VC/NVA divisions, looked ripe for the picking. And it would have been, too, except for one of those "foul-ups" which makes war the unpredictable and dicey business it is.

The 5th VC Division, badly worn from its recent victory, closed on to Quan Loi. The 9th VC Division, which was supposed to deliver the main attack on An Loc, did nothing. It just sat for almost a week—the victim of an inadequate and inflexible logistical system which simply could not get the supplies up when needed. That delay probably saved An Loc, for the South Vietnamese took full advantage of it. During an emergency meeting at the Independence Palace in Saigon on 6 April, Thieu decided to send the 21st ARVN Division from the Mekong Delta and the remaining airborne brigade (the last unit of his general reserve) to buttress the defense of An Loc. With the 21st ARVN Division now on the way, the III Corps commander was able to send two more battalions from the 5th ARVN Division into An Loc, bringing the strength of its defenders up to nearly 3,000 men.

Daily, the pressure increased on the besieged city. Supply depended entirely on helicopters and air drops from C-123 aircraft; the wounded could be evacuated only by helicopters. By nightfall of 12 April, all signs pointed to an imminent and major NVA attack to take An Loc. The blow fell early on the next morning. First, there came the heavy artillery preparatory fires. Then came the tanks unprotected by infantry, and then two regiments of infantry in a mass assault. The NVA attacked An Loc from the west, northwest, and north, with the main effort coming from the north. With the help of United States air power, all of the assaults were beaten off. Most of the tanks were knocked out by the M-72 LAW, an effective hand-held tank-killer. However, NVA troops held the northern part of the city. The 9th VC Division was a tough outfit, and it attacked again the next day, 14 April, and again it was repulsed. They tried again on the 15th with the same results. On 16 April the attacks slacked off. The first attempt to take An Loc had failed.

ARVN had been busy, too. On 13–14 April, the 1st Airborne Brigade, which had been fighting the 7th VC Division south of An Loc, was airlifted into Hill 169 and Windy Hill, three kilometers southeast of the city. The 21st Division from the Delta had reached the blocking position of the 7th VC Division south of Chon Thanh and engaged the 7th there.

On 18 April, ARVN got one of those priceless windfalls which win battles. They captured a document from the political officer of the 9th VC Division to COSVN. The report gave two reasons for the 9th's failure to take An Loc: first, the devastation wrought by United States tactical air and B-52's; and second, poor tank-infantry coordination. Even more important, the report gave detailed plans for the next attack. This time the 275th Regiment from the 5th VC Division and the 141st from the 7th VC Division would make secondary attacks on the ARVN Airborne Brigade on Hill 169 and Windy Hill. The 9th VC Division would again make the main effort to take An Loc. On 19 April, the attack occurred as planned, and in hard fighting the ARVN paratroopers lost Hill 169. The 9th VC attacked again, and could make no progress, although the NVA division still held the northern part of the town. By 23 April the attacks abated. The second attempt had failed.

So confident had the Communists been in the success of this second attempt that Radio Hanoi had announced on 18 April that the PRG would be installed in its new capital of An Loc on 20 April.

While the ARVN troops and United States air power turned back two NVA attempts to take An Loc, the defenders suffered heavily also. The enemy held the northern part of town, and ground communications into An Loc were still cut off. Due to intense NVA antiaircraft fire, food, medicine, and ammunition were running low, and evacuation of the wounded was impossible. Helicopters alone could not do the supply job, and so C-123's and C-130's were used. Initially, most of these drops fell into enemy hands, but by the end of April, improvements in delivery techniques made by American army and air force personnel kept An Loc adequately supplied throughout the siege.

The NVA had major supply problems, too. The two attacks on An Loc between 13 and 23 April had consumed all supplies in the area. So, from 23 April until 10 May, the NVA's ponderous logistical system struggled to build up adequate supplies to support another attack. The lull, however, permitted ARVN to insert into the town the 81st Airborne Ranger Group, *the* elite unit in the South Vietnamese Army. These troops took over the critical northern sector of the defensive positions. With the rangers on the north and the paratroopers on the south, An Loc was now defended by ARVN's "finest."

As April turned into May, there was no doubt on either side that the climactic battle for An Loc was fast approaching. Then, on 5 May, ARVN got another of those tactical bonanzas. An officer defector from the 9th VC Division turned himself in and told his interrogators that COSVN had severely reprimanded the CG, 9th VC Division because of his failure to take the town. According to the defector, the commander of the 5th VC Division got into the act and boastfully told COSVN and the B-2 commander that if his division could make the main effort, that he would take An Loc in two days, just as he had taken Loc Ninh. His superiors told him to go ahead. The defector reported that the plan for the attack called for the main effort to be made from the southeast (the 5th VC) while secondary assaults were made from the southwest by the 7th VC Division and from the northeast by the remnants of the

9th VC Division. The prisoner did not know the time of the attack, but said that it would come within a week—that is, before 12 May.

It came on 11 May, preceded by two days of the usual NVA probes and intensive artillery fire (7,000 rounds on 11 May). At first, the attack made some progress on the west and northeast, but at dawn the USAF fighter-bombers struck the attackers, and then at exactly 0900 hours the first pre-planned B-52 strike hit the assaulting infantry. By noon the heavy bombers had broken the back of the attack, but they continued to pound the hapless enemy, using thirty B-52 strikes in a twenty-four hour period. The strikes were awesome in their destruction. In one area the B-52's struck an NVA regiment in the open, and when the smoke and dust had settled, the regiment had simply vanished. The enemy tried again on 12 May and once more on 14 May, but the fire and punch were gone, and the NVA not only failed to make any gains, but the elite ARVN troops, emboldened by their success, counterattacked and regained most of the ground they had lost in the city. The battle for An Loc was over, a battle won by the valor of the ARVN troops, the professionalism of the American advisors, the attacks of the United States and VNAF fighter-bombers, but above all by the "big birds," the B-52 bombers of the Strategic Air Command.

The offensive on the northern front produced as its hero the South Vietnamese general, Truong, the savior of Hue; on the central front it was another South Vietnamese, the redoubtable Colonel Ba, who held Kontum. On the southern front the hero was an American, Maj. Gen. (later Lt. Gen.) James F. Hollingsworth, the III ARVN Corps senior advisor. It was he who saved An Loc. Hollingsworth strengthened the resolve of the ARVN corps commander when things looked grim. He visited An Loc daily during the worst of the shellings, encouraging both the South Vietnamese and the American advisors there. It was Hollingsworth who, realizing the criticality of American advisors, mobilized additional advisors and established the policy that the Americans stayed with the ARVN troops regardless of consequences. Above all, it was Hollingsworth who personally planned the B-52 and tactical air strikes which saved An Loc.

"Holly" Hollingsworth is an authentic character. He is a big, brash, tough, loud-mouthed Texan, given to excessive braggadocio. His bombastic statements, dogmatically delivered with supreme self-confidence to a heavy accompaniment of profanity and obscenity, infuriated many of his brother officers. His peers either admired and liked him tremendously or they disliked him intensely. His detractors accused him of consciously imitating his idol, George Patton. But what separated "Holly" from most of the rest of the Patton imitators—and the army was once full of them—is that when the bullets start to whine and the shells fall, "Holly" always made good on his boasts. He was perhaps *the* outstanding tank battalion commander in the European Theatre of World War II. His personal courage was legendary, and he came out of that war with a chest full of medals, including the Distinguished Service Cross for "extraordinary heroism." Nor was he just a big mouth with a lot of guts. He was an astute professional, actually something of a military theorist—the model of a battlefield general.

Hollingsworth had served a prior tour of duty in Vietnam as an assistant division commander in the United States 1st Infantry Division, which operated in the Lai Khe/An Loc area. He knew the country, he knew the enemy, and he grasped the often befogged truism that on the battlefield the name of the game is—in his words—"Kill Cong." To do that, he told the South Vietnamese, "You hold, and I'll do the killing," and with his careful plotting of strike areas and timing for the United States air power at his control, he did just that. A lot of people deserve credit for saving An Loc, but Jim Hollingsworth stands at the head of the list.

There remains one facet of the An Loc battle which needs to be wrapped up—the move of the 21st ARVN Division from the Delta to the relief of An Loc. Recall that Thieu ordered the division toward the beleaguered town on 6 April. By 12 April its advanced elements ran into blocking positions set up by the 7th VC Division on Highway 13. It took the 21st Division the rest of April to clear the road up to Chon Thanh, and until 13 May (when the siege of An Loc was almost broken) to get eight kilometers north of Chon Thanh. From then on, there was some skirmishing up and down Highway 13, but the 21st Division never got to An Loc. The performance of the 21st Division had been, at best, mediocre. In its defense one must say that it was attacking heavily fortified positions held by good NVA troops, and while it didn't get to An Loc, it pinned down two NVA regiments, which didn't get to An Loc either.

Just as each of the other fronts had featured NVA secondary offensives, so, too, did the southern front. This offensive was to be carried out in the Mekong Delta mainly by the NVA 1st Infantry Division, assisted by several VC Regional Force regiments. Opposing it were initially the ARVN 7th, 9th, and 21st Divisions supported by some ranger battalions and the usual array of Local Force units. The objectives of the NVA attack were: to pin the existing ARVN units in the Delta to prevent them reinforcing ARVN troops elsewhere; to raise VC morale; to set back pacification; and to capture rice supplies. The offensive began on 7 April. There was some inconclusive fighting on the border as the 1st NVA Division tried to move from Cambodia into Vietnam. By the time the NVA division had gotten into South Vietnam, the battles and air strikes had reduced it to impotence. There were other battles throughout the Delta, but when the smoke cleared, the NVA had accomplished almost nothing. With this wheeze the Easter offensive expired.

The NVA invasion on the southern front mirrored the offensives launched on the more northerly fronts. There was the same pattern of attack-lull, attack-lull, the inability to keep the required constant pressure on the defenders. Tank-infantry coordination was not only deficient, it just didn't exist. The attacks on An Loc featured the now familiar massed infantry attacks in spite of the horrible casualties United States air power constantly inflicted on such formations. Note again Giap's incapacity to grasp the potentialities of weapons systems and means of war (B-52's) with which he had had no personal experience. The B-2 Front and COSVN repeated another mistake made further north—the preoccupation with terrain objectives, again, a town. Critics of the An Loc campaign have censured Giap—and rightly so—for not containing An Loc and then bypassing it, sending his tank-infantry teams down Highway 13 toward the ultimate objective, Saigon.[7] Instead he used his tanks in a rubble-strewn town—the very worst conditions for armor employment—and then without close infantry support. While the NVA troops fought bravely, as always, the performance of the commands at division and higher level could only be rated as abysmal.

On the American side, President Nixon in early April made the decision which determined the outcome of the NVA Easter offensive. Against the recommendations of the State and Defense Departments, he ordered those United States naval and air forces in Southeast Asia to be quickly and vastly augmented to meet Giap's all-out attempt to win the war. This augmentation not only destroyed the Easter offensive, but it provided the aircraft to carry the war, once again, into North Vietnam itself. The raw numbers of the increases tell most of the story. In March 1972 the United States Air Force had only three squadrons of F-4's and a squadron of A-37's, a total of 76 fighter and attack aircraft in Vietnam. Operating off the coast were two navy attack carriers, the *Hancock* and the *Coral Sea,* each with an air wing of 90 aircraft (180 total). Present in Thailand were 114 other jets. The number of B-52's operating out of Guam and U-Tapao, Thailand, totaled 83 on 30 March 1972. By the end of May, well into the NVA invasion, USAF forces in Southeast Asia included 409 F-4's and F-5's, over double the number available on 30 March. The inventory of B-52's had risen from 83 to 171 by 20 May. The United States Navy augmented its two carriers with four others, later reduced by one, and sent several marine fighter squadrons into Vietnam and Thailand. In addition, the navy rushed surface ships into the area, and within a month the United States had one heavy cruiser, five cruisers, and 44 destroyers on station off the Vietnamese coast.

The aircraft sortie rate reflected this rapid increase in assets. In March 1972 there were 4,237 sorties flown against the enemy, and the VNAF flew 3,149 of them. In April the figure rose to 17,171; in May to 18,444; and declined slightly in June, to 15,951.

President Nixon took the decision to augment air and naval power in Southeast Asia and to hit North Vietnam amid the debates and quibbles which always seemed to surround difficult Nixon decisions. Laird, Rogers, and other "pragmatists" recommended that no augmentation be made in United States air or naval assets in Southeast Asia. They argued that the NVA invasion was the supreme test of Vietnamization, and that the South Vietnamese ought to go it with what United States support was present in-country on 30 March. Underneath this argument lay their real position, that a magnified American reaction to the NVA offensive would agitate the antiwar dissenters and the liberals in Congress. They had been down *that* wearisome road before and wanted no more of it. On the other hand, Nixon and Kissinger believed that the NVA invasion was a test, not just of South Vietnam, but of the United States as well. The future of the United States-North Vietnamese negotiations hung on the outcome of the Easter offensive. Beyond that, the whole United States foreign policy would be jeopardized by a defeat in South Vietnam. Nixon held firm against the appeasers, and by the end of April he had committed a significant part of the air and naval might of the United States in Vietnam.

President Nixon looked beyond merely aiding South Vietnam. He wanted to hit North Vietnam as well as destroy the invasion of South Vietnam. On 6 April, United States fighters struck sixty miles north of the DMZ. On 10 April, B-52's hit Vinh, a key transshipment point, 150 miles north of the DMZ, the first use of B-52's in North Vietnam by the Nixon administration. But as the situation worsened in South Vietnam, the president had to make a more painful decision—whether to send the B-52's and fighter-bombers after Hanoi and Haiphong. Kissinger contended that the North Vietnamese must not only be stopped in South Vietnam, but that Hanoi's escalation of the war must be countered by a comparable counterescalation. The most telling response to the NVA invasion would be to destroy the North Vietnamese ports, roads, bridges, storage depots, electric plants, and industrial facilities.

As usual, Laird, known by now in the Pentagon as "Chicken Hawk" (with accent on the adjective), and Rogers objected. On 15 April, the president decided to hit the two North Vietnamese cities with a two-day attack by naval bombardment and air strikes, including B-52's. Predictably, the doves in the media and Congress shrieked again that Nixon was escalating the war, and since Russian vessels were in Haiphong harbor, risking nuclear war with the Soviet Union. But the doves were not the only ones outraged by the bombings in the north. General Abrams and Ambassador Bunker strenuously objected, also. By mid-April they were in desperate straits in South Vietnam. They cared little about the big picture, they wanted all air assets targeted on *their* war in the south. Abrams and Bunker argued that the strikes in North Vietnam would have no immediate effect on the war in South Vietnam, and that if the NVA invasion succeeded, the war was lost anyway. Laird supported Abrams, and again Nixon overruled him.

Some of the liberal Senators made another argument against Nixon's renewed bombing of the North. They maintained that between 1965 and 1968 bombing had clearly been proven to be ineffective. But 1972 was not 1965–68, and this time Nixon had unleashed a real tiger. In the first place, he turned the management of the campaign over to the

JCS and the local commanders. No more would the president and his secretary of defense—military neophytes—pore over target maps and bomb tonnages. Second, Nixon removed many of the large strike-free zones, particularly around Hanoi and Haiphong, which had become sanctuaries for North Vietnamese military installations and storage dumps. Finally, the renewed attacks employed the "smart" bombs, whose guidance systems used laser beams and television to gain pinpoint accuracy. These bombs not only vastly improved the effectiveness of the new program, but permitted the attackers to go after critical targets in densely populated areas which had previously been off-limits due to the probability of hitting civilian facilities. As an example of improved effectiveness, the infamous bridge at Thanh Hoa, on which the navy from 1965 to 1968 had lost 97 aircraft without bringing it down, was destroyed in the first run of 1972 by a "smart" 2,000-pound bomb.

But in early May, Nixon's bombing campaign appeared to be inadequate. Quang Tri City had fallen, the victorious NVA forces were threatening Hue, Kontum, and An Loc, and the northern part of Binh Dinh province had been seized by the 3d NVA Division. On the same day (1 May), more bad news struck the president. In a cable reporting the fall of Quang Tri City, General Abrams told the president that the South Vietnamese had lost their will to fight, and that the war might well be lost.[8] On 2 May, Kissinger met Le Duc Tho. The Communists were riding high, confident that a great military victory was within their grasp. Tho was arrogant, insulting, and totally inflexible. In Tho's view, why negotiate about what you are going to win on the battlefield? Kissinger broke off the conference.

Something more had to be done, and that was the mining of the port of Haiphong. While it would have no immediate effect on the ground war in South Vietnam, it would send a powerful message to the Russians, Chinese, and North Vietnamese. It would tell the Russians and the Chinese that the United States meant to stay the course in Vietnam, and that the recent thaw in relations between the United States and the two Communist superpowers was hostage to the war there. To the North Vietnamese, the message was more threatening—here is another American escalation, and if that doesn't work, there will be others, each more punishing than its predecessor. So, on 8 May, the navy laid the mine field. Sea traffic in and out of Haiphong ceased.

The vast augmentation of air and naval power made their immediate impact on the battlefields of South Vietnam. Gunfire from the surface navy furnished valuable support in the battles of Quang Tri and Hue. This was a powerful concentration of artillery, extremely accurate, and available in any kind of weather through forward observer teams attached to ARVN units. The volume of fire matched the accuracy. From May to July, the United States armada fired a high of 7,000 rounds a day and a low of 1,000 rounds. From April through September 1972, the ships fired over 16,000 *tons* of munitions into the enemy.

United States air power, however, made the major American contribution in 1972 in South Vietnam. It is too trite to say that United States air power (USAF, navy, marine, and army helicopters) saved South Vietnam in 1972. South Vietnam was saved by a combination of ARVN tenacity, United States air power, and NVA inadequacies and mistakes. It *is* no exaggeration to say, however, that American air power was the main ingredient in this mix. One cannot help but be amazed in reading General Truong's monograph by the accuracy and timeliness of United States air support to the ARVN land battle. Truong summed it up well when he wrote, "Quang Tri City could not have been retaken, nor could ARVN forces have held at Kontum and An Loc, had it not been for the support provided by the United States Air Force."[9]

While the B-52's, fighter-bombers, AC-119 and 130 gunships, and helicopter gunships were saving Kontum and An Loc, it was the C-130 cargo aircraft and supply helicopters which made ARVN resistance possible. The C-130's kept the defenders supplied, first by landing in and near An Loc, and then by air drops. Army helicopters not only brought in supplies and replacements, but evacuated the critically wounded. Years later, an American officer asked the chief of the Vietnamese Air Force, Gen. Than Van Minh, about the campaign at An Loc. "At An Loc in 1972," said Minh, "the battle turned on the employment of B-52's and C-130's."[10]

According to President Nixon, who compiled his statistics from official reports, the Easter offensive cost the North Vietnamese over 100,000 dead, 450 tanks, and untold numbers of artillery pieces and trucks.[11] In the North, the damage to facilities and supplies from the bombing attacks was extensive. By July 1972, North Vietnam was almost completely cut off from Russian and Chinese assistance, due to the mining of Haiphong and the destruction of the land routes from China.

But the North Vietnamese had some gains to show for the ghastly "butcher's bill." As a result of the invasion, they held sway over territory they had never controlled before. They set back the pacification program, although this turned out to be transitory. The Communists realized another gain from their bloody misadventure: the South Vietnamese knew they had come within a razor's edge of terminal defeat, and it shook them badly. Most important, within the United States, the Easter offensive (and Nixon's reaction to it) had eroded what little support remained for the administration's war policy. So, another Communist military defeat had been converted into a political and psychological victory within South Vietnam and the United States.

On the other hand, the failure of the Easter offensive had political and military costs to North Vietnam far beyond the casualties to their men, facilities, and equipment. The Communists realized that they had been catastrophically set back, not only in striking power, but in that crucial element—time. No less an authority than Giap's chief of staff, four-star Gen. Van Tien Dung, after a post-invasion inspection trip, told the senior cadre at COSVN that there was no prospect for a quick end to the war, and that there could be no new offensive for another three to five years.

Finally, the North Vietnamese realized for the first time that they had to negotiate seriously to get the United States out of Vietnam on some mutually acceptable terms. Douglas Pike claims that the Politburo agreed prior to the offensive that if it failed, North Vietnam would enter purposeful negotiations to end the war. The North Vietnamese lost the Easter offensive and with it the opportunity to defeat militarily the United States.

There is no dearth of opinions on the subject of the hows and whys of the failure of the Easter offensive. Henry Kissinger, Sir Robert Thompson, Lewy, General Truong, Gen. Cao Van Vien (chief of the South Vietnamese Joint General Staff), and Douglas Pike all weighed in with their views of what felled Giap's Easter invasion.

Kissinger states that the offensive failed because the three major attacks could not be synchronized, and that the whole affair was too complicated to be supplied adequately. He maintains that Giap's attack-lull sequences on the three fronts permitted Saigon to shift forces to threatened points about the periphery. Other causes of the failure, accord-

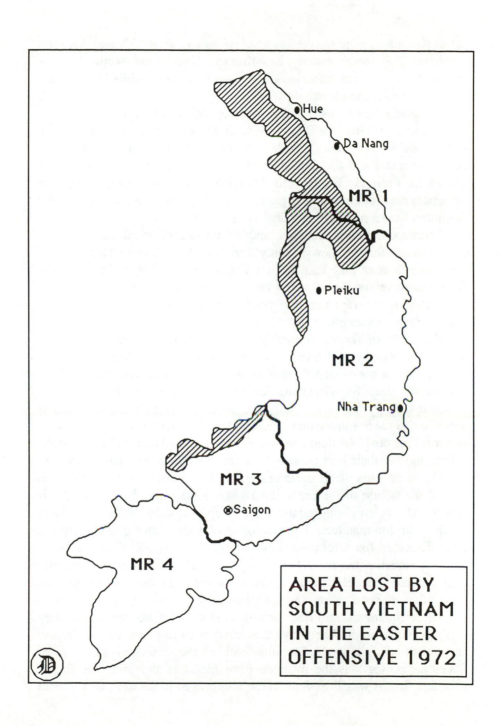

Hue

Da Nang

MR 1

Pleiku

MR 2

Nha Trang

MR 3

Saigon

MR 4

AREA LOST BY
SOUTH VIETNAM
IN THE EASTER
OFFENSIVE 1972

ing to Kissinger, were the performance of American B-52's and ARVN's combat staying power. Finally, he writes that because the North Vietnamese leaders were not experienced in handling large units, their tank-infantry coordination broke down.[12]

Douglas Pike claims that the invasion failed through a major error in judgment by Giap. In Pike's eyes, Giap erred in overestimating the NVA's ability to conduct a high-tech war, in underestimating ARVN's defensive metal and the impact of United States air power. Finally, he blames the Politburo for expecting too much from the American antiwar dissenters and for anticipating greater opposition from Russia and China to United States retaliation against North Vietnam.[13]

Thompson, Lewy, Truong, and Vien take identical views of the causes of the failure. Lewy openly attributes his views to Thompson,[14] and while Truong and Vien do not link their opinions to Thompson's, the remarkable similarity cannot be coincidental, particularly since they wrote their monographs several years after Thompson's book, *Peace Is Not at Hand,* appeared.[15]

The views of Thompson (and his echoes) are these: The Easter offensive failed because of United States air power, the fighting qualities of ARVN, and a series of mistakes made by Giap and his commanders. He blames Giap for dispersing his forces on three fronts rather than concentrating them on one, and he maintains that Giap's lack of momentum allowed the South Vietnamese to shift forces between fronts. Thompson criticizes the NVA field commanders for abysmal tank-infantry coordination and for their historic penchant for assaults of massed infantry.[16]

The consensus of all these criticisms, then, holds that three factors caused the failure of the Easter invasion. These were: United States air power, ARVN's fighting quality, and Giap's mistakes as well as those of his field commanders. The catalogue of these latter errors includes: Giap dispersed his forces; he allowed ARVN to switch forces on him; and he overestimated the NVA ability to conduct and supply a mobile, conventional war. His field commanders are charged with inadequate tank-infantry coordination and with mounting suicidal massed assaults.

These distinguished critics are all correct. The trouble is that they don't go far enough. They have described the symptoms of the disease and not the disease itself. Examine each of the factors in turn. United States air power was the most decisive factor in defeating the Easter invasion. But it was President Nixon's courageous decision to augment the air power in Vietnam which made it the dominant factor in the combat equation. He rejected the counsel of Laird and Rogers to leave things as they were in Vietnam, and he braved what he knew would be the full-throated cries of the antiwar dissenters. Credit a significant part of the victory to President Nixon.

Now, look at ARVN's staying power. The South Vietnamese were good soldiers when properly trained, equipped, and led. No derogation is implied, then, to note that it was the American advisors who played the essential role in ARVN's staying power. From Abrams in Saigon, down to the regimental (and sometimes battalion) advisors, the American officers did a magnificent job. They didn't just advise their counterparts. They plotted B-52 strikes and controlled the mass of close air support. They stiffened the morale of the ARVN commanders in times of desperate peril. In the case of John Paul Vann and Gen. "Holly" Hollingsworth, and others of lower rank, they practically commanded the units they advised. One has only to contrast the debacle of Lam Son 719 with the staunch and professional defenses against the Easter offensive to see the difference United States advisors made.

Finally, a look at the mistakes of Giap and his battlefield commanders. The charges that Giap dispersed his forces and then allowed ARVN to shift troops to meet his on-again, off-again attacks are correct—theoretically. Actually, the transfer of ARVN ground units around the perimeter was minimal and inconsequential. Much more critical was the fact that Giap's "attack-lull" tactics *did* permit the Americans to shift the weight of air power from one threatened area to another. All of these charges, however, ignore the fundamental deficiency which produced them—an inflexible and inadequate Communist logistical system. Giap could not mass his divisions on one front because he could not support them logistically. He could stockpile supplies, but his ponderous system could not push them from the base areas to the battlefield in amounts adequate to support a concentration of many divisions in one area. Besides, a dense concentration of troops and supplies would have attracted catastrophic attacks by American air power. The same inadequate logistical system accounts for his sequence of attack-lull, attack-lull. When one considers the tremendous logistical requirements of a modern army in combat, requirements measured in thousands of tons per day, one sees Giap's problem—a problem not only of voracious consumption, but one complicated by devastating American air strikes along his whole logistical chain.

Beyond Giap's logistical inadequacies lay an even deeper deficiency—neither he nor his commanders had any feel for, any experience in, or any understanding of truly mobile operations. His use of tanks is an example. Tanks may be used in close support of the infantry, in which case they become an infantry auxiliary. On the other hand, tanks may be used as a mobile arm to strike deep into the enemy's rear areas. The accompanying infantry then become the auxiliaries of the tanker. Giap chose the former method. This was not mobile war as seen in Europe in 1940 and again in 1944, but a return to the trench warfare of World War I.

Another example is Giap's preoccupation with terrain objectives, the cities Kontum and An Loc. An experienced armor commander would have loaded his infantry on the decks of the tanks and bypassed the two towns. The terrain and weather would have permitted it, and a sizable NVA armored force showing up in ARVN's rear areas would have panicked the already jittery South Vietnamese troops. The NVA columns might well have run out of gas, but the infantry could have pressed on, sowing panic and confusion as they advanced. If an Abrams or a Hollingsworth had commanded the NVA troops at Kontum or An Loc, those battles might well have gone quite differently.

The difference between a master of mobile warfare and a neophyte can be seen again in the conduct of the campaigns at Kontum and An Loc. Contrast these battles with Patton's Metz campaign of 1944. Although Patton could have surrounded Metz, he purposely left the Germans an escape route. He wanted the Germans to get out of Metz so he could get at them in the open countryside. If he surrounded them, they would just hole up, and he would have to commit a division or two in a long and bloody battle to dig them out. In contrast, when Giap surrounded Kontum and An Loc, he solidified the ARVN defenses. He put ARVN's back to the wall, and they fought with no distracting thought about escape.

In some ways it is probably unfair to censure Giap and his commanders for their inability to conduct mobile warfare. For at least twenty years they had planned and fought the set-piece battle, as at Dien Bien Phu and Khe Sanh. This involved a lengthy and careful positioning of troops and supplies. They were masters of this type of warfare. But there was nothing in their experience, in Vietnamese history, or in their culture, to prepare them for the cut and slash of an armored penetration. They

had no cavalry spirit, no mechanical tradition, and no feel for the movement of huge amounts of supplies. Absent from their history were heroes
like "Swampfox" Marion, Nathan B. Forrest, Jeb Stuart, Phil Sheridan,
or George Patton, or even the "foot cavalry" of old William Tecumseh
Sherman. Mobile warfare was not Giap's game, and he shouldn't have
tried to play it.

One last criticism: one of the few truths in modern war is that mobile
warfare cannot be conducted in the face of enemy air superiority. Tanks,
and the immense logistical support they need, are simply too vulnerable.
This truism is ten times stronger when one faces not enemy air superiority
but enemy *air supremacy*. Once again, Giap didn't understand the first
principle about what he was trying to do.

No sooner had the Easter offensive collapsed than Laird and General
Abrams began to extol Vietnamization and its results. The ARVN had
fought hard and in many cases well, but the same old faults were there,
too. Serious failures of leadership had occurred again. Two of the four
corps commanders had to be summarily fired. The 3d Division commander
was tried and found guilty by a general court-martial—probably unfairly.
The marine division commander was relieved, and the 22d Division
commander disappeared after a disastrous battle. Whole units collapsed,
and the commander of the 56th Regiment surrendered with his entire
regiment. Connected with the leadership deficiencies was the old problem
of command and control. People from Thieu on down gave orders to
lower-ranking officers without informing the intervening members in
the chain of command. In Quang Tri, Giai found himself overextended
trying to command eight or ten major units. The same overextension
occurred early in Kontum, but it eventually worked itself out.

The static nature of the so-called ARVN infantry divisions arose
again to haunt the South Vietnamese. The presence of the families with
the divisions at Quang Tri, Kontum, and An Loc hampered operations,
and in Quang Tri was a major contributor to the debacle there. The
21st ARVN Division moved from the Mekong Delta to An Loc, with
its different enemy, climate, and terrain, where it performed badly. With
the exception of the 1st ARVN Division, infantry divisions fought poorly
in the initial stages of the NVA invasion. They had become accustomed
to small-unit pacification tasks and were not prepared for large-scale
combat operations. They committed forces piecemeal and broke up the

artillery into small, largely useless, groups. The tactical and strategic reserves proved woefully inadequate. Each ARVN corps had only a ranger group. As strategic reserves, ARVN could count only the airborne and marine divisions, and they would have been immobilized except for the C-123's and C-130's of the United States Air Force.

Finally, the Easter offensive revealed South Vietnam's continued reliance on the United States. American air power saved South Vietnam. American transports shuttled troops and supplies about the country, and they saved An Loc. American advisors virtually ran ARVN combat operations. Indeed, ARVN units became so dependent on United States air power that they would not advance unless their assault was preceded by an American air strike—a harbinger of future disaster. And so, while the Easter offensive was a stern test of Vietnamization, it was not the complete test. That would come sometime later when all United States forces and support had left Vietnam. Then South Vietnam would face the real trial of Vietnamization.

The Easter offensive was Giap's last battlefield hurrah. His chief of staff and successor, Van Tien Dung, late in 1972 took command of the North Vietnamese Army, replacing Giap, who remained as minister of defense. About that same time, Giap dropped from sight around Hanoi, and intelligence reports had it that he had gone to Russia for medical treatment—an old sign that Giap was in trouble. His demotion was confirmed when, in August 1972, Dung was elevated to full membership in the Politburo. And so, after twenty-nine years as North Vietnam's preeminent soldier, a span which saw him take an ill-equipped platoon and make it into a modern field army, Giap stepped down from battlefield command.

The irony of his reduction is that here again, as he had at Tet 1968, he opposed the Easter offensive. The same high-level North Vietnamese source who told of Giap's opposition to the 1968 offensive stressed Giap's resistance to the Easter offensive. While the battlelines in the Politburo in 1972 are less clear than those prior to the Tet offensive, there are firm indications that the old fight between rebuilding the North and winning the war in the South continued.

Pike recounts that in early 1972 the Politburo bitterly debated the advantages of attempting to get a negotiated settlement versus the try for a military victory.[17] According to the high-level informant, Giap and Truong Chinh lost again. The offensive was on, and Giap planned it. When it failed, it cost him his command—finally.[18] (See note #18 for Giap's later years.)

The NVA Easter offensive and its failure determined the direction and outcome of the final negotiations between the United States and North Vietnam—another example of the old axiom that negotiations can only reflect battlefield reality.

A twist of circumstances would have it that in early March 1972 (before the NVA launched the invasion), Kissinger agreed to meet Le Duc Tho in Paris to resume negotiations on 24 April. Later the date was shifted to 2 May. From Kissinger's viewpoint, the latter date could not have been worse. Quang Tri City had just fallen, and Kontum and An Loc appeared about to go under at any time. To add to this cheerless picture, General Abrams on 1 May sent his gloomy cable informing the president and Kissinger that the South Vietnamese had lost their will to fight, and that the war could easily be lost.

At the 2 May meeting, Kissinger repeated the offers which he proposed in late 1971 and which Nixon confirmed in his "clearing the air" speech of 25 January 1972. In general, these called for United States troop withdrawal within *six* months of the signing of an agreement, internationally supervised free elections with Communist involvement, and Thieu's willingness to resign a month prior to the elections. Le Duc Tho contemptuously and arrogantly dismissed Kissinger's renewed offer and made no proposals of his own. The North Vietnamese proposition was clear—they were going to win the war militarily, which would make negotiations irrelevant.

On 8 May, Nixon went on television to announce the mining of Haiphong harbor. This announcement overshadowed his offer (made in the same speech) of the most generous terms of settlement the United States had yet made to North Vietnam—a standstill cease-fire, release of prisoners, and a total American withdrawal within *four* months. Nixon implied in his offer that North Vietnam could keep any territory they had gained during the Easter offensive. One proposal the Nixon approach did not contain, however, was any offer to dismantle the Thieu government. Nixon had ruled that out in his speech of 25 January 1972. The North Vietnamese answered Nixon's offer with the roar of tanks and 130mm guns in the south and the whoosh of SA-2's and other Soviet antiaircraft missiles in the north. The terms of the settlement were being hammered out on the battlefield.

And hammered out they were. As the tide of the NVA Easter invasion slowed, then receded, negotiations began to look more and more attractive to the North Vietnamese. In addition to their fading military fortunes, their superpower allies, Russia and China, were leaning heavily on them. In mid-June, President Podgorny of the Soviet Union paid a visit to Hanoi. He bluntly told the North Vietnamese that it was time to negotiate and then flew back to Moscow. Russia had its own needs and agenda (credit, wheat, arms agreements, and détente) and it would not let some third-rate Communist country thwart them. Red China, too, had plans which would be advanced by a settlement of the Vietnam War. With Nixon's recent visit, China found herself in a position to play the Soviet Union off against the United States, while the Taiwan question and other problems required American help. Thus Mao himself, in the summer of 1972, urged the Vietnamese Communists to be more flexible.[19] In a masterpiece of diplomacy, Nixon and Kissinger had finally succeeded in isolating North Vietnam politically.

To the North Vietnamese, these actions of Russia and China were sharp goads. Not only were the Vietnamese totally dependent on their two big allies for everything from missiles to food, but to the doctrinaire Communists in Hanoi, the withdrawal of the support of their big allies struck a serious psychological and ideological blow. According to Truong Nhu Tang, the onetime minister of justice in the PRG, "There were, as all political cadre learned by heart, three currents of revolution in every people's war. The first two currents are the ever-growing international socialist camp and the armed liberation movement within the country in question. The third is the progressive movement within the colonial, or neo-colonial, power."[20] Tang's first two currents were, in mid-summer 1972, weak indeed. The third current, American antiwar dissidence, was at full flow, but it could not make up for the feebleness of the other two. As the North Vietnamese saw things, the "correlation of forces" had shifted against them. Communist dogma indicated, therefore, a step backwards, a retreat toward serious negotiations.

This NVA move towards meaningful negotiations coincided with American interests. For while the Easter offensive had left North Vietnam's industry and armed forces in shambles, Nixon's Vietnam policies rested precariously on a disintegrating political, diplomatic, and psychological base at home. The "blame America firsters" in Congress, academia, and the elite news media were in shrill cry about the bombing and mining. Congress, particularly the Senate, edged ever closer to legislating the United States out of the war on the most craven of terms. These growing forces emasculated the administration's efforts to get a firm compromise from Hanoi, and indicated to Nixon and Kissinger that if they were to get an acceptable settlement, they would have to do it quickly.

Only Thieu in Saigon could perceive no gain from meaningful negotiations. He and his country were completely dependent on the United States, and it frightened him to see the United States trying to negotiate its way out of Vietnam. While Laird and Abrams proclaimed the successes of Vietnamization, Thieu was skeptical of its accomplishments and dubious about its prospects. Thieu realized South Vietnam would have been overrun in the Easter offensive without United States air support. But Thieu was a clever, wily Oriental. He had come to realize from the events of the preceding four years that Hanoi would not settle on terms acceptable to Nixon. Reassured by this belief, Thieu tacitly had accepted United States negotiating points with which he disagreed because he knew Hanoi would reject them anyway. Now in 1972, he saw that serious negotiations were about to begin, and that meant some form of United States/NVN compromise almost sure to endanger South Vietnam. For the first time, Thieu realized that he would have to scrutinize every negotiation ploy, whether American or North Vietnamese, with wary and searching apprehension.

So, with these diverse national currents running, *at Hanoi's request* Le Duc Tho met Henry Kissinger once again in Paris on 19 July 1972. In this meeting Kissinger sensed a subtle change in Tho's attitude. However, Hanoi made no new offers nor did it retreat from its prior positions. The conferees agreed to meet again on 1 August. At the 1 August meeting and another which followed on 14 August, Tho softened Hanoi's position regarding the details of the cease-fire and on Thieu's future. While the United States could not accept the new North Vietnamese proposals, Hanoi was moving toward an acceptable agreement. Hanoi's use of terms like "two administrations," "two armies," and "three political groupings," (referring to Thieu's government, the PRG, and the "neutrals"), implied for the first time a recognition of Thieu's government and a hint of the NVN withdrawal of this perennial obstacle to an agreement. At the meeting on 14 August, Tho and Kissinger agreed to reconvene on 15 September.

Heartened by Hanoi's perceptible softening of position, on 17 August Kissinger flew into Saigon to brief Thieu on the results of his three latest meetings with Le Duc Tho. There Kissinger hit a stone wall. Thieu, alarmed at the possibility of an agreement, objected principally to the details of the in-place cease-fire which Kissinger proposed and to the United States proposal for a Tripartite Committee of National Reconciliation, even though the committee would work on the principle of unanimity, giving Thieu veto power. Thieu launched almost a score of other objections, mostly minor. Behind this foot-dragging lay Thieu's fundamental fear—the departure of the United States forces and the advent of peace. And so, between 18 August and Kissinger's meeting with Le Duc Tho in 15 September, Thieu continued his nit-picking and procrastination, raising point after point whose only purpose was to delay and confuse the negotiating process.

At the 15 September meeting, Le Duc Tho further softened his negotiating positions, and proposed, in effect, a coalition government which Kissinger promptly rejected. At Tho's urging, Kissinger consented to reaching "an agreement in principle" by 15 October. Le Duc Tho was now obviously seeking a fast agreement and proposed a two-day meeting within a week's time. Kissinger agreed to meet again on 26 September. This meeting showed further progress. The military issues were in large measure resolved, and while Tho still tried to force his tripartite coalition government on Kissinger, he gave signs of a further weakening on this point also.

The key meeting took place outside Paris on 8 October. Here, the North Vietnamese, eager to get a quick settlement, made a proposal which went a long way towards meeting Kissinger's previous objections. Le Duc Tho proposed that there be an immediate cease-fire, a prisoner exchange, American troop withdrawal, a cessation of movement of new NVA troops into South Vietnam, and the creation of a "Council of National Reconciliation" composed of three groups, representatives from the Thieu government, the PRG, and the "neutrals." This latter group would eventually supervise elections and move South Vietnam towards peace. Here was an historic breakthrough—Le Duc Tho had dropped his previous demand for a coalition government. He accepted that a military settlement could be separated from the political settlement (the two-track negotiating device which Kissinger had urged for years). Tho's terms now closely approached Nixon's proposals of 8 May 1972.

Nevertheless, Tho's proposal presented problems to Kissinger. The North Vietnamese version of the cease-fire applied only to South Vietnam, not to Laos and Cambodia as well. Tho's language regarding a cessation of NVA infiltration after the cease-fire lacked detail; the functions of the "Council of National Reconciliation" were vague; and the NVN proposal on "An International Commission on Control and Supervision" of the cease-fire needed a great deal of fleshing out. Nevertheless, this was real progress.

More long meetings were held on 9, 10, and 11 October, and compromise positions began to appear. By 12 October, Tho and Kissinger settled all the main issues except the American replacement of equipment for the South Vietnamese forces and the release of the political prisoners held by Saigon. These would be ironed out by Kissinger and Xuan Thuy, Tho's deputy, on 17 October. Additional details of the cease-fire in Laos and Cambodia (to which Tho had agreed in principle) still required formulation. So confident were both men that their agreement would be sustained by their superiors (and in Kissinger's case by Thieu also) that they agreed to a tentative timetable of implementation: cessation of American bombing—21 October; initialing of agreement in Hanoi—22 October; formal signing of agreement in Paris—30 October.

Kissinger returned to Washington on 12 October. He briefed Nixon, who approved the tentative agreement, but he cautioned Kissinger that Thieu must be brought along, and not to make a disadvantageous settlement just to meet the election deadline. With these admonitions, Kissinger set off for his 17 October meeting with Xuan Thuy in Paris and his 18–22 October conference in Saigon with Thieu. The one-day meeting with Xuan Thuy epitomized the entire trip. Kissinger attempted to get an acceptable agreement on the replacement of equipment for both sides, on the release of political prisoners held by the South, and on the details of a cease-fire in Laos and Cambodia. The first difference (equipment replacement) was eventually settled, but the others hung fire. With this meager success, Kissinger hurried to Saigon to see the implacable Thieu.

Nor was all the action in this fateful October taking place on the diplomatic front. Both sides, foreseeing a cease-fire in place leading to a "leopard-spot" arrangement, planned to go on a "land-grabbing" expedition just before and just after the cease-fire to improve their postagreement position. Thieu's forces were not ready, but the North Vietnamese were. Anticipating a cease-fire on 30 October, on 20 October the NVA made their move. They made some minor gains, but ARVN exacted a heavy toll for their premature grab—5,000 Communists killed or captured.

The second nondiplomatic action was a massive airlift of United States military equipment into South Vietnam, an operation called EN-HANCE PLUS. Since the draft agreement specified that equipment would be replaced on a one-for-one basis, this augmentation would not only improve Saigon's postagreement military capabilities, but would provide the basis for a full and continuing resupply.

Now, back to Kissinger's Saigon visit to persuade Thieu to support the tentative agreement he had reached with Le Duc Tho. For the next four days, Kissinger would endure his Gethsemane in trying to gain Thieu's support for the agreement. In turn, Thieu was arrogant, Machiavellian, shrewd, angry, rude, and tearful. After several acrimonious meetings, Thieu's objections to the NVN/United States draft boiled down to four major points:

1. The purpose and function of the "National Council of Reconciliation and Concord" (the old "Council of National Reconciliation") was unclear. Was it an "administrative organ" or a "governmental structure," the latter implying in the Vietnamese translation a coalition government. Thieu, of course, violently objected to this latter interpretation, telling Kissinger either that Tho had tricked him (which was true) or that Kissinger and Tho had conspired to deceive him (Thieu).

2. The draft agreement referred to three Vietnamese States—North Vietnam, and South Vietnam divided into two states, that part controlled by Saigon and that portion under the PRG. Thieu objected to any such denigration of his authority over *all* South Vietnam.

3. The draft agreement required *no* withdrawal of NVA troops from South Vietnam.

4. There was no reconstitution of the Demilitarized Zone. Not only could NVA troops move over it at will, but the absence of a DMZ implied *one* Vietnam, not two sovereign states, a North Vietnam and a South Vietnam.

Thieu contemptuously pointed out to Kissinger that the negotiations had been conducted in such obvious haste that the English and Vietnamese translations were at substantive odds in several parts. This was critically true regarding the functions of the "National Council." Further, Thieu continued, there were no protocols (the detailed instruments telling how the agreement was to be carried out).

Then, in the midst of the Thieu-Kissinger confrontation, the North Vietnamese prime minister, Pham Van Dong, dropped a diplomatic bomb. In an interview with Arnaud de Borchgrave on 18 October, Dong referred to the "National Council of Reconciliation and Concord" as a "three-sided coalition of transition." With Dong's words, the old NVN concept of a coalition government had been raised again. To make matters worse, Pham Van Dong gratuitously announced that "Thieu has been overtaken by events."[21] The Dong interview, made available to Thieu on 22 October (Kissinger's final day in Saigon) along with Thieu's intransigence had, at least temporarily, wrecked the draft agreement reached between Kissinger and Le Duc Tho. On 23 October, Kissinger cabled Tho that the tentatively agreed schedule was now impossible to meet, citing "difficulties in Saigon," the "ambiguities" of the Dong interview, and signs that the Communists had embarked on a land-grabbing operation.[22] He concluded by requesting another negotiating session in Paris.

Kissinger proposed, and Nixon approved, a cessation of the United States bombing attacks above the 20th Parallel. After all, North Vietnam had not delayed the agreement and should not be punished further.

Confusion and misunderstanding in Washington, Saigon, and Hanoi rapidly turned into stormy chaos. On 24 October, Thieu went on Saigon television and roundly denounced the draft agreement, ending with a call to arms to beat back the Communists' land-grabbing operations. Thieu did reveal his rock-bottom position, however. He would accept a cease-fire in place, but he would never accede to a coalition government or the continuing presence of NVA troops in South Vietnam. Thieu's virulent broadcast triggered a reply of equal pique and animosity from North Vietnam. On 26 October, Radio Hanoi released a lengthy broadcast, revealing the details of the draft agreement and the last few rounds of negotiations between Tho and Kissinger. The broadcast concluded with a North Vietnamese *demand* that the agreement be signed on 31 October (Hanoi's new target date).

Now the whole world looked to the United States and its chief negotiator and diplomatic spokesman, Henry Kissinger, for an answer. He was in a tough spot, trapped between a rock (Thieu) who wanted no agreement, and a hammer (North Vietnam) who wanted an agreement, and wanted it immediately. He had to try to bring Thieu along while reassuring North Vietnam that an agreement was at hand. To make matters worse, there was a third party involved, the most powerful of all, President Nixon. Nixon wanted to be sure that Thieu stayed on board. The president didn't care whether an agreement was signed before the election. He knew he would beat McGovern handily.

On 26 October, Kissinger held his now-famous television press conference. He started the conference with the statement, "We believe that peace is at hand."[23] This obviously over-optimistic statement overshadowed Kissinger's later remarks in the same telecast regarding "certain concerns and certain ambiguities." These he enumerated as:

1. The NVA land-grabbing operations in South Vietnam;
2. The powers of the International Commission to oversee the cease-fire;
3. The institution of a cease-fire in Laos and Cambodia;
4. The ambiguities in the Pham Van Dong interview with de Borchgrave;
5. The "linguistic problems" involved in the phrases "administrative structure" versus "coalition government";
6. The reestablishment of the DMZ;
7. Who should sign the agreement.[24]

Kissinger concluded his television statement with two messages— one for Hanoi and one for Saigon. He said, "We will not be stampeded into an agreement until its provisions are right. We will not be deflected from an agreement when its provisions are right."[25]

Nixon recognized immediately that Kissinger's "peace is at hand" statement had eroded the United States bargaining position. Such an unambivalent statement would harden Thieu's resistance, give Hanoi a new and powerful negotiating tool, and raise expectations (and thus pressure) within the United States. Kissinger, himself, while he makes a halfhearted effort to defend his gaffe in his memoirs, afterward seems bemused that he could have made such a statement.

Critics have claimed that Kissinger knew the delusive nature of his statement that "peace was at hand," but used it anyway. After all, as a preelection ploy it neutralized McGovern's attacks on the war; it reassured Hanoi; and it threatened Thieu. In addition, there are those who claim that this modern Metternich's real purpose in making the remark was to pin Nixon to the negotiated settlement. Nixon and Kissinger had never seen eye-to-eye on the negotiations. Kissinger had always leaned toward the North Vietnamese, while Nixon held back. Kissinger "tilted" toward accommodations with Hanoi, while Nixon tended to support Thieu. Nixon, the old "Cold Warrior," thought in terms of a militarily-enforced settlement, while Kissinger thought of a "decent interval." On 26 October, Kissinger feared that Nixon might pull back from the settlement and, reinforced by an election landslide, reopen the whole negotiating process. Perhaps, there was some validity to this last point, for Nixon *was* unhappy with Kissinger's ill-chosen sentence.

On the other hand, Kissinger's unfortunate remark may have been the result of nothing more sinister than fatigue. Kissinger had flown around the world in the week preceding his televised conference. He had been taunted, "nitpicked," and frustrated by Thieu in Saigon. On the day of his unfortunate news conference he was awakened at 0200 hours, worked all morning conferring with the president and others, and then hastily prepared his speech. Then, speaking extemporaneously, he found himself confronted by a hundred adversarial reporters on television. No wonder his tongue slipped.

Regardless of Kissinger's intentions behind his ill-timed statement, the motives of the North Vietnamese for seeking a preelection settlement are clear. At first glance, this rush for a preelection agreement would seem to place the North Vietnamese in the illogical position of attempting to help Nixon, the dedicated anti-Communist, get reelected over McGovern, the dovish leftist, and a man who campaigned on the platform of abject surrender to North Vietnam. But the war had taught the NVN Politburo a good deal about domestic American politics. From the Democratic Convention on, they had tagged McGovern as a loser. They calculated that Nixon would win, probably by a large margin, and that after the election he would hold out for much harsher terms. To the North Vietnamese, then, American political developments argued for a rapid settlement.

There was a second reason for Hanoi's bid for a quick settlement: they wanted to stop the tremendous flow of United States equipment to the RVNAF. In late October, the United States still had much major equipment undelivered. If the agreement could be signed on 31 October, the equipment would remain undelivered. Thus, the Politburo spent all efforts to get the settlement by 31 October. When that fell through, some of the impetus for a quick settlement fell with it.

A third reason existed for Hanoi's rush toward a 31 October settlement. The haste of the October negotiations left many areas either ambiguous or uncovered. Even the language of the English and Vietnamese versions differed, in some cases in matters of important substance. The protocols, the detailed instruments to be drawn up to execute the agreement, were either missing or woefully inadequate. Since the North Vietnamese had no intention of abiding by the agreements, they wanted the ambiguity and confusion contained in the documents.

There was a final, and most compelling, reason to complete the negotiations prior to the election—the North Vietnamese had the essentials of the agreement they wanted. The onetime PRG minister of justice, Tang, in his book states that from the start of the negotiations in 1968, the Politburo had two primary objectives: first, get the United States out of Vietnam, preferably in such a way that they would not return; and second, get the Americans to agree to leave the NVA troops in South Vietnam. All else, according to Tang, such as Thieu's ouster, the coalition government, the status of the DMZ, were negotiable and expendable.

So, while the 31 October date for the signing slipped away, the North Vietnamese persisted in trying to bring negotiations to a conclusion. On 26 October (after Kissinger's television conference), Le Duc Tho sent him a message which left the door open for future meetings. After an exchange of mutually unacceptable dates, they agreed to meet in Paris on 20 November.

While negotiations with Hanoi were now back on track, there remained the sticky problem of Thieu. One prod to bring him into line was the continuation of the copious flow of equipment from the United States to South Vietnam—Operation ENHANCE PLUS. The other spur was a visit to Thieu on 10 November by Maj. Gen. Alexander Haig, Kissinger's assistant. Haig's talks with Thieu—half cajolery, half threats—produced no progress. Thieu still adamantly refused to accept or compromise on three major points. These were: total withdrawal of NVA troops from South Vietnam; recognition of the DMZ as a clear and permanent boundary between North and South Vietnam; and a recognition that *his* government held sovereignty over *all* of South Vietnam.

When Haig reported Thieu's recalcitrance to Nixon and Kissinger, Nixon wrote Thieu a letter in which he attempted to meet Thieu's objections to the terms of the draft agreement. Included in Nixon's letter to

Thieu of 14 November is this crucial paragraph: "But far more important than what we say in the agreement on this issue is what we do in the event the enemy renews his aggression. You have my absolute assurance that if Hanoi fails to abide by the terms of this agreement it is my intention to take swift and severe retaliatory action."[26] By this letter, Nixon committed himself and the United States to the enforcement of the agreement by military means. In the light of the prevailing opinions in Congress, the news media, and the country at large, Nixon must have known that this was a fragile commitment indeed. In spite of Nixon's assurances and Haig's explanations, Thieu doggedly opposed major portions of the draft agreement. He went even further. On 18 November, his emissary in Washington proposed sixty-nine changes to the agreement, modifying it extensively—another ploy to delay or demolish the negotiations.

Kissinger met with Le Duc Tho on 20 November. The meeting opened with an exchange of unpleasantries about who had reneged on the signing of the agreement. Kissinger then tabled Thieu's sixty-nine changes and objections; some were major, most were minor and uncontroversial. Tho said he would study them and requested an adjournment until the next day. On 21 November, Tho rejected most of Kissinger's suggested changes and to Kissinger's consternation submitted some changes of his own, including a few which withdrew some of the previous concessions he had made on 8 October.

On 22 November, Kissinger, sensing a deadlock, withdrew most of Thieu's changes and concentrated on what he (and Nixon) considered to be the keys. These were: "administrative" versus "coalition" structure; clarification of the nature of the DMZ; the fate of NVA forces in the South; clarification of procedures for introducing weapons into South Vietnam; and the functioning of the international peace-keeping body. Tho proved unresponsive.

The meeting on the next day turned out no more productive, as did additional meetings on 24 and 25 November. On 25 November, the two negotiators decided to recess until 4 December. As November ended, the prospects for an agreed settlement appeared more remote than at any time since 2 May, when the NVA Easter offensive was in full flower. Not only were the negotiations floundering, but the United States team of Kissinger and Nixon was in disarray. Each now mistrusted the other and his motives. The incongruity of their aims and means was becoming clearly apparent. Also, Kissinger's enemies in the White House and the bureaucracy, sensing blood, now leapt in, trying to discredit the "Lone Ranger of Foreign Policy." Kissinger himself described his relations with Nixon during this period as "wary and strained."[27]

Once more, on 4 December, Tho and Kissinger met in Paris. Tho led off with an abusive and condemnatory speech. Kissinger tried without success to mollify him. Tho not only shrugged off Kissinger's suggested changes, but withdrew nine of the twelve changes he had previously agreed to. On Kissinger's recommendation, the next day's conference was postponed until Wednesday, 6 December. At this meeting, which continued into 7, 8, and 9 December, things appeared brighter. Pham Van Dong's gaffe was clarified, ruling out a "coalition government" in favor of an "administrative structure." Tho gave some hints that a partial withdrawal of NVA troops from the South might be made, and he returned to his previous agreements of 8 October on several other points. By 9 December one issue separated the negotiators—the integrity of the DMZ as an international boundary. An agreement appeared (to use Kissinger's words) "tantalizingly close."

Then on 10 December, at a meeting of "technical experts," the North Vietnamese reversed course again. They presented seventeen new "linguistic" changes, some of which were not linguistic, but clearly substantive. Nor did the negotiating atmosphere improve on 11 December when Tho and Kissinger met. Kissinger raised Hanoi's seventeen "linguistic" changes. Tho refused to discuss them. Ditto for the DMZ issue and for the others. The meeting on Tuesday 12 December made some progress: the seventeen issues were reduced to two. The meeting on the next day was chaotic. The North Vietnamese introduced sixteen new "linguistic changes," four of substance. Hanoi then unveiled its protocols, the instruments by which the agreement would be carried out. Kissinger promptly labeled them "outrageous." In particular, the NVN protocol dealing with the supervision of the cease-fire provided for International Commission forces of only 250 men, dependent for all support on the government (Saigon or PRG) in whose area they were stationed. In effect, this amounted to no supervision at all. Disgusted with Hanoi's obvious intransigence, on 13 December Kissinger told Tho that he was returning to Washington. He told the press that he was leaving his experts so they could consult with Hanoi's experts—an implication of a continuity of negotiations which didn't exist. In reality, negotiations which had looked so hopeful so often in 1972 were dead in the water.

In viewing Hanoi's negotiating tactics of later November and early December 1972, a natural question arises: since the North Vietnamese were panting to sign an agreement in October, why did they stall in November and December? Nobody in the West knows for sure, but speculations abound. Most of them start with the intelligence report that for some time a serious split had existed in the North Vietnamese Politburo over the desirability of negotiating *any* agreement with the United States. Those opposed to negotiations reminded the others of the Geneva Convention of 1954 which, the "antis" contended, had deprived the Vietminh of the rewards of their victory over the French. Now, they maintained, the same thing was happening again. Nixon, the devoted anti-Communist, was attempting to deceive them. They pointed out that the United States had reneged on signing the agreement on 30 or 31 October, a reversal which had cost them 5,000 killed and captured in their premature land-grabbing operation. Further, Nixon had poured equipment into South Vietnam, building up the RVNAF into a potent *offensive* machine. United States support of Thieu's sixty-nine changes, which Kissinger tabled at the reopened session in November, were (to the North Vietnamese) a sign of Nixon's perfidy and proved that he had no intent of ever agreeing to an acceptable settlement. To the Politburo, a group of proud, hostile, old men, such deception was unacceptable. And so some said—hold out.

The second thesis accounting for the North Vietnamese tactics of November–December stresses Hanoi's reliance on the theory of "the objective correlation of forces." This speculation holds that in Hanoi's view, the "correlation of forces" had shifted against them and conditions were wrong for concluding negotiations. They had suffered a significant military setback in the Easter offensive and again in the land-grabbing operations of late October, and the massive influx of equipment to the RVNAF generated by ENHANCE had further strengthened the South Vietnamese *vis-à-vis* the VC/NVA forces. Beyond the military situation, another unfavorable development had come about. The agreements of October had been quickly—some critics say sloppily—negotiated by Kissinger and his assistants. Imprecisions of language and lack of detail favored the Communists, who had been meticulous and guileful in the use of language and translations. This duplicity had now largely vanished as the United States diplomats and experts hammered out the details of linguistic nuances and protocols.[28]

While the above speculations have some validity, they fail to explain how stalling the negotiations would improve conditions for Hanoi. In fact, the probability is that these unfavorable conditions would get worse, not better. A more acceptable explanation of Hanoi's behavior is furnished by Kissinger and Nixon. They speculate that Hanoi stalled for two reasons: one, to exploit the deep and bitter split between the United States and South Vietnam. Nixon maintains that the Politburo knew of the various American threats to cut off funds unless Thieu came around. Two, Hanoi decided to see if Congress would legislate the United States out of the war, and in fact, Congress might very well have done just that.

Regardless of the reasons impelling North Vietnam's dilatory tactics, Nixon knew on 14 December that he had to break the deadlock, and break it quickly, before his domestic support (already badly eroded) disappeared completely and before a hostile, surrender-minded Congress reconvened in early January. Nixon's only tools were the renewed bombing of North Vietnam and the remining of Haiphong harbor. On 15 December, he sent a note to Hanoi demanding that they reopen negotiations within seventy-two hours or face the consequences. The consequences were the Christmas bombing of 1972—called LINEBACKER II.

In December 1972 the news media wrote and spoke a great deal about the so-called Christmas bombing, and like the reporting of the Tet offensive of 1968, most of it was either badly distorted or dead wrong. The "Prestige Media" (*New York Times, Washington Post, Time, Newsweek,* and CBS) reported that the bombing was indiscriminate; that its purpose was to cause heavy civilian casualties; that it would stiffen Hanoi's resolve; that it would result in serious losses of United States aircraft and manpower; and that it shamed the United States in its own eyes and in the eyes of the world. All of this turned out to be false (with the partial exception of the last charge) and could have been determined as false at the time.

An objective analysis of LINEBACKER II requires a brief discussion of its purpose, the operation itself, the results, and its public handling by the Nixon administration and the news media. LINEBACKER II had *no* military purpose. President Nixon initiated it for purely psychological reasons—he wanted to send a message to the North Vietnamese to return to the negotiating table and reach an acceptable agreement to end the war. To make this message plain to Hanoi, he ordered a maximum bombing effort by fighter-bombers and B-52's. To make his intent clear to his own subordinates, he telephoned Admiral Moorer, chairman, JCS, and told him, "I don't want any more of this crap about the fact that we couldn't hit this target or that one. This is your chance to use military power effectively to win this war, and if you don't I'll consider you responsible."[29] Nixon's blunt words told the JCS that this operation was no ordinary operation. The wraps were off, and United States air power, Model 1972, was to be tested to the limit.

The operation was to be a maximum effort designed to take out all military installations in the Hanoi/Haiphong area as well as other facilities (railroad yards, bridges, roads, electric power plants, and steel works) which supported the NVA war effort. The concept called originally for attacks to be made over a three-day period. Later this was extended indefinitely or until the North Vietnamese gave some indication of returning to serious negotiations. In actual time, the attacks extended from 18 to 29 December. During this period, the air force and navy mounted 724 B-52 sorties and around 640 fighter-bomber sorties, dropping some 20,000 tons of bombs. In addition, there were more than 1,384 other sorties in support of the attacking aircraft (chaff flights, refueling flights, fighter cover, SAM suppression, and electronic countermeasure flights). Due to the characteristics of the various types of aircraft used, the B-52's generally attacked targets in the outlying areas, while the fighters (who could deliver bombs much more accurately) struck targets in and near heavily populated areas.

From the American viewpoint the results were spectacular. At the completion of the twelve-day campaign, North Vietnam's military potential, its industry, and economy lay in ruins. In fact, there were no more legitimate military targets in North Vietnam to strike. In addition, the United States raids had destroyed North Vietnam's ability to defend itself against further attacks from the air. Its airfields had been destroyed, and it had expended all of its SAM's. In fact, during the last three days, United States aircraft were virtually unfired on.

United States losses, considering the missile and other AAA defenses in the target, were slight—twenty-six aircraft were lost (including fifteen B-52's). Considering the weather (bad for all but twelve hours), the type of operations, and the density of population in the target area, civilian casualties were amazingly light. Hanoi claimed that 1,318 civilians had been killed and 1,261 wounded in the attacks.

The most important result was that Hanoi got Nixon's message, and they got it loud and clear. On 26 December, Hanoi indicated that it would resume negotiations, and on 29 December, Nixon halted the bombings. A debate rages to this day about whether the Christmas bombing drove Hanoi back to the conference table. Like so many other decisions taken by the North Vietnamese leadership, the background of this one remains shrouded in the murky shadows of the Politburo. It is my opinion that the bombing did act as a catalyst, forcing Hanoi back to negotiations.

But Hanoi was prodded back to the table by more than the bombing itself; it was the threat of what might come *after* the bombing that perturbed the Politburo. What might Nixon do next? Where would he stop? After all, he had ordered, and persisted in, a massive air campaign against North Vietnam in the face of the outcries of the American news media and Congress and in spite of the condemnations of most of the other nations of the world. Equally disquieting to the Politburo was the fact that both the Russians and Chinese had done nothing to protect them from the aerial onslaught. Nor could their big allies be relied on to prevent some future and more devastating American attack. If the bombing failed, would Nixon then go after the dikes along the Red River? This was a terrible vulnerability which had always terrified the Politburo. Or did he have something even more sinister in mind? With these nightmares, a settlement seemed preferable to waiting for the dreaded second shoe to drop.

Ironically, the American news media, which so misreported the bombings, fueled Hanoi's fears of the "second shoe." The *New York Times* and the *Washington Post* implied that Nixon might be deranged, saying in the *Times* that "Americans must now speak out for sanity in Washington,"[30] while the *Post* proclaimed that the bombings caused "Americans . . . to wonder at their president's very sanity." In the *Post* of 27 December, columnist Stewart Alsop raised the question directly. He wrote, "What would Nixon do if the North Vietnamese refused to return to the conference table? Nuke Hanoi? Hit the dikes? Or just go on bombing North Vietnam 'til hell freezes over?"[31] Eric Sevareid asked the same question on the CBS broadcast of 22 December: "What higher bargaining cards do we possess?" The inferred answer to the questions posed by Alsop and Sevareid could not have comforted the Politburo.

If the misreporting of the nature and results of the Christmas bombing followed its Tet predecessor, so too—strangely enough—did the administration's response. Just as Johnson had done at Tet, Nixon and his staff hunkered down and clammed up about the bombing. Kissinger gave one low-key news conference about the cause of the deadlock of negotiations, but no explanation was given by anyone about the purpose of the bombing, the measures taken to prevent civilian casualties, or the results. Nixon, in particular, took great pains to distance himself from the operation. In these conditions, as Johnson's actions at Tet 1968 showed, the antiwar news media and activists have free rein to shout their charges of immorality and butchery by "carpet bombing." In his memoirs, Nixon excuses his decision for silence as necessary to avoid the appearance of having given the North Vietnamese an ultimatum, which in his view would only have stiffened Hanoi's will to resist a return to the bargaining table. And yet, a few pages later, Nixon criticizes President Johnson for the same sin he himself committed in December 1972. Nixon wrote of Johnson, ". . . he quit fighting for his policies in public—he did not generate the public support for them. As a matter of fact he seemed to be running away from them."[32] Well, there is no law which says that politicians must be consistent.

Nixon's silence about the bombing was joined by another group who had been most vociferous in the past, the college students. The all-out attacks generated a limp reaction from the campuses. True, most of the students were at home celebrating Christmas, but a much more potent tranquilizer was Nixon's announcement on 28 June 1972 that no more draftees would be sent to Vietnam. When Nixon removed the students from danger, he removed their outrage at the immorality of the war. One can only conclude that the students' professed concern for the hearts and minds of the Vietnamese people was in reality a much greater concern for a lower part of their own anatomy.

Regardless of the motives which drove the North Vietnamese back to the conference table, when the "technical experts" reconvened in Paris, a new sense of urgency motivated the Communist delegates. On 8 January, when Kissinger met Tho, the latter greeted him with a bitter denunciation of the bombing, but on 9 January, the two men got down to business. By 13 January they had hammered out the basic agreement.

Some of the protocols still required work, but the differences were manageable. Kissinger, burned from his October experience with Nixon and Thieu, told Tho that he would take the agreement first to Nixon and then to Thieu for their approval. Nixon tentatively approved it on 15 January, and on 16 January, Haig arrived in Saigon with the unpleasant and unpromising task of selling the agreement to President Thieu.

When Haig presented the agreement to Thieu, he (Thieu) called it a ''surrender agreement'' and categorically refused to sign it.[33] In retaliation, Nixon launched a two-pronged attack on Thieu's recalcitrance. He admitted that the settlement was imperfect, but that its conditions could be accepted, particularly when they were backed up by his pledge to retaliate severely with force if the Communists took advantage of the agreement. Also, Nixon promised that he would push Congress to continue aid to South Vietnam. Then, turning tough, he told Thieu that the United States would sign the agreement whether Saigon did or not, and if that happened, all aid to South Vietnam would be cut off. Faced with the small carrot and the big stick, Thieu acquiesced in the agreement, which was formally ratified on 23 January 1973.

The agreement carried the following major provisions:

1. It called for a cease-fire in place.

2. It required the withdrawal of United States troops and an exchange of POW's within sixty days.

3. It prohibited both the United States and North Vietnam from sending more troops into South Vietnam.

4. Equipment could be replaced only on an item-for-item basis.

5. It created two Commissions—the Joint Military Commission (South Vietnam-NVA/VC) and the International Commission on Control and Supervision (Hungary, Poland, Indonesia, and Canada) to enforce the cease-fire and compliance with the agreement.

6. It set up a National Council of National Reconciliation and Concord to organize free elections in South Vietnam.

7. It established the integrity of the DMZ using the terms of the Geneva Accords of 1954.

There were, of course, other provisions, but the above established the fundamental structure of the agreement.

Four long years of bloodshed and hundreds of thousands of casualties had finally produced an agreement—an agreement which from the viewpoint of South Vietnam and the United States was badly flawed. Nixon candidly admitted as much; and Kissinger implied it. To see the flaws in the agreement one must start with a fundamental assumption shared by Thieu, Nixon, and Kissinger: the North Vietnamese had no intention of abiding by the settlement which they had signed. There were no illusions in either the Independence Palace in Saigon or the White House that North Vietnam would give up its long effort to subjugate South Vietnam.

Unfortunately, the agreement left the North Vietnamese in a position to do just that. In the first place, the settlement left the NVA troops not only in place in South Vietnam, but in attack positions. Second, the agreement prescribed no effective machinery for supervising the cease-fire and the future combat activities of either side. Both the Joint Military Commission and the International Commission on Control and Supervision worked on the principle of unanimity, allowing North Vietnam a veto in the Joint Commission and the Communist members of the International Commission (Hungary and Poland) the same blocking power in that body. In effect, the agreement failed to provide any real restraints on future military action by North Vietnam. In reality, the settlement only suspended major combat operations for the period necessary for North Vietnam to prepare her forces for the final offensive.

Nor did any knowledgeable individual delude himself that the RVNAF could withstand a major NVA offensive. True, ENHANCE and EN-HANCE PLUS had loaded the RVNAF with equipment, but it soon became apparent that the United States had given South Vietnam airplanes they couldn't fly, ships they couldn't man, and tanks and other equipment they couldn't maintain. Even more fundamental, little or no progress had been made in curing the basic flaws in the South Vietnamese government and in its armed forces.

Thus, Thieu, Nixon, and Kissinger believed that the primary enforcer of the peace would have to be the threat of retaliation by the United States—a most unrealistic concept. Kissinger and Nixon both realized in early 1973 that Congress was about to legislate the United States out of the war in Indochina. The Christmas bombing had produced a violent condemnation of the war from the news media and other antiwar activists. Antiwar sentiment had by December 1972 reached a new high in the United States, quieted only by the prospect of an early peace agreement. In retrospect, it is difficult to see how Nixon and Kissinger, both intelligent and pragmatic men, could have believed that Congress and the country would acquiesce in the reentry of United States air and naval forces into combat over Indochina. Nixon, himself, later admitted that he saw indications at the time of the signing of the agreement that Congress would never permit another involvement of United States forces in Vietnam. In sum, if North Vietnam could not be restrained from military action and South Vietnam could not defend herself, and the United States could not retaliate with force against North Vietnam's violations, the eventual demise of South Vietnam was assured. This left only that policy of ignominy, "The Decent Interval."

But the more one ponders this withering verdict, the more one sees it as too simplistic and too harsh on Nixon and Kissinger. In view of the mood in early 1973 in Congress, the news media, and among the American people, Nixon and Kissinger had to take the agreement they got. There was simply no public support for a tougher settlement which would have exploited the military victories which had been won by the Americans (and South Vietnamese) in the Easter offensive and the Christmas bombing. The fundamental truth is that the United States had won the irrelevant war in Vietnam, and had lost the real one—the war for the "hearts and minds" of the American people. Giap's *dich van* had won in the United States what his troops could not win on the battlefield.

Notes—Chapter 24

1. Lt. Gen. Ngo Quang Truong, *The Easter Offensive of 1972,* Indochina Monographs (Washington, D.C.: U.S. Army Center of Military History, 1980), p. 13.
2. Truong, *Easter Offensive,* p. 157.
3. Tang, *Vietcong Memoir,* p. 210.
4. Truong, *Easter Offensive,* p. 18.
5. Fulghum, Maitland, et al. *Vietnam on Trial,* p. 128.
6. Ibid., p. 150.
7. Maj. A. J. C. Lavalle, ed., *Airpower and the 1972 Spring Offensive* (Washington: USAF Southeast Asia Monographs Series, 1976), Monograph 3, Vol. 2, p. 14.
8. Nixon, *Memoirs,* p. 594.
9. Truong, *Easter Offensive,* p. 172.
10. Lavalle, *Airpower,* p. 104.
11. Richard M. Nixon, *No More Vietnams* (New York: Arbor House Publishing, 1985), p. 150.
12. Kissinger, *White House Years,* p. 1301.
13. Pike, *Marxism,* p. 277.
14. Lewy, *America,* pp. 198–200 with end notes on p. 485.
15. Truong, *Easter Offensive,* pp. 159–160; and Vien and Khuyen, *Reflections,* pp. 104–105.
16. Thompson, *Peace,* pp. 110–112.
17. Pike, *Marxism,* pp. 276–277.
18. Giap's life and career since 1972 have gone downward. His health, apparently never good, has steadily deteriorated, and reports say he suffers from the advanced stages of Hodgkin's disease. His career, no doubt adversely affected by his health, has declined also. Giap remained the titular North Vietnam minister of defense until February 1980, when he lost that post to Gen. Van Tien Dung, the conqueror of South Vietnam. Actually, Dung had replaced Giap in the late seventies in all but title. Giap held his seat in the Politburo until 1982 when Le Duan demoted him from the Politburo to the position of chief, Science and Technology Commission. In April 1984 Giap was named president of the Vietnam Commission on Demography and Family Planning. He is believed to have retained his role as chief, Science and Technology Commission.

   By 1984 he was slipping into obscurity. He was "nonprominent" at the 40th anniversary celebration of the birthday of the North Vietnamese Army (which Giap had founded alone) and was absent from the main events celebrating the thirtieth anniversary of his victory at Dien Bien Phu.

As a general, Giap gave an uneven performance, brilliant in some aspects, mediocre or worse in others. Looked at overall, Giap is a great general. After all, he won—and that is the most conclusive test of a general. MacArthur's cliché is right: there really is no substitute for victory.

19. Barbara W. Tuchman, *The March of Folly, from Troy to Vietnam* (New York: Alfred A. Knopf, 1984), p. 371.
20. Tang, *Vietcong Memoir,* p. 212.
21. Kalb and Kalb, *Kissinger,* p. 362.
22. Ibid., p. 377.
23. Kissinger, *White House Years,* p. 1399.
24. Kalb and Kalb, *Kissinger,* pp. 382–383.
25. Kissinger, *White House Years,* p. 1400.
26. Anthony T. Bouscaren, ed., *All Quiet on the Eastern Front: The Death of South Vietnam* (Old Greenwich, CT: The Devin-Adair Co., 1977), p. 159; also Nixon, *Memoirs,* p. 718.
27. Kissinger, *White House Years,* p. 1419.
28. Martin F. Herz, *The Prestige Press and the Christmas Bombing, 1972* (Washington, D.C.: Ethics and Public Policy Center, 1980), p. 13.
29. Nixon, *Memoirs,* p. 734.
30. *New York Times,* 22 December 1972.
31. Stewart Alsop, *Washington Post,* 27 December 1972.
32. Nixon, *Memoirs,* p. 754.
33. Nixon, *No More Vietnams,* p. 167.

25 An Indecent Interval

1973–1974

The signing of the 1973 Paris Agreement ended Indochina War II and initiated Indochina War III. The agreement provided for a cease-fire in place, a provision which left a large North Vietnamese force in South Vietnam. It established two control commissions to oversee the cease-fire and the execution of the agreement's military provisions, but since both commissions operated on the principle of unanimity, they were powerless. The agreement set up a National Council of Concord and National Conciliation to plan and supervise elections, but this never functioned. The agreement *did* recognize the Provisional Revolutionary Government (PRG), a Communist satellite of North Vietnam, as a legitimate government competing with the Thieu regime in South Vietnam. In retrospect, most of South Vietnam's leaders view the Paris Agreement of 1973 as the fundamental cause of the eventual destruction of the Thieu government.[1]

Immediately after the signing of the Paris Agreement, the RVNAF were stronger in South Vietnam than their Communist foes. South Vietnam had almost one million men under arms (counting Regulars, Local Forces, Militia, and Home Guards), and in Operation ENHANCE PLUS the United States had dumped vast amounts of equipment on RVNAF. Much of this equipment, however, the RVNAF could neither use nor maintain. The North Vietnamese had about 219,000 troops in South Vietnam. Their combat efficiency and morale had been dealt a savage blow by the horrendous casualties of the Easter offensive and the long-term effects of the United States air strikes and mining operations in North Vietnam. Col. Gen. Tran Van Tra, the commander of the COSVN B-2 front (an area comprising all South Vietnam south of the Central Highlands) wrote that "in 1973 our cadres and men were fatigued, we had not had time to make up for our losses, all units were in disarray, there was a lack of manpower, and there were shortages of food and ammunition . . ."[2]

These statistics of relative strengths, however, are misleading. Only about 200,000 of the 450,000 ARVN regulars were in the infantry divisions and other combat units. The rest were absorbed by the huge administrative and logistical "tail," another legacy the United States Army left ARVN. The South Vietnamese Air Force and Navy totaled another 100,000, while some 525,000 were in the Regional and Popular Forces. The NVA had about 148,000 combat troops in South Vietnam and 71,000 in support. A breakdown of enemy and friendly strength by ARVN corps area follows:

	MR1	MR2	MR3	MR4	Total
RVNAF: Ground combat troops (thousands)	145–170	143–146	155–175	246–257	689–748
In Regular units (thousands)	75–90	27–29	50–60	40–50	192–229
Regional and Popular (thousands)	70–80	116–117	105–115	206–207	497–519
Trainees, admn. and service troops, and casuals (thousands)	—	—	—	—	c.200
Divisions	5	2	3	3	13
Regiments and brigades*	16	7	9	9	48#
Regular battalions*	95	50	64	55	264
Enemy: Troops (thousands**)	96	42	41	40	219
Combat troops (thousands**)	71	25	25	27	148
NVA regulars	68	19	20	16	123
Viet Cong	3	6	5	11	25
Admn. and service troops (thousands**)	25	17	16	13	71
NVA regulars	19	9	5	1	34
Viet Cong	6	8	11	12	37
Divisions	8##	3	2	3	16
Regimental Hq*	54	11	13	16	94
Battalion Hq*	195	73	777	79	424

* Includes independent regiments and battalions.
# Total includes 7 ranger groups.
** In most cases, figures have been rounded down rather than up.
Includes an air defense division.[3]

Again, the figures can be misleading if taken without reference to other Order of Battle factors, such as organization, training, leadership, weaponry, morale, and mission—the intangibles of military strength.

Two of these intangibles were critical in any assessment of relative strength. First, North Vietnamese forces in South Vietnam, while battered and understrength, were sound and capable of restoration and expansion. In contrast, the foundation and structure of the RVNAF were rotten and askew and provided no scaffolding upon which to build an effective force. Furthermore, these fundamental RVNAF deficiencies could be cured only by tearing down the existing structure, an extremely dangerous operation requiring years, perhaps decades, of effort in the face of an implacable foe. A second factor, mission, was also important. The NVA mission was strategically offensive, although on occasion the Communists might be forced onto the tactical defensive. The South Vietnamese were on the strategic defensive, forced to defend (largely from static positions) villages, bases, and LOC's. This difference in mission gave the strategic initiative ("the Big I") to the Communists, and with it the eventual advantage of attacking when, and where, and in what strength they chose.

As they had done just before the "phony signing" in October 1972, the Communists went on a land- and people-grabbing expedition the night before the Paris Agreement went into effect (midnight Greenwich Mean Time), 27 January. This time the South Vietnamese went on a land-grab of their own, and in general they beat the Communists at their own game. The South Vietnamese picked up a few villages and hamlets and repulsed the Communists in their efforts to do the same. Local Forces on both sides did most of the fighting, which was generally on a small scale. Heavy casualties did come, however, from four division-size attacks launched by the NVA after the cease-fire went into effect. Each was aimed at gaining a piece of tactically important real estate. ARVN repulsed three of the attacks after heavy fighting, but in the fourth the Communists eventually overcame the defenders, an isolated ranger battalion.

The results of LANDGRAB 73, as the NVA operation was called, confirmed to the North Vietnamese leadership that their most immediate problem was to rebuild and reinforce their forces in South Vietnam. They did not hesitate. In the first two weeks after the signing of the Paris Agreement, they committed over 200 major violations of the Accords relating to the infiltration of men and equipment into South Vietnam. Included among these violations was the movement on 6 February of a 175-truck convoy through the DMZ and the march of 223 tanks from Laos and Cambodia into South Vietnam. By mid-April, some 7,000 NVA truck crossings of the DMZ were reported. Huge convoys rolled down the expanded and hardened Ho Chi Minh Trail system. During 1973, Hanoi infiltrated over 75,000 troops, increased its tank strength from 100 to 500, and almost doubled its heavy artillery strength. The NVA augmented its antiaircraft strength in South Vietnam drastically. By the end of April, thirteen *new* AA regiments had taken up positions in South Vietnam, and the 263d Surface-to-Air Missile (SAM) Regiment established itself at Khe Sanh.

NVA construction kept pace with the influx of men and equipment. In 1973, thirteen new airfields were built in South Vietnam. The Ho Chi Minh Trail was widened and modernized. A new all-weather road was pushed from Khe Sanh down the east side of the Annamite Chain to link up to Highway 14 down to An Loc. Altogether the NVA added 12,000 miles of roads. A fuel pipeline was built from North Vietnam deep into South Vietnam, and a modern radio net linked NVA forces throughout South Vietnam.

While the North Vietnamese made a major effort to rebuild and augment their military capability in South Vietnam, they decided that the main effort initially would be to overthrow the Thieu government by political means.[4] Actually, the Politburo could do little else. The Communist forces in South Vietnam were incapable of a major offensive, and such an attack might bring the feared United States air arm back into the fray—a consequence to be avoided at all costs. Beyond the military aspects, the Paris Agreement had legitimatized the PRG and would give it a voice in South Vietnam, and the agreement might protect their territorial gains against the stronger and more aggressive RVNAF.

In anticipation of the signing of the Paris Agreement and the cease-fire, the NVN Politburo and its operating wing in the South, COSVN, issued detailed instructions in January 1973 for the conduct of the political struggle, the *dich van* program aimed at the South Vietnamese people. This campaign called for all Communist forces in South Vietnam to undertake programs designed sequentially to: (1) motivate the population; (2) develop mass movements; (3) reform and augment the political infrastructure; and (4) adapt military procedures to the new situation. Propaganda was to play a major role in the political offensive. In keeping with their usual procedures, the Politburo aimed the propaganda campaign at three audiences: first, the "world," that is, the United States, its allies, and the Communist nations; second, the citizens and armed forces of South Vietnam; and third, the Communists' own soldiers and people.

The principal theme the Politburo beamed to the "world" was that the Communists were abiding by the terms of the agreement while the South Vietnamese aggressively and constantly violated them. It worked. Richard Nixon and others have testified that this program "succeeded in totally hamstringing the South Vietnamese. If Saigon had tried to interrupt or interdict Hanoi's buildup, the uproar in Congress would have been deafening."[5]

The propaganda campaign directed at the South Vietnamese people tried to subvert the Thieu government and to get the troops to desert or defect. As it had done in the past, it largely misfired. While desertion in ARVN was always a problem, the NVN propaganda assault failed to increase it, and desertions remained just that—not defections. The morale of South Vietnamese civilians held firm in 1973. It did begin to erode in 1974, and it collapsed in 1975, but the actions and inaction of the United States government and the South Vietnamese leadership brought that on—not Communist propaganda.

The third thrust of the North Vietnamese propaganda campaign was directed at its own civilians and soldiers. The latter posed a particularly difficult problem. The NVA soldiers had fought long and hard; they had lost comrades and battles; and with the signing of the agreement, the North Vietnamese soldiers expected to go back to North Vietnam. Now their leaders had to tell them that their work was not done, that the revolution was incomplete, and that final victory lay somewhere in the future. The leaders explained the extension of their stay in the South by attributing the prolongation of the fighting to the perfidy of the South Vietnamese. They tried to encourage the soldiers by telling them that now (early 1973) the Communists were in the strongest position they had occupied during the whole war.

The Politburo's emphasis on the political offensive over the military struggle did not last long, although how long is a matter of uncertainty. Certainly, the emphasis on political *dau tranh* was over by October

1973, and perhaps even earlier. By May, and probably sooner, Communist Party cadre throughout South Vietnam were being told by the senior leadership that victory could be obtained only by a military "blitzkrieg."

While the North Vietnamese began immediately after the cease-fire to expand both their military and political capabilities, the Thieu government did almost nothing. In place of a military-political strategy and plan, Thieu promulgated his "Four No's." They were: (1) No territory or outpost would be relinquished to the enemy; (2) No coalition government; (3) No negotiation with the enemy; and (4) No Communist or neutralist activity in the country.[6] The "Four No's" doomed the RVN to a static and defensive policy, both politically and militarily. The political "No's" denied the South Vietnamese government any attempt at exploiting the political and ideological divisions between the North Vietnamese and the Viet Cong, deep divisions now known to have existed. The military "No" (denial to the Communists of any territory or position) forced the JGS and the RVNAF into a classic "no-win" situation. The RVNAF could not shift to the offensive and "go north" due to their military incapacity. In South Vietnam they had inadequate strength to hold everything, everywhere, against NVA forces which were rapidly becoming stronger. Because of Thieu's orders, they could not surrender territory and abandon people in an effort to consolidate their forces and military assets. As a result of Thieu's inflexible and adamant stand, none of the South Vietnamese leaders could even *discuss* proposals to give up territory and people. No plans were drawn up for withdrawal in the face of a large enemy attack, and no preparations were made for this complicated and always dangerous maneuver.

Thieu has been roundly condemned, particularly by his former South Vietnamese colleagues, for his "Four No's." And yet if his assumptions and rationale of 1973 are examined, his policy becomes more understandable. Thieu envisioned that in 1973 the Communists might take one of two paths in attempting to overcome South Vietnam. One would be by a full-blown, all-out military offensive similar to, but greater than, the Easter offensive of 1972. In this case, RVNAF would resist the NVA offensive to the limit, but certainly, thought Thieu, the United States would retaliate massively against NVA forces and North Vietnam itself. The second course Thieu visualized—*and the one he thought the enemy would adopt*—would be to try to overthrow the RVN by political warfare, subversion, and low-level violence. If the North Vietnamese carried out this form of warfare prudently and patiently, the United States would probably not retaliate. If the Communists selected this option, the South Vietnamese would have to go it alone on a hundred small battlefields, resisting Communist attacks whenever and wherever they occurred, and giving up ground here and retaking it there. Thus, Thieu entered the cease-fire period with wrong assumptions about what his enemy would do, but less forgivable, wrong assumptions about what the United States, his *former* ally, would do.

In 1973, what the United States Congress, news media, and many of its people were trying to do was to put Indochina War II completely behind them. But not all Americans felt this way. In March, Henry Kissinger, alarmed by the massive infiltration of North Vietnamese troops and equipment into South Vietnam, recommended to President Nixon that the United States bomb the Ho Chi Minh Trail or the DMZ or both. Nixon, by now knee-deep in the Watergate flood, procrastinated. He simply lacked the energy and mental concentration required to wage another bitter battle in addition to Watergate. Nixon did authorize some minor and meaningless air strikes in Laos, but nothing to stop the torrent of supplies moving down the Ho Chi Minh Trail to South Vietnam. In view of the president's lack of forceful actions in retaliation for the North Vietnamese violations, the Politburo as early as April 1973 had a strong indication that the United States would not take action against even major breaches of the agreement. It is no coincidence, then, that in early May American and South Vietnamese intelligence officers began to receive reports that the North Vietnamese were beginning to plan for a "blitzkrieg."

As spring ran into summer, the United States Congress began to exert its influence on the war in Vietnam. In June 1973, Congress passed a cut-off of funds for combat action over or in Cambodia and Laos. After a great deal of legislative maneuvering and one presidential veto, on 1 July Congress passed and the president reluctantly signed a bill which prohibited direct or indirect combat activities over, on, or near Laos, Cambodia, and *both Vietnams* after 15 August 1973. With this bill, Congress freed the Politburo's hand to strike the RVN whenever it so desired.

In October, Congress struck the Watergate-wounded president another blow by passing the War Powers Act, which provided that the president must consult with Congress before using troops in any armed conflict. The president could continue such use for sixty days without congressional approval and another thirty days if he certified in writing that the safety of the employed force required it. If Congress did not then declare war or authorize continued deployment by other legislative action, the president would have to bring the forces home. President Nixon vetoed the bill on 24 October as unconstitutional and unworkable, but Congress overrode his veto on 7 November, confirming again to Hanoi that the United States would take no retaliation for a massive violation of the Paris Agreement.

Congress gave another indication of its feelings about the war in Vietnam by its actions on the Fiscal Year 1974 Military Aid Bill for Vietnam. The administration had requested $1.6 billion in aid. Congress cut this figure to $1.126 billion, giving a clear indication of the direction in which Congress was moving—away from the war and the South Vietnamese.

In October 1973, the NVN Politburo called a Plenum (the 21st) to reappraise their policy in South Vietnam. Many factors of the situation in the South had changed since the implementation of the agreement on 28 January 1973. Some were good for North Vietnam, others bad. The favorable developments had occurred in the United States. Nixon's hands had been tied by legislative action and the War Powers Act. The slash of military aid funds to South Vietnam had forced the RVNAF onto a bare sustenance basis. The North Vietnamese propaganda attack against the RVN within the United States was beginning to bear a poisonous fruit. For the NVA the unfavorable developments occurred in South Vietnam, where the Communist political offensive had faltered, and their military posture, while improving, still required additional inputs of men and equipment. As a result, the Thieu government had made incremental, but damaging, inroads into Communist control of territory and people.

At this 21st Plenum, the North Vietnamese leaders made the fundamental decision to shift from primary emphasis on political warfare to a war-winning military offensive. It is significant to note that Le Duan had in September returned from a visit to the Soviet Union. In addition to the major decision to shift to an all-out military offensive, the 21st

Plenum made several subsidiary decisions. These were: to intensify the political and propaganda offensive in the United States to cause Congress to cut aid to the RVN; to attack remote ARVN bases and outposts; to clear a "logistics corridor" down the eastern edge of the Annamite Chain from Khe Sanh to Loc Ninh (to be used as a primary LOC and base area); to take the initiative from the RVNAF; to prepare troops and logistic installations for the future offensive; to keep military pressure on Saigon and the other major South Vietnamese cities to prevent the shift of forces that would counteract other Communist actions.[7]

There is one strange and unexplained inconsistency about the 21st Plenum between the account of Gen. Tran Van Tra (the senior commander in the South) and the report of Gen. Van Tien Dung, Giap's successor as commander of all Communist forces. Dung states in his account that the 21st Plenum convened in October 1973. This is the date accepted by other knowledgeable experts, both Vietnamese and American. Tra, however, maintains in his book that the 21st Plenum met in *April 1973*. He implies that the meeting ended sometime around *1 June 1973,* and that he disseminated the results of the Plenum to his subordinates in *September 1973*—all of this *before* Dung says that the 21st Plenum even convened. Tra is probably wrong, but the conflicting reports give the 21st Plenum, at least its date, some uncertainty.

At any rate, the ARVN troops quickly began to see the results of the 21st Plenum. Communist operations began to be more aggressive. Remote outposts and bases began to come under attack, a campaign which continued into 1974. One by one, they were lost, and since one of Thieu's "Four No's" forbade their evacuation, the troops were lost with them.

As 1973 ended, the RVN still held the upper hand. The Communist political offensive in South Vietnam had fizzled, largely because the Viet Cong political infrastructure had never recovered from the Tet offensive. Militarily, by year's end the NVA had reinforced and reequipped its forces in the south, but still lacked the potential to launch a major offensive. South Vietnam had done well in 1973, riding the momentum from recent years, but the seeds of disaster had been sown—a hostile United States Congress, abysmal RVN leadership which weakened South Vietnamese morale from top to bottom, and above all, the success of the NVN propaganda campaign in the United States and the virtual certainty of no American retaliation when the North Vietnamese openly violated the Paris Agreement.

The role the United States played in Indochina War III in 1974 is central to an understanding of the events which took place that year in Vietnam. To understand the American role, one must grasp the influence and power of the Politburo's intensified political and propaganda offensive within the United States. The philosophy and concept of Hanoi's *dich van* program against the United States has been detailed by Douglas Pike, in his book *PAVN: People's Army of Vietnam*. It is Pike's thesis that during the late sixties and early seventies a number of factors coalesced within the United States to poison the body politic and to lay it open to Hanoi's political *dau tranh*. Chief among them was the antiwar dissent. From 1968 until the signing of the Paris Agreement in 1973, the antiwar dissenters exercised an increasingly powerful role in determining not only national policy, but military strategy and even operational tactics. Some of the dissenters opposed the war for moral, political, or ideological reasons, while others attacked it on purely pragmatic grounds—it was costly, and it wasn't working. Although the antiwar movement subsided after January 1973, the embers of the old fire still simmered, awaiting only the wind of some perceived American escalation or other misdeed to reignite them.

There were other factors destroying consensus on the war. Politics and personal aspirations pitted liberal Democrats (who had applauded the war under Kennedy and Johnson) against the Nixon administration. Watergate ripped the country to shreds, destroying not only Nixon's presidency, but his foreign policy and the respect for governmental authority with it. Underlying all the rest was an abysmal ignorance and almost total lack of interest about the war, its significance, and the opposing governments and forces. Most of what the country accepted as fact about the war was either false or a polyglot of misinformation and disinformation. The result of the coalescence of these factors has been shown in preceding chapters. Antiwar dissent drove the United States from the war and forced it to settle the conflict on terms which doomed the South Vietnamese to terminal defeat. This was the climate in which Hanoi in 1974 launched its intensified campaign of political *dau tranh* within the United States.

The Politburo's propaganda program within the United States had three objectives: 1. Reduce American support to the RVN, particularly military and economic aid; 2. Make sure that United States forces did not reenter the war; and 3. Build up the credibility of the PRG as a legitimate government. The program's main effort was devoted to the simple, but lethal, theme that the RVN did not deserve American support. Hanoi launched a systematic campaign to show that the RVN had consistently and aggressively violated the terms of the Paris Agreement. The North Vietnamese charged the RVNAF with attacks against "defenseless" Viet Cong villages and units, and when the NVA did the same, the Communists passed them off as a "defensive reaction." This theme stressed that Thieu and his government, "the warmongers," wanted to continue the war and bloodshed, while the Communists, the "peace lovers," wanted to bring it to a pacific conclusion. It was Communist disinformation, but it worked.

The next charge the Communists used to attack the RVN was the accusation that the South held 200,000 political prisoners. The charge was grossly exaggerated. The United States embassy studied the allegation and announced that South Vietnam held only 35,000 prisoners of *all* types, and that the total prison capacity did not exceed 50,000. Regardless of the facts, letters poured into American editorial offices keening about Thieu's "political prisoners" and their plight of torture and mistreatment. Television programs featured interviews with people who claimed to know about Thieu's "tiger cages." So effective was this propaganda thrust that Congress passed a law in late 1973 that read: "no assistance furnished under this part . . . will be used for support of police, or prison construction or administration, within South Vietnam."[8]

The third charge the Communists leveled against the Thieu government was that it obstructed the process of political accommodation called for in the agreement. This is another falsehood. In fact, neither side wanted "reconciliation and concord." The Communists wanted victory, and Thieu wanted to survive. Neither would be served by a phony reconciliation. These new charges relating to the Paris Agreement were accompanied by a litany of old ones. The news media harped on the corruption of the Thieu government. The old myth that "ARVN wouldn't fight" surfaced again and again. Stories of torture by South Vietnamese police and mistreatment of civilians by ARVN made their usual appearance. These old chestnuts were partly true, partly false, but deadly effective.

Anti-Thieu pressures on members of Congress were immense, not only through the news media but from their constituents as well. And once again—as had occurred so often during the years of Indochina War II—the Nixon administration remained silent, giving the anti-RVN propagandists the high ground. The propaganda assault on Thieu and his government went to lengths which now almost defy comprehension. For example, Congress granted a congressional conference room to Jane Fonda and her husband, Tom Hayden, for their use in promoting the North Vietnamese *dich van* program. The two gave lectures *in the Capitol itself* which at least sixty congressional aides attended. On the conclusion of the lectures, a group of thirty-five aides formed the Capitol Hill Coordinating Committee, whose purpose was to end all aid to South Vietnam.

This committee, in alliance with liberal congressmen, almost succeeded. Congress appropriated a mere $700 million for military assistance to South Vietnam for fiscal year 1975, but from this had to be subtracted shipping expenses, certain undelivered items in previous years' programs, plus $46 million for operating expenses of the Defense Attachés Office (DAO), which administered the program. This left a total of less than $500 million, half the administration's request. This drastic cut of 60–70 percent of basic requirements would have been devastating, but other factors made it catastrophic. Inflation increased the prices on all items; ammunition costs rose 27 percent while oil skyrocketed by 400 percent. The truncated appropriation actually bought only about 20 percent—*one-fifth*—the materiel furnished in previous fiscal years. The Politburo's *dich van* program aimed at RVN support by the United States had proved to be an overwhelming success.

The Politburo's program to ensure that United States forces did not reenter the war was more muted. After all, the United States Congress had done most of that job for them. Nevertheless, Hanoi tried to buttress its American antireentry supporters by a campaign reciting the terrors of aerial bombing, the most likely form of United States retaliation. Horror stories (which were untrue) of the "carpet bombing" of Christmas, 1972, were revived and promoted by Hanoi and its supporters in America. The famous picture of the small girl who had allegedly been hit by napalm continued its grisly circuit in the United States news media.

The campaign to legitimatize the PRG was conducted in not only

South Vietnam and the United States, but in the world at large. This program emphasized the agreement's confirmation of the PRG as a legitimate government and an entity equal to the RVN. The Communist propaganda drummed out the message that the PRG wanted "concord and reconciliation" and an end to bloodshed and strife.[9] This in spite of the fact that the PRG and NVA had carried out 15,000 acts of terrorism in 1973 alone.

While Hanoi's *dich van* program succeeded, probably beyond the Politburo's expectations, it is deceptive to give all, or even much, of the credit for its success to the North Vietnamese. Almost all of the "dump Saigon" propaganda was "home-grown," without Hanoi's guidance, and with only a minimum input from the North Vietnamese of the information, misinformation, and disinformation which fueled the propaganda assaults. The congressional executioners of South Vietnam didn't need or want any help from North Vietnam in destroying the Republic of South Vietnam.

As 1974 began, the South Vietnamese appeared to be holding their own, at least militarily. They held most of the territory they had occupied in January 1973, but they had lost isolated outposts and fire support bases, mostly in the Western Highlands of South Vietnam. Monstrous problems, only dimly perceived in 1973, began to surface in 1974. Some were of Saigon's making; some were made for them by the United States.

The first impact of the drastic cuts in military aid fell on the military capability of the RVNAF. The Americans had taught, trained, and organized the South Vietnamese to fight the war "American-style"—with high-tech devices, air mobility, and profuse expenditures of ammunition and other materiel. While in theory the South Vietnamese should have adapted their armed forces to the revised conditions brought on by the Paris Agreement, in reality such a reorganization and reorientation was impossible. The South Vietnamese lacked the military experience and expertise, the equipment and facilities, and the time to dismantle its armed forces and remold them. Beyond that, any such upheaval would have invited a determined attack by the NVA forces in South Vietnam.

So, in 1974, the RVNAF had to fight a rich man's war on a pauper's budget. The result was devastating. Training in each branch of the armed forces (never an RVNAF strength) ceased altogether. Strategic mobility through the use of helicopters and cargo aircraft shrank by 50 to 70 percent. The shortage of spare parts deadlined vehicles of all types, while cannibalization additionally reduced inventories, and dwindling fuel stocks imposed a further limitation on mobility. The shortage of munitions presented a major problem. All types of artillery and mortar fires were severely curtailed. Hand grenades had to be rationed and accounted for, and the allotment of rifle ammunition was cut by about 50 percent. NVA Sr. Gen. Van Tien Dung, who in 1975 would lead the final offensive on the Republic of South Vietnam, summed up the effects of the drastic aid cuts when he wrote, "Nguyen Van Thieu was then forced to fight a poor man's war. Enemy firepower had decreased by nearly 60 percent. . . . Its mobility was also reduced by half . . ."[10]

The debilitation of the RVNAF's materiel capabilities was equaled, or exceeded, by the resulting blow to ARVN morale. The decreased use of ammunition meant more ARVN casualties, and under the shortages, the wounded, particularly, suffered. Evacuation of the injured was frequently delayed, and often had to be accomplished on Honda motorbikes or by a train of four or five gasless ambulances pulled by a truck. When the wounded arrived at a hospital, they found a shortage of medicines, antibiotics, bandages, intravenous fluids, and other life-saving devices. With the advent of the wet season and the onset of malaria, the supply of insect repellent was exhausted.

The shortages ravaged soldier morale in other ways. ARVN clothing allowances, always inadequate, were cut below subsistence level: boots were replaced every nine months instead of every six months; the issue of boot socks dropped from three to two pairs per year; the issue of uniforms was rigidly controlled. The cuts also impacted directly on the ARVN soldier's family life and on his military effectiveness. A survey made by the United States Defense Attaché's office in Saigon found that the cuts (plus other economic factors) had created a hopeless situation for many soldiers. More than 90 percent of the 6,600 ARVN soldiers polled stated that their pay did not meet their family's minimum needs, and 88 percent claimed that their standard of living had declined since 1973. The DAO report concluded that "South Vietnamese military personnel are forced to live at less than reasonable subsistence levels and that performance and mission accomplishment are seriously affected. Day to day survival . . . has caused a deterioration of performance which cannot be permitted to continue, if the South Vietnamese military is to be considered a viable force."[11] And, of course, it was permitted to continue.

Not only did ARVN morale plummet, but so did its performance of duty. Men deserted at the rate of 15,000–20,000 per month to take care of their families. Others (at least 100,000) made arrangements with their commanders to work elsewhere than at their duties. The junior officers, nearly as destitute as the enlisted men, made extra money by graft, corruption, and the sale of equipment. Those men who were held on duty joined the demoralized parade by stealing equipment and by "squeezing" the farmers and merchants for food.[12] Other long-standing RVNAF deficiencies made an additional impact on soldier morale in 1974. The leadership made no effort to improve the deplorable conditions of the men and their families. In fact, through the chain of corruption, they profited from it, and the men knew it. As the fighting heated up in 1974, commanders increasingly shunned the battlefield. In 1974, as a result of the aid cuts and other factors, a paralysis began to grip the RVNAF—a lethargic acceptance that the war was going increasingly against them and would eventually be lost.

Confronted not only by the deterioration of the RVNAF, but also by the ever-increasing strength of the enemy, what were the actions of Thieu and his JGS? In a word, prayer—a prayer that if the NVA attacked, the Americans would reenter the war and save them. The leadership, from Thieu on down, clung adamantly to this illusion of American intervention even when by mid-1974 every sign indicated that the United States would *not* reenter the war under any circumstances. The JGS, always weak and cowed by Thieu, studied no other options for rectifying the degenerating situation. Passivity and prayer were its recipe.

Nor was South Vietnam civilian morale any higher than that of the military. Cuts in the purchasing power of United States economic aid plus the virtual collapse of the South Vietnamese economy hit the civilians hard, urban and rural alike. The economy of South Vietnam had for many years depended on economic aid from the United States and on the revenue resulting from the influx of American troops. Without heavy industry or manufacturing, the people in the cities had developed a service economy supported by the free-spending Americans and their war machine. Now, that source of income had departed, leaving in its place massive unemployment. The United States Agency for International Development (USAID) estimated that in 1974, one-third of the urban labor force was out of work, and that urban per capita income fell between 36 percent and 48 percent between 1971 and 1974. The reeling economy was given another blow by inflation. From January 1971 to September 1974, food prices went up by 313.8 percent, while other items soared by 333.0 percent. By 1974, inflation was running away with the economy. Prices in Saigon increased 26 percent in 1972, 45 percent in 1973, and 63 percent in 1974.

The situation in the countryside was no better. There, heavy movement of rural dwellers and refugees to the cities had created a farm labor shortage. Under United States auspices, the farmers had modernized rice production, utilizing mechanization, electrical-powered irrigation, and fertilizer. The new strains of rice (another United States import) required twice as much fertilizer as did the traditional strains. All of these innovations in 1974 backfired on the peasant and the rural economy as inflation began to stalk the rice paddies. From 1972–1974, the price of fertilizer rose 285 percent. Fuel for mechanization and irrigation increased by 250 percent. The price of rice rose 143 percent between 1972 and 1974, but the farmers still lost money. The plight of the farmers in 1974 became as desperate as that of their urban counterparts. Underlying these economic woes was the old problem of corruption. In April 1974, the "fertilizer scandal" erupted, revealing a high-level plot to hoard and sell fertilizer at inflated prices on the black market. Implicated in it were Thieu, his family, his minister of trade, and ten province chiefs. USAID in one study of the South Vietnamese economy stated that corruption was "enough to have been a key factor in the 1973–1974 recession."[13]

The drastic cut in United States aid, the worsening economic conditions, and the decline in the effectiveness of the RVNAF brought on major political problems for Thieu in 1974. In previous years, his domestic political allies had stood uneasily behind him assuming that he alone could obtain adequate United States aid. When the United States Congress dissolved this myth, Thieu's supporters began to distance themselves from him, and his coalition began to crumble. Some, principally the army officers, thought he ought to be tougher, move toward a more autocratic rule needed to oppose a totalitarian and ruthless enemy. Others argued that Thieu ought to seek some contact and accommodation with the PRG. They contended that the neutralists, the "Third Force," and the PRG were basically South Vietnamese, and that some governmental *modus operandi* might be worked out.

Then, in 1974, Thieu had trouble with the religious groups and minorities. He lost the support of his coreligionists, the Catholics. The Pope urged Thieu and the Catholics toward accommodation with the PRG. When Thieu adamantly rejected this Papal advice, the Catholics deserted him. Some went further than desertion. Father Tran Huu Thanh organized an Anti-Corruption Campaign aimed at Thieu and his senior military and civilian subordinates. One senior South Vietnamese, the RVN's last prime minister, Nguyen Ba Can, called this desertion by the Catholics ". . . the most catastrophic political move. The Vietnamese Catholic community, which was the best organized force in the country fighting Communism, now [in 1974] abandoned its will to resist and took steps toward coexistence."[14]

Not to be outdone, in 1974 the An Quang Buddhists, always a troublesome sect, increased their resistance to Thieu. They sparked movements, secret societies, violence, and riots. At the same time, the Hoa Hao sect in the Mekong Delta withdrew their previous support for Thieu. Always a militant group, the Hoa Hao armed ARVN deserters and draft-dodgers and organized them into military units to oppose Thieu. To cap things off, the Montagnards, primitive tribes who lived in the Western Highlands, turned against Thieu. Their grievances included exploitation by ARVN officers, theft of livestock, destruction of crops and villages by the soldiers, and favoritism in promotions and decorations towards ethnic Vietnamese over Montagnards.

The net political result was aptly described by Can: ". . . either because of a fatal combination of circumstances or because of some magical orchestration, the religious and political parties, the press and other influential groups such as the lawyers—even those traditionally regarded as favorable to the government—expressed their discontent and seemed united in a front of protest which brought disorder to the country, thus affecting seriously the armed forces' morale and the population's confidence."[15]

All of the woes discussed above, of course, further eroded popular morale. And to add to the troubles of their own making, the obvious abandonment of South Vietnam by the United States traumatized the people. In 1974 the fight went out of them; they sensed that the RVN was doomed; and that even without an enemy attack the Thieu regime was on the point of collapse. With this realization came the final blow—the psychological disintegration of the South Vietnamese people. As Can put it, "the war had lasted too long, had been too costly, and had offered too few prospects of favorable termination."[16]

As 1974 began, the Politburo, beguiled by the product of the 21st Plenum, its 21st Resolution, failed to see clearly the signs of the approaching disintegration of the South Vietnamese government, its social fabric, and its armed forces. Hanoi simply couldn't believe that the RVN might well collapse from its own afflictions. One of the factors which blinded the North Vietnamese to the erosion of the Thieu government was the weakness of their own PRG, particularly in the cities. In fact, the PRG itself was laced with major problems of manpower and morale. Ironically, the Politburo—the self-appointed experts at combining military, political, and psychological *dau tranh*—nearsightedly pursued the path established by the 21st Plenum, a path posted by three landmark decisions: 1. to intensify the NVN political *dau tranh* against South Vietnam and the United States; 2. to complete NVA preparations for a major offensive scheduled tentatively for 1976; and 3. to conduct more aggressive military operations during 1974. In March 1974 the NVN Military Committee and NVA General Staff recommended to the Politburo (which approved) that in 1974 the NVA forces in South Vietnam intensify its attacks on isolated ARVN outposts, bases, and communication centers. The military committee called this tactic "strategic raids."

Taking a longer look, the committee intensified preparations for the upcoming offensive. NVA divisions in northern South Vietnam were withdrawn north of the DMZ and refitted, reinforced, and given new equipment such as tanks, artillery, and antiaircraft guns and missiles. Logistic arrangements to support a large, mobile, conventional army group were escalated. NVA engineers completed the eight-meters-wide hard-surface road east of the Annamites from the DMZ to Loc Ninh. Another NVA group finished the gasoline pipeline from the DMZ through the Central Highlands to Loc Ninh. NVA signal personnel strung a total of 20,000 kilometers of telephone lines throughout South Vietnam. In base areas throughout Laos, Cambodia, and South Vietnam, NVA logistic personnel established and expanded giant depots, training centers, hospitals, and repair facilities. Hanoi at last realized that logistics had always been the NVA's "Achilles' heel," and that a modern conventional army requires a modern and effective logistical system. Such a modernized logistical system was *the* key to battlefield success. When it was in readiness, the final invasion would be launched.

To prepare the striking force for the great offensive, the NVA General Staff in the late spring of 1974 began a major reorganization of combat units. Separate Regional and Main Force battalions were formed into regiments, and separate regiments were amalgamated into divisions. Most significantly, the divisions became part of NVA corps. I (First) Corps was organized from divisions around Hanoi in May 1974; II Corps was formed of units around the DMZ and the two northern provinces of South Vietnam in July 1974; IV Corps was established in the southern Highlands and Cambodia; later, III Corps was formed in the Central Highlands. So, to a vastly increased logistic capacity, the NVA General Staff added a streamlined, modern command system.

While the NVA General Staff designed these long-range improvements and reorganizations to implement the projected general offensive, the "strategic raids" concept was being carried out in 1974. The NVN Military Committee and its subordinate headquarters intended these strategic raids to accomplish both general and specific goals. The general goals were: 1. to regain the initiative, which ARVN had generally held in 1973; 2. to gain control of additional territory and people; 3. to attrite ARVN forces; 4. to lower South Vietnamese morale by a combination of aggression and attrition; and 5. to sharpen the combat edge of their troops and staffs in preparation for the 1975 offensive.

The specific goals of the strategic raids varied by area. In the Mekong Delta, they possessed little more significance than grabbing for land and people. In and around Saigon, the raids assumed a more focused aspect. They were intended for two purposes: one, cut Saigon off from the Mekong Delta on the south, from the sea at Vung Tau on the southeast, and from central South Vietnam on the north; two, erase ARVN outposts which blocked Communist LOC's and future avenues of NVA advance from remote areas toward Saigon. The urgency of these dual-purpose attacks is revealed by COSVN's order that they be continued through the wet season (May–October) in contrast to the practice which the Communists had followed for some two decades.

To isolate Saigon, Gen. Tran Van Tra, the B-2 Front commander, ordered the 5th NVA Division (the old 5th VC) to attack from Cambodia southeast towards Highway 4 south of Saigon to cut the principal route

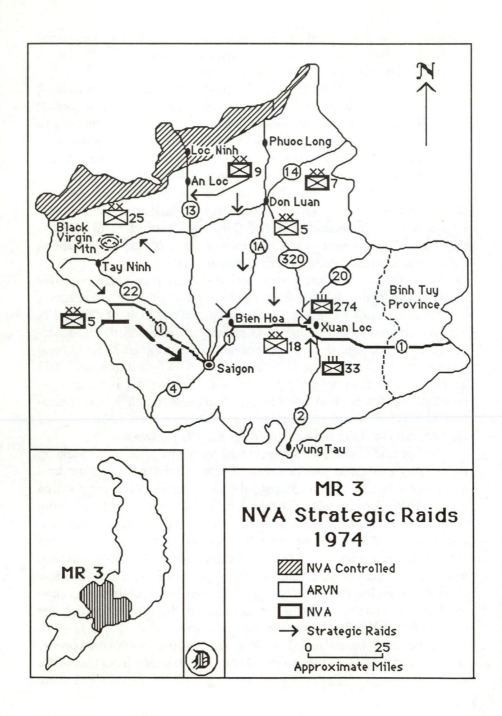

MR 3
NVA Strategic Raids
1974

between the capital and the Mekong Delta. After heavy fighting, the attack was repulsed. In another effort to isolate Saigon, Tra pushed a major attack by two NVA separate regiments toward Xuan Loc, a major communications hub, thirty-seven miles northeast of Saigon. Xuan Loc was critical since through or near it ran Highway 1, which connected Saigon to central South Vietnam, Highway 2, which led from Saigon through Xuan Loc to the sea at Vung Tau, and Highway 20, which led to the Highlands and the produce-rich gardens of Da Lat. After weeks of inconclusive fighting in the ARVN outposts surrounding Xuan Loc, the enemy was repulsed.

In addition to his efforts to isolate Saigon, Tra made several raids to shorten his LOC's and his future avenues of approach to Saigon. To grasp this aspect of Tra's concept of "strategic raids," one must be privy to Tra's long-range plans for the seizure of Saigon in the culminating offensive to be launched in 1975 or 1976. His plan for the reduction of Saigon—incidentally, the identical plan he had tried (and failed with) at Tet 1968—envisioned a five-prong attack on the RVN capital. One prong would advance from the northwest along the general line Tay Ninh/Saigon; another from the north from An Loc; another from the northeast via Bien Hoa; a fourth from the south; and the fifth, and last, from the west. To prepare the ground for his eventual five-pronged assault, he attacked a series of ARVN outposts northwest, north, and east of Saigon to clear the way for his future offensive. He took most of the outposts he attacked (with overwhelming numbers) and succeeded by the fall of 1974 in bringing his forces into position much nearer Saigon.

The NVA's strategic raids in MR2 (the Central Highlands and the country between Nha Trang and Da Nang) followed a purposeful pattern also. Like Tra's attacks farther south, the assaults in this area had two missions; one, to eliminate the ARVN outposts in or near the NVA "logistic corridor" from the DMZ down the east side of the Annamite Chain to Loc Ninh; two, to push the ARVN outposts and units out of the foothills onto the narrow coastal plain and to move NVA units into advanced positions near the major coastal cities. To accomplish the first mission (clear the "logistic corridor"), the NVA launched attacks in overwhelming numbers against ARVN outposts at Dak Pek, Tieu Atar, and Plei Me in the Highlands. The first two outposts fell, while the third, Plei Me, managed to hold on after heavy fighting. The second

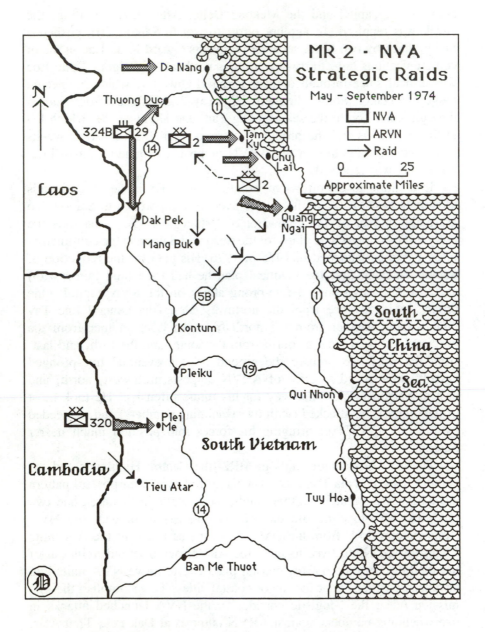

MR 2 · NVA
Strategic Raids

May – September 1974

NVA
ARVN
→ Raid

0   25
Approximate Miles

Da Nang
Thuong Duc
324B 29
2
Tam Ky
Chu Lai
2
Quang Ngai
Laos
Dak Pek
Mang Buk
Kontum
Pleiku
Qui Nhon
Plei Me
320
South Vietnam
Cambodia
Tieu Atar
Tuy Hoa
Ban Me Thuot

South China Sea

mission of the raids in middle South Vietnam (pushing up to the coastal plain) featured a series of NVA west-to-east attacks and movements in the northern portion of the area. Most of these NVA attacks were costly, but successful. The end of the wet season saw NVA units within artillery range of every major city (Da Nang, Quang Ngai City, and Qui Nhon) in the central region.

In the northern third of South Vietnam, the NVA devoted the main effort of their strategic raids to the isolation of the old Imperial capital, Hue. Lieutenant General Truong, the ARVN I Corps commander, as usual, handled his forces skillfully. There were a series of hard fights southeast of Hue in which ARVN gave as good as it got, but the ring around Hue did contract.

The NVA's strategic raids carried out from March through October 1974 were successful. Looking first at their general purpose, one sees that the raids did seize the initiative, did regain territory and population, did attrite ARVN and lower South Vietnamese morale, and did sharpen the combat effectiveness of the NVA troops. The raids accomplished, by and large, their specific goals also. The NVA "logistic corridor" was cleared; NVA units throughout South Vietnam opened strategic lines of advance to future major objectives; and in some cases, units had even arrived on or near their "jump-off points" for the major offensive.[17]

The success of the "strategic raids" and the signs of the increasing disintegration of the RVN persuaded Le Duan to call for a shift in strategy. From July 1974 until October, the Politburo debated what action to take in the dry season of 1974–1975. By the end of October the Politburo had tentatively decided on a strategy for 1975 and 1976. For 1975, the concept called for intensified attacks in the Mekong Delta as the main battlefield, and a conservation of forces throughout the rest of South Vietnam by employing more small-scale strategic raids to open avenues towards critical target areas and to widen the "logistic corridor" east of the Annamites. The Politburo intended to mount the big, war-winning offensive in 1976.

The Politburo had obviously chosen a conservative strategy, in fact, a downright timid one, and there were reasons for this timidity. First, the North Vietnamese had been burned twice by premature "Great Offensives, Great Uprisings,'' once at Tet in 1968 and again in 1972. There had been no uprisings, great or small, and the ''Great Offensives'' had only brought monstrous casualties. So, now, in 1974, they were understandably reluctant to put the issue again to a major test of arms. Another factor contributed to the Politburo's reluctance to go all-out in 1975—it overestimated the strength of the RVNAF. The NVA ''strategic raids'' of the first half of 1974 revealed some decline of ARVN capabilities, but the General Staff believed that RVNAF, technically at least, still held a superiority of overall combat strength.

The third factor which stayed the Politburo's hand was its perception that the NVA troops in South Vietnam lacked adequate logistic support for a major offensive. In November 1974, Le Duc Tho, by this time the second-most powerful man in North Vietnam behind Le Duan, told the COSVN delegation that ''Our materiel stockpiles are still very deficient, especially with regards to weapons and ammunition. . . . Therefore, we must limit the fighting in 1975 in order to save our strength for 1976, when we will launch large-scale attacks. . .''[18] A final factor pushed the Politburo towards caution—the possibility of United States reentry into the war. Hanoi agreed as of October that 1974 American reentry was improbable, but the North Vietnamese lacked total conviction that the United States would stay out. Only events which took place in December 1974 and January 1975 would provide that necessary certainty.

In late October 1974, the Politburo called to Hanoi the major field commanders and political chiefs from the battle areas to brief them on the strategic concepts for 1975–1976. And this call initiated a burlesque of military decision-making, for one of those summoned to the briefing was Gen. Tran Van Tra, commander of the B-2, ''Bulwark'' Front, the front comprising the southern half of South Vietnam.

To understand what happened in Hanoi in November and December 1974, one must know something about Tran Van Tra. Tra was a Southerner, having been born in 1918 in Quang Ngai province.[19] He had converted to communism in 1940, and, like many of his comrades, spent a couple of years in French prisons. During Indochina War I, he remained in South Vietnam in a relatively obscure post while Giap and Van Tien Dung, among others, fought the French and eventually won the major victory at Dien Bien Phu. He ''regrouped'' to the North after the Geneva Accords, where he worked his way up to be a major general in 1958. In 1963 Tra came south again. By 1968, he had become the commander of the B-2 Theatre with the rank of lieutenant general. In 1968, he sold the Politburo on making a major attack on Saigon. It failed with heavy losses, and Tra's star faded with it.

In fact, by 1974, Tra was a "maverick" in the Communist military hierarchy. He was a die-hard Southerner in an "establishment" dominated by Northerners and transplanted Southerners who had "turned Yankee." Their victory over the French in 1954 had solidified Giap, Dung, and company into a homogeneous clique, to which Tra, who had sat out Indochina War I in some unimportant Southern command, could not hope to join. Tra had a galling self-confidence, a mountainous ego, and a "wiseass" attitude. Finally, Tra was obsessed with *his* concept of how to win the war. He devoutly believed that the war in the South would *not* be won by attacks around the DMZ and Hue, *not* by attacks in Cambodia and the Mekong Delta. With a true believer's faith, he saw victory resulting *only* from an all-out massive assault on Saigon, to make "the final attack on the enemy's headquarters lair and conclude the war," as he put it.[20]

In the summer and early fall of 1974, Tra and his comrades at COSVN hammered out a plan to carry out his concept of winning the war by an assault on Saigon. Tra envisioned an open-ended concept for his operation in 1975, featuring hard, intensified combat throughout his theatre, particularly around Saigon. If things went well, he *might* end up assaulting Saigon in 1975. If obstacles appeared, he would just prepare the way, waiting until 1976 to attack the RVN capital. No matter how his plan turned out, several preliminary operations had to be under-taken early in 1975 (see map p. 754). He had to clear the Tay Ninh/Saigon avenue of approach and take Mount Ba Den (the Black Virgin), a black symmetrical mountain dominating the Tay Ninh plain which provided an essential ARVN signal communications relay and observation site. Second, Tra proposed to take several key towns north and northwest of Saigon as staging areas for the eventual attack on the city from those directions. Third, and most critical, Tra wanted to take the ARVN-held key road junction and town of Don Luan (sometimes called Doan Duc or Dong Xoai). He had to clear Don Luan so that he could move supplies and troops from Cambodia and the "logistic corridor" to the east of Bien Hoa to establish a base for his eastern thrust at Saigon. As an afterthought, Tra noted that "if conditions permitted," the fall of Don

Luan would isolate the province of Phuoc Long and make it an easy target.[21]

It was Tra and this plan which would set in motion a Mack Sennet scenario within the Politburo and the NVA General Staff—a comedy of actions, reactions, reversals, double-dealings, and old-fashioned ward-heeling politics. Tra's account reveals a performance which would blast forever the Communist pomposity about their scientific approach to decision-making in war, as trumpeted by Marx, Lenin, Mao, and Giap.

According to Tra's chronicle of events, in late October, the Politburo invited Tra and his political boss, Pham Hung, the number one man in COSVN, to motor from his headquarters in Cambodia to Hanoi. Tra and Hung left on 13 November. On about this same date, the General Staff in Hanoi and General Dung himself dispatched an NVA major general, who had been hospitalized in Hanoi, to go to COSVN and the B-2 Theatre and give those headquarters the decision of the Politburo of the strategic concepts for the years 1975 and 1976. At the same time, the General Staff fired off a message telling Tra and Hung to stay at home. Tra claims that the two leaders never received the message—so much for the 20,000 kilometers of NVA communications. Tra wrote in his brash way that even if he had gotten the message, he and Hung would have gone to Hanoi anyway. Fact is, he probably did get it. This message is significant in that it shows the antipathy of the General Staff towards Tra. Not only was Tra a maverick and a "Johnny one note" (Take Saigon!), but in October he had brassily asked the General Staff to send him four divisions *immediately* to carry out *his* plan. Hanoi promptly refused. So, in November, it was obvious that Hanoi's military establishment did not want Comrade Tra around screwing up their plans.

Tra and Hung arrived in Hanoi on 22 November, and the rodeo began. The operations officer of the General Staff, Major General Hien, briefed Tra and Hung on the approved concepts for 1975 and 1976. Tra saw immediately that his ambitious plan for the B-2 Theatre in 1975 was in jeopardy. Contrary to Tra's plan, the NVA General Staff put forth a cautious strategy. Tra immediately objected, arguing that it did not take advantage of the opportunities furnished by ARVN's declining capabilities and the devastating problems of the Thieu government.

A couple of days after the initial briefing, the General Staff dealt Tra another blow. *Without telling him,* Gen. Van Tien Dung (acting on Le Duan's orders) sent a message to COSVN and the B-2 headquarters (which in turn informed Tra) canceling the Don Luan operation, Tra's key operation for the early 1974–1975 dry season campaign. And worse was to follow. The General Staff ordered the NVA 7th Infantry Division (with which Tra had planned to take Don Luan) and the 429th Sapper Regiment (an elite commando-type unit) to the B-3 Front in the Southern Highlands. With these two decisions, the General Staff thoroughly shredded Tra's plans for the B-2 Theatre in 1975.

The actions of the NVA General Staff (and Dung) confound any experienced military professional. Their action violated not only every axiom governing staff work and command relations, every custom and courtesy of any army, but common sense as well. What kind of army would issue orders to a major command behind the commander's back, especially when he is present in the issuing headquarters? What kind of an army would countenance such an insult to a major commander without summarily relieving him? What kind of an army was this? And this overall question becomes more pointed because Tra (and Hung) accepted this abuse as if it were commonplace—at least that is what Tra implies in his account.[22]

But Tran Van Tra hadn't gotten to be a theatre commander and a lieutenant general by taking such double-dealing passively. He mobilized Pham Hung and together they wangled a meeting with the NVN Military Committee to present the viewpoint of COSVN and the B-2 Theatre and their plan for operations in 1975. The meeting took place on 3 December, with Tra arguing for his old plan and for retaining the 7th Division under his command. Tra, never shy, asked not only to keep the 7th Division, but brazenly asked again for additional divisions from other theatres. After considerable and heated discussion, Tra was told that he could keep the 7th Division, but that he must send the 429th Sapper Regiment to the Highlands. The Military Committee also informed Tra that a decision would be made later on his now-suspended Don Luan attack.

Then matters took another unconventional twist. A few nights later (somewhere around 6 December), Hung received a telephone call from Le Duan, asking that he and Tra meet him that night at his home. After the preliminary pleasantries, Le Duan turned the conversation to

Tra's proposed Don Luan operation. Tra bluntly asked Le Duan why he had canceled the operation. Le Duan told him that the General Staff had informed him (Le Duan) that Tra's plan involved the use of large Main Force units at the start of the dry season, and that he had canceled it to conserve forces. Tra explained that his plan didn't envision the use of large forces to take Don Luan—a lie, incidentally, since Tra planned to use four regiments in the operation. After some more discussion, Le Duan approved the operation and told Tra to carry it out. Tra, of course, sent a message immediately to that effect to his command. So now, there was a Grade-A mess in which the NVA General Staff had canceled an operation and taken troops from a major commander without telling him, then halfway reversed itself, and then the political chief reversed the General Staff without *its* knowledge or input. An example—to quote Tra—"of the era of revolution and science with the leadership of a Marxist-Leninist Party . . . ."?[23]

Sooner or later, such haphazard and unprofessional decision-making is paid for by the troops in the field, and that was the case here. By the time the second change arrived, the NVA troops (the 7th NVA Division) scheduled for the Don Luan operation were moving to the Highlands. The tanks and 130mm artillery (which were to support the attack on Don Luan) had been sent back to the base area in Cambodia. With the Don Luan operation now approved, the troops had to countermarch back towards Don Luan and the operation had to be prepared all over again. As a result, the attack on Don Luan had to be delayed until 22 December. On 26 December, following a 1,000-round artillery preparation, elements of the 7th NVA Division captured Don Luan. Tra now had his corridor to the east, and Phuoc Long province and its capital, Phuoc Long City, were ripe for the plucking. And Comrade Tra had a plan for that plucking.

He planned to keep the ARVN III Corps commander so busy throughout his area of responsibility that he could not send significant reinforcements to Phuoc Long. Accordingly, Tra launched the newly formed 6th NVA Division in an attack in Binh Tuy province, east of Saigon. Near Tay Ninh City, northwest of Saigon, the 205th NVA Regiment, reinforced with artillery, attacked outlying posts and Mount Ba Den. ARVN repulsed the attacks after heavy fighting, although the South Vietnamese company holding the Black Virgin Mountain eventually had to withdraw. Tra's diversionary attacks accomplished their purpose. The

III ARVN Corps commander, General Dong, was so busy putting out fires all over his Corps area that he could devote little of his attention or limited resources to avoid the approaching disaster in Phuoc Long.

As General Dong saw the noose tightening around Phuoc Long, he managed to scrape up one battalion of the 7th ARVN Infantry Regiment of the 5th ARVN Division and airlift it into the city. So, when the battle began, this reinforcement, the only regular unit in or near the city, plus two good Regional Force battalions, had to try to hold Phuoc Long City. In addition, there were about 3,000 disorganized South Vietnamese Regional and Popular Force troops which the NVA units had driven into the city from surrounding outposts. These troops were a net deficit.

The NVA assault forces had massive superiority. Tra used two infantry divisions, the 7th NVA Division and the newly formed 3d NVA Division, reinforced by two separate infantry regiments, an antiaircraft regiment, an artillery regiment, and a tank regiment, all under the command of IV NVA Corps. The result of this one-sided battle was foregone. The ARVN fought well, but had no chance against the smothering NVA artillery fire and the overwhelming tank-supported infantry attacks of about three infantry divisions. On 6 January 1975, Phuoc Long City fell to Tra and his IV Corps.

The RVNAF could do little to prevent the disaster. The South Vietnamese Air Force was impotent, lacking planes, combat expertise, and the stomach to come in low enough to furnish the embattled garrison adequate close air support. Since the NVA held all roads in Phuoc Long City, any reinforcement and resupply had to be by air and the ARVN airlift capability simply wasn't there. To cap matters off, the JGS had no major units in reserve. The usual strategic reserve, the marine division and the airborne division, were tied down in the I ARVN Corps area far to the north. The JGS belatedly ordered the only unit available, the 81st Airborne Rangers, to send two companies into Phuoc Long City. They landed just in time to become grist for the NVA mill which had already ground up the other ARVN units in the town. ARVN suffered heavy casualties in the debacle. Out of the 5,400 men of different units committed, fewer than 850 survived. The two companies of rangers lost all but 85 men, the ARVN infantry battalion all but 200. The civilian officials who were captured were summarily executed.

The casualties plus the loss of a whole South Vietnamese province further demoralized the already disheartened people of South Vietnam. ARVN and the Thieu government had clearly revealed their impotence to avert the disaster. On the other side, the NVA had shown not only overwhelming strength, but an heretofore unseen professionalism in the conduct of its attacks. Beyond this contrast between the two contenders, the battle for Phuoc Long demonstrated to both the North and the South that regardless of provocation, the United States would not intervene to save South Vietnam. This was the Republic of South Vietnam's last hope, and with its death, both sides drew the same conclusion—the North would win the war.

Notes—Chapter 25

1. Gen. Cao Van Vien, *The Final Collapse,* Indochina Monographs (Washington, D.C.: U.S. Army Center of Military History, 1982), p. v; and Stephen T. Hosmer, Konrad Keller, Brian M. Jenkins, *The Fall of South Vietnam: Statements by Military and Civilian Leaders* (Santa Monica, CA: Rand Corp., 1978), p. 6.
2. Col. Gen. Tran Van Tra, *Vietnam: History of the Bulwark B-2 Theatre, Vol 5: Concluding the 30-Years War* (Ho Chi Minh City: Van Nghe Publishing Plant, 1982), p. 33.
3. William E. Le Gro, *Vietnam From Cease-Fire to Capitulation* (Washington, D.C.: U.S. Army Center of Military History, 1981), p. 28.
4. William J. Duiker, *The Communist Road to Power in Vietnam* (Boulder, CO: Westview Press, 1981), p. 301.
5. Nixon, *No More Vietnams,* p. 184.
6. Hosmer, Keller, and Jenkins, *The Fall,* p. 43.
7. Sr. Gen. Van Tien Dung, *Great Spring Victory* (Foreign Broadcast Information Service, *Daily Report: Asia and Pacific,* Vol. 4, No. 110, Supplement 38, 7 June 1976), I:1–2; Vien, *Final Collapse,* pp. 38–39; Tra, *Bulwark,* pp. 53 and 65; Tang, *Vietcong Memoir,* p. 229.
8. Public Law 93-189, 17 December 1973.
9. Tang, *Vietcong Memoir,* p. 227.
10. Dung, *Great Spring Victory,* I:5.
11. Anthony B. Lawson, "Survey of the Economic Situation of RVNAF Personnel, Phase III," report by the DAO Special Studies Section, pp. 2–17; quoted in Stuart A. Herrington, *Peace with Honor* (Novato, CA: Presidio Press, 1983), pp. 86–87.
12. U.S. Committee on Foreign Relations, *Vietnam: May 1974,* a staff report, 93d Congress, 2d Session, 5 August 1974, p. 6.
13. Gabriel Kolko, *Anatomy of a War: Vietnam, the United States, and the Modern Historical Experience* (New York: Pantheon Books, 1985), p. 493.
14. Hosmer, Keller, and Jenkins, *The Fall,* p. 19.
15. Ibid., p. 20.
16. Ibid., p. 60.
17. For a detailed and excellent discussion of the NVA "strategic raids," see Le Gro, *Vietnam from Cease-Fire to Capitulation,* pp. 96–132.
18. Tra, *Bulwark,* p. 106.
19. Pike, *PAVN,* p. 359. The bulk of the biographical material on Tra is from Pike's *PAVN.*

20. Tra, *Bulwark,* pp. 93, 96–98.
21. Ibid., pp. 100–101.
22. Ibid., p. 108.
23. Ibid., p. 112.

26 Defeat

Beginning on 18 December 1974, a week before the attack on Don Luan, the North Vietnamese Politburo and Military Committee met once more to determine the operational concepts governing its 1975 campaign. The NVA General Staff remained cautious, tentatively selecting a series of attacks which would expand its "logistic corridor" east of the Annamites. The staff selected as its main effort a three-division attack on Duc Lop, a minor post on Highway 14 in the Southern Highlands. Although the Highlands area was not his responsibility, the irrepressible Gen. Tran Van Tra gave the General Staff the benefit of his strategic acumen anyway. He told them that Duc Lop was unimportant, and that *if* the General Staff planned to use three divisions, that it should use them against something significant, and suggested Ban Me Thuot. And Ban Me Thuot *was* significant. It sat astride Highway 14, the main north-south road inland, and Highway 21, which connected Ban Me Thuot to the sea at Nha Trang and Phan Rang. It was a large town, the capital of Darlac province, and the site of an RVNAF air base.

General Hien, the operations officer of the NVA General Staff, stung by Tra's kibitzing, huffily stated that if the NVA was going to grab a major city in the Highlands that it should mount a multidivision thrust at Kontum, followed by an attack on Pleiku (the two key cities). This offensive would clear the whole Highlands area. But Tra, always the smart-ass, had a ready rejoinder, which he describes: "I disagreed. I smiled and said in a pleasant voice . . . 'I think that to attack Kontum and Pleiku is to attack where the enemy is strongest, . . . the enemy would be on guard. . . . But to attack Ban Me Thuot would be to completely surprise the enemy and to attack the enemy's undefended rear. . . . If their rear area was taken, the enemy in the forward area would be perplexed and shaken.' "[1] With this and other debates going on, the conference on the NVA concept of operations for 1975 dragged on through December 1974 into January 1975. There were other reasons for delay. The Politburo wanted to see: first, how the fighting at Phuoc Long was going to come out; and more critically, if the United States would intervene to save that doomed city and province. On 6 January, the North Vietnamese leaders had the critical answer. The United States would not intervene, and now the concept for 1975 could be solidified.

On 8 January, Le Duan concluded the conference by giving the Politburo's guidance for the 1975 campaign to the Military Committee and the General Staff. The main effort, he said, would be made in the Central Highlands with attacks, not *against,* but *toward* Ban Me Thuot and Tuy Hoa on the coast. Binh Dinh province, continued Le Duan, would be cleared of ARVN forces and this "liberated area" extended northward. On the B-4 Front (the Quang Tri-Thua Thien area), the NVA would seize control of the area between Hue and Da Nang.

Le Duan's guidance of 8 January had been transparently indecisive concerning the attack on Ban Me Thuot. Tra, ever the opportunist, collared Le Duan after the conference and again made his pitch for attacking Ban Me Thuot. Le Duan said nothing. On the Ban Me Thuot controversy Le Duan was caught between General Dung and the General Staff on the one hand, who didn't want to attack Ban Me Thuot, and the more aggressive clique of Southerners led by Le Duc Tho and Tra, who did. So, Le Duan equivocated, intending originally to leave the matter up to the Military Committee. Then, on the night of 8 January, Le Duc Tho and his supporters began to hammer on Le Duan, and eventually Le Duan caved in to the "attack Ban Me Thuot" group.

On 9 January, the Military Committee, chaired by Giap, met to carry out the indecisive guidance Le Duan had given it the previous day. Shortly after the conference opened, Le Duc Tho strode in unannounced. He fixed the group with a cold stare and announced, "It would be absurd if with almost five divisions in the Central Highlands we could not attack Ban Me Thuot."[2] Tho then stalked out. The Politburo had spoken. Giap, somewhat shaken, went on to flesh out the details of the concept and issue (along with Dung) supplemental instructions for the campaign, now code-named "Campaign 275."

As of 9 January, then, Tran Van Tra (according to *his own book*) had bested the Military Committee and the General Staff in several substantial confrontations. He had driven them off their cautious strategic concept for 1975; he had forced them to reinstate and permit him to carry out *his* plan for the Don Luan attack and the reduction of Phuoc Long; and he had pushed them away from Duc Lop as an objective, and then away from Kontum and Pleiku, onto *his* original choice, Ban Me Thuot. A notable string of triumphs for Tra, and in the process he exposed as a fraud the "scientific decision-making of Marx and Lenin" as carried out by the North Vietnamese Politburo, its Military Committee, and the NVA General Staff.

There is a postscript to Tra's unmasking of his superiors which requires a leap forward in time. Tra escaped retribution for his undoing of Dung and the General Staff for some years, rising to positions of increasing responsibility in the postwar regime. Then, in 1982, he published his book, *History of the Bulwark B-2 Theatre, Vol. V,* revealing the unprofessional and unscientific performance of the North Vietnamese hierarchy. When Tra's book hit the streets of Hanoi and Ho Chi Minh City (Saigon), the North Vietnamese "establishment" exploded. They first tried to confiscate all the copies and tried particularly to prevent any copies from leaving Vietnam. In this they were unsuccessful, but they did even the score with Brother Tra. In 1982 or early 1983, he vanished, either into house arrest or into the Vietnamese gulag of "Reeducation Camps."[3] Toward the end of his rash book, Tra prophetically wrote about the receipt of a prestigious appointment he had not expected: ". . . I was certain that I had not been surprised for the last time. There would be many more surprises, both good ones and bad ones."[4] Brother Tra was right again—or at least half right.

While the battle of Phuoc Long marked a major turning point in Indochina War III by demonstrating the impotence of both ARVN and the United States, it was ARVN's loss of Ban Me Thuot which marked the beginning of the end for the RVN. Ban Me Thuot lay in the II ARVN Corps area, also known as RVN Military Region 2 (MR 2), which had always been a formidable area for ARVN to defend. It was a large area, mountainous, with an inadequate road net subject to easy interdiction and ambush. In the Western Highlands lived the Montagnards, usually in varying stages of rebellion against any Vietnamese government in power. In the east, the populous coastal plain of Binh Dinh province had been a hotbed of communism going back to the Vietminh days. Six key towns and cities constituted the strategic points in the corps area. In the Western Highlands these were Kontum, Pleiku (the site of the corps headquarters), and Ban Me Thuot, each province capitals, key road centers, and sites of a major airfield. On the coast, the three critical cities were Nha Trang, Tuy Hoa, and Qui Nhon—province capitals, major ports, and airfield sites. The immense distances between these strategic areas, the undependable road net, and the airfields placed a high premium on good, timely intelligence and on rapid reinforcement by air.

The importance of these factors was magnified by the overall scarcity of ARVN combat troops and resources in the corps area. ARVN stationed two divisions in the II ARVN Corps area, plus seven ranger groups (regiments) and one armored brigade. The 22d ARVN Division of four regiments held the coastal lowlands of Binh Dinh and Phu Yen provinces. The 23d ARVN Division defended the Highlands with three regiments at Pleiku, one at Ban Me Thuot. Most of the ranger groups were arrayed west of Kontum City, although one ranger group and some Regional Force units defended Ban Me Thuot. The ARVN troops were short of supplies of all kinds and of questionable morale.

The NVA forces in the area totaled five Main Force divisions (the 3d, F-10th, 320th, 968th, and 316th). The 3d was stationed in the coastal lowlands of Binh Dinh province, the 968th Division stood opposite Kontum, while the 10th, 320th, and 316th could concentrate against Ban Me Thuot. In addition to the NVA divisions, there were fifteen regiments of tanks, artillery, antiaircraft, and engineers in the area, a total of 75,000 to 80,000 men. The NVA troops were eager, well supplied, and well led. The overall commander was Giap's successor, Sr. Gen. Van Tien Dung, who had been sent by the Politburo to organize and conduct the attack on Ban Me Thuot, probably to assuage his ego after Comrade Tra had demolished his 1975 strategic concept.

Dung's plan for the attack on Ban Me Thuot was simple. He would secretly concentrate an overwhelming force against the city. He would attack elsewhere in the II ARVN Corps area to divert attention from his objective. Then he would cut the roads leading into the city and capture the airfield to prevent reinforcement by ground or air. Coincidentally, he would overpower the defenders within the city.

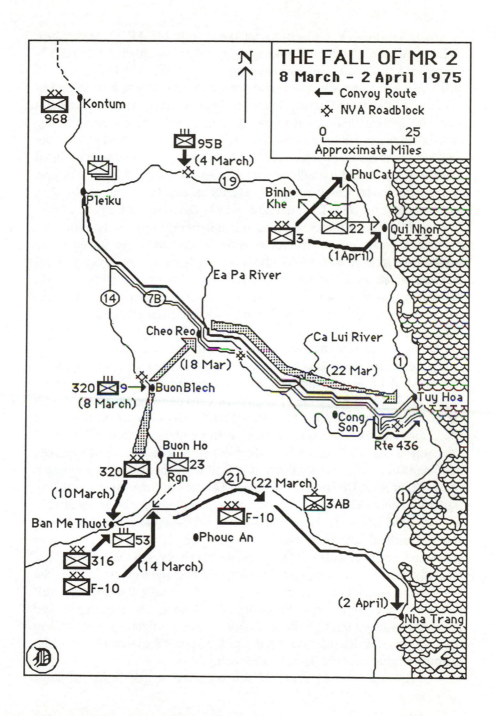

THE FALL OF MR 2
8 March – 2 April 1975
← Convoy Route
✧ NVA Roadblock

0   25
Approximate Miles

968
Kontum
95B
(4 March)
19
Pleiku
Binh Khe
Phu Cat
22
3
Qui Nhon
(1 April)
Ea Pa River
Ca Lui River
14
7B
Cheo Reo
(18 Mar)
(22 Mar)
320 9 Buon Blech
(8 March)
Tuy Hoa
Cong Son
Rte 436
Buon Ho
320
23
Rgn
(10 March)
21 (22 March)
F-10
3 AB
Ban Me Thuot
53
Phouc An
316
(14 March)
F-10
(2 April)
Nha Trang

As usual, the NVA attack got an assist from the ARVN leadership. Thieu's inflexible policy of holding everywhere doomed the II ARVN Corps to a scattered, piecemeal defense while the RVNAF's lack of airlift made it impossible to move major reserves, which didn't exist anyway, to threatened areas. The corps commander, Maj. Gen. Pham Van Phu, contributed his bit to help Dung. In spite of estimates by his own intelligence officer and the J-2, JGS, that Dung intended to make Ban Me Thuot his main objective, Phu believed up until the final moment that the NVA would assault Pleiku or Kontum, their customary targets in the Highlands. Only around 1 March would Phu grudgingly shift one regiment, the 53d, from the 23d ARVN Division, to Ban Me Thuot.

Much has been made of Phu's misjudgment, but it is doubtful that it made a great deal of difference. Phu lacked adequate forces to do what Thieu ordered him to do—hold everywhere and yet meet a three-division attack by the NVA. And if there was no way for Phu to win, there was almost no way for Dung to lose. He had the initiative, and he had the superior force. All he had to do was pick a target and concentrate his forces against it.

Dung writes that the battle for Ban Me Thuot began on 1 March with a series of minor attacks west of Pleiku to draw Phu's attention to that area. Most other authorities state that the Ban Me Thuot campaign began on 4 March when the NVA troops cut Highway 19 in two places between Qui Nhon and Pleiku. On 5 March, Highway 21 between Ban Me Thuot and the coast was blocked in three places by the 320th NVA Division. Thus the two roads leading from the coast to the Highlands had been cut in twenty-four hours. On 8 March, the 9th NVA Regiment of the 320th NVA Division cut Highway 14 north of Buon Blech, isolating Ban Me Thuot. The way had now been prepared for the main attack.

At 0200 hours on 10 March, the NVA assaulted Ban Me Thuot and the airfield east of town at Phuong Duc. NVA artillery fire was heavy and accurate, and by 1000 hours, the 320th NVA Division, attacking from the north, was well into the city. By the night of 10 March, the NVA had captured the center of the city, but heavy fighting was still going on west, south, and east of Ban Me Thuot. The fighting around the city continued through the next day. Although fighting continued in the outskirts, particularly around the airfield, on 12 March General Phu announced that Ban Me Thuot had fallen.

Sometime during 11 or 12 March occurred one of those incidents for which ARVN became infamous. The 23d ARVN Ranger group had been stationed before the attack at Buon Ho, about twenty miles north of Ban Me Thuot. As the NVA assault on Ban Me Thuot developed, the ranger group moved towards the city against light Communist opposition. It reached the outskirts of Ban Me Thuot and was driving the NVA ahead of them into the city, which at that time the 320th NVA Division held lightly. At this juncture, the division commander of the 23d ARVN Division, Brig. Gen. Le Van Tuong, halted the ranger attack and ordered them to secure a landing zone outside the town, to protect the evacuation of his wife and children by helicopter. After the evacuation, the ranger group returned to the attack on Ban Me Thuot, only to find the way now blocked by sizable enemy forces. Thus, Tuong squandered the only chance to get back into the city before the NVA troops could consolidate their hold on it.

On 12 March, President Thieu ordered General Phu to retake Ban Me Thuot. To do this, the JGS flew its last reserve unit, the 7th Ranger group, to Kontum to replace the 44th and 45th ARVN Regiments of the 23d ARVN Division. These latter units were to be airlifted to Phuoc An, from where they were to counterattack to the west to retake Ban Me Thuot and the airfield (still being held by a battalion of the 53d ARVN Regiment). The commander of the 23d ARVN Division, General Tuong, the same man who had used the rangers to cover the evacuation of his family, was to conduct the counterattack.

The ARVN counterattack jumped off on 15 March and immediately fell into chaos. There was no tank or artillery support for the ARVN infantry and little close air support. There was a shortage of all types of supplies, and none could be brought in along Highway 21, which was blocked. These factors, as important as they usually are, turned out this time to be minor causes of the disintegration of the counterattack. The element which proved catastrophic was the presence of the soldiers' families in Ban Me Thuot, the rear base of the 23d ARVN Division. When the soldiers landed in their helicopters at Phuoc An, instead of forming up to fight, they broke ranks and ran to find their wives and children. When they found them, the ARVN soldiers threw away their uniforms and weapons and started with their families for Nha Trang. And so, before it even got started, the ARVN counterattack collapsed ignominiously.

The JGS should have known better. They should have remembered the disaster the "family syndrome" caused in Quang Tri in 1972 and in several other operations before that one. And while the JGS fumbled its one play, the ARVN leaders on the scene performed poorly throughout the battle. The corps commander, Phu, misjudged the situation. He guessed incorrectly as to enemy intentions, and he made a serious mistake in judging his capability to retake Ban Me Thuot. The 23d Division commander, Tuong, who had fouled up the ranger counterattack, was even worse. On 16 March, he received a slight facial wound. Instead of slapping a Band-aid on it and going on with his job, he had himself evacuated to the safety of a hospital in Nha Trang. From Thieu on down, ARVN leadership reaped the whirlwind which eventually befalls the inflexible, the incompetent, and the cowardly.

The RVNAF, already driven to the edge of disaster, got the final shove into oblivion from a decision made by Thieu himself. There is some background for this fatal decision. By early March 1975, events in the United States had convinced Thieu that the United States would not intervene to save the RVN and that American military aid would be cut ever deeper in the future. Faced with these harsh realities, in early March, Thieu began to weigh desperate alternatives. His dire reflections were galvanized on 10 March when the three NVA divisions opened their assault on Ban Me Thuot. On 11 March, he called to the Independence Palace for a "working breakfast" the prime minister, Tran Thien Khiem, his security adviser, Lt. Gen. Dang Van Quang (known as "Fat" Quang), and Gen. Cao Van Vien, the chief of the JGS.[5] After the food was served, Thieu produced a small-scale map and calmly stated that the RVNAF could not hold everywhere and that the forces must be redeployed to protect the most vital and productive areas of South Vietnam. Thieu then showed his subordinates the map.

Thieu wanted to try to hold all territory south of an east-west line from just north of Tuy Hoa on the coast to the Cambodian border, some of which would have to be recaptured. This area contained the bulk of South Vietnam's resources and people. Farther north, most of the Highlands (including Kontum and Pleiku) would be given up. In MR 1, Thieu's concept became more ambiguous. In this area he would try to hold Hue, but if that could not be done, he would attempt to hold Da Nang. If that failed, there was Quang Ngai City, or Qui Nhon, and lastly, the final defensive position north of Tuy Hoa. Interestingly,

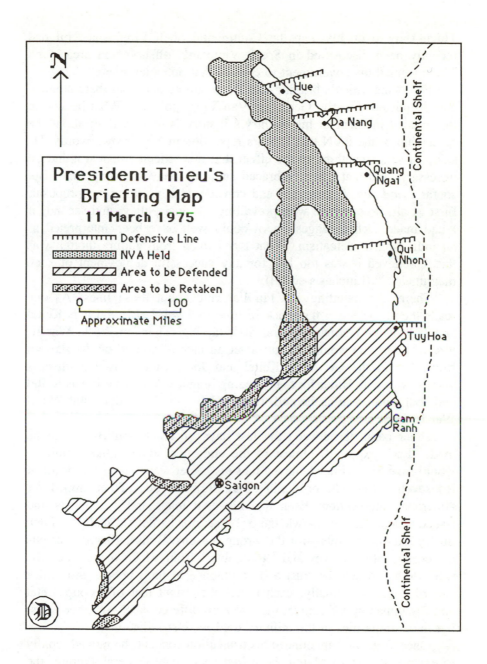

President Thieu's
Briefing Map
11 March 1975

Defensive Line
NVA Held
Area to be Defended
Area to be Retaken

0   100
Approximate Miles

Hue
Da Nang
Quang Ngai
Qui Nhon
Tuy Hoa
Cam Ranh
Saigon

Continental Shelf
Continental Shelf

N

Thieu showed on his map the Continental Shelf Line, since oil had recently been discovered in South Vietnam's offshore sea areas, and Thieu wanted his government to control that potential asset.

Following Thieu's briefing, his three subordinates sat there stunned and disquieted. Finally, Gen. Cao Van Vien spoke up. What he said at this crucial moment in his country's history is so revealing about the leadership of the RVN that it bears repetition in Vien's own words. He said, "I said something to the effect that this redeployment was indeed necessary, and that I had embraced such an idea for a long time. But so far *I had kept it to myself* and considered it an improper proposal. First of all, it conflicted with prevailing national policy, and second, if I had made such a suggestion, it could well have been interpreted as an indication of defeatism. What I *refrained* from adding though was that I believed it was too late for any successful deployment of such magnitude."[6] (Emphasis added)

There is a haunting and familiar ring about those lines. As one reads them, there is a flashback in time to 1944–1945, and it is Keitel and Jodl of the German General Staff talking. Then, in World War II, it was Hitler who would not surrender an inch of ground on the Eastern front. It was the Germans, Keitel and Jodl, who refused to discuss withdrawals with Hitler for fear of being branded defeatists. It was Keitel and Jodl who, even at the end, refrained from telling Hitler that World War II was lost.

Other parallels between the last days of Thieu and Hitler can be made. Each expected, almost to the end, that some unlikely miracle would save him. Hitler believed that his secret weapons or the death of Roosevelt, Churchill, or Stalin might turn the tide; Thieu hoped for American intervention. Each had his own maps and sycophants and issued orders without knowledge or regard for battlefield realities. Each mistrusted his generals—for the wrong reasons. Both harbored concepts of retiring into enclaves and "Redoubts" from which to continue the war. Both had lost the trust and confidence of their people and senior subordinates. And finally, each lived in constant fear of a coup d'état and assassination. Of course, the two men differed vastly in other ways, but their similarities in the military field were striking.

Once Thieu had announced his truncation concept, he moved rapidly to execute it. On 13 March, he called Lieutenant General Truong, the I ARVN Corps commander, to Saigon and told him that his corps would now give up everything except Da Nang and enough territory nearby to hold it. Truong said nothing, but later reported that he was "disturbed" by the order. He remembered 1972 and its problems, particularly those caused by fleeing refugees and military dependents. But Truong had some time to do the detailed planning such an operation requires, which was more than was given the next recipient of Thieu's truncation order, General Phu, the unfortunate commander of II ARVN Corps.

Thieu ordered Phu to meet him at the American-built air and naval base at Cam Ranh Bay on 14 March. At the meeting, Thieu asked Phu if he could retake Ban Me Thuot. Phu weaseled and said that he needed reinforcements. Thieu told him (as Phu already knew) that there were none. Then Thieu unloaded his truncation concept on Phu and ordered him: 1. to withdraw the *Regular* Forces only from Kontum and Pleiku and move them to the coast, there to be reconstituted as a force to retake Ban Me Thuot; 2. to abandon the Regional and Popular Forces, dependents, and civilians in the Pleiku-Kontum area; 3. to keep the movement secret and to execute it as soon as possible; and 4. to withdraw down Provincial Route 7B, a broken-up track which had not been used for years. (See map p. 771)

If Thieu desired to bring on a catastrophe, those four orders would be hard to beat. Taking the Regulars and leaving the other forces and civilians was bound to bring on a major panic and a frenzied flight by everyone down the same road the troops had to use. The order to make the withdrawal secret and immediate negated any prior planning, an absolute requirement in this most complex and hazardous of operations. Finally, the decision to use Route 7B was a major factor in the impending disaster. Never more than a narrow track, it had long been abandoned to the jungle. The bridges over the major streams had been destroyed and the South Koreans, who held the area prior to their departure in 1972, had mined the eastern end of the road. And when the Koreans mined a road, it "stayed mined."

As was to be expected, the withdrawal was a debacle from the start. The 20th ARVN Engineer Group moved out of Pleiku on 15 March as the lead element. This made some sense, for a great deal of engineer work would be needed to make route 7B passable. The trouble was that the engineer group had neither the training nor the right equipment to do what had to be done. On 16 March the chaotic withdrawal of the main body began. Some of the units who were supposed to leave Pleiku and Kontum didn't get the word. Others got it only at the last minute and picked up what they could quickly lay their hands on and took off, leaving vast stores of undestroyed equipment and supplies. The local troops (mostly Montagnard units) who were to be left behind rioted—killing, raping, and pillaging. The civilians and dependents, panic-stricken, joined and impeded the withdrawing columns. It was ARVN at its worst. Phu and most of the other senior officers of II Corps abandoned the troops and flew back to Nha Trang before the operation even started. The deputy corps commander, a brigadier general, flew to Tuy Hoa. Leadership and discipline rapidly disappeared. It was every unit for itself, and then every man for himself.

To complete the disaster, the NVA hit the disorganized and demoralized column. On 18 March, the column jammed up around the town of Cheo Reo because the ARVN engineers up ahead could not get a bridge across the Ea Pa River. In this defenseless state, artillery fire from the 320th NVA Division inflicted heavy casualties on both military and civilians. To add to the misery, no one was available to attend the wounded. Hundreds of damaged or destroyed vehicles lay around the town or in it.

But the tormented column staggered on. People were run over by trucks and tanks. Troops, dependents, and civilians were thoroughly intermingled. Food and water were exhausted, and when it seemed matters could get no worse, they did. The South Vietnamese Air Force, attempting to relieve NVA pressure on the column, and flying too high (as usual), hit the column, destroying four tanks, killing and wounding civilians, and virtually destroying a ranger battalion. And still the agonized column struggled on. The lead elements got over or through the Ca Lui River west of Cong Son and kept pressing onward. Then east of Cong Son, the wretched survivors ran into the next nightmare—the ARVN engineers could not clear the numerous Korean mines from the remaining route to Tuy Hoa. The engineers had to detour the column into local Route 436 and after great difficulty got a bridge across the broad Ba River.

Now the column faced the final test. The NVA, seeing the direction the column must take, set up five roadblocks between the bridge and Tuy Hoa. Here, the column was stopped again, until the 34th Ranger Battalion in a series of gallant actions cleared the roadblocks and led the "column of sorrow" into Tuy Hoa. The battalion, however, was destroyed.

The cost to ARVN and the RVN was almost beyond measure. Only 20,000 of the 60,000 troops which started for Tuy Hoa made it, and they were unfit for combat. Of the 7,000 rangers, only 700 came through. After the battle of Ban Me Thuot and the withdrawal, II ARVN Corps virtually ceased to exist as a combat force. Of the 400,000 civilians who attempted to flee the Communists, only 100,000 reached Tuy Hoa.

Of Thieu's fatal decision and of Phu's execution of that decision criticism abounds. Both Phu's execution of Thieu's decision and his own conduct were reprehensible. He was professionally incompetent and a personal coward. But Phu deserves a little better than that harsh verdict. He was a very sick man (he had tuberculosis)—a man with a good record as a division commander, but with no capacity for independent corps command. Underlying everything else, Phu had been captured by the Vietminh at Dien Bien Phu and had a horror of recapture by the NVA. In fact, senior South Vietnamese generals report that he killed himself when the Communists entered Saigon rather than be captured.[7]

As to Thieu's decision, in war as in life itself, timing is crucial. Thieu's truncation concept *might* have worked if it had been carried out in 1973, or perhaps even in early 1974. Even then, enormous military, political, and psychological problems would have plagued any such operation, requiring the most sound and detailed planning and preparation. And such planning was probably beyond the capabilities of the JGS. Of course, Thieu had another course of action—he could have left the troops in place and let them fight it out. In retrospect, this would seem to have been the better course—at least the results couldn't have been any worse than what Thieu tried to do. In all probability, however, such action (leaving the troops to fight in place) at best would only have prolonged RVN's death agony.

The disaster at Ban Me Thuot and in the Central Highlands was followed by a similar catastrophe in the I ARVN Corps area. And like the debacle in II Corps, the one in I Corps was also of Thieu's making. It will be recalled that Thieu had called Lt. Gen. Ngo Quang Truong, the I ARVN Corps commander, to Saigon on 13 March and had given him orders to give up most of the I ARVN Corps area, but to hold Da Nang and enough nearby territory to defend it. By that order Thieu confronted Truong with a most formidable task. Thieu had already dealt the defense of MR 1 a devastating blow, when on 10 March he ordered

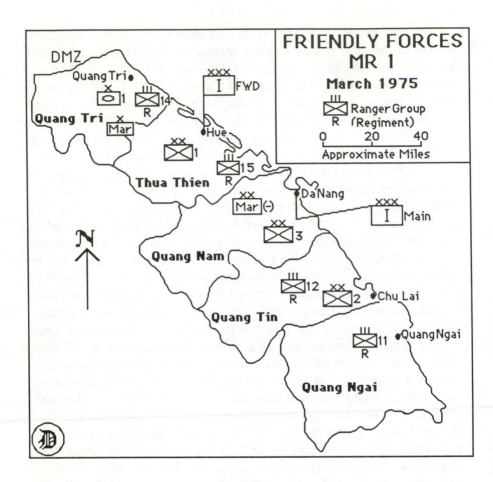

the airborne division, then operating south and west of Da Nang, to be returned to Saigon. In addition to weakening Truong's forces, this troop shift would of itself initiate a catastrophic series of events in the MR 1. After Thieu's recall of the airborne division, Truong's forces were disposed as follows: the 1st ARVN Division, one armored brigade, and one marine brigade held Quang Tri and Thua Thien provinces; the marine division (minus a brigade) had replaced the airborne division and with the 3d ARVN Division protected Da Nang. The 2d ARVN Division defended Quang Tin and Quang Ngai provinces including the big, American-built base of Chu Lai. At most, Truong's forces totaled about four or five divisions.

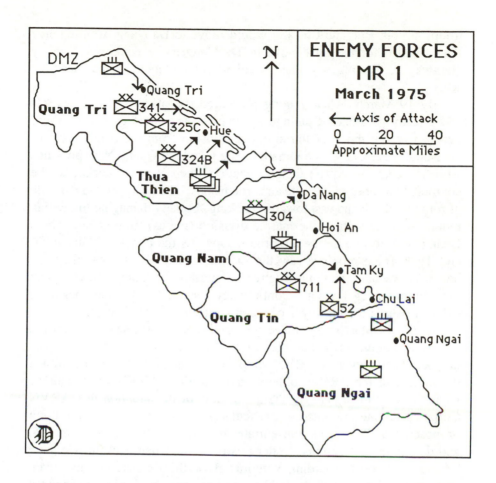

ENEMY FORCES
MR 1
March 1975
← Axis of Attack
0   20   40
Approximate Miles

DMZ
Quang Tri
Quang Tri 341→
325C Hue
324B
Thua
Thien
Da Nang
304
Hoi An
Quang Nam
Tam Ky
711
Chu Lai
52
Quang Ngai
Quang Tin
Quang Ngai

Confronting the ARVN troops in I Corps area were five NVA Main Force divisions, nine separate infantry regiments, three sapper regiments, three tank regiments, eight artillery regiments, and twelve antiaircraft regiments, an equivalent of around eight or nine divisions. The NVA plan to reduce the I ARVN Corps called for simultaneous, concentric attacks from the north, west, and south to drive all ARVN forces into Da Nang and there to destroy them.

To oppose this expected NVA operation, Truong drew up two plans, which he presented to Thieu on 19 March. Both proposed as opening ARVN moves to concentrate forces initially in three defensive centers—Hue, Da Nang, and Chu Lai. Both plans envisioned that eventually the troops at both Hue and Chu Lai would move to Da Nang. Contingency Plan I called for the final move to Da Nang to be made overland by Highway 1; Contingency Plan II called for the move to be made by sea.

By 19 March, when Truong presented the plans to Thieu, events had already overtaken Contingency Plan I. The most critical of these events was the move of the airborne division from south and west of Da Nang to Saigon. This traumatized the people of Quang Nam province who had come to equate their protection, their very existence, to the continued presence of the elite airborne troops. The move started a trickle of refugees north and east toward Da Nang. Equally damaging to civilian morale was the shift of the marine division (minus) from Quang Tri to Quang Nam to replace the airborne troops. As the people of Quang Tri and Thua Thien province saw the marine division move out, they too began to evacuate, jamming Highway 1 north of Da Nang. To complete the demolition of Truong's Contingency Plan I, NVA forces began to exert pressure on Highway 1 between Chu Lai and Da Nang.

At the 19 March conference, General Truong stressed to Thieu the seriousness of the refugee problem. He told the president that the refugees hampered and prevented ARVN troop movements; that their panic sapped the morale of the ARVN soldiers; and that the I ARVN Corps had no means to control or care for them. In view of the situation in I ARVN Corps as Truong presented it, particularly the refugee problem, Truong proposed that his troops concentrate at Hue, Da Nang, and Chu Lai and defend those locations. Under this pressure Thieu buckled. He gave Truong no orders regarding withdrawal or the defense of any given area, telling him merely to hold on to whatever he could. He ignored Truong's refugee problem, although his government was the only agency remotely capable of doing anything about it.

At this same conference, Truong raised another demoralizing problem which beset him—rumors of a ''deal'' between Thieu and the Communists in which the northern provinces would be ceded to North Vietnam. These rumors, plus the withdrawal and shift of the airborne and marine divisions, coupled with the debacle in II ARVN Corps, demoralized both soldiers and civilians in the I Corps area. These rumors had been cleverly planted and spread by the Communists as part of their *dich van* program among the South Vietnamese people and their *binh van* program among the ARVN soldiers. The effectiveness of these psychological attacks was enhanced by the silence of the Thieu government. Thieu made a few ineffectual appearances on television and radio, but by and large the rumors went unanswered—a clear and important victory for the Communist political *dau tranh* offensive.

The final factor driving the refugees toward Da Nang (their perception of safety) was the deep-seated fear of what the NVA troops would do to them if captured. Those South Vietnamese living in Quang Tri and Thua Thien provinces, particularly, remembered Hue in 1968, where thousands of innocent people were brutally murdered by the NVA. This terror propelled hundreds of thousands onto the roads toward Da Nang.

Another momentous event occurred on this day of 19 March—the NVA launched a series of attacks throughout the I ARVN Corps area, one striking south of Da Nang, another between Da Nang and Hue, and a third over the cease-fire line in Quang Tri province. By that night, all of Quang Tri province was in NVA hands, and Highway 1, both north and south of Da Nang, had come under heavy Communist pressure. On 20 March, Thieu went on TV, assuring the people of Hue that the ARVN troops there would defend them. While Thieu was giving this assurance, the JGS, at his order, was sending a flash message to General Truong, telling him he need only defend Da Nang. The people of Hue, rightly suspicious of Thieu's speech, continued to evacuate south towards Da Nang. By 22 March, the NVA had cut Highway 1 between Hue and Da Nang.

The deterioration of the ARVN situation north of Da Nang was mirrored by the disaster south of that city. On 22 March, Tam Ky, the capital of Quang Tin province, came under heavy attack. On 24 March, it fell to the NVA, and Truong ordered what was left of the ARVN force at Tam Ky to assemble at Chu Lai; only a small portion of the force made it. At the same time he ordered all troops in Quang Ngai province to move to Chu Lai. The Quang Ngai troops never went to Chu Lai, but were eventually sealifted to Re Island some twenty miles offshore. The abandonment of these two southern provinces of MR 1 started another flood of refugees toward Da Nang. There, the situation was rapidly sliding toward catastrophe. By 24 March, 400,000 refugees had crowded into Da Nang, and hundreds of thousands more were pushing panic-stricken toward the city.

On 24 March, Truong decided to evacuate his troops from Hue by sea. Truong's plan called for part of the force to move to an inlet north of Hue where the South Vietnamese Navy would evacuate them to Da Nang. The second element would move to another inlet southeast of Hue for evacuation. Both evacuations were costly failures. Many soldiers were drowned, thousands were killed or wounded by NVA artillery fire, many were left on the beaches, and all heavy equipment was abandoned. The troops that did reach Da Nang were demoralized and disorganized, and on reaching that city promptly deserted.

The evacuation of Chu Lai was equally ruinous. After dark on 25 March, the sealift of ARVN troops from Chu Lai to Da Nang began, and almost immediately panic ensued as the troops fought to get in the first boats. Eventually, only about 7,000 men reached Da Nang.

By 27 March, Da Nang was beyond salvation. Over a million and a half refugees had flooded into the city, where the chaos and disorder were indescribable. The police deserted, soldiers killed and pillaged, and NVA artillery fire killed and wounded soldiers and civilians alike. Thousands drowned in the surf trying to get aboard outgoing boats. Others were trampled to death in the streets and on the tarmac of the airport. On the night of 28 March, the NVA shelled and attacked Da Nang, and by 29 March, the NVA forces were in the outskirts of the city. Truong ordered ARVN troops to evacuate Da Nang by sea, and as Truong later recalled, "Not many got out."[8] Truong himself had to swim through the surf to be evacuated. By 30 March, the NVA troops held Da Nang and all of ARVN Military Region 1.

MR 1 fell easily to the Communists. There was no heavy and prolonged fighting, no calamitous ARVN casualty lists, no great destruction—ARVN just collapsed. Analysts who have studied the campaign, including men like Truong and Vien and members of the staffs who participated in it, generally agree about the causes of the catastrophe. First, the NVA had overwhelmingly superior forces—not just in numbers, but in morale, leadership, firepower, and logistics. Second, the pernicious effects of rumors, refugees, and the "family syndrome" destroyed the morale and effectiveness of the ARVN units. Third, Thieu's faulty orders and indecision were fatal. Finally, there was an almost total lack of air support, both tactically and logistically. In short, in MR 1 as in MR 2 the only thing which might have saved the area was the reentry into the war by United States air power.

*   *   *

By April 1, the NVA held MR 1 in the far north of South Vietnam and were prepared to liquidate what remained of II ARVN Corps in MR 2. Most of II ARVN Corps forces had been lost in the disaster at Ban Me Thuot and the catastrophic withdrawal from the Central Highlands; however one division, the 22d ARVN Division, along with other forces, both Regulars and Local Forces, held on to the MR 2 coastal areas, controlling the three large towns of Qui Nhon, Tuy Hoa, and Nha Trang. The 22d ARVN Division, with four regiments, had one regiment north of Phu Cat, one at Binh Khe, one at Qui Nhon, and one around Nha Trang. This division had been heavily engaged north of Qui Nhon initially against the 3d NVA Division, which was later joined by the 95B NVA Regiment and the 968th NVA Division from the west. Still later, the victorious NVA forces moving south from Quang Ngai province in MR 1 got into the fight. In contrast to other ARVN units in MR's 1 and 2, the 22d Division not only "fought well, but valiantly" until overpowered by NVA reinforcements.[9]

On 1 April, out of supplies and overwhelmed, the 22d ARVN Division had to be evacuated by sea. Only about 2,000 officers and men got away. Two of the regimental commanders pled with the division commander to stay and fight. When the division departed, these two colonels refused to leave and committed suicide.[10] Binh Dinh province, an area which had been hotly contested for a quarter of a century, was now for the first time completely NVA.

The deterioration in Binh Dinh was reflected farther south. The defeat at Ban Me Thuot exposed the provinces south and southeast of that city. These areas, always lightly held by ARVN troops, quietly slipped under NVA domination with scarcely a shot fired. On Route 7B, the route of the disastrous withdrawal from the Highlands, the 320th NVA Division continued its pursuit of the demoralized stragglers of that dismal march. With scarcely a stop, the 320th NVA Division attacked Tuy Hoa and on 2 April, against almost no resistance, took it.

A tougher fight loomed, however, on Route 21, the road from Ban Me Thuot to Nha Trang. On this route, the 10th NVA Division was attempting to force its way into Nha Trang. It was opposed by elements of the ARVN 23d Division (thoroughly beaten at Ban Me Thuot) and the 3d ARVN Airborne Brigade, which had been evacuated from Da Nang destined for Saigon, but pulled off the boats at Nha Trang and sent to reinforce ARVN troops in the fight with the 10th NVA Division

at Khanh Duong. After a week of heavy fighting, the ARVN troops at
Khanh Duong were overrun. Only 300 paratroopers survived. On that
same day (2 April) the 10th NVA Division seized Duc My and Ninh
Hoa.

Now, in early April, the enemy was poised to take Nha Trang. As
in Da Nang, refugees flooded Nha Trang. The police disappeared, prisoners broke out of jail, soldiers and officers deserted or pillaged. Military
staffs, including II ARVN Corps Headquarters, simply melted away. It
was the old ARVN game, literally, of "follow the leader." When a
commander took off, his staff and troops deserted too. With little to
oppose them, the NVA troops completed the seizure of MR 2 by mid-
April. The climactic event of the war was about to begin.

Indochina War III ended not with a great heroic Götterdämmerung,
but with a craven, every-man-for-himself scuttle for the exits. For ARVN,
the war had been lost in MR's 1 and 2—in Hue, Da Nang, Ban Me
Thuot, and along Route 7B. The RVN had sacrificed their best troops
in these debacles, and the refugees, flooding south like the plague they
were, plus the "family syndrome," destroyed what military discipline
was left. The defeats in the north had thoroughly demoralized the South
Vietnamese people, from Thieu down to the lowest ARVN private and
the simplest peasant. For South Vietnam in late March 1975, the only
hope—which many of the leaders persisted in holding—lay in American
intervention with massive air power. Bewitched by this will-o'-the-wisp,
the JGS and the RVN leaders did little to shore up the defenses of
Saigon and nothing towards continuing the war after the predictable
loss of the capital.

Nor were the South Vietnamese the only ones to sense the imminence
of their own doom. The North Vietnamese Politburo, at last, discerned
the terminal prostration of the Thieu regime. On 25 March, seeing the
demise of ARVN in MR's 1 and 2, the Politburo ordered Gen. Van
Tien Dung to liberate Saigon before the arrival of the Southwest Monsoon
(about mid-May). And for this decision some credit must be given to
Giap, now the commander in chief, Emeritus. It was Giap in the December
1974 Politburo conference in Hanoi who, while agreeing with the others
on the concept of the two-year campaign (1975–1976) to subdue South
Vietnam, stressed, "Our planning must provide for the contingency that
it could end in 1975 . . ."[11]

When Dung received the Politburo's directive to take Saigon and end the war, he suggested to the Politburo that the final campaign be called the Ho Chi Minh Campaign. The Politburo approved his recommendation, and with that name, no Vietnamese Communist would dare fail. Nor was there much possibility of Communist failure. Depending on the time frame of participation, the NVA employed the equivalent of from thirteen to twenty divisions against Saigon. This force was supported by sappers, tanks, artillery and antiaircraft units, and in the final stages,

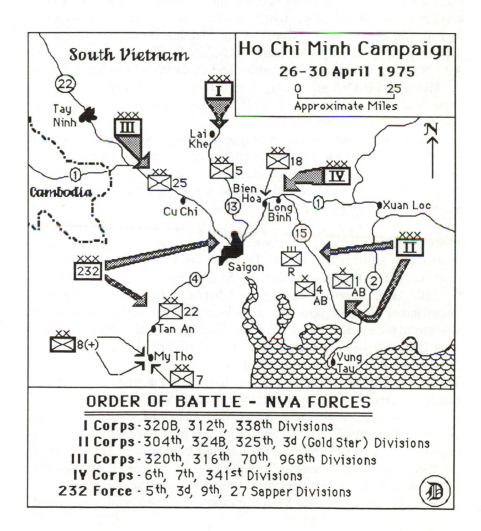

ORDER OF BATTLE - NVA FORCES

I Corps - 320B, 312th, 338th Divisions
II Corps - 304th, 324B, 325th, 3d (Gold Star) Divisions
III Corps - 320th, 316th, 70th, 968th Divisions
IV Corps - 6th, 7th, 341st Divisions
232 Force - 5th, 3d, 9th, 27 Sapper Divisions

even by a hastily improvised tactical air force. This awesome army was organized into five corps, the I, II, III, and IV Corps, and Group 232, a corps-size force of four divisions. More impressive than sheer numbers was the fact that the NVA could at last adequately supply this huge force, and that its morale was sky-high.

To oppose this overpowering NVA force, the South Vietnamese could field only the three organic divisions of III ARVN Corps (the 5th, 18th, and 25th) plus a reconstituted division from MR 2 (the 22d) and what was left of the armor brigade, the airborne division, the marine division, and some beat-up ranger groups. There were three organic divisions in the ARVN IV Corps in the Mekong Delta, but they were able to participate only marginally in Saigon's defense. Many of the ARVN troops had endured the battles and evacuation from MR's 1 and 2. ARVN suffered from shortages of supplies, defensive plans were vague and *ad hoc,* and their morale was low. The South Vietnamese Air Force was in equally bad shape.

The ARVN forces defending Saigon were disposed to cover the five main roads leading into Saigon. North of Saigon, the 5th ARVN Division defended against an enemy attack down Highway 13. Northeast of the capital, the 18th ARVN Division held Xuan Loc covering Highway 1 and the city and air base of Bien Hoa. Southeast of Saigon, two airborne brigades and a ranger group (all at about 50 percent strength) defended against an enemy thrust up Highway 15. Southwest of Saigon, the reactivated and refitted 22d ARVN Division sat astride Highway 4, the main route from the Mekong Delta to Saigon. Finally, in the northwest, the 25th ARVN Division held Route 1 between Tay Ninh and Saigon. These initial blocking positions were located some seventeen to thirty miles from the edges of Saigon. General Truong, who after his evacuation from Da Nang became deputy chief of the JGS in charge of Saigon's defense plans, saw that there could be no real defensive line around Saigon. The defensive circle was too large and the troop strength too meager. Yet to move the defensive circle closer to Saigon meant surrendering valuable real estate and huge cantonments (built by the American army) at Bien Hoa, Cu Chi, and Lai Khe, plus the principal ARVN logistic base at Long Binh, and the huge air base at Bien Hoa. Also, if the JGS brought the defensive lines too close to Saigon, it exposed the city to the devastating artillery fire of the NVA's 130mm guns.

The NVA plan to seize Saigon mirrored the ARVN plan to defend it. Dung adopted with minor alterations Tran Van Tra's plan of a five-pronged concentric drive on the South Vietnamese capital. Dung remembered that there had been considerable devastation in Saigon during the Tet offensive. He wanted to prevent that destruction, and more importantly, he did not want to compress the ARVN forces into a "cornered-rat" defense inside Saigon. Accordingly, he devised a plan which he hoped would overcome the problems presented by ARVN's dispositions. First, he gave each of his five corps a principal axis of advance. Second, he ordered the corps to attempt to surround or annihilate the ARVN defenders in their outer defensive positions, thus averting a last ditch defense in Saigon itself. Third, he gave his troops five critical targets in Saigon. These were: Independence Palace (the South Vietnamese White House), the headquarters of the JGS (near Tan Son Nhut "TSN" air base), TSN air base itself, the National Police Headquarters, and the headquarters of the Capitol Zone, whose commander controlled troops in and around Saigon. Dung reasoned that if these installations were captured quickly before serious fighting in Saigon began, the battle for Saigon would be over.

And being North Vietnamese Communists, they had to have a plan for a Great Uprising in Saigon to accompany the Great Offensive. In spite of the fact that a plan for an uprising was totally unnecessary, and that none of the uprisings planned for Tet 1968 or 1972 had remotely succeeded, the Communists drew up an elaborate plan for political *dau tranh* involving a *dich van* program among the South Vietnamese people and a *binh van* program (troop proselyting) aimed at the RVNAF.

Before the Communist drive on Saigon could begin, the NVA had to undertake two preliminary operations—the seizure of Xuan Loc and the cutting of Highway 4. The Communists wanted to cut Highway 4 to prevent the movements of ARVN reinforcements from the Delta to Saigon and to secure a staging area for a later attack on the capital itself. Xuan Loc was a more significant NVA objective. It anchored the eastern end of the outer defenses of Saigon. In addition, the town controlled the roads from the east to Saigon, Bien Hoa, and Vung Tau, and covered the two big air bases at Bien Hoa and Tan Son Nhut. Both sides considered Xuan Loc to be the key to the defense of Saigon.

Neither of these preliminary operations went well. The NVA effort to cut Highway 4 sputtered and faltered, cutting Highway 4 and then being driven off by effective ARVN counterattacks. The battle for Xuan

Loc produced one of the epic battles of any of the Indochina wars, certainly the most heroic ARVN stand in Indochina War III. On 9 April, Dung attacked the 18th ARVN Division (reinforced) with the entire IV NVA Corps consisting of three infantry divisions (eventually reinforced to four) plus tanks and artillery. The fighting featured mass NVA infantry attacks supported by extremely heavy artillery fire (the ARVN troops at Xuan Loc took over 20,000 rounds of artillery and rockets). ARVN held out until 22 April and then had to withdraw. The 18th ARVN Division lost about 30 percent of its strength (almost all its riflemen) while destroying 37 NVA tanks and killing over 5,000 Communist attackers.[12] In this final epic stand ARVN demonstrated for the last time that, when properly led, it had the "right stuff."

But after Xuan Loc, it was a slide into the abyss for the South Vietnamese. The combination of demoralization and apathy had become fatal. On 21 April, Thieu resigned and fled to Taiwan, and his resignation completed the paralysis of the RVN government. Vice President Tran Van Huong, who succeeded Thieu, was a well-meaning man, but totally inadequate to the emergency. As April ended, evacuations of Americans and senior South Vietnamese officials swelled to flood proportions. Panic gripped the South Vietnamese Congress, and on 28 April, they voted to make Gen. Duong Van Minh the president.

Due to his six-foot height—unusually tall for a Vietnamese—the general was called "Big" Minh. He had been in and out of the shadows of South Vietnamese military politics since at least 1964, when he led the coup that overthrew President Diem. Most of the other South Vietnamese generals, especially Thieu and Ky, mistrusted him, and during the late sixties and early seventies kept him under close surveillance. Not only was Minh personally ambitious, but he had a following and was suspected of having contacts in the Communist camp. (This latter suspicion proved to be true.)[13] Minh's selection as president was motivated by his eleventh-hour admission that he had these Communist connections. Through these contacts the RVN Congress thought that Minh might be acceptable to the North Vietnamese as a negotiator. The South Vietnamese and Minh himself firmly believed that the North Vietnamese would negotiate a settlement. This was pure illusion; the Communists had no need to negotiate with Minh or any desire to do so. On 26 April, the NVA began its assault on Saigon, and by 28 April the Communist troops were in the outskirts of the capital. At 1130 hours, 30 April, NVA troops ran up their red banner over Independence Palace. The war was over.

The fall of Saigon triggered an avalanche of explanations about its causes. Many were self-serving, many politically or ideologically motivated; most of them were partially right and partially wrong. The answer to this still unsettled question—why did the RVN collapse?—is complex. No one cause brought about South Vietnam's fall. Its demise resulted from a number of causes, all interrelated and interwoven into a single, inescapable net.

It is overly simple to attribute the fall of the RVN to the incompetence of Thieu, the JGS, and the RVNAF. Of course, these South Vietnamese leaders and agencies played a major role in their own demise, but the collapse of the RVN would not have occurred without dynamic NVA action. It was the NVA attack on Ban Me Thuot which precipitated Thieu's fatal plan for truncating South Vietnam. It was the Communist pursuit in MR's 1 and 2 which destroyed the flower of the South Vietnamese armed forces. And finally, it was the rapid shift of NVA forces to the south and their subsequent assault on Saigon which ended the war before the South Vietnamese could regroup and reorganize to defend the capital.

The North Vietnamese accomplished these feats by fielding an overwhelming force, not only in numbers, materiel, and firepower, but in the intangibles of leadership, training, and morale. Most important, for the first time in this twentieth century Thirty Years' War, the North Vietnamese managed to establish and operate a modern, first-class, and completely adequate logistical system. The Easter offensive of 1972 had finally taught Giap, Dung, and their cohorts the criticality of logistics, and the North Vietnamese finally overcame their historic Achilles' heel by launching in 1973 a monumental two-year logistical buildup in South Vietnam.

The overpowering and sudden success of NVA arms in March and April 1975 obscured a major, but hidden, contribution to the Communist victory—North Vietnamese strategy. Throughout Indochina War III the Politburo held to a clear and concrete mission, developed flexible and innovative concepts employing all facets of power to accomplish this mission, and executed these concepts and plans with skill and resolution. In particular, its concept of launching political *dau tranh within the*

United States to destroy American political and psychological support for the RVN and to forestall the reentry into Vietnam of United States armed forces was a master stroke in the field of grand strategy.

Every observer who has commented on the fall of South Vietnam has assigned a major portion of the blame to the South Vietnamese themselves. First and foremost, there was throughout Indochina War III an abysmal failure of South Vietnamese leadership. Throughout 1973–1975, Thieu and his principal subordinates made catastrophic military decisions. First, they tried to hold everywhere. When they couldn't do that, Thieu suddenly decided to abandon large segments of the country in the face of the enemy. When this brought on a debacle, paralysis set in, and with it defeat. The system by which Thieu maintained his power, "purchased support," guaranteed that inept political supporters and incompetent cronies would be in positions of leadership, while the all-prevalent corruption undermined discipline and morale. The only factor which might have saved South Vietnam—dedicated and competent leadership—was (with very few exceptions) lacking.

To this leadership void must be added other serious debilities. Training, always an RVNAF stepchild, never reached adequate levels. Then there were the materiel and supply shortages in the final year of the ARVN's existence, brought on by the reductions in aid by the United States Congress. These shortages severely hampered military operations, produced excessive casualties, and demoralized the troops. But this cut in military aid did not in itself bring about the collapse of South Vietnam. Even if the United States had continued its military assistance at the 1972–1973 level, the combination of the inherent debilities of the Thieu government and the power and determination of the North Vietnamese would have eventually destroyed the RVN.

The Joint General Staff (JGS) was another source of weakness. Cowed by Thieu, it failed to exercise any initiative in developing concepts and plans which might save the country. It held to the American style of high-tech, lavish-expenditure war when obviously the RVNAF had neither the materiel nor the training to fight it. The JGS prated constantly about the lack of an adequate general reserve, yet never attempted to establish one. It never even did its primary job—the development of a coherent, workable strategy to fight the war and contingency plans to counter an expected NVA offensive.

The one factor which accounted for most of this South Vietnamese apathy and lack of initiative was the fantastic mind-set of all South Vietnam's leaders that the United States would eventually intervene with massive air power. They held to this myth after the fall of Phuoc Long, after the debacle in MR's 1 and 2, after the defeat at Xuan Loc, and they continued to believe it as twenty NVA divisions closed in on Saigon. They believed it after numerous senior American officials had told them there would be no intervention, and even after the United States Congress had passed a law forbidding it.

The South Vietnamese held this chimerical hope because *they* realized that the only way South Vietnam could be saved was by United States military power. They knew what Laird, Abrams, and the others would never admit—that Vietnamization was a failure. They knew that time had run out for them; in fact, they knew all along that adequate time would never be available. They knew that only Uncle Sam riding at the head of a long column of B-52's could save South Vietnam.

But the B-52's were not coming, and a few hours before the North Vietnamese flag went up over the palace, an obscure American radio operator in the United States Embassy sent this message, "It's been a long and hard fight and we have lost . . . Saigon, signing off." The United States of America had lost its first war.

Notes—Chapter 26

1. Tra, *Bulwark*, pp. 121–122.
2. Dung, *Great Spring Victory*, I:9.
3. Pike, *PAVN*, p. 358.
4. Tra, *Bulwark*, p. 214.
5. The account of the ''Working breakfast'' of 11 March is taken from Vien, *Final Collapse*, pp. 75–82.
6. Vien, *Final Collapse*, p. 78.
7. Hosmer, Keller, and Jenkins, *The Fall*, p. 96.
8. Ibid., p. 111.
9. Ibid., p. 98.
10. Vien, *Final Collapse*, p. 118.
11. Tra, *Bulwark*, p. 125.
12. Vien, *Final Collapse*, p. 132; Hosmer, Keller, and Jenkins, *The Fall*, p. 123.
13. Vien, *Final Collapse*, p. 145.

27 Why We Lost the War

In my introduction I stated that I wrote this book in an attempt to learn how the most powerful nation in the world won every battle in Vietnam, but lost the war. Now, some eleven years later, I know the answer—at least, to my own satisfaction. But to be candid, I submit this answer with considerable misgiving. Indochina War II was a complex war, the most unusual one we Americans ever fought. It was a war critically influenced by events far removed from the battlefield, not only in space, but in discernible connection. Above all, it was a war waged in a critical, but indeterminate manner, in the uncharted depths of the American psyche and in the obscurity of our national soul.

Of all the so-called "lessons" reaped from Vietnam's wars, the one most debated is: how did the Communists win? The answers derived to this cataclysmic question vary greatly. The ideologues on the left hold that the United States was automatically condemned to defeat by its very entrance into a nationalistic war for freedom by a xenophobic people. Those on the right maintain that defeat was not foreordained, and in fact, that the United States won Indochina War II by early 1973, but that the war was lost in the next two years.

Few commentators pinpoint the primary reason for the Communists' victory: *they had a superior grand strategy*. (Grand strategy is defined as "the employment of all facets of national power to achieve a political objective.") From the beginning to the end of the Indochina wars, the Communists had one national objective—the independence and unification of Vietnam, and eventually of all of French Indochina. They achieved this national objective by the conception, development, and implementation of a coherent, long-term, and brilliant grand strategy—the strategy of revolutionary war. This strategy was the key ingredient of the Communist victory.

Now, no one strategy is innately better than any other strategy. In some circumstances the strategy of attrition may be the best strategy; under other conditions limited war strategy or revolutionary war strategy may be superior. *The superior strategy is the one which is best fitted to the actual conditions under which the war is waged.* More specifically, *the superior strategy takes advantage of the enemy's vulnerabilities and one's own strengths while neutralizing the enemy's strengths and one's own vulnerabilities.*

This is the sense in which the strategy of revolutionary war proved superior to the strategy we used against it. And a superior strategy wins wars. The North Vietnamese have an old axiom they often cite. It is this:

1. "When the tactics are wrong and the strategy is wrong, the war will be quickly lost.

2. When the tactics are right, but the strategy is wrong, battles may be won, but the war will be lost.

3. When the tactics are wrong, but the strategy is right, battles may be lost, but the war will be won.

4. When the tactics are right, and the strategy is right, the war will be won quickly."[1]

While this obviously oversimplifies a complex subject, it does contain, like most axioms, a solid kernel of truth. Looking at Indochina War II, the American conduct of the war falls into Case 2, while the North Vietnamese can be placed in Case 3.

This superior grand strategy used by the North Vietnamese Communists has been described before, but its overwhelming criticality in our defeat, and the probability of its future use somewhere else, justifies a summary.

The key aspects of revolutionary war are:

1. Revolutionary war is waged *to gain political control* within a state. One or both sides may be aided openly or covertly by an outside power; nevertheless, in its essence, revolutionary war is *political warfare.*

2. Revolutionary war is *total war.* It mobilizes and uses *all* the people to support its cause. It integrates and uses to the utmost every

available facet of power—military, political, diplomatic, economic, demographic, and psychological.

3. Revolutionary war is waged with *total unity of effort*. It features close coordination and tight control of the employment of all facets of power by a small group of leaders, who by experience are not only military theorists but political scientists, psychologists, and diplomats.

4. Revolutionary war stresses *ambiguity*. Words and concepts are used to confuse an enemy, to alter his perceptions of reality, and thus, to lead him into faulty countermeasures.

5. Revolutionary war is a *protracted war*. Time is the ally of the revolutionary since time is required to build a political base and to develop his military power. Protracted war erodes an opponent's will to persist by presenting a grim picture of an endless war, one without measurable goals and with no prospect of surcease.

6. Revolutionary war is a *changing war*. By its nature it normally will start an almost purely political war with a small guerrilla-type force. As the military force grows, it assumes a more key role, but the political side is still predominant. Eventually the guerrilla force grows into a combination of a conventional army and a large guerrilla force, with an equality of effort between the political and military thrust. In its final stages it becomes almost purely a conventional military effort with only a minimal regard for the political aspects.

This strategy of revolutionary war was the *key* ingredient of the Communist victory. One might argue that crediting the Communist triumph in Vietnam to a superior strategy is overly simplistic. A critic might contend that other factors, such as massive aid from China and Russia, the use of the Cambodian and Laotian sanctuaries, the weakness of the South Vietnamese government and leaders, and the incredible martial spirit of the North Vietnamese soldiers were significant factors. And this is true, *but* the factor which welded and focused the Communist effort from first to last was the strategy of revolutionary war. Without it, there would have been no Communist victory.

If the United States was to win the Vietnam War it had to develop a strategy superior to that of revolutionary war. Returning to the first law of strategy, the United States had to find some way to take advantage of its own strengths and the Communist vulnerabilities while negating its own weaknesses and their strengths. Our principal vulnerability was the weakness inherent in democracy itself—the incapacity to sustain a long, unfocused, inconclusive, and bloody war far from home, for unidentified or ill-defined national objectives. We had other weaknesses, but that was our Achilles' heel.

We had many strengths, but our principal advantage over the enemy lay in our tremendous military superiority. In theory, at least, the American strategy in the Vietnam War should have been to avoid a protracted war and to strike the Viet Cong and North Vietnam as soon as possible with enough military force to bring the war to a quick and satisfactory solution. This does not mean the use of nuclear weapons (which would have been militarily unnecessary and politically disadvantageous). It means the use of whatever overwhelming force was needed to bring the war to a quick and satisfactory end. Such an attack with overwhelming force would not only have achieved United States objectives in South Vietnam, but when compared to the protracted war we fought, it would have been a more humane conflict. A short war would have reduced casualties on both sides, avoided much of the destruction of a long war, and saved billions of dollars, which could have been used to better human conditions, both at home and abroad.

As we know, President Johnson and the other American leaders rejected the above course of action. If the United States was not going to exploit its great military power in a quick, overwhelming effort, then it had to develop a counterstrategy which would neutralize the North Vietnamese version of revolutionary war. As old Sun Tzu put it over two millennia ago, "What is of supreme importance in war is to attack the enemy's strategy."

This task would not have been easy. Indeed, Douglas Pike, in his book *PAVN,* wrote of revolutionary war ". . . that it is a strategy for which there is no known counterstrategy."[2] While one hesitates to disagree with an authority of Pike's eminence, in my opinion there is no such thing as an invincible strategy. But Pike has a point, and while it is *theoretically* possible to develop a counterstrategy to revolutionary war, neither the United States or France, for that matter, produced one during their wars with the Vietnamese Communists.

There were reasons for this failure. Up until at least the advent of the Nixon administration, the United States could never determine clearly its national objective in Vietnam. From the late fifties until early 1964, there was a vague understanding that the purpose of the United States advisory effort was to help the RVN defend itself against the Viet Cong insurgency. Not until March 1964 did NASM 288 proclaim the United States national objective to be "a stable and independent non-Communist government in South Vietnam." This objective had several faults. It was so broad that it could be, and was, interpreted in a variety of ways. The attainment of this objective depended in large measure on the South Vietnamese government and that government was a weak reed, and improving it was largely beyond the power of the United States. The statement of the United States objective was essentially defensive in nature, did not define "success" or "victory," and lacked any appeal around which the American people could rally.

With such a vague statement of the national objective, is it any wonder that the principal executors of the Johnson policy were confused? General Westmoreland says that as COMUSMACV he deduced his mission (and the national mission) to be ". . . punishing the Communists until they would come to the conference table." Gen. Maxwell Taylor in 1966 gave another interpretation of the national objective. Testifying before Congress, he said that we were not trying to "defeat" the North Vietnamese, but only "to cause them to mend their ways."

The Nixon administration did have an objective, although not a very heroic one: to withdraw from the Vietnam War while preserving the integrity of American commitments. Nixon and Kissinger camouflaged this withdrawal behind a facade featuring Vietnamization and negotiations. They got the United States out of Vietnam, but the final and ignominious collapse of the RVN spelled failure for that part of the objective seeking to preserve the integrity of United States commitments.

While no grand strategy can be devised without a clear national objective, other massive failures doomed the United States. The greatest failing was that the United States violated Clausewitz's fundamental dictum: "The first, the supreme, the most far-reaching act of judgment that the statesman and commander have to make is to establish . . . the kind of war on which they are embarking; neither mistaking it for, or trying to turn it into, something which is alien to its nature. This is the first of all strategic questions and the most comprehensive."[3] The American failure to meet "this first, this supreme, this most far-reaching" act of judgment defeated the United States.

The American leadership grasped only vaguely the broad principles of revolutionary war and never understood its nuances. Robert Komer confirmed this, writing, "While many perceived the essentially political and revolutionary nature of the conflict, we miscalculated both its full implications and what coping with it required."[4] And that is the best that can be said for the American grasp of revolutionary war. Giap put it more bluntly. He said about the Americans, "They can't get it into their heads that the Vietnam War has to be understood in terms of the strategy of a People's War, that it's not a question of men and materiel, that these things are irrelevant to the problem."[5] And since the Americans never understood the war in those terms, they responded inappropriately and ineptly. To confirm this unsparing verdict, this chapter will examine the American response to each of the facets of revolutionary war.

First, revolutionary war is a *political* war. Its aim is to achieve political dominance within a state, and military power is a tool by which to gain this political end. Yet the United States perceived and fought the war, from beginning to end, as a predominantly military struggle. At the American bureaucratic level, the war was conducted not under the aegis of the State Department (or by a group chaired by State), but by the Defense Department and the JCS. Weighed on every scale available—leadership attention, media coverage, or dollars expended—the purely military effort overwhelmed all other aspects of the American war effort.

The United States failure to recognize the primacy of the political side of the war is further confirmed by the history of the pacification program. Here was the most important political tool available to the American government. About many of the political problems in South Vietnam the United States could do little, but it could make a major contribution in pacification. But as recorded earlier, our pacification program drifted haplessly between agencies and individuals from the early sixties until 1967, when Komer energized the program, titularly under Westmoreland's command. Even then, it was a stepchild. The emphasis, both in Saigon and Washington, was on the big-unit war and on ROLLING THUNDER.

Throughout the war both the United States and South Vietnam gave little thought to the political, economic, and psychological effects of their military operations. Actions were condoned which resulted in civilian casualties and needless destruction, both of which brought on adverse political effects. Very little attempt was ever made to indoctrinate ARVN in its political role or the requirement for it to help and support the South Vietnamese people.

Finally, the United States never *acted* on the principle that victory in the political war in South Vietnam required major reforms within the government of South Vietnam. Oh, the Americans spoke constantly about the critical need to reform the South Vietnamese government if it was to win the battle for the loyalty of the South Vietnamese people, but when the RVN leaders rebuffed or eluded our suggestions, we pusillanimously withdrew them. Yet these reforms were absolutely essential to a successful countereffort to the strategy of revolutionary war.

The second characteristic of revolutionary war is its *totality*. Its aim is victory, not some vague middle ground. It is waged by *all* the people and *all* the agencies under the control of the revolutionaries. The people are relentlessly indoctrinated, tightly organized, and grossly exploited to support the revolutionary war effort. As a result, the North Vietnamese and the Viet Cong took casualties and destruction which would have appalled and defeated a Western nation. And yet the Vietnamese Communists persevered. In the deepest meaning of the phrase, to them, "there was no substitute for victory."

In addition to the totality of commitment to the war, the North Vietnamese Politburo conducted it with a totality of effort, a meshing of all facets of state power aimed at a given end. Pike calls it a "seamless web," in which the various facets blend into a single whole. Truong Nhu Tang, the onetime PRG minister of justice, describes this totality of effort thusly, "Every military clash, every demonstration, every propaganda appeal was seen as a part of an integrated whole; each had consequences far beyond its immediately apparent results."[6] When the North Vietnamese used a tool of power, they used it to its utmost limits. They employed every division (except one) and every separate regiment (except four) in the 1972 Easter offensive. The Communists drove equally hard in negotiations with the United States. They used tirades, cajolery, tears, threats, silences, tricks of language and translation, and even feigned illness to carry their negotiating positions, and in the end the North Vietnamese got the treaty they wanted.

The United States responded to this totality of Communist commitment with a faltering and confused resolve. Instead of defining "victory" and then pursuing it with resolution, the United States leaders saw the war in terms of "limited objectives" requiring something less—a good deal less—than total dedication to settling the war on terms favorable to this country. In fact, Johnson purposely tried to fight the war without arousing the American people and without demanding sacrifices from the population as a whole. It didn't work. Dean Rusk once said, "You can't fight a hot war in cold blood."

When the United States employed a tool of state power, it used it piecemeal and irresolutely. We never employed more than a small fraction of our tremendous military power. We never called up the Reserves or went after North Vietnam's greatest vulnerability—the dikes on the Red River. Pressed by war dissenters, and, eventually, by Congress, our negotiators gave away point after point to Le Duc Tho and his colleagues, and in the end we gave away South Vietnam.

The American response to the "seamless web" of the North Vietnamese was equally futile. The third facet, unity of effort of revolutionary war, can only be countered by unity of effort. And this the United States was never able to do—either in Washington or in Vietnam. The American leadership never waged the war as a unified whole. There were sometimes three, sometimes four American "wars," each carried out by separate headquarters or agencies with little regard for the others and little coordination. United States bombing raids in the North deflowered MARIGOLD and some of the other diplomatic approaches to negotiations. The pacification program and the military effort were never really coordinated. The battle for the "hearts and minds of the American people" was never seen as an integral—and *the* crucial—battlefield of the war. Robert Komer, who labored in both Washington and Saigon, wrote, "who was responsible for conflict management of the Vietnam War? The bureaucratic fact is that below presidential level everybody and nobody was responsible for coping with it in the round."[7]

There were several reasons for this lack of a unified effort in Washington. The Johnson administration slid gradually into the war. For a long time it conducted the war on a "business as usual" basis, which means reacting to the problems at hand, rather than taking a long look at what had to be done, and then reorganizing to do it. Indeed, Johnson consciously decided that the government would function in a normal way to prevent jarring the American people from their complacency. And so up until the Tet offensive of 1968, there was never any sense of urgency in Washington, never any sense that the situation required new and radical organizations and procedures. When the shock of the Tet offensive hit Washington, it generated not an escalation of the war effort with a sense of urgency and a tightening of control, but a psychological retreat from the conflict.

The greatest enemy of unification of effort within the Johnson administration, however, was bureaucratic compartmentation. Unity of the American effort could have been obtained *only* by cutting across traditional bureaucratic command lines and prerogatives. To unify the national effort, special committees and task forces would have had to be developed and given great power. Such a reorganization would destroy traditional chains of authority and wrench operating procedures and staff loyalties— all unsettling and distasteful to military and civilians alike. Such a massive uprooting of institutional procedures and values daunted both the Johnson and Nixon administrations. As a result, the Johnson administration accepted this compartmentation, thus insuring fragmentation of response, competition among programs, wasted effort, and the inability to see and respond to the overall situation and to Giap's strategy of revolutionary war.

President Nixon took another tack. He tried to unify the American effort by concentrating all decision-making power in himself and Henry Kissinger, aided by a small staff. While such an arrangement improved unity of effort, it, too, had serious defects. It overburdened the staffs of the national security adviser and the National Security Council, neither of which is supposed to be an operating agency. This high degree of centralization deprived the president of much of the advice and information that the military, foreign policy, and intelligence agencies of the government could have provided. Finally, the limited staff support available to the national security adviser, plus the exclusion of the normal operating agencies from the decision-making procedure, prevented adequate follow-up to insure compliance with presidential directives.

Washington's disjointed approach was mirrored and magnified in the American effort in Vietnam. The United States fought three sub-wars in Vietnam almost totally uncoordinated with each other. COMUS-MACV ran the ground war within South Vietnam; CINCPAC ran the air war beyond the borders of South Vietnam (with a separate input by the B-52's under SAC); and pacification, titularly under COMUSMACV, was, in practice, carried out as a separate fiefdom of Bob Komer, and later of Bill Colby. Harold Brown, a secretary of the air force and later secretary of defense, once proclaimed, "Certainly, the command chain in Vietnam was the most fouled up thing in recent history."[8] While there is an obvious element of hyperbole here, Brown is close to the truth.

The uncoordinated effort of the United States was reflected by the RVN. The South Vietnamese attempted to combat the strategy of revolutionary war through an array of inefficient, archaic, and competing ministries, loosely coordinated at the top. Pacification was run by one of the ministries, while military operations were conducted, nominally, by the Joint General Staff, but in actuality by President Thieu and his corps commanders.

This disunity within the individual efforts of the United States and the RVN was magnified in the conduct of allied (combined) operations. The reasons, both open and covert, for not establishing a unified U.S./RVN/Allies military command have been discussed. But in the broader picture of countering revolutionary war, the need for a unified military command assumes secondary importance—"nice to have," but not essential. What *was* essential—and totally absent—was a Supreme War Council. Such a council should have been composed of senior representatives (perhaps even heads of state) of contributing Allied powers who would coordinate military, political, diplomatic, psychological, and economic efforts to defeat the Communists' revolutionary war. While the establishment and operation of such a council would have posed gargantuan problems, the defeat of revolutionary war demanded no less.

Failing to create a Supreme War Council, the United States should have appointed a "pro-consul" for South Vietnam (Sir Robert Thompson's conception) with authority over all American military, political, economic, and psychological agencies and operations in the country. Such a man would probably have to have been a senior military figure of immense reputation and prestige—a Matthew Ridgway, Maxwell Taylor, or Earle Wheeler. In fairness to the Johnson administration, it tried to set up a "pro-consul" when the president appointed General Maxwell Taylor as ambassador in June 1964. In a letter written at the time of Taylor's assumption of his duties, the president gave him full authority over all United States activities in country, specifically including the United States military. Taylor refused to exercise this authority, believing that it would conflict with the military responsibilities of CINCPAC and the JCS and force Westmoreland (as COMUSMACV) to serve two masters. When Henry Cabot Lodge returned as ambassador in 1965, he, too, received similar authority, but also refused to use it. President Johnson then let the concept die, unfortunately.

To conclude this section on the essentiality of unity of effort in combating revolutionary war, one need only look at the two recent examples in which revolutionary war has been defeated—Malaysia and the Philippines. In passing, obeisance must be paid to the admonition that all wars are unique, and that these two insurgencies had probably as many differences from Vietnam as they had similarities. Nevertheless, they speak forcefully of the need for unity of effort. In Malaysia, Sir Gerald Templer, a distinguished soldier, unified all aspects of the counterinsurgency effort under his direction. He and his predecessor, Lt. Gen. Sir Harold Briggs, established War Executive Committees at district, state, and national levels where all operating agencies (police, military, political, economic) were molded into a single command structure.

In the Philippines, the key factor bringing about unity of effort was the personality and leadership of Ramon Magsaysay. He started out as minister of national defense battling the Communist insurgents, known by the short title of Huks. He reformed the army and the constabulary, and then, seeing the need for control of the political effort as well as the military, simply usurped that authority.

The fourth characteristic of revolutionary war is its ambiguity. Twisted words and disinformation are used as weapons to confuse the enemy, thereby causing him to misdirect his response. To counter revolutionary war this ambiguity must be swept away, and the United States failed to do that. It permitted North Vietnamese aggression to be called a "southern insurgency" or "liberation," deluding United States leaders into concentrating on the Viet Cong insurgency within South Vietnam instead of on the aggression from North Vietnam. Until Nixon assumed the presidency, the United States adhered to the fiction created by the North Vietnamese that Cambodia and Laos were neutral countries and thus immune from ground attack, and in the case of Cambodia from air attack as well. Even when Nixon attacked the North Vietnamese forces in Cambodia and Laos, his domestic adversaries, deluded (perhaps?) by this fiction, accused *him* of enlarging the war. None of Nixon's foes bothered to note that the NVA had used the territory of these two nations for several years prior to the American and South Vietnamese raids.

Another masterpiece of ambiguity was the so-called "understandings" which the North Vietnamese and the Johnson administration agreed to in 1968 in return for the cessation of United States bombing north of the 19th Parallel. The NVN agreed not to use the DMZ, not to mount large-scale ground attacks in South Vietnam, not to attack South Vietnamese cities with rockets, and to permit aerial reconnaissance flights over North Vietnam. At North Vietnamese insistence these "understandings" were never put into writing, and they were promptly and consistently violated by the Communists. When the American representative to the peace conference complained about the infractions, the North Vietnamese blandly told him that no such "understandings" existed.

The United States not only accepted the Communist ambiguities but turned out a few of its own. We called United States air strikes "protective reactions" and the invasion of Cambodia an "incursion." The greatest ambiguity, however, was the Gulf of Tonkin Resolution. While it was overwhelmingly approved by both houses of Congress, none of the congressmen who voted for it were sure what it really meant. The intent of the document became increasingly confused when it later came under partisan fire, and even later, when it was "repealed." These ambiguities confused not only the American leaders, but the American people as well. War was no longer war, but something else, and no one rallies to the call of such an uncertain trumpet.

The fifth characteristic of revolutionary war is its protraction. This protraction is one of its great strengths, particularly when the enemy is one of the Western democracies. If the protraction of the war is a revolutionary war strength, then obviously its foe should attempt to shorten the conflict. But the United States made no attempt to do this. *On the contrary, it adopted the very concept which would protract the hostilities— the strategy of limited war.*

"Limited War" is the brain-child of a group of academic theorists who believe that a war can be fought with limited means for a limited objective. Its style is to apply "force skillfully along a continuous spectrum . . . in which adversaries would bargain with each other through the medium of graduated military responses. . ."[9] This "gradualism" played into the hands of Giap and his strategy of revolutionary war. He wanted to prolong the war because this allowed him to strengthen his forces while at the same time eroding the morale and resolution of his enemy.

For the United States, there were other disadvantages to fighting a limited war in Vietnam. The "signals" the "limited warriors" sent the NVN Politburo were often missent, misread, misunderstood, or ignored. Often, the North Vietnamese read the signal of United States restraint as a sign of weakness or lack of national resolve. Another disadvantage of limited war is that it is the most subtle of strategies, requiring the acme of fine tuning and coordination of effort by the United States government—both extremely difficult, if not impossible. Perhaps the greatest deficiency of limited war for the United States was that it not only misled the North Vietnamese, but confused and eventually dismayed the American people. The subtle "signals," the indirect use of military power, persuaded the American people that the government was not serious about the war or resolute in its prosecution. Beyond that, as the war went on without signs of obvious progress, the people became convinced that it was unwinnable, and thus, best abandoned.

Finally, revolutionary war is a changing war. To combat this its foe must be aware of the various phases of the struggle and of its changing nature. The counterinsurgent must not only adjust to these changes but anticipate them as well. Here, again, the United States failed, and the American/South Vietnamese experience provides a clear example of that failure. During the later fifties and early sixties, the threat to the RVN was from a Phase I Communist insurgency. Yet during that period the American advisors and the South Vietnamese leaders organized and trained heavily equipped regiments and divisions primarily designed to repel a North Vietnamese attack. What they needed, of course, were light infantry units to battle the guerrillas. But more than any military might, they needed to concentrate on and win the political struggle.

As the conflict moved into the second stage of revolutionary war, what was required was a force roughly half antiguerrilla and half anticonventional. But here again, ARVN stayed wedded to its heavy, cumbersome, immobile divisions, unable to counter effectively either guerrillas or conventional forces—and in 1964 South Vietnam almost lost the war. When the American ground forces took over the war against the NVA and VC Main Force units, thereby freeing ARVN for antiguerrilla duty, the South Vietnamese forces remained in their inappropriate divisional organization.

In 1968 and 1969, when the NVA reverted to sapper-guerrilla warfare, the United States troops amended their tactics to meet the change, but

ARVN changed neither its tactics nor its organization. In 1970, as United States troops began to withdraw, neither ARVN nor its American advisors saw clearly the need not just for South Vietnamese divisions to oppose the NVA divisions, but a mobile, modernized force of all arms capable of fighting a sustained, large-scale, conventional war.

The adjustment to and anticipation of the changing phases of revolutionary war carries beyond organization. It goes into such connected areas as strategy, tactics, armaments, and intelligence. Thieu's 1973–1974 strategy of holding everywhere made sense if he was fighting an insurgency, but it was strategic suicide to adopt it when faced with a massive conventional challenge. Thieu failed to realize that the North Vietnamese had long ago gone into the final phase of revolutionary war, and that the danger was not a political insurgency, but an invasion by massive, modern, conventional forces.

Armaments were affected, too, by the changing nature of the war. Heavy weapons, such as artillery, tanks, and jet aircraft are largely useless against guerrillas, but an absolute requirement against a conventional foe. Operations, training, and intelligence activities are all fundamentally determined by the phasing of revolutionary war. Tactics vary greatly by phases and thus so must training. Intelligence targets change along with intelligence collection methods and agencies. Again, remember Clausewitz's counsel—"know what kind of war you're fighting; don't try to make it something different"—yet that is what we persistently tried to do.

Finally, one aspect of revolutionary war is so critical that it deserves special attention—the *dich van* program of the North Vietnamese aimed at shattering the support for the war by the American people. The NVN program was *of itself* largely ineffectual, but its objectives were brilliantly achieved by the Communists' unwitting American allies. But beyond that specific program, Giap's whole strategy after Tet 1968 was aimed at one decisive objective—to attack the greatest American vulnerability, its will to continue the struggle. The protraction of the war, the propaganda, the inconclusive negotiations, the ambiguities, and the military actions which produced American casualties were blended and used to strike at this American weakness.

The exploitation of this critical American vulnerability elevated Vo Nguyen Giap into the first rank of grand strategists. By his attacks on the American will to continue the war, he produced a dual strategy which B. H. Liddell Hart, the foremost strategic theorist of this century, claims is the essence of military genius: he employed the indirect approach, and he placed the United States on the horns of a strategic dilemma. After 1968, Giap avoided direct attack on our forces in Vietnam in favor of striking at the will of the American people. By this strategy he not only matched his strength against our weakness, but transferred the principal battlefield from the rice paddies of Vietnam to the streets of the United States—a classic example of the indirect approach. He forced the United States into a no-win strategic dilemma by these same attacks on the American home front. If the American leadership prosecuted the war forcefully, it risked losing domestic support to continue the war. If the United States attempted to assuage its war critics by restraining military initiatives and measures, it had to forego the hope of winning in Vietnam. Any American attempt to walk the fine line between the extremes, or to bound back and forth between them (as Nixon did), only guaranteed eventual defeat—a brilliant strategic triumph for the former high school history teacher.

But Giap must share this triumph with circumstances peculiar to the United States in the late sixties and early seventies. Underlying the American government's failure to maintain the support of its people for the war was a lack of consensus among the intellectuals, the news media, and political elite. Since at least the fifties there has been in America a schism over what the nation's foreign policy objectives should be, and what place the use of military force should play in attaining them. This lack of unity was sharpened by ideological extremism, partisan politics, and personal ambition. The gap widened as the war wore on, particularly after Nixon's election, which freed the liberal element of the Democratic party from its loyalty to Lyndon Johnson and *his* war. Eventually, this chasm of national unity became so wide and so deep that in the end, the anti-war elements in Congress became the most powerful ally of the North Vietnamese Politburo. Nor has this canyon yet been bridged.

But Congress, by and large, only reflected the views of the American people, who by late 1968 had given up on the war. The failure here was one of leadership. The American leaders, President Johnson in particular, made little effort to accomplish the prime job they *had* to do—the continuous education of the American people about why the United States was in Vietnam, what it was trying to do there, and how it intended to do it. To make matters worse, the Johnson administration stumbled into the "credibility gap." It tripped here not through any intent to lie to the American people. It fell into the gap because, not understanding revolutionary war, it kept reporting what the administration thought were indices of success when in fact these indices were peripheral to the outcome of the war.

In retrospect, the Johnson administration should have committed Congress, and through it, the American people, to the war by asking for and getting, not a Gulf of Tonkin Resolution, but a declaration that a state of war existed between the United States and North Vietnam/Viet Cong. Not only does such a declaration commit the Congress and the people, but it brings into force other laws, regulations, and executive orders needed to fight a war (censorship, for example). It also gains certain belligerent rights under international law. As seen previously, a declaration of war sweeps away one of the ambiguities with which revolutionary war is waged. If Congress had refused to declare war, then the president would know that he did not have the support of the people, and that the war could not be won. He would then have had to back off from Vietnam or to adopt some other line of action.

The news media played their part in demolishing popular support for the war. They misreported the war, sometimes intentionally, more often unintentionally. After all, the media understood the strategy and nuances of revolutionary war even less than the American leaders. In the latter stages of the war the news media had a bias against the RVN, and since the United States supported the RVN, against their own government as well. The media, largely unknowingly, were effective practitioners of Giap's *dich van* program within the United States.

Television contributed heavily to the destruction of the American will to prosecute the war. The constant fare of destruction, suffering, and blood brought into American living rooms horrified and dismayed the American people. The Johnson and Nixon administrations never realized that in this age the "control of images and information is central to the exercise of political power."[10] The United States government never clearly realized that the hearts and minds of the American people had become the critical battlefield, and that it had to protect the nation here as surely as it did its armed forces in combat. Some form of voluntary censorship should have been adopted if possible, but involuntary censorship if necessary, not just in Vietnam, but in the United States as well.

Finally, the greatest erosion of the American spirit to win the war came from the increasing American casualties as the Vietnam War ground on. In 1983, Professor Lawrence W. Lichty said, "If one does a fairly detailed statistical analysis, the support for the war is a precise, inverted relationship to the number of people getting killed. It was Americans coming home in boxes that tended more than anything else to turn public opinion against the war."[11] This relationship of American casualties to home-front support is confirmed by another expert who studied not only the Vietnam War, but the Korean War as well. Daniel Hallin, quoting John E. Mueller, stated that ". . . public support for the shorter and less costly limited war in Korea also dropped as its costs rose, despite the fact that television was in its infancy, censorship was tight, and the World War II ethic of the journalist serving the war effort remained strong."[12] This is the most powerful of all arguments for a short, conclusive war.

To sum it all up, the United States lost the war in the way all wars are lost—to a superior strategy which availed itself of our political and psychological vulnerabilities while negating our great military strength. We failed to take advantage of the Communist vulnerabilities, and, in fact, fought the war in such a way as to intensify enemy strengths and our own weaknesses. We lost because the United States government was unable to comprehend the strategy of revolutionary war, and thus, unable to counter it. Even if the American leaders *had* understood revolutionary war, the United States government for political, psychological, institutional, and bureaucratic reasons would have been unable to combat it effectively.

Sad to say, we cannot counter revolutionary war even now—our defeat in Vietnam has taught us nothing. After a lengthy study of "low-intensity conflict" (which includes revolutionary war) a high-level Joint Study Group (army, navy, air force, marines, and civilians) concluded in a study dated 1 August 1986 that "The United States does not understand low-intensity conflict nor does it display the capability to adequately defend against it."[13]

Notes—Chapter 27

1. Lung, *Strategy and Tactics,* p. 130.
2. Pike, *PAVN,* p. 213.
3. Von Clausewitz, *On War,* p. 133.
4. Komer, *Bureaucracy,* p. 5.
5. Giap, *Military Art,* pp. 329–330.
6. Tang, *Vietcong Memoir,* p. 86.
7. Komer, *Bureaucracy,* p. 75.
8. John Morrocco and eds. of the Boston Publishing Co., *The Vietnam Experience. Rain of Fire, Air War, 1969–1973* (Boston, MA: Boston Publishing Co., 1985), p. 183.
9. Osgood, *Limited War,* pp. 10–11.
10. Daniel C. Hallin, *The "Uncensored War"* (New York: Oxford University Press, 1986), p. 214.
11. Lawrence W. Lichty, speech to U.S. Army public affairs officers, March 1983.
12. Hallin, *"Uncensored War,"* p. 213.
13. Report prepared by the Joint Low-Intensity Conflict Project (Fort Monroe, VA, 1 August 1986), p. 1.

Glossary

Agrovilles   South Vietnam resettlements.

AA   Antiaircraft (also AAA).

AAA   Antiaircraft Artillery.

AgitProp   Communist term meaning revolutionary agitation and propaganda.

AID   Agency for International Development (see USAID).

AK-47   A Russian and Chicom assault rifle.

Annam   Central Section of Vietnam.

AO   Area of Operation.

Apparatchiks   Communist bureaucracy.

ARVN   Army of the Republic of Vietnam (South Vietnam).

AWOL   Absent Without Leave.

BA   Communist base area where supplies and facilities were stored and maintained.

Bac Bo   A Communist term for North Vietnam.

Beehive   A U.S. antipersonnel artillery round containing steel slivers or darts.

BEP   *Bataillon Etranger de Parachutistes* (French); Foreign Legion Parachute Battalion.

Binh Trams   North Vietnamese logistic units.

Binh Van   Communist political action among the enemy military.

BMI   *Bataillon de Marche Indochinois* (French); Indochinese Light Infantry Battalion.

BPC   *Bataillon de Parachutistes de Choc* (French); Parachute Assault Battalion.

BPC   *Bataillon de Parachutistes Coloniaux* (French); Colonial Parachute Battalion.

BPVN   *Bataillon de Parachutistes Vietnamiens* (French); Vietnamese Parachute Battalion.

Cao Dai   A religious sect centered around Tay Ninh, South Vietnam.

C & GSC   U.S. Army's Command and General Staff College, Ft. Leavenworth, Kansas. Referred to familiarly as "Leavenworth."

CG   Commanding General.

Chicom   Chinese Communists.

Chieu Hoi   South Vietnamese program to encourage the Viet Cong to defect.

CIA   Central Intelligence Agency.

CINCPAC   Commander in Chief, United States Pacific Command.

COMUSMACV   Commander, United States Military Assistance Command, Vietnam.

CORDS   Civil Operations and Revolutionary Development Support (Pacification).

COSVN   Central Office South Vietnam (Headquarters controlling all political and military operations in Central and South Vietnam. Subordinate to NVN Politburo.)

CP   Command Post—a tactical headquarters.

Crachin   Fog and drizzle, from French term *crachat,* meaning spit.

CSA   Chief of Staff, Army.

CTZ   Corps Tactical Zone.

Dan Cong   Communist supporters, no combat capability.

Dan Cong du Kich   Communist guerrillas.

Dan Van   Communist *agitprop* among people under their control.

DIA   Defense Intelligence Agency.

Dich Van   Communist *agitprop* among the people under enemy control.

Dinassauts   (Division Navale d'Assaut) French river craft.

DMZ   Demilitarized Zone separating North and South Vietnam.

DOD   Department of Defense (the entire United States military establishment).

DRV   Democratic Republic of Vietnam (North Vietnam).

DSCOPS   Deputy Chief of Staff, Operations. Chief staff officer dealing with tactical plans and operations.

DZ   Drop Zone—preplanned landing area for paratroopers and/or parachuted equipment.

Field Force   United States corps-type headquarters in Vietnam.

Fragging   The murder of an officer or NCO by a man of lower rank, generally by a hand grenade.

FSB   Fire Support Base (a protected artillery position).

FWF   Free World Forces.

G-1 Section   Military personnel staff division.

G-2 Section   Military intelligence staff division.

G-3 Section   Military operations staff division.

G-4 Section   Military logistics staff division.

GAP   *Groupement Aeroporte* (French); Airborne Battle Group.

Group Mobile   A French regimental combat team, generally three infantry battalions and an artillery battalion.

Grunt   Nickname for United States combat infantryman or combat marine.

GVN   Government of Vietnam (South).

HES   Hamlet Evaluation System.

Hoa Hao   A militant Vietnamese religious sect concentrated in the Mekong Delta.

Hoi Chanh   A VC defector.

"Hot"   Dangerous, as a "hot LZ."

I & E Program   Indoctrination and Education Program (Communist).

I (Eye) Field Force   United States corps headquarters controlling American operations in South Vietnam MR-2.

II Field Force   United States corps headquarters controlling American operations in South Vietnam MR-3.

III MAF   III Marine Expeditionary Force, corps headquarters controlling American operations in South Vietnam MR-1.

ISA   International Security Affairs section in OSD.

JCS   (United States) Joint Chiefs of Staff.
JGS   Joint General Staff (equivalent of United States JCS in RVNAF).
Joint Staff   Staff organization of JCS.
J-2   Chief, Joint Intelligence Section, MACV (highest United States military intelligence officer in Vietnam).
J-2, JGS   Chief, Joint Intelligence Section, JGS (senior South Vietnamese military intelligence officer).

Karst   Limestone pinnacles found in Laos and Vietnam.
KIA   Killed in Action.

Lao Dong   (also Vietnamese Worker's Party) Communist Party in North Vietnam.
LAW   M-72 light antitank weapon (United States).
LOC   Line of Communication.
LZ   Landing Zone, for helicopters.

MAAG   Military Assistance Advisory Group.
MACV   Military Assistance Command Vietnam.
Main Force   Regular Army forces of North Vietnam, Vietminh, and Viet Cong.
MIA   Missing in Action.
MIG   Communist aircraft.
MR   Military Region.

Nam Bo   A Communist term for South Vietnam.
Napalm   A jellied incendiary used by French and Americans.
NATO   North Atlantic Treaty Organization.
NLF   National Liberation Front (Communist).
NVA   North Vietnamese Army.
NVN   North Vietnam (or Vietnamese).
NSAM   National Security Action Memorandum.
NSC   National Security Council.
NSSM   National Security Study Memorandum.

OB   Order of Battle (a listing of military units).
OCO   Office of Civil Operations.
OPLAN   Operation Plan.

OSD   Office, Secretary of Defense (the secretary of defense and his immediate staff).

OSS   Office of Strategic Services (United States WWII spy organization).

PACAF   United States Pacific Air Force.

PACFLT   United States Pacific Fleet.

Pacification   Program by governments of South Vietnam and United States to win allegiance of South Vietnamese people and eradicate Viet Cong influence.

PACOM   United States Pacific Command.

PAVN   People's Army Vietnam (NVN designation for NVA).

PF   Popular Forces.

PFIAB   President's Foreign Intelligence Advisory Board (United States).

PHOENIX   A United States/South Vietnam program to detect and neutralize the Viet Cong Infrastructure.

POL   Petroleum, oil, and lubricants.

PRG   Provisional Revolutionary Government.

PROVN   Program for the Pacification and Long-Term Development of South Vietnam (developed by United States Army).

PSDF   People's Self Defense Forces.

Punji stake   A sharpened bamboo stake covered with feces and placed in the bottom of a pit.

POW   Prisoner of War.

RCP   *Regiment de Chasseurs Parachutistes* (French); Parachute Light Infantry Regiment.

RF   Regional Forces.

ROTC   Reserve Officer Training Corps.

RVN   Republic of Vietnam (South).

RVNAF   Republic of Vietnam Armed Forces.

SA   Systems Analysis.

SA-2   Medium-range Communist surface to air missile.

SAC   Strategic Air Command.

SAM   Surface to air missile.

Sapper   Communist commando, expert at penetrating defenses.

SEATO   Southeast Asia Treaty Organization.

SHAEF   Supreme Headquarters, Allied Expeditionary Force (WWII).

SOG   Studies and Observation Group (United States), a clandestine operation unit.
SHAPE   Supreme Headquarters, Allied Powers Europe.
Sortie   An operational flight by one aircraft.
SVN   South Vietnam.

TAOR   Tactical Area of Responsibility.
TCK-TKN   (*Tong Cong Kich-Tong Khoi Nghia*) General Offensive, General Uprising (Tet offensive, North Vietnamese term).
TF   Task Force.
TOT   Time on target.
Trung Bo   A Communist term for Central Vietnam.
TSN   Tan Son Nhut airbase.
TTC   (*Tong Tan Cong*) General Counteroffensive (Giap's 1951–1952 campaign).

USAID   United States Agency for International Development.
Uhlan   German Cavalryman of World War I.
USAF   United States Air Force.
USARPAC   United States Army, Pacific.
USARV   United States Army, Vietnam.
USIA   United States Information Agency.
USMC   United States Marine Corps.
UCMJ   Unified Code of Military Justice (United States code of military law).

VC   Derived from term Viet Cong Son (meaning Vietnamese Communist).
VCI   Viet Cong Infrastructure—shadow government of the VC.
Viet Bac   A Communist redoubt area in NVN near the China border.
VNAF   Vietnamese Air Force (South).
VNN   Vietnamese Navy (South).
VNQDD   Vietnam *Quoc Dan Dang* (preindependence, nationalistic Vietnamese political party).
VVAW   Vietnam Veterans Against the War.
VWP   Vietnamese Worker's Party (see *Lao Dong*).

WIA   Wounded in Action.
WIEU   Weekly Intelligence Estimate Update (strategy session, MACV).

Bibliography

Albright, John; Cash, John A.; and Sandstrum, Allan W. *Seven Fire Fights in Vietnam*. Washington, D.C.: Office of the Chief of Military History, United States Army, 1970.

Asprey, Robert Brown. *War in the Shadows*. 2 vols. New York: Doubleday, 1975.

Blaufarb, Douglas S. *The Counter-Insurgency Era: U.S. Doctrine and Performance, 1950 to the Present*. New York: The Free Press, 1977.

Bodard, Lucien. *The Quicksand War: Prelude to Vietnam 1950 to the Present*. Trans. by Patrick O'Brian. Boston, MA: Little, Brown & Co., 1967.

Bouscaren, Anthony T., ed. *All Quiet on the Eastern Front: The Death of South Vietnam*. Old Greenwich, CT: The Devin-Adair Company, 1977.

Bowman, John S., ed., *The Vietnam War, An Almanac*. New York: World Almanac Publications, 1985.

Braestrup, Peter. *The Big Story*. 2 vols. Boulder, CO: Westview Press, 1977.

Buckley, Kevin P. "General Abrams Deserves a Better War," *The New York Times Magazine*. 5 October 1969.

Burchett, Wilfred G. *Vietnam Will Win*. New York: Monthly Review Press, 1970.

Buttinger, Joseph. *Vietnam: A Dragon Embattled*. 2 vols. New York: Frederick A. Praeger, 1967.

_____. *The Smaller Dragon: A Political History of Vietnam*. New York: Frederick A. Praeger, 1968.

819

Cao Van Vien. *The Final Collapse*. Indochina Monographs. Washington, D.C.: United States Army Center of Military History, 1982.

Cao Van Vien and Dong Van Khuyen. *Reflections on the Vietnam War*. Indochina Monographs. Washington, D.C.: United States Army Center of Military History, 1980.

Charlton, Michael, and Moncrief, Anthony. *Many Reasons Why, The American Involvement in Vietnam*. New York: Hill and Wang, 1978.

Clifford, Clark M. "A Vietnam Reappraisal—The Personal History of One Man's View and How It Evolved," *Foreign Affairs*. July 1969.

Collins, James Lawton. *The Development and Training of the South Vietnamese Army, 1950–1972*. Vietnam Studies. Washington, D.C.: Department of the Army, 1975.

de Gaulle, Charles. *The Edge of the Sword*. New York: Criterion Books, 1960.

Devillers, Philippe, and Lacouture, Jean. *End of a War: Indochina, 1954*. Trans. by Alexander Lieven and Adam Roberts. New York: Frederick A. Praeger, 1969.

Dodge, Theodore Ayrault. *Great Captains*. New York: Houghton Mifflin, 1889.

Draper, Theodore. *Abuse of Power*. New York: The Viking Press, 1967.

Duiker, William J. *The Communist Road to Power in Vietnam*. Boulder, CO: Westview Press, 1981.

Elegant, Robert. "Looking Back at Vietnam: How To Lose A War," *Encounter*. August 1981.

Fall, Bernard B. *Hell in a Very Small Place: The Siege of Dien Bien Phu*. New York: J. B. Lippincott, 1967.

————. *Viet-Nam Witness 1953–66*. New York: Frederick A. Praeger, 1966.

————. *Street Without Joy*. Harrison, PA: The Stackpole Co., 1967.

Fallaci, Oriana. *Interview With History*. 1974 Trans. by John Shepley. Milan: Liveright Publishing Corp., 1976.

Fanning, Louis A. *Betrayal in Vietnam*. New Rochelle, NY: Arlington House, Publishers, 1976.

Fishel, Wesley R. *Anatomy of a Conflict*. Itasca, IL: F. E. Peacock Publishers, 1968.

Fulghum, David, Maitland, Terrence, et al. *The Vietnam Experience: South Vietnam on Trial Mid 1970 to 1972*. Boston, MA: Boston Publishing Co., 1984.

Furguson, Ernest B. *Westmoreland: The Inevitable General*. Boston, MA: Little, Brown & Co., 1968.

Gelb, Leslie H., and Betts, Richard K. *The Irony of Vietnam: The System Worked*. Washington, D.C.: The Brookings Institution, 1979.

Giap, Vo Nguyen. *The People's War, People's Army: The Viet Cong Insurrection Manual for Underdeveloped Countries*. New York: Frederick A. Praeger, 1962.

_____. *Dien Bien Phu*. Hanoi: Foreign Languages Publishing House, 1964.

_____. *Nhan Dan*. "The Big Victory, The Great Task." Hanoi: 14–16 September 1967.

_____. *Nhan Dan*. 7 May 1964. Quoted in JCS *Study*, 31 January 1968.

_____. *The Military Art of People's War*, ed. Russell Stetler. New York: Monthly Review Press, 1970.

_____. *Banner of People's War, The Party's Military Line*. New York: Frederick A. Praeger, 1970.

Gravel, Mike, ed. *The Pentagon Papers*. 5 vols. Boston, MA: Beacon Press, 1971.

Halberstam, David. *The Best and the Brightest*. Greenwich, CT: Fawcett, 1969.

Hallin, Daniel C. *The "Uncensored War."* New York: Oxford University Press, 1986.

Herrington, Stuart A. *Peace With Honor?* Novato, CA: Presidio Press, 1983.

Hersh, Seymour M. *The Price of Power, Kissinger in the Nixon White House*. New York: Summit Books, 1983.

Herz, Martin F. *The Prestige Press and the Christmas Bombing, 1972: Images in Reality in Vietnam*. Washington, D.C.: Ethics and Public Policy Center, 1980.

Hoang Ngoc Lung. *General Offensives of 1968–69*. Indochina Monographs. Washington, D.C.: United States Army Center of Military History, 1981.

_____. *Strategy and Tactics*. Indochina Monographs. Washington, D.C.: United States Army Center of Military History, 1980.

Hoang Van Chi. *From Colonialism to Communism: A Case History of North Vietnam*. New York: Frederick A. Praeger, 1964.

Ho Chi Minh. *On Revolution*. New York: Frederick A. Praeger, 1967.

Hoopes, Townsend. *The Limits of Intervention*. New York: David McKay, 1969.

Horne, Alistair. *A Savage War of Peace, Algeria 1954–1962*. New York: The Viking Press, 1977.

_____. "A British Historian's Meditation," *National Review*. 23 July 1982.

Hosmer, Stephen T.; Keller, Konrad; Jenkins, Brian M. *The Fall of South Vietnam: Statements by Military and Civilian Leaders*. Santa Monica, CA: The Rand Corporation, 1978.

Johnson, Lady Bird. *A White House Diary*. New York: Dell Publishing, 1970.

Johnson, Lyndon Baines. *The Vantage Point, Perspectives of the Presidency, 1963–1969*. New York: Rinehart and Winston, 1971.

Kahn, Herman, and Armbruster, Gastil. *Can We Win in Vietnam*. New York: Frederick A. Praeger, 1968.

Kalb, Marvin, and Kalb, Bernard. *Kissinger*. Boston, MA: Little, Brown & Co., 1974.

Kalb, Marvin, and Able, Elie. *Roots of Involvement: The U.S. and Asia 1784–1971*. New York: W. W. Norton, 1971.

Karnow, Stanley. *Vietnam, A History: The First Complete Account of Vietnam at War*. New York: The Viking Press, 1983.

Kearns, Doris. *Lyndon Johnson and the American Dream*. New York: Harper & Row, 1976.

Kinnard, Douglas. *The War Managers*. Hanover, NH: University Press of New England, 1977.

Kissinger, Henry B. "The Vietnam Negotiations," *Foreign Affairs* 47. January 1969.

_____. *The White House Years*. Boston, MA: Little, Brown & Co., 1979.

_____. *Years of Upheaval*. Boston, MA: Little, Brown & Co., 1982.

Kohler, Foy D. *Understanding The Russians: A Citizen's Primer*. New York: Harper & Row, 1970.

Kolko, Gabriel. *Anatomy of a War: Vietnam, the United States, and the Modern Historical Experience*. New York: Pantheon Books, 1985.

Komer, Robert W. Memo To President Johnson. LBJ Library, Austin, TX, Guam Conference File Notes, 18 March 1967.

_____. *Bureaucracy Does its Thing: Institutional Constraints on U.S.– GVN Performance in Vietnam.* Santa Monica, CA: The Rand Corporation, 1972.

Lancaster, Donald. *The Emancipation of French Indochina.* London: Oxford University Press, 1961.

Latimer, Thomas. *Hanoi's Leaders and Their South Vietnam Policies, 1954–68.* Unpublished Ph.D. thesis: Georgetown University, 1972.

Lavalle, A. J. C., ed. *Airpower and the 1972 Spring Offensive.* Vol. 2, Monograph 3. Washington, D.C.: USAF Southeast Asia Monograph Series, 1976.

Lawrence, T. E. *Seven Pillars of Wisdom.* New York: Dell Publishing, 1966.

Le Gro, William E. *Vietnam From Cease-Fire to Capitulation.* Washington, D.C.: United States Army Center of Military History, 1981.

Lewy, Guenther. *America in Vietnam.* New York: Oxford University Press, 1978.

Liddell Hart, Basil H. *Strategy,* 2d ed. New York: Frederick A. Praeger, 1967.

Lipsman, Samuel; Doyle, Edward; and eds. of the Boston Publishing Co. *The Vietnam Experience: Fighting for Time.* Boston, MA: Boston Publishing Co., 1983.

McGarvey, Patrick J. *Visions of Victory: Selected Vietnamese Communist Military Writings 1965–1968.* Stanford, CA: Hoover Institute on War, Revolution and Peace, 1969.

Mao Tse-tung. *On Protracted War.* English trans. Peking: Foreign Languages Press, 1960.

_____. *Mao Tse-Tung, An Anthology of His Writings,* ed. Anne Freemantle. New York: The New American Library of Literature, 1962.

Momyer, William W. *Air Power in Three Wars (WWII, Korea, Vietnam).* Washington, D.C.: United States Government Printing Office, 1978.

Montgomery, Bernard. *Paths of Leadership.* New York: G. P. Putnam, 1961.

Morris, Roger. *Uncertain Greatness. Henry Kissinger and American Foreign Policy.* New York: Harper & Row, 1977.

Morrocco, John, and eds. of the Boston Publishing Co. *The Vietnam Experience: Rain of Fire, Air War, 1969–1973.* Boston, MA: Boston Publishing Co., 1985.

Mueller, John E. "A Summary of Public Opinion and the Vietnam

War,'' *Vietnam as History,* ed. Peter Braestrup. Washington, D.C.: University Press of America, 1984.

Navarre, Henri. *Agonie de L'Indochine.* Paris: Plon, 1958.

Ngo Quang Truong. *The Easter Offensive of 1972.* Indochina Monographs. Washington, D.C.: United States Army Center of Military History, 1980.

Nguyen Chi Thanh. ''Ideological Tasks of the Army and People in the South,'' *Hoc Tap.* Hanoi: July 1966.

Nguyen Duy Hinh, *Lam Son 719.* Indochina Monographs. Washington, D.C.: United States Army Center of Military History, 1979.

_____. *Vietnamization and Cease-Fire.* Indochina Monographs. Washington, D.C.: United States Army Center of Military History, 1983.

Nixon, Richard. *RN: The Memoirs of Richard Nixon.* New York: Grosset & Dunlop, 1978.

_____. *The Real War.* New York: Warner Books, 1980.

_____. *No More Vietnams.* New York: Arbor House Publishing, 1985.

O'Ballance, Edgar. *The Indo-China War 1945–1954: A Study in Guerrilla Warfare.* London: Faber & Faber, 1964.

Oberdorfer, Don. *Tet!* New York: Doubleday, 1971.

O'Neill, Robert J. *General Giap—Politician and Strategist.* New York: Frederick A. Praeger, 1969.

Osgood, Robert E. *Limited War Revisited.* Boulder, CO: Westview Press, 1979.

Palmer, David Richard. *Readings in Current Military History.* West Point, NY: Department of Military Art, USMA, 1969.

_____. *Summons of the Trumpet: U.S.-Vietnam in Perspective.* San Rafael, CA: Presidio Press, 1978.

Palmer, Bruce, Jr. *The Twenty-five Year War: America's Military Role in Vietnam,* Lexington, Ky: University of Kentucky Press, 1984.

Pearson, Willard. *The War in the Northern Provinces 1966–1968.* Vietnam Studies. Washington, D.C.: Department of the Army, 1975.

Pike, Douglas. *War, Peace, and the Viet Cong.* Cambridge, MA: The MIT Press, 1969.

_____. *Marxism, Communism, and Western Society, A Comparative Encyclopedia.* ''Vietnam War.'' Cambridge, MA: The MIT Press.

_____. *PAVN: People's Army of Vietnam.* Novato, CA: Presidio Press, 1986.

Pisor, Robert. *The End of the Line: The Siege of Khe Sanh*. New York: W. W. Norton, 1982.

Porter, Gareth. *Vietnam: The Definitive Documentation of Human Decisions*. 2 vols. New York: Earl M. Coleman Enterprises, 1979.

President's Foreign Intelligence Advisory Board. *Intelligence Warning of the Tet Offensive in South Vietnam*. Washington, D.C.: 11 April 1968. Declassified 3 December 1975.

Prugh, George S. *Law at War: Vietnam 1964–1973*. Vietnam Studies. Washington, D.C.: Department of the Army, 1975.

Reedy, George. *Lyndon B. Johnson, A Memoir*. New York: Andrews and McMeel, 1982.

Rogers, Bernard William. *Cedar Falls-Junction City: A Turning Point*. Vietnam Studies. Washington, D.C.: Department of the Army, 1974.

Rosen, Stephen. "After Vietnam: What the Pentagon Has Learned," *The American Spectator*. October 1979.

Rostow, Walt W. *The Diffusion of Power: 1957–1972*. New York: Macmillan, 1972.

Roy, Jules. *The Battle of Dien Bien Phu*. Trans. by Robert Baldick. New York: Harper & Row, 1965.

Salisbury-Jones, Guy. *So Great A Glory*. New York: Frederick A. Praeger, 1955.

Schandler, Herbert Y. *The Unmaking of a President: Lyndon Johnson and Vietnam*. Princeton, NJ: Princeton University Press, 1977.

Shaplen, Robert. *The Lost Revolution: The U.S. in Vietnam, 1946–1966*. New York: Harper & Row, 1965.

————. *Time Out of Hand*. New York: Harper & Row, 1969.

Sharp, U. S. Grant, and Westmoreland, William C. *Report on the War in Vietnam*. Washington, D.C.: United States Government Printing Office, 1969.

Sharp, U. S. Grant. *Strategy for Defeat—Vietnam in Retrospect*. San Rafael, CA: Presidio Press, 1978.

Shub, David. *Lenin, A Biography*. Baltimore, MD: Penguin Books, 1966.

Shulimson, Jack, and Wells, Edward F. "First In, First Out: The Marine Experience in Vietnam, 1965–1971." Charles R. Shrader, ed. Proceedings of the 1982 International Military History symposium, "The Impact of Unsuccessful Military Campaigns on Military Institutions,

1860–1980.'' Washington, D.C.: United States Army Center of Military History, 1984.

Shy, John, and Collier, Thomas W. "Revolutionary War," *Makers of Modern Strategy,* ed. Peter Paret. Princeton, NJ: Princeton University Press, 1968.

Summers, Harry G., Jr. *On Strategy: The Vietnam War in Context.* Carlisle Barracks, PA: Strategic Studies Institute, 1981.

Sun Tzu. *The Art of War.* Trans. by Samuel B. Griffith. New York: Oxford University Press, 1963.

Szulc, Tad. *The Illusion of Peace, Foreign Policy in the Nixon Years.* New York: The Viking Press, 1978.

Tanham, George Kilpatrick. *Communist Revolutionary Warfare: The Vietminh in Indochina.* New York: Frederick A. Praeger, 1961.

Taylor, Maxwell D. *Swords and Plowshares.* New York: W. W. Norton, 1972.

Thies, Wallace J. *When Governments Collide: Coercion and Diplomacy in the Vietnam Conflict, 1964–1968.* Berkeley, CA: University of California Press, 1980.

Thompson, Sir Robert. *No Exit from Vietnam.* New York: David McKay, 1969.

_____. *Peace is Not at Hand.* New York: David McKay, 1974.

Thompson, W. Scott, and Frizzell, Donaldson D., eds. *The Lessons of Vietnam.* New York: Crane, Russak & Co., 1977.

Tolson, John J. *Airmobility 1961–1971.* Vietnam Studies. Washington, D.C.: Department of the Army, 1973.

Tran Dinh Tho. *Pacification.* Indochina Monographs. Washington, D.C.: United States Army Center of Military History, 1980.

_____. *The Cambodian Incursion.* Indochina Monographs. Washington, D.C.: United States Army Center of Military History, 1983.

Tran Van Don. *Our Endless War: Inside Vietnam.* San Rafael, CA: Presidio Press, 1978.

Tran Van Tra. *Vietnam: History of the Bulwark B-2 Theatre, Vol 5: Concluding the 30-Years War.* Ho Chi Minh City: Van Nghe Publishing Plant, 1982.

Truong Chinh. *Primer for Revolt: The Communist Takeover in Viet Nam.* New York: Frederick A. Praeger, 1963.

Truong Nhu Tang. *A Vietcong Memoir—An Inside Account of the Vietnam*

War and Its Aftermath. New York: Hartcourt Brace Jovanovich, 1985.

Truong Son. *Quan Doi Nhan Dan*. "On the 1965–1966 Dry Season." Hanoi: July 1966.

Tuchman, Barbara W. *The March of Folly, from Troy to Vietnam*. New York: Alfred A. Knopf, 1984.

United States Embassy (USIS), Saigon. Vietnam Documents and Research Notes No. 38. "The Sixth Resolution, Central Office of South Vietnam." Saigon: United States Embassy, July 1968.

_____. Vietnam Documents and Research Notes No. 67. "An Elaboration of the Eighth Resolution: Central Office of South Vietnam." Saigon: United States Embassy, September 1969.

_____. Vietnam Documents and Research Notes No. 81. "COSVN Resolution No. 14 (October 30, 1969)." Saigon: United States Embassy, July 1970.

_____. Vietnam Documents and Research Notes No. 82. "A Preliminary Report on Activities During the 1969 Autumn Campaign." Saigon: United States Embassy, August 1970.

_____. Vietnam Documents and Research Notes No. 96. "Central Office of South Vietnam." Saigon: United States Embassy, July 1971.

Van Dyke, Jon M. *North Vietnam's Strategy For Survival*. Palo Alto, CA: Pacific Books, 1972.

Van Tien Dung. *Great Spring Victory*. Foreign Broadcast Information Service, Daily Report: Asia and Pacific, Vol. 4, No. 110, Supplement 38, 7 June 1976.

Von Clausewitz, Carl. *On War*. Michael Howard & Peter Paret, eds. Princeton, NJ: Princeton University Press, 1976.

_____. *Principles of War*. Ed. and trans., Hans W. Gatzke, Harrisburg, PA: The Military Service Publishing Company, 1942.

Westmoreland, William C. *A Soldier Reports*. New York: Doubleday, 1976.

Index